D0218134

Introducing Language and Intercultural Communication

Introducing Language and Intercultural Communication is a lively and accessible introduction for undergraduates who are new to the study of intercultural communication, with a particular emphasis on the language dimension.

Incorporating real-life examples from around the world and drawing on current research, this text argues against cultural stereotyping and instead provides students with a skill-building framework to enhance understanding of the complexities of language and intercultural communication in diverse international settings. Readers will learn to become more attuned to power relations and the ways in which sociopolitical forces can influence language choice/ attitudes and the intercultural communication process.

Features new to this edition include:

- Revised in-text discussion questions and the addition of multiple exercises and examples that aim to engage students and provide a more interactive experience
- New material that takes account of key social, cultural, and political events such as the refugee crisis, Brexit and the rise of populism in many parts of the world
- Updated theoretical constructs that reflect recent trends in this area of study such as criticality in intercultural communication
- An updated Companion Website featuring suggested readings, links to media resources and real-world intercultural scenarios for students, as well as additional in-depth instructor resources featuring test materials, PowerPoints, key terms, extended chapter outlines, and sample assignments and syllabi
- Refreshed references and glossary to enhance understanding of key terms and concepts

This is the essential text for undergraduate students who are new to the field of intercultural communication.

Jane Jackson, an experienced intercultural educator, is Professor of Applied Linguistics at the Chinese University of Hong Kong.

'This is an excellent introduction to the field of intercultural communication, as equally useful for anybody working internationally as to the university classroom. New material for this edition can be a bridge to contemporary history and current events.'

– Allan Goodwin, Nagoya University of Foreign Studies, Japan

'The new edition of Jackson's textbook addresses topics of urgent interest to the intercultural communicator. While the book was already a comprehensive guide to moving across and between cultures, the additional material responds to the rise of nationalist populism, hate speech on social media, and the demonisation of the "Other." Educators will find this a timely and wide-ranging resource that tackles difficult issues in challenging times.'

– John Corbett, University of São Paulo, Brazil

'Jackson's text is a comprehensive, fresh look at today's exceedingly complex intersection of intercultural communication, global competence, identity, and language. Relevant to students and intercultural communication practitioners, Jackson offers both breadth and depth when it comes to major concepts, frameworks, and highly applicable real-world examples.'

– Whitney Sherman, Council on International Educational Exchange (CIEE)

Introducing Language and Intercultural Communication

Second Edition

JANE JACKSON

Routledge
Taylor & Francis Group

LONDON AND NEW YORK

Second edition published 2020
by Routledge
2 Park Square, Milton Park, Abingdon, Oxon, OX14 4RN

and by Routledge
52 Vanderbilt Avenue, New York, NY 10017

Routledge is an imprint of the Taylor & Francis Group, an informa business

© 2020 Jane Jackson

The right of Jane Jackson to be identified as author of this work has been
asserted by her in accordance with sections 77 and 78 of the Copyright,
Designs and Patents Act 1988.

All rights reserved. No part of this book may be reprinted or reproduced or
utilised in any form or by any electronic, mechanical, or other means, now
known or hereafter invented, including photocopying and recording, or in
any information storage or retrieval system, without permission in writing
from the publishers.

Trademark notice: Product or corporate names may be trademarks or
registered trademarks, and are used only for identification and explanation
without intent to infringe.

First edition published by Routledge 2014

British Library Cataloguing-in-Publication Data
A catalogue record for this book is available from the British Library

Library of Congress Cataloging-in-Publication Data
Names: Jackson, Jane, 1954– author.
Title: Introducing language and intercultural communication / Jane Jackson.
Description: Second edition. | London ; New York, NY : Routledge, 2019. |
    Includes bibliographical references and index.
Identifiers: LCCN 2019026165 | ISBN 9781138482012 (hardback) |
    ISBN 9781138481619 (paperback) | ISBN 9781351059275 (ebook)
Subjects: LCSH: Intercultural communication.
Classification: LCC P94.6 .J33 2019 | DDC 306.44—dc23
LC record available at https://lccn.loc.gov/2019026165

ISBN: 978-1-138-48201-2 (hbk)
ISBN: 978-1-138-48161-9 (pbk)
ISBN: 978-1-351-05927-5 (ebk)

Typeset in Times New Roman
by Apex CoVantage, LLC

Visit the Companion Website: www.routledge.com/cw/jackson

Contents

List of plates   ix
List of figures   xiii
List of tables   xiv
Preface   xv
Acknowledgments   xix

Chapter 1 Why study language and intercultural communication?   1

Introduction   1
Definitions   2
Imperatives to study language and intercultural communication   4
The characteristics of an ethical intercultural communicator   23
Summary   24
Discussion questions   24
Activities   24
Further reading   25
Companion Website   25

Chapter 2 Culture and the primary socialization process   26

Introduction   26
Conceptions of culture   27
Facets of culture   28
The text's conception of culture   49
Summary   50
Discussion questions   50
Activities   50
Further reading   52
Companion Website   52

Chapter 3 Language, communication, culture, and power in context   53

Introduction   53
Definitions of human communication   54
The components of human communication   55
Communication properties   56
Language, culture, and verbal communication styles   71

Characteristics of an effective intercultural communicator
   in second language situations   76
Summary   77
Discussion questions   77
Activities   78
Further reading   79
Companion Website   79

Chapter 4 Language and nonverbal communication   80

Introduction   80
The nature of nonverbal communication   81
The importance of nonverbal communication   81
The relationship between verbal and nonverbal communication   82
Functions of nonverbal communication   83
Culture and types of nonverbal communication   90
The nonverbal expectancy violation theory   105
Nonverbal intercultural communicative competence   106
Summary   108
Discussion questions   108
Activities   109
Further reading   109
Companion Website   110

Chapter 5 Language and identity in intercultural communication   111

Introduction   111
Characteristics of identity   112
Types of identities   118
Summary   140
Discussion questions   140
Activities   141
Further reading   141
Companion Website   142

Chapter 6 Ethnocentricism and Othering: barriers to intercultural communication   143

Introduction   143
Social categorization and Othering   144
Ethnocentricism   146
Stereotyping   147
Bias and prejudice   150
Discrimination   152
Racism   156
Terrorism and genocide   159
Xenophobia   160
Combatting ethnocentricism and identity biases   161
Summary   164
Discussion questions   164

Activities		165
Further reading		165
Companion Website		166

Chapter 7 Intercultural transitions: from language and culture confusion to adaptation ... 167

Introduction ... 168
Types of migrants ... 168
Transitioning to a new culture: Long-term and short-term adaptation ... 174
Types of transition shock (confusion) ... 178
Language and culture shock (confusion): Sources, symptoms, and degrees of ... 180
Stages of culture shock and adjustment ... 193
An integrative communication theory of cross-cultural adaptation ... 201
Optimizing intercultural transitions ... 203
Summary ... 204
Discussion questions ... 205
Activities ... 205
Further reading ... 206
Video and online resources ... 207
Companion Website ... 207
Note ... 208

Chapter 8 Language and intercultural relationships ... 209

Introduction ... 209
Interpersonal communication and intercultural relationships ... 210
Crossing boundaries in intercultural relationships ... 211
Benefits of intercultural relationships ... 217
Intercultural friendship and diverse social networks ... 221
Intercultural romance and marriage ... 237
Enhancing intercultural relationships ... 240
Summary ... 241
Discussion questions ... 241
Activities ... 242
Further reading ... 242
Companion Website ... 243

Chapter 9 Language and intercultural conflict ... 244

Introduction ... 244
The nature and characteristics of conflict ... 245
Types of conflict ... 247
Cultural dimensions of conflict situations ... 251
Intercultural conflict styles ... 255
Facework and intercultural conflict resolution ... 258
Intercultural conflict competence ... 260
Managing language and intercultural conflict situations ... 262

Summary   265
Discussion questions   265
Activities   266
Further reading   266
Companion Website   267

Chapter 10 Language and intercultural communication in the global workplace   268

Introduction   268
Globalization and diversity in the workplace   269
Englishization, identity, and the global workforce   270
The benefits of diversity in the workplace   271
The challenges of diversity in the workplace   275
Cultural difference frameworks and the global workplace   282
Alternative approaches to intercultural business research,
    education, and practice   288
Enhancing intercultural communication in today's global workplace   289
Summary   292
Discussion questions   292
Activities   293
Further reading   294
Companion Website   295

Chapter 11 Language, interculturality, and global citizenship   296

Introduction   297
Global citizenship   297
Global competency   303
Intercultural competency   304
Models of intercultural competence   309
Second language proficiency and intercultural competence   315
Requisite competencies for today's global society   317
Enhancing intercultural (communicative) competence
    and global citizenship   318
Summary   323
Discussion questions   324
Activities   324
Further reading   325
Companion Website   326

References   327
Glossary   357
Index   390

Plates

1.1 Tourism in China has increased in recent years and there has also been
     a dramatic rise in the number of Mainland Chinese who are visiting
     other countries.   6
1.2 While some nations are benefiting economically from globalization,
     inequality and poverty persist in many regions.   7
1.3 Advances in communication technologies (e.g., smartphones) and social
     media (e.g., Facebook) are making it possible for people to maintain social
     ties with intercultural friends in other countries.   12
1.4 Buddhist monks are guided by a code of ethics or precepts linked to their
     religious beliefs.   20
1.5 Muslims perform salat, that is, they pray five times a day facing Mecca. 21
1.6 The Hajj (Arabic ‎ﺞﺣ) is one of the largest annually occurring pilgrimages in
     the world. One of the five pillars of Islam, it is a religious duty that is to be
     carried out at least once by all able-bodied Muslims who can afford to do so. 21
2.1 To celebrate the Galungan festival, the triumph of Dharma over Adharma
     or good against evil, Balinese Hindus make offerings to ancestors and line
     the streets with bamboo poles (penjor) that are embellished with beautiful
     coconut leaf decorations.   30
2.2 In traditional Chinese culture, red is an auspicious or lucky color. At this
     Beijing temple, red cards are decorated with images or symbols that are
     designed to bestow luck, health, and prosperity.   31
2.3 In Turkey, nazars, or charms, are worn or hung on walls to ward off the curse
     of the evil eye, that is, the negative energy that is directed toward you
     (e.g., envy, jealousy).   32
2.4 Prayer wheels (Tibetan འཁོར་ལོ།) play an essential role in Tibetan Buddhist
     traditions and have been used for over a thousand years.   33
2.5 Christmas is an annual commemoration of the birth of Jesus Christ that
     is celebrated by millions of Christians on 25 December (or by Orthodox
     Christians in early January). Popular modern customs associated with this
     holiday vary in the world and may include Christmas Eve services in a
     church, large family gatherings with special food and decorations
     (e.g., turkey and cranberry sauce, plum pudding), carol singing, gift-giving,
     Christmas pageants, nativity scenes, the decoration of a Christmas tree,
     and streetlights.   34

2.6 Incense burning, an ancient religious ritual common to East Asia, Egypt, and India, is steeped in symbolism. For Buddhists, the act demonstrates respect to Buddha and one's ancestors. The fragrant smoke also reminds practitioners to burn away negative qualities within themselves to seek clarity and purity. 35

3.1 These signs may easily be understood by a Spaniard but mystify newcomers who are unfamiliar with Spanish language and culture. 59

3.2 The Arabic language is a code made up of symbols (script). It is written from right to left in a cursive style and includes 28 letters. 60

3.3 Khmer, the primary language of Cambodia, is written left to right, similar to Thai and Lao, the languages spoken in Thailand and Laos, respectively. 60

3.4 In Hanoi, Vietnam, this sign is posted near a public park. If you cannot read Vietnamese, can you figure out what the message is? 62

3.5 Demonstrating their close friendship, these Chinese women walk arm in arm. 70

4.1 In many countries, attitudes toward smoking have changed significantly. This bilingual anti-smoking message is posted throughout Japan. Would you understand the nonverbal message if you did not know Japanese or English? What anti-smoking signs, if any, are posted in your neighborhood? Would they be understood by newcomers? 86

4.2 Greetings vary in different parts of the world. In Thailand, the wai (traditional greeting of respect) consists of a slight bow, with the palms pressed together in a prayer-like fashion. This Buddha statue illustrates the wai hand position. 88

4.3 Emotions are often expressed nonverbally. This Filipina seller is making a gesture to the photographer. Can you identify the meaning of the nonverbal emblem and discern his affective state? 91

4.4 This woman is selling vegetables in a market in Siem Reap, Cambodia. Can you read her state of mind? Is a smile a universal marker of happiness? 92

4.5 In Beijing, houses in hutongs (narrow streets or alleys) are very close together. How might the use of space influence social relations? 98

4.6 Wherever we live, we become accustomed to a certain amount of personal space. In a small island in the Philippines, locals crowd into jeepneys to get around. How would you feel in this situation? Would you be willing to climb onboard? 99

4.7 In some countries people generally move from one place to another in vehicles with only one or a few people inside. If you were used to a lot of personal space how would you feel if you were studying or working in an environment where you had to travel in a crowded subway each day? 100

5.1 Cultural and religious identities may be expressed through nonverbal means (e.g., dress, adornments). 119

5.2 How is this Scotsman's cultural identity conveyed? 122

5.3 In Beijing, this hostess in a restaurant that is frequented by tourists greets people wearing traditional dress. What identities are projected through her attire and demeanor? If she was wearing jeans and a t-shirt would your impression differ? Why is it important to consider the context and situation when forming ideas about identities? 124

5.4 Uniforms can convey professional identities. When you see this Turkish guard what is your perception of him and his duties? 125

5.5   Religious identities may be marked by one's appearance. This monk conveys
his devotion to Buddhism through his bright orange robe and shaved head.   135

6.1   While some immigrants thrive in their new environment, others face
discrimination and harsh living conditions, and struggle to rebuild their life.   153

6.2   Some parts of the world have benefited greatly from globalization, whereas
in other regions people still live in abject poverty and have not yet realized
the dream of economic independence. For some, the effects of decades of
racism and repression linger.   158

6.3   This racist sign was posted in South Africa during the apartheid era.   159

6.4   During apartheid, taxi drivers who were not white were required to park in a
separate area. Inequality was pervasive.   159

7.1   In many parts of the world, tourism is a major industry, bringing people
from diverse linguistic and cultural backgrounds into contact with one another.   169

7.2   Tourists typically stay a short time in the host environment and have varying
degrees of contact with host nationals.   170

7.3   In Bali, tourists are invited to join locals in Hindu temples (Pura in
Balinese), where they may mediate and bathe with devotees who believe that
these acts can bring about good fortune and health.   173

7.4   The majority of students who study abroad do so in a second language, with
English the most common language of internationalization.   174

7.5   This street painting depicts the daily life of early Chinese immigrants in
North America.   176

7.6   The lives of early Chinese immigrants in Western Canada are captured in
this street painting in Chinatown in Victoria, British Columbia.   177

7.7   We may experience culture shock or confusion in a new environment due to
the loss of the familiar and uncertainty about local social norms and practices.   183

7.8   Newcomers can easily be overwhelmed by unfamiliar scents, sights, sounds,
and choices.   184

7.9   In a new environment, tasting unfamiliar foods is part of the experience.
© Jane Jackson.   192

8.1   The number of intercultural (interfaith, interracial, interethnic) friendships is
on the rise in most parts of the world.   211

8.2   Intercultural friendships can expose you to new ideas and practices. A Cambodian
chef is showing her Hong Kong friends how to make fresh spring rolls.   219

8.3   Romance and marriage between people who have a different linguistic and
cultural background are becoming more common and accepted in many regions.   238

9.1   The Israeli-Palestinian conflict, which began in the mid-20th century, is one
of the world's longest-running and most controversial conflicts.   249

9.2   Intercultural conflicts are exacerbated when individuals or groups have
divergent ideas about conflict and ways to deal with discord.   252

9.3   While conflict is a natural part of life, intercultural conflict competence
can help people deal more constructively with conflicts that arise
with individuals or groups who have a different linguistic and cultural
background.   262

10.1 Diversity can enrich the global workplace and also benefit one's social
life, potentially bringing about significant personal growth and intercultural
sensitivity.   272

10.2 Efforts to enhance one's intercultural communication skills and develop an open mindset can help to cultivate and maintain good working relationships in multicultural organizations. 289

11.1 As a consequence of war, famine, and persecution, individuals and groups may be compelled to flee their home country and be afraid to return. In their new environment, how can global citizens help refugees feel safe and at home? 298

11.2 Global citizens are troubled by social injustice and inequality and take steps to make the world a more equitable and sustainable place. 301

11.3 Learning another language and improving one's intercultural communication skills can lead to a broadening of one's sense of self. 306

11.4 What knowledge, skills, and attributes are essential for today's graduates to be 'global-ready'? 319

Figures

3.1	A process model of communication	56
3.2	Linguistic codes/symbols for the word 'house'	61
4.1	Examples of culture-specific emblems	95
4.2	The seven universal facial expressions of emotion	96
7.1	The U-curve adjustment model	194
7.2	The W-curve adjustment model	195
9.1	A model of intercultural conflict style	257
11.1	Global citizenship conceptual model	299
11.2	The components of intercultural communicative competence	310
11.3	Process model of intercultural competence	315
11.4	Requisite competencies for today's global citizens	318

Tables

1.1	World Internet users and population statistics	13
1.2	Top ten languages on the Internet	14
3.1	Properties and definitions of communication	54
3.2	Contexts that influence the communication process	65
4.1	Characteristics of monochronic and polychronic time systems	105

Preface

As more and more people are on the move (e.g., immigrants, refugees, tourists, education abroad students, expatriates) and societies across the globe are becoming increasingly diverse, there is a pressing need for all of us to push past an 'us vs. them' mentality, which privileges people who appear to look, dress, think, speak, and act in ways similar to us. In today's interconnected world it is incumbent on all citizens to reject the boundaries and hate-fueled 'Self vs. Other' ideologies that seek to divide us. With enhanced language and intercultural communication skills, we can take steps to create a more inclusive planet. Mutual intercultural understanding and respect are essential to foster peace and security.

With these and other imperatives in view, institutions of higher education recognize the need to offer courses and experiences that foster the requisite knowledge, skills, and attitudes for ethical intercultural communication and global citizenship. Introductory courses in intercultural communication are now being offered in baccalaureate degrees in a range of disciplines; however, few books are truly international in scope and the language dimension of intercultural communication is often given little attention.

This introductory book is written in an accessible, user-friendly style for undergraduates across the globe who are new to this area of study. It is designed to provide a basic skill-building framework to enhance understanding of the complexities of language and intercultural communication in diverse domestic and international settings. The book raises awareness of the implications of English as a lingua franca in today's globalized world and also underscores the benefits of mastering other languages.

After putting forward a case for the enhancement of language and intercultural communication skills, this practical book introduces foundational concepts in this area of study (e.g., culture, communication, intercultural communication) and explains the stance underpinning the chapters. As readers work through the book they are encouraged to explore and interact with others to develop a deeper understanding and appreciation of what it means to be intercultural. Core issues related to language and intercultural communication are linked to real life examples from around the world (e.g., photos of diverse cultural scenes, student narratives in different cultural/linguistic contexts, critical incidents involving study abroad students, excerpts from interviews with international exchange students).

Critical self-awareness is essential for effective intercultural communicators. Accordingly, throughout the book readers are prompted to learn more about themselves (e.g., reflect deeply on their preferred self-identities, values, beliefs, communication styles). They are encouraged to challenge assumptions about other worldviews and ways of being (e.g., attitudes toward unfamiliar accents and cultural practices). The text strives to avoid the essentialization of people and behaviors, that is, the tendency to put people into boxes and overlook variations *within* cultures. A constructive, open mindset is vital for mutually satisfying intercultural relations, and this is promoted throughout the book.

The chapters aim to sensitize readers to the ways in which external elements (e.g., economic and sociopolitical forces, power relations, societal attitudes) can affect language choice/use and the intercultural communication process (e.g., interpersonal relations, management styles, discourse, nonverbal communication, the willingness to communicate). Attention is drawn to the cognitive, affective, and behavioral dimensions of intercultural (communicative) competence and the qualities associated with ethical global citizenship. The chapters also underscore the lifelong nature of intercultural competence development.

Ultimately, *Introducing Language and Intercultural Communication* is intended to serve as a valuable resource for students both in their home environment and abroad. My wish is that as readers become more confident, competent intercultural communicators, they will initiate more intercultural interactions and build meaningful relationships with individuals who have a different linguistic and cultural background. Finally, with more awareness of the elements associated with ethical global citizenship, I hope that the book will inspire readers to make a positive difference in the world around them and beyond.

NEW TO THIS EDITION

Since I wrote the first edition, driven by a tide of rising nationalism and self-interest, and deeply rooted fears of cultural difference, the world has become increasingly polarized. In many countries, hate-filled, divisive rhetoric (e.g., anti-immigration, racist speech) that was once deemed unacceptable in mainstream society now permeates political discourse in the media as well as interactions on social networking platforms (e.g., Facebook, Twitter). With mounting fears of the 'Other' (e.g., people who worship differently, immigrants, and refugees in general), we have witnessed more terrorist attacks (e.g., the massacre of Muslims in New Zealand and Jews in the United States), which have made a book of this nature even more imperative. Reflecting these worrying developments, this edition includes discussion of the impact of the rise of populism, identity politics, and racist right-wing ideology on peoples' attitudes toward individuals who have a different linguistic and cultural background.

This edition has also been updated to incorporate new insights in the field and more international examples that illustrate key concepts. In addition to discussion questions, each chapter now includes suggested activities to promote deeper engagement with the content. More attention is also drawn to the challenges of online intercultural communication. To allow for the presentation of new material, information about the historical development of the field of intercultural communication has been reduced, with discussion largely centering on shifts over time in conceptions of culture.

CHAPTER-BY-CHAPTER OVERVIEW OF THE BOOK

Chapter 1 introduces definitions of key constructs (e.g., intercultural communication, interpersonal communication) and raises awareness of the many imperatives for studying language and intercultural communication in today's globalized, interconnected world. The importance of understanding what it means to be a responsible global citizen is explained. This chapter also draws attention to the need to view intercultural competence development as a lifelong endeavor. The text's definition of intercultural communication is presented.

Chapter 2 examines the concept of culture and enculturation, the process of first language and cultural socialization in one's home environment. Discussion centers on definitions and shifting conceptions of culture and the various qualities and dimensions that are associated with this construct (e.g., culture as learned, culture as shared, culture as relative, etc.). The definition of culture that is adopted in the text is explained.

Chapter 3 delves into the nature of communication and the many factors that can influence the communication process (e.g., culture, context, power). After describing the characteristics and properties of communication, discussion centers on variations in communication styles and the potential influence of cultural elements. Suggestions are offered for ways to become a more effective intercultural communicator in interactions with a second language speaker. Many of the ideas will also be useful in intercultural situations involving speakers who have the same first language.

In Chapter 4, we examine the vital role of nonverbal communication in intercultural encounters, whether in face-to-face interactions or online. The forms and functions of nonverbal communication are reviewed, with attention drawn to universal and culture-specific dimensions. The relationship between language and nonverbal codes is also explored. Suggestions are offered to enhance the nonverbal dimension of one's intercultural communication.

Chapter 5 explores identity in relation to language and intercultural communication. Discussion addresses such topics as the effect of enculturation on identity formation; language as an emblem of identity; intercultural contact and identity change; multiple types of identity (e.g., social, personal, cultural, racial, global, hybrid); the relational, dynamic, and sometimes contradictory nature of identity; and the complex relationship between language, identity, and culture.

Chapter 6 centers on identity biases (e.g., ethnocentricism, stereotypes, discrimination, prejudice, racism) and their potential harmful impact on intercultural relations. Suggestions are offered for ways to cultivate a more open, inclusive perspective. The importance of self-awareness (e.g., sensitivity to one's preferred self-identities) and the need to recognize and respect the preferred self-identities of one's communication partners are emphasized.

Chapter 7 focuses on intercultural transitions, that is, the movement of individuals from their home environment to an unfamiliar linguistic/cultural setting. After discussing different types of border crossers (e.g., immigrants, sojourners), attention shifts to issues related to the challenges of adapting to a new environment. Examples from interviews with education abroad students are presented. Several models of culture shock (confusion) and adjustment are reviewed and critiqued. The chapter concludes with suggestions to optimize intercultural transitions.

Chapter 8 explores various types and dimensions of intercultural relationships (e.g., interethnic, interfaith). Discussion centers on the benefits and challenges of forming and maintaining interpersonal relationships (e.g., friendships, romance, marriage) with individuals from another cultural and/or linguistic background. The chapter offers suggestions to enhance intercultural relationships.

In Chapter 9 we examine intercultural conflict. After identifying multiple domains and types of conflict, discussion focuses on variations in the way conflict is viewed and managed. Intercultural conflict styles and taxonomies are examined, along with the role of face and facework in conflict resolution. The chapter concludes with suggestions to resolve language and intercultural conflict through peaceful dialogue and skillful intercultural communication/mediation.

Chapter 10 focuses on intercultural communication in the global workplace and raises awareness of communication challenges that may occur in both domestic and international workplaces when people from different cultural backgrounds interact (e.g., divergent communication styles, a language barrier, discrimination, etc.). The use of cultural difference frameworks in intercultural business education is also examined and critiqued. The chapter ends with suggestions to enhance intercultural communication in workplace contexts.

Finally, Chapter 11 examines the characteristics of global citizenship and explores what it means to be globally and interculturally competent in today's increasingly diverse and interconnected world. Several models of intercultural (communicative) competence are reviewed, and suggestions are offered to become a more effective intercultural communicator and ethical global citizen. This chapter serves as a review of key elements in the text and reinforces the notion that the road toward interculturality involves a lifelong journey.

Throughout the text key terms are in bold. These terms are explained in the text and also defined in the glossary at the end of the book.

ANCILLARY MATERIAL

Students may access the Companion Website (student pages). This resource includes support material that has been designed to deepen and extend learning related to issues and concepts presented in each chapter. On this site, the students will find the glossary of key terms.

Instructors' resources are available online for qualified adopters of the book. These online materials include the following: additional discussion questions, PowerPoint presentations, suggested teaching resources (e.g., films, video/YouTube links, print material), 'real-world' excerpts (e.g., cultural identity narratives, critical incidents, interview excerpts), interactive student activities, and a test bank (questions and answers for each chapter).

Acknowledgments

This book would not have been possible without the editorial assistance and encouragement provided by the Routledge team, especially Nadia Seemungul-Owen, Elizabeth Cox, and the copy editor. I also wish to thank the anonymous reviewers (intercultural educators in Australia, Italy, the UK, and Hong Kong) and my own students who provided constructive feedback on the first edition of the text. Their suggestions helped me to refine the content and sequence the material.

For many decades, I have taught intercultural communication courses at the undergraduate and postgraduate levels in several countries and am deeply indebted to my students who have shared their intercultural stories and ideas with me both in and out of class. In particular, their cultural identity narratives and reflective intercultural journals offered a window into their language use/learning and intercultural understandings.

My research on education abroad has also helped to shape this book. In particular, I have drawn on my ethnographic investigations of short-term sojourners as well as mixed-method studies of the international exchange experiences of university students from diverse ethnic backgrounds who participated in semester or year abroad program.

With the support of teaching development grants at my institution, I developed and researched an intercultural transitions course for students with recent or current international experience and, more recently, a fully online intercultural communication course for international exchange students to take while in their host country. Their generous sharing of their experiences enabled me to gain deeper insight into their intercultural learning. With their permission, some of the voices and photos of students are featured in the book and in the Companion Website.

I appreciate the support of my institution, the Chinese University of Hong Kong, especially the Department of English, throughout the writing of this book. Undergraduate and postgraduate students have conducted library research, processed student data, and helped to gather examples of intercultural interactions. In particular, I would like to thank Ms. Tongle Sun and Dr. Chan Sin Yu (Cherry) for their valuable assistance. I also appreciate the help of junior research assistants who gathered material for the website: Joyce Cheung, Serena Kwok Ho Ching, Flora Leung Yat Chi, Siu Ho Yan (Yancy), and Wong Po Yee (Bowie). A number of local and international students at my institution kindly agreed to be photographed using common gestures in their home cultures. Their contribution is very much appreciated.

Finally, I wish to acknowledge the support of my extended multicultural family. Their enthusiasm, intercultural stories, and photos have enriched my life as well as this book.

The author and publisher appreciate the permission granted to reproduce the copyright material in this book:

Table 1.1 Adapted from Internet World Stats – www.internetworldstats.com/stats.htm.
Table 1.2 Adapted from Internet World Stats – www.internetworldstats.com/stats7.htm 2018 Miniwatts Marketing Group

Figure 10.1 Taken from M. Hammer (2005) 'The intercultural conflict style inventory: A conceptual framework and measure of intercultural conflict resolution approaches', *International Journal of Intercultural Relations*, 29: 691.

Figure 11.1 Taken from D. B. Morais and A. C. Ogden (2011) 'Initial development and validation of the global citizenship scale', *Journal of Studies in International Education*, 15: 447.

Figure 11.3 An updated version of an image that originally appeared in M. Byram (1997) Teaching and Assessing Intercultural Communicative Competence, Clevedon, UK: Multilingual Matters.

Figure 11.4 Taken from D. K. Deardorff (2006) 'Identification and assessment of intercultural competence as a student outcome of internationalization', *Journal of Studies in International Education*, 10(3): 256.

CHAPTER 1

Why study language and intercultural communication?

In the globalized world, effective intercultural communication is an increasingly essential requirement in the critical efforts to ensure world peace, improve relationships between co-cultures and the dominant cultures within each country, assure resource sustainability, and promote ecological viability.

(Samovar *et al.* 2017: 3)

As globalization and localization intensify in every corner of the world, however, this field [intercultural communication] is increasingly confronted by more fundamental issues of identity, community, and humanity. In effect, intercultural communication is the only way to mitigate identity politics, social disintegration, religious conflicts, and ecological vulnerability in the global village. Human survival and flourishing depends on our ability to communicate successfully across differences.

(Asante *et al.* 2014: 1)

learning objectives

By the end of this chapter, you should be able to:

1   Define intercultural communication, interpersonal communication, and cross-cultural communication
2   Identify and describe eight imperatives for studying language and intercultural communication
3   Explain how studying language and intercultural communication can lead to increased self-awareness and understanding of people who have a different linguistic and cultural background
4   Explain why intercultural competence entails a lifelong process
5   Describe the characteristics of an ethical intercultural communicator

INTRODUCTION

This chapter begins by introducing various understandings of 'intercultural communication', 'interpersonal communication', and 'cross-cultural communication'. We then examine eight imperatives for studying language and intercultural communication: globalization;

internationalization; advances in transportation and communication technologies; changing demographics; the rise in populism, localism, and xenophobia; conflict and peace; ethics; and personal growth and responsibility. We then review the characteristics of an ethical intercultural communicator.

DEFINITIONS

There are many definitions of intercultural communication. Each reflects the author's disciplinary roots and understandings of communication and culture, core elements that are explored in more detail in the next three chapters.

Intercultural and interpersonal communication

Speech communication specialists have offered various definitions of **intercultural communication**. Rogers and Steinfatt (1999) define it straightforwardly as 'the exchange of information between individuals who are unalike culturally' (p. 1), while Jandt (2018) refers to it as 'communication between people and groups of diverse culture, subculture, or subgroup identifications' (p. G-4). Samovar and colleagues (2012) provide a more precise definition, drawing attention to elements in the communication process: 'Intercultural communication involves interaction between people whose cultural perceptions and symbol systems differ enough to influence the communication event' (p. 8).

Applied linguists have also offered their understandings of intercultural communication, accentuating the linguistic dimension. For Müller-Jacquier (2004), intercultural communication denotes 'a peculiar communication situation: the varied language and discourse strategies people from different cultural backgrounds use in direct, face-to-face situations' (p. 295). Jack and Phipps (2005) understand intercultural communication to be 'a participatory set of actions in the world', that is, 'dialogical and material exchanges between members of cultural groupings' (p. 181). Their definition highlights the interpersonal, dynamic nature of intercultural dialogue and interaction. For these applied linguists, **cultural membership**, or affiliation with a cultural group, is 'marked variously by race, ethnicity, nationality, language, class, age and gender' (p. 181). (The complex relationship between language, culture, and identity is explored in Chapter 5.)

An example of intercultural communication is a South Korean university student in Seoul interacting in English with a Swedish exchange student. In this intercultural situation, neither of them is using a first language and both have been socialized in a different linguistic and cultural environment. In another example, an American exchange student in Oxford is chatting on Skype with an Australian friend in Brisbane. While both speakers are using their first language, they have been socialized in different cultural contexts and are using a different variety of English, so this, too, is an intercultural encounter. In another scenario, an elderly Buddhist monk in Siem Reap is conversing with a young Cambodian female who is a devout Christian and a chef by profession. While they share the same nationality and ethnicity, these interlocutors have different religious backgrounds and also differ in terms of age, occupation, and gender. This, too, is an example of intercultural communication.

Conceptions of intercultural communication have shifted over time, and today more scholars are embracing critical notions of both culture and intercultural communication. **Critical**

intercultural communication studies examine the role of power and positioning in language and intercultural communication within a particular context (e.g., sociopolitical, historical, linguistic, cultural). Critical intercultural communication scholars (e.g., Adrian Holliday, Ingrid Piller, Kathryn Sorrells) reject static notions of culture and cultural groups. Advocating broader, more flexible conceptualizations, they rally against the **culture as nation perspective**, in which nations (or large communities) are depicted as homogeneous, largely ignoring the diversity within.

For this text, **intercultural communication** generally refers to interpersonal communication between individuals (or groups) who have been socialized in different cultural (and, in most cases, linguistic) environments. Cultural differences may include such aspects as age, class, gender, ethnicity, language, race, nationality, and physical/mental ability. **Interpersonal communication** denotes 'a distinctive, transactional form of human communication involving mutual influence, usually for the purpose of managing relationships' (Beebe *et al.* 2018: 3). Therefore, this form of communication is concerned with the personal dimension in human interactions such as how people use verbal and nonverbal cues (e.g., discourse strategies, gestures) to communicate their ideas and feelings and accomplish their personal and relational goals (e.g., develop and maintain friendships).

Intercultural interaction may occur in face-to-face encounters, through written discourse, or online (e.g., Skype, Facebook, WeChat) through the use of innovative technology and social media. Intercultural communication often involves a second language, with either one or both interlocutors using a language that is not their mother tongue. Even if the individuals speak the same first language, if they have been socialized in different communities in different parts of the world, variations in accents, expressions, politeness norms, and worldviews may influence the communication process.

Genuine intercultural communication goes well beyond narrow, simplified notions of cultural membership. In the 'culture as nation' orientation, people from a particular country (or community) are assumed to possess the same characteristics. This reductionist stance can easily lead to overgeneralizations (e.g., the Japanese are modest; Germans are overly direct). For mutually satisfying intercultural relations, it is vital for us to regard ourselves and others as complex cultural beings with multiple identities and attributes. (Chapter 6 delves into the 'dark sides of identity', including the harmful effects of stereotyping.)

Cross-cultural and intercultural communication studies

While the terms 'cross-cultural' and 'intercultural' are often used interchangeably, different research foci are associated with each. **Cross-cultural communication research** typically compares and contrasts native discourse and communication behaviors (or styles) in one cultural context with those in another (Gudykunst 2003). For example, the conflict negotiation strategies employed by Japanese administrators in a hospital in Tokyo may be compared with those of Irish administrators in a Dublin hospital. In another cross-cultural communication study, a researcher might examine the discourse communication strategies of Dutch business students in English-medium case discussions in Amsterdam and compare them with the discourse communication strategies of Taiwanese business students in English-medium case discussions in Taipei.

In contrast, **intercultural communication research** typically investigates interpersonal interaction between individuals (or groups) from diverse linguistic and cultural backgrounds. This intercultural contact may be face to face or involve communication through written discourse. With advances in technology, more researchers are also investigating intercultural interactions that take place online (e.g., Skype calls, chat groups, email, second language classes with online intercultural exchange). In their research, scholars may examine the verbal or nonverbal behavior of people engaged in intercultural communication or perhaps focus on the language and intercultural attitudes and perceptions of the interlocutors.

Using a variety of techniques, intercultural communication researchers may also observe and analyze classroom interactions involving students from diverse backgrounds. At a university in Finland, for example, academic discussions between Chinese, Dutch, and Finnish business majors in English-medium classes may be video recorded. To better understand elements that appear to influence the communication process, transcriptions of this intercultural event may then be subjected to **discourse analysis**, that is, 'the close study of language in use' (Taylor 2001: 5). Paltridge (2012: 2) offers a more detailed explanation of this mode of research:

> *Discourse analysis* examines patterns of language across texts and considers the relationship between the social and the cultural contexts in which it is used. Discourse analysis also considers the ways that the use of language presents different views of the world and different understandings. It examines how the use of language is influenced by relationships between participants as well as the effects the use of language has upon social identities and relations. It also considers how views of the world, and identities, are constructed through the use of discourse.

As they examine transcripts, discourse analysts may seek to understand how intercultural communication is facilitated or hindered by the discourse (e.g., communication strategies) of the participants. Alternatively, scholars may review the videotapes and focus their attention on nonverbal dimensions (e.g., gaze, gestures, touching).

An intercultural researcher could also track the language and intercultural learning of young people who move temporarily from one geographic setting to another in the pursuit of higher education. Cultural adjustment/adaptation, social networks, intercultural friendships and romance, identity negotiation, and culture/language learning strategies in a new environment are just some of the many interests and concerns of interculturalists. All of these topics (and many others) are explored in this text.

IMPERATIVES TO STUDY LANGUAGE AND INTERCULTURAL COMMUNICATION

There are many reasons to become more knowledgeable about intercultural communication and the role(s) of language in intercultural relations. Because of globalizing forces, internationalization, transportation and technological advances, conflict situations, changing demographics, a rise in populism, and the fear or hatred of foreigners, ethical intercultural communication is more imperative than at any time in the history of humans. We need to learn how to adapt and thrive in unfamiliar situations and contribute to our planet in a constructive, peaceful manner. Through interactions with people from diverse linguistic and cultural backgrounds, we can learn more about ourselves, reduce our fear of the unfamiliar, and discover respectful ways to build and nurture constructive intercultural relationships.

Globalization

No matter where we live, we are impacted by globalizing forces. While the exchange of ideas, goods, and people is not new, in the last few decades we have been experiencing an intensification of economic, cultural, political, linguistic, and social ties (Fairclough 2006; Steger 2017). This phenomenon, **globalization**, involves 'a process of removing government-imposed restrictions on movements between countries in order to create an "open", "borderless" world economy' (Scholte 2000: 16). Rogers and Hart (2002: 12) characterize globalization as 'the degree to which the same set of economic rules applies everywhere in an increasingly interdependent world'. Europe's Maastricht Treaty and the USMCA (the United States-Mexico-Canada) agreement, for example, were created to reduce barriers to trade with neighboring countries.

Knight (1997: 6) offers a much broader conceptualization of globalization, defining it as 'the flow of technology, economy, knowledge, people, values, [and] ideas . . . across borders', while Appadurai (1990) simply refers to it as 'a dense and fluid network of global flows'. Inda and Rosaldo's (2006) understanding is particularly relevant to our study of language and intercultural communication. Acknowledging the cultural dimension, these social scientists characterize globalization as

> spatial-temporal processes, operating on a global scale that rapidly cut across national boundaries, drawing more and more of the world into webs of interconnection, integrating and stretching cultures and communities across space and time, and compressing our spatial and temporal horizons.
>
> (Inda & Rosaldo 2006: 9)

Their description draws attention to the interconnectedness of people from different cultural backgrounds across the globe. As a consequence of this 'intensification of worldwide social relations', Giddens (1990: 64) observes that, 'local happenings are shaped by events occurring many miles away and vice versa'. In modern societies, humans are affected by 'the decisions and actions' of people in other regions that they may never meet (Gerzon 2010). For example, an economic recession in one part of the world can have serious consequences for people on other continents.

In addition to closer ties in trade and commerce, globalizing forces are triggering profound changes in the social, cultural, political, and linguistic dimensions of communities across the globe. This interdependence is influencing language policies on all continents (e.g., the designation of English as the medium of instruction in institutions of higher education in non-English speaking countries). Globalization is also altering linguistic codes. For example, in some quarters, there has been a marked increase in code-mixing (e.g., the use of English expressions together with a local language or dialect), especially among bilingual youth. More broadly, **code-mixing** refers to the mixing of two or more languages or language varieties in speech.

As a consequence of colonialism and globalization there are more varieties of English in the world today than in the past century, and most scholars now refer to **World Englishes**, rather than 'World English'. As Sharifian (2012: 310) explains, 'English has not "spread" as a monolithic code, but has become a pluricentric language: many new varieties have developed, and are still being developed'. Around the world, the number of localized or indigenized varieties of English (e.g., Cameroon English, Hong Kong English, Indian English, Malaysian English, Nigerian English) continues to grow. There has also been a gradual shift in ownership of English away from native speakers of standard English to anyone who speaks the language, irrespective of their linguistic and sociocultural background (Canagarajah 1999; McKay & Bokhorst-Heng 2008).

Ryan (2006: 28) argues that 'globalization could not happen without its own language, and that language is unquestionably English'. In this age of rapid globalization, in many regions, English has become widely used as a **lingua franca**, that is, 'a language which is used in communication between speakers who have no native language in common' (Trudgill 2003: 80). In 2010, David Crystal, an English language expert, observed that non-native speakers of English outnumbered native speakers by three to one.

Globalizing forces are also creating more interest in the learning of other languages. For example, in the late 1970s, China's Open Door Policy and subsequent entry into the World Trade Organization (WTO) in 2001 led to a significant increase in the number of non-Chinese studying Mandarin (Putonghua) around the world. In 2004, the government of the People's Republic of China began establishing Confucius Institutes across the globe to encourage trade ties and promote Chinese culture and language abroad. By 2018, there were more than 500 Confucius Institutes and over 1,000 Confucius classrooms in 142 countries and regions. Additionally, 67 countries have incorporated Chinese studies as part of their national education systems, and Chinese courses are offered in more than 170 countries (Xinhua 2017). As China's global influence in trade, international politics, tourism, and finance is on the rise, the number of second language speakers of Chinese will likely continue to grow in the years ahead.

McGrew (1992: 65) argues that these 'patterns of human interaction, interconnectedness, and awareness are reconstituting the world as a single social space' (e.g., global community). On a personal level, events, behaviors, and values from far away are affecting many aspects of

Plate 1.1 Tourism in China has increased in recent years and there has also been a dramatic rise in the number of Mainland Chinese who are visiting other countries. © Jane Jackson

our daily habits or **ways of being** (e.g., the products we buy, the language and expressions we use in online chats, the clothes we wear, the food we eat, the music we listen to, the television programs we watch, the Internet sites we access).

While some view this growing interdependence of societies and cultures as 'an opportunity to be embraced, allowing people to break free from the stifling restrictions of nationality and tradition' (Ryan 2006: 26), others consider globalization to be 'a threat, removing the security of familiar local networks and imposing an unwanted external uniformity' (ibid: 26). Critics also point to the widening gap between the 'haves' and the 'have-nots' and argue that the historical legacy of colonization and globalizing forces have exacerbated **inequality**, that is, unequal access to power and resources (e.g., cultural, economic, educational, linguistic, political, social, technological) (Bremmer 2018; Sorrells 2016; Stiglitz 2018). They maintain that the process of **homogenization** is leading to the loss of linguistic and cultural distinctiveness (e.g., the McDonaldization and Anglicization or Englishization of the world). For some, the global domination of American culture is taking place at the expense of traditional ways of being, including the use of the local language.

Differential opportunities to learn English can also divide societies. For example, proficient speakers of this global language may gain admission to more prestigious institutions of higher education. After graduating, these same individuals may be offered better-paying jobs and the chance to rise to much higher ranks in their careers (e.g., civil service, business, education). Conversely, in some parts of the world, those who do not have access to quality English language education (and education, more broadly) are left behind.

Plate 1.2 While some nations are benefiting economically from globalization, inequality and poverty persist in many regions. © Jane Jackson

Whether one's conception of globalization is positive or negative, it remains the most powerful force shaping our world today and in the foreseeable future. This phenomenon is bringing about more frequent intercultural contact and the need for well developed intercultural communication skills and knowledge of more than one language, especially one with an international status. Whether your career path lies in applied linguistics, TESOL (teaching English to speakers of other languages), the civil service, law, tourism, business, international relations, healthcare, the legal profession, or a completely different line of work, in our interconnected world, intercultural understanding and skills are apt to be necessary for your future career as well as your social life. In this highly competitive world, bilingualism or multilingualism is also a requirement for many and an advantage for most.

Internationalization

Accelerating globalization has resulted in increased investment in training for **knowledge industries** (organizations or industries dependent on a workforce with advanced scientific or technological knowledge and skills) and second or foreign language teaching. ELT (English language teaching), for example, has become a global industry. Higher levels of interconnectedness on campus and in the wider community are pushing educational institutions to devote more attention to international and intercultural dimensions of learning, teaching, and research. There is now a high demand for well educated, technologically advanced, bilingual, or multilingual individuals who can interact effectively with people from diverse cultural backgrounds and perform well in the competitive, global marketplace.

Sensitive to increasing global interdependency and the complex challenges facing graduates in all disciplines, institutions of higher education around the world have been revisiting their mission and responsibilities. In the process, most have confronted a range of challenging questions: How can they best prepare students to become responsible global citizens and professionals in today's diverse world? What skills and attributes do students need to be 'global-ready'? What steps can be taken to foster **intercultural competence**, that is, 'the ability to communicate effectively and appropriately in intercultural situations based on one's intercultural knowledge, skills and attitudes'? (Deardorff 2006: 249). What actions are needed to diversify their campus and attract students and faculty from other countries? What initiatives might help faculty and staff enhance their intercultural sensitivity and develop a more open, inclusive mindset?

Leaders in teacher education are asking how they can best ready pre-service teachers for classrooms with linguistically and culturally diverse learners. Those charged with the preparation of second language educators (e.g., TESOL professionals) seek the most effective ways to deal with the cultural and intercultural dimensions of language learning and teaching. As schools become increasingly diverse in many parts of the world, regular classroom teachers must also be better equipped to deal with a multicultural classroom. Administrators in educational institutions have also become more aware of the need for all staff (e.g., librarians, registration clerks, cafeteria workers, counselors) to become more interculturally sensitive. Whether in applied linguistics, general education, business, healthcare, law, science, or other disciplines, educators are grappling with similar demands.

The policy-based response of many tertiary institutions is **internationalization**, which Kälvermark and van der Wende (1997: 19) define as 'any systematic sustained effort aimed at making higher education more responsive to the requirements and challenges related to the globalization of societies, economy and labor markets'. Within the context of higher education, de Wit and Hunter (2015) describe this phenomenon as

> the intentional process of integrating an international, intercultural or global dimension into the purpose, functions and delivery of post-secondary education, in order to enhance the quality of education and research for all students and staff and to make a meaningful contribution to society.
>
> (p. 2)

While most internationalization efforts focus on higher education, in a growing number of regions, primary and secondary schools are incorporating international, intercultural learning into their curricula, especially in contexts where there is a large immigrant population.

Internationalization at home (IaH)

The term **internationalization at home (IaH)** refers to 'the purposeful integration of international and intercultural dimensions into the formal and informal curriculum for all students within domestic learning environments' (Beelen & Jones 2015: 69), with the aim of raising the global awareness, cultural understanding, and intercultural competence of faculty and students, both mobile and non-mobile. You may be using this text in an intercultural communication course that is designed to help meet the IaH aims of your institution.

To provide local students with more exposure to diverse languages and cultures, many institutions of higher education are taking steps to draw international students to their home campus (e.g., semester- or yearlong exchange students, full-degree students) (Knight & de Wit 2018; Proctor & Rumbley 2018). Whether motivated by economic necessity or the desire for a more multicultural environment, tertiary institutions in non-English speaking countries are increasingly offering courses and even full degrees in English, the de facto language of internationalization. In Europe there has been a significant increase in the number of English-taught degree programs in non-English-speaking nations (Lam & Wächter 2014). Among them, in 2018, the Netherlands, Germany, Sweden, Denmark, and Spain were offering the most English-medium courses (www.mastersportal.com/articles/1717/non-english-european-countries-with-most-english-taught-degrees.html). On campuses in these contexts, more and more international students are arriving with little or no knowledge of the local language or dialect.

Throughout Asia we are also witnessing an increase in the number of educational institutions conducting courses in English (Ota & Horicuhi 2018). At my university in Hong Kong, which has a bilingual (Chinese-English) policy, more courses are being taught in English to accommodate inbound semester- and yearlong exchange students as well as full-degree students who are unfamiliar with Cantonese, the local language. Newcomers are also encouraged to take courses in Chinese language and culture.

Educators and administrators have discovered that a greater number of international students on campus does not ensure meaningful intercultural interactions or more opportunities for foreign language learning. Contrary to the aims of internationalization, students (both locals and newcomers) may spend much of their time with **conationals** and valuable opportunities for language and intercultural learning are lost (Arkoudis *et al.* 2018; Jackson 2018a). Accordingly, international educators and administrators are designing innovative activities and events to prompt meaningful intercultural communication (e.g., informal outings, social gatherings, international clubs, a 'buddy system' linking local and international students/ language partners). Educators are urged to prompt more meaningful intercultural engagement in their courses (e.g., facilitate discussions and group projects with students from diverse backgrounds) (Arkoudis & Baik 2014; Jackson & Oguro 2018). On campus, administrators of student accommodation (e.g., hostels, dormitories) may encourage local and international students to share rooms or common areas (e.g., lounges) and interact with each other in extra-curricular events.

Ultimately, in addition to fostering inclusivity on campus, these IaH activities aim to prepare individuals (students, faculty, staff, administrators) for life in an interconnected world whereby interaction with people from diverse linguistic and cultural backgrounds is increasingly the norm.

Education abroad

Besides 'internationalization at home' (IaH) initiatives, there has been a dramatic increase in the number of students who are gaining some form of **education abroad**, that is, education outside their home country (e.g., study abroad, internships, work, volunteering, directed travel with learning goals) (https://forumea.org/resources/glossary/). In 1975, there were approximately 0.8 million higher education students being educated transnationally (OECD) 2015). According to the UNESCO Institute for Statistics, there were over five million in 2018, with the number of participants expected to rise to eight million by 2025 (UNESCO 2018; see http://uis.unesco.org/en/uis-student-flow).

At your institution you may find a range of education abroad options to choose from. Perhaps you can join a year abroad or semester-long international exchange program. If you have an advanced level of proficiency in the medium of instruction in the host institution you may study alongside host nationals in regular subject courses and then, with the necessary approval, transfer credits to your home institution.

Other options may include a language and cultural studies tour, an intensive summer language immersion program, a regional or international conference for students (e.g., intercultural citizenship or global leadership forum, peace camp), or volunteering. You might also do a practicum, internship, or fieldwork abroad (e.g., anthropology, business, global health, language teacher education). Increasingly, university students are choosing to take part in **short-term sojourns**, ranging from four to seven weeks, or **micro-sojourns** lasting three weeks or less (e.g., language enhancement programs). If you have already participated in some form of international education, take some time to reflect on what you gained from it and share your language and intercultural journey with classmates. The chapters in this book can help you to 'unpack' your experiences and set new language and intercultural learning targets.

Following the emergence of English as the global language of internationalization, as noted earlier, more non-English-speaking countries now offer education abroad students exposure to local (and global) course content through English than in past decades (Jackson 2018a; Jenkins 2013; Rumbley *et al.* 2012). Business majors from Vietnam, for example, may take English-medium courses in management or marketing in Sweden or the Netherlands. In Hong Kong, inbound international exchange students from Germany and Malaysia may do all of their coursework in English and also study the local language (e.g., Cantonese). Whatever the medium of communication, meaningful intercultural interaction both inside and outside the classroom (e.g., communication between local and international students) should be an important dimension of education abroad.

The amount of support for education abroad participants varies greatly. In faculty-led, short-term programs, participants may receive predeparture preparation, ongoing support during their stay abroad, and guided debriefings when they return home. This level of support is not common, however, and longer-term education abroad participants usually receive less guidance, if any. Most institutions offer only brief predeparture orientation sessions for international exchange students, which largely focus on logistics (e.g., the transfer of credits, safety and security). As educators and administrators familiarize themselves with education abroad research findings, they are becoming aware of the need for and potential benefits of more intensive, systematic programing (Jackson & Oguro 2018). For example, intercultural communication courses, like the one you may be taking now, are increasingly being offered to students in all disciplines to help them make the most of their time spent in their host country. Courses of this nature can also help participants develop the (inter)cultural knowledge and skills that are essential for successful intercultural interaction in in all areas of life (e.g., academic, social, professional).

As educational institutions play a central role in the formation of citizens and future professionals, intercultural education is vital to help prepare students for responsible intercultural citizenship in our global community, whether in the home setting or abroad. **Intercultural education** is defined by the National Council for Curriculum and Assessment (NCCA) as an 'education which respects, celebrates and recognises the normality of diversity in all areas of human life. . . . It is education, which promotes equality and human rights, challenges unfair discrimination, and promotes the values upon which equality is built' (NCCA 2005: 3). (International, intercultural education and global citizenship are discussed in more detail in Chapter 11.)

Advances in transportation and communication technologies

Innovations in transportation and communication technologies now link the far corners of the globe. Reductions in the physical barriers of time and distance have greatly facilitated the exchange of people, commodities, information, and ideas. Today, modern transportation systems (e.g., air, rail, road, water, underground) enable the movement of people and goods within countries, and from one country to another; vast geographic distances can be covered in far less time than in past years, with less cost and greater ease. Rapid trains, jet aircrafts, modern highways, high-speed ferries, and other advanced forms of transport are all making it possible for travelers, services, and products to move between countries and continents in record numbers. These transportation enhancements are bolstering economic growth and sociopolitical ties, and allowing for more intercultural contact (e.g., tourism, business, educational exchange) within nations and across borders. Undoubtedly, technological developments in transport and communication are making it possible for people from diverse language and cultural backgrounds to interact more easily and frequently than ever before. Nowadays, individuals have more contact with people from diverse cultural backgrounds than at any time in human history.

Telecommunication (e.g., communication through telephones, telegraphs, the Internet) and the mass media are also enabling the dissemination and exchange of information over significant distances. **Mass media** refers to a message created by a person or a group of people sent through a transmitting device (a medium) to a large audience or market (e.g., books, newspapers, magazines, recordings, radio, television, movies, the Internet) (Campbell *et al*. 2017). The mass media and rapid advances in digital communication technology are enabling more people to connect in virtual space, while they are in their home environment or abroad.

In 1962, Marshall McLuhan, a Canadian educator, philosopher, and scholar, coined the term **global village** to refer to the way the world is 'shrinking', as people become increasingly interconnected through media and other communication advances. He predicted that the ease and speed of electr(on)ic technology would have a profound impact on global communication, and he was certainly right! Today, people from different parts of the world can interact with each other through instant messaging, Facebook, email, blogs, and websites on the internet, as well as through older technology such as fax machines and voicemail.

Information and communications technology (ICT) refers to the role of unified communications and the integration of telecommunication (e.g., wireless signals), computers, and middleware, as well as necessary software, storage- and audio-visual systems, which allow users to create, access, store, transmit, and manipulate information. ICT consists of **information technology (IT)** as well as telecommunication, broadcast media, all types of audio and video processing, and transmission and network-based control and monitoring functions (Frick 2017).

By December 2017 there were more than 4 billion Internet users, more than half of the world's population (www.internetworldstats.com/stats.htm). While the number of users in developing countries has increased, as Table 1.1 illustrates, the highest density of users is still in developed countries (e.g., 95% of North American households), with less affluent regions lagging far behind (e.g., only 35.2% of households on the African continent).

Plate 1.3 Advances in communication technologies (e.g., smartphones) and social media (e.g., Facebook) are making it possible for people to maintain social ties with intercultural friends in other countries. © Jane Jackson

Table 1.1   World Internet users and population statistics

World regions	Population (2018 est.)	Internet users latest data	Penetration (% population)	Users % of table
Africa	1,287,914,329	453,329,534	35.2	10.9
Asia	4,207,588,157	2,023,630,194	48.1	48.7
Europe	827,650,849	704,833,752	85.2	17.0
Middle East	254,438,981	164,037,259	64.5	3.9
North America	363,844,662	345,660,847	95.0	8.3
Latin America/ Caribbean	652,047,996	437,001,277	67.0	10.5
Oceania/Australia	41,273,454	28,439,277	68.9	0.7
WORLD TOTAL	7,634,758,428	4,156,932,140	54.4	100

Source: Adapted from Internet World Stats (www.internetworldstats.com/stats.htm) (Accessed 16 January 2019)

Table 1.2 shows the top ten languages used in the Internet in December 2017. English was used most frequently, followed by Chinese, as the number of users in Greater China and elsewhere has grown exponentially in recent years. As English is a dominant international language, many of the users of English that are represented in the table are second language speakers.

The majority of international websites are in English and this has implications for information-sharing and intercultural interactions online. Even with the emergence of more websites in other languages (e.g., Chinese, Spanish, Arabic, Portuguese, etc.), a large number of academic/professional international sites remain in English. People who have little (or no) proficiency in English or another international language have fewer opportunities to access international information or interact online. This, in turn, may limit their international, intercultural contact in cyberspace, especially if their first language or dialect is not widely known outside their home environment.

Advances in digital communication technology are playing a critical role in educational, professional, social, and personal settings, especially in countries that have benefited economically from globalization. The emergence of a range of new technologies is providing more opportunities for social interaction and collaboration. **Social media** is defined as 'a group of internet-based applications that build on the ideological and technological foundations of Web 2.0, and that allow the creation and exchange of User Generated Content' (Kaplan & Haenlien 2010: 61). **Web 2.0**, the second generation of the worldwide web encompasses 'the revolutionary new ways of creating, collaborating on, editing, and sharing user-generated content online. It's also about ease of use' (Discovery Education n.d.). Recent computer-mediated interactive and social tools include Facebook, FaceTime, Myspace, Instagram, Twitter, Google Groups, WeChat, blogs, Wikis, Skype, LinkedIn, and multimedia (such as YouTube), among others.

Social networking sites are having a profound impact on contemporary social life and activity. With access to the internet, mobile devices (e.g., smart phones) are enabling Facebook users and Twitter followers to continuously stay in touch with local and international friends and family wherever they are in the world. Interactive social tools are facilitating the rapid dissemination and sharing of information and viewpoints with conationals as well as individuals or groups in other countries. Social tools are affording the exchange of diverse views about local and global issues, and in some regions these technological advances are being credited with changing or at least influencing history (e.g., the Arab Spring).

Table 1.2 Top ten languages on the Internet

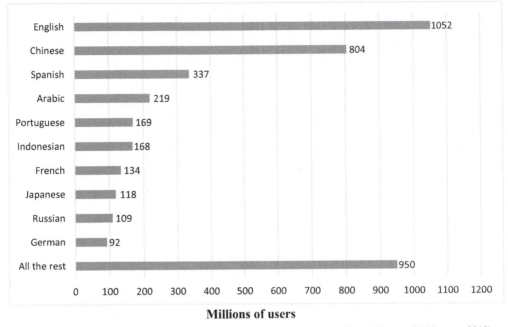

Millions of users

Source: Adapted from Internet World Stats (www.internetworldstats.com/stats7.htm) (Accessed 16 January 2019)

Estimated no. of Internet users is 4,156,932,140 as of 31 December 2017

Copyright © 2018, Miniwatts Marketing Group

Web 2.0 applications are revolutionizing the ways we interact with each other and opening up more possibilities for intercultural connections and collaborative projects in education and other domains (e.g., business, healthcare, government) (Pacansky-Brock 2017). Social media allows users to work together to create and develop content (e.g., wikis, podcasts, blogs). People from diverse linguistic and cultural backgrounds can share knowledge, information, and opinions online using web-based applications and tools. These innovations have radically changed our perceptions and use of communication.

Increased intercultural contact, facilitated by technological advances in transportation and communication, underscores the necessity of intercultural sensitivity and the benefits of acquiring proficiency in an additional language. It is also important to acknowledge, however, that not everyone is benefiting from modernization. Economic disparity is resulting in unequal access to communication technology and efficient transportation systems. Political control (e.g., censorship of websites/social media) and little or no proficiency in an international language (e.g., English) are still serving as barriers for many people across the globe.

Changing demographics

Human migration entails physical movement by people from one place to another, sometimes over long distances. While only a few groups have retained a nomadic lifestyle in modern times, various forms of migration have persisted and even increased in the last few decades.

This movement of individuals, families, or large groups is bringing about more diversity and, all contemporary urban societies are culturally plural. This is creating more opportunities for daily interaction with people from diverse linguistic and cultural backgrounds and another reason why intercultural communication knowledge and skills have become vital. (See Chapter 7 for more discussion about migration, education abroad, and intercultural transitions.)

Migration can take many forms. It may involve voluntary movement within one's region, country or beyond, and be driven by a range of aspirations (e.g., higher education opportunities, better job prospects, residence in a more peaceful environment, intercultural marriage, life in a warmer climate). Sometimes, however, migration is involuntary such as in the case of **ethnic cleansing** (e.g., the violent removal of an ethnic or religious group by another) and **human trafficking**/the modern slave trade (the illegal trade of human beings for sexual exploitation or forced labor).

Individuals may be displaced by war, economic crises, religious persecution, natural disasters or other calamities. The United Nations 1951 Convention Relating to the Status of Refugees, as amended by the 1966 Protocol, defines a **refugee** as an individual who:

owing to well-founded fear of being persecuted for reasons of race, religion, nationality, membership of a particular social group or political opinion, is outside the country of his nationality and is unable or, owing to such fear, is unwilling to avail himself of the protection of that country; or who, not having a nationality and being outside the country of his former habitual residence, is unable or, owing to such fear, is unwilling to return to it.

(UNHCR 2011: 10)

Immigration, that is, moving from one's home country to reside in another, is on the rise as a consequence of economic instability and armed conflicts. In 2019, according to the International Organization for Migration (IOM), 244 million people were residing in a country other than their country of birth; up by 41% since 2000, representing the highest number of migrants ever recorded, with most moving to high-income countries (http://gmdac.iom.int/global-migration-trends-factsheet). If this trend continues, there could be 405 million international migrants in 2050. Disturbingly, more than 5,700 migrants died or went missing during migration in 2015, an increase of about 9% compared to 2014 (IOM 2019).

In countries with a large immigrant population, romantic intercultural (e.g., interracial, interethnic) relationships are becoming much more common. Consequently, more children of mixed heritage (who may have some knowledge of more than one language) are entering school systems. This development has significant implications for educational institutions as educators, students, and administrators need to acquire the requisite knowledge and skills to communicate effectively and appropriately with culturally and linguistically diverse people.

As well as a long-term change in residence (e.g., immigration), people flows may be transitory (e.g., tourist trips, pilgrimages, education abroad). In some host countries, international students are regarded as probationary immigrants and are permitted to stay and work after graduation if they get a job offer. This policy is also contributing to long-term linguistic and cultural diversity within receiving nations.

Current demographic trends are creating more opportunities for intercultural interactions in educational institutions, in the workplace, and in one's social life. 'With the world becoming more and more linked by immigration, communication, media, economy, and transportation', Kim (2010: 170) speculates that 'cultural mixing is likely to further increase multiculturalism and within-culture variance in the future' (ibid: 170). With these developments comes the imperative for enhanced intercultural communication skills and understanding.

The rise in populism, localism, and xenophobia

While diversity, multiculturalism, and inclusivity goals may be embedded in national policies, in some parts of the world, economic recession, a widening gap between the haves and have nots, a rejection of globalization and the global elite (e.g., the bankers of Wall Street, the leaders of the European Union, career politicians), and mounting questions about the benefits of democracy are spurring a rise in **populism**, which basically refers to words and actions that appeal to ordinary people, who believe that their concerns are ignored by established groups in power.

The term 'populism' is hotly contested and definitions tend to have a regional, historical dimension (e.g., ties to fascism in Europe or right-wing nationalism and anti-immigration policies in the U.S., UK, Austria, and elsewhere) (Mudde & Kaltwasser 2017). This phenomenon is closely linked to the intensification of **localism**, that is, a range of political philosophies and strategies that prioritize the local (e.g., the production and consumption of domestic goods, local control of government, the promotion of local culture and identities) (Katz & Nowak 2018). Claiming that they are guided by the will of the people, populist leaders typically seek to oust the political establishment and replace it with a new world order which privileges domestic concerns and issues (Moffitt 2016).

When international financial bodies like the World Trade Organization (WTO) or the International Monetary Fund (IMF) meet, loud, and sometimes violent, protests may erupt, providing an outlet for deeply felt concerns about growing poverty among people who have not benefited from globalization (e.g., local blue collar workers). In the United States some groups rally against free trade agreements and call for more protectionism and a reduction in the number of immigrants. In a referendum in June 2016, slightly more than half of the participating UK electorate voted for the UK to leave the European Union (EU), in a move that has been viewed by some as a rejection of globalization (e.g., free trade) and immigration policies. Brexit (a merging of the words 'Britain" and 'exit' to indicate the departure of the UK from the EU) has involved years of contentious, protracted negotiations, which have exacerbated bitter divisions in UK society (Culkin & Simmons 2019).

Contemporary populism is inflaming anti-immigration sentiments, stoking resistance to international free trade agreements, and testing long-held global alliances (e.g., North Atlantic Treaty Organization (NATO), the United Nations (UN)). Resisting some of the tenets of democratic governance (e.g., a free press), populists are using new media technologies and social networking sites (e.g., Twitter, Facebook, Instagram, WeChat, Snapchat) to spread their message. In the United States, populism has led to the branding of unfavorable press reports as 'fake news' and the labeling of the press as 'the enemy of the people'. Concerns about border security and an elevated fear of foreigners (e.g., refugees from war-torn regions, economic migrants, Muslims) have helped to elect right-wing governments in Austria, Brazil, and other nations.

Of particular concern to interculturalists, populism has triggered a dramatic increase in divisive, highly emotive, 'us vs. them' discourse and **xenophobia**, that is, a fear or hatred of foreigners. For example, on a daily basis, in some nations, people are bombarded with polarizing political discourse that incites fear of the 'Other' (e.g., minorities who are not fluent in English, certain ethnic or religious groups), while ingroup members (e.g., working class whites) are exalted. Wodak (2015) offers her views about the roots of this phenomenon:

> Currently, we observe a normalization of nationalistic, xenophobic, racist and antisemitic rhetoric, which probably works with 'fear': fear of change, of globalization, of loss of

welfare, of climate change, of changing gender roles; in principle, almost anything can be constructed as a threat to 'Us', an imagined homogeneous people inside a well-protected territory.

(p. x)

Populism is closely tied to identity politics and belongingness (e.g., nationalism). Anxiety about change (e.g., shifting demographics, increasing linguistic and cultural diversity), fear of cultural difference, and economic disparity enable charismatic leaders to sow division. Persuasive rhetoric can inspire followers to reject intercultural dialogue and inclusivity (e.g., multiculturalism policies). Discriminatory rhetoric (e.g., anti-Muslim or anti-Semitic discourse) and policies (e.g., the separation of immigration families at the Mexico-United States border) have emboldened racists to spew their hatred of people who do not share their ethnicity, religion, or political views. Inspired by hate-filled rhetoric and doctrine, extremists have carried out vile terrorist attacks in many parts of the world (e.g., the killing of Muslims in mosques in Christchurch, New Zealand; the murder of Jews in a synagogue in Pittsburg, USA, the slaughter of Christians in churches in Sri Lanka). More than at any time in history, truthful, responsible journalism and intercultural education are imperative to overcome ethnocentric, racist tendencies and combat **terrorism** (the unlawful use of violence and intimidation, especially against civilians, in the pursuit of a political agenda). (Chapter 6 discusses the harmful effects of heightened ethnocentricism and Othering and explains how identity biases can lead to stereotyping, bias, prejudice, discrimination, racism, xenophobia, and, in extreme cases, terrorism and genocide.)

Conflict and peace

> The fault lines that divide us as peoples and nations have become deeper, more raw, and more lethal in our nuclear age. It is essential that we enhance our understanding of conflict and its terrain so that we can navigate the physical, psychological, and spiritual chasms that threaten to swallow us, creative potential and all.
>
> (LeBaron & Pillay 2006: 12)

Divisions between nations and conflict between 'co-cultures and the dominant cultures within each country' (Samovar *et al.* 2017: 3) have led to a troubling rise in intercultural and interracial tension. 'The fault lines that divide us' (LeBaron & Pillay 2006: 12) threaten stability, peace, and indeed the future of our planet. As communities become more diverse and the world more interdependent, the mutual understanding of people from diverse linguistic and cultural backgrounds becomes even more vital to cooperation, harmony, and stability. For Peck (1978), the key to community and world peace is 'the acceptance, in fact, the celebration of our individual and cultural differences'. More than four decades later, his words still ring true.

Conflict is an unavoidable feature of human interaction. Whether in a family setting, among friends or colleagues, in educational or health institutions, in the workforce (e.g., businesses), in government bodies, in international organizations, or in regional/national/international negotiations, disagreements, and disputes between individuals and groups may fester and grow. Although technological advances and globalizing forces are enabling more interactions between people from different parts of the world, 'wars, terrorism, environmental devastation, and massive changes in the world economic order have resulted in greater political and social fragmentation' (Scollon *et al.* 2012: xiii).

One of the most pressing problems confronting humans today concerns shifts in our **climate**, that is, 'the long-term regional or even global average of temperature, humidity and rainfall patterns over seasons, years or decades' (NASA n.d.). **Global warming** refers to the long-term warming of the planet, especially since the late 1970s, which is widely attributed to a rise in fossil fuel emissions following the Industrial Revolution (e.g., the burning of coal). Although the terms global warming and climate change are sometimes used interchangeably, their meanings differ. **Climate change** refers to 'a broad range of global phenomena created predominantly by burning fossil fuels, which add heat-trapping gases to Earth's atmosphere'; consequences include a rise in sea levels, ice mass loss in glaciers, shifts in flower/plant blooming, and extreme weather events such as droughts, floods, etc. (NASA n.d.).

Climate change, the dramatic increase in the earth's population (already exceeding 7.5 billion), globalizing forces, global economic crises, migration, and fierce competition for limited natural resources are all contributing to increased contact, stress, and conflict between linguistically and culturally diverse people. Therefore, it is imperative that all of us acquire the knowledge, respect, and skills necessary to mediate intercultural disagreements in an effective, appropriate, and peaceful manner.

Intercultural conflict is defined by Ting-Toomey (2012: 279) as 'the perceived or actual incompatibility of cultural values, situational norms, goals, face orientations, scarce resources, styles/processes, and/or outcomes in a face-to-face (or mediated) context'. Divergent behaviors (e.g., unfamiliar communication styles, different expressions of politeness) can make intercultural negotiations more stressful and even more complicated when a second language is involved. In situations like this, van Meurs and Spencer-Oatey (2010: 59) warn that 'conflict cannot be managed effectively without simultaneously considering both culture and communication'.

Intercultural conflict frustrations may boil over if we do not know how to deal with culture- or language-based conflict communication issues in a competent manner. Consequently, '[t]he need to summon creativity and exercise the choice to cooperate has never been more urgent' (LeBaron & Pillay 2006: 12).

If inappropriate or ineffective **conflict negotiation strategies** are continuously employed, misunderstandings can quickly evolve into a complicated and protracted intercultural conflict situation. Unfortunately, it is not difficult to identify long-standing domestic or international disputes that necessitate effective intercultural communication knowledge and skills to bring about a just, ethical resolution (e.g., the intractable Israeli-Palestinian conflict). Consequently, Kim and Ebesu Hubbard (2007) argue that on the world stage **intergroup relations** is arguably the most serious of all the problems confronting 'humankind, and is the single most vital domain in which intercultural communication has important ideas, theories, and facts to contribute' (p. 233).

In today's globalized world, learning to manage intercultural conflicts appropriately and effectively is not just an imperative for world leaders. In our academic, social, and professional lives it is becoming increasingly important for all of us to develop **intercultural conflict competence**, that is, 'the mindful management of emotional frustrations and conflict interaction struggles due primarily to cultural, linguistic, or ethnic group membership differences' (Ting-Toomey 2012: 279–80). To accomplish this, LeBaron and Pillay (2006) argue that we need both '**conflict fluency**' and '**cultural fluency**'. The former entails 'recognizing conflict as a difference that offers us choices and growth', while the latter, refers to recognizing that culture is 'a series of underground rivers that profoundly shape not only who we are, but how we cooperate and engage conflict' (ibid: 12). (See Chapter 9 for more discussion on intercultural conflict mediation and resolution.)

Ethics

> Significant global and regional problems of climate change and environmental degradation, poverty, disease, and war point to the necessity of meaningful communication across cultural boundaries. Addressing problems like these require decision makers to communicate ethically their concerns about what is right, good, or virtuous across cultural boundaries and to understand others who communicate their concerns in return.
>
> (Tompkins 2019: 211)

The world we live in is increasingly interrelated, and this means that individuals of different ages, genders, languages, socioeconomic status, races, religions, and ethnicities must coexist on our planet. As well as opening up exciting possibilities for collaboration and enrichment, this contact can present challenging ethical issues and concerns in all arenas of life (personal, legal, medical, political, professional, recreational, religious, business, etc.).

The term 'ethics' stems from the Greek word 'ethos', which refers to the character and sentiment of the community. Basically, **ethics** refers to 'the study and practice of what is good, right, or virtuous' (Tompkins 2019: 4), that is, the principles of conduct that help determine or govern the behavior of individuals and groups within a particular cultural context. Ethics provide direction for how we live our life, and this can vary depending on our environment.

Blackburn (2009) explains that the moral or ethical environment in which we live

> determines what we find acceptable or unacceptable, admirable or contemptible. It determines our conception of when things are going well and when they are going badly. It determines our conception of what is due to us, and what is due from us, as we relate to others. It shapes our emotional responses, determining what is a cause of pride or shame or anger or gratitude, or what can be forgiven and what cannot. It gives us our standards – our standards of behavior.
>
> (p. 1)

A **code of ethics** consists of guidelines that spell out what is 'right' or 'wrong' behavior in everyday life as well as in professional contexts (e.g., educational, business, healthcare, legal). These fundamental principles stem from core beliefs and the ancient wisdom of religion, as well as its teachers and traditions. We also continuously receive messages from our families, friends, and coworkers about what constitutes ethical behavior.

Throughout the world, religious codes of ethics serve as life guides for believers (Fasching *et al.* 2011; Gudorf 2013). In Christianity, for example, the 'Ten Commandments' is a set of biblical principles. As well as instructions to worship only God, keep the Sabbath (the holy day), and honor one's parents, the Commandments include prohibitions against idolatry (the worship of a physical object as a god), blasphemy (irreverence toward religious or holy persons or things), murder, theft, envy, and adultery (sexual infidelity to one's spouse). Jews are guided by ten commandments that are similar to those adapted by Christians. The 'Five Precepts of Buddhism' (do not kill, steal, lie, misuse sex, consume alcohol or drugs) are somewhat similar to the second half of the Ten Commandments in Christianity, although they are considered recommendations, not commandments.

Muslims are guided by the 'Five Pillars of Islam', which the Qur'an (holy book) presents as a framework for worship and a sign of commitment to the faith. They include (1) the shahada (creed), the declaration of faith linked to the belief that the only purpose of life is to serve and obey God, which is achieved through the teachings and practices of the Last Prophet, Muhammad,

Plate 1.4 Buddhist monks are guided by a code of ethics or precepts linked to their religious beliefs. © Jane Jackson

(2) prayers five times a day (salat), (3) fasting during the holy month of Ramadan (sawm), (4) almsgiving to the poor (zakāt), and (5) the pilgrimage to Mecca, a holy place in Saudi Arabia, at least once in a lifetime (hajj). Believers recite prayers in Arabic, the language of the Qur'an. Although only the majority of Muslims do not speak Arabic as a first language, all believers are expected to learn the basics to be able to say prayers and read the holy book (Begley 2009).

Hinduism also has a strict code of conduct that followers are expected to abide by in their daily lives. It consists of ten restrictions (yamas) (nonviolence, truthfulness, no stealing, sexual moderation, patience, perseverance, compassion, honesty, moderation of the appetite, cleanliness) and ten observations (niyamas) (e.g., show remorse, be content, give wisely, worship) (Boyett 2016; Smith 2009).

In Sikhism, 'Rahit' refers to the precepts for pious moral, spiritual, and ethical life. As well as prohibitions against the cutting of body hair, eating meat, using intoxicants, and committing adultery, believers are required to meditate upon only one Waheguru (Naam Simran). Sikhs also must perform daily prayers (Namm Japna); earn an honest and truthful living (Kirat karni); share money, food, affection, and time with the needy (Wand Chhakna); maintain special articles of clothing (the 5 Ks, or Karars); respect all people including those from all religions and races; and control their lust, anger, greed, ego, and attachment to worldly goods (Singh 2011).

Followers of other religions or sects also have their own rules or codes to live by. And for some devotees, 'ethics is not only tied up with religion, but is completely settled by it. Such people do not need to think too much about ethics, because there is an authoritative code of instructions, a handbook of how to live' (Blackburn 2009: 9). By contrast, other 'believers' may only observe some of the commandments or recommendations, and this may vary throughout their lifetime. Individuals who do not belong to any official religion or sect may consider themselves spiritual beings and follow their own code of ethics.

In truth, all of us are guided by ethical principles, whether religious in orientation or not. Atheists (nonbelievers in the existence of deities), for example, have beliefs that guide their daily

Plate 1.5 Muslims perform salat, that is, they pray five times a day facing Mecca. © Jane Jackson

Plate 1.6 The Hajj (Arabic ﺣﺞ) is one of the largest annually occurring pilgrimages in the world. One of the five pillars of Islam, it is a religious duty that is to be carried out at least once by all able-bodied Muslims who can afford to do so. © Jane Jackson

life. While some ethical principles may be below our level of awareness, they are still giving us messages about what is appropriate or inappropriate. As noted by philosopher Carl Wellman,

> An ethical system does not solve all one's practical problems, but one cannot choose and act rationally without some explicit or implicit ethical system. An ethical theory does not tell a person what to do in any given situation, but neither is it completely silent; it tells one what to consider in making up one's mind what to do. The practical function of an ethical system is primarily to direct our attention to the relevant considerations, the reasons that determine the rightness or wrongness of any act.
>
> (Wellman 1988: 305)

Fundamental notions about what is right and wrong not only affect our behavior in our personal and professional life (e.g., business/educational/legal/ medical practices), they impact our attitudes toward those who have divergent beliefs and traditions. Uncomfortable with difference and feeling under threat, people may disrespect the preferred identities of others and resort to using unethical, harmful language that is racist or sexist. Fear of difference can lead to **Othering** or **Otherization**, that is, the labeling and degrading of people who are different from oneself (Dervin 2012; Holliday 2012, 2016). As Jandt (2007: 42) warns, the 'collective pronouns *us* and *them* become powerful influences on perceptions' and can lead to the use of oppressive language and racist, exclusionary behavior, which, in turn, can cause emotional and physical distress to those who are singled out for this abuse. (See Chapter 6 for more discussion on racism and racist discourse.)

Personal growth and responsibility

> Through the course of our lives, we have many opportunities to learn about others – their cultures, their ways of being in the world, and their diverse stories and meanings. We can choose to go toward these opportunities or move away from them. We can live amidst differences and ignore them, or notice the differences that divide us and plumb them for their richness.
>
> (LeBaron & Pillay 2006: 11)

When we encounter individuals who have different ideas about what is right or wrong, this may cause us to question our own beliefs, values, and patterns of behavior. While this can be very uncomfortable and even seem threatening at times, it can also be an opportunity for learning. As we become more aware of different codes of ethics and ways of being, we may think more deeply about our own beliefs, identities, and position in society. Learning more about oneself is an essential part of becoming an ethical intercultural communicator.

The study of language and intercultural communication offers significant possibilities for personal growth and expansion. When we encounter linguistic and cultural difference in our personal, educational, or professional life, whether on home soil or abroad, we are afforded opportunities to discover more about ourselves and people who have been socialized in a different environment. Exposure to different beliefs and practices coupled with critical reflection on our own intercultural attitudes, knowledge, and behaviors can gradually propel us to higher levels of intercultural sensitivity and adaptability *if* we are truly open to this possibility. It is also vital to bear in mind that intercultural competence development should continue throughout one's lifespan.

Enhancing our intercultural communication understanding and skills necessarily means building awareness of ourselves as well as learning more about individuals who speak a different first language and have different values and habits. As Rothman (2008: 15–16) states:

> A commitment to intercultural competence is not only a commitment to learning more about other cultures and to the development of culturally appropriate communication skills. It also involves the commitment to personal awareness, to personal growth, to understanding, and to unlearning (as possible) any biases, stereotypes, or prejudices . . . the complete elimination of *all* biases within ourselves will remain an elusive, though always worthwhile, goal to pursue.

Throughout our life, the acquisition of (inter)cultural knowledge and skills, accompanied by critical reflection on 'real world' intercultural interaction (face to face and online) can lead to a broadening of our sense of self and facilitate the development of more satisfying intercultural relations. (In the chapters that follow, we explore ways to cultivate an open mindset and develop more effective language and intercultural communication skills.)

THE CHARACTERISTICS OF AN ETHICAL INTERCULTURAL COMMUNICATOR

A number of interculturalists (e.g., Chen & Starosta 2005; Hall *et al.* 2018) have proposed guidelines or principles for universal ethical intercultural communication. That is, they have suggested behavior we can adopt in intercultural interactions to make the world a better, more equitable place.

The following are traits of an individual who is an ethical intercultural communicator:

1 Regards people as equal, even when their beliefs or values differ
2 Actively seeks out and interacts with persons of diverse backgrounds (e.g., ethnic, religious, gender, linguistic, physically disabled, etc.)
3 Listens attentively and refrains from making snap, negative judgments about the behaviors of people who have a different cultural or linguistic background
4 Patiently asks questions to confirm the intended meaning
5 Recognizes that misunderstandings may arise due to linguistic and/or cultural differences
6 Seeks and provides (verbal and nonverbal) feedback to ensure that messages were received as intended
7 Makes a genuine effort to learn about the language and cultural practices of people who have been socialized in a different cultural context
8 Works from the perspective that the behavior of people who have a different cultural background is apt to be rational when understood in its situational and cultural context
9 Values intercultural cooperation and peaceful conflict mediation/resolution
10 Recognizes diversity within cultural groups and acknowledges that no individual can serve as a representative of an entire community or culture
11 Seeks to include all voices in intercultural interactions
12 Treats all people with respect and dignity, irrespective of their linguistic and cultural background.

(adapted from Chen & Starosta 1998)

With enhanced self-awareness and more understanding and acceptance of other worldviews and practices (e.g., cultural, linguistic), we have the potential to enrich ourselves, our families, and the world around us. All of us can and should make a difference. Throughout the text we explore ways to communicate in productive and ethically responsible ways in intercultural situations. As you work through the chapters that follow, it is also important to be mindful of the lifelong nature of intercultural learning.

SUMMARY

In this chapter we examined eight imperatives for studying language and intercultural communication today: globalization; internationalization; transportation and technological advances; changing demographics; the rise in populism, localism, and xenophobia; conflict and peace; ethics; and personal growth/responsibility. All of us can take steps to become more open, ethical intercultural communicators, a necessity in today's increasingly interconnected and multicultural world. It is also helpful to recognize that intercultural competence entails a lifelong process. In the chapters that follow we explore many of these issues in more depth.

discussion questions

1   What are some reasons why people might be reluctant to communicate with people who have a different linguistic and cultural background?
2   In what ways is the region where you live changing demographically? What do you think the population will be like in 20 years? Do you think the need for bi(multi) lingualism and intercultural competence is increasing?
3   Why are you interested in learning more about language and intercultural communication? What do you hope to gain by exploring the issues and themes in this text?
4   In what ways is populism increasing the need for intercultural education?
5   What does it mean to be an ethical intercultural communicator? Discuss your understanding with a classmate.

activities

1   This chapter identified eight imperatives for studying language and intercultural communication today. With a partner identify three additional reasons.
2   Think about your typical day. How many intercultural encounters do you have? In what contexts and situations?
3   In this chapter, many imperatives for people to enhance their intercultural communication skills. What are the most important reasons for you personally?
4   Individually or with a partner, interview three to four people from diverse backgrounds about their understandings of intercultural competence. How do their views resonate with or differ from your own?

5   Identify a current event or incident that involves interaction between individuals or groups who have a different linguistic and cultural background. Access news reports (in print, on television, or online) about the event or incident from at least two different sources. How do the reports differ? Why do you think this is the case? What are the implications for readers/viewers?

6   Review the propositions for ethical intercultural communication. Are there any that you disagree with? Which ones do you think would be the most difficult to follow? Why? Are there any propositions that should be added to the list?

7   Find a conversation buddy who has a different linguistic and cultural background from you who is willing to chat with you as you work your way through the topics in this book.

further reading

Boyett, J. (2016) *12 Major World Religions: The Beliefs, Rituals, and Traditions of Humanity's Most Influential Faiths*, Berkeley, CA: Zephyros Press.

This accessible book explores the teachings and tenets of the world's 12 most influential religions.

Hall, B.J., Covarrubias, P.O. and Kirschbaum, K.A. (2018) *Among Cultures: The Challenge of Communication*, New York and London: Routledge.

The third edition of this introductory text includes a chapter devoted to ethics. The authors also discuss the importance and benefits of studying intercultural communication.

Sorrells, K. (2016) *Intercultural Communication: Globalization and Social Justice*, 2nd edn, Thousand Oaks, CA: Sage.

Following a social justice approach, this revised edition examines intercultural communication within the geopolitical, economic, and cultural context of globalization, and offers a dynamic and complex understanding of culture to help address challenges in modern life (e.g., discrimination, racial profiling, ethnic conflict, wealth disparities).

Young, W.A. (2013) *The World's Religions*, 4th edn, Upper Saddle River, NJ: Pearson.

Surveying the historical development and worldviews of the major world religions, this text explores the ways they respond to contemporary ethical issues.

Companion Website: continue your journey online

Visit the Companion Website for a variety of tools and resources to support and extend your intercultural learning. (Instructors who are qualified adopters of the text may access additional resources on this site.)

CHAPTER 2

Culture and the primary socialization process

Culture is one of the two or three most complicated words in the English language.

(Williams 1981: 3)

Cultures are not somehow embedded in our DNA, but are learned, whether it is early (i.e., during primary socialization) or later in life . . . culture is broadly conceived as an inclusive concept which facilitates entrée into a social system with its own commonplace – but not absolute – norms, values, and attitudes.

(Komisarof & Hua 2016: 198)

learning objectives

By the end of this chapter, you should be able to:

1 Identify functions and characteristics of culture
2 Explain the primary language and cultural socialization process
3 Define and give examples of subcultures/co-cultures
4 Describe at least seven facets of culture
5 Define and provide an example of cultural beliefs, values, and worldviews
6 Define what is meant by a 'cultural script' and provide an example
7 Explain why culture is a difficult construct to pin down

INTRODUCTION

This chapter explores ideas or assumptions about the fundamental nature of culture and linguistic and cultural socialization. It does not aim to provide the definitive interpretation of culture; rather it draws attention to various elements that merit our attention. Drawing on literature from a broad range of disciplines we explore the following facets of the culture concept: culture as learned; culture as shared (group membership); culture as relative; culture as dynamic and mediated; culture as individual, fragmentary, and imaginary, culture as contested; and culture as communication. Each perspective provides a focus for thinking about culture, language, and intercultural communication.

CONCEPTIONS OF CULTURE

The word '**culture**' stems from the Latin word *cultura*, which literally means to till or cultivate the ground. When the concept of culture first emerged in 18th-century Europe, it was associated with the process of cultivation or improvement, as in agriculture or horticulture. By the mid-19th century, however, some scholars were using the word to denote a universal human capacity (Levine 1971). Over time, the term began to refer to the fulfillment of national ideals and the enhancement of the individual, especially through education. In 1869, Matthew Arnold, an English poet and cultural critic, wrote that 'having culture' meant to 'know the best that has been said and thought in the world'. This notion of '**high culture**' was linked to the arts (e.g., fine paintings, classical music, literature) and individuals who are refined, well educated, and/or wealthy (the elite). In contrast, '**low culture**' ('popular culture' or 'folk culture') was associated with elements in society that have mass appeal, that is, the sports, food, dress, manners, and other habits of the 'common people' (the masses) who have less education, money, and sophistication.

In his book *Primitive Culture* (1871), English anthropologist Edward Burnett Tylor defines culture as 'that complex whole which includes knowledge, belief, art, morals, law, custom, and any other capabilities and habits acquired by man as a member of society' (p. 1). This broad conception, which encompasses elements associated with both 'high' and 'low' cultures, served anthropologists well for 50 years. Since then numerous definitions and interpretations have been formulated by scholars in diverse disciplines. In 1952, Kroeber and Kluckhohn published a critical review of more than 162 notions of culture, ranging from 'learned behaviour' to 'ideas in the mind', and so on. They then put forward the following definition, which is still widely quoted today:

> Culture consists of patterns, explicit and implicit, of and for behavior acquired and transmitted by symbols, constituting the distinctive achievements of human groups, including their embodiments in artifacts; the essential core of culture consists of traditional (i.e. historically derived and selected) ideas and especially their attached values; culture systems may, on the one hand, be considered as products of action, and on the other as conditioning elements of further action.
>
> (Kroeber & Kluckhohn 1952: 181)

Characterizing culture as a 'system', Kroeber and Kluckhon's (1952) definition emphasizes the transmission of elements (e.g., beliefs, values) that help group members interpret their social worlds and function in their daily life. For these cultural anthropologists, culture is displayed through patterns of behavior, symbols, products, and **artifacts** (things created by humans, usually for a practical purpose) (Merriam-Webster online n.d., a). A **symbol** is 'a sign, artifact, word(s), gesture, or nonverbal behavior that stands for or reflects something meaningful' to individuals in a particular context (Ting-Toomey & Chung 2012: 309). (Chapters 3 and 4, respectively, discuss verbal and nonverbal symbols that may be employed in the communication process.)

Scholars have continued to reflect on and debate the qualities and dimensions of this core construct, and in a more recent publication, Baldwin *et al.* (2006) examined more than 300 definitions of culture from a wide array of disciplines (e.g., anthropology, cultural and social psychology, cultural studies, education, international business, linguistics, political science). Their review demonstrates how our understandings of culture have evolved over time.

Today, the concept of culture remains complex, variable, and difficult to define. In fact, Williams (1981: 3) describes culture as 'one of the two or three most complicated words in the English language'. To help you make sense of this elusive construct, the following section examines some basic ideas or assumptions about the qualities and fundamental nature of culture. Discussion centers on seven perspectives: culture as learned; culture as shared (group membership); culture as relative; culture as dynamic and mediated; culture as individual, fragmentary, and imaginary; culture as contested; and culture as communication.

FACETS OF CULTURE

Culture as learned

Our cultural orientation begins at birth. As we grow and learn our first language (or multiple languages simultaneously), we become accustomed to particular **ways of being** (e.g., modes of verbal and nonverbal behavior, philosophy of life). The process of learning about the ins and outs of one's culture (e.g., social rules of behavior, values) is referred to as **enculturation** or **primary socialization**. This process entails 'observation, interaction, and imitation and is both conscious and unconscious' (Fortman & Giles 2006: 94). Children discover how to adjust their behavior depending on their interlocutor (e.g., parent, sibling, teacher) and learn to behave in ways that are deemed appropriate in particular settings in their home environment (e.g., at school, in a place of worship).

Enculturation is a lifelong process. As people mature and enter the workforce, they continue to be exposed to social conventions in settings that are new to them, both inside and outside the workplace. For example, a fresh graduate who begins to work for a large accounting firm is inducted into the organizational culture at her place of employment, where she encounters communication styles and strategies that are unfamiliar to her. After work, she may socialize with coworkers that afford her exposure to informal discourse and ways of communicating that are new to her.

Socialization, a concept from sociology, refers to 'the process by which we all come to believe that there is a "right" way to think, express ourselves, and act' (Cushner & Brislin 1996: 5). Put another way, socialization is 'the process by which a person internalizes the conventions of behavior imposed by a society or social group' (Kramsch 1998: 131). Brown and Eisterhold (2004) explain the process in this way: 'Through interaction, members of a given culture socialize and are socialized by others. Culture emerges through action while it is simultaneously organizing action, offering its members a perspective on the meaning of that action' (p. 25).

Language naturally plays a vital role in enculturation. As Clyne (1994: 1), an applied linguist, explains:

> Language represents the deepest manifestation of a culture, and people's value systems, including those taken over from the group of which they are part, play a substantial role in the way they use not only their first language(s) but also subsequently acquired ones.

Children acquire language and culture together in what is basically an integrated process. At an early age, we learn sociocultural content by way of language-mediated interactions (e.g., verbal and nonverbal communication with caregivers) (Ochs & Schieffelin 1984; Ottenheimer & Pine 2019). It is through **enculturation**, the process of language and cultural socialization, that our primary cultural beliefs, values, rules of behavior, and worldviews are learned and internalized to varying degrees.

Beliefs

Acquired through socialization, **beliefs** are learned interpretations that provide direction for cultural members to determine what is and what is not functional, logical, and valid (Bhawuk 2015). In essence, beliefs are the basic assumptions we make about ourselves, about others in the world, and about how we expect life to be. Many core beliefs are religious in nature and central to a person's sense of self. In Islam, for example, Muslims believe that there is no God but Allah, and Muhammad is His messenger. Devotees are guided by messages in the Qur'an (holy book). Christians believe that Jesus is the Son of God and the savior of humanity. A fundamental belief of Buddhism is reincarnation, that is, the concept that people are reborn after dying. Atheists do not believe in a divine being, whereas followers of some religions worship multiple deities.

Some core beliefs relate to health and wellness (e.g., ideas about the source of illnesses and appropriate treatments). One of the core beliefs in traditional Chinese medicine, for example, is that certain foods (e.g., garlic, chili peppers, chocolate, French fries) have a 'hot' (heat-inducing) quality, while others (e.g., watermelon, lemon, seaweed) have a 'cold' or chilling effect on one's organs and 'energy' level. An imbalance of natural 'heat' and 'cold' in one's body is thought to cause disease or make one more susceptible to illness. In this belief system, the eating of too many 'hot' (Yang) foods can cause a rash or fever, while the consumption of too many 'cold' (Yin) foods can bring about stomach pains or diarrhea. Thus, believers strive to maintain a balance of Yin and Yang forces in their diet. Healthcare providers who are unfamiliar with this system may understand the individual words used to explain an illness but fail to grasp the concept and its significance to the patient. In today's multicultural world, familiarity with diverse cultural beliefs (and communication styles) is necessary to facilitate optimal healthcare interactions, interventions, and outcomes.

Beliefs may also be **peripheral**, that is, they may simply relate to personal perceptions and tastes (e.g., ideas about the best way to learn a foreign language or prepare for the TOEFL, an English language proficiency test). Peripheral beliefs may also be superstitious in nature. A **superstition** is 'a belief, half-belief, or practice for which there appears to be no rational substance' (Encyclopedia Britannica n.d.). Believing a 'lucky' coin will help you perform well on the TOEFL would be an example.

Many people have nonscientific beliefs about ways to ward off misfortune, foretell the future, or prevent/cure minor ailments. Throughout history, folk traditions (e.g., belief in curses or the 'evil eye' in Turkey and Egypt) have been found in most parts of the world. Some superstitions and folk traditions are limited to a particular country, region, or village, or to a specific social group. For example, the number '4' is considered unlucky by many Hong Kongers, as it can be read as *shi* in Chinese, which is a homophone for death. Consequently, some high-rise residential buildings avoid the use of the number '4' when numbering floors (e.g., no 4th, 14th, 24th floors). Compared with core beliefs, peripheral beliefs may be more easily reflected upon and changed through education and life experience.

Plate 2.1   To celebrate the Galungan festival, the triumph of Dharma over Adharma or good against evil, Balinese Hindus make offerings to ancestors and line the streets with bamboo poles (penjor) that are embellished with beautiful coconut leaf decorations. © Jane Jackson

Values

Values are shared ideas about what is right or wrong, fair or unfair, just or unjust, kind or cruel, or important and unimportant. Though primary socialization, we learn to think that things ought to be or people ought to behave in a particular way. It is during this process that we form views about the nature and significance of human qualities such as honesty, integrity, and openness. **Valence** refers to the positive or negative nature of a particular

Plate 2.2 In traditional Chinese culture, red is an auspicious or lucky color. At this Beijing temple, red
cards are decorated with images or symbols that are designed to bestow luck, health, and pros-
perity. © Jane Jackson

value, while **intensity** points to its importance or strength for the individual. As discussed
in Chapter 1, values affect one's sense of ethics and, to varying degrees, serve as guiding
principles in one's daily life.

Worldviews

Cultural values and beliefs cover many aspects of society (e.g., equality, freedom, the right to
pursue happiness, the meaning of life and death); together they form an individual's perception
of the world. An intercultural **worldview** signifies 'fundamental assumptions and beliefs concerning a conception of how the world works' (Dodd 2018). For McDaniel and Samovar (2015:
13) it is 'what forms an individual's orientation toward such philosophical concepts as God, the
universe, nature, and the like'. More simply, it is our overall way of looking at the world. It is
a bit like viewing life through an invisible pair of glasses or contact lenses, which serves as a
filter to help us make sense of humanity. As one's worldview usually operates at a subconscious
level, we are not fully aware of how it is affecting our psyche.

As noted by Samovar *et al*. (2010), worldviews cover a broad range of weighty concerns
and issues, e.g., 'What is the purpose of life, Is the world ruled by law, chance or "God"?,
What is the right way to live? How did the world begin? What happens when we die?' (p, 98).
Our worldviews form a complex framework of ideas and beliefs, which influence the way we

Plate 2.3 In Turkey, nazars, or charms, are worn or hung on walls to ward off the curse of the evil eye, that is, the negative energy that is directed toward you (e.g., envy, jealousy).

perceive and communicate with others. When we interact with individuals who have been socialized in a different context, we may be surprised, or even shocked, to discover conflicting views about fundamental life questions. (Chapter 9 explores intercultural conflict situations that may stem, in part, from the collision of divergent worldviews, values, or beliefs.)

Infants are not born with a worldview. Our understandings of life form during the social-ization process and continue to evolve as we mature. Religion often plays a fundamental role in shaping worldviews, including one's ideas about nature, deities (divine or supreme beings), and the origin of life on earth. For example, while Muslims, Jews, and Christians believe that the universe was created by God, Buddhists and Taoists worship multiple gods or god-like beings. According to the Taoist creation theory, the beginning of the universe consisted of yin and yang forces that consolidated to form the earth in the center. Hindus believe there is one

Plate 2.4 Prayer wheels (Tibetan འཁོར་ལོ) play an essential role in Tibetan Buddhist traditions and have been used for over a thousand years. © Jane Jackson

Divine Power with multiple forms, whereas atheists (nonreligious people) do not recognize a divine power as the creator of nature.

Religion can also shape one's ideas about sin (violations of the accepted moral code) and the consequences for what happens after death. Notions of judgment and punishment (and forgiveness) for violations committed during one's lifetime are core elements in many religions. Religious (and nonreligious) worldviews related to sin, mortality, and the afterlife can affect how people lead their lives.

Buddhists believe that each life continues after death in some other form (human, divine or animal) depending on one's behavior on earth. Believers in the afterlife, Hindus maintain that due to the actions in one's present life, the soul may be reborn in either a higher or lower physical form after death. Through devotion or correct behavior, devotees believe it is possible to ascend through the orders of reincarnation, achieve liberation from the cycle of rebirth, and be reunited with the Divine Power.

Christians, Jews, and Muslims believe there is only one life, and there are differing views about what happens after death. Some believe the soul may ascend to heaven and be judged by God or the soul and the body may be raised on the Day of Judgment at the end of time and will then be judged. Muslims, for example, maintain that paradise awaits those who have lived by the will of Allah and those who have not done so cannot enter Paradise.

Religious beliefs can also influence one's perception of time. For example, in Islam, Christianity, and Judaism, time is viewed as linear (e.g., life has a beginning, middle, and end)

whereas in Buddhism, Hinduism, and Sikhism cyclical dimensions of time are emphasized (e.g., the process of creation moves in cycles and is never ending). Notions of life, death, and time together influence one's worldview and shape how one sees and interprets life.

Followers of a particular religion or sect may accept some religious beliefs and reject others. This means that an individual's worldview is not necessarily aligned with the fundamentals of a single religion, if any. In today's multicultural world, we are exposed to diverse beliefs, practices, and worldviews. As we mature, we carry with us a tapestry of different notions about life, which draw on our unique, varied experiences and evolving understandings of the world.

Traditions

Throughout our life, we are exposed to both religious and nonreligious traditions. Culturally shared **traditions** are customs or rituals that have been passed down from one generation to another. Each tradition has its own rituals and practices, some of which are linguistic in nature (e.g., the use of a specific language, dialect, or expressions on certain occasions such as prayers and funerals). Influenced by the culture's core beliefs and values, traditions may take the form of festivals or other celebrations. In Taoism, for example, there are hundreds of local festivals such as *Ching Ming*, the veneration of the dead, the *Hungry Ghosts' festival*

Plate 2.5   Christmas is an annual commemoration of the birth of Jesus Christ that is celebrated by millions of Christians on 25 December (or by Orthodox Christians in early January). Popular modern customs associated with this holiday vary in the world and may include Christmas Eve services in a church, large family gatherings with special food and decorations (e.g., turkey and cranberry sauce, plum pudding), carol singing, gift-giving, Christmas pageants, nativity scenes, the decoration of a Christmas tree, and streetlights, etc. © Mary Jackson

for the release of the restless dead, and the *moon festival* to celebrate the autumn harvest. In Christianity, the main festivals celebrate the life of Jesus Christ: His birth at *Christmas* and His death and resurrection at *Easter*. In Islam, *Ramadan* is the holy month of fasting, while *Eid al-fitr* marks the end of Ramadan and the giving of the Qur'an (the holy book) to Muhammad, the messenger of Allah (God). Other religions have special days and observances that are meaningful to devotees.

Cultural traditions also include healing rituals, folk art, handicrafts, myths, legends, the singing of folk songs in a certain dialect, funeral rites, and celebrations of birthdays/weddings/anniversaries/the coming of age/the birth of a child, etc.

When a baby is born into a Sikh family, the Mool mantra, the core teaching of Sikhism, is whispered into the baby's ear. The baby is then named at the gurdwara, or place of worship. The Guru Granth Sahib is opened and the first letter of the first word on the page gives the first letter of the baby's name. At death, the body is cremated and the ashes thrown into running water (OABITAR [Objectivity, Accuracy, and Balance in Teaching About Religion] n.d.; Smith 2009).

Before birth and in the first months of life, Hindus organize many ceremonies, including the reciting of scriptures to the baby while still in the womb, the casting of the child's horoscope shortly after birth, and a gathering to mark the cutting of the baby's hair for the first time. At death, bodies are cremated and the ashes thrown onto a sacred river. The River Ganges, a trans-boundary river in India and Bangladesh which is named after a Hindu goddess called Ganga, is the most sacred river of all (Boyett 2016; OABITAR n.d.; Smith 2009).

In Taoism, horoscopes are cast at birth. After a month a naming ceremony is held. At death, the body is buried, and paper models of money, houses, and cars are burnt to help the soul in the afterlife. After about ten years the body is dug up and the bones buried again in an auspicious site. In Theravada Buddhism, funerals are occasions for teaching about the impermanence of human life and for chanting paritta (protection) for the deceased.

Plate 2.6   Incense burning, an ancient religious ritual common to East Asia, Egypt, and India, is steeped in symbolism. For Buddhists, the act demonstrates respect to Buddha and one's ancestors. The fragrant smoke also reminds practitioners to burn away negative qualities within themselves to seek clarity and purity. © Jane Jackson

Many Christians are baptized into the Church while they are babies, although this can be done at any time in life. At death, Christians are laid to rest in the hope of the resurrection of the dead. Cremation and burial are both considered acceptable.

In Judaism, baby boys are circumcised eight days after birth. The names of girls are announced in the synagogue on the first Sabbath after birth. As for death, burial takes place within 24 hours of death and cremation is quite rare. The family is in full mourning for seven days and, for 11 months, the special prayer Kadish is recited every day.

In Islam, the call to prayer is whispered into the baby's ear at birth. After seven days, the baby is given a name, shaved, and baby boys are circumcised. At a person's death, the body is washed as if ready for prayer and then buried as soon as possible. Cremation is not permitted.

With the passage of time, the significance of cultural traditions may change, along with the ways they are enacted. Within the same context, some individuals may have a strong attachment to a certain tradition or custom, whereas others (e.g., family members from a different generation) may be more ambivalent. People may gradually have little or no understanding of the origins of certain customs but still have an emotional attachment to them and a desire to share them with their own children when they become parents.

Cultural norms

During the process of enculturation or primary socialization, elders (e.g., parents, religious figures, teachers) and the media (e.g., television) convey messages about what is expected (e.g., forms of address, communication styles, nonverbal behavior) in various situations and contexts (e.g., familial, religious, social, academic, professional). At an early age, we learn what is considered polite (and impolite) behavior (e.g., 'good manners'), that is, we discover what we can and cannot say (or do) in certain situations. Implicit or explicit messages are also relayed about social hierarchies and one's positioning (and possibilities) in specific settings, such as interactions with grandparents/elders/authority figures or people of a different gender/cultural background/socioeconomic status. **Cultural norms** are shared ideas about what behaviors (e.g., communication styles, language usage) are deemed appropriate or 'normal' in a particular situation and context (e.g., interactions with elders). **Politeness** refers to 'showing awareness and consideration of another person's public self-image' (Yule 2017: 327), that is, acting in ways that are deemed respectful and considerate. Sociolinguists Wardaugh and Fuller (2015) regard culture as 'the "know-how" that a person must possess to get through the task of daily living' (p. 10). We are not born with this knowledge; it is learned in particular sociocultural and linguistic contexts.

Cultural schema

A **cultural schema** refers to 'a mental structure in which our knowledge of the world is organized so that it can be efficiently used in thinking, communication, etc.' (Spencer-Oatey 2008a: 336). Through enculturation, we become habituated to expect certain arrangements (e.g., procedures) and behaviors (e.g., discourse, social norms of politeness) in specific situations and settings (e.g., a bank, a restaurant, a family dinner, a classroom). Basically, over time, through observation and experience we gradually form mental pictures of various scenes. These 'patterns of typicality' help people to 'organize the world around them so that events become more meaningful and understandable' (Shahghasemi 2018: 570). Schema enable us to cope with the complex world in which we live.

In Mumbai, India, a lecture schema has a lecturer standing behind a podium delivering a formal speech on an academic topic using PowerPoint; students sit in rows facing the front and raise their hands when they wish to ask a question. In other cultural settings, this schema may vary a little or considerably (e.g., in Sydney, Australia, the organization of the room may differ, including the type and placement of the furniture and the positioning of the lecturer; the dress and behavior (degree of formality) of the lecturer and students may also be different).

Language socialization: Cultural scripts, discourse, and politeness

This 'acquisition of linguistic, pragmatic, and other cultural knowledge through social experience' is referred to as **language socialization** (Duff 2010: 427). This is a core element in enculturation. While we are socialized by and through language into the practices of our own community (and others), we gradually develop cultural and communicative competence in these settings. This process entails lifelong learning. As we mature and gain exposure to situations that are unfamiliar to us, we learn new 'rules of speaking' from more experienced individuals (e.g., discover what is expected in workplace situations). Ochs and Schieffelin (2014) maintain that '[l]anguage socialization begins as the developmental point at which members of a community recognize that a person enters into existence and continues throughout the life course until a person is viewed as no longer a living social being' (p. 3).

Through the primary socialization process, we learn 'norms of interaction, which are basically "rules" of how interactants are supposed to behave, for example, who should talk and when, how turns might change' (Kiesling 2012: 81). As we gain exposure to various social worlds, we learn 'cultural scripts' and the style of communication that is deemed appropriate in specific contexts (Goddard 2004; Wierzbicka 2006). A **cultural script**, which is a type of schema, refers to 'a pre-existing knowledge structure for interpreting event sequences' (Yule 2008: 134). Essentially, it entails a sequence of actions that is associated with a particular event or situation. One learns these scripts by way of observation and experience, that is, through enculturation.

In Tokyo, for example, a visit to a public bathhouse (sentō) might start with the payment of an entrance fee to the attendant, followed by disrobing in a change room that is reserved for members of one's sex. Then one may sit on a stool near faucets to wash. It is only after one is thoroughly clean, that one steps into the communal bath (same sex), which is usually quite hot. One may chat with other bathers or simply relax in silence. After soaking, one gets out of the water, rinses, dries off, gets dressed, and heads home. Embedded in this schema are notions of what is proper in this context. For individuals who are new to the sentō and not used to public nudity, this may be a shocking event! A trip to a public bathhouse in other parts of the world (e.g., Finland, Germany, Hungary, South Korea, Turkey) would not be the same experience due, in part, to different 'event sequences' or procedures that stem from variations in etiquette (norms of politeness) and attitudes toward such aspects as sex, gender, nudity, cleanliness, and communication. If unfamiliar with the prevailing 'cultural script', one may feel like a fish out of water.

Very often, a cultural script entails 'cultural rules of speaking'; that is, one learns to expect and use certain expressions (e.g., verbal/nonverbal forms of politeness) and other forms of discourse in particular situations. Scripts for particular situations and events may vary from one cultural context to another, as the following examples illustrate:

> *A Russian cultural script*
> [*Many* people think like this]
> when I feel (think) something
> I can say to other people what I feel (think)
> it will be good if someone else knows what I feel (think)

> *A Malay cultural script*
> [*Many* people think like this]
> when I feel (think) something
> I can't always say to other people what I feel (think)
> it will be good if I think about it before I say it.
> (Wierzbicka 2006: 308)

> *A high-level Anglo cultural script connected with 'personal autonomy'*
> [*Many* people think like this]
> When a person does something, it is good if this person can think about it like this:
> 'I am doing this because I want to do it'.
> (Goddard 2006: 6)

(N.B. The qualifier 'many' was added to draw attention to the fact that these understandings may be shared by many people in a particular context but not by everyone.)

Cultural scripts offer insight into localized assumptions and expectations about social inter-action but they are not definitive, prescriptions for real life events, as Goddard (2004: 7–8) explains:

> A cultural script is not intended as a description of actual behaviour, but as a depiction of shared assumptions about how people think about social interaction. Individuals may or may not follow the cultural guidelines; they may follow them in some situations but not in others; they may defy, subvert or play with them in various ways; but even those who reject or defy culturally endorsed modes of thinking and modes of action are nonetheless aware of them. It is in this sense that cultural scripts can be regarded as part of the inter-pretive backdrop of actual social interaction.

While cultural scripts can influence how particular encounters unfold in a specific setting, there will naturally be variations in the behavior (e.g., speech, nonverbal communication) of individ-uals, in part, due to differing levels of **sociopragmatic competence.** 'Sociopragmatic compe-tence in a language comprises more than linguistic and lexical knowledge. It implies that the speaker knows how to vary speech-act strategies according to the situational or social variables present in the act of communication' (Harlow 1990: 328). The sociocultural context and the status of the interlocutors will largely determine the appropriate form of a particular **speech act** (apology, request, refusal, etc.). Thus, the notion of sociopragmatic competence encompasses one's knowledge about the social distance, social status between the speakers involved, the cul-tural knowledge, and linguistic awareness. **Social distance** denotes 'the degree of closeness' or 'solidarity' between people (Swann *et al.* 2004: 288); **social status** refers to the honor or prestige attached to an individual's position in society. Over time, children develop an awareness of what actions are socially appropriate through observations, trial and error, and messages that they receive from others (e.g., elders, older siblings, teachers).

When an individual behaves in ways that deviate from accepted norms of behavior, social sanctions may be imposed. **Social sanctions** are 'the measures used by a society to enforce its rules of acceptable behavior' (Mosby 2009). For example, if children use profanity in class or when talking with their grandparents, they would likely be considered rude; for punishment, they might be verbally reprimanded or excluded from activities. Similar to values and beliefs, unwritten rules about what is acceptable behavior (actions and responses) can differ amongst cultures as well as *within* cultural groups. Among individuals and groups, both the intensity and significance of cultural norms are variable. This means that there are apt to be differences in the use of cultural scripts and expressions of politeness, including **honorifics** (a style of form of address that conveys respect toward a social superior). For example, in some contexts, individuals may be addressed using titles that reflect their occupation and status. In the United States, judges may be addressed as 'Your Honor' in courts of law or as 'Your Lordship' in Britain. In some languages (e.g., Japanese, Korean), honorifics are embedded in the grammar, with honorific stems added to verbs and some nouns, depending on the formality and position of the interlocutor. Newcomers who are unaware of the prevailing use of honorifics in a particular situation or context may unintentionally cause offense.

In the environment where we are born and raised, our culture 'facilitates entrée into a social system with its own commonplace – but not absolute – norms, values, and attitudes' (Komisarof & Hua 2016: 198); however, we may largely be unaware of the ways in which enculturation is influencing our ways of being. For this reason, many scholars describe our primary culture as 'invisible' or 'silent' (Furstenberg *et al.* 2001; Hall 1959, 1966; Kramsch 1993). Further, as today's world becomes increasingly interconnected and diverse, the number of children who are in contact with multiple languages and cultures, both at home and in the wider community, is becoming more common. Hence, the primary socialization process is increasingly multicultural and, in many cases, bi- or multilingual. (Second language socialization and acculturation are discussed in Chapter 7 when we explore intercultural transitions.)

Culture as shared

All of us live out our lives as members of groups. Initially, the groups to which we belong are decided by others (e.g., our parents and other elders). In our formative years, our family, community, religion (if any), school, and home country serve as sources for our primary cultural orientation, promoting certain beliefs, values, traditions, languages, and norms either directly or indirectly. As we mature and experience life, we gradually make more choices for ourselves.

This notion of culture as 'shared' among group members is conveyed in many definitions, including the one formulated by Lindsay *et al.* (1999: 26–7):

> Culture is everything you believe and everything you do that enables you to identify with people who are like you and that distinguishes you from people who differ from you. Culture is about groupness. A culture is a group of people identified by the shared history, values, and patterns of behavior.

This perspective draws attention to the idea of membership and community. It raises questions such as how people identify with particular groups/communities, how outsiders identify individuals with these groups/communities, and how different groups view and interact with others (Baldwin *et al*. 2006; Hecht *et al*. 2005).

Race

Cultures may be distinguished from one another by a wide variety of means such as geographical location, language, race, ethnicity, sexual orientation, religious or political affiliation, clothing, food, and so on. Definitions of **race** have varied over time and across cultures. Today, race is a very politically charged, controversial term that is often used interchangeably with 'ethnic group'. As Samovar *et al*. (2017) explain, race is 'a social construct arising from historical attempts to categorize people into different groups' (p. 248). Anthropologists originally divided people into groups (e.g., Caucasoid, Mongoloid, Negroid) based on physical appearance (e.g., skin color, facial features). Modern science, however, has found few genetic variations between members of 'different races' and with more interracial marriages, this classification system is regarded by many as obsolete.

> Most people think of 'race' as a biological category – as a way to divide and label different groups according to a set of common inborn biological traits (e.g., skin color, or shape of eyes, nose, and face). No consistent racial groupings emerge when people are sorted by physical and biological characteristics. For example, the epicanthic eye fold that produces the so-called "Asian" eye shape is shared by the Kung San Bushmen, members of an African nomadic tribe. Race is not a biological category, but it does have meaning as a social category. Different cultures classify people into racial groups according to a set of characteristics that are *socially* significant. The concept of race is especially potent when certain social groups are separated, treated as inferior or superior, and given differential access to power and other valued resources.
>
> (United States Department of Health and Human Services,
> Office of the Surgeon General 2001: 9)

While the term 'race' is still 'frequently used in everyday discourse in some parts of the world, cross-cultural psychologists Smith *et al*. (2006) argue that it has 'no defensible biological basis' (p. 278). Accordingly, they prefer to refer to ethnic identification in their research and practice.

Ethnicity

Similar to race, **ethnicity** is a social construct; however, it is 'a broader and more flexible cultural description than the biologically based or inflected categorization by race' (Brooker 2003: 92). In the United States, many contemporary scholars refer to 'ethnic groups' instead of race when discussing groups such as African Americans, Asian Americans, or Hispanics (Samovar *et al*. 2017; van de Vijver 2018a).

Zenner (1996: 393–4) defines an **ethnic group** as 'a group of people of the same descent and heritage who share a common and distinctive culture passed on through generations'. **Heritage** refers to aspects that are inherited or linked to the past (e.g., language, rituals, preferences for music, certain foods, dress). Ethnic groups may be distinguished by a wide range of characteristics, such as ancestry, language or accent, customs or traditions, physical features, a common sense of history, family names, diet, forms of dress, and religion. Perceptions of ethnic differences are not inherited; they are learned. Examples of ethnic groups are Indigenous Australians, Italian Americans, Malays, and Chinese. Individuals of mixed heritage may not fit neatly into these categories and claim affiliation with more than one group. Alternatively, they may not feel connected to any ethnic group. (Racial, ethnic, and hybrid identities are discussed further in Chapter 5.)

Subcultures

As well as dominant cultures, numerous smaller cultures coexist in the same environment. Identifiable groups within the larger cultural context are referred to as subcultures, subgroups, or co-cultures. Liu *et al.* (2011: 293) define a **subculture** as '[t]he smaller, coherent collective groups that exist within a larger dominant culture and which are often distinctive because of race, social class, gender, etc.'. Subcultures may also be delimited by age (e.g., youth culture, Generation Z), appearance (e.g., dress, body piercings), behavior (e.g., geeks, nerds), language (e.g., use of slang, terminology, code-mixing), nonverbal actions (e.g., use of certain gestures), physical disability (e.g., deaf culture), profession (e.g., legal culture, business culture), sports (e.g., football culture), technology (e.g., online/digital culture), and many other attributes. Some scholars prefer to use the term **co-culture** to make it clear that no one culture is inherently superior to others.

Closely related to the notion of 'co-cultures', is Holliday's (2011) conception of 'small and large cultures'. In his framework, 'large' refers to generalized, monolithic concepts of ethnic, national, or international cultures and 'small' denotes the multiple cohesive social groupings we engage with daily and which are 'the basic cultural entities from which all other cultural realities grow' (p. 3). The latter is a good fit with Kramsch's (1998) depiction of subcultures as 'a discourse community that shares a common social space and history, and common imaginings' (p. 10).

Speech communities

A **speech community** refers to a group of people or 'individuals who share the same language variety, and have shared ways of interpreting and using that language' (Stanlaw *et al.* 2018: 380). Speech communities typically share vocabulary and grammatical conventions, speech styles and genres, and norms for how and when to speak in certain contexts. Accordingly, Senft (2009: 6) refers to language as 'a mirror of the culture of its speech community'. Membership in a speech community is acquired through 'local knowledge of the way language choice, variation, and discourse represents generation, occupation, politics, social relationships, identity, etc.' (Morgan 2006). It is through living and interacting together that people in a speech community come to understand and share a particular set of norms for language use. Put another way, they develop **sociopragmatic awareness**, that is, that is the awareness about how and why language is used in certain ways in a particular sociocultural context. Through this process, individuals learn how to function in ways that are deemed appropriate in specific situations in their environment. Thus, speech communities may emerge among any groups that interact frequently and share certain norms and belief systems.

Ingroups and outgroups

Individuals tend to be aware of 'the critical attributes of the group with which they identify' (Fortman & Giles 2006: 96). In other words, we usually know rather quickly whether we are 'insiders' or 'outsiders' in relation to a particular group or community. We may have a strong sense of belonging and feel at easy when in the company of certain people (our 'ingroup'), whereas we may sense little or no personal connection to outsiders. In some situations, we may experience resistance or rejection in the company of outgroup members, which intensifies our connection to our ingroup. **Ingroups** refer to groups that we feel emotionally attached to (e.g., family, cultural or ethnic group members, a religious group), whereas, **outgroups** are groups that you feel distant from and may even feel in competition with when there are limited resources.

Individuals are not entirely free to move in and out of groups/subgroups at will. One's religious or political affiliation, gender, age, socioeconomic status, ethnicity, physical appearance (e.g., dress, adornments such as tattoos and body piercings, skin color, disability), and other attributes/aspects may exclude one from becoming a member of a particular cultural group or community. Language may also play a leading role in enabling or negotiating entry. For instance, one's **accent** (the way one pronounces words when one speaks) or **dialect** (variety of language used in a specific region) can signify and reinforce membership in a particular group. These same linguistic features may also serve as a barrier in other situations and prevent individuals from being accepted by other groups or communities.

In Hong Kong, speaking Cantonese can serve as glue to bond local Chinese youth and distinguish them from Mainland Chinese who speak Putonghua (Mandarin) and expatriates (e.g., American-born Chinese) who speak English. In some informal contexts the use of English by local Cantonese speakers is frowned upon; those who insist on conversing in this second (or third) language risk being labeled as 'weird' or branded as 'show-offs' by their Chinese peers (Jackson 2010). Fear of being 'out-grouped', that is, being rejected or rebuked by members of one's cultural group (one's 'ingroup'), can compel people to conform (e.g., adhere to familiar cultural scripts; use a certain language, accent, or dialect). The desire to fit in and nurture one's sense of belonging in a group can be powerful motivating factors in many contexts, whereas in other settings, individuals may be less concerned about standing out.

As explained in the previous section, cultures as groups adopt particular practices and behavior (e.g., linguistic codes, cultural scripts, etiquette) which involve explicit or implicit rules and codes of conduct that are generally understood and shared by members. Even if one adopts these practices, however, one may not be welcomed or accepted by other members either formally or informally. Membership is not solely in the hands of the potential participant; it is subject to the varied and subtle ways in which the group chooses to accept or reject members. Receptivity to new group members can vary significantly from one cultural context to another.

Discourse communities

As we grow, learn another language, travel or study abroad, join the work force, and interact with people from other cultures, subcultures, and/or speech communities, we become members of diverse groups. For example, we may join multiple **discourse communities**, which Hewings and Hewings (2005) define as 'groups of people who share particular registers and use the kinds of text (both spoken and written) in which these registers occur' (p. 37). **Registers** are 'linguistically distinct varieties in which the language is systematically determined by the context' (Davies 2005: 114). For example, environmental engineers, business executives, English for Specific Purposes (ESP) teachers, golf enthusiasts, and writing specialists tend to use a particular register when interacting with peers. Naturally, within each of these communities, there will also be individual variations in cultural practices (e.g., discourse, communication styles), an element that is discussed further in Chapter 3.

Whereas 'speech communities' are 'sociolinguistic groupings with communicative needs such as socialisation and group solidarity', 'discourse communities' are 'groupings based on common interests' (Swann *et al.* 2004: 84–5). Applied linguists from Australia, Taiwan, Spain, and Egypt could belong to the same discourse community (e.g., be affiliated with the same professional group), though they may individually be members of four distinct speech communities (e.g., Australian English, Taiwanese Hokkien, Spanish, Egyptian Arabic).

As we join more groups and become exposed to diverse ways of being, further layers or levels may be added to the complex cultural mix that forms our evolving sense of self. (The complex relationship between language, identity [e.g., cultural, ethnic, hybrid, linguistic, personal, racial, social], and belongingness [e.g., group membership] is explored in more detail in Chapter 5.)

Culture as relative

> The reason man does not experience his true cultural self is that until he experiences another self as valid, he has little basis for validating his own self. A way to experience another group is to understand and accept the way their minds work. This is not easy. In fact, it is extraordinarily difficult, but it is of the essence of cultural understanding.
>
> (Hall 1976: 213)

The notion of 'culture as relative' refers to the belief that a culture can really only be understood or appreciated when reference is made to another. As mentioned earlier, one's primary culture is sometimes described as 'invisible', as much of what we have learned from our parents (and other members of our community) is below our level of awareness and simply accepted as 'normal' (e.g., beliefs, cultural scripts, values).

Agar (2006: 8) maintains that 'culture becomes visible only when differences appear with reference to a newcomer, an outsider who came into contact with it'. This means that our cultural frameworks may remain largely unexamined until we encounter other ways of being. This exposure can raise our awareness of unique aspects of our cultural group(s). Initially, we may only notice visible differences (e.g., dress, food, language). Gradually, with more intercultural contact *and* critical reflection, we are apt to become more aware of less obvious aspects that differ from what we have grown accustomed to (e.g., different beliefs, practices, values, worldviews, linguistic norms of politeness). Through this process of discovery, we begin to understand that culture is not an absolute concept. Rather, it is relative, that is, culture may only be truly understood in relation to another.

Ethnocentricism

The natural process of contrasting and comparing cultures can be helpful in raising awareness of ourselves as cultural beings, while simultaneously learning about other perspectives and ways of life. It can also be highly problematic, however, as there is a natural tendency to resort to an 'us' vs. 'them' perspective, whereby 'us' is viewed very favorably (e.g., the home culture, familiar ways of being) and the unfamiliar is continuously cast in a negative light (or vice versa). In this state, ethnocentric discourse, like the following, usually prevails: '*We*'re always so polite but *those people* are just plain rude. . . . Why are they doing it that way?! Those guys are really weird!'). **Ethnocentricism** is defined by Neuliep (2018a) as 'the natural tendency to employ the values, attitudes, beliefs, and behaviors of one's own cultural or ethnic group as the standard to judge and evaluate other cultural and ethnic groups' (p. 752). An **ethnocentric** or **monocultural mindset** does not foster the respect that is essential for cordial intercultural relations.

When encountering cultural difference, individuals may make snap judgments about unfamiliar behaviors and resort to a '**culture as nation' perspective**, that is, 'a view of peoples within national boundaries as essentially homogeneous, possessing certain core characteristics' (Martin *et al.* 2012: 18). For instance, at the beginning of a semester-long sojourn in Madrid, Singaporean exchange students may observe the boisterous behavior of a few local teenagers who are drinking alcohol and conclude that all Spanish youth are loud, jovial alcoholics. In case discussions at a Swedish university, local business students may note the reticence of a few Chinese exchange students and decide that all Asian students are shy and lacking in confidence. In both scenarios, the observers are making assumptions about the behaviors of others, which may be quite inaccurate. Not all Spanish teenagers drink alcohol to excess; many are very quiet. The Chinese business students may have different notions of participation and may be actively engaged in the discussion by listening attentively. They may also be very outgoing, self-assured, and expressive in their first language when hanging out with their friends outside of class.

In these examples, the observers are using very broad categories (e.g., Spanish youth, 'Asian' students) and making sweeping generalizations, ignoring individual variations. They are overlooking the very real possibility that they have misinterpreted the behavior they have witnessed. The Singaporean and Swedish students are also assuming that the way they behave and the way people from 'the other cultural group' act are common to all members of their respective cultural groups.

In both scenarios, the observers are using a contrastive approach to try to make sense of unfamiliar behaviors. Without critical awareness, however, this approach may reduce culture to monolithic, static categories, ignoring the diversity within. **Essentialism** and **reductionism** occur 'when one treats a heterogenous collection as homogenous' (Holliday 2012; Holmes 2012), e.g., 'as if, all those of a single nation or even subgroup have the same cultural characteristics. This obscures the differences within culture. Second, these definitions can obscure the dynamic nature of culture' (Hecht *et al.* 2006: 56). With limited intercultural awareness and sensitivity, individuals may resort to using even broader categories (e.g., regional, ethnic) to label people (e.g., Asians are . . . Arabs are . . . Africans are . . . etc.). (See Chapter 6 for more discussion about the roots of and negative consequences of stereotyping.)

Ethnorelativism

As we live in an increasingly diverse world, it is important for all of us to negotiate intercultural encounters with an open mind. For this reason, many interculturalists advocate the development of an ethnorelative perspective.

> Fundamental to **ethnorelativism** is the assumption that cultures can only be understood relative to one another and that particular behavior can only be understood within a cultural context. There is no absolute standard of rightness or "goodness" that can be applied

to cultural behavior. Cultural difference is neither good nor bad, it is just different. . . . One's own culture is not any more central to reality than any other culture, although it may be preferable to a particular individual or group.

(Bennett 1993: 46)

An **ethnorelative mindset** is basically the opposite of an ethnocentric stance. In the former, the experience of one's own beliefs and behaviors is recognized as just one version of reality among many other possibilities. An ethnorelative orientation does not mean that one must accept all cultural differences or no longer prefer a particular worldview. In contrast with an ethnocentric perspective, however, it does imply that 'ethical choices will be made on grounds other than the ethnocentric protection of one's own worldview or in the name of absolute principles' (Bennett 1993: 46). Ethical reasoning and choice should begin with an open mindset and be informed by knowledge of diverse cultural norms, practices, and worldviews, including our own. (Chapter 6 delves further into the dangers of essentializing cultures and identities by looking at the world through an ethnocentric or monocultural lens.)

Culture as dynamic and mediated

An essentialist perspective largely overlooks 'the dynamic nature of culture' (Hecht *et al.* 2006: 56). With more recognition of the complexity and sociopolitical nature of life, there has been a shift away from a product-oriented view of culture as static and unitary. Most scholars now regard culture as dynamic and mediated through discourse. Berger (1969), for example, argues that '[c]ulture must be continually produced and reproduced. . . . Its structures are, therefore, inherently precarious and predestined to change' (p. 6). Markus *et al.* (1996) reinforce this notion of culture as fluid and emergent through interaction in particular contexts:

Cultural influence does not just involve a straightforward transmission of the 'way to be.' If entering a conversation, it matters what the conversant brings to the conversation, and whether and how the cultural messages and imperatives are accepted, or rather resisted and contested.

(p. 863)

For this reason, Street (1993) and Scollon *et al.* (2012) prefer to depict culture as a verb. For these applied linguists, 'culture is not something that you think or possess or live inside of. It is something that you *do*. And the way that you do it might be different at different times and in different circumstances' (Scollon *et al.* 2012: 5). Culture is created and challenged through discourse. Thus, in their intercultural work, instead of focusing on cultural facts, products, artifacts, or patterns of thinking, these scholars examine 'people doing things' using systems of culture. For example, they conduct critical analyses of the discourse in intercultural business meetings in English with Chinese and American managers.

Scollon *et al.*'s (2012) view of culture contrasts sharply with Matthew Arnold's (1869) notion of people 'having culture' and Geert Hofstede's (1991) depiction of culture as 'software of the mind', that is, 'mental programming' or 'patterns of thinking, feeling, and potential acting which were learned throughout [one's] lifetime' (Hofstede 1991: 4). Hofstede (1991) maintains that the 'collective programming of the mind' distinguishes the members of one group of people from another. Nowadays, however, there is more recognition of the limitations of intercultural and cross-cultural research that 'categorizes people and characteristics as set, unchanging, and unconnected to issues of gender, class, and history' (Martin & Nakayama 2000: 61). Simply put, we can no longer ignore the dynamic, mediated nature of culture. Over time, all cultures shift and change in some ways and people are unique individuals.

Our own cultural profile is not fixed or static. Complex, varied, and dynamic, it continues to evolve as we mature and experience life (e.g., engage in intercultural discourse, live abroad). As Skelton and Allen (1999: 4) explain, 'any one individual's experience of culture will be affected by the multiple aspects of their identity – race, gender, sex, age, sexuality, class, caste position, religion, geography, and so forth – and it is likely to alter in various circumstances'. (See Chapter 5 for a discussion of identity in relation to intercultural communication.)

When we encounter people who have been socialized in other linguistic and cultural environments, we are naturally exposed to unfamiliar ways of being (e.g., discourse, cultural scripts, nonverbal codes, worldviews). This contact need not be face to face; in today's interconnected world, we may also participate in online cultures (e.g., chat rooms, Facebook). All of these experiences will be filtered by our frame of reference, which draws on our cultural knowledge and life experiences. **Intercultural interaction** (e.g., communication with individuals associated with a different subculture, speech community or discourse community, etc.) offers the potential for further self-expansion, *if* we are genuinely open to this possibility.

Culture as individual, fragmentary, and imaginary

Culture is a variable concept. Within cultural groups, perceptions of cultural elements vary from individual to individual. Even the ways we choose to display our cultural membership may differ. A particular language/dialect or our choice of dress may be used to mark our affiliation with a group. For example, the use of Welsh in Wales or Gaelic in Ireland can serve as powerful markers of one's cultural identity.

Referring to culture 'as a process not a thing', Freadman (2004) argues that 'what we call our "own" culture is incomplete and fragmentary', explaining that it is 'traversed by ignorance' and 'imperfectly owned' (p. 16). An individual's interpretation of his or her own culture (or subgroup) will necessarily be subjective, personal, and partial. New cultural insights and understandings that arise as we learn and grow will always be subject to filtering by each individual. Further, we can never fully grasp all of the knowledge and practices associated with any cultural group that we belong to. Our understandings of 'our culture' (any cultural group that we belong to) are incomplete and dependent on our experience, level of cultural knowledge and awareness, and our individual point of view.

Culture is variable and continuously produced through discourse and nonverbal means. Language interaction is central to how culture evolves within and between groups at every level (Scollon *et al.* 2012). As Geertz (1973) explains, social reality is constantly being constructed and mediated by individuals through the exchange of messages in particular sociocultural contexts. These messages may be transmitted through both verbal and nonverbal means.

Benedict Anderson, an international studies scholar, coined the term **imagined community**, which helps us to understand how notions of culture are socially constructed and subject to individual interpretation. Anderson (1983, 1991, 2006) refers to nationhood and national identity as socially constructed images that are 'imagined' by people. As none of us will ever meet the vast majority of members of the nation in which we live, he questions how we can regard ourselves and others as belonging to a particular 'national culture'. What does 'national culture' actually mean? Anderson (1983, 1991, 2006) suggests that we belong to an 'imagined community' in which we *assume* that other members follow norms, practices, and beliefs similar to our own. People who belong to the same religion or gender, or share a common language, descent and/or history (e.g., an ethnic group) may also feel or *imagine* this sense of community or nationhood.

Along similar lines, Moon (2008) challenges conceptions of 'culture as nation', in which 'differences within national boundaries, ethnic groups, genders, and races are obscured, and hegemonic notions of "culture" are presented as "shared" by all cultural members' (p. 17). **Hegemony** refers to 'domination through consent where the goals, ideas, and interests of the ruling group or class are so thoroughly normalized, institutionalized, and accepted people consent to their own domination, subordination, and exploitation' (Sorrells 2016: 258). Within the contexts of nations, there may be strong political agendas and forces (overt or covert), which push nationals to perceive of themselves as possessing common traits and agendas (e.g., a 'national culture').

In reality, culture is multiple, complex, variable, and layered. It is also imagined and subject to individual interpretation and enactment. Therefore, a nuanced understanding of culture is needed. As Hecht *et al.* (2006: 56) warn, 'structural definitions of culture, especially those that frame culture merely as a list of aspects, run the risk of essentializing cultures'. Critical intercultural communication scholars argue that the unit of analysis should not be limited to a single national culture, largely ignoring diversity within subgroups or co-cultures as well as among individuals (Martin & Nakayama 2018a; Holliday 2019). In today's increasingly interconnected, relativistic world, cultural boundaries are becoming blurred and intermingled, which make the homogenizing notion of 'national cultures' obsolete. In many intercultural communication texts, however, national groups (or even people who live on the same continent) are still treated as homogeneous, as if all members have the same cultural characteristics. For example, Asians are often portrayed as passive collectivists, while Americans and Australians are depicted as proactive individualists with little concern for family. (See Chapter 6 for more on stereotypes and ways to reduce the common tendency to engage in this practice.)

Culture as contested

Notions of culture as contested or subject to different, sometimes conflicting, interpretations have emerged from such scholarly areas as critical pedagogy, critical theory, and cultural studies, as well as postmodernist thought in relation to culture (Baldwin *et al.* 2006; Nakayama & Martin 2018). From this perspective, culture is viewed as 'an apparatus of power within a larger system of domination where meanings are constantly negotiated' (Sorrells 2016: 255). Giroux (1988: 171), an American cultural critic, refers to culture as:

> the representation of lived experiences, material artefacts, and practices forged within the unequal and dialectical relations that different groups establish in a given society at a particular historical point. In this case, culture is closely related to the dynamics of power and produces asymmetries in the ability of individuals and groups to define and achieve their goals. Furthermore, culture is also an arena of struggle and contradiction, and there is no one culture in the homogeneous sense. On the contrary, there are dominant and subordinate cultures that express different interests and operate from different and unequal terrains of power.

Moving away from a product-oriented, static, and unitary perspective of culture, there is growing recognition among scholars that culture is multiple and contested at many levels, both externally and from within. It may be contested at the level of the nation state (e.g., protests against long-established cultural practices and beliefs, differing imaginings of what constitutes 'national culture') or within subgroups (e.g., rejection of particular forms of verbal or non-verbal behavior, differing understandings of what membership means). Culture may also be contested at the discourse level (e.g., differing conceptions and use of terms, expressions, communication styles). At the individual level, one may also question one's values and practices when encountering cultural difference. For these reasons, Giroux (1988: 97) depicts culture 'as a terrain of struggle'.

Critical scholars, such as Giroux (1988), Holliday (2012, 2019), and Sorrells (2012, 2016), among others, recognize that human behavior (e.g., communication) is always constrained by societal structures (e.g., political hierarchies, the legal system, the economic system, the educational system, religious hierarchies (ranked clergy), family structures, the healthcare system, language policies, etc.), which may privilege some individuals and disadvantage others. 'Culture is not a benignly socially constructed variable, but a site of struggle where various communication meanings are contested within social hierarchies' (Martin *et al.* 2012: 28). Cultural systems may categorize people according to language, race, social or economic status, etc., resulting in an unequal distribution of power, privilege, and resources.

Critical discourse analysts investigate the ways in which discourse practices reproduce and/or transform power relations within cultural groups (Fairclough 2010; Scollon *et al.* 2012). **Discourse** here refers to 'particular uses of language in context' as well as 'the world views and ideologies which are implicit or explicit in such uses' (Swann *et al.* 2004: 83). **Critical discourse analysis (CDA)** is an interdisciplinary form of discourse analysis which has 'the clear political aim of attempting to reveal connections of hidden relationships encoded in language that may not be immediately evident, in order to bring about social change' (Llamas *et al.* 2007: 210). Critical discourse analysts often explore the social practices and interactions of disadvantaged groups such as minorities (e.g., the discourse of second language immigrant children and teachers from the majority culture in an inner city school in New York). Ultimately, the aim of their work is to bring about positive change (e.g., identify constructive ways to enhance the education of minority members).

Power (unequal relations between individuals and groups) (Schirato and Yell 2000: 191) is an element that cannot be overlooked when discussing culture. '**Power relations** (an imbalance of power between individuals or groups) are arguably part of every communicative event or practice, and every social relation, whether or not they are explicitly or overtly at stake' (ibid: 191). Consequently, critical interculturalists view culture as 'a site of struggle' between the discourses and ideologies of the interactants (Moon 2010; Nakayama & Martin 2018). **Ideology** is 'a system of ideas which promote the interests of a particular group of people' (Holliday 2011: 198). (In relation to communication, power is discussed further in Chapter 3.)

Culture is not simply passed from one generation to the next; rather it is 'a contested zone' in which different groups struggle to define issues with their own interests in mind (Nakayama & Martin 2018). Consequently, Hannerz (1996) describes cultures as dynamic 'organizations of diversity' that intersect national and regional boundaries. This conception of culture 'simultaneously acknowledges the overlapping nature (i.e., sharedness) of various cultural realities within the same geographical space, while recognizing that cultural realities always have some degree of difference' (Moon 2002: 15–16).

When you learn another language, interact with people who have been socialized in a different environment, or move to another country to live, your understandings of culture may be contested or challenged as you encounter differing belief systems, ideas, and values. As the unfamiliar is compared and contrasted with the familiar, both consciously and subconsciously, you may initially feel insecure about your place in the world. As Chapter 7 explains, you may experience disequilibrium or confusion while adjusting to a new environment. In this process of personal discovery and expansion, your beliefs, values, worldviews, and self-identities may be challenged, reoriented, and modified.

Culture as communication

> Culture is a code we learn and share, and learning and sharing require communication. And communication requires coding and symbols, which must be learned and shared. Communication and culture are inseparable.
>
> (Smith 1966: 7)

Culture is developed, shaped, transmitted, and learned through both verbal and nonverbal forms of communication. It is through the act of communication that cultural characteristics (e.g., customs, norms, roles, rituals, laws) are created and shared by humans. Individuals may not set out to create a culture when they interact in relationships, groups, organizations, or societies, but cultures naturally take shape and evolve through social discourse and interaction. Communication and communication media make it possible to preserve and pass along cultural elements from one place and time to another (e.g., from one generation to the next).

The reverse is also true; that is, communication practices are largely created, shaped, and transmitted by culture. Over time, through communication and interaction, members of a culture develop history, patterns, customs, and rituals that distinguish them from other groups and influence how they interact with each other as well as outsiders. While creating this set of shared experiences, group members develop specific ways of communicating verbally and nonverbally (e.g., discourse norms, cultural scripts). Consequently, E.T. Hall (1959: 186) states that 'Culture is communication and communication is culture'. The communication-culture relationship, which is by nature very complex and personal, is explored in more detail in the next chapter.

THE TEXT'S CONCEPTION OF CULTURE

The conception of culture that prevails in the remainder of this text draws on the many facets described herein, with an emphasis on contemporary, critical notions. Culture, in part, involves membership in a community or group that shares a common history, traditions, norms, and imaginings in a particular **cultural space** (e.g., a neighborhood, region, virtual space). Much of this is below our level of awareness and may not become apparent until we encounter cultural difference. In other words, culture is relative.

Culture is not just about the group, however. Recognizing the perspective of the individual in relation to the group is also an important dimension of the culture concept. In addition to being a manifestation of a group or community, culture is subject to an individual's unique experience within it, or apart from it. Culture is dynamic, multiple, and contested. It is a very complex construct that is difficult to pin down.

SUMMARY

The purpose of this chapter was to introduce the concept of culture and the process of language and cultural socialization to lay the foundation for the remainder of the text. We examined many definitions and conceptions of culture, and considered some important qualities or dimensions associated with it (culture as learned; culture as shared (group membership); culture as relative; culture as dynamic and mediated; culture as individual, fragmentary, and imaginary; culture as contested; and culture as communication). It will be helpful to keep these dimensions in mind when digesting the chapters that follow.

discussion questions

1   In relation to intercultural communication studies, why is it important to reflect on your understanding of culture? Discuss your ideas with a partner.
2   What are the limitations and potential dangers of the 'culture as nation' perspective?
3   Define subculture and co-culture. Discuss examples of subcultures/co-cultures that you are familiar with in your context. What are some ways in which membership is enacted?
4   Giroux (1988) describes culture as 'an arena of struggle and contradiction'. With a partner, discuss the meaning of this statement and provide relevant examples in contexts that you are familiar with.
5   What does Senft (2009) mean when he says that '[l]anguage is a mirror of the culture of its speech community' (p. 6)? Can you think of examples to support this view? Discuss your ideas with a partner.
6   How are culture and communication related?

activities

1   This chapter has presented many definitions of culture. Write your own and explain why you have included certain elements.
2   Compare and contrast the following conceptions of culture. Which of the definitions (or elements in the definitions) do you feel are the most useful? Are there aspects that you disagree with or find confusing?

   a   'Culture is the fabric of meaning in terms of which human beings interpret their experience and guide their action' (Geertz 1973: 24).
   b   'Culture is a verb' (Scollon *et al.* 2012: 5).

    c   Culture is 'the totality of communication practices and systems of meaning' (Schirato & Yell 2000: 1)

    d   Culture is 'the collective programming of the human mind that distinguishes the members of one human group from those of another. Culture in this sense is a system of collectively held values' (Hofstede 1981: 24).

    e   Culture is 'the shared patterns of behaviors and interactions, cognitive constructs, and affective understanding that are learned through a process of socialization. These shared patterns identify the members of a culture group while also distinguishing those of another group' (Center for Advanced Research on Language Acquisition, CARLA), University of Minnesota, n.d.).

    f   Culture is 'the membership in a discourse community that shares a common social space and history, and a common system of standards for perceiving, believing, evaluating, and acting' (Kramsch 1998: 127).

    g   Culture is 'the process by which people make sense of their lives, a process always involved in struggles over meaning and representation' (Pennycook 1995: 47).

    h   'In action in social life, culture constitutes the unwritten rules of the social game' (Hofstede n.d.)

    i   'Culture is an ideological construct called into play by social actors to produce and reproduce social categories and boundaries' (Piller 2017: 10).

    j   Culture is 'the social cement of all human relationships; it is the medium in which we move and breathe and have our being' (Scovel 1994: 205).

3   Select an event that you are familiar with (e.g., a birthday party, a post-class meeting with a professor, a visit to a medical clinic, a tutorial) and identify a cultural script that is associated with it in your environment. Have you ever been to another cultural context, where a different cultural script was more common for a similar event? If yes, how did you react?

4   Identify an ethnic food dish in your environment that is new to you. (If you are studying abroad, you could go to a cafeteria, grocery store, market, restaurant, or canteen where that food is readily available and ask a server, cook, customer, or local friend about it and its significance in the host environment. If you live on campus, you could talk to someone in your hostel or dormitory who is cooking an ethnic dish that is unfamiliar to you.) Try the dish and share what you have learned with your classmates.

5   Meet with someone who has a different linguistic and cultural background from you. Identify three values (e.g., integrity, family, success) and share what they mean to each of you. Provide examples to illustrate and explain your ideas. In what ways do your values converge or differ?

6   Proverbs are phrases or sayings which encapsulate values that are prevalent in a culture at a particular time. Identify proverbs that are associated with your cultural context but are now outdated. In the United States, for example, the proverbs 'Children should be seen and not heard' and 'Spare the rod and spoil the child' do not represent contemporary values. In your examples, identify the values that have changed. What does this exercise suggest about culture and cultural change?

further reading

Baldwin, J.R., Faulkner, S.L., Hecht, M.L. and Lindsley, S.L. (eds.) (2006) *Redefining Culture: Perspectives Across the Disciplines*, Mahwah, NJ: Lawrence Erlbaum.

This volume presents over 300 definitions of culture from a wide array of disciplines. The authors examine how the definition of culture has changed historically.

Gardiner, H. (2018) *Lives Across Cultures: Cross-Cultural Human Development*, 6th edn, Harlow: Pearson.

Differences in the primary language and cultural socialization process in diverse cultural contexts are discussed.

Hall, E.T. (1976) *Beyond Culture*, New York: Anchor Books.

This book is written by the scholar who is regarded by many as the founding father of the scholarly field of intercultural communication. In this volume, he describes the many influences of culture on the way people live and interact, with a special emphasis on nonverbal codes.

Companion Website: Continue your journey online

Visit the Companion Website for a variety of tools and resources to support and extend your intercultural learning. (Instructors who are qualified adopters of the text may access additional resources on this site.)

CHAPTER 3

Language, communication, culture, and power in context

The way people communicate is the way they live. It is their culture. Who talks with whom? How? And about what? These are questions of communication and culture.

(Smith 1966: 1)

The fact is, when two or more languages come together, two or more peoples have come together and the result is always about power and identity.

(Morgan 2002: 12)

To be mindful intercultural communicators, we need the knowledge of both verbal and nonverbal communication in order to communicate sensitively across cultural and ethnic boundaries.

(Ting-Toomey & Dorjee 2019: 309)

learning objectives

By the end of this chapter, you should be able to:

1 Define communication
2 Describe the process of human communication
3 Identify nine properties of communication
4 Explain the relationship between language, communication, culture, power, and context
5 Identify and describe high-context and low-context verbal communication styles
6 Explain the communication accommodation theory (CAT) and the difference between 'convergence' and 'divergence'
7 Identify the elements in the audience design framework and explain its relationship to the CAT
8 Explain the merits and limitations of communication style typologies
9 Identify the traits and behaviors of an effective intercultural communicator

INTRODUCTION

As discussed in Chapter 2, the relationship between culture and communication is not straightforward, rather it is multifaceted, personal, and intertwined. Accordingly, E.T. Hall (1959: 186) famously states that 'Culture is communication and communication is culture'. To be an effective intercultural communicator, it is essential to understand the process of human communication and the impact of cultural dimensions and power in communicative events that take place within a particular environment.

To better understand the role of communication in intercultural interactions, this chapter examines the nature, properties, and components of communication. After reviewing the process of human communication, we examine individual and cultural variations in communication styles (e.g., direct, indirect, formal, informal). We primarily focus on verbal communication as the next chapter centers on nonverbal codes. Finally, we review the characteristics of an effective intercultural communicator in second language situations.

DEFINITIONS OF HUMAN COMMUNICATION

Similar to culture, human **communication** is difficult to define, and, over time, scholars have put forward a wide array of definitions. Table 3.1 presents some of the most common elements associated with communication, along with definitions that illustrate the dimension that is emphasized. As one might expect, there is some overlapping, with elements from one definition appearing in another.

Table 3.1 Properties and definitions of communication

1 Process	Communication is 'a symbolic process whereby reality is produced, maintained, repaired, and transformed' (Carey 1989: 23). 'Communication can be defined as the symbolic process by which we create meaning with others' (Moon 2002: 16).
2 Dynamic	'Because we view communication as a process, we also perceive it to be dynamic, ever-changing, and unending' (Barker & Barker 1993: 3). 'Communication is the process by which we understand others and in turn endeavor to be understood by them. It is dynamic, constantly changing and shifting in response to the total situation' (Anderson 1959: 5). 'Communication is dynamic. This means that communication is not a single event but is ongoing, so that communicators are at once both senders and receivers' (Martin & Nakayama 2008: 36).
3 Interactive/-transactive	Communication is 'message exchange between two or more people' (Guirdham 2011: 381). Communication is 'the process by which individuals try to exchange ideas, feelings, symbols, meanings to create commonality' (Schmidt et al. 2007: 59). 'Communication in face-to-face encounters can be seen as constituted by interactive exchanges of moves and countermoves involving speakers and listeners who actively co-operate in the joint production of meaningful interaction' (Gumperz & Cook-Gumperz 2012: 66).
4 Symbolic	Communication is 'the transmission of information, ideas, emotion, skills, etc., by the use of symbols – words, pictures, figures, graphs, etc. It is the act or process of transmission that is usually called communication' (Berelson & Steiner 1964: 527). 'The symbolic nature of communication means that the words we speak or the gestures we make have no inherent meaning. Rather, they gain their significance from an agreed-upon meaning. When we use symbols to communicate, we assume that the other person shares our symbol system . . . these symbolic meanings are conveyed both verbally and nonverbally' (Martin & Nakayama 2018b: 92).

5 Intentional and unintentional	'In the main, communication has as its central interest those behavioral situations in which a source transmits a message to a receiver(s) with conscious intent to affect the latter's behaviors' (Miller 1966: 92).
	'Unintentional messages are not purposeful, but may be transmitted by action as well as by words' (Tubbs 2009).
	'Communication does not have to be intentional. Some of the most important (and sometimes disastrous) communication occurs without the sender knowing a particular message has been sent' (Martin & Nakayama 2008: 36).
6 Situated and contextual	'Communication involves the creation, constitution, and intertwining of situated meanings, social practices, structures, discourses, and the nondiscursive' (Halualani & Nakayama 2010: 7).
	'Communication is dependent on the context in which it occurs' (Neuliep 2012: 14).
7 Pervasive	Communication is 'the process through which participants create and share information with one another as they move toward reaching mutual understanding. Communication is involved in every aspect of daily life, from birth to death. It is universal. Because communication is so pervasive, it is easy to take it for granted and even not to notice it' (Rogers & Steinfatt 1999: 113).
	'We cannot not communicate' (Watzlawick et al. 1967: 49).
	'If two humans come together it is virtually inevitable that they will communicate something to each other . . . even if they do not speak, messages will pass between them. By their looks, expressions and body movement each will tell the other something, even if it is only, "I don't wish to know you: keep your distance"; "I assure you the feeling is mutual. I'll keep clear if you do"' (Argyle & Trower 1979).
8 Power-infused	'Communication is the mechanism by which power is exerted' (Schacter 1951: 191).
	'Power is always present when we communicate with each other although it is not always evident or obvious' (Martin & Nakayama 2008: 48).
9 Cultural	'Culture is communication and communication is culture' (Hall 1959: 186).
	'Communication is a process of utilizing cultural resources' (Sorrells 2013: 10).
	'Every cultural practice is a communicative event' (Kress 1988: 10).

THE COMPONENTS OF HUMAN COMMUNICATION

Before we examine the properties of communication and their implications for intercultural interactions, it is helpful to identify the key components in the communication process. As illustrated in Figure 3.1, the basic elements are: sender, encoding, message, channel, noise (interference), receiver, decoding, receiver response, feedback, and context.

In this process model, the components may be defined as follows:

Sender: The person who is sending a message (verbally or nonverbally), which may be intentional or unintentional. A sender is 'someone with a need or desire, be it social, work, or public service to communicate with others' (McDaniel & Samovar 2015: 8).

Encoding: The process of putting an idea or message into a set of symbols (e.g., words, gestures).

Message: What is conveyed verbally (e.g., in speech, writing) or nonverbally from one person (the sender) to one or more persons (the receiver(s)). The form and content of the message may differ. In a spoken apology, for example, the *message form* is how the apology is made (e.g., type of sentence structure, use or nonuse of politeness discourse markers, type of intonation) and the *message content* is the substance of the apology (e.g., regret about an overdue assignment).

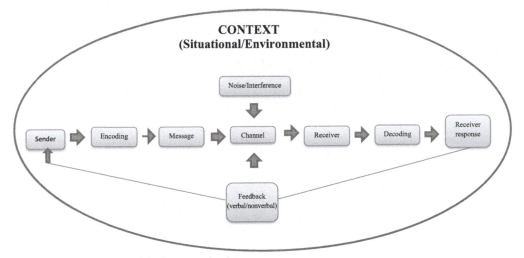

Figure 3.1 A process model of communication

Channel: The way in which a message is conveyed from one person to another. The most common channels or paths of communication are speech, writing, and nonverbal signals.

Noise (Interference): Any disturbance or defect which interferes with or distorts the transmission of the message from one person to another (e.g., background sounds, fatigue, lack of concentration on the message, feeling unwell, unfamiliar jargon, use of specialized professional terminology, a hearing impairment, an unfamiliar accent, etc.).

Receiver: The person (or persons) who is receiving the message that is being sent, whether intentional or not.

Decoding: The process by which the receiver tries to understand the meaning of a message that is being sent, that is, the receiver translates or interprets the meanings of the symbols.

Receiver response: The verbal or nonverbal reaction, if any, of the receiver after decoding the message.

Feedback: Verbal or nonverbal signals which receivers give to a speaker to indicate they have processed what the speaker has said (e.g., smiles, nods, grunts, comments). These may be intentional or unintentional (below the level of awareness of the sender).

Context: The overall environment in which the communication occurs (e.g., physical, psychological, sociocultural, political, sociorelational, etc.).

COMMUNICATION PROPERTIES

To better understand human communication and its implications for intercultural interactions, we now take a closer look at the key properties of communication that are identified in Table 3.1. When appropriate, reference is also made to Figure 3.1.

Property 1: Communication as a process

Most scholars view communication as a process, that is, it involves 'an interrelated, interdependent group of elements working together to achieve a desired outcome or goal' (Barker & Barker

1993: 10). As Figure 3.1 illustrates, the communication process entails multiple components and steps (e.g., people who are sending and receiving a message, the ideas and emotions that are being communicated, the channel through which the communication takes place, the context).

Although individual (verbal/nonverbal) messages and interactions have definite beginnings and endings (e.g., greetings and words of farewell), the overall process of communication does not. How two individuals interact with each other on a particular day is very much influenced by how they interacted previously. As a Russian proverb says, 'Once a word goes out of your mouth, you can never swallow it again'.

Think about the last time you had a disagreement with one of your friends. You may have said some things that you now regret. Communication, however, is irreversible. You cannot take back what you have said or done. An apology may soothe hurt feelings and help repair the relationship; however, expressions of regret cannot erase past interactions (e.g., previous verbal and nonverbal behavior). This also means that the messages you communicate now can affect your interpersonal relationships and future interactions.

This communication process also applies to intercultural interactions. When you are interacting with someone who has been socialized in a different linguistic and cultural environment, the history you are developing together impacts any communication that you have today and in the future. When the communication process goes well and both speaker and receiver feel respected and understood, relationships are enhanced. Conversely, when the communication process is unsuccessful (e.g., 'noise' interferes with the message), misunderstandings may occur, which adversely affect the interpersonal relationship and curb the desire for further contact. Hence, the communication process influences interpersonal relations (e.g., relationship building). (This element that is discussed in more detail in Chapter 8.)

Property 2: Communication as dynamic

Communication, like culture, is characterized by energy or action; it is always developing and never passive or static. A model, like the one depicted in Figure 3.1, can identify the elements involved in communication; however, because communication is a flexible, dynamic, and adaptive process, it is not possible to fully capture its essence in a graphic model or written definition. At best, models are representations that raise our awareness of the complexity of the steps and elements involved.

In intercultural interactions, the various elements in the communication process are also interdependent, variable, and dynamic. In addition to being irreversible, intercultural communication is time-bound and flexible. No two interactions will be exactly alike. Factors such as time, location, topic, and circumstances (e.g., attitudes toward the other communicator, the tenor and quality of the previous communication) influence the dynamic communication process, rendering it complex and impossible to replicate.

Property 3: Communication as interactive and transactive

Although people may engage in **intrapersonal communication**, that is, they may talk to themselves (e.g., work through ideas in their head or out loud), most scholars maintain that a fundamental dimension of communication is interaction between two or more people. Active participation means that people are consciously directing their messages to someone else. Thus, the communication is **transactive**. Because individuals both send and receive (and interpret) messages, communication is a two-way process; this makes it **interactive**, as illustrated by the multi-directional arrows in Figure 3.1. Face-to-face communication entails 'interactive exchanges of moves and countermoves involving speakers and listeners who actively co-operate in the joint production of meaningful interaction' (Gumperz & Cook-Gumperz 2012: 66).

In a communicative event, you may send verbal and nonverbal messages to another person, who is likewise communicating thoughts, ideas, and emotions to you. The receiver's body language, facial expression, eye contact, and tone in her voice give you an indication of how your message is being received and interpreted. Thus, as the model shows, each person in an interactional setting simultaneously sends (encodes) and receives (decodes) messages.

Consider the following scenario. Your friends have just seen *Roma*; they give the movie a glowing review and encourage you to go and see it. When they are speaking, it is clear to you that they are sending you messages (e.g., recommending that you see the movie). Even if you do not utter a single word, you are transmitting messages to them, although you may not be aware you are doing so. For example, your eye contact, smiles (or frowns), raised eyebrows, and other nonverbal reactions are communicating your interest (or disinterest) in what is being said. Both you and your friends are sending and receiving messages simultaneously. If you have a shared history and have been socialized in a similar linguistic and cultural environment, you may understand one another quite easily. When you interact, you may not even need to finish each other's sentences. What happens, however, when the communicators do not share these common understandings?

If you are interacting with someone who is not fluent in the language that you are using and unfamiliar with the cultural environment where the conversation is taking place, the verbal messages you are sending may be misunderstood. As Gumperz and Cook-Gumperz (2012) explain, in many intercultural communicative events, 'inferences necessary to understand it [the message] rest on familiarity with a complex body of social relational assumptions that reveal culturally specific knowledge acquired through participation' (p. 66). What this means is that the possibility of miscommunication may rise if the receiver has been socialized in a different cultural context and does not share the same background knowledge as you. Your communication partner may understand the words but not the intended meaning. Nonverbal signals may also be misinterpreted or ignored.

If you are using a second language in unfamiliar situations in a cultural context that is new to you, you may become quite frustrated at times and feel misunderstood by locals. As you become more proficient in the language and more knowledgeable about the cultural context and prevailing **sociopragmatic norms** (rules governing the appropriate use of discourse in social situations), the transmission and decoding of messages should become much easier and more efficient. Familiarity with the prevalent **cultural scripts** (local conventions of discourse), politeness markers, and nonverbal codes that are prevalent in particular settings may ease your anxiety and help you to make communication choices that are more appropriate. This awareness can facilitate both interactive and transactive dimensions of communication. As Ting-Toomey and Dorjee (2019) observe, '[t]o be mindful intercultural communicators, we need the knowledge of both verbal and nonverbal communication in order to communicate sensitively across cultural and ethnic boundaries' (p. 309).

Property 4: Communication is symbolic

Communication is also symbolic. A **symbol** is a sign, word(s), gesture, or other nonverbal behavior that represents something meaningful to people in a particular linguistic and cultural context. It is during the primary socialization process that these verbal and nonverbal symbols are learned. Through language or gestures and other forms of nonverbal communication individuals convey their emotions and ideas to another person. Outside of this environment, these symbols may mean something different or nothing at all. Consequently, symbols may easily be misunderstood or simply overlooked in intercultural interactions.

Among the symbols, it is the use of words that distinguishes humans from other animals. Kress (1988: 183) observes that language is 'the most fully articulated of all media of human communication'. **Language** is 'a system comprised of vocabulary and rules of grammar that allows us to engage in verbal communication' (West & Turner 2011a: G-6). A verbal language (e.g., Arabic, Chinese, English, Russian) is a code made up of symbols. For example, the letters of the English alphabet (e.g., 'a, b, c') are a set of symbols that represent sounds. When we combine individual symbols into words (e.g., 'h+o+u+s+e'), they become meaningful to English speakers. By using symbols, people can represent their thoughts and ideas orally or through writing. Once an idea has been encoded with symbols, it becomes a message, following the process displayed in Figure 3.1. When verbal communication is employed, people ('senders') encode their thoughts and send them to someone else (the receiver) in the form of words, which may be accompanied by nonverbal behaviors. The individual then listens to the verbal message and translates or decodes it along with nonverbal information. **Interaction**, then, is the process of encoding and decoding messages. While people who speak different languages may use different codes, the process is the same.

Some languages are '**phonetic**', that is, there is a direct relationship between the spelling (symbol) and the sound, as in Slavic languages, for example. That means you can look at a written word and know how to pronounce it, or you can hear a word and know how to spell it. Other languages (e.g., Chinese, Japanese) are not phonetic; there is no relationship between the written symbols and the way you say the words.

Plate 3.1   These signs may easily be understood by a Spaniard but mystify newcomers who are unfamiliar with Spanish language and culture. © Jane Jackson

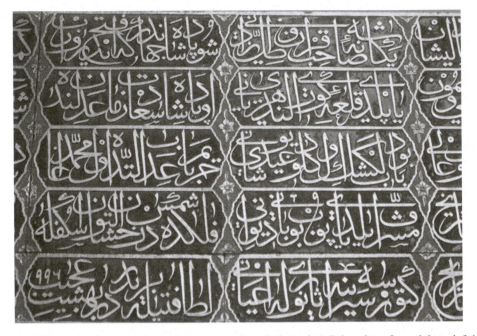

Plate 3.2   The Arabic language is a code made up of symbols (script). It is written from right to left in a cursive style and includes 28 letters. © Jane Jackson

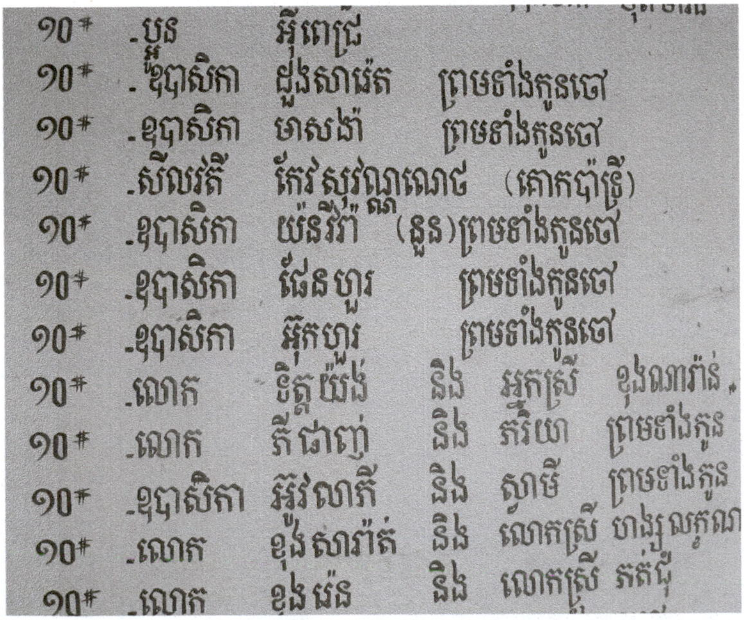

Plate 3.3   Khmer, the primary language of Cambodia, is written left to right, similar to Thai and Lao, the languages spoken in Thailand and Laos, respectively. © Jane Jackson

To facilitate the second language learning of phonetic languages, the International Phonetic Association devised the **International Phonetic Alphabet (IPA)**, an alphabetic system of phonetic notation based primarily on the Latin alphabet (International Phonetic Association n.d.). The IPA represents the qualities of speech that are distinctive in spoken language: phonemes, intonation, and the separation of words and syllables. It serves as a standardized representation of the sounds of spoken language, and is widely used today by linguists, translators, and foreign language speakers. This system aids intercultural communication by helping second language speakers express themselves in ways that are comprehensible to others.

Human languages also use different linguistic codes or symbols for writing. In English, for example, the verbal symbols (letters) that form the word 'h+o+u+s+e' have no natural connection with 'a building that serves as living quarters for one or a few families' (Merriam-Webster Online n.d., b). In other languages, as Figure 3.2 illustrates, different symbols (e.g., letters, characters) have been arbitrarily chosen to signify the meaning of 'house'. Moreover, what this actually means in different cultural settings varies, depending, in part, on the experiences of the people in that particular context. For example, when Filipinos say the Tagalog word for 'house' ('bahay'), they may visualize something quite different from first language speakers of English in Scotland, or Arabic speakers in the Sudan who say the word for 'house' in their first language. In other words, conceptions may vary along with the words (symbols) used.

Language	Original form/ script	Transliteration (if the Roman alphabet is not used)	Illustrations of a 'house' (many possibilities in different cultural contexts)
Arabic	بَيْت	beyt	
Chinese	家	Jiā	
French	maison		
German	haus		
Hebrew	תיב	Beit	
Hindi	घर	ghar	
Italian	casa		
Japanese	宅	taku	
Korean	집	Jip	
Norwegian	hus		
Polish	dom		
Portugese	casa		
Russian	дом	dohm	
Slovenia	hiša		
Swahili		nyumba	
Swedish	hus		
Tagalog	bahay		
Urdu	مكان	makaan	

Figure 3.2 Linguistic codes/symbols for the word 'house'

Similar to language, **nonverbal codes** (e.g., gestures) are arbitrary. Raising your fist in the air with knuckles pointed outward is an expression of victory in Argentina. In Britain, however, the sign for victory is an erect forefinger and middle finger in the shape of the letter V. This same movement symbolizes the number '2' in the United States, and, in Australia, it may be seen as an insult! Nonverbal symbols may have a particular meaning in one context but mean something entirely different in another part of the world, or they may not communicate anything at all.

On the field, football players use different symbols (e.g., gestures) to communicate with each other. To be effective, one's communication system should only have meaning for members of one's own team and especially not one's opponents! People smugglers and drug dealers also have an elaborate linguistic and nonverbal code that allows them to share information about their illegal activities, without disclosing information to law enforcement. Twins and other siblings may develop their own communication codes that are incomprehensible to their

Plate 3.4 In Hanoi, Vietnam, this sign is posted near a public park. If you cannot read Vietnamese, can you figure out what the message is? © Jane Jackson

parents. (Chapter 4 explores forms and functions of nonverbal communication, including gestures and other symbols that may be culture specific.)

In the previous examples, the verbal and nonverbal symbols are only meaningful to people who have learned to associate them with particular ideas. In our everyday life, all of us are surrounded by specialized symbols that carry meaning for 'ingroup members' who have been socialized in a particular cultural group. Consequently, 'outgroup members' may easily misinterpret or fail to notice messages that are being transmitted. As one might expect, the interpretation of verbal and nonverbal communication is an aspect that can pose challenges when the communicators have been socialized in different linguistic and cultural contexts.

Property 5: Communication is both intentional and unintentional

Communication can be intentional or unintentional. An example of **intentional communication** is a situation in which two or more people consciously engage in interaction with a specific purpose in mind. For example, if Jessica says to Heejun, 'Would you like to go to the basketball game tonight?' and he replies, 'Sure. What time should we leave?' intentional communication has occurred, and they'll soon head off to the event together. **Unintentional communication** may also be taking place, however. For example, Heejun may believe that Jessica is asking him to go to the game because she is romantically interested in him, when, in fact, she just wants to go with him as a friend.

Communication is not always straightforward. When we hear a message, we also interpret, and possibly misinterpret, the intention and meanings that lie behind the verbal and nonverbal communication. When interactants do not share the same background and experiences, there are more possibilities of miscommunication, especially when a second language is involved.

If you go abroad to work or study, or you engage in intercultural interactions in your home environment, you may find yourself in situations in which you either misinterpret or are unsure of your communication partner's intentions. When a second language is involved, you may understand each word that is spoken (or written) but still find it difficult to figure out what the speaker's motives or intentions are (e.g., what lies behind the words). This is also the case for nonverbal modes of communication.

In intercultural situations, the communication process may be complicated by a range of factors: divergent understandings of when and how to convey messages (e.g., variations in communication styles, including the degree of directness), disparate views about gender relations, and differing expectations about what constitutes 'appropriate' verbal and nonverbal behavior in a particular situation and context. **Cultural schema** (mental representations of a context or situation) and **cultural scripts** (cultural rules of speaking and interpretation) are apt to vary somewhat in different linguistic and cultural settings and, initially, newcomers may find the communication process confounding. They may find it difficult to 'read' the intentions of their communication partner. (See Chapter 2 for examples of cultural scripts and schema.)

Our behavior, whether intentional or not, communicates ideas and attitudes to others. This means that we need to be mindful of the messages that we are sending and the possibility that our verbal and nonverbal actions are not being understood in the ways that we have intended or would like them to be. Mindful intercultural communicators need to have a grasp of both verbal and nonverbal communication to communicate sensitively and effectively with individuals who have a different cultural background. Even if you are trying your best to be pleasant and polite, you may, inadvertently, be giving a very different impression to people who have been socialized to regard your behavior as unacceptable or rude. When we lack awareness of prevailing norms (e.g., cultural scripts), we may unintentionally violate accepted social rules of behavior and misinterpret the behaviors of our intercultural communication partners.

In intercultural encounters, especially those that take place in a second language, it is essential to recognize that all of us have been socialized in particular environments, which have given us ideas about what is acceptable (and unacceptable) behavior in certain contexts. The socialization process guides us to react and interpret behaviors in specific ways. In intercultural interactions, it can be helpful to bear in mind that individuals with a different language and cultural background are usually not behaving in a particular way to deliberately annoy you! With more intercultural awareness and understanding, you can suspend your judgment and allow more time to figure out why someone is communicating in this way. You can also reflect more on how your own behavior is being interpreted by others.

Property 6: Communication is situated and contextual

As Figure 3.1 illustrates, all communication takes place within a particular context or environment. In many ways, the context defines the meaning of any message as it influences the form and interpretation of both verbal and nonverbal communication. For Hall and Hall (2002: 166), **context** is 'the information that surrounds an event; it is inextricably bound up with the meaning of that event'.

In interactions, Cruse (2006: 35) regards the following contextual elements as essential to interpret utterances and expressions:

1   Preceding and following utterances and/or expressions ('co-text')
2   The immediate physical situation
3   The wider situation
4   Knowledge presumed shared between speaker and hearer

Communication may be complicated, in part, due to different perceptions about what constitutes appropriate or polite behavior in a particular context. Differing understandings of who should speak and what may be said can complicate intercultural interactions.

At the health clinic at my university in Hong Kong, for example, the context of the doctor's office dictates where the patient will sit (e.g., in a chair alongside the physician's desk) and the kind of communication that will occur (e.g., disclosure of medical problem following questions by the physician). In other words, there is a particular cultural script for this situation and context; certain behaviors are expected of both interlocutors. When I lived in Egypt, I discovered that the cultural schema and script in medical clinics differed somewhat, so I learned to adjust my expectations and some of my behaviors.

In secondary schools in rural Malaysia, as in other parts of the world, students learn to expect certain roles and responsibilities of teachers and students. If the Malaysian students go on exchange to Australia, they may be quite surprised when they encounter differences in the academic environment (e.g., variations in classroom interaction patterns and perhaps a more informal style of communication between teachers and students). In their home environment, teachers may do most of the talking in English language lessons and students are very quiet. In Australia, the newcomers may, initially, find it quite strange if their classmates ask many questions in class and respond to the comments of other students in discussions. In effect, they are exposed to different cultural scripts and schema or 'cultures of learning', a notion that is discussed further in Chapter 7.

These examples illustrate the potential effect of the environment on communication. As Table 3.2 shows, there are many types of context and contextual elements that can influence the communication process (e.g., cultural/microcultural, environmental/ physical, perceptual, psychological, (socio)relational, situational, temporal, etc.). The chart provides descriptors and examples of multiple contextual elements that can impact communication.

Table 3.2 Contexts that influence the communication process

Type of context	Descriptor	Examples
Cultural	all of the factors and influences that make up one's culture, that is, all the learned behaviors and social norms that affect interaction and hierarchy (e.g., status and positioning of the communicators)	If you have been socialized to believe it is rude to make direct eye contact with authority figures, out of politeness you likely avoid this. If your communication partner has been socialized to believe that direct eye contact signals trustworthiness and respect, there is the potential for misunderstanding.
Environmental	the physical environs where you are communicating, including the location, distance between interactants, noise level, temperature, seating arrangement, technology, furniture, temperature, season, etc.	Communicating in a hot, noisy construction site differs from interaction that takes place in a quiet, air-conditioned office.
Perceptual	the individual characteristics of the interactants: the motivations, intentions, and personality traits people bring to the communication event	When you are asking your professor for an extension for an overdue paper, you are apt to have a very different demeanor and intentions from when you are asking a close friend to go out for a bite to eat.
Physiological	the health, well-being, illness, and disabilities (e.g., hearing loss) of you and the other interactant(s)	Communicating with someone who is hearing impaired and feeling unwell differs from communicating with a healthy person who has excellent hearing.
Psychological	who you are and what you bring to the interaction, e.g., your needs, desires, values, personality, attitudes, feelings, emotion, perceptions, pressure, stress level, trauma, self-concept, views, bias, stereotypes, prejudice, and prior experience	If you have an ethnocentric mindset, the way you communicate with someone from another culture may be disrespectful (intentionally or unintentionally).
Relational	the personal relationship between you and the other person (e.g., your history together, the feelings you and the other person have about each other and the relationship)	You are apt to be more guarded and less open when interacting with someone you do not trust. Past disagreements may affect current interactions.
Situational	the psychosocial environs, that is, the location where you are communicating within a particular sociohistorical, political context	An interaction that takes place in a lecture theater is very different from one that takes place in a karaoke lounge.

Table 3.2   continued

Type of context	Descriptor	Examples
Social	power, hierarchy, the social relationship between you and the other person, social distance, cultural rules of behavior, politeness norms, formality, history of relationship, and gender	The power distance and social relationship between you and your professor differs from that of the power distance and social relationship between you and a close friend or family member.
Sociorelational	social roles and group memberships (e.g., demographics), age, gender, religious affiliation, education level, and socioeconomic status	The way you communicate with a monk or priest differs from the way you interact with a close friend of the same age, ethnicity, and gender.
Temporal	Time and timing of the interaction; moment in history when the communication occurs	The way you interact may differ depending on whether the interaction is at 5 am, noon, or midnight.

Source: N.B. 'You' refers to both participants (sender and receiver) in the communicative event

Property 7: Communication as pervasive

'We cannot not communicate' (Watzlawick *et al.* 1967: 49). This means that anytime you are perceived by another person, you are communicating messages about yourself and your emotions, even though they may be below your level of awareness. For example, the clothes you wear, your hairstyle, your tattoos or body piercings, your jewelry, your facial expressions, your body type (e.g., athletic), your body movements, your posture, your perfume or cologne, and your tone of voice are just some of the many ways in which you are conveying messages about yourself to others. (More elements are explored in Chapter 4 when we focus on nonverbal communication.)

Communication is a human endeavor. As communication is symbolic and continuous, it is impossible for us not to communicate. Argyle and Trower (1979: 4) explain:

> If two humans come together it is virtually inevitable that they will communicate something to each other. . . . Even if they do not speak, messages will pass between them. By their looks, expressions and body movement each will tell the other something, even if it is only, "I don't wish to know you: keep your distance"; "I assure you the feeling is mutual. I'll keep clear if you do".

As communication is a normal feature of everyday life, it can easily be taken for granted.

Property 8: Communication as power-infused

Although not always obvious, power influences the communication process and the ways in which people present themselves (e.g., display certain aspects of their identities and status through language and nonverbal means). Communication is rarely between individuals with the same amount of power and prestige. In most interactions, it is the person (or persons) with more power and status who determines how the communication process unfolds (e.g., which language or dialect is used, the communication style that is accorded more respect, who speaks when and for how long). Whether aware of it or not, people in power may create and perpetuate ways of communicating that reinforce their status and positioning. They may also accept or fail to recognize the preferred identities of their interlocutors. (See Chapter 5 for more on ascribed and avowed identities.)

Morgan (2002) asserts that 'when two or more languages come together, two or more peoples have come together and the result is always about power and identity' (p. 12). When individuals or groups from different linguistic and cultural backgrounds interact they do not share an equal **power status**. Kubota (2014: 97) maintains that 'actual intercultural interactions are largely influenced by where one is positioned in the power hierarchy in terms of race, ethnicity, gender, age, language, physical ableness, sexual identity, and other social categories'. One's accent, adaptive ability, communication style, nationality, and other characteristics (e.g., personal, social, cultural) may also have a bearing on one's degree of power or positioning in a communicative event. Therefore, in intercultural interactions it is incumbent on us to be mindful of 'whose communication styles, both verbal and nonverbal communication, and whose behaviors are seen as "normal" as well as how communication is used to marginalize and exclude' (Sorrells 2015: 235).

In many contexts around the world, women struggle for respect when communicating in a male-dominated environment, as their language use and speech style may differ from those of men in power. Deborah Tannen, a American sociolinguist who has written widely on gender, language, culture, power, and communication, claims that as females are socialized to believe that 'talk is the glue that holds relationships together' (Tannen 2001: 85) they tend to engage in '**rapport-talk';** in conversations they 'try to seek and give confirmation and support, and to reach consensus' (ibid: 25). In contrast, Tannen (2001) maintains that boys learn to view conversations as '**report-talk'** (e.g., the transmission of information) and, as men, they negotiate to maintain the upper hand in verbal interactions in order to protect their status or authority (p. 24). As women try to advance in society (e.g., move up the corporate ladder, run for public office), they may feel pressured to conform to the dominant, male-oriented styles of communication and, even if they do, they may be regarded as 'bitchy' or overly aggressive (ibid). While this is certainly changing as women gain more equality and assume leadership positions in various sectors of society, these barriers are still an issue in many contexts.

Ethnic minority group members may face similar obstacles in communicative events involving people from the majority culture. As they struggle to make their voices heard, they may feel disrespected and disempowered by those who have a more prestigious accent and style of communication or other characteristics that are valued in that context. Individuals and groups can resist (e.g., withdraw, avoid interacting with 'outgroup' members except when absolutely necessary, use their first language), but, in the process, they may be sidelined and have fewer opportunities to advance.

In intercultural encounters the use of a particular language or language variety is often power-laden. For example, if you speak English as a first language and are conversing with someone who is not fluent in the language, you have an advantage. You can speak more quickly, make jokes, and employ a much wider range of vocabulary and verb tenses without much effort. Your communication partner, however, may not fully understand your accent or the vocabulary that you use and, in particular, have trouble making sense of idioms, slang, sarcasm, and humor. Your rapid rate of speech and communication style may also pose a challenge. All of these factors make the communication process more challenging and exhausting for a second language speaker who is not proficient in the language. In situations like this, your higher level of confidence and facility in the language accord you more power and prestige, although you may be unaware of this.

Learning another language can enable you to appreciate what it is like to struggle to express one's ideas and emotions in a second language. It can help you to become a more empathetic communicator, who is sensitive to the needs of your communication partner (the receiver). Becoming bilingual or multilingual can also open up more possibilities to communicate with people from diverse linguistic and cultural backgrounds.

Property 9: Communication as cultural

As noted in Chapter 2, culture shapes communication (and vice versa). 'Communication and culture are so closely bound together that virtually all communication engaged in by humans is culturally linked' (Prosser 1976: 417). Through **enculturation**, the process of primary language and cultural socialization, we learn how to communicate in ways that are deemed appropriate in various settings and situations in our culture. Even if we do not always follow prevailing norms of communication in our home environment, we are apt to be familiar with them since we are continuously exposed to them in daily life. The verbal and nonverbal symbols we use to communicate with our 'ingroup' members (e.g., close friends and family members, people who share the same language, ethnicity, and religion) are strongly influenced by our linguistic and cultural socialization. 'The way people communicate is the way they live. It is their culture. Who talks with whom? How? And about what? These are questions of communication and culture' (Smith 1966: 1). For these reasons, Hall (1976) refers to communication as 'internalized culture' (p. 69).

People from different linguistic and cultural backgrounds have been socialized to communicate in ways that are deemed appropriate in their environment (e.g., use honorifics and specific styles of communication with people of a certain age and status). Through enculturation, we learn to view and communicate in ways that follow conventions or norms that are prevalent in specific contexts in our culture. For example, we learn expressions of politeness and cultural scripts for particular social situations.

In intercultural interactions, one of the most obvious communication differences may be language, especially if one or both of the speakers is using a second language (or a different dialect). Edward Sapir (1921) and his student Benjamin Whorf (1956) hypothesized that differences in the way languages encode cultural and cognitive categories significantly affects how users of a particular language view the world around them. The **Sapir-Whorf hypothesis** played a foundational role in early studies of language and intercultural communication.

Linguistic determinism, the strong form of this theory, posits that our language *determines* our ability to perceive and think about objects. 'If we don't have a word for something in our language, this theory predicts that we won't think about it or notice it' (West & Turner 2011a: G-6). For example, if your first language does not have words for certain colors or types of snow, this theory suggests that it would be very difficult to recognize or identify them.

Contemporary scholars have widely rebuked the strong version of the Sapir-Whorf hypothesis. Scollon *et al.* (2012: 17), for example, wrote: 'We do not take the extreme deterministic position that a language solely determines the thought patterns of its speakers . . . reality is far too complex to allow for such a simple statement'. Yule (2017) argues that while the language we use can 'influence the organization of our knowledge in some way', as humans, 'we also inherit the ability to manipulate and be creative with that language in order to express our perceptions' (p. 304). Further, he points out that a member of a remote tribe who sees a computer for the first time and does not have a word for it, would still be able to perceive it. As experiments have generally not supported the strong version of the hypothesis, a weaker version was put forward.

'**Linguistic relativity**', the weaker version, posits that the language one speaks *influences* our thinking patterns and, potentially, our communicative behavior (Holmes & Wilson 2017; Neuliep 2018b) (emphasis added). Scollon *et al*. (2012: 17) explain that 'languages, like all cultural tools, have various built-in affordances and constraints which limit and focus the kinds of meanings that can be expressed with them'. How we view or see the world is affected in some ways by the grammar or structure of our language (e.g., lack of the future tense will affect how we understand and express this dimension). Therefore, if we don't have a word for an object in our language, linguistic relativity suggests that 'it will be difficult, but *not* impossible, to think about it or notice it' (West & Turner 2011a: G-6). (emphasis added)

LoCastro (2003) has also reflected on the complex connection between language, thought, worldview, culture, and communication:

> the linguistic social action of speakers of a particular language mirror the underlying worldview of the speakers; manifestations of the cultural models of thought are embedded in talk both in the micro features and at the macro level. The list of micro behaviors includes prosodic features, listener behavior, turn-taking, conversational routines, constituents of an activity type, conventional indirectness, nonverbal cues, and speech act realizations.
>
> (p. 227)

While cultural elements are embedded in the languages we speak, individuals who speak the same first language may possess different worldviews and values that may be conveyed through the communication process. They may associate different meanings with the same verbal and nonverbal symbols, which naturally impacts the communication process. For example, although English is the dominant language spoken in the United States and Britain, many words and phrases have different meanings in American and British English; there are also differences between these language varieties with regard to pronunciation, punctuation, and spelling. The British also use colloquialisms (informal language in relaxed, everyday speech) and slang (words used only by specific groups such as teenagers or military personnel). These words or expressions may not be well understood by Americans, just as their British interlocutors may be confounded by some American words. English has been acquired and shaped in different cultural environments and this has led to variations in the language.

Today, English is an **international language** with many varieties around the world (e.g., Indian English, Nigerian English, Singaporean English) and, as one might expect, among World Englishes, there are many differences in pronunciation, punctuation, spelling, and idiomatic expressions. Local cultural elements, including other languages in use, influence the way each variety has developed over time. In addition, culture influences the style of communication that is used in different contexts (e.g., degree of directness).

Culture also influences nonverbal communication. Nonverbal symbols, gestures, and perceptions of personal space and time vary significantly from culture to culture. In Canada, for example, adults of the same sex who are not romantically involved with each other generally stand about two-and-a-half feet, or an arm's length, away from each other when communicating. By contrast, in many Middle Eastern cultures, two same sex friends generally stand closer to one another when interacting. In the Sultanate of Oman, two male friends walking together may hold hands or touch each other's arms as a sign of trust and solidarity. In China, two female friends may do the same. If unfamiliar with this behavior, an observer may jump to the wrong conclusions and misinterpret what you are seeing (e.g., assume that the individuals are gay). As Schmidt *et al.* (2007: 61) explain, 'even it were possible to send a message without any cultural influences, the receiver will automatically interpret it through the filter of their own cultural conditioning'. (See Chapter 4 for a more in-depth discussion of nonverbal communication and its implications for intercultural relations).

In sum, the communication process is influenced by the linguistic and cultural socialization process in one's home environment. Through enculturation we become habituated to expect certain verbal and nonverbal behavior in specific situations and contexts. To complicate matters, while many of our messages are sent intentionally, many others (e.g., nonverbal actions) are unintentionally influencing how others perceive us.

Plate 3.5 Demonstrating their close friendship, these Chinese women walk arm in arm. © Jane Jackson

LANGUAGE, CULTURE, AND VERBAL COMMUNICATION STYLES

So far, we have examined various properties of communication and core elements in the communication process. Many interculturalists maintain that our preferred ways of communicating are influenced by our cultural background and the language(s) we speak, that is, each of us is affected by enculturation. Let's take a look at variations in speech and communication styles and their potential implications for intercultural interactions.

Styles of speech

Linguistic style refers to an individual's 'characteristic speaking pattern', which includes such features as degree of directness or indirectness, pacing and pausing, word choice, and the use of such elements as jokes, sarcasm, figures of speech (e.g., metaphors, irony, hyperbole), stories, questions, silence, and apologies (Holmes & Wilson 2017; Tannen 1995). For Tannen (1995), linguistic style is 'a set of culturally learned signals by which we not only communicate what we mean but also interpret others' meaning and evaluate one another as people' (Tannen 1995: 139). One's **speech style** is made up of choices regarding a range of linguistic elements (e.g., vocabulary, syntactic patterns, volume, pace, pitch, register, intonation).

While studying speech styles in the U.S., Tannen (1995, 1996, 2001) concluded that gender differences are built into language: 'because boys and girls grow up in what are essentially different cultures . . . talk between women and men is cross-cultural communication' (Tannen 2001: 18). In her work, she attributed linguistic variations to the primary socialization process and culturally embedded notions of gender. 'Each person's life is a series of conversations, and simply by understanding and using the words of our language, we all absorb and pass on different, asymmetrical assumptions about men and women' (ibid: 243).

Tannen's publications drew attention to gender variations in linguistic styles in interpersonal communication and their potential impact on gender relations, power relations, and intercultural relationships. Shi and Langman (2012: 169), however, caution that

> all research that examines "women" and "men" as members of groups will invariably lead to stereotyping of behavior and essentializing of the categories of "men" and "women" in ways that assume that there are no differences among women as a whole, and men as a whole, and, in contrast, vast differences between women and men.

(Gender, identity, and stereotyping are discussed further in Chapters 5 and 6)

Communication accommodation theory (CAT)

Language and social psychologists are also interested in the relationship between language, speech behaviors, and culture. Howard Giles and his associates have developed the **communication accommodation theory (CAT)** to describe and explain why individuals may modify their speech communication practices depending on who they are talking to. More specifically, this framework explores the reasons for, and consequences arising from, speakers *converging* toward and *diverging* away from each other (Giles *et al.* 2012; Zhang & Giles 2018). CAT has received empirical support when examined in diverse languages and cultures, as well as in applied intercultural settings and electronic interaction.

To win approval, speakers often accommodate their speech to that of their addressee through the act of **convergence**. More specifically, individuals sometimes shift their style of speech (e.g., adjust their speech rate, accent, content) to become more similar to that of their addressees to emphasize solidarity and reduce **social distance** (the degree of closeness or separation between groups) (Giles *et al.* 2012). Convergent moves are generally received favorably by recipients and this satisfaction may then generalize to more positive feelings about the entire culture or group to which the converger belongs (Zhang & Giles 2018).

Conversely, speakers may choose to maintain their style of speech to emphasize their affiliation with their ingroup and differentiate themselves from the addressee (or a particular group). By accentuating language (and cultural) differences, this strategy of **divergence** (e.g., switching to an ethnic dialect or language when speaking to a host national) leads to an increase in social distance (Giles *et al.* 2012; Zhang & Giles 2018). Such moves are often viewed negatively by communication partners and taken rather personally.

In sum, this social psychological theory of language and social interaction posits that style shifts in intercultural discourse may have consequences for interpersonal relations, with the act of convergence bringing interactants closer together and divergence having the opposite effect. (CAT is discussed further in Chapter 5 in relation to identity and language use.)

Speech style as audience design

A related theory of speech style has been developed by Allan Bell, a sociolinguist in New Zealand. For this scholar, **speech style** is 'the dimension of language where individual speakers have a choice' (Bell 2007: 95). He explains:

> We do not always speak in consistently the same way. In fact we are shifting the way we speak constantly as we move from one situation to another. On different occasions we talk in different ways. These different ways of speaking carry different social meanings. They represent our ability to take up different social positions, and they affect how we are perceived by others.
>
> (ibid: 95)

Relevant to this discussion is the sociolinguistic term **style shifting**, which refers to the process of adjusting or changing from one style of speech to another (Eckert & Rickford 2001; Holmes & Wilson 2017). Most typically, style shifts are automatic or unconscious reactions to a situation, an audience, or a topic, although they may also be deliberate. For example, a speaker may intentionally switch to another dialect or style of speech to enhance social relations (e.g., lessen the distance between herself and her listener). **Code-switching** involves changing between different languages, whereas style shifting occurs within the same language.

To explain observed variations in speech styles, Bell (2007) developed the **'audience design framework'**, which incorporates the following notions:

1 Style is what an individual speaker does with a language in relation to other people.
2 Style derives its meaning from the association of linguistic features with particular social groups. The social evaluation of a group is transferred to the linguistic features associated with that group.
3 Speakers design their style primarily for and in response to their audience. (This aspect relates to the notions of 'convergence' and 'divergence' in the communication accommodation theory (CAT).)

4   Audience design applies to all codes and levels of a language repertoire: monolingual and multilingual.

5   Style variations in speech between different social groups are normally greater than differences within individual speakers of a particular group.

6   Speakers are able to design or adjust their style of speech for a range of different addresses.

7   Style shifts according to topic or setting derive their meaning and direction of shift from the underlying association of topics or settings with typical audience members.

8   A style shift in language initiates a change in the situation, that is, language helps shape the situation.

9   The linguistic features associated with a group can be used to express affiliation with that group. An individual may employ a particular style or language variety to demonstrate a sense of belonging to another group.

(adapted from Bell 2007: 97–8)

The CAT and the 'audience design framework' both suggest that speakers can make choices about their speech styles that influence their interpersonal, intercultural relationships (e.g., bring them closer together or pull them further away from their interlocutors). It is also necessary to bear in mind that power relations, positioning, and situational/contextual constraints can also influence the communication process and inhibit the agency of individuals. Messages conveyed in intercultural interactions may also not be received as intended.

Communication style

While linguistic style focuses on patterns of language use, the term 'communication style' is more broad. Saphiere *et al.* (2005) define **communication style** as 'the way in which we communicate, a pattern of verbal and nonverbal behaviors that comprises our *preferred ways* of giving and receiving information in a specific situation' (p. 5) (emphasis added). More specifically, for Barnlund (1975: 14–15), communication style refers to:

> the topics people prefer to discuss, their favorite forms of interaction – ritual, repartee, argument, self-disclosure – and the depth of involvement they demand of each other. It includes the extent to which communicants rely upon the same channels– vocal, verbal, physical – for conveying information, and the extent to which they are tuned to the same level of meaning, that is, to the factual or emotional content of messages.

For Zhu (2011: 419), communication style is simply 'the way individuals or a group of individuals communicate with others'. In other words, 'if the message content is the *what* and the communicators the *who*, then communication style is the *how*' (Saphiere *et al.* 2005: 5).

Our preferred ways of communicating include **speech style preferences**, that is, the speech we are most comfortable using in interactions. One's communication style and speech style preferences can affect how we behave in communicative events, including intercultural encounters. In particular, our communication style may influence:

1   How we organize and present information (e.g., how we structure an argument to persuade others of our viewpoint or position)

2   How we give praise and how we react to receiving praise (e.g., how often we give compliments, the ways in which we compliment others, how we respond when someone compliments us)

3 The timing and manner of **self-disclosure** (the sharing of personal details that our listeners would not normally know about us) and how we respond to the personal information that others reveal to us

4 How we express agreement or disagreement and how we respond to the way our interactant communicates agreement or disagreement to us

5 How we build interpersonal relationships (e.g., develop a close connection with others, establish intimacy with a romantic partner, build trust with someone from another linguistic and cultural background)

6 How we convey politeness (and impoliteness) (e.g., our use of discourse markers or expressions of politeness) and how we perceive politeness (impoliteness) in the communicative actions of others

7 How we negotiate (e.g., mediate conflict situations) and respond to the negotiation or conflict management style of our interactant (e.g., our willingness to adjust the way we communicate, that is, our willingness to converge in negotiations to reach an amicable settlement) (Conflict negotiation strategies are discussed in Chapter 9.)

8 How we make decisions and solve problems or disputes, and how we respond to the problem solving approach of others

9 How and when we interrupt and prefer to be interrupted (and how often) as well as how we respond to being interrupted

10 How we apologize and make requests or refusals (and other speech acts) and how we respond to the speech acts of others in various contexts and situations.

(adapted from Saphiere *et al.* 2005: 5)

In our cultural environment we learn to expect certain patterns of communication (e.g., cultural scripts, cultural schema) in particular settings (e.g., at home, in the doctor's office, in the classroom, in a restaurant). Through enculturation, we learn norms of social discourse and preferred ways of interacting with others, taking into account such aspects as social status, age, gender, power, positioning, and context. Over time, we become accustomed to expressing ourselves in particular ways. Naturally, there are variations in communication styles in diverse linguistic and cultural contexts.

High-context vs. low-context communication

The anthropologist E.T. Hall (1976, 1983) drew attention to the influence of culture on communication styles and categorized cultures into two broad types: 'high-context' and 'low-context' (McKay-Semmler 2018). For Hall (1983), contextual elements and communication styles are closely correlated with the cultural dimensions of **individualism** and **collectivism**. On the individualism-collectivism continuum, collectivist cultures tend to emphasize the following traits: 'community, collaboration, shared interest, harmony, tradition, the public good, and maintaining face' (Anderson *et al.* 2003: 77). In contrast, individualistic cultures place more emphasis on 'personal rights and responsibilities, privacy, voicing one's opinion, freedom, innovation, and self-expression' (ibid: 77).

In **high-context communication** most information is communicated through indirect means (e.g., nonverbally, through the use of indirect discourse), and there is a reliance on mutually shared knowledge (e.g., awareness of cultural norms, scripts, and social customs) (Hall 1976; Nam 2015). In this form of communication, the context, 'the information that surrounds an event', is 'inextricably bound up with the meaning of that event' (Hall & Hall 2002:

166). In **indirect communication**, implicit verbal messages and subtle nonverbal behaviors (e.g., pauses, silence, tone of voice, the use of space, gestures, avoidance of eye contact) are frequently employed to convey a message.

High-context communication is common in cultures that stress communication through 'the context of the social interaction' (e.g., the speakers' social roles, gender, age, status, and other cultural elements), and interlocutors pay close attention to 'the physical environment in which the interaction is taking place' (DeCapua & Wintergerst 2004: 71). They are also mindful of their relationship with their communication partner(s) and the need to maintain harmony. Hall (1976) observed that this style of communication was common in 'collectivist-oriented' nations such as China, Japan, Kuwait, Mexico, Nigeria, Saudi Arabia, South Korea, and Vietnam.

By contrast, in **low-context communication**, most information is clearly stated 'in the transmitted message in order to make up for what is missing in the context' (Hall 1976: 101). In **direct communication**, the speaker's intentions, ideas, and opinions are made explicit through the use of 'direct, specific, and literal expressions' (Sorrells 2016: 262). Individuals who have been socialized in a context which favors clarity in speech are accustomed to people 'speaking their mind' or 'telling it like it is' in both oral and written forms of communication. In low-context communication, '*what* (content) is said is of primary importance' (Nam 2015: 378), whereas in high-context communication, '*how* the message is delivered often matters more' (ibid: 378).

The context (e.g., sociocultural, physical) still influences the communication process in environments where low-context communication is widely used; however, 'the primary responsibility for ensuring that listeners correctly receive and interpret verbal messages rests on speakers' (DeCapua & Wintergerst 2004: 71). To try to ensure that sent messages are interpreted as intended, low-context communicators tend to employ elaborate, direct verbal modes of communication. Hall (1976) observed that low-context communication styles are most prevalent in more 'individualistic-oriented' nations, e.g., Australia, Canada, Denmark, Germany, the UK, the U.S., Switzerland, and Sweden.

Early communication scholars pointed to a number of implications of these observations for intercultural interactions. In environments that favor low-context communication, much of the information in interactions is expressed verbally, and directness, precision, clarity, and lack of ambiguity are valued. To someone who is used to high-context communication receiving very detailed information may make the person feel as if she is being treated as a child. Conversely, when interacting with someone who is employing a high-context communication style, individuals who have been socialized in context where low-context communication is the norm may fail to understand subtle messages that are being transmitted (e.g., through the tone of voice, silence). Initially, interactions between low-context and high-context communicators may be frustrating and lead to mistrust and anxiety.

Limitations of communication style typologies

Many interculturalists (e.g., Bill Gudykunst, Y.Y. Kim, Stella Ting-Toomey) have been greatly influenced by E.T. Hall's continuum of high- and low-context styles of communication, and it is still widely referred to in intercultural communication texts and other publications. While this framework provides a general, broad indication of communication styles and patterns that are common in particular contexts, we must be cautious and not assume that everyone in a particular part of the world behaves in certain ways. For example, not all Japanese favor indirect styles of communication, just as not all Germans have a very direct style of communication. Not all Chinese business executives prefer a formal style of communication in meetings, just as not all American executives adopt an informal style in their meetings. The degree of directness and formality can differ among individuals who are affiliated with the same culture.

People may also favor one communication style over another in particular situations (e.g., use more indirect communication with family members and more direct communication in the workplace). For these reasons, Saphiere *et al.* (2005) have misgivings about 'an oversimplified relationship portrayed between high context and indirect communication and between low context and direct communication' (p. 263). While communication typologies may help us to make sense of the ways people interact in our own and other environments, they are limiting.

Our communication style preferences reflect not only our linguistic and cultural socialization but our individual, personal preferences and unique experiences. While much of our language use and nonverbal behaviors are learned through enculturation, each of us makes creative use of language and speech/communication styles. Consequently, the classifications of people from large groups (e.g., nations) are rebuked by critical scholars (e.g., Dervin 2012, 2016; Holliday 2012, 2019) who argue that this approach overlooks individual differences and leads to essentialism. (Reductionism and stereotyping are discussed further in Chapter 6, while the use and limitations of 'cultural difference' frameworks are explored in Chapter 10.)

CHARACTERISTICS OF AN EFFECTIVE INTERCULTURAL COMMUNICATOR IN SECOND LANGUAGE SITUATIONS

In intercultural interactions, you may find yourself in situations where you are using your first language to communicate with someone from a different linguistic and cultural background. The following are some suggestions to become an effective intercultural communicator in such situations:

1 Be patient. Allow more time for the interaction.
2 Try to avoid the use of idioms that may be easily misunderstood; bear in mind that jokes and sarcasm often do not translate well across cultures.
3 Pay attention to the content meaning of the messages you are sending and receiving.
4 Be aware of your rate of speech and speak more slowly *if* this appears to help your listener.
5 To gauge how your message is being received, be attentive to the other person's verbal and nonverbal behavior (feedback). Remember, that you are also sending messages nonverbally, which may not be interpreted in the way you expect.
6 Whenever feasible, use culture-sensitive probing questions to check to see if your message has been understood in the way that you intended.
7 Listen attentively and pay attention to both verbal and nonverbal messages of your communication partner before responding.
8 Be mindful of the power dynamics and their potential impact on intercultural relations and the communication process (e.g., the advantages you may have as a first language speaker).
9 Be sensitive to the benefits of convergence and the potential negative consequences of divergence in terms of your speech/communication style and language choice.
10 Be sensitive to the cultural beliefs, values, gender differences, and politeness norms that may underlie different styles of communication. Remember that all of us have been socialized to expect certain speech/communication styles and cultural scripts in particular situations although we may not always adhere to these norms.
11 Recognize your personal style of communicating and make an effort to determine how your communication partners are perceiving you. Effective intercultural communication requires a high level of self-awareness and listener sensitivity.

12 To further enhance intercultural relations, build up your repertoire of communication styles (e.g., familiarity with direct-indirect, formal-informal communication strategies). Adapting your communication style to put your interactant at ease may help you to create a positive impression and facilitate your communication.

13 Bear in mind that miscommunication may be due to language barriers rather than cultural difference (and vice versa).

While these strategies have been suggested with second language situations in mind, many may also enhance your interaction with people who share your first language but differ from you in terms of age, ethnicity, gender, religion, etc. As a sensitive and respectful intercultural communicator you can take steps to reduce the power gap and cultivate more equitable, satisfying relationships. (Throughout the text, more suggestions are offered to enhance intercultural relations; Chapter 11 examines core elements in intercultural [communicative] competence.)

SUMMARY

Communication is a complex, dynamic process that entails the encoding and decoding of verbal and nonverbal messages within a particular cultural, physiological, sociorelational, and perceptual environment. As well as multiple dimensions of context, the relationship between culture and communication is complex and influenced by many factors (historical relations, gender, language, power, etc.). An understanding of the elements in the communication process and the potential impact of variations in speech/communication styles can help you to become a more effective, listener-sensitive, intercultural communicator. It can enhance your interpersonal, intercultural relationships and communication in second language situations.

discussion questions

1 Describe the relationship between language, culture, and power. Share your ideas with a partner.

2 Why is context important in any discussion of language, culture, and power?

3 Do you agree with Frederico Fellini (1920–1993), an Italian film director and writer, that 'a different language is a different vision of life'? Why or why not?

4 How can knowledge of the communication process help you to become a more effective intercultural communicator? Discuss your ideas with a partner.

5 With regard to intercultural interactions, why does Ingrid Piller (2012) caution us 'not to mistake language problems for cultural problems' (p. 11)?

6 Saphiere *et al.* (2005) maintain that typologies of communication styles are 'useful, yet limiting'? Do you agree? Why or why not?

7 Think about an intercultural encounter in a second language that did not go well. What did you learn in this chapter that might have helped to enhance the communication process? In future intercultural interactions, what might you do differently?

activities

1 Offer a definition of human communication. Identify and explain the basic elements of communication to a classmate.

2 With a partner, identify five strategies to employ to become a more effective intercultural communicator, especially in situations where one of the communicators is not fluent in the language being used.

3 Describe your style of communication. Does it vary depending on the context or situation? If yes, how? How might this knowledge enhance your intercultural interactions?

4 Visit a place on campus (e.g., cafeteria, library, sports center) and observe international students interacting with each other. Do you notice any similarities or differences in the way they communicate (e.g., degree of directness in discourse) in comparison with your own style of communication? Do you observe any gender or age differences in the ways they interact? Reflect on your reaction to what you observe.

5 Imagine that you are working in a group in a context where indirect discourse and maintaining harmony are favored. The following statements are characteristic of direct communicators. Rephrase the statements so that the style of communication is less direct.

    a   I don't think that's a good solution.
    b   I disagree.
    c   I think that our group should. . .
    d   That's not a sensible idea.
    e   What's your view, Bianca? (Can you find out what she thinks without asking her a direct question?)

6 Now imagine that you are in a setting where clear, direct discourse is the norm. Read the following statements that are characteristic of an indirect style of communication and rephrase them so that they are more forthright.

    a   Shall we move on to the next task?
    b   I will try my best.
    c   Your suggestion may work.
    d   That's an interesting idea.
    e   Have you ever tried this approach?

7 With a partner discuss the benefits of expanding your repertoire of communication styles to become a more flexible, competent intercultural communicator.

8 Write a short essay about how enculturation has affected your intercultural attitudes and communication style, and identify personal goals to enhance your intercultural competence.

further reading

Bonvillain, N. (2013) *Language, Culture and Communication*, 7th edn, Upper Saddle River, NJ: Prentice Hall.

Using data from cultures and languages throughout the world, this book explores the connections between language, culture, and communicative meaning.

Kramsch, C. (1998) *Language and Culture*, Oxford: Blackwell.

This compact book offers an accessible survey of key language concepts such as social context and cultural authenticity, using insights from such fields as linguistics, sociology, and anthropology.

Remillard, V. and Williams, K. (2016) *Human Communication Across Cultures: A Cross-Cultural Introduction to Pragmatics and Sociolinguistics*, Sheffield and Bristol: Equinox.

This introductory text explores how language is used in social interactions in various cultural contexts, drawing attention to differences due to such aspects as gender, age, race/ethnicity, religious background, social class, and level of education.

Saphiere, D.H., Mikk, B.K. and Devries, B.I. (2005) *Communication Highwire: Leveraging the Power of Diverse Communication Styles*, Yarmouth, ME: Intercultural Press.

The authors introduce the notion of communication styles and explain how communication style preferences reflect our personal and cultural upbringing, and also vary depending on the context and cultural setting.

Companion Website: Continue your journey online

Visit the Companion Website for a variety of tools and resources to support and extend your intercultural learning. (Instructors who are qualified adopters of the text may access additional resources on this site.)

CHAPTER 4

Language and nonverbal communication

Fie, fie upon her!
There's language in her eye, her cheek, her lip,
Nay, her foot speaks; her wanton spirits look out
At every joint and motive of her body.
                    William Shakespeare (1914)

> When the eyes say one thing, and the tongue another, a practiced man relies on the language of the first.
>
>   (Emerson 1930: 118)

learning objectives

By the end of this chapter, you should be able to:

1   Define nonverbal communication
2   Describe the relationship between verbal and nonverbal communication
3   Identify the characteristics and functions of nonverbal communication
4   Identify different types of nonverbal codes
5   Explain the influence of culture on nonverbal communication
6   Explain how nonverbal elements can affect intercultural communication

INTRODUCTION

Learning to communicate effectively and appropriately in intercultural interactions requires knowledge of both verbal and nonverbal code systems. Just as our verbal behaviors (e.g., language use, communication styles) are influenced by the cultural socialization process that was described in Chapter 2, many of our nonverbal actions (e.g., use of space, gestures, volume of speech) are affected by our linguistic and cultural environment.

In this chapter we begin by delving into the nature and importance of nonverbal communication, and then examine the relationship between verbal and nonverbal communication and consider how they differ. Discussion then centers on the characteristics and functions of nonverbal communication. Next, we review various types of nonverbal codes and discuss the influence of culture on nonverbal forms of communication, drawing attention to universal nonverbal cues as well as cultural variability. We then discuss the implications of the non-verbal expectancy violation theory for intercultural communication. The chapter concludes with a discussion of practical ways to enhance the nonverbal dimension of intercultural interactions.

THE NATURE OF NONVERBAL COMMUNICATION

Similar to verbal communication, there are multiple conceptions of **nonverbal communica-tion**. van de Vijver (2018b) define it straightforwardly as 'a socially shared coding system of communication beyond language', adding that it is broader than the earlier term 'body lan-guage' (p. 1617). Along similar lines, Moore *et al*. (2014) and Matsumoto and Hwang (2015) state that nonverbal communication is concerned with the transmission and reception of mes-sages that does not include words. Drawing attention to the process involved, Eaves and Leath-ers (2018) describe nonverbal communication as: 'the use of interacting sets of visual, vocal, and invisible communication systems and subsystems by communicators with the systematic encoding and decoding of nonverbal symbols and signs for the purpose(s) of exchanging con-sensual meanings in specific communicative contexts'.

Nonverbal communication takes place 'when a message is decoded (or interpreted) as hav-ing some meaning, *regardless of the sender's intent*' (Hickson *et al*. 2004: 11–12) (emphasis in original). It can occur through the speaker's dress, voice, and social distance, the receiver (posture, facial expression, distance kept from the speaker), and the situation as perceived by the interactants (the social context, the environment, the time of the interaction). Therefore, Hickson *et al*. (2004: 482) depict nonverbal communication as 'a process whereby people, through the intentional or unintentional manipulation of normative actions and expectations, express experiences, feelings, and attitudes in order to relate to and control themselves, others, and their environments'.

What all of these definitions of nonverbal communication have in common is the notion that nonverbal acts are communicating a message, whether on purpose or not. The receiver's perception of some form of intent is sufficient for a nonverbal act to be deemed communication.

THE IMPORTANCE OF NONVERBAL COMMUNICATION

Why study nonverbal communication? In his play *Troilus and Cressida* (1914), the great play-wright William Shakespeare drew attention to the diverse ways in which our whole body is engaged in the communication process (e.g., our eyes, cheeks, lips, feet, joints, posture). As Cressida spoke, her facial features and body movements gave her away. 'There's language in her eye, her cheek, her lip. Nay, her foot speaks. Her wanton spirits look out at every joint and motive of her body'. Through nonverbal means, we, as social actors, may disclose our emo-tions, attitudes, and thoughts – whether we are aware of it or not.

Nonverbal communication specialists assert that nonverbal communication is the sin-gle most powerful form of human communication. Albert Mehrabian (1982), a body lan-guage specialist, claims that the vast majority of meaning and emotional intent is actually transmitted through nonverbal channels (e.g., body movements, facial expressions, vocal qualities). 'Depending on the study, the estimated amount of information conveyed nonverbally ranges between 65% and 95% of the total messages conveyed' (Matsumoto & Hwang 2015: 513). Further, most nonverbal communication scholars maintain that nonverbal acts are a more accurate indicator of the true meaning than the actual words (e.g., Eaves & Leathers 2018; Moore *et al.* 2014). As Emerson (1930) observes, '[w]hen the eyes say one thing, and the tongue another, a practiced man relies on the language of the first' (Emerson p. 118).

Many nonverbal acts are **innate** (existing in one from birth) and **universal**, that is, people in different cultures share a similar understanding of particular cues (e.g., facial expressions of fear). Other elements and dimensions of nonverbal communication vary depending on the cultural context (e.g., head nods, some gestures). Considering the significance of **nonverbal codes** (all symbols that are not words, e.g., bodily movements, use of space and time, clothing and adornments, and sounds other than words), the field of intercultural communication studies benefits from studies in a variety of cultural contexts that carefully document and interpret nonverbal acts, both alone and in connection with verbal communication.

THE RELATIONSHIP BETWEEN VERBAL AND NONVERBAL COMMUNICATION

When individuals interact face to face, their communication typically consists of both verbal and nonverbal components. Therefore, Knapp *et al.* (2014) argue that nonverbal communication should be regarded as 'an inseparable part of the total communication process' (p. 28). As individuals transmit and receive messages, nonverbal codes often interact with verbal forms of communication (e.g., the use of sounds and words). For example, **gestures** (movements of part of the body to express an idea or meaning) and **facial expressions** (facial motions that convey one's emotional or affective state) may accompany words. Speech may also vary with regard to such aspects as accent, rate, tone, and volume, all of which are considered nonverbal features. To complicate matters, verbal and nonverbal codes may communicate meaning together or separately, as Hickson *et al.* (2004: 9) explain:

> Nonverbal communication is complex because it creates communication by use of nonverbal behaviors, either by themselves or combined with words. It may be shared *between* people (interpersonally) or *within* a person (intrapersonally). It may be intentional or unintentional. It may also be used without words, or it may take on meaning only when it is used in combination with words.
>
> (emphasis in the original)

Both verbal and nonverbal channels of communication consist of symbols and patterns that are learned over time. Just as different societies and cultures may have different languages or dialects, some of their nonverbal codes and norms of behavior (e.g., accepted patterns or rules) may vary across cultures and differ depending on the context and situation.

Through **enculturation**, the primary socialization process, individuals develop the ability to appropriately use and interpret verbal and nonverbal cues in particular cultural contexts. As children mature they acquire their first language (and perhaps others), that is, they learn the meanings of words and expressions along with rules of verbal communication (e.g., the politeness norms of speech, cultural scripts for greetings/requests/refusals). Over time, through observations and experimentation, they also become more attuned to nonverbal cues and learn the norms for nonverbal communication (e.g., emotional display, use of space) that are prevalent in various situations. While children learn some grammar rules and vocabulary through formal language education, most of the learning of nonverbal cues is implicit, that is, they discover how to use and interpret nearly all nonverbal cues by observing and imitating the actions of others rather than through direct instruction.

Many communication specialists maintain that nonverbal communication is more important than verbal communication in face-to-face situations. Why might this be the case? Even if adults are not aware they are doing so, they continuously use and observe nonverbal cues (e.g., eye movements, posture, facial expressions) and form judgments about speakers and their messages (verbal and nonverbal), drawing on what they have learned during the socialization process (e.g., ideas about what is appropriate and inappropriate). (This aspect is discussed further in this chapter when we turn our attention to the nonverbal expectancy violation theory.)

Nonverbal communication specialists Mark Hickson *et al.* (2004) maintain that 'most verbal communication carries with it a greater amount of intent, but nonverbal communication tends to be more primitive and less controllable than its verbal counterpart' (pp. 11–12). As people are thought to have less control over their nonverbal actions, adults generally consider the nonverbal message to be more truthful and accurate when contradictory messages are sent through verbal and nonverbal channels. In contrast, children typically rely on verbal expressions for meaning as they have not yet developed the ability to interpret nonverbal acts and read between the lines. With less awareness of nonverbal cues, young children tend to depend on the literal meaning of words and are generally more trusting of the verbal message.

FUNCTIONS OF NONVERBAL COMMUNICATION

Nonverbal communication can serve a number of functions. While many messages are conveyed nonverbally without the awareness of the senders, in other situations, the use of nonverbal codes is intentional and purposeful. Some nonverbal functions are associated with verbal forms of communication (oral or written), while others are not. To communicate effectively, whether in **intracultural interactions** (the exchange of messages between people who share the same cultural background) or intercultural situations, it is helpful to be aware of the various functions of nonverbal communication.

Self-presentation

We routinely use nonverbal signals to let other people know who we are, that is, we convey aspects of our identities and personality through nonverbal means. Through **self-presentation**, we disclose information about ourselves through our physical appearance, our tone of voice, our posture, our mode of dress, and our adornments (e.g., body piercings, tattoos, make-up). Personal dimensions of ourselves (e.g., our personality, degree of openness, values) are conveyed through our use of time, body odor, use of space, the ways we decorate our homes (or dorm rooms), and many other nonverbal means.

At times, our nonverbal behavior is intentionally designed to manage the impressions that others have of us. For example, the outfit you wear to a job interview may be carefully selected to send a message to the interviewer about your maturity, sense of responsibility, and seriousness. When you go out on a date, your clothes, perfume, and accessories may also be chosen to showcase your personality, emphasize your best features, and demonstrate your interest in your romantic partner. Whether intentional or not, every day we continuously disclose details about ourselves through nonverbal channels. This means that if we are attentive we can learn a great deal about others by paying close attention to the way they present themselves nonverbally.

Conveying relationship messages

Through nonverbal means we reveal our relationship with others, whether we realize it or not. We demonstrate how we feel about someone through our facial expressions (e.g., smile, frown, raised eyebrows), the tenor or loudness of our voice (e.g., aggressive tone), and how closely we stand or sit by him or her, and so on. For example, in some cultural settings we may walk arm in arm with a romantic partner and when sitting, lean forward and frequently touch each other as we chat. We may also convey intimacy by using a soft tone of voice and whispering into each other's ears. Conversely, we may reveal our distrust, dislike, or lack of interest in another person through other nonverbal actions, such as by avoiding eye contact, folding our arms, leaning away, or by keeping a large physical distance between us when standing.

Nonverbal communication can also indicate and reinforce the power dimension or status differences in relationships. For example, in a work situation, an employer may stand further away from her employees than she would her close friends. To emphasize her authority she may also talk in a louder, more assertive voice with subordinates. In a formal dinner, seating/serving arrangements may also nonverbally communicate status and **power** (authority or strength). At a formal banquet in Mainland China, for example, the attendees may gather at a round table and sit in assigned places according to their status; the guest with the highest rank is usually positioned to the right of the host and is the first person to be offered a serving from the communal dishes. In a similar event in Canada, the attendees may sit at an oblong table and be served individual meals. Whereas the guest with the highest position may be seated next to the host at the head of the table and be served first, the other attendees may sit anywhere they like regardless of rank or status. When guests are expecting certain formalities and conventions, it can be confusing when different procedures are followed. Unintentionally, hosts may not display the degree of respect and formality that international guests have become accustomed to in their home environment, and if individuals are not flexible, relationships can be put in jeopardy.

Replacing verbal messages

Nonverbal messages can also be used as a substitute for verbal messages. For example, instead of verbally telling students to be quiet, a primary teacher may simply hold a finger to her lips and as long as the students understand this gesture (and are willing to comply), this simple action may be quite effective.

In some situations, using words to communicate may not be a viable option. When conducting an orchestra in a concert hall, a conductor uses gestures (e.g., hand movements) to transmit messages to a large number of musicians who are playing different instruments. If there is a major event at your university, the campus police may use hand signals or put up signs to direct traffic as talking to each motorist individually would be impractical.

With advances in technology we are also witnessing the emergence of new forms of nonverbal communication. In online communication (e.g., emails, Facebook, web forums, Instagram) it has become commonplace to insert **emoticons**, pictorial representations of facial expressions (e.g., punctuation marks and letters, images), to convey the tone of a message. Instead of relying solely on words, in Internet-mediated interactions, people often use emoticons to alert others to their mood or reaction to what has been posted (e.g., ☺ for happiness).

Throughout the world, a range of signs and symbols are used to regulate behavior and draw attention to hazardous situations (e.g., steep slope ahead, kangaroo crossing, slippery road when wet). Many symbols and illustrations are clearly linked to what they represent (e.g., pictures of related objects, lines in the shape of a particular object, a smile indicating a happy person), while other symbols are arbitrary and may not be interpreted as intended by people who have been socialized in a different cultural environment.

Repeating verbal messages

Nonverbal messages may also be used to repeat what we say verbally. For example, in emails emoticons may accompany the written word (e.g., a statement about feeling depressed may be accompanied by the image of a person with a sad face, a hostile comment may be followed by an emoticon of an angry facial expression). If a visitor asks you where the cafeteria is you may say that it is next to the campus bookstore while using your finger or arm to point in that direction. In this scenario, your nonverbal cue is repeating your words.

When using a second language that you are not fluent in, you may frequently use gestures to accompany your words, especially if you lack confidence in your oral skills and are concerned that your verbal message will not be understood. Of course, your gestures might also be misinterpreted by your communication partner, especially if he or she has been socialized in a different cultural environment.

Emphasizing verbal messages

Nonverbal messages may be used to emphasize the emotions or depth of feelings that lie behind the words we are speaking. For example, a furrowed brow can convey concern as you verbally tell a friend that you are sorry that her pet has died. A look of surprise (e.g., wide eyes, raised eyebrows) can emphasize your shock when you exclaim that you cannot believe that one of your friends is getting married to someone she has dated for only three weeks. In both examples, the verbal and nonverbal codes are in sync and apt to transmit a clear message to a close friend, who is very familiar with you and the way you communicate nonverbally.

Plate 4.1 In many countries, attitudes toward smoking have changed significantly. This bilingual anti-smoking message is posted throughout Japan. Would you understand the nonverbal message if you did not know Japanese or English? What anti-smoking signs, if any, are posted in your neighborhood? Would they be understood by newcomers? © Chan Sin Yu

Relaying awkward messages

Ideas or messages which are difficult or awkward to express verbally may sometimes be communicated more easily and effectively through nonverbal means. For example, when someone has passed away it is not easy to find the right words to say to the person's relatives or close friends. In lieu of words, sympathy and solidarity may be conveyed through a facial expression, a gentle touch on the arm, or by being sitting silently beside the bereaved in a memorial service.

Nonverbal channels may also be used to avoid awkward verbal communication encounters. For example, when you come across someone you don't wish to talk to, instead of giving a lengthy verbal excuse that does not ring true, you may keep on walking slowly and nonverbally indicate that you are in a rush to get somewhere. You could tap your watch, shrug your shoulders or raise your hands in the air to indicate that the situation is not in your control. As you smile, you keep on moving without exchanging a single word.

In contexts where very direct discourse (saying exactly what's on your mind) is considered overly aggressive and rude, individuals who are asked if they agree with a suggestion may remain silent and keep their eyes downcast to avoid an unpleasant, awkward confrontation. People who have been socialized to understand this indirect form of communication are apt to quickly realize that the idea that has been put forward is not supported, whereas individuals who are used to direct discourse may miss these nonverbal cues and continue to press for a verbal response. When a clear response does not come, both parties may be perplexed and irritated.

Regulating interactions

Nonverbal codes are frequently used to regulate conversations and other communicative events. Ekman and Friesen (1969: 82) coined the term '**regulators**' to refer to:

> actions which maintain and regulate the back-and-forth nature of speaking and listening between two or more interactants. They tell the speaker to continue, repeat, elaborate, hurry up, become more interesting, less salacious, give the other a chance to talk, etc. They tell the listener to pay special attention, to wait just a minute more, to talk, etc.

Through the use of these regulators (e.g., hand gestures, head nods, forward leans, gaze, other body movements) we can tell others to do or not to do something while we talk. We can give young children a stern look when we want them to stop poking each other or fidgeting while we are talking with them.

In interactions, we may use nonverbal means to direct **turn-taking** (e.g., indicate when to start or finish a conversation). In a small group project meeting, for example, you may use a hand gesture to signal that you are giving the floor to someone else. Alternatively, you can nonverbally indicate that you wish to speak by leaning forward or touching the arm of the person who is talking. The politeness norms associated with turn-taking vary depending on the cultural setting, the situation (e.g., formal event, informal chat), and the characteristics or attributes of the interactants (e.g., age, gender, cultural background, status) and the relationship between them (e.g., power distance, difference in status).

Displaying emotions

Nonverbal communication may also reveal our emotions, attitudes, and mental state. The term **emotional display** refers to the expression of our emotions (e.g., through gestures and expressiveness) (Altarriba & Kazanas 2018). When bored in a lecture, for example, we may yawn frequently, and our shoulders may slump. If we are happy, we may smile broadly. When we are very familiar with people and their habits, we may ascertain their state of mind simply by observing their nonverbal behavior. Words are not usually needed to know when a close friend is depressed, sad, or worried. Even if she says she is fine, we may rely more on nonverbal messages to gauge her mood. The better we know someone and the cultural context, the more likely we are to accurately interpret his or her affective state. This awareness can help us to respond appropriately.

Keltner and Ekman (2003: 412) explain that 'emotions are expressed in multiple channels, including the face and voice, and through words, prosody, and grammatical devices'; touch and body language (e.g., posture) may also disclose our affective state. At a basic level, emotions do not differ significantly across cultures; however, some variations in the ways people display their feelings (e.g., disgust, fear, guilt, pride, shame) may confound individuals who have been

Plate 4.2 Greetings vary in different parts of the world. In Thailand, the *wai* (traditional greeting of respect) consists of a slight bow, with the palms pressed together in a prayer-like fashion. This Buddha statue illustrates the wai hand position. © Jane Jackson

socialized in another cultural context (Altarriba & Kazanas 2018; van de Vijver 2018b). Mis-understandings about relationships may arise when these nonverbal cues are misunderstood. Keltner and Ekman (2003: 413) also observe that '[i]ndividuals vary, according to their personality, in how they express emotion in the face and voice'. While we may recognize some emotions (e.g., anxiety, happiness) in people who have a different cultural background, the situations in which they display these emotions may differ.

More recently, nonverbal communication scholars have turned their attention to the use of emotional expressions in online communication, including intercultural interactions (Altarriba & Kazanas 2018). Researchers have investigated the graphic representations of facial expressions in social networking sites (e.g., Twitter, Facebook, Instagram) and blogs and found interesting differences among people who have a different cultural background with regard to the preference for particular emotions (e.g., positive, negative, or ambiguous; eye-oriented vs. mouth-oriented) and the frequency of their use (Eaves & Leathers 2018). More research is needed to more fully understand the nonverbal dimension of online intercultural communication.

Emotion regulation, that is, the degree of control over one's emotions, may vary among individuals who have been socialized in a different cultural environment. For example, researchers have discovered that children in Japan learn from an early age that it is important to refrain from overtly expressing their feelings (van de Vijver 2018b). While many aspects of emotional display are universal, others are culturally variable and subject to individual differences within cultural groups.

Rituals

All cultures have **rituals** (sets of actions or rites performed for symbolic meaning) that include nonverbal actions. It is common for nonverbal acts to feature in demonstrations of patriotism (e.g., saluting the flag), national holidays, public ceremonies, parades, religious activities (e.g., praying, worship, baptisms), weddings, funerals, etc. Over time, related actions or activities become routinized and passed from one generation to another. People may still perform certain rites but no longer fully understand the reasons that lie behind them.

Even the ways people greet each other often involve nonverbal codes and these may vary from one cultural setting to another. In Thailand, for example, the traditional greeting referred to as the *wai* in Thai (ไหว้, pronounced [wâːj]) consists of a slight bow, with the palms pressed together in a prayer-like fashion. The higher the hands are held in relation to the face and the lower the bow, the more respect or reverence the giver of the *wai* is showing. This salutation is traditionally used when formally entering and leaving a house; the *wai* may also be used to convey gratitude or to apologize.

In Argentina, people usually give each other a peck on the cheek when they greet friends, family, and even acquaintances. Men may also hug and kiss their friends, both male and female, and in a more formal situation, shake hands, at least when meeting for the first time. In other parts of the world, different nonverbal actions or rituals may be performed to greet people. Within particular cultural contexts, the rituals may differ in some ways depending on the age, gender, and social status of the communicators.

CULTURE AND TYPES OF NONVERBAL COMMUNICATION

There are numerous types or forms of nonverbal communication. In this chapter, we review the following:

1   Paralanguage (vocalics)
2   Kinesics (body language)
3   Oculesics (eye contact or movement)
4   Proxemics (social distance)
5   Haptics (touch)
6   Olfactics (smell)
7   Physical appearance and artifacts
8   Chronemics (time)

Paralanguage

Paralanguage (also called **vocalics**) is concerned with the study of vocal or paralinguistic cues, that is, the nonphonemic qualities of language which convey meaning in verbal communication (Matsumoto & Hwang 2015; Moore *et al*. 2014). This area of research encompasses 'the nonverbal messages of the voice that add to the meaning of verbal communication, or that stand alone as a meaning-making entity' (Hickson *et al*. 2004: 258). It is important to pay attention to these nonlinguistic features of communication as they are 'often what give verbal messages their full meaning' (ibid: 258). It is through enculturation that we learn to recognize and interpret paralanguage in our home environment (e.g., develop an understanding of what vocal cues and behaviors are appropriate in particular situations). Therefore, when we engage in intercultural communication we are apt to encounter unfamiliar paralinguistic cues, or perhaps not notice them.

Nonverbal communication specialists have identified multiple characteristics of sound that contribute to the vocalic meaning associated with speech, including loudness (the volume and degree of intensity of the voice), pitch, duration (how long a particular sound is made), quality, regularity, articulation, pronunciation, and silence (e.g., Eaves & Leathers 2018; Moore *et al*. 2014). Belching, crying, gasping, grunting, laughing, sighing, whining, and yawning are also of interest as long as these sounds transmit messages.

The use and interpretation of paralinguistic cues can vary depending on the cultural context, which can complicate intercultural communication. For example, vocal qualifiers such as volume, pitch, rhythm, and tempo may differ among people who have been socialized in diverse regions. In some contexts, speaking loudly indicates sincerity, whereas in others it is interpreted as aggressive. Vocal segregates (utterances such as mmmm, uh-huh, oooo), vocal rate (the speed at which people talk), and vocal characterizers (e.g., laughter, belching, grunting) may also differ in diverse cultural contexts and be interpreted differently. For example, belching during or after a good meal is a common and accepted practice in some parts of the world and yet considered vulgar and inappropriate in other contexts.

Even the use and meaning of silence are influenced by culture. For example, among indigenous people in Northern Canada, it is not unusual for friends to enjoy each other's company by sitting together for long periods without uttering a word. Visitors who are not used to this practice may be uncomfortable with the 'dead air' and feel compelled to speak. Additionally, in face-to-face discussions attitudes can be expressed through silence, and this, too, can vary and be misinterpreted. For example, in contexts where high-context communication is common, messages are usually conveyed indirectly, and silence may indicate disapproval rather than the acceptance of an idea or proposal.

Not surprisingly, variations in paralanguage can lead to miscommunication. What is deemed polite behavior in one cultural context may be considered weird or rude in another, and this can easily lead to negative valuations of people who are communicating in ways that are unfamiliar. When vocal cues are misinterpreted or overlooked, intercultural communication may falter and hamper relationship building.

Kinesics

Kinesics is a broad category of nonverbal actions. It encompasses the study of body movement (**body language**), e.g., body posture, gestures, facial expressions, and eye movements. Basically, kinesics is concerned with the messages that are conveyed through physical movement, either by the body as a whole or by specific parts (e.g., the face, hands, arms). It also encompasses **posture** (the ways people stand and sit) and **eye movements** (e.g., the rolling of the eyes, the arching of eyebrows) that convey meaning to others, whether intentional or not. Kinesics includes the study of **affect displays**, that is, the use of physical movement (e.g., facial expressions, posture) to convey the intensity of an emotion (Altarriba & Kazanas 2018). As noted by William Shakespeare, people can 'speak' through body movements, including facial expressions.

Plate 4.3 Emotions are often expressed nonverbally. This Filipina seller is making a gesture to the photographer. Can you identify the meaning of the nonverbal emblem and discern his affective state? © David Jackson

Body language communication varies from one cultural setting to another. In Egypt, for example, vigorous hand movements and body gestures are often used to express anger. In Japan, locals may be just as furious (or even more so) but as their nonverbal behaviors are more contained or less expressive to an Egyptian, for example, they may appear to be less agitated. Not surprisingly, this dimension can potentially lead to miscommunication.

Kinesics also includes communication through the use of smiling, frowning, giggling, and so on; these nonverbal cues may differ among and within cultures. Around the world, a smile usually signals happiness; however, in some cultural contexts it can also mask sadness or be used to conceal embarrassment. For example, in some East Asian nations people may smile or even laugh or giggle in situations they find awkward or overly personal (e.g., when they are embarrassed about a mistake they have made at work, when someone reveals that a close

Plate 4.4   This woman is selling vegetables in a market in Siem Reap, Cambodia. Can you read her state of mind? Is a smile a universal marker of happiness? © Jane Jackson

friend has just passed away). Communication partners from other cultural backgrounds who are unfamiliar with this nonverbal behavior may mistakenly interpret the smile or laugh as uncaring, rude, and a bit strange. Misunderstandings like this can hamper the development of constructive intercultural relations.

Gestures

Gestures are typically hand or facial movements that are used to illustrate speech and convey verbal meaning. Ekman and Friesen (1969) identified five types of gestures:

Illustrators: Shape/illustrate what is being said (e.g., pointing, outlining a picture of a referent)
Emblems: Direct replacements for words (e.g., OK signal in U.S.)
Affect displays: Convey the intensity of an emotion (e.g., frown, dropping shoulders to signify sadness/empathy)
Regulators: Control the flow of conversation (e.g., hand gestures, head nods)
Adaptors: Used unintentionally to relieve tension (e.g., scratching, smoking)

Speech illustrators are gestures or movements that are directly linked to speech, that is, they illustrate or emphasize the verbal message, even though the user may not be conscious of their use (Ekman & Friesen 1969; Matsumoto & Hwang 2012, 2015). Drawing on the work of Efron (1968), Ekman (2004: 41) classified illustrators into the following categories:

Batons (movements that emphasize a particular word or phrase)
Ideographs (movements that draw a thought or outline a path)
Deictic movements (e.g., pointing to draw attention to someone or something)
Kinetographs (e.g., to illustrate bodily action)
Spatial movements (e.g., to illustrate spatial relationships)
Pictographs (e.g., to draw a picture of their referent)
Rhythmic movements (e.g., to illustrate the pacing of an activity or event)

Most of these illustrative gestures are performed with the hands, and all of them may be linked to verbal behavior (e.g., volume of speech, speech context, verbal meaning) as it occurs in real time. Except for the first two types, batons and ideographs, illustrators have meaning even without language (Matsumoto & Hwang 2012).

Cultural differences are evident in the amount, type, and frequency of the illustrative gestures that are used in different parts of the world. In Latin and North African cultures, for example, large, illustrative gestures often accompany speech, that is, individuals are inclined to be highly expressive in their gesticulation. In contrast, from an early age, children in East Asian cultures are discouraged from using such gestures in public so they tend to be relatively less expressive in their use of gestures (Matsumoto & Hwang 2012, 2016; van de Vijver 2018b). Naturally, there are also variations *within* cultures as a consequence of individual differences and contextual elements.

Emblems or **emblematic gestures** are used to convey messages without speech. Every culture has emblematic gestures which are associated with particular words or phrases. Ekman

(2004) maintains that '[e]mblems are the only true 'body language', in that these movements have a set of precise meanings, which are understood by all members of a culture or subculture' (p. 39). Within cultures, some of these gestures are gender-specific (e.g., in traditional cultures, obscene gestures may primarily be used by males in the company of other men and if used by females they are considered very shocking.) Examples of emblems are the peace sign (two fingers up, palm facing outward), and the OK sign (thumb up, hand in fist), which are generally understood by people who have been socialized in the U.S. and Canada. Emblems like these permit communication across distances when verbal messages cannot be easily heard or when speech is not permitted or safe.

Since emblems are culture-specific, their meanings can vary in different cultural settings. A gesture that has a positive connotation in one context may be deemed offensive in another. For example, the American A-OK sign has sexual implications in many parts of Europe and is regarded as an obscene gesture. In other cultural settings, it may have no meaning at all. The American inverted peace sign – two fingers up in a fist pointed inward toward oneself – is interpreted as an insult in England and Australia. (See Figure 4.1 for examples of emblems that are culture specific.)

While emblems tend to be culture-specific, David Matsumoto and other nonverbal researchers observe that due to the influence of the mass media (e.g., television, film, the press) and advances in technology and social media (e.g., Facebook, films, YouTube) common American emblematic gestures for 'hello', 'good-bye', 'yes', and 'no' are now widely understood on all continents (Hwang *et al.* 2010; Matsumoto & Hwang 2012).

Posture

While vocal cues (e.g., tone, volume of voice) and facial expressions (e.g., frowns, smiles) can convey specific emotions (e.g., anger, fear, happiness), body **posture** is more likely to disclose an individual's general state of mind and attitude (e.g., mood, emotion, feeling). For example, the way we stand can reveal whether we are interested or disinterested in someone and whether we are being attentive or not. Our posture can indicate if we are open or closed to what our communication partner is saying. How we stand can also signal our status or positioning in relation to another speaker (Matsumoto & Hwang 2012, 2015; Mehrabian 1969). For instance, we are apt to stand in a more upright position when communicating with someone of a higher status.

Facial expressions and emotional display

The English naturalist Charles Darwin (1872) stated that all humans possess the ability to express emotions in exactly the same ways, primarily through their faces. Anthropologist Margaret Mead (1930), however, argued, that facial expressions of emotion are culture-specific and learned in each culture like verbal language. This issue has been debated for decades. In a series of studies conducted in the 1960s by Paul Ekman and his colleagues, participants from different parts of the world were shown images of facial expressions. Interestingly, all of them agreed that the following emotions were conveyed in the faces they viewed: anger, disgust, fear, happiness, sadness, and surprise, lending support for the notion of universal facial expressions (Ekman 1972, 1973; Ekman & Friesen 1971; Izard 1971). Later, a seventh facial expression – contempt – was found to be universally

Had too much to drink (France)

Anger (Japan)

Come here (Japan)

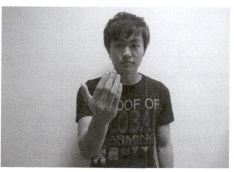

Come here (U.S.)

No! (U.S.)

Don't do that! (France)

Money (U.S.)

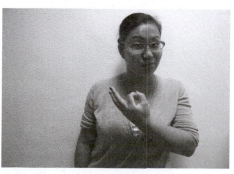

Money (Japan)

Figure 4.1 Examples of culture-specific emblems

Source: Reprinted with permission from ©Jane Jackson, author

recognized (Ekman & Heider 1988; Matsumoto 1992). These findings led Ekman (2009: 1) to the following conclusion:

> In business and in life, it doesn't matter what language you speak, where you live, what you do for a living – the facial expressions you show for anger, fear, sadness, disgust, surprise, contempt and happiness will be the same. You share these expressions with all human beings, and many of them with the great apes.

Over the past four decades there have been well over 100 judgment studies that have demonstrated the pancultural recognition of these seven expressions; more than 75 studies have found that these facial expressions are spontaneously produced by individuals all over the world to convey similar emotions (Matsumoto *et al.* 2008). These findings provide strong evidence for the universal facial expressions of emotions that are depicted in Figure 4.2. The implication is that these expressions are biologically innate.

Despite the existence of universal facial expressions of emotion, people around the world express certain emotions differently. Nonverbal communication specialists Ekman and Friesen (1969) coined the term **cultural display rules** to account for cultural differences in facial expressions of emotion. At a young age, through the primary socialization process, we learn to manage and modify our emotional expressions in particular situations and social contexts.

Ekman and Friesen (1969) identified six ways in which expressions may be managed when emotion is aroused:

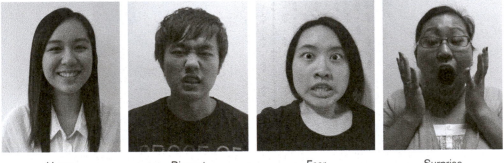

Happy   Disgust   Fear   Surprise

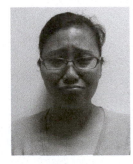

Sadness   Contempt   Anger

Figure 4.2 The seven universal facial expressions of emotion

Source: Reprinted with permission from ©Jane Jackson, author

1   Individuals can express emotions as they feel them with no modification.
2   They can amplify (exaggerate) their expressions, e.g., feelings of sadness may be intensi-fied (amplification) at funerals.
3   They can minimize their expressions, e.g., limit displays of sadness at weddings to avoid upsetting others.
4   People can mask or conceal their emotions by expressing something other than what they feel, as when physicians hide their emotions when communicating with patients with ter-minal illness.
5   Individuals may also learn to neutralize their expressions, expressing nothing, e.g., when playing poker.
6   They can qualify their feelings by expressing emotions in combination, e.g., when feelings of sadness are intermingled with a smile, with the smile commenting on the sadness, say-ing 'I'll be OK'.

Studies of spontaneous expressive behaviors have identified all of the behavioral responses that have been previously described (Cole 1986; Ekman & Rosenberg 1998). Based on their own work and that of other nonverbal communication specialists, Matsumoto and Hwang (2012, 2016) concluded that when emotions are aroused, displays may be *either* universal *or* culture-specific, depending, in part, on the context.

Oculesics

Oculesics is concerned with eye behavior as an element of communication (e.g., eye contact, dynamic eye movement, pupil dilation, static/fixed gaze, gaze direction and intensity). The term **gaze** refers to the act of looking at someone or something. It can be a powerful form of nonverbal communication, and, to complicate matters, its use and interpretation may vary in different cultural settings and contexts, and among genders.

Research on humans and non-human primates has revealed that gaze serves multiple func-tions; for example, it can express emotions, intentions, or attitudes. Gaze can also convey group membership and empathy (Argyle & Cook 1976) as well as dominance, power, or aggression (Fehr & Exline 1987). Matsumoto and Hwang (2012) note that in North America the power of gaze is evident in 'the staring game', in which two people stare at each other to see who can outlast the other; the one who smiles or looks away first is the loser, whereas the one who stares longer is declared the winner.

To foster group membership, unity, and stability, cultures develop unwritten rules or norms for gazing behavior in specific situations and contexts. Not surprisingly, there are cultural dif-ferences in gazing rules and visual behavior, which can lead to misunderstandings in intercul-tural interactions. In the United States, for example, **direct eye contact** (looking into the eyes of the other person) is common about 40% of the time while talking and 70% while listening, whereas in Japan, it is more common to look at the throat of the other person (Matsumoto & Hwang 2012). From an early age, U.S. American children are taught to look directly into the eyes of their older interlocutor to demonstrate respect. In North Asia, however, this same behavior is deemed disrespectful and children are expected to look away (e.g., downward) to show deference to their elders. Individuals who are expecting direct eye contact may find it dif-ficult to 'read' the situation when their communication partner does not make eye contact with them; they may view gaze avoidance as disrespectful, insincere, or even deceitful. Conversely, individuals who are not expecting direct eye contact may judge people who gaze directly at them as aggressive or arrogant; feeling under threat, they may be unwilling to engage further.

In Arab cultures it is common for male speakers and listeners to look directly into each other's eyes for long periods of time, indicating keen interest in the conversation. In Mediterranean societies men may gaze intensely at women for long periods of time, which may be interpreted as intrusive and impolite by women from other cultural backgrounds (Eaves & Leathers 2018; Moore *et al.* 2014). As cultural norms for gazing vary, one's nonverbal behavior may not be interpreted as intended, resulting in intercultural misunderstandings.

Proxemics

Proxemics is concerned with the social use of space in a communication situation. As well as the effective use of space in businesses, homes, and other social settings (public or private), it encompasses the arrangement of space (e.g., furniture, architecture) to encourage or inhibit

Plate 4.5   In Beijing, houses in hutongs (narrow streets or alleys) are very close together. How might the use of space influence social relations? © Jane Jackson

communication and also the use of space in human interactions. The term '**interpersonal distance**' refers to the psychological 'bubble' or the preferred space that separates individuals from their communication partners in a particular cultural context. The distance between interlocutors helps to regulate intimacy by controlling exposure to the senses (sight, smell, touch); the closer people are to each other when they interact, the greater the sensory stimulation (smells, sights, touch) (Hall 1963, 1968). Further, the interpersonal distance that people find comfortable varies, in part, due to what they have grown accustomed to during the socialization process.

In *The Hidden Dimension* (1966), Hall proposed a theory of proxemics based on the notion that human perceptions of space are shaped and patterned by culture. He observed and analyzed the personal spaces that people form around their bodies as well as their culturally shaped expectations about how streets, neighborhoods, housing estates, and cities should be organized spatially. Hall (1966) concluded that the ways people in various cultures define and organize space are internalized at an unconscious level.

Hall's (1959, 1966) classic work on proxemics identified four levels of interpersonal space use in the United States, which vary depending on the type of social relationship involved: intimate, personal, social, and public. He then placed these spatial zones on a continuum, ranging from **intimate space** (reserved for private situations with people who are emotionally close to us, such as family members and very close friends, 0–18 inches), to **personal space** (informal distance reserved for close friends, colleagues, and some acquaintances, 18 inches to 4 feet), to

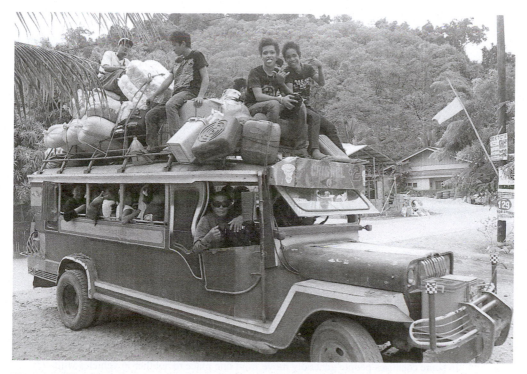

Plate 4.6 Wherever we live, we become accustomed to a certain amount of personal space. In a small island in the Philippines, locals crowd into jeepneys to get around. How would you feel in this situation? Would you be willing to climb onboard? © David Jackson

social space (formal distance between acquaintances at a social function such as a party, 4–12 feet), and **public space**/distance (less personal contact in public situations (e.g., when talking to a large group), beyond 12 feet). Violations of these zones can cause discomfort and anxiety.

Enculturation plays a significant role in determining what distance we consider to be appropriate in certain social situations (Høgh-Olesen 2018). While people from all cultural backgrounds appear to use space according to the four major distinctions proposed by Hall (1959, 1966), they differ in the amount of space or distance linked to each category. In Latin America, for example, people who are complete strangers may greet one another by kissing on the cheeks and then sit very close to each other. In contrast, North Americans may shake hands with a stranger but stand several feet apart when interacting for the first time.

There are also cultural variations in interpersonal space related to gender. For example, it is acceptable in Western countries for men and women to sit or stand close to each other when talking, whereas in some Muslim countries it is taboo for there to be interaction between males and females in certain social situations. These nonverbal 'rules' vary within nations and regions and depend on the context, gender, and relationship between the interactants. They are also subject to culture change (e.g., adjustments due to exposure to other practices.)

Through the primary socialization process, children develop expectations about what is socially acceptable in terms of interpersonal distance, and this can vary in different cultural settings. Hall (1968: 88) observed that 'physical contact between two people . . . can be perfectly correct in one culture, and absolutely taboo in another'. Not surprisingly, when people who have a different cultural background interact, conflicting expectations of spatial behavior can lead to misunderstandings, which hamper intercultural relations. For example, if a Northern

Plate 4.7   In some countries people generally move from one place to another in vehicles with only one or a few people inside. If you were used to a lot of personal space how would you feel if you were studying or working in an environment where you had to travel in a crowded subway each day? © Jane Jackson

European woman is greeted by a Latin American male she barely knows, she may feel as if her space is being invaded if he kisses her on both cheeks and stands close to her. She may feel a bit threatened and consciously or subconsciously step back to regain her physical space and sense of security. Although unintentional, her actions may be considered rude by the Latin American. If the woman does not accept the kiss and extends her hand instead he might view her actions as standoffish or impolite.

As the previous example illustrates, individuals from different cultural backgrounds may have divergent ideas about what spatial distances are appropriate in a given situation. Being sensitive to such differences is critical to successful intercultural communication. It is also important to be mindful of individual variations and not stick to preconceived ideas about people affiliated with a particular culture. If we are observant we can become more attuned to the comfort level of our communication partners and adjust our use of social space, accordingly.

Haptics

Haptics refers to the use of touch in communication, including the type of contact as well as its frequency and intensity. Touch can send multiple messages, many of which are affective or emotional in nature. In a communicative event, for example, touch can disclose one's attitude toward one's communication partners, including distinct emotions such as anger, fear, disgust, love, gratitude, and sympathy. Touch can also be used to provide support and encouragement, display intimacy, signal approval, or, alternatively, convey dislike, distrust, and/or rejection. In addition to attachment, bonding, or protection, touch can indicate compliance and mark differences in power, status, and prestige.

Like many other elements of nonverbal communication, haptics is very much influenced by enculturation. From a young age, through the primary socialization process, we learn rules for touching in various situations (e.g., the type and amount of touching considered appropriate when interacting with parents, siblings, teachers, acquaintances of the opposite sex, romantic partners). When, how, where, and whom we feel comfortable touching varies considerably among diverse cultural contexts.

After observing cultural differences in the use of touch, E.T. Hall (1966) drew a distinction between what he termed **high-contact** and **low-contact communication**. In the former, people tend to display considerable interpersonal closeness or immediacy, e.g., encourage touching and touch more often than those in cultures that favor low-contact communication. High-contact communication is common in warmer countries near the equator (e.g., Columbia, Egypt, Indonesia, Western Africa), while low-contact communication is more prevalent in cooler climates farther from the equator (e.g., Britain, South Korea, Sweden) (McKay 2018; van de Vijver 2018b).

In Latin American, Mediterranean, and Middle Eastern contexts, (high-contact or high-touch cultures), Hall (1966) observed that people tend to employ a lot of social touching in greetings and conversation (e.g., hugs, hand-holding, kisses) with members of the same gender. In moderate-touch cultures (e.g., the United States, Sweden), touching (e.g., handshakes, back slapping, sporadic shoulder or arm touching) is used less frequently. In low-contact cultures such as those in North Asia, social touching among acquaintances is generally not as common as in high-contact cultures.

Research in diverse cultural settings has demonstrated that the way touch is used and interpreted may differ depending on one's socialization and degree of intercultural awareness and sensitivity (Hertenstein *et al.* 2009). Violations of cultural rules or norms for touch and personal space likely have negative consequences. In business situations in different cultural contexts, handshakes may vary in terms of the strength of the grip, arm movements, and duration of the contact. In some Asian countries, handshakes tend to be less firm than in North America and Northern Europe. Consequently, a tight grip and prolonger, vigorous handshake may be considered rude and overly aggressive. Conversely, businesspeople in Belgium or Germany who are expecting a firm handshake may be confused when they receive a brief, weak handshake from a Japanese businessman, and they may regard him as insecure or disinterested.

It is important to recognize, however, that the cultural and social rules governing touch are situational and vary *within* cultures. Touching behaviors can also change over time, in part, as a consequence of exposure to other norms of touching in the multicultural workplace, the mass media, films, and firsthand intercultural contact in one's social life. Further, the amount, type, frequency, and meaning of touch may differ depending on the gender, age, and situation, as well as the relationship between the people involved. For example, while some Mainland Chinese may be reserved when interacting with acquaintances, they may use a significant amount of social touching in conversations and interactions with family members and close friends of the same gender. While classification systems can provide a general picture of nonverbal behaviors, we must be aware of and sensitive to possible variations in different situations and contexts.

Olfactics

Olfactics (also known as olfaction) is the study of smells (e.g., perfumes, spices, body odor, deodorant), including how they are perceived. Some studies indicate that there is a universal preference for certain scents, which is likely due to biological makeup and evolution (Liu *et al*. 2019). Fragrances such as jasmine, lavender, and rose, for example, tend to communicate a soothing and relaxing feeling to individuals no matter the cultural background. Other research points to interesting cultural differences regarding smell that may affect intercultural relations.

How people perceive and react to body odor can vary due to our eating habits and attitudes that are prevalent in our cultural environment. People who eat a lot of meat tend to have a different body odor than vegetarians, although they are very likely unaware of this. Individuals who are raised in an environment where meat is not consumed may be sensitive to the smell of meat and meat-eaters, and this may influence how they respond to them. The converse may also be true.

In some parts of the world, through the primary socialization process, people learn to conceal body odor (e.g., perspiration, bad breath) through the use of deodorants, colognes, mouth wash, breath mints, and other means, whereas, in other cultural contexts, the smells that the body emits are accepted as natural and fewer hygiene products appear on the shelves of local markets. In addition to personal odors, the foods we prepare and eat affect the smells in our homes, although we are not likely to notice as we are so used to them. When someone who has been socialized in another cultural environment visits us, they may be sensitive to unfamiliar odors and react to them.

In some cultures, certain smells communicate social class and power, and they may be used to categorize people. Synnott (1993), for example, observed that perceived foul odors are one of the criteria by which negative identities are attributed to some social or ethnic groups. In Germany the strong odor of sweat may be linked to manual labor and a lower status (e.g., immigrant construction workers), whereas the wearing of an expensive perfume, cologne, or after-shave can signal status and wealth (e.g., professionals). In Hong Kong, the smell of curry is associated with South Asians, and this can sometimes be used as the basis for discrimination (e.g., refusals to rent apartments to people from India and Pakistan). More olfactics research is needed in various cultural contexts to more fully understand the ways in which smell can play a role in communication, including intercultural interactions.

Physical appearance and artifacts

Physical appearance is also considered a form of nonverbal communication among human beings. In addition to **physical features** (e.g., body type, deformities, eye shape, gender, height, skin color, weight), this type of nonverbal code includes **artifacts** (objects created or shaped by humans) such as various forms of **decorative ornamentation** (e.g., accessories, body piercings, brand names and logos, choice of color, clothes, grooming, hairstyle, jewelry, makeup, tattoos) used to enhance one's appearance. What we wear (e.g., designer watches, eyeglasses, clothes, purses) or surround ourselves with (e.g., expensive cars, pets) sends messages about our preferred self-identities and personal nature. Whether we are aware of it or not, our physical appearance and related artifacts may convey information about our gender, social class, status, personality, and group memberships (e.g., affiliations with our ethnic group or a subgroup such as a student organization).

Appearance messages are generally the first nonverbal codes we process and, as such, they can have a profound impact on any verbal communication that follows. When we first meet people we often form judgments about their personality, abilities, and other attributes based on the way they look and what they wear, among other things. We quickly form an impression about their degree of similarity to us (e.g., age, dress, adornments, skin color) and assess such aspects as their social standing, credibility, financial status, and general attractiveness (Moore *et al.* 2014). These first impressions can affect our desire to interact and form personal relationships. More specifically they can influence our comfort level and our subsequent willingness to disclose our ideas and feelings. For example, we may be less inclined to develop friendships with people we perceive as very different from ourselves. Of course, just as we are judging others, our observers are forming opinions about us (e.g., our identities, manners, positioning or status, sense of style).

Our perceptions of what is attractive, beautiful, or appropriate (e.g., adornments, dress) are influenced by our culture and the media (e.g., television, magazines, social media) as well as our intercultural experience and degree of openness. Through enculturation we build up expectations of what physical appearance and attire are acceptable in certain situations and contexts. We may not be consciously aware of how we are reading visual cues (e.g., dress, body shape, weight), but the messages and our reactions can be quite powerful. For example, police and military uniforms subliminally communicate the authority of those wearing them. In some contexts they can instill fear rather than respect. Well-groomed executives wearing tailored suits project success, whereas adults wearing wrinkled, soiled sportswear in a business setting may transmit messages of failure (e.g., limited education, a poor work ethic, low status), which lessens their credibility. People who are obese may be perceived as lazy and unproductive, while blondes may be viewed as sexually permissive and lacking in intelligence. In some quarters, Muslim women who wear the veil may be perceived as subservient, religious fanatics, whereas in others they may be accorded more respect than women who are uncovered.

Culture clashes may erupt in intercultural situations due to differing ideas about what is appropriate attire in certain social situations. In the United Arab Emirates, local women launched a Twitter campaign to object to 'scantily clad' women from other countries who visit the shopping malls and other public places (e.g., foreigners wearing short shorts and halter tops). In another example, a French law on secularity and conspicuous religious symbols bans the wearing of conspicuous religious symbols in public (i.e. government-operated) schools in France. This includes the niqab, a veil that covers a woman's face so that only her eyes are exposed through slits. Mismatches between traditional and modern values about what is appropriate attire may lead to intercultural misunderstandings and conflict.

Although subliminal messages about physical appearance are below our level of awareness, they are often more powerful than conscious, overt messages. Advertisers take advantage of this to persuade us to buy certain products to become more attractive, slimmer, whiter, etc. Young, beautiful people usually appear in advertisements to communicate the subconscious message that the advertised product is associated with youth and beauty (according to prevailing views about what this actually is). As a consequence of globalization, many beauty brands and products are now sold around the world with implicit or explicit notions about what it means to be beautiful (usually a Western image). Influenced by these messages, some people are taking drastic steps to alter their appearance. Young models may develop an eating disorder as they strive to obtain a weight well below what is normal for them. In an effort to conform to prevailing standards of beauty, in many cultural settings, strict diets and exercise programs abound. Some Asian women have plastic surgery to add a crease to their upper eye lid so that their eyes will look larger and, in some cases, more Westernized.

The colors we wear can also send messages to others, whether intentional or not. Some colors may have a particular meaning in certain cultural contexts, while in others they may mean something completely different or signify nothing at all. If someone is dressed in black from head to toe, for example, it might indicate the person is in mourning, while in another context it might signify an individual's membership in a gang, or it might simply serve as an indicator of the person's degree of sophistication and style. The color one chooses to wear may simply be linked to personality traits and preferences rather than cultural norms.

Chronemics

Chronemics is the study of how people use, view, and structure time. The way that we perceive and value time, organize our time, and respond to time influences the communication process (Berglund 2015). To complicate matters, all of these elements may vary depending on the cultural environment and what individuals have become accustomed to during the socialization process.

Time perception, which includes punctuality and willingness to wait, may play a significant role in the nonverbal communication process in intercultural communication. The use of time can affect one's lifestyle, daily routine, rate of speech, movements, and how long one is willing to listen or wait for others. Time can also be used to reinforce one's status. In most companies the boss can interrupt progress to hold an impromptu meeting in the middle of the workday, yet the average worker is likely to have to make an appointment to see a supervisor.

Monochronic and polychronic time orientations

Some intercultural scholars have categorized cultures into two time system categories: **monochronic** and **polychronic** (Hall & Hall 1990; Kaufman-Scarborough 2018). The characteristics associated with each are presented in Table 4.1.

Table 4.1 Characteristics of monochronic and polychronic time systems

In a monochronic time system, people tend to:	In a polychronic time system, people tend to:
do one thing at a time	do many things at once
concentrate on the job	be highly distractible and subject to interruptions
take time commitments (deadlines, schedules) seriously	consider an objective to be achieved, if possible
be low-context and need information	be high-context and already have information
be committed to the job	be committed to people and human relationships
stick to plans	change plans often and easily
be concerned about not disturbing others; follow rules of privacy and consideration	be more concerned with those who are closely related than with privacy
show great respect for private property; seldom borrow or lend	borrow and lend things often and easily
emphasize promptness	base promptness on the relationship
be accustomed to short-term relationships	have strong tendency to build lifetime relationships

In a monochronic time orientation tasks are done one at a time, and time is segmented into precise, small units so that one's day is scheduled, arranged, and managed. Time is basically like a commodity; hence, the common saying, 'Time is money'. Monochronic cultures include Canada, East Asia, England, Japan, Germany, Northern Europe, and the United States. Individuals who have been socialized in these contexts typically value schedules, tasks, and 'getting the job done'. In workplace situations individuals are committed to regimented schedules and may view those who do not subscribe to the same perception of time as disrespectful and disorganized.

In a polychronic time orientation multiple tasks can be performed simultaneously, and schedules follow a more fluid approach. Latin American, African, Asian, and Arabic cultures generally follow the polychronic system of time. Unlike Americans and most northern and western European cultures, individuals from these cultures are much less focused on the preciseness of accounting for each and every moment. In contrast with monochronic cultures, polychronic cultures prioritize tradition and relationships over tasks. Consequently, individuals are not ruled by schedules and have a more informal, elastic perception of time. They may arrive late for events with family or close friends and, as they may schedule multiple appointments simultaneously, it is difficult to keep to a tight schedule. Polychronic cultures include Egypt, India, Mexico, Pakistan, the Philippines, and Saudi Arabia. As one might expect, intercultural misunderstandings may arise when people familiar with different time systems interact. It is also vital to be attentive to individual variations and not assume that people will view time in a particular way because they have grown up in a particular part of the world. Being observant in intercultural situations can help you to discover how your communication partners' view and use time.

THE NONVERBAL EXPECTANCY VIOLATION THEORY

The **nonverbal expectancy violation theory**, which was developed by Judee Burgoon (1978), suggests that during the socialization process we build up expectations (mostly subconscious)

about how others should behave nonverbally in particular situations and contexts. In other words, from an early age we learn certain social norms of nonverbal behavior and become comfortable with certain **nonverbal cues** (informative behaviors that are not purely linguistic in content), just as we become accustomed to particular verbal expressions of politeness (e.g., greetings, cultural scripts).

When our nonverbal expectations are violated, we are apt to react negatively. As Høgh-Olesen (2018) explains, '[i]f the level of intimacy is greater or lesser than expected, the person withdraws; if it equals, reciprocation occurs' (p. 1670). When someone stands too close to us or stares at us longer than we are used to, we likely feel uneasy and even threatened. We may then cast this person and the relationship in a negative light. We may even extend this valuation to all perceived members of this individual's culture. As nonverbal communication often takes place at a subconscious level, we likely have little awareness that we are making positive or negative judgments about others based on their violation of our expectations of certain nonverbal behaviors (Burgoon 1995; Floyd *et al.* 2008).

The expectancy violation theory, which has been applied to a wide range of nonverbal behavior such as body movement, facial expression, eye contact, posture, touch, and time management, helps explain common reactions to unexpected nonverbal behavior in intercultural interactions (Burgoon 1978). When expectations are not met, the violation can impact people's impressions of one another and, this in turn, can influence the outcomes of their interactions. 'Stable exchanges occur when discrepancies are small, and unstable exchanges occur when discrepancies are great' (Høgh-Olesen 2018: 1670). This theory has significant implications for ways to enhance intercultural relations. In particular, it raises awareness of the importance of becoming more attuned to one's expectations of nonverbal behaviors. It is also vital to recognize that differing norms may prevail in different cultural contexts. Additional ways to enhance one's nonverbal interactions in intercultural interactions are explored in the next section.

NONVERBAL INTERCULTURAL COMMUNICATIVE COMPETENCE

Although studying nonverbal communication cannot ensure competence in interpersonal communication, more awareness of nonverbal codes and the potential variations across and within cultures can help to enhance your interaction with people who have been socialized in a different cultural environment. The following are some practical suggestions to optimize nonverbal communication in intercultural interactions.

1 Become more attuned to your own nonverbal behavior and expectations in diverse settings, as well as your attitudes toward nonverbal behavior that differs from your own.
2 Recognize that people communicate on many levels (e.g., multiple nonverbal channels). Be attentive to voice qualities (e.g., volume, tone), eye contact, facial expressions, hand and feet movements, body movement and placement, gestures, posture, gait, and appearance. In a new environment carefully observe nonverbal communication in specific settings. Becoming more aware of the nonverbal communication of your hosts can help you to recognize and better understand the messages they are sending.
3 In intercultural interactions, note the nonverbal behaviors of your communication partners, and check to see if their nonverbal communication is telling you that they understand or misunderstand you. Your ability to read nonverbal communication can improve with practice.

4   If individuals say something verbally and their nonverbal communication conveys another message, seek verbal clarification.

5   Be aware that you are often being evaluated by your nonverbal communication. When people meet you for the first time they are observing your appearance, gestures, voice qualities, and other nonverbal codes and forming an impression of you. For example, in an interview (e.g., for scholarships, study abroad, a job) the interviewers may assess your nonverbal behaviors as well as your verbal comments. Through nonverbal channels you are sending signals about your degree of self-confidence, level of interest and motivation, attitude toward the interview, emotional state, and many other personal attributes and characteristics. Think about the messages that your posture, eye contact, and other nonverbal behaviors are sending.

6   Check your perceptions of others' nonverbal behavior to see if you are accurate or if you are misreading (or overlooking) nonverbal cues.

7   Seek verbal clarification for unexpected nonverbal behavior instead of rushing to judgment.

8   Expand your nonverbal communication repertoire. In new cultural settings, for example, observe and practice new nonverbal behaviors and see what you are comfortable with.

9   Become more aware of your prejudicial assumptions related to nonverbal behavior. When you have an adverse reaction to someone from another cultural background, reflect on the basis for it. Is unfamiliar nonverbal behavior the source of your discomfort? For example, is the person standing very close to you and making you feel uneasy? Has he or she been socialized to be more familiar with less personal distance between people?

10   Never assume that individuals who have a different linguistic and cultural background understand your nonverbal messages. When in doubt use verbal checks to ensure that your meaning has been interpreted as intended.

11   Be flexible and adaptable in your nonverbal communication in intercultural encounters. At times, in a respectful way, try synchronizing your behavior to that of your communication partners, as this may communicate respect and the desire to cultivate the relationship.

12   When working in a diverse group or leading a meeting with people from different cultural backgrounds, be attentive to nonverbal cues as they can tell you:

  ■   When you've talked long enough or too long
  ■   Whether it is appropriate to interrupt a speaker as well as the accepted ways to do so
  ■   When someone else wishes to speak or take the floor
  ■   The mood of the group
  ■   Their feelings about your comments and suggestion

Listening attentively and observing the nonverbal behavior of group members can help you to be a more effective group member and communicator.

13   Whenever possible, try to accompany your nonverbal messages with some type of verbal follow-up that reiterates or emphasizes your nonverbal message.

14   Be aware that your physical appearance and attire are continuously sending out messages about who you are and how you feel about the people around you.

15   Finally, remember that your cultural background plays a significant role in the nonverbal messages you send and how you interpret nonverbal messages.

Similar to verbal codes, nonverbal acts vary among people who have a different cultural background, and these differences can sometimes lead to misunderstandings and conflict. To become a competent intercultural communicator it is important to recognize the multiple dimensions of nonverbal communication that can affect interpersonal relations. Making an effort to enhance and expand your nonverbal communication repertoire is vital for effective intercultural interactions.

Your nonverbal communication skills can improve with practice and, ultimately, strengthen relationships with individuals who have been socialized in a different cultural setting.

SUMMARY

While our language system is undeniably a vital component of communication, nonverbal actions that occur on their own or accompany spoken messages can be even more significant and powerful. Nonverbal cues account for most of the communication we have with others in face-to-face interactions, and when there is a discrepancy between verbal and nonverbal messages, adults tend to believe the latter. Although nonverbal communication and verbal communication differ in many ways, the two systems often function together. It is important to recognize that we both send and receive nonverbal information through multiple sensory channels (e.g., visual, auditory, smell, touch) with or without speech.

This chapter introduced many different functions and types of nonverbal codes (e.g., haptics, kinesics, oculesics, olfactics, physical appearance and attire, proxemics, paralanguage). While some elements appear to be universal, the use of nonverbal codes can vary among individuals from different cultural backgrounds (e.g., differing gestures as well as norms and interpretations of nonverbal actions). The nonverbal expectancy violation theory suggests that when we encounter unfamiliar nonverbal behaviors we may instinctively react in a negative way and not even realize why. To become a competent intercultural communicator in today's globalized world, it is imperative that we enrich our knowledge of nonverbal communication and expand our repertoire of nonverbal behaviors and strategies so that our communication is more appropriate and effective in diverse contexts and situations.

discussion questions

1   As an intercultural communicator, why is it helpful to become more knowledgeable about nonverbal communication? Discuss your ideas with a partner.

2   What are the major differences between verbal and nonverbal communication?

3   Explain how culture, language, and nonverbal communication are connected. Share your understandings with a partner.

4   In your home environment, do males and females use nonverbal communication in different ways? Have you observed any gender differences in nonverbal communication in other cultural contexts? Provide examples in various situations and cultural settings. Share your ideas with a partner.

5   Through the process of primary socialization, we learn to speak at a preferred volume in certain situations and contexts. Can you think of any examples in which you have negatively judged people who have a different cultural background from you who speak much louder or more softly than what you are used to?

6   This chapter identified many forms of nonverbal behavior. Which ones do you think are the most challenging for you in intercultural interactions? Why?

7   After reading this chapter, do you think you will respond differently when someone from another linguistic and cultural background violates your expectations for nonverbal behavior? Please explain.

activities

1   Identify five ways in which we communicate nonverbally and provide examples of each.

2   Observe one of the spaces where you often hang out (e.g., a cafeteria, a karaoke lounge, a sports bar, a library). Note the furnishings, the décor, the architecture, and the nonverbal actions of the staff. What values are conveyed by the furniture and décor (e.g., the ways in which tables are arranged, the color scheme)? What have you discovered about the use of space that you did not notice before?

3   Visit a cultural scene in your community and pay close attention to nonverbal forms of communication. Do you observe any gender or age differences in the ways people communicated? What gestures do they use, if any (with or without words)? Can you tell what they meant? How close are the people to each other? Do they touch each other often? How are the individuals you observe expressing elements of their identity through verbal or nonverbal means? Based on your observation, how would you characterize the relationship of the people you are observing? Do any of the nonverbal actions you witness surprise, confuse, or shock you? Drawing on this fieldwork, reflect on the connection between language, culture, and nonverbal communication.

4   Drawing on your own intercultural experience, give examples of cultural variations in nonverbal communication (e.g., gestures, facial expressions, touching) that you have observed. How do you feel when someone behaves in ways that you do not expect? How might this influence the way you respond? What are the implications for the enhancement of your intercultural communication skills?

further reading

Eaves, M.H. and Leathers, D. (2018) *Successful Nonverbal Communication: Principles and Applications*, 5th edn, New York: Routledge.

Drawing on theory and research, the authors review the major forms, functions, and uses of nonverbal communication and offer valuable suggestions to enhance one's nonverbal communication.

Hall, E.T. (1984) *The Dance of Life: The Other Dimension of Time*, New York: Anchor Books.

This book, which was written by a foundational figure in intercultural communication studies, explores the cultural nature of time.

Hall, E.T. (1990) *The Hidden Dimension*, New York: Anchor Books.

This classic explores variations in the use of space across cultures and discusses how that use reflects cultural values and norms of behavior.

Matsumoto, D. and Hwang, H-S (2012) 'Nonverbal communication: The messages of emotion, action, space, and silence', in J. Jackson (ed.) *The Routledge Handbook of Language and Intercultural Communication*, London and New York: Routledge, pp. 130–47.

In this chapter, the authors review the key findings of research that has examined the influence of culture on various nonverbal behaviors (e.g., facial expressions, gestures, gaze, voice, interpersonal space, touch, posture, gait).

Moore, N-J., Hickson, M. and Stacks, D.W. (2014) *Nonverbal Communication: Studies and Applications*, 6th edn, Oxford: Oxford University Press.

Balancing theory and practice, this volume is designed to help students understand how nonverbal communication impacts 'real world' interactions.

Companion Website: Continue your journey online

Visit the Companion Website for a variety of tools and resources to support and extend your intercultural learning. (Instructors who are qualified adopters of the text may access additional resources on this site.)

CHAPTER 5

Language and identity in intercultural communication

'Where are you from?'
'What is your nationality'?
'You have an accent.'
'But, I never think of you as. . .'
'I didn't know you were. . .'
                    (James 2001: 1)

The nature of identity is highly subjective . . . the fixed categories that have sufficed to describe features of identity in the past are hardly adequate to explain the processes that individuals experience during intercultural encounters of all kinds.

                                                                    (Temples 2015: 573)

Identity is not something one has, but something that develops during one's whole life.
                                                                    (Beijaard *et al.* 2004: 107)

learning objectives

By the end of this chapter, you should be able to:

1   Define identity
2   Identify and discuss multiple characteristics of identity
3   Explain how identities are shaped and formed
4   Identify, define, and provide examples of different types of identity
5   Describe ways in which people communicate their identities to others
6   Explain how individuals negotiate their identities in intercultural interactions
7   Explain how and why identities may be contested or challenged
8   Describe the relationship between language, culture, and identity

INTRODUCTION

Identity is a principal area of concern in the study of language and intercultural communication. Our sense of self and positioning in the world affects the quality of our life and interpersonal ties, including intercultural unions (e.g., friendships, romance, work relationships). The language we use and our cultural socialization influence how we see ourselves and communicate with people who have different backgrounds (e.g., linguistic, cultural, religious).

After defining what is meant by identity, this chapter explores how the socialization process plays a role in identity development and reconstruction. We then turn our attention to other characteristics and facets of identities that can influence intercultural relations. Next, we explore some of the major types of identities (e.g., personal, social, cultural, racial, ethnic, language, multicultural/ multilingual, gendered, sexual, age, religious, physical ability, national, regional, global, organizational, virtual) that can affect our language use and intercultural communication. Throughout, attention is drawn to the complex connection between language, culture, and identities.

CHARACTERISTICS OF IDENTITY

Identity is defined by Schaetti (2015a) as 'a person's largely unconscious sense of self, both as an individual and as part of the larger society' (p. 405). Basically, this term refers to our self-concept or self-image. Identity defines how we see ourselves and our place in the world. It is influenced by both internal and external elements (e.g., others' perceptions of us) (Jackson 2018b).

Before we examine various types of identities, it is helpful to have an understanding of shifts in conceptions of this important construct. Contemporary scholars have generally concluded that identities are: (1) developed through primary socialization, (2) formed in different ways in different parts of the world, (3) multiple and complex, (4) both dynamic and stable, (5) both chosen and ascribed, (6) variable in strength and salience, and (7) conveyed through verbal and nonverbal means. Now, let's examine each of these characteristics in more detail.

Identities are formed during the socialization process

In infancy we begin to form our sense of self through **enculturation**, the primary socialization process. Social institutions (e.g., the family, the education system, religious organizations), media technologies (e.g., television, radio, digital), and social media (e.g., Facebook, Instagram) all play a role in determining how we develop as social beings. Thus, as we mature and gain life experience our sense of self is socially constructed. As young children we continuously receive messages about who we are and how others see us. Over time, through observation and social interaction, we acquire the means to identify with or relate to our peers, our neighbors, the communities in which we live, and the people we come across in our everyday life and online. 'Through others we become ourselves' (Vygotsky 1997: 105). We also form ideas about individuals and groups who differ from us.

While establishing our own identities we learn what makes us similar to some people and different from others (e.g., gender and age affiliations, ethnic and religious bonds). In the process we develop the knowledge and skills necessary to form and nurture social connections with members of the various groups we are affiliated with. Our vision of ourselves affects who we feel close to and what communities and groups we spend most of our time with. Messages from those who are closest to us can influence our choice of friends, who we develop a romantic relationship with, and who we may eventually choose as a life partner. Dominant values and beliefs can affect our views about intercultural marriage, homosexuality, and a range of other sensitive social dimensions of identity. Cultural and social identities can provide a sense of belonging in an increasingly complex world; however, attitudes toward non-group members can also serve as barriers to successful intercultural interactions, an aspect that is explored in the next chapter.

Identities are shaped in diverse ways in different cultural contexts

The primary socialization process differs among and within cultures. This is significant, as the ways in which young children are socialized influences how they view and position themselves. Enculturation can affect how individuals engage with ingroup members as well as people from different linguistic and cultural backgrounds.

Some cultural contexts stress **individualism** ('the rights and independent action of the individual' (Jandt 2018: G4)), and young children are encouraged to develop a strong sense of self (e.g., to figure out and verbally express their personal preferences, to assume responsibility for their own actions). Individualists possess 'an independent concept of self, they have their goals independent from their ingroups, their social behaviors are attitudes-, values, and belief-driven, and they emphasize rationality in evaluating and choosing their social relationships' (Bhawuk 2018a: 921).

In the U.S., for example, an **independent self-construal** tends to be promoted, that is, 'the representation of the self as separate from the social context, bounded, unitary, and stable' (Smith *et al*. 2013). Parents strive to foster self-reliance and a strong, independent identity in children so that they will develop into mature, responsible adults who can fend for themselves and make a worthwhile contribution to society. Elders may offer advice and guidance; however, young adults generally choose their post-secondary education path, life partners, and careers. There is an emphasis on 'finding yourself' and being 'true to yourself'. While autonomy, self-reliance, and separateness from others are emphasized, family is still very important in U.S. societies.

In cultures that tend to be more **collectivist**, 'interdependence, groupness, and social cohesion' are valued (Jandt 2018: G-2), and 'we' rather than 'I' is emphasized. Bhawuk (2018a) states that collectivists have an interdependent concept of self, their goals are compatible with those of their ingroups, their social behaviors are norm-driven, and they are relational in their social exchange with other people (Triandis 1995).

In many Asian, African, and Latino societies, for example, an **interdependent self-construal** is fostered, that is, 'the representation of the self as closely connected to others, embedded in, and varying across, contexts' (Smith *et al*. 2013: 402). Throughout one's life, family tends to dominate, and children are generally encouraged to view themselves in relation to others. The involvement of parents and grandparents in their children's life decisions (e.g., choice of major/university, selection of spouse, the timing of one's marriage, career path, place of residence) may continue well into adulthood. Several generations of a family may live together and family duties and responsibilities (e.g., the duty to care for one's elderly parents) are emphasized (e.g., filial piety in China).

Although the process of identity formation may differ among and within cultures, all of us develop a sense of who we are and how we fit in society (e.g., independent self-construal, interdependent self-construal) through messages we receive from the world around us. To varying degrees, we are all influenced by the primary socialization that is prevalent in our environment.

Identities are multiple and complex

Rather than a single, fixed identity, people have many dimensions to their sense of self. Identities are multifaceted, complex, hybrid, and sometimes contradictory. Oetzel (2009: 369) argues that it is this 'constellation of identities that makes us who we are'.

As Mort (1989: 169) explains,

> We carry a bewildering range of different, and at times conflicting, identities around with us in our heads at the same time. There is a continual smudging of personae and lifestyles, depending where we are (at work, on the high street) and the spaces we are moving between.

Individuals may assert different identities in diverse social and cultural contexts and circumstances. A 21-year-old male, for example, may define himself primarily as a caring son and elder brother in his family in New York, as a devoted Jew in his religious community, as a hard-working bilingual (English-Hebrew) English major on his home campus at NYU (New York University), as a fun-loving American exchange student while taking part in a semester abroad program at a university in Edinburgh, as a faithful gay partner in his sexual life, and as a clever comedian and tattoo artist when in the company of his closest friends. He may also convey different messages about himself in different social spaces in an online environment (e.g., project a particular image in a chat group and another on his Facebook account). This example illustrates the complexity of identities, reminding us that it is possible for people to emphasize different facets of themselves in different social situations. Whether we are aware of it or not, each of us has multiple dimensions to our identities that become salient at different times and in particular social situations and contexts, including in online environments.

Identities are dynamic

Early identity scholars tended to portray identity as singular and fixed by the time children reach adolescence, with one's social and cultural group membership clearly defined through the process of socialization (Erikson 1968). While some aspects of our identity may remain stable after we reach maturity, contemporary identity researchers recognize the dynamic or fluid nature of identities and the potential for the development of hybrid selves. That is, they acknowledge that many dimensions may change or evolve over time. As Temples (2015) explains 'the nature of identity is highly subjective. . . . The fixed categories that have sufficed to describe features of identity in the past are hardly adequate to explain the processes that individuals experience during intercultural encounters of all kinds' (p. 573). Through first-hand experience (e.g., meaningful intercultural interactions) and our own imagination, we may create new images of ourselves and our place in the world (e.g., imagine ourselves as fluent, sophisticated speakers of another language).

Beijaard et al. (2004: 107) maintains that 'identity is not something one has, but something that develops during one's whole life'. The meanings that young adults or middle-aged people attribute to certain aspects of their identity (e.g., age, ethnicity, gender, language, nationality) may be quite different from when they were young children or adolescents. Both fluidity and hybridity may influence the way individuals enact their identities in different situations and contexts (Beinhoff & Rasinger 2016).

Recognizing the dynamic nature of identity, cultural theorist and sociologist Stuart Hall (1990: 222) writes:

> Identity is not as transparent or unproblematic as we think. Perhaps instead of thinking of identity as an already accomplished fact, which the new cultural practices then represent, we should think instead of identity as a 'production,' which is never complete, always in process and always constituted within, not outside representation.

Identities are created and co-created through discursive practice (e.g., social interactions) and our participation in imagined communities, in which we create the possibility of divergent selves. Further, people may give little thought to their ethnicity, language use, and other facets of their identities until they travel or study abroad and/or experience life as a minority for the first time. Being different from the majority may stimulate deeper reflection on multiple dimensions of one's identities (e.g., cultural, ethnic, linguistic, religious, national). When Hong Kong Chinese students venture outside Asia they are often misidentified as Japanese, Koreans, or Mainland Chinese. This experience tends to raise their awareness about the personal meaning of their regional, ethnic, and linguistic identities. In this situation, some decide to present themselves as Chinese instead of insisting on recognition of their Hong Kong identity. Much to their surprise, some become more nationalistic, that is, for the first time in their life they feel some attachment to the 'Motherland' (Mainland China). Feeling disrespected and misunderstood, others cling more tightly to their Cantonese selves and unique Hong Konger identity (Jackson 2008, 2010).

As we mature and gain life experience whether in our home environment or abroad, we may express our evolved sense of self in a variety of ways. For example, we may strive to convey a more cosmopolitan, global identity through the use of an international language we have mastered in adulthood (e.g., English). We may also alter our nonverbal behaviors to reflect changes in our socioeconomic status and social identities. Youth may wear casual clothing most of the time but after they graduate and begin their career, they may don formal business suits for work and hold themselves in a more erect way to emphasize their professional identity. Their communication style and language choice may also change as they strive to project a sophisticated image to people they wish to impress (e.g., supervisors, colleagues).

Other aspects of one's identity (e.g., gender, ethnicity, religion) may also have different meanings and significance at certain stages in one's life. As an adult, a Nepalese male may feel a strong emotional attachment to his Buddhist self and yet have given this little thought as a child. While in a refugee camp in Bangladesh, a Rohingya woman may become more strongly connected to her first language and ethnic identity.

The identities that people claim and the significance they attach to them may change as a consequence of personal, economic, political, and social circumstances (e.g., study abroad, more intimate intercultural interactions, a higher level of education and wealth, deeper reflection on one's place in the world, more exposure to other groups and societies, interethnic marriage, travel, encounters with racists, forced mobility, etc.). A dramatic increase in the prevalence of electronic social media (e.g., FaceTime, Instagram, Twitter) and the frequency of intercultural contact can also influence how individuals view their identities. People are affected by happenings in the world around them (e.g., changes in societal views about gay marriage, mental and physical disabilities, homosexuality, interracial marriage, political freedom, immigration, and diversity).

A shift in societal attitudes and perceptions may also bring about the use of different **identity labels**. For example, in the U.S., the terms 'African American' or 'Black' are now used instead of 'colored' or 'Negro'. In the 1950s and 60s, American Civil Rights leaders objected to the word Negro, which was associated with a long, painful history of slavery, segregation, and discrimination, and this brought about a shift in terms. In Canada and Greenland, many natives now consider the label 'Eskimos' to be pejorative and prefer to be referred to as 'the Inuit'. In other parts of the world, group identity labels are changing as people who were oppressed fight for more recognition and respect.

Identities are both avowed and ascribed

Identity is concerned with the way individuals or groups see, define, and express themselves, as well as how other individuals or groups define or label them. Our **avowed identity** is the one that we wish to present or claim in an interaction, whereas an **ascribed identity** is the one that others give to us (or we give to someone else).

Avowal refers to 'the process of telling others what identity(ies) you wish to present or how you see yourself' (Oetzel 2009: 62). Individuals and groups can freely select some dimensions of their identities that they wish to present to others. For example, we may choose to convey a particular image through our dress, adornments, speech, and mannerisms. In Britain, Jameela, an immigrant from Pakistan, may proudly wear shalwar kameez (a long tunic and pants with embroidery that is distinctive of her home village) that conveys her strong attachment to her ethnic identity. In contrast, her more rebellious cousin, Sharifa, wears jeans and t-shirts, to display her more Western persona.

Through language we may also verbally declare dimensions of our identity that are especially meaningful or important to us (e.g., 'I am a British Pakistani', or 'I'm a vegan', or 'I am lesbian', or 'I am a dentist'). How people feel about their identities may change, and individuals who are affiliated with the same group may have different ideas about what this means to them personally. For example, being Japanese may be a source of great pride for Tomoko but of little importance to Katsumi, even though both women have been socialized in the same city and are affiliated with the same ethnic group.

We are not entirely free to adopt any identities we want. The perception of others can affect how we are labeled and positioned in a specific situation and context. **Ascription** refers to 'the process of assigning in another person what you think his or her identity should be' (Oetzel 2009: 62). Factors such as age, language, accent, ethnicity, skin color, social class, dress, communication styles, and sex (etc.) can influence how others see and categorize us. Thus, our preferred identities may not be the ones that are recognized by others.

Let's look at some examples. After many years abroad, an international student may feel at home in her new world and consider herself a member of the host community; yet, her physical appearance, second language accent, temporary status, and lack of familiarity with local social norms distinguish her from locals who persist in treating her like an outsider. A Latino woman may wish to be identified primarily as a department head rather than as a Latino or a woman. Her colleagues and students, however, may persist in defining her in terms of her ethnicity and gender characteristics. Consequently, she may find it a struggle to assert her preferred identity and authority. Similarly, a fresh graduate in a new job may aspire to be seen as a capable adult, but in the eyes of his older, more experienced supervisor, he is still a mere child. Conversely, a physically active and mentally sharp retiree in her late sixties may consider herself a vibrant being; much to her dismay, however, she is regarded as 'over the hill' by younger members of the community and talked to in a patronizing way. Failing to acknowledge and respect the preferred identities of individuals and groups can have negative consequences for intercultural interactions and relationships, an aspect that is explored in the next chapter.

Identities are variable in salience and intensity

While all of us have multiple identities, this does not mean that each dimension is of equal importance to us at all times. Depending on the context and situation, there will naturally be aspects or dimensions that we wish to accentuate more than others or that other people will consider more important. For example, as Fong and McEwen (2004: 166) observe, our perception of our cultural identity may vary:

> Some members will identify with particular communicative cultural practices, while other members may choose not to partake and identify themselves as enacting the same expressions, rituals, and so forth because of differing preferences, values, attitudes, beliefs, and so.

Identity salience is 'the degree to which an identity is prominent or stands out to us in a given situation' (Oetzel 2009: 59). When we are in an environment where the majority of people speak a different language and are visibly different from us, our ethnic, language, or national identity may become more salient. A devout Muslim exchange student in New Zealand during Ramadan (the holy month of fasting) may find that her religious affiliation has become even more meaningful to her, especially if none of her classmates are fasting. In a similar situation, feeling under pressure to conform to the behavior of the majority, another Muslim student may distance himself from his religious affiliation and choose not to fast in order to fit in with his new peers.

Elements of our identity may become more evident and significant to us when they are contested or challenged. The term **contested identity** refers to facets or elements of one's identity that are not accepted by the people we are in contact with.

> 'Where are you from?'
> 'What is your nationality'?
> 'You have an accent.'
> 'But, I never think of you as. . .'
> 'I didn't know you were. . .'
>   (James 2001: 1)

These are just some of the many questions that Carl James and other minority members or newcomers experience. It can be very unsettling to discover that you are not viewed as you see yourself or wish to be identified.

Identity intensity refers to the degree of significance of a particular identity (Collier 1994). The strength of one's attachment to a facet of one's identity can vary depending on the circumstances. For example, minority members who have a weak ethnic identity may demonstrate little interest in being affiliated with other individuals from their ethnic group and may shun related cultural events. They may insist on using a different language, they may wear jeans instead of ethnic dress and live a different lifestyle from the majority of people who have the same ethnicity. In contrast, individuals with a strong ethnic identity may wear clothing and eat certain foods that visibly link them to their ethnic group; they may actively participate in functions linked to their ethnic group (e.g., religious services, community celebrations, weekly social gatherings). They may also primarily use the language(s) associated with their ethnicity (e.g., a Sri Lankan international exchange student in London may use Tamil instead of English as much as possible when not in classroom situations).

Identities are expressed verbally and nonverbally

On a daily basis, we intentionally express and negotiate our identities through a range of verbal and nonverbal means, depending, in part, on what messages we wish to send about ourselves to others. We continuously convey information that is below our level of awareness, especially through nonverbal channels. In face-to-face interactions, our communication partners are interpreting our actions and processing our appearance, while making assessments about who we are and what groups we belong to. Their perception of our identities may differ from our own.

Our language and communication styles can express multiple dimensions of our identity. For example, the use of one's mother tongue can serve as a marker of one's cultural or regional affiliation. When far away from home in an alien environment, familiar accents and expressions can provide a sense of comfort and belonging. Regional accents and dialects can bind people together and foster harmony among community members; they can also intentionally or unintentionally segregate individuals and groups who speak in a different way or use a different language.

Bilingual or multilingual individuals may feel they are conveying different dimensions of their identities depending on the language they are using. For example, a young woman who speaks French at home, German with her boyfriend, English in the workplace, and code-mixes online may project different self-images in various situations and contexts, and, occasionally, some elements may conflict with each other.

We also express ourselves through a variety of nonverbal messages. For example, our appearance (e.g., clothing, jewelry, tattoos, hairstyle) communicates aspects about our identities that we wish to convey to others. For Sikhs, five items of dress and physical appearance (the 'Five Ks') represent discipline and spirituality: kesh (uncut hair and the wearing of a turban), kirpan (a ceremonial sword), kangha (a small wooden comb), kara (a steel bracelet), and kachera (cotton boxer shorts). Together, these five items signify a unique Sikh identity.

Following the cultural tradition of their family and community, some Muslim girls may wear the hijab (head covering) to school. While this mode of dress is common in some Islamic countries, it has been banned in some secular nations (e.g., France) as it is interpreted as a religious marker of identity that can separate people from each other. (In Chapter 6 we explore identity barriers and discriminatory practices that can hinder intercultural relations.)

TYPES OF IDENTITIES

As we develop and mature, we identify with many different groups based on such dimensions as age, language, gender, religion, ethnicity, social class, occupation, and so on. Some aspects of our identity are linked to our personal interests, career, and preferences, while others are influenced by our geographic location and the messages we receive from those around us (e.g., political campaigns that promote a particular language and national, ethnic, or regional identity). In this digital, global age, new forms of identity (e.g., virtual or cyber identities, e-identity) are also emerging. All of these dimensions reveal who we are and can influence how we present

Plate 5.1 Cultural and religious identities may be expressed through nonverbal means (e.g., dress, adornments). © Tongle Sun

ourselves and interact in different contexts and situations. Let's take a look at some of the many types of identities that can affect our intercultural interactions and influence the quality of the relationships that develop.

Personal identity

Personal identity may be defined simply as an individual's unique self-perception that develops throughout the course of his or her life. De Fina (2016) explains that personal identities 'capture characteristics and attributes that the individual regards as defining her/himself as a particular and unique kind of person' (p. 163). When describing personal identities, scholars generally emphasize aspects or dimensions that distinguish individuals from other people (e.g., our age, personal interests and pursuits, personality, gender, age, religion). Oetzel (2009), for example, observes that personal identities consist of the 'unique qualities of ourselves such as personality and relationships' (p. 369).

Social identity

According to **social identity theory (SIT)** (Tajfel 1981, 1982), **social identity** consists of our social group membership affiliations, including their emotional significance. De Fina (2016) refers to social identities as 'membership into social groupings that may be based on gender, age, ethnicity, place of origin and so forth' (p. 163). Emphasizing the affective dimension, Liu *et al.* (2019), define social identity as 'those parts of an individual's self-concept which derive from his or her knowledge of membership in a social group together with the value and emotional significance attached to that membership'. In addition to cultural or ethnic membership, social identities may form through attachments to others due to age, political or religious affiliation, disability, gender, sexual orientation, social class, and professional or relational identities within ones' family. For Ting-Toomey (2015a), social (or sociocultural) identities can encompass 'ethnic membership identity, social class identity, and family role issues' (p. 418).

Basically, social identity relates to how we feel socially connected to other people due to what we have in common. For example, we can identify ourselves according to our religion (Taoists, Jains, Christians), place of origin, (Gibraltar, Macau, North Korea), political affiliation (Green Party, Independent, Muslim Brotherhood), profession or educational status (university student, English language teacher, civil engineer), language and accent (Yorkshire accent, Singlish, Tagalog), or relationship (step-mother, great-aunt, first cousin, friend, lover). Some social identities are stigmatized in mainstream society (e.g., drug addicts, homeless people, the unemployed, high school dropouts).

Most social identities are multiple (e.g., a multilingual, gay British Indian male student may be a devout Hindu and belong to Green Peace). Together, all of our diverse roles and attributes help us to realize our overall social identity, which continues to evolve throughout our life as our preferences, interests, financial situation, job status, marital situation, and other social dimensions change.

Our social identity can provide us with a sense of self-esteem and a framework for socializing as it influences how we chose to interact with and behave in social contexts (e.g., respond to other people). In experiments carried out by social psychologists Henri Tajfel and John Turner, people were found to favor members of their own social group. As well as affecting how you view yourself and your ingroup, aspects of your social identity can have negative consequences, e.g., people may treat you with disrespect when they have little regard for your language and social status. (Ingroups and outgroups were discussed in Chapter 2; the 'ingroup favoritism principle' is examined in Chapter 6.)

Cultural identity

Social scientists and intercultural communication scholars have put forward numerous definitions of **cultural identity**, in part, due to differing understandings and conceptions of culture. For Wintergerst and McVeigh (2011: 230), cultural identity refers to 'that part of identity determined by one's cultural background or way of life', whereas Chung (2015) describes it as 'the emotional significance and sense of belonging that individuals attach to the larger culture' (p. 305). Adopting a more fluid stance, Sorrells (2016: 11) depicts cultural identity as 'our situated sense of self that is shaped by our cultural experiences and social locations'.

Our emotional attachment to a particular culture is affected by how we believe others perceive and value it:

> Cultural identities are more than just collections of cultural values, attitudes, beliefs, and norms. Cultural identities also include emotional evaluations of others' perceptions of our cultural groups. During communicative interactions, individuals may apply various communicative strategies to negotiate cultural identities that are positive and fulfill social needs.
>
> (Bradford *et al.* 2004: 315)

Similar to Bradford *et al.* (2004), Ting-Toomey and Dorjee (2019) stress the affective dimension of cultural membership. For these speech communication specialists, cultural identity refers to our emotional attachment or sense of belonging to the culture. Through the process of primary socialization, individuals internalize, to varying degrees, the sociocultural value patterns of their community. Through shared experiences and teachings, members of a cultural group develop a sense of belonging in a process that is referred to as **cultural identity formation.**

Multiple elements and conditions may affect the development of one's cultural identity. For example, language, physical appearance, race, history, gender, sexuality, religious beliefs, ethnicity, and other shared attributes can bind people together. In diverse multicultural nations where there is considerable ethnic and linguistic diversity (e.g., Australia, Canada, England), cultural identity may be based primarily on social values and beliefs that are perceived to be shared (e.g., multiculturalism ideology).

As affiliation with a group can provide a sense of security and comfort, cultural identity may contribute to one's well-being. It can facilitate access to social networks where individuals share similar values, ethics, and aspirations. While these attachments can be beneficial, strong cultural identities also have the potential to serve as barriers between groups and can lead to 'us vs. them' discourse. Minorities may feel excluded from the majority culture and individuals may become less accepting and tolerant of cultural practices and beliefs that differ from their own.

Racial and ethnic identity

Before we define what is meant by racial and ethnic identities, it is important to have an understanding of what is meant by 'race' and 'ethnicity'. As noted in Chapter 2, although some people use these terms interchangeably, there are differences in their meaning:

> Race and ethnicity both involve drawing boundaries between people. A conceptual distinction can, however, be made between race and ethnicity. While racial boundaries are drawn on the bases of physical markers, ethnic boundaries are drawn on the basis of cultural markers.
>
> (Pilkington 2003: 27)

Plate 5.2 How is this Scotsman's cultural identity conveyed? © Jane Jackson

Cross-cultural psychologists Smith *et al.* (2006: 278) point out that while race is 'a term frequently used in everyday discourse and social perception', it has 'no defensible biological basis'. For this reason, they prefer to use the term 'ethnicity'. Parker and Mease (2009: 315) concur, arguing that '[t]he classifications that constitute references to "race" – Asian, Black, White, etc. – are social and historical constructions that have economic and political functions, but no biological determinant'. Accordingly, they define **race** as 'a product of human social and historical processes that have arbitrarily (but purposefully) created categories of people that are positioned differently in society' (ibid: 315). Socially constructed racial hierarchies elevate some racial groups (e.g., Whites) at the expense of others (e.g., Blacks). **Racial identity**, which is also a contested notion, refers to one's 'biological/genetic make-up, i.e. racial phenotype' (Block 2007: 43) (e.g., Black, White, biracial).

Ethnicity denotes groups of people who share common geographical origins, values and beliefs, and customs and traditions. In contrast with the notion of 'race', ethnicity is not based on supposed innate biological differences; rather, it implies similarities derived from belonging to, or being brought up as part of a specific group. Puri (2004: 174) explains:

> Ethnicity is . . . a form of collective identity based on shared cultural beliefs and practices, such as language, history, descent, and religion. Even though ethnicities often allude to enduring kin-based and blood ties, it is widely recognized that they are cultural, not bio-logical ties.

Ethnic identity refers to one's perceptions and emotions regarding one's affiliation with one's own ethnic group(s) (Fong 2004). Chung (2015) defines it straightforwardly as 'the subjective sense of belonging with an ethnic group' (p. 305). The following dimensions of ethnic identity have been identified by Martin and Nakayama (2018b): self-identification with a particular ethnic group; knowledge about the ethnic group's customs, traditions, values, and behavioral norms; and a sense of belonging or attachment to the group. For immigrants, an ethnic identity may involve a shared sense of origin and history with ancestors and ethnic groups in distant cultures in Asia, Europe, South America, or other parts of the world. A **minority identity** refers to one's sense of belong to a minority group, whereas a **majority identity** is one's identification with the dominant or majority group.

While ethnicity may be very important to some, for others, it is of little concern. Individuals who are affiliated with the majority ethnic group (e.g., Han Chinese in Mainland China, White Anglo Saxons in Britain) may not think much about their ethnic identity, whereas ethnicity may be a core part of the identity of minority members (e.g., Miao, Utsuls, Uyghurs, Tibetans in China; Rohingya in Myanmar; South Asians in Britain). Minority members may speak a different home language, practice a different religion, wear clothing that is particular to their group, and maintain customs and traditions that distinguish them from the majority. These differences may be a source of great pride, and minorities may resist policies and practices that conflict with or diminish the status of their first language, religious beliefs, and customs. Other minority members may choose to downplay their ethnicity and blend in with the majority if the wider community is open to them. Over time, their offspring may have little emotional connection, if any, to their ethnic group and scant knowledge of the first language of their parents or grandparents. (Chapter 7 further discusses the identities and diverse adaptation strategies of immigrants.)

The notion of ethnic membership or affiliation has also become much more complex as a consequence of increasing intercultural contact. With more romances and intermarriage among individuals from different ethnic backgrounds, the number of people of dual or mixed heritage is becoming increasingly common, especially in parts of the world where there are many immigrants. Offspring of mixed heritage do not fit neatly into traditional ethnic (or racial) groups. For example, former U.S. President Barack Obama is of mixed heritage. His mother was a White American, secular humanist (nonreligious) with predominantly English roots, as well as some German, Scottish, Welsh, and Irish ancestry, while his father, a Black man, was a Muslim Luo Kenyan from Africa. Mariah Carey, an American singer, has both Irish roots from her mother and Hispanic-African heritage from her Venezuelan father.

Similar to 'race', the terms 'ethnic' and 'ethnicity' are sometimes contested and emotionally charged as they can be used to categorize and marginalize people (e.g., differentiate them

Plate 5.3 In Beijing, this hostess in a restaurant that is frequented by tourists greets people wearing traditional dress. What identities are projected through her attire and demeanor? If she was wearing jeans and a t-shirt would your impression differ? Why is it important to consider the context and situation when forming ideas about identities?
© Jane Jackson

from the majority). In Britain, for example, 'ethnic dress', 'ethnic languages', 'ethnic food', and 'ethnic music' may be used to single out people who are different from the perceived White British norm. Ironically, this majority is actually ethnically diverse (e.g., a mix of people with English, French, Irish, Italian, Scottish, Welsh heritage). (This notion of 'Otherization' is explored further in Chapter 6.)

Class identity

One's socioeconomic status may also play a role in one's identity makeup and, subsequently, affect intercultural relationships. **Class identity** refers to a sense of belonging or attachment to a group that shares a similar social, economic, or occupational/professional status. A core element in ingroup identification, it may influence who we identify with and wish to spend our time with. Social class identity can shape our perceptions and reactions to language use (e.g., accents, dialects) and communication or speech styles in particular settings and contexts.

While often below our level of awareness, we are continuously communicating our economic, social, and occupational status through our verbal and nonverbal behaviors. For example, our class identity is revealed through our dress and adornments (e.g., tattoos, jewelry, business suits, designer bags) as well as our posture/stance and even the cologne or perfume we use. Some schools require children to wear uniforms to downplay class differences and build up a shared sense of belonging to the institution. In the military, where hierarchy is pivotal, personnel often wear different uniforms and other **emblems of identity** (e.g., badges, medals) to indicate their rank or position. Individuals may also be addressed differently according to their status (e.g., more formal greetings and titles for senior ranking officers). In some business contexts, senior staff may only appear in formal business suits, while entry-level workers wear more casual clothing.

A person's prestige, social honor, or popularity in a cultural group may be linked to his or her level of education, intellect, or talent rather than economic status or material possessions. In some cultures, for example, authors with limited financial resources are admired for their clever use of words and expressions in poetry and novels. Gifted musicians, painters, and other artists who have little money may be accorded a high status, and people may use honorifics or

Plate 5.4 Uniforms can convey professional identities. When you see this Turkish guard what is your perception of him and his duties? © Jane Jackson

terms of respect when addressing them. In many other contexts financial wealth largely determines one's social status.

Our class status or economic position in society is often reflected in our language use and the ways in which we communicate (both verbally and nonverbally). In particular, the vocabulary, accent, and dialect that we use may reveal our level of education and social standing. In professional work situations, senior managers may use more direct forms of discourse and less slang than entry-level workers. People with a higher level of education may employ a wider range of vocabulary and, in some cases, may be multilingual as they have had more opportunities to study other languages and travel to other countries.

Individuals who are similar to the majority in terms of economic, education, or social status may give little thought to their class identity until they are in the company of people who have a much higher or lower status. Differences in dress, accent, dialect, or behavior can affect intercultural communication. In the company of individuals or groups who possess a higher class status, for example, people may feel compelled to adjust their communication style, accent, or mode of dress in an effort to fit in and gain more power and respect. While they may initially feel like they are wearing a mask, over time they may become more comfortable and proficient in another style of communication as they negotiate their identities and positioning. Individuals may use an informal, colloquial style when hanging out with friends and family and switch to a more formal code at work. They may also interact in one language in a work situation and switch to a different language or dialect during their free time.

In the presence of people with a higher social status, individuals from a lower social class may also follow a different path. They may retain their usual communication style and refrain from adopting behaviors that make them feel like imposters. Some may even employ creative strategies to avoid personal contact with people of a higher status.

Language identity

While some people remain **monolingual** (fluent in only one language) throughout their life, many others become **bilingual** (proficient in two languages) or **multilingual** (able to speak multiple languages). Our linguistic competence and familiarity with diverse languages and cultures can influence how we see themselves and our place in the world. Block (2007: 40) defines **language identity** as 'the assumed and/or attributed relationship between one's sense of self and a means of communication which might be known as a language (e.g., English), a dialect (e.g., Geordie) or a sociolect (e.g., football-speak)'. Similar to Block, Chowdhury (2016) cautions that '[l]anguage identity, if seen through the lens of hereditary endowment or by belonging to a particular community only, is restricting in scope as it undermines the possibility of choice or agency in shaping one's language identity' (p. 478–9). Language may be passed to children in the home environment or acquired in a school setting (or elsewhere); however, expertise in a language is not inherited. Individuals may master a language as a necessity or by choice and possess varying degrees of emotional attachment to the language(s) they speak. The relationship between language, culture, and identity is complex and dynamic.

Language identity encompasses such variables as **language expertise** (one's degree of proficiency in a particular language), **language affiliation** (one's 'sense of attachment' or bonding to the language), and **language inheritance** (being born into a family or community where the language is spoken) (Block 2007; Chowdhury 2016). The language identities of individuals may be influenced by sociocultural, linguistic, political, historical, and religious messages in their environment. For example, governmental discourses may promote a particular language or dialect (e.g., the language of the majority or those in power) and actively discourage the learning and use of minority languages.

The language(s) we speak help to define who we are and how we are perceived by others. Thus, language identity is associated with the notions of avowal and ascription that were explained earlier in this chapter. For example, individuals may wish to be affiliated with a particular social or cultural group through the use of their second language (avowed identity), but first language speakers may persist in viewing them as outsiders no matter how well they master the language (ascribed identity).

Many dimensions of our social and cultural identities (e.g., gender, class, nationality, ethnicity) are shaped by the language(s) we speak. During the socialization process, language becomes strongly intertwined with culture and identity. Within a particular environment, at a certain period of history, language develops according to the needs and interests of the inhabitants. Over time, social and cultural groups develop certain ways of being, including communication styles and linguistic norms (e.g., cultural scripts, use of particular discourse markers of politeness). In essence, identities emerge from linguistic practice and linguistic performance. Language can provide a sense of belonging and serve as a powerful marker of identity, especially when individuals find themselves in situations where the majority use a different language, dialect, or sociolect.

Drawing on their extensive fieldwork in the Creole-speaking Caribbean and among West Indian communities in London, sociolinguists Le Page and Tabouret-Keller (1985) observed that people's utterances may serve as '**acts of identity**', that is, dimensions of their identities (e.g., age, gender, social class, nationality, ethnicity, personal) are conveyed through language choice and use (e.g., accent, code-mixing, idiomatic expressions) in particular sociocultural settings and situations. With each **speech act** (e.g., request, apology, refusal), individuals perform 'acts of identity' to varying degrees; in the process, they disclose their social or ethnic solidarity with (or separation from) the people they are communicating with.

Related to 'acts of identity' is the **communication accommodation theory (CAT)**, which posits that language may be used as an identity marker to either draw us closer to or further apart from interlocutors who have a different linguistic and cultural background (e.g., individuals who possess different social and cultural identities from ourselves) (Giles *et al.* 2012). **Convergence** occurs when individuals adjust their speech patterns to more closely fit with those of their communication partners who are affiliated with a different linguistic and cultural identity. For example, second language sojourners may adopt a less direct style of speech that is similar to host nationals. **Divergence** happens when individuals (e.g., second language speakers) accentuate speech and nonverbal differences between themselves and people who are affiliated with another group (e.g., first language speakers who have a different ethnic background from them).

Similar to other types of social and cultural identities, language identities can change during the course of one's lifetime. Learning an additional language, for example, can alter the way you view yourself and your place in the world. You might learn Tagalog as a child in the Philippines and immigrate to Australia in your twenties, where you live and function in English in your social and professional life. You may marry an Australian first language speaker of English and have children who speak only that language. Over time, your proficiency in English grows to the extent that you feel very confident and at ease when using it in your daily life as well as at work. As you form strong ties with Australian speakers of English, you develop a sense of belonging in that linguistic community and spend most of your time conversing in this language. In some circles, however, you discover that the identity you wish to project (e.g., your English language self) is contested, that is, it is not recognized and accepted by locals. No matter how fluent you are in English, you may still be positioned as a second language speaker since your accent and other linguistic (and nonlinguistic) features differ from that of individuals who grew up in Australia. In addition to raising awareness of the potential tension and conflict between avowed and ascribed identities, this scenario draws attention to the potential loss of an immigrant's first language and attachment to his or her cultural roots.

Learning a second language (or more) need not lead to the loss of one's first language, heritage, and cultural identity, however. While some immigrant parents may decide to only use the dominant language in their new country of residence, others may promote **heritage language learning** (the acquisition of a minority or indigenous language at home that typically is incomplete). Cummins (1994) distinguishes between **subtractive bilingualism** in which a second language is added at the expense of the first language and culture, and **additive bilingualism**, whereby the first language and culture continue to be nurtured as a second language develops. In the latter, the individual is enriched by learning two or more languages and ways of being, and, over time, may develop a more broadened sense of self.

Multicultural and multilingual identities

What does it mean to 'be multicultural' or to possess a multicultural identity? Nowadays, in many regions, individuals have more interaction with people who have a different linguistic and cultural background, whether through immigration, higher education (e.g., more diverse campuses due to internationalization policies), travel, education abroad, marriage (e.g., interethnic, interreligious unions), employment, long-term volunteer work (e.g., missionaries), adoption, or birth (e.g., parents with diverse multicultural backgrounds).

Individuals who have sustained contact with people who have diverse linguistic and cultural backgrounds (e.g., expatriates, immigrants) may develop a sense of attachment to multiple ethnic groups and linguistic communities. Others may feel as if they have no ties or affiliation with any group in particular. Martin and Nakayama (2018a: G-4) define a **multicultural identity** as '[a] sense of in-betweeness that develops as a result of frequent or multiple cultural border crossings'. Individuals who have many intercultural experiences may acquire 'an identity that transcends one particular culture'; over time, they may 'feel equally at home in several cultures' (ibid: 112). Those who are proficient in more than one language may develop a **bilingual** or **multilingual identity**, a hybrid sense of self that is linked to the use of the languages that they speak.

Over time, individuals who have sustained contact with diverse cultures and languages may form **hybrid (mixed) identities** that meld multifarious cultural elements and linguistic codes (Kraidy 2005; Kramsch 1993, 2009). For example, they may develop a broad repertoire of communication styles and strategies, draw on both local values and global perspectives, and frequently code-mix or code-switch to more freely express themselves. Their expanded sense of self may help them to function and indeed thrive in today's multicultural, multilingual world.

> When asked who they are and where they belong, transnational migrants are not likely to answer by naming a single country or a single national or ethnic identity, but rather, they will describe an identity constructed of elements mixed from the region of origin and the region of destination, and convey a sense of belonging to more than one spatial setting, social group, or national state.
>
> (Meier 2015: 617)

Marginality or a state of inbetweenness may also develop through intense exposure to other cultures in one's family or community, whether at home or abroad. This is especially the case for **global nomads**, individuals who have an international lifestyle (e.g., mobile individuals who live and work outside their home country for a long period of time and find it difficult to put down roots). This may include **third culture individuals (TCIs)** (also referred to as **third culture kids, TCKs**), that is, individuals who have grown up in a country other than their country of citizenship because their parents have lived abroad (e.g., diplomats and other foreign service staff, the military, expatriate professionals, aid workers, missionaries, etc.) (Barker 2018; Schaetti 2015b). Enculturation in multiple cultural contexts may foster a third culture, that is, the blending of the values, communication styles, and other ways of being associated with their home and host cultures. Barker (2018) explains:

> Unlike people who acculturate as adults, who already have a cultural identity and a more or less established worldview when moving abroad, TCIs become socialized into their home culture and host culture simultaneously and develop their individual identity while influenced by several different cultural frameworks.
>
> (p. 1904)

Children who are raised in many different cultural environments (or in multicultural households) may experience a more complex form of primary socialization than those who grow up in a setting where they are part of the majority in terms of ethnicity, first language, religion, etc. At a young age, TCIs may receive mixed messages from those around them (e.g., ideas about what is 'right' and 'wrong', 'fair' and 'unfair'), and have more contact with differing social norms of behavior (e.g., linguistic) and communication or speech styles.

When individuals are exposed to cultural values, practices, and identities that sometimes conflict with each other, it can be very disquieting and, in some, it can lead to **identity confusion**. For example, the following was written by a young Chinese woman who grew up in Mainland China, moved to Hong Kong as an adolescent, and then attended university in Hong Kong, England, and Ireland before becoming an ESL teacher in Hong Kong:

> A person's sense of identity is often greatly influenced by the cultural background he/she grows up with. In my case, traditional Chinese culture plays an important role during my early years. Later, Hong Kong culture and Western culture also greatly influenced me . . . as a result of growing up and having different experiences my perception about who I am changes over time. I am now still a little bit confused about myself.

Nguyen and Benet-Martínez (2010: 96) explain that '[t]he process of negotiating multiple cultural identities is complex and multi-faceted' and, in some individuals, intense feelings of loss and inbetweenness may emerge. In this state, individuals may feel torn between different cultural worlds, identities, and languages. Some may experience difficulty making life choices and feel on the margin of all of the languages and cultures they are in contact with.

While some border crossers may suffer from identity confusion and fragmentation, others may thrive and take full advantage of the opportunities that their mobility and multicultural, multilingual experiences afford them. With a positive, open mindset, they may recognize and embrace their ability to comfortably and appropriately interact in different cultural settings in multiple languages. Sparrow (2000), for example, explains her adaptable multicultural identity in this way:

I think of myself not as a unified cultural being but as a communion of different cultural beings. Due to the fact that I have spent time in different cultural environments, I have developed several cultural identities that diverge and converge according to the need of the moment.

(Sparrow 2000: 190)

Increasingly, process-oriented studies of multicultural individuals is exploring the ways in which culture is negotiated through intercultural interactions. This work is drawing attention to 'the complex interplay among identity, language, and contextual factors' (Liu 2018: 829).

Gendered identities

When asked to describe our identity, it is natural to mention one's gender. It is also one of the ways that others often categorize us, drawing on their own ideas, experiences, and expectations. **Gender**, which comes from the Latin word *genus*, meaning kind or race, refers to one's identification as male, female, or, less commonly, both male and female or neither. Gender may be based on such aspects as one's legal status, personal preferences, physical appearance, public persona, activities and interests, and social interactions, among others.

Because gender is such a basic category, it is inevitable that there are numerous meanings associated with it. For example, developmental psychologists have linked the following dimensions to gender categories: 'personality traits (e.g., being competitive or being aware of the feelings of others), role behaviors (e.g., taking care of children or assuming leadership roles), physical characteristics (e.g., having broad shoulders or a soft voice), and a host of other associations' (Deaux 2001: 1060).

Language use has also been tied to gender. Differences in vocabulary and communication styles may serve as markers of one's gender (Jones 2016; Samovar *et al*. 2010). In some settings, for example, females use more hedging devices (e.g., expressions like 'maybe', 'sort of', 'what I mean to say is') and rising intonation than males. Certain words may be used exclusively by males, with females using other expressions or nonverbal codes to convey similar emotions and meanings. If females express themselves in ways similar to the men they may, in some contexts, be regarded in a very negative way (e.g., as overly aggressive, vulgar) (Coates 2016; Tannen 2001).

To better understand the notion of gender, it is helpful to consider how the World Health Organization (WHO) defines it. For the WHO (n.d.), gender refers to 'the socially constructed roles, behaviors, activities, and attributes that a given society considers appropriate for men and women'. In this definition, attention is drawn to enculturation and variations among cultures.

A number of definitions of **gender identity** have also been put forward by international organizations and scholars in various disciplines. For example, Liu *et al*. (2019: 345) define gender identity as 'part of a person's self and social identity', whereby 'the term "gender" entails social roles established for the sexes'. Noting that gender identity differs from biological sex or sexual identity, Ting-Toomey and Chung (2012: 69) define gender identity as 'the meanings and interpretations we hold concerning our self-images and expected other-images of femaleness and maleness'. An individual's understanding of gender develops at an early age during the socialization process. As this occurs in particular sociocultural, historical contexts, it is not surprising that there are variations in the gender-related behaviors that are encouraged and deemed appropriate. Further, these understandings may change over time as a consequence of globalization, the social media, intercultural contact, education, and other forces.

Instead of viewing gender as a single social category, some scholars prefer to use the term **gendered identities**. The plural form acknowledges that 'multiple identities are shaped by one's gender, and that social identities can intersect and overlap with one another' (Deaux 2001: 1061). Rather than being singular and fixed, gender identities are multidimensional and constructed in particular social contexts through the process of **gender socialization**. For example, relationships (e.g., wife, husband) and professions (e.g., nursing, engineering) frequently have multiple gender implications within particular cultures. To complicate matters, expectations of roles and responsibilities evolve over time and vary in different cultural settings, even among people who are categorized as belonging to the same gender. An individual's identity as a female, for example, may differ depending on whether she sees herself as a traditional woman or feminist. With increasing interconnectedness in the world, the roles of women, in particular, are changing, along with communication styles, language use, and values. Nowadays, women in many cultures are in professions that were once reserved for males, and vice versa.

Just as gender-related behaviors vary among individuals and within cultures, notions of what it means to be male or female or masculine or feminine also differ. As Sorrells (2016: 56) explains:

> Differences between masculinity and femininity are symbolically embodied, performed, and communicated within our specific cultural contexts through the way we walk; through our gestures, speech, touch, and eye contact patterns; through the way we use physical space and the gendered activities we participate in; through our hairstyles, clothing, the use of makeup or not; and through colors, smells, and adornments.
>
> (Butler 1990; Wood 2005)

Within cultures, gender roles and identities may also differ from what is prevalent in the mainstream society. For example, **gender-crossing** (e.g., beginning life as a male and assuming female behaviors and characteristics) has existed in societies for generations (e.g., Hijaras in Pakistan, Fafafinis in Samoa). People who are categorized as neither male nor female (either by themselves or by social consensus) may sometimes be labeled as a **third gender**. In Samoa, the Fa'afafine, for example, are biological males who are raised to assume female gender roles in society. **Transgender** refers to 'people whose gender identities differ from the social norms and expectations associated with their biological sex' (Sorrells 2016: 56). When societies develop fixed expectations of gender roles and behavior, those who do not fit the norm may be subjected to gender inequality and oppression, an aspect that is explored further in the next chapter.

Sexual identity

To understand the relationship between sex and identity, it is essential to first distinguish between what is meant by 'sex' and 'gender'. As discussed in the previous sub-section, gender is associated with culturally influenced perceptions of masculine and feminine attributes, roles, and behaviors. In contrast, **sex** refers to the biological and physiological characteristics that define men and women (WHO, n.d.). Whereas 'male and female' are sex categories, 'masculine' and 'feminine' are gender classifications. Gender characteristics and functions (e.g., roles and responsibilities) may differ considerably among and within cultures; however, sexual characteristics and functions are much less variable. For example, females menstruate, and have internal and external sexual organs and widened hips, which enable childbirth. As their bodies produce more estrogen, they have enlarged breasts that can produce milk to feed their babies. In males, testosterone increases the size and mass of muscles, deepens the voice, stimulates the growth of facial hair, and affects the shape of the face and skeleton. Males have sexual organs on the outside of the body which can produce sperm and impregnate females.

Contemporary scholars distinguish **sexual identity** from gendered identities. The former refers to how one thinks of oneself in terms of who one is sexually and romantically attracted to. While related to sexual identity and sexual behavior (e.g., actual sexual acts), one's **sexual orientation** refers to desires, fantasies, and attachments to sexual partners. Sexual identity may or may not relate to one's actual sexual orientation (e.g., individuals may be attracted to members of the same sex but project a sexual identity that differs from this orientation).

Sexual orientation implies an enduring pattern of attraction (e.g., emotional, romantic, sexual) to members of the opposite sex, the same sex, or both sexes, and the genders associated with them. In North America and Europe, these attractions are usually referred to as **heterosexuality** (sexual attraction to members of the opposite sex), **homosexuality** (sexual attraction to members of the same sex), and **bisexuality** (sexual attraction that is not limited to individuals of one particular sex). People who are attracted to more than one sex may identify themselves as bisexual, pansexual, queer, or fluid, or prefer not to use a label.

Cultures may use diverse terms and definitions of sexualities and the attitudes toward those who differ from the majority vary considerably. The ways that people view themselves and their sexual orientation may also differ. For example, in regions where gays and lesbians have gained more rights and respect, more people are willing to claim a sexual identity that embraces their homosexuality. In homophobic environments people may try to conceal their homosexual or bisexual identities for security reasons, for example, fear of being outgrouped (rejected by ingroup members), discriminated against (e.g., job loss), or worse (e.g., physical abuse, imprisonment, death by stoning).

The way you view and categorize sexualities may differ from that of individuals who have been socialized in a different cultural environment. The language used to identify people according to their sexual preference (e.g., identity labels) can also vary. These terms or labels offer insight into an individual's or society's value judgments and degree of openness to people who are different from ourselves.

Age identity

In most cultures, age is an important element for individuals, groups, and societies. Age can influence one's self-image, personality, language use, attitudes, and communication with others. It can also determine one's positioning and status in family, work, leisure, and social settings (e.g., religious, political, and secular community organizations).

Age identity refers to how people feel and think about themselves and others based on age. It is concerned with the inner experience of a person's age and the aging process. Westerhof (2008) defines age identity as 'the outcome of the processes through which one identifies with or distances oneself from different aspects of the aging process' (p. 10). From a poststructuralist perspective, Andrew (2016) observes that 'the experience of ageing and the construction of age identity can only occur through language and the competing discourses of a particular culture, including gender, ethnicity, social class and other discourses' (p. 338).

In scientific research, a person's age identity is typically measured by responses to such questions as 'How old do you feel?', 'To which age group do you belong?', 'How do you perceive and understand your own aging process?', and 'In what ways do you communicate your age to others?' Age identity is often linked to such social dimensions as ethnicity, gender, and professional roles (Andrew 2016).

Several dimensions of age identity have been scrutinized, including how people feel, act, look, behave (e.g., functional capacities, interests, hobbies, social roles and activities), think (e.g., cognitive and linguistic functioning, attitudes, values), and express themselves (e.g., language use, colloquialisms) at different stages of their life. Researchers on aging are examining how individuals from different cultural backgrounds: (1) identify with or classify themselves into particular age groups, (2) compare themselves to peers of the same age (e.g., ingroup identification), (3) perceive and distinguish themselves from other age groups (e.g., outgroups), (4) communicate verbally and nonverbally with individuals from their own and other age groups. Their work is helping us to better understand how age identities may differ in various cultural contexts and affect intercultural relations.

The relationship between language, age, and culture is of particular interest to intercultural communication specialists who are concerned with the adjustment of immigrants and temporary residents (e.g., education abroad students, expatriates) in new linguistic and cultural environments. As noted by many cross-cultural psychologists, it is not unusual for people of different generations to have disparate values, worldviews, philosophies, and ways of speaking. In immigrant families, members of older generations (e.g., from the 'old country') may use a dialect, expressions, or colloquialisms that are foreign to younger members of their families who have grown up in the receiving country. While children may learn the primary language of the 'new country' at school and informally in the wider community, parents or grandparents may have little or no command of the language and, not surprisingly, intergenerational communication problems may arise.

Older immigrants who had senior professional positions in their home country may find themselves in occupations with a much lower status. Without a good command of the new country's language they may feel devalued, depressed, and sidelined. Their young children, who have more proficiency in the local language and more informal exposure to local cultural practices, may serve as interpreters or cultural brokers for their elders, which further challenges traditional notions of age, status, and power.

Perceptions of age and the aging process vary among cultures and shape one's expectations of roles, status, and responsibilities as well as everyday social interactions in later life. Ideas about aging are conveyed to us by family members, religious organizations, schools, and peers, as well as through advertisements, the television, the Internet, and other forms of mass media and social networks. In traditional, less industrialized contexts, the wisdom and life experiences of older people are prized. In tribal areas in Northern Thailand, for example, as a marker of respect, younger people may use relationship titles or honorifics when addressing their elders.

In industrialized nations, senior posts in most fields and industries (e.g., higher education, business, healthcare, politics) tend to be filled by people who have a lot of experience; however, in some sectors, the technological revolution has propelled young people to very lucrative, powerful positions early in their career. For example, Mark Zuckerberg, an American computer programmer, co-founded the social networking site Facebook when he was only 19. In 2010, at the age of 26, he was identified by *Time Magazine* as one of the most influential men in the world. As the chairman and chief executive officer (CEO) of Facebook, Inc. he is now worth billions. There are many other entrepreneurs who have played a role in the digital revolution and become very successful at a young age.

Undeniably, youth is highly valued in Western cultures. This is evident in the marketing campaigns that bombard people with messages about the significance of looking young and staying fit. Annually, millions of dollars are spent on cosmetic products and surgical procedures in an effort to fight against the natural aging process. Due to technological advances (e.g., social media) and globalizing forces these notions are spreading across the globe and challenging traditional perceptions of age and the aging process. As people are living and working longer in modern societies, views about what it means to be old are changing.

Religious identity

In many parts of the world, affiliation with a religion is a core dimension of one's identity, and this can have a profound impact on one's daily life. **Religious identity** refers to one's sense of belonging to a particular religious group. Similar to other aspects of identity, a religious identity may mean different things to individuals, and the significance of one's religious affiliation may change over time with exposure to other beliefs and practices. In some cultural settings, one's religious affiliation is a private matter, and there is a clear separation of religion and government, whereas in other contexts, religion permeates all dimensions of life.

Religious identity formation is concerned with the process by which individuals decide what their relationship to religion will be. In many contexts, messages from family and religious figures begin at a very early age and are reinforced through various rituals (e.g., prayers, weekly sermons which have messages about moral behaviors) and ceremonies (e.g., baptism and confirmation for Christians, the bar mitzvah to mark a Jew's coming of age). One's affiliation with a particular religion may also be conveyed and reinforced through one's dress (e.g., the wearing of a skull cap or long robes of a particular color), adornments/jewelry (e.g., wearing a necklace with a cross), personal grooming (e.g., the growing of a beard by male devotees), and the eating of special foods (e.g., kosher foods by Jews, halal food by Muslims). The use of a particular language or dialect may also reveal one's affiliation with a religion (e.g., Arabic in Islam; the holy book, the Qur'an, was written in this language).

Membership in a religious group can offer believers a sense of community and provide inner fulfillment. While a religious identity can be a great source of strength and provide a purpose or direction for one's life, in some situations it can serve as a barrier to intercultural communication. For example, people may refuse to socialize or interact with atheists or followers of a different faith. When individuals in positions of power have little respect for the religious beliefs and practices of a different religious group, disputes and even wars may result. (Discrimination is discussed further in Chapter 6; interfaith conflict is examined in Chapter 9.)

Physical and mental ability identity

All people have a **physical ability identity** as each of us has both physical capabilities and limitations. No human is perfect. We may be limited in some ways by our height, weight, body shape, chronic illness, or other physical features. Throughout our life we may strive to overcome multiple dimensions of our physical ability, especially as we age. Some people are temporarily disabled (e.g., broken leg or jaw), while others are born with disabilities (e.g., cerebral palsy, blindness, deafness, inability to speak). Individuals may become permanently disabled through illness or accidents, or they may develop chronic conditions (e.g., multiple sclerosis, Parkinson's disease) that affect their quality of life and impede their communication with others. Enculturation influences how individuals in a particular context view and respond to individuals who have a physical disability.

We also have a **mental ability identity** that is linked to our cognitive abilities (e.g., degree of intelligence), mental health (e.g., stable, depressed), and ability to function in everyday life.

Plate 5.5 Religious identities may be marked by one's appearance. This monk conveys his devotion to Buddhism through his bright orange robe and shaved head. © Jane Jackson

Some people are of above average intelligence (e.g., intellectually gifted), while others are below average (e.g., intellectually challenged, developmentally delayed). Some individuals have been born with less cognitive ability, whereas others experience a loss in their mental capacity as a consequence of illness, drug use, an accident, or the aging process. Individuals may also suffer from a mental illness or disorder (e.g., autism, bipolarism, schizophrenia).

How people view their mental state, cognitive ability, and physical capabilities affects their sense of self and positioning in society. Individuals with disabilities, whether mental or physical, may regard themselves as members of a special cultural group with their own values, practices, language, and communication patterns (e.g., deaf culture, blind culture). Group members who share similar perceptions, concerns, and aspirations may work together to fight for more respect and recognition in the wider society. Attitudes toward people with mental and physical difficulties can vary tremendously across cultures and result in significant differences in their quality of life and opportunities to participate in their community. (Chapter 6 discusses prejudicial attitudes and discriminatory practices related to the treatment of people with physical and mental disabilities.)

National identity

Most people have a **national identity**, which refers to their affiliation with and sense of belonging to a particular state or nation. While some scholars limit this type of identity to official citizenship, others refer to it as the feeling one shares with a group of people in a nation, regardless of one's citizenship status. For example, illegal immigrants who have spent much of their life in a particular country may possess a sense of belonging to their adopted home even if they have no legal papers to formalize this sentiment. Accordingly, Liu *et al.* (2019: 348) prefer to describe national identity as a type of identity that is 'characterized by one's individual self-perception as a member of a nation'.

An individual's national identity may be associated with specific symbols (e.g., flags, flowers, colors), language(s) (e.g., dialects, code-mixing, bilingualism policy), ethnicity, music (e.g., national anthem in a particular language or languages, folk songs), cuisine (e.g., local dishes, a special type of cooking), political system (e.g., democracy, communism), religion(s), television stations (and other forms of media), heroes (e.g., Olympians, war heroes), special feats (e.g., inventions), a shared history, and so on. Verbal and nonverbal symbols may serve as a bond for many nationals; however, it is important to recognize that people within a nation may have very different understandings and emotions in relation to each symbol (e.g., use of 'official' language, oath of allegiance, national anthem).

The strength or salience of one's national identity may vary over time. When under threat, whether real or imagined, one's national identity tends to strengthen and draw individuals closer to other people from the same nation. National identity can be a great source of pride and provide individuals with a sense of belonging; however, it can also lead to negative perceptions and mistreatment of people who are affiliated with other nations. These identity markers may serve as the basis for people from other countries to treat nationals in a particular way (e.g., display admiration, convey disrespect and hostility).

Regional identity

Linked to national identity is the notion of **regional identity**, which refers to an individual's affiliation with and connection to a particular region. In many nations, people from particular regions have distinct identities, which may vary in importance among the inhabitants. For some, regional identities may be even more meaningful and significant than their national affiliation. Other individuals, of course, may distance themselves from a regional label, preferring to be linked to a broader, more national, or even international persona.

Regional identities may be inspired by cultural, ethnic, religious, linguistic, or political ties as well as geography. For example, people who live on an island or in an isolated, mountainous region may develop bonds and habits (e.g., linguistic, cultural, religious) that distinguish them from people in other parts of the country. If the inhabitants do not feel understood or respected at the national level, regional ties can sometimes be a powerful motivating force that drives independence movements. In some cases, this has led to the creation of autonomous regions or states (e.g., Bosnia, Herzegovina, Slovenia, Namibia).

In many regions, people are distinguished from the rest of their nation by their own unique linguistic and cultural identities, which are accompanied by special forms of dress, artwork, food, and social norms such as unwritten rules of politeness (e.g., verbal and nonverbal greetings). Because of ethnic or religious ties, inhabitants in a particular region may feel a stronger connection with each other than people in other parts of their nation. Regional accents and dialects may identify people as being from a particular region. For example, in Britain someone from Yorkshire typically has a very different accent compared with a lifelong resident of London. In Canada, French is the primary language of the province of Québec, and for many French-speaking Québécois, their regional identity is stronger than their national identity. This is also the case in many other regions of the world (e.g., the Basque region of Spain, the Kurdish region of Iraq).

Besides geography, regions may be emotionally separated from the rest of a nation due to political, linguistic, and historical reasons. For example, after being a colony of Britain from 1843 to 1997, Hong Kong reunited with Mainland China and will be a Special Administrative Region (SAR) in this populous nation until 2047. After that date, it will be more integrated into the 'Motherland'. The use of Cantonese distinguishes Hong Kong Chinese from Mainlanders who speak Putonghua (Mandarin), the official language of the 'Motherland', or another Chinese dialect. Similar to other types of social identity, the meaning and significance of regional identities may change over time. In particular, factors such as the sociopolitical climate, the economic situation, and language policies may influence the strength of regional identifications.

Global, transnational identity

Chapter 1 discussed how globalization has made our world increasingly interconnected, facilitating mobility and interaction between people from diverse backgrounds. In addition to national, regional, or local identities, more and more individuals are developing a **global** or **transnational identity** that affords them a sense of belonging or connection to a worldwide or global culture (Arnett 2002).

A global identity is often associated with the use of an international language. For example, as mentioned earlier in the Chapter, individuals who speak English as an additional language may feel connected to speakers of the language in distant lands and, over time, develop a global persona. Third culture individuals (TCIs) and other multicultural individuals who are open to what the world has to offer welcome diverse intercultural and linguistic experiences. As they acquire a more cosmopolitan, inclusive outlook, they may nurture both local and global selves.

Through a global identity (and global language), we can recognize and appreciate our connection with people in other parts of the world. Our broadened mindset can help us to solve the pressing issues facing us today (e.g., food shortages, global warming, territorial disputes, racism). As noted by Gerzon (2010: xvii), 'we human beings are now being challenged to realize that we are something more than citizens of separate nations, members of different races, and followers of different religions. We are also global citizens'. (In Chapter 11 we discuss global citizenship and ways to nurture a more intercultural, global mindset, whether in one's home environment or in an international setting.)

Organizational identity

People may also develop an **organizational identity**, that is, a sense of attachment to organizations, whether in their social, educational, religious, or professional life. For example, my university follows a college system and all undergraduates and professors are affiliated with a particular college. In a large institution like this, it is easier for people to get to know one another in smaller groups and the colleges arrange activities designed to build up a sense of belonging among members. For many students, their college identity becomes so strong that it persists well after graduation. Through social media, graduates may maintain contact with each other and regularly attend college-affiliated alumni gatherings after leaving our campus.

When people enter the workforce, they are often employed by a company or organization, and, through a variety of activities, they become inducted into the culture of that organization. Over time, they may build up a degree of loyalty and pride in the organization and acquire a company identity. In some contexts, individuals spend their entire career with a single company, and their primary identity is work-related. In many parts of the world, however, people are changing jobs and relocating much more frequently for a variety of reasons (e.g., economic recessions, more opportunities for advancement). As one might expect, this influences organizational identities and bringing about more diversity in the workplace, an aspect that is discussed further in Chapter 10.

Within an organization or workplace, language can serve as a powerful marker of one's membership or affiliation. For example, the use of specialized terms and informal discourse that is only fully understood by members of one's organization (or work team) can reinforce the distinctiveness of one's group and bolster one's sense of belonging to the company or work unit.

Organizational identity can also be linked to the notion of '**community of practice**' **(CoP)** (Lave & Wenger 1991), which Eckert and McConnell-Ginet (1992: 464) define as 'an aggregate of people who come together around mutual engagement in an endeavor'. Through social and professional interaction with more experienced members, newcomers form an understanding of their roles and responsibilities, that is, they learn about particular '[w]ays of doing things, ways of thinking, ways of talking, beliefs, values, power relations – in short practices' (ibid: 464). While engaging in the practices of their organization (or other type of group), members gradually move from 'apprentices' to 'experts'; in the process, they construct identities in relation to the group or community.

Identities are partly shaped and conditioned by social interaction and social structure (Block 2007, 2014). Similar to many other types of identity, the salience and strength of one's organizational identity may change over time depending on such factors as perceived benefits of the affiliation, desire and need to/pressure to fit in, attitude toward the organization, and outsider perceptions of the organization, among others. As economies come under pressure and more mobility options emerge, people in many parts of the world are less likely to be tied to the same employer for their entire working career. Consequently, in some contexts, loyalty to a particular organizational identity may be weaker than in previous generations.

Professional identity

Related to the notion of organizational identity, is the formation of a **professional identity**, which refers to an individual's sense of belonging in a particular profession (e.g., teaching, nursing, business, etc.). This form of identity encompasses beliefs, attitudes, and understanding about one's roles within the context of work and is characterized by the use of specialized terms (e.g., jargon) and communication styles.

Professional identity formation refers to how individuals develop a sense of what it means to be a member of a particular profession, and how this identity distinguishes them from other professional groups. This developmental process is closely tied to the notion of 'communities of practice' that was previously described (Lave & Wenger 1991). For example, if you decide to become an English as a second language teacher you will attend teacher education and applied linguistics courses and likely participate in a practicum (e.g., practice teaching in a school) as an 'apprentice'. By observing and interacting with experienced professionals ('experts'), you develop an understanding of the worldview (e.g., beliefs and attitudes) that is emphasized in your chosen profession, as well as the theories and methodologies that one is expected to master. As your professional identity takes shape, you discover the boundaries of the teaching profession and the ways to behave or interact with other teachers and students (e.g., the language and communication styles that are appropriate in different situations).

Virtual (cyber and fantasy) identities

In this era of advanced information technology, **cyberculture** (Internet culture) has emerged from the use of computer networks for communication, business, and entertainment. The Internet, gaming, and multi-user domains (MUDs) are spawning new types of identity. An **Internet identity (virtual, cyber, online)** refers to 'the infinitely changeable online representations of individuals and groups using words, pictures, and other images, and music and other sounds, which can be outside the control of the actual person or group being represented' (West 2015: 557).

In online virtual communities (e.g., online chat rooms, online multi-player games, social gaming, social media, and texting), a user's online identity serves as an interface between the physical person and the virtual person that other users view on their computer screen. Users may create a persona that is far different from who they are in real life. Further, the language they use and the way they express themselves may differ considerably from their communication style in face-to-face interactions. In essence, through language and nonverbal means individuals can perform multiple identities online (Darvin 2016; West 2015).

When you become a member of an online community, you usually have some control over how much personal information, if any, you wish to reveal about yourself. You can choose to let other users see how you actually look, or you can be deceptive and post the photo of someone else. You can also decide if others can hear your voice. Suler (2002: 455) explains that 'the desire to remain anonymous reflects the need to eliminate those critical features of your identity that you do NOT want to display in that particular environment or group'. Advocates of cyber communication maintain that this allows people to engage in intercultural communication with individuals they might never meet in real life. As people may not see your physical characteristics, they are reliant on the personal details you provide about yourself in texts (e.g., your age, ethnicity, first language), the images (e.g., photos, artwork) you post, as well as your use of emoticons (pictorial representations of facial expressions and other symbols that are meant to convey particular emotions).

Cyberculture and the possibility of anonymity have significantly altered the ways many people communicate on a day-to-day basis. Spending too much time immersed in virtual reality with one's cyber identity(ies) can cause some to lose touch with the real world. In Japan and South Korea, for example, psychologists are counseling a growing number of young people who are addicted to online gaming. Lost in a fantasy world, some find it difficult to communicate with people in direct physical interactions and feel like outsiders in their home environment.

In all cultures, there are also forms of **fantasy identities**, which center on characters from anime, manga (comic books), and science fiction film (Samovar *et al.* 2017). Annually, Hong Kong hosts one of the world's largest animation and comic book fairs, attracting thousands of fans who bring superheroes (e.g., Thor, Spiderman, Captain America, Optimus Prime) to life through colorful costumes. These events bring together young people and adults from different backgrounds who share a passion for particular fantasy characters. In the United States, *Star Wars* conventions also attract people who dress up like their favorite characters. There are many ways in which individuals express diverse facets of their self-identities.

SUMMARY

Identity is a core element in intercultural interactions. We all have multiple identities (e.g., age, ethnic, gender, religious, national, cyber) that affect how we see ourselves and others. Identities are dynamic and influenced by the language and cultural socialization process, our sociocultural environment, and our desire to fit in with particular groups. Identities are complex and subject to negotiation; they may be contested or challenged in diverse contexts. While we may wish to project a certain identity, others may view us in a different way, which can be very disconcerting. Our affiliations with particular groups can provide us with a sense of belonging; however, our identities and attitudes toward outgroup members can also serve as barriers to intercultural communication, an aspect that is explored in Chapter 6.

discussion questions

1   How have your perceptions of your language identity changed since you were in primary school?
2   What does it mean to say that the process of identity construction is 'complex, multifaceted, dynamic, and dialogic' (Schecter & Bayley 2002: 49)?
3   According to Mary Fong (2004), each and every speech community is layered with the multiple identities of its individual members. What does she mean by this? Do you agree?
4   How do you define yourself in your home environment? Does this change when you are outside your home country or region? Provide examples.
5   Why do bi-and multilingual speakers sometimes feel like they have different identities when speaking different languages? Reflecting on your own experiences, describe your sense of self when using different languages in diverse contexts.
6   Have you ever been in a situation in which your preferred identities were not recognized or respected? Describe your emotions and response.
7   Why is it important to recognize and respect the preferred self-identities of the people we are communicating with? Discuss your ideas with a partner.
8   Reflect on what you have learned about identity in this chapter. What are the implications for intercultural relations? How might this knowledge impact the way you communicate with people with a different linguistic and cultural background? Share your understandings with a partner.

activities

1   Who are you? Make a list of ten statements about your identity. (I am. . .). Write as many statements about yourself as you can possibly think of in ten minutes. What do these statements reveal about your cultural identity? Personal identity? Ethnic identity? Regional identity? What other facets of your identity have you disclosed? How has your linguistic and cultural background influenced who you are today and who you hope to be in the future?

2   In a small group, discuss how language use and gender identity/roles may differ in different cultural contexts.

3   Identify features of your language or language usage that may signal your ethnic identity.

4   Chat with two bi- or multilingual speakers (e.g., local or international students who are not from your ethnic group) and informally discuss language, culture, and identity issues with them. What languages do they speak? Do they feel more connected to a specific culture or group when they use a particular language or dialect (or code-mixing)? Does language use serve as an identity marker for them? Do they sometimes feel as if they have different identities when speaking a different language? Do they feel they have a more global identity when they use an international language like English? What elements of their stories and emotions are similar to your own? What aspects are different? From this task, what did you discover about the connections between language, culture, and identity, and the implications for intercultural communication?

5   Explain what is meant by 'contested identities'. The following is an excerpt from an interview with a Hong Kong Chinese international exchange student: 'In Germany, the Japanese said I was Korean, the Koreans said I was Japanese, and the Mainland Chinese wouldn't say I was Chinese. I felt, well, a bit helpless'. Have you ever been misidentified (or misidentified others)? How did this affect you emotionally? How can situations like this hamper intercultural relations?

6   Write a language and cultural identity paper in which you reflect on how your identities and the languages you speak affect your intercultural attitudes and interactions. Reflect on the implications for intercultural relations and the enhancement of your intercultural communication skills.

further reading

Block, D. (2009) *Second Language Identities*, London: Continuum.

Drawing on social science theory, the author discusses identity formation and change in foreign language learners, adult migrants, and study abroad students.

Jandt, F. (2018) *An Introduction to Intercultural Communication: Identities in a Global Community*, 9th edn, Thousand Oaks, CA: Sage.

This introductory text discusses the ways in which culture and language influences identities and intercultural communication.

Noels, K.A., Yashima, T. and Zhang, R. (2012) 'Language, identity and intercultural communication', in J. Jackson (ed.) *Routledge Handbook of Language and Intercultural Communication*, Abingdon: Routledge, pp. 52–66.

In this chapter, the authors critically examine how scholars in social psychology, communication, and applied linguistics define identity; their review highlights the complex relation between language and identity in intercultural communication.

Pollock, D.C., Van Reken, R.E. and Pollock, M.V. (2017) *Third Culture Kids: Growing Up Among Worlds*, 3rd edn, Boston: Nicholas Brealey Publishing.

Drawing on interviews and personal writings, this book explores the challenges and benefits of being Third Culture Kids (TCKs), young people who have spent a significant part of their developmental years abroad.

Shi, X. and Langman, J. (2012) 'Gender, language, identity, and intercultural communication', in J. Jackson (ed.) *Routledge Handbook of Language and Intercultural Communication*, Abingdon: Routledge, pp. 167–80.

In this chapter the authors discuss the major topics and theoretical approaches that have shaped language, gender, and identity studies.

Companion Website: Continue your journey online

Visit the Companion Website for a variety of tools and resources to support and extend your intercultural learning. (Instructors who are qualified adopters of the text may access additional resources on this site.)

CHAPTER 6

Ethnocentricism and Othering

Barriers to intercultural communication

'I'm not racist, but. . .'
'It's just a joke.'
'Some of my best friends are. . .'
       – (James 2001: 1)

> It is not our differences that divide us. It is our inability to recognize, accept, and celebrate those differences.
>
>   (Lorde 1986: 197)

Change your thoughts and you change your world.
            Norman Vincent Peale, minister and author (Peale 2007: 233)

---

learning objectives

By the end of this chapter, you should be able to:

1   Explain the process of social categorization
2   Discuss the negative consequences of Othering for intercultural relations
3   Explain the ingroup favoritism principle and its potential impact on intercultural communication
4   Describe the nature of ethnocentricism and explain why it can serve as a barrier to intercultural communication
5   Distinguish between a generalization and a stereotype
6   Define and give examples of the harmful effects of stereotyping, bias and prejudice, racism, and xenophobia on intercultural relations
7   Identify ways to combat ethnocentric tendencies and biases

---

INTRODUCTION

In the previous chapter, we examined the nature, characteristics, and types of identities that exist in today's complex world. While identity can provide us with a sense of belonging, it can also serve as the basis for negative perceptions of and reactions to people who are different from us. We are naturally drawn to individuals and groups who share a similar language, culture, and ways of being. Unconsciously or consciously, we may shy away from those who do not belong to our ingroup. As Samovar *et al.* (2017: 200) explain, '[o]ur preference for things we understand and are familiar with can adversely influence our perception of and attitude toward new and different people and things. Left unchecked, this can lead to stereotyping, prejudice (e.g., Islamophobia, Anti-Semitism), racism, and ethnocentrism'. In extreme cases it can inspire terrorist attacks and even genocide.

Social categorization and ethnocentrism lie at the heart of identity biases and discrimination. Consequently, this chapter begins by examining these processes, which all too often create barriers to successful, equitable intercultural interactions. We then examine what lies behind racist and xenophobic behavior (e.g., racist discourse, exclusion). Finally, we discuss ways to overcome ethnocentrism and identity biases.

SOCIAL CATEGORIZATION AND OTHERING

Social categorization refers to the way we group people into conceptual categories in order to make sense of our increasingly complex social environment. This entails the act of **perception**, that is, 'becoming aware of, knowing, or identifying by means of the senses' through a three-step process involving selection, organization, and interpretation (Jandt 2018: 431). Throughout each day we are continuously exposed to a variety of perceptual stimuli (e.g., sights, sounds, smells) that can be overwhelming. To cope, we try to reduce information to manageable forms. In the process, we typically place people into different groups and categories based on our current understandings, perceptions, and experience (Allport 1954; Landis 2018). In other words, we make inferences about individual behavior in relation to group patterns. Unfortunately, this can easily lead to essentialism, 'an assumption that any entity (a group of people, geographic place, observable behavior, or physical object) has a set of requisite attributes that is essential to its form and function' (Strauss 2018: 730). This reductionist ideology assumes that 'groups can be clearly delimited' and 'group members are more or less alike' (Bucholtz 2003: 400).

Essentialism refers to situations in which 'social groups are assumed to share universal and homogenous characteristics without consideration for variation across cultures, within groups, or over time' (Sorrells 2015: 298). 'Assumptions that cultures are determinate, bounded, and homogeneous manifest essential thinking' (ibid: 298). Essentialism and other negative consequences of Othering can be very harmful to intercultural relations as noted by many critical interculturalists, including Prue Holmes (2012: 468):

> the cognitive activities of categorization and generalization that occur normally in the human brain are an important way of making sense of the world around us. Although such categorizations are useful as sense-making strategies for human behavior, if unchecked, they can lead to more extreme understandings of cultural difference, such as ethnocentrism, stereotyping, and prejudice – the roots of racism.

Othering or Otherization is a form of social representation which involves 'the objectification of another person or group' (Abdallah-Pretceille 2003). Through this process, arbitrary, abstract characteristics are ascribed to Others by those 'who have the power to control the subject/Other' (Chawla 2018: 1649). Culture is used to account for all of the views and behaviors of 'the other', largely ignoring the complexity and diversity within (e.g., individual variations in thoughts, emotions, actions) (Holliday 2012, 2019; Dervin 2012, 2016). Instead of seeing people who have a different cultural and linguistic background as complex individuals like themselves, an ethnocentric person sees them simply as representatives of a particular culture and tied to a rigid set of characteristics and behaviors. This reductionist orientation is not conducive to the formation of meaningful intercultural ties.

Social categorization and Othering are linked to the **social identity theory** that was developed by Henri Tajfel and John Turner in the 1970s and 80s to explain intergroup behavior (Tajfel 1982; Tajfel & Turner 1979, 1986). This theory posits that individuals tend to categorize people in their social environment into ingroups and outgroups (Schmid 2018; Stephan & Stephan 2015). Ting-Toomey and Chung (2012: 303) define **ingroup members** as 'people with whom you feel connected to or owe a sense of loyalty and allegiance, such as family members, close friends, or familiar others within the community'. An ingroup can offer security and provide its members with a sense of belonging in exchange for loyalty.

Ingroups typically consist of family members, people from the same perceived ethnic or religious group, or peers of the same age, gender, class, political affiliation, or occupation, etc. This also means that we usually belong to multiple ingroups at the same time and one's ingroups may change at different stages of one's life. In contrast, **outgroup members** are 'those with whom one feels emotionally and psychologically detached, such as strangers, unfamiliar others, or members who belong to a competitive or opposing group' (Ting-Toomey & Chung 2012: 306). Who we perceive as outsiders may change as we gain more life experience (e.g., engage in more intercultural interactions at home or abroad, diversify our social circle).

In her home environment, prior to studying abroad, a student wrote the following in her intercultural reflections journal, offering insight into how she defined one of her most important ingroups. Her comments reveal how negative perceptions and attitudes can serve as barriers to engagement with outgroup members.

> I strongly recognize myself as belonging to a religious group, and I find my particular religion a concrete and absolute thing in culture that conspicuously differentiates me from nonbelievers. . . . The way I choose friends and socialize with other people is very much based on my religion, too. I see nonbelievers as human beings belonging to their flesh. Thus, I share no common points with them in their spiritual aspects, and I should not adopt their thoughts and behaviors.

Not surprisingly, her social network consisted solely of individuals who shared her religious beliefs.

The social identity theory posits that it is natural for people to seek ways to 'strengthen their self-esteem' and to 'strive to achieve or to maintain a positive social identity' (Tajfel & Turner 1979). Positive ingroup membership can help to accomplish these aspirations by providing a sense of belonging and camaraderie among those who are thought to share similar beliefs, values, and traditions or ways of being (e.g., communication styles). As individuals gain positive self-esteem from their group memberships, they tend to view their ingroup more favorably than other groups.

Group characteristics are developed over time within specific social, historical, linguistic, religious, political, and geographic contexts. By observing how other members of our ingroup behave (e.g., use language and nonverbal means of communication), we discover what attributes and actions are valued. The typical characteristics and behaviors of the group gradually become norms that guide our own behavior, reinforcing our ties to the group. This learning is part of the socialization and identity formation processes that were discussed in Chapters 2 and 5. The emotional and cognitive significance of our ingroup membership becomes salient and is often strengthened when in the presence of outgroup members, especially when there is discord or rivalry between groups. In times of heightened tension and conflict, emotive 'us' vs. 'them' discourse may prevail as individuals seek to defend their group.

Individuals with a strong ingroup identification tend to more fully adopt the values, behaviors, and practices that they associate with their particular ingroup(s). In addition to influencing thoughts and actions, the group's norms serve as a basis for Othering, that is judging outsiders (outgroup members) by one's own standards. People who have a more intense connection with their ingroup identity see themselves as more typical group members and are more apt to evaluate the performance of ingroup members more favorably than outsiders (Schmid 2018; Tajfel &Turner 1979).

Ingroup favoritism (sometimes called **ingroup bias**) refers to situations in which people give preferential treatment to those who are perceived to be in the same ingroup. If ingroup members feel under threat from outsiders, ingroup favoritism may be accompanied by outgroup derogation (e.g., 'us' vs. 'them' discourse, whereby us is positioned more favorably). Insufficient or inaccurate information about outsiders coupled with negative perceptions and expectations can heighten one's anxiety level and reduce the desire to interact with people outside one's ingroup. It is not surprising that overly favoring one's ingroup can lead to the negative consequences of Othering (e.g., prejudice, discrimination, sexism, ageism, and racism).

ETHNOCENTRICISM

Through the process of primary socialization, children develop expectations and shared understandings about the most appropriate ways to behave in particular situations and contexts. From our parents, teachers, and religious leaders, we learn the social rules and ways of being (e.g., linguistics norms of politeness) that are preferred by members of our particular ingroup (e.g., ethnic group, religious group). We are exposed to the worldviews of those who are closest to us and form ideas about what is 'right' and 'wrong', 'fair' and 'unfair', etc. If we have limited contact with people who have a different cultural background, we may also assume that everyone does things as we do.

The **ingroup favoritism principle** is closely linked to the notion of ethnocentrism, which derives from the Greek words *ethnos*, meaning 'nation' or 'people', and *kentron*, meaning *center*. The term ethnocentrism was coined by William G. Sumner, an American sociologist, who observed the tendency of people to differentiate between their ingroup and outsiders in a way that privileges their own group members. He defined **ethnocentricism** as '[t]he sentiment of cohesion, internal comradeship, and devotion to the ingroup, which carries with it a sense of superiority to any out-group and readiness to defend the interests of the ingroup against the out-group' (Sumner 1911: 11).

While ethnocentrism can foster 'ingroup survival, solidarity, conformity, cooperation, loyalty, and effectiveness' (Neuliep 2018a: 753), tight ingroup ties can also lead to the distrust and denigration of outgroup members. Individuals with an ethnocentric or monocultural mindset may display empathy and concern about the well-being of ingroup members but view outsiders as inferior or insignificant and exhibit little concern about them. Ethnocentric behavior may be characterized by arrogance, vanity, and even contempt for people who do not belong to one's ingroup.

Ethnocentric thinking may cause us to make false assumptions and premature judgments about people who have been socialized in a different cultural environment. When we only draw on our own cultural (and linguistic) norms to evaluate unfamiliar practices (e.g., cultural scripts, sociopragmatic norms, customs, ethics, religious traditions), we are engaging in Othering and behaving in an ethnocentric way. We are 'assuming that the worldview of one's own culture is central to all reality' (M.J. Bennett 1993: 30) and that our ways are the *only* proper ways to think and behave. Emotional, negative reactions to cultural difference can reduce the willingness to expend the additional energy that may be required to make sense of unfamiliar cultural messages. An ethnocentric, monocultural mindset can hold one back from cultivating healthy intercultural relationships.

Ethnocentric tendencies can affect the way we communicate with people who are different from ourselves. Monolingual, monocultural individuals who converse with minority members who are second language speakers may convey a lack of respect or indifference toward their interlocutors through both verbal and nonverbal means. Using a patronizing tone of speech, for example, they may position adult second language learners as young children or adults who lack intelligence and sophistication.

Ethnocentric individuals may also make comments that disparage people who they perceive to be from a lesser group or category. For example, they may denigrate people from another region who speak with a different accent. To create social distance from outsiders they dislike, fear, distrust, or simply disrespect, ethnocentric individuals may avoid intercultural interactions, which, in turn, limits their intercultural learning.

In stark contrast, **cultural relativism** refers to the view that beliefs, value systems, and social practices are culturally relative, that is, no culture is inherently superior to another. From an ethnorelative perspective, 'different cultures are perceived as variable and viable constructions of reality' (M.J. Bennett 1993: 66). This position acknowledges that there is no absolute standard to compare and contrast different ways of being. Individuals who adopt an ethnorelative orientation make an effort to understand unfamiliar cultural ways of being from the perspective of their interlocutors. As noted in the first chapter, this does not mean that one must accept practices that harm others. Later in this chapter we discuss how to minimize the ethnocentric tendencies that exist in all of us.

STEREOTYPING

Ethnocentrism often results in **stereotyping**, a strong tendency to characterize people from other cultural backgrounds unfairly, collectively, and usually negatively. A **stereotype** is a preconceived idea that attributes certain characteristics (e.g., personality traits, intelligence), intentions, and behaviors to all the members of a particular social class or group of people (Holliday 2010; Kochman & Mavrelis 2015). Hummert (2018) further explains that stereotypes are 'culturally shared person perception schemata or cognitions that associate particular trait and behavioral characteristics, some positive and some negative, with members of a defined group' (p. 1852).

Before we go further, it is important to distinguish between stereotypes and generalizations. A **generalization** is 'a statement about common trends within a group, but with the recognition that further information is needed to ascertain whether the generalization applies to a particular person' (Galanti 2000: 335). Although stereotypes and generalizations may seem similar, they function in different ways. For example, if you meet a Sudanese man and assume that he has many children and do not allow for other possibilities, you are stereotyping him. If, on the other hand, you say to yourself, 'Many Sudanese have many children, I wonder if Mr. Salama does' and leave open the possibility that he does not, you are generalizing. A stereotype imposes one's assumptions on others based on commonly held beliefs, whereas a generalization is a starting point and you understand that much more information is needed to determine if your ideas or perceptions apply to a particular individual (or group) or situation.

We are not born with stereotypes, we learn them during the process of socialization by way of messages about outgroup members from parents, grandparents, teachers, the clergy, etc. As we mature, we are influenced by portrayals of different groups in society (e.g., television dramas, sitcoms, movies, comedy shows, newspapers, the Internet, political campaigns, social media) as well as our own life experiences (e.g., intercultural encounters, travel, study abroad). Stereotypes may also emerge out of fear, ignorance, or distrust of people who are different from ourselves (e.g., physical attributes, intelligence, color of skin, etc.).

There are many reasons why people resort to stereotyping: to quickly process new information about a person or situation, to organize previous experiences, to stress differences between themselves and other individuals or groups (e.g., to convey that 'us' is superior to 'them'), to make predictions about other people's behavior, to simplify their busy life, and so on.

The process of stereotyping typically involves the following steps:

1   Often individuals are categorized, usually on the basis of easily identifiable characteristics such as sex or ethnicity.
2   A set of attributes is ascribed to all (or most) members of that category. Individuals belonging to the stereotyped group are assumed to be similar to each other, and different from other groups, on this set of attributes.
3   The set of attributes is ascribed to any individual member of that category.

(Hewstone & Brown 1986: 29)

Groups may be stereotyped based on a wide range of characteristics (e.g., language/accent, ethnicity, physical appearance, nationality, religion, geographic location, class, age, sex, gender, etc.). The following list provides a few examples of people or groups that are frequently stereotyped in the mass media, comedy shows, and films:

- Cities (Beijingers, New Yorkers, Parisians, Singaporeans, Berliners)
- Regions within countries (Newfies in Canada, Northerners, Yorkshire folk)
- Dialects (Ebonics in the U.S., Yakuzas in Japan)
- Race (African Americans, Caucasians, Hispanics, Native Hawaiians)
- Religion (Atheists, Buddhists, Christians, Jews, Muslims, Hindus, Sikhs)
- Ethnic groups (Chinese, Black Africans, Arabs, Hispanics)
- National groups (U.S. Americans, Iranians, Irish, Italians, North Koreans)
- Age (youngsters, adolescents, teenagers, middle-aged, senior citizens)
- Vocations (teachers, garbage collectors, clergy, newscasters, football players)
- Social class (poor, white collar, blue collar, upper middle class, the corporate rich)
- Physical attributes (obese, anorexic, dwarfs, tall, jocks)
- Disabilities (deafness, blindness, mentally disabled)
- Gender (masculinity, femininity)

When people stereotype, they typically apply a commonly held generalization of a cultural group to all people who are associated with it. For example, in many parts of the world, U.S. Americans are stereotyped (e.g., in the media, movies) as friendly but arrogant and ignorant about world affairs, while British people are considered uptight and love to drink alcohol to excess, etc., etc. In Hong Kong, Mainland Chinese are often stereotyped as loud, aggressive, and lacking in manners, whereas in Mainland China, Hong Kongers are sometimes branded as materialistic and devoid of culture. In the following excerpt from a written narrative, a Hong Kong student discloses the stereotype she harbors of Mainland Chinese:

> From my own experience of the Mainland, I have a bad impression that people there are less civilized than Hong Kong people. They are untrustworthy, unfair, and unjust. Bribery and corruption are all around in court, in schools, in companies, and even in streets. . . . They are less educated in the concepts of hygiene: they squat in toilets, spit around the streets, and throw rubbish all around. . . . It is not surprising there are a lot of contagious diseases. The Mainland Chinese are just inferior to us Hong Kong people. Hence, it is a torture for me to visit my relatives in the Mainland.

Individuals who have only encountered a few people from a particular group may overgeneralize what they have observed and this, too, can lead to stereotyping. For example, if you interact with a Frenchman for the first time in your life and you perceive him to be very rude, you may erroneously conclude that all French lack manners. Similarly, if you chat with an Indonesian girl who appears to be very shy and reticent, you may draw the incorrect conclusion that all Indonesians (or even Asians) are poor conversationalists.

Stereotypes are often infused with emotion, and usually portray individuals or groups in a negative light (e.g., 'Don't employ Mexicans; they're all lazy', 'Women are not as intelligent as men', 'Males are not good at learning foreign languages'). Some overgeneralizations may actually stress positive characteristics or behaviors. For example, Asians are often assumed to excel in mathematics and the learning of musical instruments (e.g., the violin, piano). In reality, not all Asians students are good in math and many have no musical talent. When a stereotype overgeneralizes the positive characteristics attributed to a particular group, individuals who do not fit the mold are disadvantaged.

Gender-related stereotyping is common in many parts of the world. The behavior, conditions, or attitudes that promote stereotypes of social roles based on gender is referred to as **sexism**. As men are most often in positions of power, this typically entails sexist behaviors that foster prejudice and discriminate against females. **Gender stereotyping** refers to simplistic overgeneralizations about the gender characteristics, differences, and roles of males and females. For example, believing that a woman is incapable of holding public office because 'females are too emotional' is a gender stereotype. Denying men the opportunity to teach in a primary school because 'males are not good with young children' is another example. Stereotypes like this are typically expressed through **sexist language**, that is, the use of words or phrases that unnecessarily emphasize gender, or ignore, belittle, or stereotype members of either sex.

Sexist language is linked to power and oppression. As males tend to hold more power, not surprisingly, sexist discourse often portrays females in a negative light. For instance, when two professors are formally introduced in a conference meeting as Dr. Martin Shore and Mrs. Nakano, the male lecturer is accorded more respect. His academic title is verbally acknowledged, whereas her status is ignored – even though she also has a Ph.D. and a higher academic rank. In this scenario the language used privileges the male professor and diminishes the professional status of Professor Nakano. The introduction also discloses her marital status, which is a personal detail that is not relevant to the meeting. Notably, similar information is not conveyed about her male colleague.

Ageism refers to the stereotyping or discrimination of a person or group of people due to their age. As Hopkins (2010: 8) observes, ageism 'works to create and sustain assumptions about aged individuals and their behaviors, attitudes, and values'. **Ageist stereotyping** involves categorizing individuals into groups according to their age and then ascribing certain characteristics and behaviors to all people of that age group (e.g., teenagers, Generation X, senior citizens, post-millennials). In many cases, these overgeneralizations can be harmful to people. For example, not all teenagers are irresponsible, immature, and selfish; in fact, many are quite the opposite. Further, not all people who are over 65 are too old and feeble to work.

Ageist language can be used to convey stereotypes of people based on their age. For example, older people are portrayed as mentally and physically challenged when labels such as old-timers, old folks, and golden agers are used. Stereotypical language and images like this can diminish people and lead to exclusion and other discriminatory practices.

Interculturalists (e.g., Samovar *et al*. 2017, Sorrells 2016) have identified a number of ways in which stereotypes can become engrained and serve as barriers to intercultural communication:

1 Stereotypes can lead us to accept a commonly held belief as true, when it actually is not.
2 Stereotypes may compel us to only accept information that is in accord with our previous perceptions of a particular outgroup. Even if we meet an individual who does not fit our preconceived ideas, we may choose to ignore this new information.
3 Stereotypes are difficult to change, in part because many were formed in childhood through messages from people we love and respect, as well as through portrayals in the media (e.g., television, movies). Therefore, we may fail to modify the stereotype even when it no longer fits with our actual observations and experience.
4 When we stereotype we assume that all members of a group possess the same characteristics and fail to recognize or acknowledge individual variations.
5 Stereotypes generally reduce people to a single trait, characteristic or dimension, overlooking the dynamic and multifaceted nature of identities.
6 When we stereotype, we send and interpret messages in ways that do not recognize the unique, individual characteristics of others; instead, we rely on oversimplified, overgeneralized perceptions which is not fair to the people we are communicating with as it reduces them to mere 'cultural representatives'.
7 Stereotyping can lead to the use of language that diminishes the worth of individuals, perpetuates overgeneralizations, and leads to inequality (e.g., sexist language, ageist discourse).
8 Stereotyping devalues individuals and groups, and can result in or perpetuate inequality (e.g., gender inequality, age inequality, religious inequality, and so on), which is very damaging to intercultural relations.

Intergroup communication is affected in negative ways by the common practice of stereotyping and Othering. Later in this chapter we explore ways to cultivate more respectful, equitable intercultural relations.

BIAS AND PREJUDICE

To become a more mindful intercultural communicator it is imperative to have an understanding of what is meant by bias and prejudice; like stereotyping, these are common phenomena that can impede intercultural relations. We all have biases as we tend to view the world in terms of what we know and are comfortable with. A **bias** is a personal preference, like or dislike, which can interfere with our ability to be objective, impartial, and without prejudice. For example, some people have a bias against blondes and do not regard them as intelligent; hence, the pejorative term 'blonde bimbo'. Others are biased toward people with body art and fail to recognize the positive, unique qualities in individuals with tattoos and piercings. Conversely, individuals may have a bias toward people who share their religious beliefs and offer preferential treatment to them.

In his text, *The Nature of Prejudice*, Gordon Allport (1954) defined **prejudice** as 'an antipathy based upon a faulty and inflexible generalization. It may be felt or expressed. It may be directed toward a group as a whole, or toward an individual because he is a member of that group' (p. 10). While originally focused on negative dimensions, more recently, prejudice is conceptualized as 'a positive or negative attitude toward and individual that is based on beliefs about the outgroup' (Awad & Rackley 2018). Basically, prejudice means 'to prejudge' (McLoud-Schingen 2015: 691).

Prejudicial thoughts are closely linked to rigid and faulty stereotypes that typically form during enculturation. Children are not born with prejudicial thoughts. Soon after birth, they are influenced by the messages or images that they receive from those who are closest to them (e.g., parents, religious figures, teachers), and the media (e.g., news reports, films). Prejudice can ensue when children learn to dislike, distrust, or even hate a person or group who is (are) different from themselves. During the socialization process, children may also develop strong ingroup preferences that reinforce ethnocentric tendencies.

Prejudice is common all over the world as it serves many economic, psychological, and social functions (Allport 1954; Awad & Rackley 2018). Individuals may experience prejudicial thoughts and emotions for a variety of reasons:

- *To 'fit in' and feel more secure.* For example, Ali was born in Australia to immigrant parents from Yemen, who have become successful merchants in Melbourne. To fit in with the majority culture, he might display disdain for Arab immigrants (e.g., make derogatory comments about newcomers) and refuse to learn Arabic or use the language in public, fearing he would be treated as an outsider (immigrant) if he did so.
- *To provide a scapegoat for troubling times (e.g., economic, social, interpersonal).* In Manchester, England, for example, Sven, a 28-year-old skinhead (an unemployed white supremacist who dropped out of secondary school) blames his unemployment status on immigrant workers; at the same time, he denigrates their work ethic, skills, and output.
- *To boost their self-image and self-esteem.* For example, a well-to-do homemaker without higher education may give orders to her amah (live-in nanny) and frequently criticize and disrespect the young woman (e.g., her second language accent, ethnicity, work ethic, appearance, etc.) to feel more powerful and in control. Her Filipino helper may, in fact, have a university degree but be forced to work abroad because of poor economic conditions in her home country.
- *To strengthen ingroup bonds and gain social distance from outgroups.* To feel closer to other believers, a devout Catholic may only socialize with other Catholics and harbor prejudice against other branches of Christianity (as well as other religions) and portray Catholic doctrine as far superior.
- *To justify a group's domination over another.* In some countries, beliefs about the lack of mental toughness and 'emotional nature' of females allows men to exclude women from certain occupations and positions (e.g., senior administrative posts, posts within the military).

Many forms of prejudice can hamper intercultural relations. For example, individuals may possess negative prejudice toward people who have a different accent, second language speakers, individuals with a different sexual orientation/preference, devotees of another faith (or individuals who are atheists, nonbelievers), minority group members, foreigners, and people who have a different skin or hair color, etc.

Ignorance and fear are often at the root of prejudice and extremist acts. For example, people who have limited intercultural experience may fear interactions that could lead them to unchartered waters. It is also easier to blame others than acknowledge limitations in oneself or ingroup peers.

Prejudice may be expressed overtly or in indirect ways (e.g., be implied) (Awad & Rackley 2018; McLoud-Schingen 2015). Individuals may have negative **attitudes** (a learned tendency to evaluate a person, behavior, or activity in a particular way) toward people who differ from them in terms of age, class, language, skin color, sex, gender, ethnicity, level of education, physical abilities, etc., but not act on these feelings. Instead of actively discriminating against outgroup members they may keep their prejudicial thoughts and biases hidden, recognizing that it is not politically correct to openly disparage others based on religion, gender, sexual orientation, etc. With the rise in populism and negative attitudes toward outsiders, however, prejudicial discourse has become more prevalent and accepted in mainstream society in some countries.

Convinced of the superiority of their ingroup, ethnocentric individuals may display overt prejudice toward people who are not ingroup members. They may express prejudice by employing ethnocentric speech to denigrate outgroup members, that is, they may talk in a way that is demeaning or disrespectful of other groups or outgroup members (e.g., use sexist/ageist language, derogatory terms). People who are prejudiced may adhere to stereotypes even when confronted with evidence that conflicts with their negative perceptions. Undoubtedly, prejudice is destructive and very harmful to intercultural relations.

DISCRIMINATION

Discrimination stems from prejudice. As Awad and Rackley (2018) explain, '[w]hereas prejudice refers primarily to attitudes, discrimination is characterized by behavior. Therefore, discrimination involves some sort of action' (p. 1715). Essentially, discrimination involves the prejudicial or unequal treatment of certain individuals based on their membership or *perceived* membership, in a particular group or category.

The United Nations International Convention on the Elimination of all forms of Racial Discrimination (ICERD) (1989) defines **racial discrimination** as

> any distinction, exclusion, restriction, or preference based on race, colour, descent, or national or ethnic origin, which has the purpose or effect of nullifying or impairing the recognition, enjoyment, or exercise, on an equal footing, of human rights and fundamental freedoms in the political, economic, social, cultural, or any other field of public life.

Discrimination can take many forms and encompass multiple issues. Individuals or groups may be discriminated against (e.g., receive fewer benefits or be denied opportunities) based on their age, language, accent, sex, gender, pregnancy, race/color of skin, religion, national origin, medical condition (e.g., AIDS, cerebral palsy, bipolarism), mental or physical ability, and so on. Individuals or groups (e.g., ethnic minorities) who are discriminated against do not enjoy the same privileges and respect as the rest of society. The term **human rights** refers to

Plate 6.1 While some immigrants thrive in their new environment, others face discrimination and harsh living conditions, and struggle to rebuild their life. © Jane Jackson

the basic rights and freedoms to which all humans are entitled, including the right to life and liberty, freedom of thought and expression, and equality before the law.

Discrimination may occur in all domains of life (e.g., in the workplace, at social functions, in public transportation, housing, education, etc.).

The following scenarios illustrate discriminatory practices:

- A second language speaker with a high proficiency in English is denied a job as a clerk because she is not a native speaker of the language. She is more than capable of doing the required tasks and is more competent than the native speaker who is offered the post.
- A security guard refuses to allow a blind woman to enter the library with her seeing-eye dog.
- A Muslim woman applies for a job as a secretary. Even though she is the best applicant she is not given a contract due to her religion.
- An HIV-positive student is not accepted by a private school as the administrators fear that he will eventually get AIDS and this will endanger others and harm the reputation of the school.
- A junior high school teacher only encourages boys to major in physics and chemistry as he believes that hard sciences are too difficult for girls.

■ After discovering that a tenant is gay, a homophobic landlord accuses him of making too much noise and evicts him even though the heterosexual tenants are much noisier.

■ Young girls wish to attend school like their brothers, but the village men refuse to allow females to be educated.

■ An Indian couple wishes to rent an apartment that was advertised in the local newspaper, but the landlord tells them that he no longer has any vacancies. This was not true and later the same day he rents the apartment to a white applicant.

■ A high school graduate with an impressive academic record is invited to a selection interview for a prestigious college; when the Chinese interviewers discover she has a Filipina mother and her parents are divorced, they choose a Chinese candidate instead, even though that person's qualifications are not as impressive.

■ A very energetic, physically fit 55-year-old man applies for a job that he is well qualified for; however, he is rejected as he is considered too old by the potential employer.

■ A university graduate who has cerebral palsy applies for a job with a company, and even though she is physically and intellectually able to perform the required tasks, the interviewer cannot see past her disability and refuses to offer her the post.

■ Only males are allowed to participate in study abroad programs even though female students are also keen to go abroad to further their education.

These examples highlight the diverse ways in which people in positions of power may discriminate against others.

Individuals may also believe that they are the victims of discrimination when it may not actually be the case. When members of a minority group are visibly different from the majority, they may understandably feel insecure and when intercultural encounters do not go well they may attribute it to discrimination. A Chinese student who was suffering from acute homesickness and having difficulty adjusting to England wrote the following in her study abroad diary:

> The British don't accept us to be in their country. Discrimination is still there, though there may be laws to protect you. . . . Now, I feel more about my Chinese identity. It will never equal to western people. We are too different. We don't understand, or refuse to understand each other fully. They are too far ahead of us. (I notice the use of 'we', 'I; versus 'they' here; there is really a distinction).

Perceptions of discrimination, whether real or imagined, need to be acknowledged and processed as they will, inevitably, affect intercultural relations and the willingness for further intercultural encounters. This aspect is discussed further at the end of this chapter.

Discriminatory language

Discrimination may manifest itself through language use. **Discriminatory language** may take many forms (e.g., derogatory labels, offensive terms, stereotypes, trivializing language). People who are different from ourselves may be labeled in a pejorative way, largely ignored, or verbally referred to in a demeaning way, which can be very hurtful to the group or individuals that are targeted. In Australia, for example, the term 'abos' is sometimes used for Indigenous Australians, 'pooftas' for gay men, 'queue jumpers' for refugees or asylum seekers, 'welfare cheats' for the unemployed, 'wogs' for European immigrants and their children, 'spazzes' for people living with cerebral palsy, and 'geriatrics' for older people (Equal Opportunity Unit

2005; Pauwels 1991). Referring to a woman as 'just a housewife' or 'just a girl' is also dismissive; expressions of this nature foster unequal treatment and disrespect.

In many cultural settings, individuals with mental illnesses are ostracized and stigmatized. The pejorative terms used to depict people with mental illness or cognitive impairment reflect the level of ignorance and lack of tolerance that are present in the community. Undeniably, language plays a powerful role in perpetuating discrimination.

Discriminatory practices

What lies behind discriminatory practices? Why do people use discriminatory language and engage in other acts that deny individuals and groups the rights and privileges that they themselves enjoy? Discrimination can be motivated by many factors. People may feel compelled to promote and protect their ingroup and also seek to feel more powerful by putting others down.

Discriminatory beliefs and practices are often driven by fear and ignorance, and the craving of power over others. In contexts where superstitions prevail, individuals with mental illness and physical abnormalities (e.g., albinism) may be considered a curse (e.g., a consequence of the sins of parents) and marginalized by mainstream society or even killed. Able-bodied individuals may not make eye contact with people who are disabled and refrain from interacting with those who have mental or physical disabilities.

Discrimination has also been linked to the potential dark side of identities (Samovar *et al.* 2010). Strong ingroup affiliations can foster ethnocentric practices, including discrimination and exclusion (e.g., hostility and even hatred of perceived members of a particular outgroup).

Combatting discrimination

Perceptions and attitudes toward difference and disabilities can and do change over time. For example, with more education, superstitions diminish and there is more awareness and recognition of the valuable contributions that disabled people can make in society (e.g., in their home environment, in the workplace). The pejorative labels used to identify people who are physically and mentally different from the majority are then considered unacceptable. To eradicate barriers to equality, people in many parts of the world are fighting discriminatory language and other practices.

In some regions, individuals and groups are pushing for equal education benefits. In 2012, Malala Yousafzai, a 15-year-old Pakistani schoolgirl, survived a murder attempt by the Taliban (Islamic fundamentalists) as she fought for the right of girls to attend school in the Swat Valley of Pakistan. She survived the attack and, in 2013, became the youngest nominee for the Nobel Peace Prize. Today, as a university student at Oxford, Malala continues to press for women's rights and education for all children. Inspired by her courage, young people and adults all over the globe are joining her crusade to combat gender discrimination.

In October 2017, Alyssa Milano's online posts against sexual harassment, violence, and discrimination spread virally. While the '#Me Too movement' did not start with the American actress, her tweet put the spotlight on this struggle for respect and equality. Tarana Burke, an African American survivor of sexual violence, actually coined the phrase #Me Too in 2006 when she created the nonprofit 'Just Be Inc.' to empower young women of color. Since then the hashtag has been used to share personal experiences of sexual harassment and violence in the United States, Canada, Australia, the United Kingdom, India, Israel, China, and Japan, and many other countries (Chicago Tribune Staff & Hawbaker 2019). These stories and the work of many courageous activists have drawn attention to the harmful effects of gender discrimination and sexual violence in all sectors of society. Attitudes are shifting and even powerful figures in the media and other industries are being brought to justice for related crimes.

Across the globe, individuals and groups are working to combat various forms of discrimination. Some strive to protect language rights (e.g., promote mother tongue teaching, advocate for bilingual policies in government, create more opportunities for lower income children to learn an international language), while others advocate for equal pay/compensation (e.g., equal pay for women and minorities). In addition to the #Me Too Movement, activists strive to create legislation to combat sexual harassment (bullying or coercion of a sexual nature), etc. Some also fight for disabled individuals to have more opportunities to actively contribute to society (e.g., in the workplace). Medical professionals (e.g., mental health experts, rehabilitation specialists, physicians) and, in some cases, caregivers may play a role in advocating for the rights of those who are affected by mental and physical disabilities. Groups may lobby against the use of degrading labels (e.g., mentally retarded) and other forms of language that undermine the dignity of individuals with mental or physical limitations.

To change attitudes and approaches to persons with disabilities, in 2006, the United Nations adopted the Convention on the Rights of Persons with Disabilities. Moving away from the perception of persons with disabilities as dependent 'objects of charity', this agreement regards them as individuals with rights, 'who are capable of claiming those rights and making decisions for their lives based on their free and informed consent as well as being active members of society'. (United Nations Disability n.d.)

The Convention reaffirms that persons with disabilities must be accorded all human rights and fundamental freedoms.

A growing number of nations are passing **anti-discrimination legislation** to protect the rights of individuals and promote equality among people regardless of their differences (e.g., sex, gender, religion, ethnicity, social class, physical ability). In the U.S., through **affirmative action** (known as **positive discrimination** in the U.K.), education, business, or employment policies have been enacted to redress the negative, historical impact of discrimination in hiring/promotion situations (e.g., the use of such factors as race, sex, religion, gender, or national origin to reduce opportunities for certain applicants/employees). In some educational and employment settings, **racial quotas** have been set, that is, there are numerical requirements for the selection and promotion of individuals from a group that is deemed disadvantaged (e.g., African American students, females). Applicants from disadvantaged groups may be admitted to college with a lower entrance standard than the norm. This policy is controversial, and opponents refer to it as **reverse discrimination**, that is, unfair treatment of the majority (or group that is generally considered to have more power and privilege).

RACISM

As explained in the previous chapter, '**race**' is a contested term that 'has no defensible biological basis' (Smith *et al*. 2006: 278). It is a social construction that has historically been used to privilege people who wish to retain positions of power (e.g., Whites in Britain, Australia, and the United States, etc.). Based on the notion that superiority is biologically determined, 'race has always been established as relationships of domination, oppression, and privilege that position people differently in society' (Parker & Mease 2009: 316). The social category of race has long been associated with colonialism and the abuse of power (e.g., the dominance of White rulers in British colonies).

Scholars and human rights advocates rally against the use of race for social categorization; however, in many parts of the world, perceived racial differences continue to be used to classify groups and explain or predict people's behavior. Census takers (e.g., those who are officially counting the population in a nation) usually ask survey respondents to declare their race from a predetermined list of categories (e.g., Black, Caucasian, Chinese, Hispanic, Japanese, mixed race, and so on). While this information may be used in a positive way (e.g., to determine areas of need for healthcare services), racial categories, which are largely arbitrary, and census data can be used by prejudiced individuals and institutions as a basis for treating people less favorably.

When power, hatred, and oppression accompany prejudicial attitudes and discrimination, racism may prevail. **Racism** refers to both 'the belief that races are populations whose physical differences are linked to significant cultural and social differences within a hierarchy' and 'the practice of subordinating races believed to be inferior' (Golash-Boza 2018). The placing of racial groups in a hierarchy in society stems from ethnocentric perspectives, ignorance, and prejudice. When people in power assume that an individual's ability to succeed in society depends on genetic characteristics instead of the quality of his or her schooling, for example, qualified applicants may be denied opportunities based on their race. More broadly, racists may treat individuals or groups unjustly become of color, physical features, or ethnicity, associating them with deficient biological, cultural, psychological, or social attributes.

Ethnocentric attitudes and feelings of superiority can lead to racist behaviors, which have dire consequences for oppressed people in all areas of life (e.g., educational, social, political, employment, religious). In extreme cases, this hatred can lead to persecution, violent acts, and even the loss of life.

Types of racism

Racism can exist on different levels, e.g., individual, institutional, systemic. **Individual racism** refers to a person's attitudes, beliefs, and actions, which can support or perpetuate racism; these racist thoughts and behaviors may be below the person's level of awareness. Individuals may enact their racist beliefs through the telling of racist jokes or by using racial slurs. They may also express their belief in the inherent superiority of their racial group in less direct ways (e.g., by only interacting with members of their racial or ethnic ingroup or by remaining silent when others use racial slurs). All the while, they may deny they are racists and become very upset when their behaviors are labeled as such. They may make routine statements of denial such as – ' "I have nothing against. . ., but", "my best friends are. . ., but", "we are tolerant, but" ' (Wodak 2008: 65). " 'I'm not a racist, but . . ." "It's just a joke." "Some of my best friends are" ' (James 2001: 1).

Racism may also be present and even pervasive in public organizations and corporations (e.g., schools, businesses, government bodies). **Institutional racism** is defined as a form of racism which can occur in social, economic, political, or educational institutions and result in differential access to the goods, services, and opportunities of society. This form of racism emerges '[w]hen a practice or policy results in discrimination against specific racial groups' (Hayles 2015: 717).

Economic, social, and political structures, and institutional systemic policies and practices may privilege a particular racial or ethnic group and place others (e.g., minorities) at a disadvantage. Racism in schools, for example, can lead to unequal treatment for second language, minority children (e.g., lack of access to linguistic, cultural, and material resources, premature streaming into vocational certificate programs instead of university-bound academic tracks

Plate 6.2 Some parts of the world have benefited greatly from globalization, whereas in other regions people still live in abject poverty and have not yet realized the dream of economic independence. For some, the effects of decades of racism and repression linger. © Jane Jackson

even if the students are very bright). In hospital settings, patients from a minority racial or ethnic group may not receive the same care and attention as members of the majority group (or whatever group is most privileged).

Systemic racism can lead to the mistreatment of people on a wide scale (e.g., minorities in a particular nation may suffer injustices in all aspects of life due to racist policies). In the United States, for example, from the 1400s to 1865, African Americans (previously labeled as 'negroes') were subjected to slavery, and some were even murdered (e.g., the victims of mob lynchings or hangings) as a direct consequence of racist beliefs and practices, which are still an issue in contemporary U.S. American society. In South Africa, from 1948 to 1994, apartheid, a system of **racial segregation** (the separation of people into racial groups in daily life), was enforced through legislation until multiracial democratic elections eventually brought it to an end. The legacy (e.g., poverty, unequal job opportunities) of this dark period, however, persists.

Racist discourse and behaviors

Racists, individuals who believe that people who have a different skin color (or ethnicity) are inferior, may convey their hatred and bigotry in their speech (both oral and written) and nonverbal behavior. Through their actions they may express, confirm, legitimize, and reinforce oppressive power relations and **racist ideologies** (beliefs) related to the dominant group.

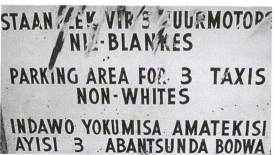

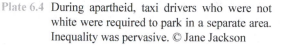

Plate 6.3 This racist sign was posted in South Africa during the apartheid era. © Jane Jackson

Plate 6.4 During apartheid, taxi drivers who were not white were required to park in a separate area. Inequality was pervasive. © Jane Jackson

Wetherell and Potter (1992: 70) define **racist discourse** as 'discourse which has the effect of categorizing, allocating and discriminating between certain groups . . . it is discourse which justifies, sustains and legitimates. . . (racist) practices'. Racist speech may be directed at individuals or groups who are racially or ethnically different or it may include derogatory comments about ethnically different others by those in positions of power. It may take the form of insults, disrespectful forms of address, slurs, taunts, and other expressions that convey the speaker's feelings of superiority.

Although there are now more regulations protecting human rights in many parts of the world (e.g., **anti-racist legislation** governing schools, the workplace), racism is still widespread and people may convey racist beliefs in a more subtle way. For example, those in positions of power may frequently interrupt ethnic minority speakers, give them little time to speak, and/or insist on discussing topics that embarrass or belittle them. Their intonation, facial expressions, and posture may also convey a lack of respect of outgroup members (e.g., people who are perceived to be members of a different 'race' or ethnic group with lower social standing).

Whether overt or covert, racism can be extremely detrimental to intercultural relations and world peace. It can threaten the fabric of social harmony and be harmful to society.

TERRORISM AND GENOCIDE

Individuals or groups who are full of hatred for outgroup members may act on racist, religious beliefs and even commit terrorist attacks, killing or maiming innocent victims. **Islamophobia** refers to the fear and hatred of, and/or the prejudice, discrimination, or racist acts against the Islamic religion or Muslims in general, especially as a political force, while **anti-Semitism** encompasses prejudice, discrimination, or racist acts against Jews. As a consequence of right-wing ideology, a fear of immigrants, and a rise in extremism (e.g., White supremacy) in some countries, we have witnessed a rise in both Islamophobia and Anti-Semitic discourse, which has turned to violence (e.g., terrorist attacks on worshipers). On 27 October 2018, Jews who were attending Shabbat morning services in a synagogue in Pittsburgh, USA, were gunned down by an anti-Semitic terrorist. On 15 March 2019, Muslim worshipers in two mosques in Christchurch, New Zealand, were the victims of a mass shooting carried out by a white supremacist who despised immigrants and Muslims. In some regions, **anti-Christian sentiments** (opposition to or objection to Christians and the practice of Christianity) are also giving rise to prejudice, discrimination, racism, and/or terrorist acts against Christians. On 2 November 2018, Islamic militants murdered Christian pilgrims in Egypt. In another senseless attack, on 21 April 2019 (Easter Sunday), Christians were the targets of terrorist attacks in Sri Lanka. Followers of other faiths have also been victims of violence. In all of the incidents previously cited, the perpetrators harbored deep-rooted fears and loathing of people who held religious beliefs and/or racial identities that differed from their own.

In extreme cases, racial hatred and bigotry can culminate in **genocide**, the intentional partial or complete destruction of a racial, ethnic, religious, or national group (Jones 2017). In the **Holocaust**, for example, millions of people who were deemed racially (or otherwise) inferior (e.g., Jews, the Roma (gypsies), the mentally or physically disabled, Slavic groups) were massacred in the 1930s and 1940s by Adolf Hitler and the German military. Mass atrocities have also taken place in Bosnia-Herzegovina (1992–1995), Cambodia (between 1.7 and 2 million Cambodians died in the Khmer Rouge's 'killing fields'), and other parts of the world.

Worldwide, strong ingroup preferences, feelings of superiority based on perceived 'racial' or biological differences, and the abuse of power can lead to racist discourse and other acts (e.g., vandalism, violent physical attacks, ridicule, name calling, arson, spray painting symbols of hate on buildings linked to minority group members), including genocide. When there is a power imbalance, individuals or groups with racist attitudes may deny the rights of those they consider 'inferior'. Often these racist thoughts and actions are driven by fear and ignorance, feelings of superiority (or inferiority) and entitlement, and a desire to control others.

XENOPHOBIA

Xenophobia is a severe aversion to or irrational fear (phobia) of 'foreigners' or 'strangers', that is, basically anyone who is different from oneself or one's ingroup, especially in terms of culture (ways of being), language, and politics. While racism is linked to prejudice based on ethnicity, ancestry or race, xenophobia is broader; it encompasses any kind of fear related to an individual or group perceived as being different. The target of this hostility may be a group that is not accepted by mainstream society (e.g., minorities, immigrants, members of other ethnic groups).

Xenophobic individuals do not recognize that their beliefs are rooted in deep insecurities (e.g., the perceived threat of losing one's own identity, culture, and positioning). Gripped with anxiety, individuals in this state may fear the loss of their imagined superiority or racial purity. They may rally against interracial marriage and immigration and support the segregation of people from different races. On a regional or national level, this may lead to discriminatory policies and anti-immigration legislation. Xenophobia is dangerous as it has the potential to spawn hostile and violent reactions (e.g., mass expulsion, brutal killings of immigrants or particular ethnic groups), such as the atrocities that have taken place in Bosnia, Nazi Germany, Darfur, and Myanmar, to name a few.

COMBATTING ETHNOCENTRICISM AND IDENTITY BIASES

In this chapter, we have explored the negative consequences of social categorization and Othering, especially in situations where individuals cling to a rigid sense of self, resist other ways of being, and do not respect the preferred identities of others. Ethnocentricism, prejudice, discrimination, racism, and xenophobia can destroy opportunities for dialogue and genuine friendship with people who have been socialized in a different environment.

In today's interconnected world, it is important for all of us to develop more awareness of the multiple dimensions of identities – our own *and* others. 'Reflecting on one's own identity and identity construction is foundational to understanding others' identities and how they are constructed' (Temples 2015: 576). As we become more attuned to our own multifaceted sense of self, it is imperative that 'a deeper awareness is gained of the complex, multifaceted identities of culturally different others' (Chung 2015: 308). This, in turn, can facilitate our intercultural communication.

'Intercultural communication involves people from dissimilar cultures, and this makes difference a normative condition. Thus, our reaction to, and ability to manage, those differences is key to successful interactions' (Samovar *et al.* 2010: 169). It is essential to develop an understanding of the ways in which our cultural perceptions and attitudes can influence our interactions with people from outside our ingroups. Understanding and appreciating cultural difference is a necessity in modern life.

To be a competent intercultural communicator it is vital to develop an awareness of how the socialization process and life experiences have influenced our identities, actions (verbal, nonverbal), and attitudes toward people who are different from ourselves. What messages about your identities and cultural membership did you receive from your parents, grandparents, religious figures, teachers, the media, etc.? What were you taught about the appropriate ways to use language and various nonverbal codes in particular situations? What did you learn in your history lessons? What experiences have you had that have affected your views about individuals who have a different linguistic and cultural background from you? How would you characterize your intercultural attitudes? These are just a few of the questions that are important to consider.

It is natural to make generalizations to cope with the complex environment in which we live but this common practice can lead to stereotyping if we are not vigilant. What stereotypes have you been exposed to throughout your life? What messages did you receive about people from other linguistic and cultural backgrounds (outgroups) that you now recognize as stereotypes? Also, critically reflect on your language usage and that of others (e.g., peers, family members, politicians, news reporters). Do you or any of your friends use terms or make jokes that might be offensive to people from other cultures? In what situations have you used the categories of your own culture to judge and interpret the behaviors of people who are culturally (and linguistically) different from you? What messages have you received about cultural difference in the media? Have you processed this information in a critical way?

With regard to intercultural relations, Lorde (1986) asserts that '[i]t is not our differences that divide us. It is our inability to recognize, accept, and celebrate those differences' (p. 197). To be mindful intercultural communicators, it is imperative to recognize the harmful effects of ethnocentricism and stereotyping, and to take steps to acknowledge, accept, and appreciate cultural difference. As the following student explains, it takes time and conscious effort to move away from a monocultural orientation and embrace a more ethnorelative mindset:

I think the most challenging aspect of communicating with someone from another cultural background is the cultural differences. People need to move away from their own culture's perspectives to see things from the partner's point of view . . . To gain new perspectives, one may have to reduce one's self-centeredness and pay more effort to build up the relationship. One needs to remove one's prejudices and stereotypes of people from other cultural backgrounds. It takes time and energy to remove the cultural barrier and build up intercultural relationships.

To enhance intercultural interactions, it is important to recognize the dimensions of our identities that are meaningful to us (e.g., ethnicity, gender, religion, nationality). Are there any aspects that you are particularly sensitive about (e.g., age, sexual orientation, gender, cultural)? How do you define yourself and how would you like others to define you? How do you communicate this to others? How do you feel when others do not recognize or appear to respect your preferred identities? Do you think you clearly indicate how you wish to be viewed or identified?

It is also essential to critically reflect on the following questions and respond in an honest way: Do you respect the identities of others? Are you attentive to messages that individuals from other linguistic or cultural backgrounds send about their preferred identities? Do you avoid the use of sexist or ageist language? If an intercultural encounter does not go well, do you automatically assume that someone from another culture is discriminating against you? Do you quickly label the individual as a racist or do you take time to reflect on other possible explanations for the miscommunication? After unsatisfactory intercultural interactions do you reevaluate your own actions and responses or do you tend to always blame the negative outcome on your communication partners?

While discrimination, prejudice, racism, and xenophobia exist everywhere in the world, it is unhelpful to attribute every negative encounter to these phenomena. In intercultural incidents, it is more constructive to begin by considering a range of possibilities (e.g., an emotional reaction to the omission of discourse markers of politeness, lack of recognition or respect for one's preferred identities). Differing linguistic/cultural norms and ignorance (e.g., lack of knowledge of cultural beliefs, values, practices) may lie at the heart of the miscommunication rather than malice or ill-will.

Identifying and making an effort to understand intercultural differences that annoy or trouble you can help to reduce negative feelings. You can also become more attuned to your own intercultural attitudes, knowledge, and actions that may be negatively affecting your communication. Identify stereotypes that have become entrenched in your mind so that you can take steps to push past them. Be mindful of the language you use (e.g., avoid the use of terms and jokes that belittle people from other linguistic and cultural backgrounds). Do you make an effort to recognize and respect the preferred self-identities of people you interact with? Are you making an effort to be more open to unfamiliar ways of being? Critical self-awareness and a positive mindset are key characteristics of successful intercultural communicators.

All of us experience emotional, visceral reactions to the world around us. It is natural. As we respond to perceptual stimuli (sights, sounds, smells, touch), we often reveal our attitudes and prejudices toward 'outgroup members'. If we are sensitive to our own emotions and behaviors when interacting with people from a different culture we are better positioned to recognize the messages that we are sending. It can also help us to be more attuned to the identities and emotional needs of our interlocutors. (Emotional intelligence is discussed further in Chapter 8).

In an intercultural situation, if you react negatively to something or someone, reflect on what may be the source of your displeasure or discomfort. For example, were you socialized to expect a larger personal distance between speakers than your communication partner? Did the person stand very close to you and invade your personal space? Were you expecting the person to speak more quietly? Were you expecting to hear 'excuse me' or 'I'm sorry' when he or she brushed up against you? Recognizing that someone from another cultural (and perhaps linguistic) background may have learned different social norms can diminish some of the negative feelings that arise. Realizing that your interlocutor is not deliberately trying to annoy you is a good start! You can then make an effort to be more accommodating and less hasty in making negative evaluations. A Hong Kong university student offers the following helpful advice:

> Opening our eyes to see cultural differences is one thing. Opening our heart to accept and respect the differences is another thing. To be open-minded and competent in intercultural contacts, we have to set aside our cultural biases, perceptions about beliefs, values and norms and our expectations on others. This process often involves a lot of internal struggles and anxieties. A way to cope with these internal struggles is to lighten up a bit and be able to laugh about ourselves. The key to deal with cross-cultural communication is to have a sense of humor.

If you are reacting strongly to some aspect of another culture, consider ethnocentric preferences that you developed during the primary socialization process. Bear in mind that people who have been socialized in another cultural context will not necessarily behave in the same way that you do. Their beliefs, values, and practices may differ. Instead of interpreting and evaluating anything new based on your own social and cultural norms and values, try to understand how a concept, product, or practice fits into the other culture. When people act differently from what you expect, try to avoid making snap judgments, e.g., labeling anything different as 'strange', 'weird', or 'wrong'. Acknowledge differences and try to understand what lies behind these differences.

> When interacting with people from a different culture, we may need to adjust our behaviors. I'm still learning to put myself into others' shoes and interpret others; behaviors from their cultural perspectives instead of mine. When I come across people of other cultures violating the rules of our culture, I step back and see the causes of problems in miscommunication before I make negative comments on others. How can we judge anyway if the standard is not the same?
>
> (University student)

Making a genuine effort to develop friendships with people from a different linguistic and cultural background can be one of the best ways to enhance one's intercultural understanding. Fiona, a student who had very negative views about people from Mainland China, was dismayed to learn that her hostel had assigned her a roommate from Beijing. The stereotypical image that was entrenched in Fiona's mind gradually faded away as she got to know the young woman as a person.

> When I knew I had to stay with a Beijing girl for the whole semester, I was quite nervous and disappointed because of my prejudice towards Mainlanders. Nonetheless, after nearly a month of getting along together, I found that there were many things valuable in her mind that we don't have. For instance, she is hard-working and just sleeps very little. She is polite and sweet to everyone. She is not so uncivilized or dirty as I had imagined. She baths every day, though not usually at night like me. Still, she keeps personal hygiene and her things are clean and packed tidily. . . . I realized how unfairly my prejudice made me look down upon our Mainland fellows.

After this positive experience, Fiona resolved to overcome her tendency to stereotype: 'I'm trying to move from a critical perspective to a sympathetic view, to understand more from the perspectives of Mainlanders and to appreciate their valuable, genuine and sincere characters rather than to criticize their place'. She also recognized that this would not be easy as prejudicial thoughts about the 'Motherland' had been built up in her mind since childhood.

Recognizing one's prejudicial thoughts (that exist in all of us) is a very important first step. A shift in attitude, a willingness to learn about other ways of being, and a strong desire to develop meaningful, equitable intercultural ties can also propel individuals to higher levels of intercultural competence. While it is difficult to avoid social categorization and stereotyping, these are steps that all of us can take to ensure more mutually beneficial and respectful intercultural relations. With more self-awareness and self-monitoring, you can avoid an 'us' vs. 'them' mentality and become a more mindful intercultural communicator.

SUMMARY

While ingroup affiliations provide us with a sense of belonging, our identities, attitudes, and mindset can also serve as significant barriers to intercultural communication. Ethnocentrism, the belief that one's own culture is superior to all others, leads us to categorize and judge the world around us using our own cultural frame (e.g., beliefs; values; social, cultural, and linguistic norms or rules of behavior) as a guide or yardstick. Ethnocentrism can result in even more serious reactions to cultural difference, such as stereotyping, discrimination, and prejudice, which lie at the heart of racism, whether overt or covert. In extreme cases, it can also lead to terrorist acts and xenophobia, an intense, irrational dislike or fear of people who are different from us (e.g., foreigners, immigrants). When the lessons or history are misunderstood, forgotten, or ignored, there is fertile ground for further injustice and atrocities (e.g., mass killings of ethnic groups).

This chapter discussed the potentially harmful consequences of ignoring our ethnocentric tendencies. Even if we are well intentioned, our verbal and nonverbal behaviors can convey a lack of respect of people who differ from us in some way (e.g., age, gender, language, ethnicity, skin color, religion, sexual orientation). This can then impede the development of positive intercultural relations and we will miss out on many of the opportunities that our diverse world offers us. This chapter suggests a different path. 'Change your thoughts and you change your world' (Peale 2007: 233). All of us can take steps toward a more ethnorelative mindset and reap the rewards of constructive, mutually satisfying, intercultural interactions.

discussion questions

1 How might your perceptions of your cultural identity influence your communication with people who have a different linguistic and cultural background? Discuss your ideas with a partner.
2 What factors influence attitudes toward people who speak a different language or have a different accent?

3   In some parts of the world, xenophobia and violence are sometimes linked to football (soccer) or other sports. Why do you think this is the case? Do you think sports officials have a responsibility to address this? If yes, what steps should be taken? Share your ideas with a partner.

4   Why are immigrants and minority groups often the targets of prejudice and discrimination? How can this be combatted?

5   How can one's accent serve as an identity marker? Provide examples of situations in which it may serve as a barrier. Discuss your ideas with a partner.

6   In this chapter we examined numerous ways to combat ethnocentric tendencies and biases. What other suggestions do you have to foster a more ethnorelative perspective in intercultural interactions?

7   Why is it essential to engage in critical thinking when listening to the messages conveyed by authority figures (e.g., politicians) about minorities?

activities

1   Define ethnocentricism and explain how it can lead to stereotyping and prejudice.

2   Identify a linguistic and cultural group in your community (or host country) that you do not belong to. What are your attitudes toward individuals who are linked to this group? How have these attitudes been formed? Do you think your views might change in the future? If yes, how and why?

3   In a small group, discuss your reaction to the following comment by Gordon Allport (1954) in his book *The Nature of Prejudice*: 'Most of the business of life can go on with less effort if we stick together with our own kind. Foreigners are a strain'. Do you agree or disagree with this statement?

4   Reflect on the roots or causes of prejudice. Cite examples from your personal experience and identify ways to push past prejudicial thoughts and behavior.

5   Identify three types of racism and provide an example of each. With a partner, identify concrete steps that can be taken to combat racism and xenophobia.

6   Discuss the causes and consequences of discrimination with two people who have a different ethnic background from you. Have they ever been discriminated against? If yes, how did they react? What suggestions do they have to combat discrimination? Do any of your own experiences or views resonate with theirs?

further reading

Brown, R. (2010) *Prejudice: Its Social Psychology*, 2nd edn, West Sussex: Wiley-Blackwell.

From a social psychological perspective, the author analyzes the prejudices and stereo-types of individuals as part of a pattern of intergroup processes. Numerous examples of prejudice in everyday life are examined.

Jones, J.M., Dovidio, J.F. and Vietze, D.L. (2014) *The Psychology of Diversity: Beyond Prejudice and Racism*, Oxford: Blackwell.

This volume presents a social psychological examination of diversity, offering insight into the historical, political, economic, and societal factors that shape the way people think about and respond to cultural difference.

Kivel, P. (2017) *Uprooting Racism: How White People Can Work for Racial Justice*, 4th edn, Gabriola Island, BC: New Society Publishers.

This volume explores the historical roots of racism and puts forward suggestions to move toward equality and justice for all.

Lippi-Green, R. (2012) *English with an Accent: Language, Ideology, and Discrimination in the United States*, London: Routledge.

The author discusses the ways in which discrimination based on accent functions to both support and perpetuate social structures and unequal power relations.

Companion Website: Continue your journey online

Visit the Companion Website for a variety of tools and resources to support and extend your intercultural learning. (Instructors who are qualified adopters of the text may access additional resources on this site.)

CHAPTER 7

Intercultural transitions

From language and culture confusion to adaptation

> Exposure to a foreign culture presses sojourners to adjust on many different levels to the strange, exciting, exasperating, and sometimes threatening encounters embedded in everyday living.
>
> (Savicki *et al.* 2008: 173)

> Undertaken with awareness, travel surely is one of the most available and most effective means to nourish, broaden, and quicken the soul. The destination does not matter as much as the attention we give to the understanding that all travel is inner travel.
>
> (Dispenza 2002: 5)

> Perhaps travel cannot prevent bigotry, but by demonstrating that all peoples cry, laugh, eat, worry, and die, it can introduce the idea that if we try and understand each other, we may even become friends.
>
> (Maya Angelou 1928–2014, quoted in Fieber 2013)

learning objectives

By the end of this chapter, you should be able to:

1 Identify and describe types of migrants
2 Explain the process of acculturation and second language socialization
3 Describe four patterns of acculturation in immigrants
4 Identify factors that can facilitate or hinder acculturation and second language socialization
5 Define transition shock (confusion) and identify five types
6 Describe the causes, symptoms, and potential benefits of transition shock (confusion)
7 Describe the stages in the curve adjustment models
8 Describe the causes and symptoms of reverse (reentry) culture shock or confusion.
9 Identify weaknesses in the curve models of adjustment
10 Describe the core elements in the integrative communication theory of cross-cultural adaptation
11 Discuss the role of language in cross-cultural adjustment and adaptation
12 Identify and discuss strategies to enhance intercultural transitions (e.g., cope with language and culture confusion)

INTRODUCTION

Each year, millions of people cross borders to study, work, perform military duties, represent their government, conduct business, do volunteer work, take part in peace missions, or engage in tourism. Some willingly choose to make another territory or country their new home; others are forced to seek temporary or permanent refuge in a foreign land. When people leave all that is familiar and enter a region that is new to them, they naturally come into contact with people who have a different linguistic and cultural background. During the process of **adaptation**, newcomers are apt to encounter unfamiliar languages or dialects, values, norms, beliefs, and behaviors (e.g., verbal, nonverbal). Increased contact with cultural difference can be both exhilarating and confounding. A myriad of individual and environmental factors can influence the transition to a new environment.

This chapter begins by describing and contrasting several types of migrant groups. The next section focuses on the long-term acculturation and adaptation of immigrants and other settlers before our attention shifts to the short-term adjustment and adaptation of sojourners. After describing several types of transition shock, discussion centers on language and culture confusion (causes, symptoms, degree of difficulty, and potential benefits). Several of the most well-known models of sojourner adjustment (e.g., the U- and W-curve adjustment models) are then reviewed and critiqued. Next, Kim's (2018) integrative communication theory of cross-cultural adaptation, which is relevant for both long-term and short-term migrants, is explained. The chapter concludes with practical, research-inspired suggestions to optimize intercultural transitions.

TYPES OF MIGRANTS

All over the world, more and more people are on the move, leaving behind the familiarity and security of their home environment for new, unchartered terrain (e.g., tourists, education abroad students, business people, expatriate workers and their families, military personnel, diplomats, third culture individuals (TCIs), immigrants, asylum seekers, refugees, indigenous peoples). Before we examine the process and potential consequences of cross-cultural transitions (e.g., psychological, cultural, linguistic, physiological, social), it is helpful to be familiar with the following basic dimensions that can differentiate migrants: 'voluntary-involuntary' and 'permanent-temporary'.

Voluntary-involuntary

Nowadays, people venture abroad with diverse motives (e.g., for adventure, pleasure, work, economic necessity/benefits, family unification, a better quality of life, a safer environment, etc.). Some individuals or groups decide to travel or move abroad of their own free will, whereas others are compelled to do so, often because of circumstances that are well beyond their control. Whether the move is voluntary or involuntary can profoundly impact the nature and quality of the transition to the new environment.

Voluntary transitions

Voluntary migrants are those who willingly chose to travel abroad. 'In voluntary cases, one make's contact with another (others), driven by one's interest in a cultural Other (e.g., travel) or the needs of social life and survival (e.g., trade)' (Kramsch & Uryu 2012: 212). Typically, this category includes tourists, travelers or other temporary visitors, education abroad students, businesspeople, expatriates, missionaries, and immigrants. Among these groups, tourists are the most numerous.

The United Nations World Tourism Organization (UNWTO) (2018) defines **tourism** as 'a social, cultural and economic phenomenon which entails the movement of people to countries or places outside their usual environment for personal or business/professional purposes'. In 2017, there were 1,322 million international tourist arrivals worldwide, a growth of 7% compared to the previous year (United Nations World Tourism Organization [UNWTO] 2018).

The number of secondary and tertiary students who choose to undertake all or part of their studies in another country is also on the rise. **International education** broadly refers to 'the knowledge and skills resulting from conducting a portion of one's education in another country' or, more generally, 'international activity that occurs at any level of education (K-12, undergraduate, graduate, or postgraduate)' (Forum on Education Abroad n.d.). International students may take all or part of their tertiary education in a country other than their own. For example, they may complete full degrees at the host institution or choose to study for a summer, a semester, or an academic year. Some students voluntarily travel abroad with the aim of improving their second language skills and (inter)cultural understanding, whereas others seek to enhance their subject matter knowledge and bolster job prospects. Others may also be motivated to gain international educational experience for different reasons (e.g., to decide if they would like to do postgraduate studies abroad or perhaps live and work in another country after graduation).

International education can take many forms. **Education abroad** denotes 'education that occurs outside the participant's home country. Besides study abroad, examples include such

Plate 7.1   In many parts of the world, tourism is a major industry, bringing people from diverse linguistic and cultural backgrounds into contact with one another. © Jane Jackson

Plate 7.2 Tourists typically stay a short time in the host environment and have varying degrees of contact with host nationals. © Jane Jackson

international experiences as work, volunteering, noncredit internships, and directed travel, as long as these programs are driven to a significant degree by learning' (Forum on Education Abroad, n.d.). In the U.S., **study abroad** is considered 'a subtype of Education Abroad that results in progress toward an academic degree at a student's home institution. . . . (In many other countries the term study abroad refers to, or at least includes, such study)' (Forum on Education Abroad n.d.). In Europe this may be referred to as 'credit mobility'.

Education abroad typically includes such activities as classroom study, research, internships, and **service learning** (community-engaged learning). A service learning program is 'a form of experiential education in which students engage in activities that address human and community needs together with structured opportunities for reflection designed to achieve desired learning outcomes' (Jacoby 2015: 1–2). For example, a group of Canadian university students may participate in a semester-long service learning project in Guatemala, in which they work with the homeless, tutor EFL students, volunteer in an orphanage, or assist human rights workers under the supervision of a faculty member.

Individuals may also choose to work abroad temporarily. Others migrate to another country to seek a better life (e.g., earn more money, procure more educational, professional, and social opportunities for themselves and their families, join family members who have immigrated earlier). Immigrants are a very diverse group (e.g., differing aspirations and expectations for their new life, disparate levels of education and linguistic competence). The majority voluntarily move to a country where host nationals speak a different language and have customs, worldviews, and habits that differ from what they are accustomed to in their country of origin.

Involuntary transitions

Not all migration is voluntary. For a variety of reasons, individuals or groups may become **involuntary migrants,** that is, they may be compelled to move to a different region or country.

> in involuntary cases, intercultural contacts are often driven by rather negative elements such as power struggles between different ethnic or cultural groups (e.g., war) or a powerful group's political, economic, ideological, and cultural imposition and domination of the less powerful Other (e.g., colonization).
>
> (Kramsch & Uryu 2012: 212)

As noted in Chapter 1, migration is sometimes forced on individuals or groups. In 2017, according to the United Nations High Commissioner for Refugees (UNHCR) there were 68.6 million forcibly displaced people worldwide, representing the 'highest levels of displacement on record'. Among this figure, there were 40 million internally displaced people, 25.4 million refugees, and 3.1 million asylum seekers, with over half of the refugees under the age of 18. Additionally, the UNHCR estimates that 10 million stateless people have been denied a nationality and have no access to basic rights including education, employment, healthcare, and freedom of movement (UNHCR 2018). Humanitarian crises and unstable political and socioeconomic situations are bringing about a significant rise in the number of displaced people across the globe.

Refugees and asylum seekers involuntarily, and often quite suddenly, find themselves in an alien environment in order to escape wars, abuse, political/sexual/religious/ethnic persecution, famine, earthquakes and other natural disasters, or oppression in their homeland. Whereas the term **refugee** refers to a person who has been granted protection in a country outside his or her homeland, an **asylum seeker** is seeking protection as a refugee and is waiting for his or her claim to be assessed by a country that has signed the Geneva Convention on Refugees (UNESCO). If successful, permission may be granted to settle in the new country. Those who are denied the right of abode, even after multiple appeals, are usually repatriated or sent to another country. The review process can be very protracted and the outcome uncertain.

Not surprisingly, unlike voluntary migrants, refugees may have more conflicted emotions about being in a foreign land and face more stress and uncertainty about what lies ahead. As noted by Berry *et al.* (2011: 311):

> most involuntary migrants live with the knowledge that "push factors" (rather than "pull factors") led them to flee their homeland and settle in their new society; and, of course, most have experienced traumatic events, and most have lost their material possessions.

Instead of carefully planning their new life abroad, some have fled their home country in great haste without a clear vision of their future. They may have entered a refugee camp without knowing if, when, or where they will be relocated. Reluctant to leave their homeland, some refugees spend much of the remainder of their life in their new country dreaming of a return home, which may never be possible. While some migrants voluntarily cross borders and come into contact with people from the host culture, this is not the case for refugees. All of these elements play a role in the transition to a new way of life (e.g., the quality of one's adjustment).

Temporary-permanent

In addition to the nature and purpose of the visit, migrants may be distinguished by the length of their stay in the new environment. Tourists and travelers typically visit for only a few days or weeks and have little interaction with host nationals, whereas international students and expatriates may stay for a longer period of time (e.g., several months or years) before returning to their home country, going on to another destination, or deciding to apply for permanent residency in the host country (if possible). Immigrants or refugees may remain in the receiving country for the rest of their life.

Temporary

A **sojourn** refers to 'a period of time spent living in a cultural setting different from one's own' (Forum on Education Abroad 2011: 15). **Sojourners** are individuals who are in the new environment temporarily for a specific purpose (e.g., study, work, business) and often for a particular length of time (e.g., several days, months, or years). When they arrive in the new environment, they already plan to return to their home country or go on to another destination at some point. The term 'sojourner' includes many subcategories, such as tourists, international students, 'third culture individuals' (TCIs) or global nomads, business executives and other expatriate workers, international civil servants or diplomats, aid workers, missionaries, military personnel, and guest workers.

Tourists are the most numerous group of sojourners. They usually stay abroad for only a short time (e.g., a few days to several weeks or months) to sight-see, enjoy themselves, and get a taste of a different linguistic and cultural environment. Several subgroups of tourists have focused goals, such as eco-tourists who travel to explore nature and backpackers who travel for an extended period and seek out interactions with locals. Thus, while tourists are temporary visitors, they may differ in terms of their motivation, expectations, activities, and degree of contact with host nationals.

Expatriates are individuals who are engaged in employment abroad (e.g., EFL teachers from Australia in Malaysia, American bankers who work for a multinational firm in Tokyo, British surveyors employed in Libya). Expatriate workers may or may not be accompanied by family members and the amount of contact they have with host nationals varies considerably. Some expatriates reside and work in a compound that is segregated from the local population (e.g., American engineers in Saudi Arabia), whereas others live, work, and spend most of their free time with host nationals.

As explained in Chapter 1, with the advent of globalization, more and more institutions of higher education (and secondary schools) have officially or informally adopted an

Plate 7.3 In Bali, tourists are invited to join locals in Hindu temples (Pura in Balinese), where they may mediate and bathe with devotees who believe that these acts can bring about good fortune and health. © Jane Jackson

internationalization policy which has created more opportunities for young people (and teachers) to travel abroad (Proctor & Rumbley 2018). Some students join 'year abroad' or semester-long exchange programs; an even greater number take part in short-term sojourns, ranging from four to seven weeks, or micro-stays lasting three weeks or less. Students may also decide to do their full undergraduate or graduate degrees at institutions outside their home country. The majority of international students study in a second language, either by taking language enhancement courses or by attending subject matter courses that are offered in that language. As the de facto language of internationalization is English, many non-English speaking countries now offer full-degree programs in this language (Ota & Horicuhi 2018).

Permanent

Whereas sojourners are only temporarily in the host environment, immigrants and refugees may settle in a country that is not their place of birth. Immigration is not a new phenomenon but the number of people who are leaving their home country to permanently reside in another has never been greater. Whether due to 'push' or 'pull' factors, these migrants end up calling another nation their home. Some become permanent residents and eventually gain citizenship in their adopted country. While some immigrants are able to hold dual or multiple citizenships, in some countries they are required to renounce their original citizenship if they adopt a new one.

Plate 7.4 The majority of students who study abroad do so in a second language, with English the most common language of internationalization. © Jane Jackson

The multidimensional nature of migration

To understand the process and impact of intercultural transitions, we must consider the motivation for migration (e.g., forced or voluntary), the duration of the stay (e.g., short-term or long-term), the nature of the move (e.g., tourism, study, work) and the frequency of crossings (e.g., habitual crossings, degree of exposure to other languages and cultures, first-timers). Differences in status, power, size of the group, rights, and resources (e.g., economic, political, social) influence how newcomers perceive and interact in the new environment. Individual characteristics or attributes such as attitudes, motives, values, personality, and abilities (e.g., proficiency in the host language) also play a role in determining how newcomers respond to their new environment and host nationals.

Individuals (e.g., education abroad students, expatriates) may also change their status from temporary sojourners to permanent residents or immigrants. For example, international exchange students may remain abroad to work after their studies are finished. This life-changing decision is apt to affect their perceptions of their adopted land (and country of origin), as well as their intercultural relationships and self-identities.

TRANSITIONING TO A NEW CULTURE: LONG-TERM AND SHORT-TERM ADAPTATION

Exposure to an unfamiliar linguistic and cultural environment can have a profound, long-lasting impact on both temporary and permanent migrants. In the last few decades, educators and researchers from a variety of fields have devoted considerable attention to the linguistic, socio-cultural, psychological, and physical challenges that newcomers face in a foreign land. Early theories and explorations tended to focus on long-term settlers (e.g., immigrants and refugees); however, with an increase in temporary stays in another culture there is now considerable interest in the intercultural contact and transitions of sojourners.

Long-term adaptation: Immigrants and other settlers

For many decades, social psychologists, communication specialists, applied linguists, and other scholars have studied the adaptation of immigrants and refugees who settle in a new cultural environment more or less permanently, either voluntarily or due to circumstances beyond their control. Their work has drawn attention to variations in attitudes toward linguistic and cultural difference, the quality and degree of contact with people in the host environment, language and culture learning strategies, differences in the desire or ability of settlers to 'fit into' the new environment, and variations in the attitudes of host nationals toward newcomers.

Acculturation and second language socialization

In Chapter 2, you learned about **enculturation**, the process by which individuals acquire the knowledge, skills (e.g., language, communication), attitudes, and values necessary to become functioning members in their primary culture. **Acculturation** refers to the process of adaptation or change that can occur when individuals are exposed to another culture or co-culture, such as when moving to an unfamiliar country. Kim (2015) defines it as 'the process of change in individuals whose primary learning has taken place in one culture and who learn, acquire, and internalize traits from another culture' (p. 792). As noted by Berry *et al.* (2011), intercultural contact may bring about psychological and behavioral changes in both newcomers and host nationals.

Closely tied to acculturation, **second language socialization** refers to the process by which novices in an unfamiliar linguistic and cultural context gain intercultural communicative competence by acquiring linguistic conventions, sociopragmatic norms, cultural scripts, and other behaviors that are associated with the new culture (Jackson 2018a; Kinginger 2017). This transformation entails knowledge gains in social, cultural, and linguistic domains and is closely tied to the notion of identity reconstruction or expansion that was described in Chapter 5. For example, in a new environment one can acquire a deeper understanding of one's strengths and weaknesses, as alluded to by James Baldwin, an American author and civil rights activist who traveled abroad: 'I met a lot of people in Europe. I even encountered myself'. Enhanced self-awareness has the potential to bring about personal transformation, an aspect that is explored further in this chapter when we examine Kim's (2001, 2018) integrative communication theory of cross-cultural adaptation.

Acculturation patterns

Researchers have discovered that the ways in which individuals and groups respond to intercultural contact and the process of acculturation can differ significantly. This is partly attributed to variations in the desire to develop a sense of belonging in the new culture (acquire a local identity, master the host language, make friends with host nationals) as well as differences in the

Plate 7.5 This street painting depicts the daily life of early Chinese immigrants in North America.
© Jane Jackson

degree of longing to maintain one's own culture and language (e.g., cultural identity, mother tongue, traditions, values, practices).

Cultural maintenance refers to the effort to sustain elements of one's culture or heritage by preserving core values, traditions, ways of being, etc., especially when faced with pressure to adopt a more dominant culture (e.g., the majority culture) (Berry 2006). **Language maintenance** refers to 'the preservation of a language or language variety in a context where there is considerable pressure for speakers to shift towards the more prestigious or politically dominant language' (Swann *et al.* 2004: 172). An example would be the maintenance of Arabic as the home language by Egyptian immigrants in an English-speaking country. The ways that individuals and ethnocultural groups or communities respond to the process of acculturation are referred to as **acculturation strategies**.

John Berry (1974, 1997, 2003, 2015), a cross-cultural psychologist, developed an acculturation theory to illustrate the cultural and psychological dimensions of acculturation and variations in the retention or reshaping of cultural identities. In his framework, he identifies four different strategies or modes of acculturation that long-term settlers may adopt in the new environment: assimilation, integration, separation, and marginalization.

Assimilation occurs when individuals do not retain their original cultural identity and link to their heritage/culture; instead, they seek close interaction with the host culture and adopt the cultural values, norms, and traditions of the new society. People who assimilate into the new culture may focus on mastering the host language and rarely use their first language, spurred by the desire to quickly 'fit in' and get ahead. When they have children they may use their second language at home and their children may grow up knowing very little about their heritage and the first language of their parents and grandparents.

Integration occurs when people take steps to maintain their cultural heritage and original cultural identity while developing harmonious relationships with people in the receiving country. People who adopt this strategy aim to integrate into the new society. In countries that have a large multilingual and multicultural population, immigrants may continue to use their first language at home and among members of their ethnic community but also master the primary language of their new country and engage in intercultural interactions both in and outside of work. As they integrate into the new environment, they take on some characteristics and behaviors associated with the host culture but retain elements of their original culture that they value.

Separation (segregation) refers to the acculturation strategy in which individuals strive to maintain their cultural heritage and avoid participation in the larger society of their new country. They do not wish to be closely linked to the host culture (e.g., be associated with values and

Plate 7.6   The lives of early Chinese immigrants in Western Canada are captured in this street painting in Chinatown in Victoria, British Columbia. © Jane Jackson

traditions they do not accept) and may resist or, at least, not invest in learning the dominant language of the community. Much of their time is spent interacting in their first language with people from their ethnic group and they live on the periphery of the mainstream culture in their new country.

Marginalization refers to the acculturation strategy in which people do not nurture their cultural heritage (and first language) and resist interacting with people in the larger society in their new country. Marginalized and isolated individuals reject both the new and old culture. They display little or no interest in maintaining the identity of their own cultural group and make no effort to develop a cultural identity linked to the dominant culture. This form of acculturation tends to be characterized by isolation and confusion.

Within the context of acculturation, Berry *et al.* (2011), define **adaptation** as the process of coping with the experiences and strains of acculturation. Many cross-cultural psychologists distinguish between **psychological adaptation** (feelings of personal well-being and self-esteem) and **sociocultural adaptation** (competence in dealing with life in the larger society) (Ward *et al.* 2001). As individuals gain exposure to unfamiliar ways of being, they may experience varying degrees of **acculturative stress**, which Berry *et al.* (2011: 465) define as 'a negative psychological reaction to the experiences of acculturation, often characterized by anxiety, depression, and a variety of psychosomatic problems'.

Short-term adaptation: Sojourners

Most investigations of short-term sojourners (e.g., international exchange students, expatriates) have focused on adjustment challenges and the ability of the newcomers to quickly adjust to the host environment. Much of the literature on this population has put forward practical ways to facilitate adjustment and optimize temporary stays abroad (e.g., learn the host language, communicate in culturally appropriate ways with host nationals, cope with culture difference). The next section focuses on the challenges that short-term sojourners may face before, during, and after their stay abroad.

TYPES OF TRANSITION SHOCK (CONFUSION)

Transition shock is a broad construct which refers to the state of loss, disorientation, and identity confusion that can occur when we enter a new situation, job, relationship, or physical location and find ourselves confronted with the strain of adjusting to the unfamiliar (e.g., novel perspectives, different roles) (Bennett 1998). Moving from secondary school to university or from one's family home to a dormitory are examples. Starting a new job or becoming single after a long-term romance has ended are other life transitions that people may experience. Events like these can have an emotional, psychological, behavioral, cognitive, and physiological impact. Several subcategories of transition challenges are especially relevant to our discussion of migration: culture shock or confusion, role confusion, language confusion, and identity confusion.

Culture shock (confusion)

'Exposure to a foreign culture presses sojourners to adjust on many different levels to the strange, exciting, exasperating, and sometimes threatening encounters embedded in everyday living' (Savicki *et al.* 2008: 173). When sojourners cross borders, they travel with the language, values, beliefs, and habits that they developed in their home culture through the process of enculturation that was described in Chapter 2. In an unfamiliar linguistic, physical, and social environment, it is quite common to experience stress and confusion when confronted with new ideas and behaviors. This experience can be very unsettling for sojourners (and long-term settlers) and how they respond can have a profound impact on the quality and lasting impact of their stay abroad.

In 1950, anthropologist Cora DuBois used the term **culture shock** to refer to the disorientation that many anthropologists often experience when entering a new culture to do field work (LaBrack & Berardo 2007). A few years later, another anthropologist, Kalvero Oberg (1960), extended the term to encompass the transition of any individuals who travel outside their home environment and face challenges adjusting to a new culture. Since then many definitions have been put forward. For Peter Adler (1975: 13), culture shock is 'a set of emotional reactions to the loss of perceptual reinforcements from one's own culture, to new cultural stimuli which have little or no meaning, and to the misunderstanding of new and diverse experiences'. It is perceived as 'a natural reaction to the clash and collision of cultural order' (Neuliep 2018c) which can happen to anyone who travels to another linguistic and cultural environment (e.g., immigrants, study abroad students, tourists).

As societies have become increasingly diverse and the world more interconnected digitally, individuals in their home environment have more exposure to cultural difference. For this reason, some scholars maintain that the term culture shock is too negative or extreme, ignoring the learning potential of this experience. Coleen Ward, a cross-cultural psychologist who has extensively researched and written about intercultural transitions, explains her reservation about the use of this term:

> the term culture shock is very limiting in terms of advancing our understanding of the process and outcomes of cross-cultural transition. 'Shock' overemphasizes the negative and threatening aspects of novel situations and the pathological reactions to the unfamiliar. It also ignores the positive growth experiences that can result from intercultural contact and change.
>
> (Ward 2015: 209)

Hottola (2004) prefers to use the term **'culture confusion'** to refer to the adjustment challenges that may arise when tourists are exposed to cultural difference. Neuliep (2018c) also maintains that 'culture confusion more accurately describes the process of cultural orientation among sojourners' (pp. 624–5).

Role shock (confusion)

Role shock or confusion is characterized by lack of knowledge and confusion about the norms of behavior in a new culture (e.g., the social 'rules' of politeness, business etiquette) (Byrnes 1966). When you enter a new, unfamiliar situation you are apt to be exposed to roles and responsibilities that diverge from what you are used to in your home environment. For example, you may encounter different expectations for the behavior of males and females in particular contexts. In an unfamiliar country, students may be surprised to discover that the roles of teachers and learners differ from what they have become accustomed to. In a new job in an unfamiliar country, it can be disorienting and stressful to discover that the relationship between employer and employee is much more formal (or less formal) than expected, and the duties that you are assigned differ from what is customary in your home country.

Language shock (confusion)

Migration frequently involves exposure to a language that is not one's mother tongue. **Language shock or confusion** refers to the challenge of understanding and communicating in a second language in an unfamiliar environment (Smalley 1963). Hile (1979) describes it as 'the frustration and mental anguish that results in being reduced to the level of a two-year-old in one's ability to communicate'. Not having enough language skills to perform simple daily tasks can be very frustrating and humbling. Even if you speak the same first language as host nationals, differences in accent, cultural scripts, norms of politeness, dialects, humor, vocabulary, slang, and communication styles can impede communication. In the host environment, nonverbal behaviors (e.g., body language, paralanguage) can be confounding for newcomers. Language and culture confusion can lead to temporary disorientation and discomfort in unfamiliar surroundings.

Identity shock (confusion)

Crossing borders can also raise awareness of one's sense of self and even challenge self-identities that have long been taken for granted. **Identity** or **self-shock** refers to 'the intrusion of inconsistent, conflicting self-images', which can involve 'loss of communication competence', 'distorted self-reflections in the responses of others', and 'the challenge of changing identity-bound behaviors' (Zaharna 1989: 501). As newcomers try to make sense of their new environment and communicate who they are, they are sometimes dismayed to discover that they are not perceived as they would like. Zaharna (1989: 518) explains:

> For the sojourner, self-shock is the intrusion of inconsistent, conflicting self-images. At a time when we are searching for meaning "out there," our own internal axis for creating meaning is thrown off balance. Our frustration becomes not so much trying to make sense of the Other (i.e. culture shock) but rather the Self (i.e. self-shock).

Communicating one's preferred identities through a second language can be frustrating and easily misunderstood. When exposed to new ways of being in daily life, newcomers may feel uncertain about who they are and how they fit into the world around them.

Identity shock (confusion) may arise when we realize that our usual ways of conveying our sense of self are misunderstood by others and we may lack the knowledge and skills to change the situation. In an alien environment, it can be very upsetting to realize that our preferred self-labels are not understood or accepted. For example, Korean or Japanese students may be identified as Chinese when abroad and vice versa. Second language speakers who are very fluent in the host language may be dismayed when constantly reminded that they are foreigners because of their accent or vocabulary choice.

LANGUAGE AND CULTURE SHOCK (CONFUSION)

Sources

Moving from one linguistic and cultural environment to another can cause stress, anxiety, and confusion. What are the main sources of language and culture confusion? Furnham (2015), Furnham and Bochner (1986), Neuliep (2018c), Oberg (1960), Ward *et al.* (2001), and many other scholars have offered a range of explanations:

Unrealistic, romantic expectations

If you have decided to move to a new environment expecting it to be perfect (e.g., an idyllic, stress-free oasis), it can be quite unsettling to discover that it is not as you had pictured in your dreams. Similar to home, there are bound to be elements in the new environment that are not pleasing to you. Idealistic, romantic notions of host nationals that have been formed by reading novels or watching movies are unlikely to match reality. For example, Elsa, a student sojourner made the following comments in her diary as she traveled from Asia to England:

> During the flight, the images, or, I should say, my imagination about what England is like and how British people look like, kept lingering in my mind. In my opinion, Britain is quite a traditional, old-fashioned country. People there are all with perfect propriety. Gentlemen and ladies in nice suits and gowns are the most outstanding images that first come to my mind whenever I think of England.

A few weeks later she was much less enthusiastic when she wrote:

> I used to think that all English were polite and gentle. Some are gentlemen but a lot are not. . . . From reading books, I thought that all the British people are very cultured, going to the theatre and reading literature but I was too naïve. That makes me a little bit disappointed as I expected that the whole country was very cultured.

Ward *et al.* (2001) observe that sojourners who hold unrealistic expectations about the host country may become disillusioned and some withdraw when confronted with reality.

Inadequate preparation

If you experience language and culture confusion soon after your arrival in a new country, it may come as a surprise if you have given little thought to what life will be like in the host culture. You may not have considered language and culture learning strategies that could help you adjust and make connections with host nationals. Without adequate preparation and limited understanding of culture shock or confusion, you may be ill-equipped psychologically to deal with the natural ups and downs of adjustment.

Abrupt change

Nowadays, with advances in transportation we can easily travel from our home environment to distant lands in a matter of hours. In our journey we may cross several time zones and arrive in a place with a very different climate as well as many unfamiliar practices (e.g., cultural, dietary, linguistic, religious, political, social, etc.). This can be a shock to one's system, as noted by Wood and Landry (2010: 48):

> Change feels too fast. Contact with difference, the unfamiliar, the strange and the 'Other' . . . can be and usually is unsettling in spite of the occasional speck of delight and surprise. The abrupt loss of the familiar and moving from one environment where one has

learnt to function easily and successfully to one where one cannot is dramatic for both [short-term and long-term sojourners].

Lack of familiarity with signs and symbols

In our home environment we are surrounded by physical and social signs that help us to make sense of our world and enable us to function in everyday life. When we enter an unfamiliar milieu we are suddenly exposed to verbal and nonverbal cues and social behaviors (e.g., words, communication styles, gestures, customs, cultural scripts) that are foreign to us. Our inability to comprehend these signs and symbols can induce acculturative stress, especially in individuals with limited intercultural experience. Oberg (1960: 177) explains:

> Culture shock is precipitated by the anxiety that results from losing all our familiar signs and symbols of social intercourse. These signs or cues include the thousand and one ways in which we orient ourselves to the situations of daily life: when to shake hands and what to say when we meet people, when and how to give tips, how to give orders to servants, how to make purchases, when to accept and when to refuse invitations, when to take statements seriously and when not. Now these cues which may be words, gestures, facial expressions, customs, or norms, are acquired by all of us in the course of growing up and are as much a part of our culture as the language we speak or the beliefs we accept. All of us depend for our peace of mind and our efficiency on hundreds of these cues, most of which we do not carry on the level of conscious awareness.

Loss

When you move to a new environment, you leave behind much of what is familiar to you. As Swallow (2010) observes, 'everything is unfamiliar, weather, landscape, language, food, dress, social roles, values, customs, and communication- basically, everything you're used to is no longer there'. Some sojourners experience intense feelings of grief and loss as they miss their first language, people, places, possessions, and other aspects (e.g., food, expressions of courtesy, sounds, smells) that are dear to them in their home environment.

Sensory overload

In unfamiliar surroundings and situations it is not unusual to feel overwhelmed and overstimulated by the multitude of new sights, sounds, and smells that you experience. Pulled in many different directions, you may feel pressured to deal with too many things at once. According to Nancy Arthur (2004: 27–8), a cross-cultural psychologist and counselor, '[i]n familiar cultural environments, cognitive and sensory processes normally operate through automatic and unconscious processing of information. However, in unfamiliar cultural environments, a conscious and deliberate effort must be made to process and understand the meaning of new information'. Not surprisingly, newcomers may experience sensory and cognitive overload and fatigue as they expend a considerable amount of energy continuously processing new information.

Plate 7.7 We may experience culture shock or confusion in a new environment due to the loss of the familiar and uncertainty about local social norms and practices. © Jane Jackson

Unfamiliar ways of being

In a new cultural environment you are bound to encounter unfamiliar worldviews and ways of doing things. You may be confronted with different ideas about what is appropriate behavior for males and females. Religious practices (e.g., interrupting work for daily prayers) may be new to you. Modes of transportation may also be very different from what you are used to.

Plate 7.8 Newcomers can easily be overwhelmed by unfamiliar scents, sights, sounds, and choices. © Jane Jackson

If you choose to study abroad you may also encounter '**cultures of learning**' that differ from what you have grown accustomed to in educational settings in your home country. As Cortazzi and Jin (1997: 83) explain:

> a culture of learning depends on the norms, values and expectations of teachers and learners relative to classroom activity. . . . It is not simply that overseas students encounter different ways of teaching and different expectations about learning; rather such encounters are juxtaposed with the cultures of learning they bring with them.

For example, you may find that you are expected to speak up in class much more than you are used to, and teachers may provide less support (e.g., no PowerPoint slides, lecture notes, or other handouts) or vice versa (Jackson 2013; Jackson & Chen 2018). These new behaviors can be very confusing and difficult to accept at first.

Feeling trapped

People who stay abroad for less than three weeks (**micro-term sojourners**) and even tourists who are abroad for longer know that if they are really uncomfortable in the new environment they can seek refuge in their hotel room or hostel and will soon escape to the safety and security of home. **Short-term sojourners** (e.g., those who will stay several months) and certainly **long-term sojourners** (e.g., expatriates who live abroad for many years) face a different situation. Newcomers who study, live, or work alongside host nationals need to be able to function in the host culture. As Nolan (1999: 78) explains, 'you can't turn off your new country, not even for a second. It's always there, pushing in on you in a thousand ways, all at once'. In extreme cases, sojourners who are unable to cope may take flight and head for home earlier than planned.

Ambiguity and uncertainty

It can be very frustrating to discover that your usual ways of accomplishing daily tasks and interacting with people do not work well in the new culture. Initially, you may be quite unsure about when and what will happen (e.g., who speaks first, what responses are deemed appropriate in a particular situation). **Cultural scripts** (e.g., local conventions for apologies, requests, refusals) may be mystifying. Displays of emotion, gender relations, and the rules for social interactions may be quite different from what you are accustomed to and in many situations you may not know how to respond. You may also be surprised at the ways in which people react to what you say and do. **Tolerance of ambiguity** refers to one's ability to cope with situations that are ambiguous. Individuals who have a low tolerance of ambiguity and limited resilience may find adjustment more difficult than those who are more at ease in situations and contexts that they do not fully understand. **Resilience** denotes an individual's ability to cope with stress and adversity. (These characteristics are linked to the uncertainty reduction theory and the uncertainty/anxiety management theory, which are discussed in Chapter 8.)

Loss of socioemotional support

Crossing linguistic and cultural boundaries can be very stressful. If this is your first foray abroad and you are on your own, there are bound to be times when you find life difficult. When you feel blue you likely miss the support of your family members and confidants who are far away. Until you make new friends and develop a support system (e.g., ties with locals and other international students), you are surrounded by strangers in a foreign environment.

No matter where you are in the world, you can suffer personal disappointments, worries, and hardship (e.g., relationship breakups, health problems, the serious illness of family members or friends, financial difficulties, academic failure). Events that would be unsettling in your home environment can seem more overwhelming in a foreign land, especially if you are not physically close to any of your loved ones. In a vulnerable state, even minor difficulties that would easily be dealt with at home can seem insurmountable.

Standing out

In your home environment, you can easily blend in if you are visibly similar to other members of the majority culture. If you display similar identity markers (e.g., religious clothing, tattoos), speak the same first language or dialect as the majority, and use nonverbal behaviors familiar to home nationals, you can go about your business without attracting attention. If you cross borders and become a visible minority for the first time in your life, it can be quite jarring as this novice sojourner from Hong Kong discovered:

> The scene in Heathrow Airport, when I was suddenly surrounded only by foreigners (mostly 'giant' Westerners whose skin, eye and hair colours were different from mine; speaking English or other foreign languages) struck me a great deal. And due to these intrinsic differences between them and me, psychologically I felt distanced from them though all of us were now under the same roof . . . my mind was occupied by uncertainty, curiosity and my effort to force out the courage to face the new.

Even if you can physically blend into a new environment, you may discover that eyebrows are raised as soon as you utter a few words. Your accent, nonverbal behavior, and communication style can signal that you are a stranger. Your clothing and adornments (e.g., body piercings, jewelry, short skirts, head scarf) may be commonplace in your home environment but set you apart in another cultural context. Being stared at (and even ridiculed) can be unnerving and can make you feel insecure, elevating concerns about your safety.

Discrimination or perceptions of discrimination

If you have grown up in an environment where you are a member of the group that has the most influence and prestige, it can be disquieting to enter a world in which you are a minority member with less status and power. When intercultural interactions do not go well you may feel that people in the host environment are treating you unfairly because of your accent, ethnicity, race, gender, religion, nationality, etc. In some situations, your instincts may be valid, whereas in others, your perception of discrimination or racism may be a consequence of your elevated stress level and a lack of understanding of local linguistic and cultural norms. For example, the annoyed look of a host national may be due to your unintentional breaking of social norms (e.g., omitting the word 'thank you') rather than prejudice. Whether real or imagined, negative encounters like this can lead to withdrawal from the host culture. 'being discriminated against can turn people inwards and cause a sense of isolation or diminished self-importance' (Wood & Landry 2010: 48).

Language confusion

If you have entered a new linguistic environment and do not speak the local language or your proficiency is at the beginner's level, you can feel helpless and dependent. You may have a basic grasp of the local language but lack familiarity with **sociopragmatic norms** (e.g., cultural scripts for social situations, routinized expressions of politeness); this can be a significant barrier to communication and hamper your adjustment. Even if you have studied the language in an academic setting for many years and attained a high score on a language proficiency text, it can be disquieting to discover that your speech (e.g., accent, style of communication) is not easily understood by locals. Your formal language lessons at school may not have equipped you for informal, social situations. Initially, you may find idiomatic expressions, humor, satire, social discourse, and communication styles impenetrable. Body language and other nonverbal codes may also be difficult to decipher. Second language socialization can be challenging.

Language fatigue

Interacting with people in a second language can be very exhausting, especially if you are not used to functioning in the language on a daily basis. '**Language fatigue** occurs when, trying to use a second language constantly, you become physically and psychologically drained by speaking, listening, and finding meaning in, until now, a little used "new" language' (La Brack 2003). If your proficiency is not advanced you may find that you need to translate oral speech in your head and then struggle to come up with a suitable response. As the comments of this second language sojourner reveal, this process can be very taxing until your proficiency improves:

> I really think that my English is not okay. I need time to translate what I want to say: grammar and articles and tenses are all wrong. . . . And it's so tiring to use English all day. I find that my English vocabulary is not enough. . . . And the translation is really killing me! . . . It is getting harder and harder for me to translate and I feel tired. I just speak Cantonese by instinct. . . . I think my mind will burst. . . . It's really killing me. My mood is on the drop. Maybe there is a maximum capacity of learning a foreign language that is preventing my further improvement.

Miscommunication

If you enter a new linguistic environment with little or no proficiency in the dominant language it can be very challenging to express your needs, ideas, and emotions in verbal and nonverbal ways that are meaningful to your hosts. To complicate matters, if you arrive with an advanced level of proficiency in the host language your hosts may assume that you are able to speak and interact in ways that are considered appropriate in that context. In other words, they may expect you to have much more sociopragmatic awareness and knowledge than you actually possess. A language barrier can lead to frustration and misunderstandings for both newcomers and host nationals.

Conflict in values

When you travel to a new environment you bring with you the values and worldviews that have been nurtured in your home country during the process of enculturation. In your new surroundings, you are bound to encounter people who do not necessarily share your perspective. Unless managed with skill, conflicting values and expectations can serve as a barrier to intercultural relations. (Conflicts in interpersonal relations are examined further in Chapter 9.)

Change in status or positioning

As a stranger or newcomer, you may discover that you have lost your status and positioning in the host culture. Back home, you may have been accorded respect as a top undergraduate with excellent academic results. In the new environment you may find yourself in classes with many students who are more proficient in the language of instruction and have more background knowledge about the local culture, which helps their performance in class. Until you find your feet, this loss in status can shake your self-confidence.

Symptoms of language and culture shock (confusion)

Cross-cultural psychologists, counselors, educators, and other scholars (e.g., Arthur 2004; Furnham 2015; Neuliep 2018c; Ward 2015; Ward *et al.* 2001) have identified a number of cognitive, psychological (emotional), and physiological symptoms that may arise as a consequence of language and culture shock or confusion. Their research suggests that when you enter another culture to live, work, or study, you *may* experience some of the following symptoms:

■ A change in sleep patterns (e.g., experience trouble falling asleep (insomnia) or sleep much more than usual)
■ Frequent mood swings and heightened irritability (e.g., be easily bothered by things that would normally not trouble you)
■ Feeling vulnerable, powerless, lost, and insecure (e.g., preoccupation with your safety, constant fears about being robbed, cheated, or exploited)
■ Excessive worrying about one's state of physical or mental health
■ Continuous concern about the purity of the water and food (e.g., you develop an obsession about cleanliness manifesting in excessive washing of hands)
■ Unfamiliar body aches and pains (e.g., skin rashes, hives, headaches, stomach aches, allergies) and frequent illnesses (e.g., colds, general malaise)
■ Loss of appetite or overeating (e.g., significant weight loss or gains)
■ Feeling sad and lonely even when in the company of other people
■ Homesickness (e.g., constant, deep longing for your family and friends back home)
■ Utopian, unrealistic views about your home culture and language
■ Fear of trying new things, meeting local people, or going to unfamiliar places (e.g., continually declining invitations to go out, staying inside more than usual)
■ Feelings of inadequacy (e.g., loss of self-confidence due to the inability to express yourself clearly in the host language and perform basic tasks)
■ Increased consumption of alcohol or drugs
■ Frequent perceptions of being singled out, overlooked, or discriminated against (e.g., not treated with the same respect as locals)
■ Pressing desire to interact with people just like yourself (e.g., individuals from the same linguistic and cultural background who 'really make sense' and 'understand you')
■ Cognitive impairment (e.g., difficulty concentrating and making decisions, inability to solve simple problems)
■ Frequently questioning your decision to go abroad and counting the days until you return home
■ Constantly comparing the new environment with your home culture, with the former cast in a negative light (e.g., constant complaints about the local weather, food, people, customs, accommodations, etc.)

- Hostility toward members of the host culture and frequent 'us' vs. 'them' discourse (e.g., negative stereotyping of host nationals)
- Resentment and lack of desire to interact with host nationals (and/or international students who have a different linguistic and cultural background from you)
- Loss of identity or confusion about who you are and how you fit into the world
- Refusal to learn/use the host language and interact with locals

Degree of language and culture shock or confusion

Not all migrants suffer from transition shock or confusion in the same way or to the same degree. Many scholars (e.g., Adler (1975), Furnham and Bochner (1986), Jackson 2018a; Neuliep 2018c, Ward 2015, Ward *et al.* 2001) have identified a range of factors that may account for disparate experiences:

Quality of information (degree of fact finding, amount and caliber of information about new environment, knowledge about the process of intercultural adjustment)

Individuals who enter a new environment armed with current information about the host country (e.g., language, history, climate, 'cultures of learning', politics, religious practices, customs, etc.) and the process of adjustment are better equipped to deal with culture shock or confusion than those who arrive without having done any groundwork.

Cultural similarity (degree of dissimilarity between one's home culture and the host culture in terms of language, values, beliefs, diet, nonverbal behaviors, customs, 'cultures of learning', religion, etc.)

Cultural distance (or ethnic proximity) refers to 'the level of homogeneity or heterogeneity between the interactants' in intercultural communication (Kim 2018: 322). Cultural distance may also encompass differences in cultural values, language, and communication styles (verbal and nonverbal) between an individual's home environment and another cultural context. When the cultural distance is great, the adjustment challenges and ensuing malaise may be more severe. For example, students from Wuhan, China may find it more challenging to adjust to Berlin than Singapore. A Brazilian may find it easier to adjust to Lisbon than Nairobi, although this is not always the case, especially if newcomers do not anticipate any difficulties and do little to prepare for the new environment.

Linguistic similarity (the degree of similarity between one's first language and the host language)

Sojourners who speak a romance language like French may find it easier to cope in a Spanish-speaking environment than in an environment where a Semitic language (e.g., Arabic) is the dominant medium of communication. When the language or dialect is from the same family (e.g., Romance languages), it is easier to pick up the rhythm of the language as well as the script (written form).

Communication style similarity (the degree of similarity between one's communication style and the common communication styles in the host culture)

For example, Japanese nationals who are most familiar with an indirect style of communication are apt to find it less challenging to move to an environment where a similar style is widely used. If they transfer to Germany or another country where more direct styles of communication are favored they may find adjustment more difficult.

Interpersonal dimensions (e.g., age, fortitude, independence, previous travel, proficiency in the host language, resourcefulness, tolerance of ambiguity)

All of these traits or personal characteristics can affect one's ability to deal with difficulties that arise. Individuals who are more resilient and tolerant of ambiguity are better positioned to cope with the strains of adjustment.

Physiological factors (mental and physical condition, medical or dietary issues, ability to tolerate changes in temperature/time zones, resilience)

Individuals who are less physically robust (e.g., become ill easily, are susceptible to changes in the weather/diet) and not emotionally stable may be more affected by the adjustment process.

Socioemotional support (friendship circles, intracultural and intercultural relationships, family support)

The strength of one's bonds with other people (e.g., friends in the host culture) and the amount of **socioemotional support** (warmth and nurturance) they provide can have a significant impact on how one's sojourn unfolds. Those who shy away from host nationals and spend all of their time with people from their home country may benefit from the camaraderie and suffer less culture shock or confusion; however, this **avoidance strategy** can limit their personal development (e.g., second language/ culture learning) and integration. Conversely, those who make more of an effort to develop friendships with host nationals may suffer from more culture shock due to more exposure to the host culture. On the plus side, they may benefit more from their stay abroad (e.g., become more proficient in the host language, develop a deeper understanding of the host environment, experience more personal growth) (Jackson 2018a; Mitchell *et al.* 2017).

Degree of control (amount of control over such aspects as one's move abroad, living conditions in the new environment, sojourn duration, free time, selection of courses, etc.)

Individuals who have chosen to go abroad are apt to be more motivated than those who venture abroad for the sole purpose of fulfilling a program or job requirement. The degree of autonomy in other aspects (e.g., housing, selection of courses/host institution/destination) can result in differences in the ways individuals view and respond to acculturative stress.

Geopolitical factors (relationship between the home country and the host nation; international, national, regional, or local tensions)

If sojourning in a region that has strong, favorable ties with one's country of origin, the host country is likely cast in a positive light. Feeling secure, the newcomer may feel well received by host nationals. Conversely, if the host country has tense or hostile relations with one's home country, one may be apprehensive about entering the new environment. Whether real or imagined, locals may be perceived to be less than welcoming.

Agency (the capacity to make choices)

Two sojourners with a similar background can be in the host environment at the same time. One may take advantage of every opportunity possible to interact with locals and practice the host language, whereas the other person may constantly pine for home and spend all of his free time on Skype complaining to friends and family back home about the weather, food, local people, housing, etc., in his first language. While one sojourner is overwhelmed with feelings of homesickness, the other is willing to try new things, makes friends with host nationals, and begins to 'fit into' the new environment. This disparate outcome evokes a well-known quote from the American author James A. Michener: 'If you reject the food, ignore the customs, fear the religion and avoid the people, you might better stay home'.

Duration and spatial factors (length of stay, location of residence, geographical locale)

Sojourners who reside in an apartment with home nationals and only stay a short time in the host culture likely have less opportunity to develop interpersonal relationships with host nationals than those who stay longer and live in a homestay or dormitory with locals. The amount and quality of exposure to the host culture can affect the degree of language and culture shock or confusion that one experiences.

Positive and negative effects of language and culture shock (confusion)

Early conceptions of culture shock were largely negative. In fact, Oberg (1960: 177) referred to it as 'an occupational disease of people who have been transplanted abroad'. For many decades, 'disease' oriented perceptions persisted and pre-sojourn orientations usually emphasized practical ways to avoid culture shock. Nowadays, there is growing recognition of the positive dimensions, and the focus has shifted to productive ways to manage the stress and confusion that naturally occur as one enters and adjusts to a new environment (Hottola 2004; Neuliep 2018c; Ward 2015).

Plate 7.9 In a new environment, tasting unfamiliar foods is part of the experience. © Jane Jackson

Contemporary scholars are placing more attention on the potential for language and culture stress to lead to deeper levels of **'whole person' development** (e.g., emotional intelligence and resourcefulness, interpersonal communication skills, intercultural competence, independence, maturity) and **identity expansion** (e.g., a broadened, more inclusive sense of self, the development of a global outlook) (Jackson 2018a; Kinginger 2009). Neuliep (2018c) comments that 'while culture shock is generally considered unpleasant, it often presents an individual with an opportunity to learn more about a particular culture and to develop personally' (p. 618). For example, grappling with transition challenges can bring about new, deeper understandings of oneself and more motivation to persevere in the host culture.

> In the encounter with another culture the individual gains new experiential knowledge by coming to understand the roots of his or her own ethnocentrism and by gaining new perspectives and outlooks on the nature of culture. . . . Paradoxically, the more one is capable of experiencing new and different dimensions of human diversity, the more one learns of oneself.
>
> (Adler 1975: 22)

While language and culture shock or confusion can be unnerving, and even debilitating for some, it can also lead to significant learning and personal growth, as noted by Lantis and DuPlaga (2010: 60–1):

> By getting "culture shocked," you are challenging yourself, surpassing your comfort zone, and becoming much more aware of your identity and of the world around you. You are building skills, gaining confidence, and forging relationships that surpass your former boundaries. Ultimately, you are learning what it means to be a global citizen.

When newcomers immerse themselves in the host culture they gain more access to host nationals and local practices (CoP) or ways of doing things. **Communities of practice (CoP)** are 'groups of people who share a concern or a passion for something they do and learn how to do it better as they interact regularly' (Wenger-Trayner & Wenger-Trayner 2015) (e.g., a group of marketing majors working on similar projects, a network of students who are exploring their passion for digital photography, a student organization devoted to public service, a rowing team). Significant contact with local language and cultural practices can certainly be exhausting and stressful at times; however, the discomfort can also lead to more awareness and understanding of both Self and Other. For example, firsthand exposure to new communities of practice can compel individuals to reflect on and even question their behaviors, self-identities, values, and beliefs. It can motivate newcomers to master the host language and enhance their intercultural competence to better 'fit into' the new environment. As sojourners become more tolerant of ambiguity and develop more effective intercultural communication skills, they are apt to experience more success in overcoming difficulties. Successfully dealing with language and culture adjustment issues can be a source of pride and can help sojourners become more self-confident and independent.

STAGES OF CULTURE SHOCK AND ADJUSTMENT

The U-curve adjustment model

Scholars have created various models to try and depict the stages of culture shock and adjustment that sojourners may experience in an unfamiliar cultural environment. One of the earliest and most well-known models is the **U-curve adjustment model** (Lysgaard 1955), which is illustrated in Figure 7.1.

The U-shaped model includes four stages, which have been given various names by different scholars (e.g., Lysgaard 1955; Oberg 1960; Neuliep 2018c):

1 The honeymoon stage (initial euphoria): Fascination and excitement about the new culture, curiosity about linguistic and cultural differences, and an emphasis on cultural similarities

2 Culture stress and shock (Crisis and frustration): Confrontation with different values and behaviors, confusion and anxiety, and criticism/rejection of the new language and culture

3 Adjustment (Integration or recovery): Learning new linguistic, social, and cultural norms, an increase in one's level of comfort and well-being, and respect for the new culture (e.g., different ways of being) and language

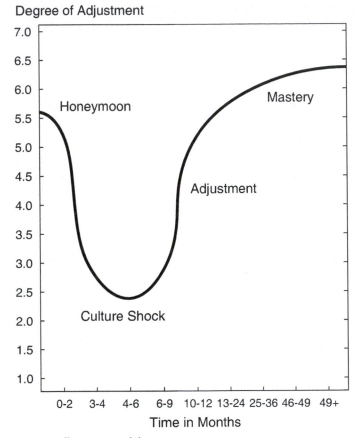

Figure 7.1 The U-curve adjustment model

4 Mastery (Adaptation and acceptance, biculturalism): Awareness and understanding of cultural differences, an increase in autonomy and satisfaction, a dual cultural/linguistic identity

Reentry and the W-curve adjustment model

Gullahorn and Gullahorn (1963) maintain that returnees often experience a similar period of adjustment when they return home so they extended the U-curve model by adding two stages: **reentry or reverse culture shock** and **resocialization**, the process of readjusting one's attitudes and behaviors to feel at ease in one's 'home environment' after a period away (See Figure 7.2). Since then many versions of their W-curve adjustment model have been proposed by interculturalists (e.g., Furnham & Bochner 1986; Neuliep 2018c; Tong-Toomey & Dorjee 2019).

As variations of this model are still widely used today, the proposed stages are explained along with relevant 'real world' examples from student sojourners.[1]

The honeymoon phase (initial euphoria)

When sojourners first arrive in the host culture, the curve model suggests that most are excited and looking forward to what lies ahead. Similar to the early stage of a romance, newcomers

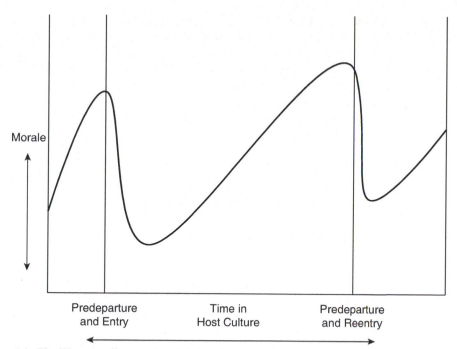

Figure 7.2 The W-curve adjustment model

may initially overlook negative aspects of the host culture and take delight in discovering new sights, sounds, and smells. This buoyant mood is captured in a diary entry written by a second language sojourner soon after her arrival in the host culture:

> Waking up this morning, I could hardly believe I was in England. It was all like a dream, a dream that came true finally. . . . I looked around my bedroom and then viewed through the window: the air was still and quiet amidst birds' chatter, everything was clear like a framed picture, with no sign of impurities or pollution which very often surround my living place back home. The colours of my room, the neighbouring houses, the trees and the sky, were plain, fresh and lively. A sense of satisfaction ran through my heart.

Hostility phase

In the model, the second phase is sometimes referred to as 'culture shock', 'crisis stage', or 'disintegration'. After the initial euphoria fades away, sojourners may feel uncomfortable in the new environment, especially if they are a visible minority or they stand out in some way (e.g., speak with a different accent, wear different clothing, eat different food, have different values). For example, in a study abroad exit interview, an international exchange student disclosed the following:

> You feel that you are different from the people there – your skin color, your language, and your thoughts. Everyone likes to be with people who are like them. I felt isolated and a bit depressed because they were all familiar with each other and I knew nobody. . . . I had difficulties with communication and felt unwelcome by locals. That was far from my expectation before going on exchange. I was desperate to go home at that time.

Newcomers may also be overwhelmed and frustrated by the psychological, cognitive, and physical demands of the new culture and the disintegration of almost everything familiar. Bombarded by stimuli that are difficult to process, excitement may be replaced by confusion and disappointment. In an irritable state, differences between the home culture and host environment are viewed as problems. For example, student sojourners may discover that their roommates have values and practices that they find difficult to accept. In this hostile phase, much of their discourse may be replete with 'us' vs. 'them' comments, with host nationals portrayed unfavorably, as in the following stereotypical comments by a disgruntled international exchange student:

> I think people in North America lead a really dissolute life. They tend to treat sex casually. They also don't have any goals. They just drink, take drugs and have sex all the time. All the students have the characteristics of a typical North American. They don't know what they are doing in their life. People said foreigners are polite but I don't think so. I think they're rather rebellious and impolite.

Sojourners may also discover that their second language skills are not as well developed as they had assumed. Unexpectedly, they may experience difficulty communicating with people from the host culture, especially in informal situations where colloquialisms are frequently used: 'Although my English isn't good enough to express myself fully, it wasn't a big problem in my coursework. The language problem was more apparent when I chatted with my classmates as I didn't understand their jokes or know how to respond'. In addition to being mentally and physically exhausting at times, using a second language can make it more challenging to cultivate intercultural relationships, an issue that is explored further in Chapter 8.

When classes get underway, education abroad students may come face to face with differing expectations and learning and teaching styles and long for familiar 'cultures of learning'. For example, a Chinese exchange student in the U.S. said:

> Sometimes the professor might look at you to force you to answer her questions, but when I had no idea what she was talking about I had to avoid having any eye contact with her. It was so embarrassing. Also, it was so hard for me to fit in. Students kept raising their hands! The most general arguments had been said and then I could not follow their flow so I had no choice but to stay quiet. Once the professor came to me and told me that I was too passive in class. She suggested that I ask more questions instead of answering them but it wasn't easy as I am a passive person and I just wasn't used to this fast pace.

In this stage, homesickness may set in and the newcomers may question their decision to go abroad. A small number who suffer severe symptoms of language and culture shock may head home.

Humorous stage

This third phase is sometimes termed the 'reorientation and re-integration phase' or 'adjustment and recovery'. The curve model suggests that sojourners in this phase have regained their sense of humor. They have begun to realize that many of the problems that they have experienced in the new environment are due to cultural difference (including their response to it) or language problems rather than deliberate attempts by locals to annoy them. While comparisons are still made between their home and host cultures, this model suggests that the sojourners are more balanced in their views by this stage. They are more aware of linguistic or cultural differences that may have led to misunderstandings.

With a more positive mindset, they are better able to interpret subtle linguistic and cultural cues, and those who are using a second language find it easier to express themselves in the language. A female exchange student in the Netherlands remarked:

> I had difficulty communicating with locals in the beginning but after many weeks had passed, I found that they were nice people. It's just that they dared not to speak in English. Also, by then I knew more about their culture and began to like this country. True, I did experience culture shock at the beginning but I learned to overcome it.

At the host university, student sojourners may have started to form friendships with other international students and perhaps some local students as well. These interpersonal connections help them to feel a bit more connected to the local scene. Although better able to function in the host culture, they may still experience difficult days (e.g., occasional bouts of homesickness).

The 'at home' stage

This phase is sometimes referred to as 'adaptation' or 'resolution'. The curve model suggests that by this stage education abroad students generally feel more at home and happy in the host environment. In a more relaxed frame of mind, they demonstrate more understanding and appreciation of the host language and culture and their new way of life. A semester-long international exchange student in London said:

> Midway through the semester, my life took a turn. By then, I'd made more friends, including some English mates, and had even begun to dream in English! I realized I'd developed a sense of belonging to Bloomsbury, my neighborhood. From the Indian restaurant to the corner shop to my residence hall, social bonds began to form. Overcoming adversities with positivity allowed me to see more and discover more, and with the positive energy this generates, others could feel this. . . . Studying abroad is not easy. It is a test of the strength of your character but if you champion it and open yourself up, it can change your life completely.

When using the host language in daily life, education abroad students are better able to communicate their ideas and feelings in ways that are context-appropriate as their sociopragmatic awareness has increased. They may actively participate in activities and have a diverse circle of friends they can rely on and confide in, including host nations. This, in turn, boosts their self-confidence and sense of belonging in the new environment.

By this time, student sojourners may have become more receptive to new 'cultures of learning' as they better understand what lies behind different practices. For example, a Chinese exchange student who spent a semester in the U.S. revealed the following in a study abroad exit interview:

> In the Human Resources Management course, I didn't like the professor in the beginning. He didn't teach much. Instead, he assigned the teaching job to groups with each group

responsible for teaching one chapter. I thought, "You are the professor, why don't you teach?" Gradually, I noticed that he made additional comments to what the students taught. This helped the students to think and learn more. . . . The interaction between the teacher and the students took up almost the whole class and you had to think independently. Soon everybody was in a heated discussion and the students would come up with all kinds of answers, including ones you cannot think of, and those you feel too shy to voice out. But they just did! In the beginning, you might not be willing to participate but gradually in such an environment, I became better in communication. One of the benefits is that I no longer get nervous in these situations. I became accustomed to thinking, discussing, and speaking up in a group environment. This is the greatest thing I gained. This helped me to develop one of the most important skills in the business field. In this field, you always need to communicate with others. My communication and cooperative skills are much better after this experience. In the past, I wouldn't dare to challenge others whenever I had a different point of view. I've become bolder to speak out my views and add to the points of others, although my attitude is still not very aggressive.

With enhanced self-confidence, sojourners in this stage may employ more culturally appropriate problem solving and conflict mediation techniques. By this stage, they are more adept at coping with challenges that arise in their daily life.

This model also suggests that some sojourners may feel that they have developed a bilingual and bicultural identity by this stage. **Biculturalism** is characterized by proficiency and comfort with both one's original culture and the culture of the new country or region (Fantini 2012a; de Groot 2018). Bilingual individuals may incorporate various languages and cultural dimensions into their sense of who they are. Like the following student, sojourners who develop a broadened sense of self may believe that they have been 'transformed' into a more open-minded person while abroad.

When you go to a multicultural, multilingual country to study, you have the chance to get to know people with different nationalities who speak many languages. . . . You can learn to think from different angles. After spending a year abroad, I've become much more open-minded. I embrace other cultures and languages, and no longer see the world from a single angle.

(A yearlong international exchange student)

Reentry or reverse culture shock

Reentry refers to the process of returning home after spending time abroad (Martin & Harrell 2004; Neuliep 2018c). The **W-curve model** suggests that many returnees experience ups and downs that are similar to what they experienced abroad. **Reentry** or **reverse culture shock** may be defined as 'the process of readjusting, reacculturating, and reassimilating into one's own home culture after living in a different culture for a significant period of time' (Gaw 2000: 83–4).

Returnees may experience disorientation, surprise, and confusion when they do not easily fit back into their home environment. This malaise may be due to a variety of reasons (e.g., a shift in perspectives, boredom with the familiar, appreciation of the host country's customs or values, idealized images of the home country formed while abroad). The reentry phase can sometimes be more severe and painful than the initial culture confusion in the host country, in part because it is not expected (LaBrack 2015; Martin & Harrell 2004; Szkudlarek 2010). After all, one is returning 'home'.

In the reentry phase, those who more fully integrated into the host culture (e.g., made close friends with host nationals or other international students) and functioned well in the host language in their daily life, may initially find it more difficult to readjust to their home culture and first language use in daily life. They may miss their more independent lifestyle and friends made abroad and find it difficult to fit back into the rhythm of local life. One returnee said:

> My adjustment on reentry has been more difficult than what I experienced abroad. I'm still not fully readjusted now. The whole living schedule and sleeping times have changed. Before going on exchange I was able to sleep very little and do a lot of things during the day but now I find this living style is very tiring. I wish I was living the comfortable Norwegian lifestyle but if I do, I won't have enough time to get everything done! I don't know how to cope with that. I'm still working on this . . . still adjusting to being back.
>
> (Yearlong exchange student)

While excited to share their experiences, returnees may find that their friends and family quickly tire of their international stories. Disillusioned, returnees may consider conationals boring and provincial; they may long for the life they had during the sojourn and view it through rose-colored glasses. They may miss not being able to converse as much in their second language as they did while abroad. Their discourse may be full of complaints about their home culture. This time, 'us' vs. 'them' discourse may elevate all aspects in the host culture and denigrate local ways of being. (See Chapter 11 for more on 'reversal'.)

Returnees may realize they have changed but find it difficult to put into words. They may feel torn between the values and behaviors of the host country and their home environment. Some may suffer from **identity confusion** or misalignments, that is, they may feel as if they are caught between two distinct worlds, the one they left behind and the one they have returned to. They may not feel that they fit into either. Like the following returnee, many feel unsettled in this stage:

> While abroad, I missed home quite a lot in the beginning but now that I'm back, I feel estranged. I feel my existence here is meaningless. In the U.S., I had a great time with my boyfriend, my roommates, and my newly met friends. Here, I feel alone. Although I'm physically back, my memories remain in L.A.

(See Chapter 5 for more discussion about cultural marginality or inbetweenness.)

Resocialization stage

The final phase in the model is sometimes referred to as 're-integration', 'the independence stage', or 'acceptance and understanding'. In this stage, returnees are beginning to feel more at home and are better able to communicate effectively and appropriately with their family members, friends, and colleagues. Similar to recovery and adjustment phases in the host country, the returnees start to readjust to the home country and reintegrate into the local way of life. The initial reentry shock has subsided, and they are better able to find a sense of balance between their 'new old' home and the culture they have just left. A returnee recounted this process in an interview:

> It took me some effort to get used to the local lifestyle again as I'd become accustomed to the way of living in Korea. When I came back home I had to readjust to many things. I had such a wonderful and splendid life in Korea but when I came back, I felt . . . umm . . . it was just . . . so different! I have had to accept it and adapt. You have to try your best to adjust since there's no choice for you! And gradually you feel like you fit in. Now, I am in a better place in my head. I'm doing more things with my friends and I'm happy. I'm also keeping in touch with my friends in Seoul through Facebook.

While returnees may experience stress as they renegotiate their identities in their home environment, some may realize and appreciate that they have developed a hybrid, multicultural identity through international educational experience. They may display more interest in both international and local happenings that they had prior to their sojourn. The W-curve model suggests that individuals in this stage are able to identify and appreciate multiple ways in which they have changed for the better due to their international and intercultural experiences. They may also make an effort to diversify their social networks to include both local and international friends and maintain contact with friends made abroad. Feeling more stable and self-confident, they may make plans for more international experience, like the following year abroad returnee:

> Before this sojourn, I never considered working overseas but after experiencing the lifestyle in the U.S., I've started to consider a career abroad. My worldview broadened and I have a more global mindset now. I can view things from a global perspective instead of just looking at them from my home city's perspective.

Criticisms of the U- and W-curve adjustment models

While the U-curve and W-curve adjustment models (or variations of them) are still used to prepare students for education abroad, a growing number of researchers have found that many sojourners experience developmental trajectories that differ from what is portrayed in these models. Many contemporary scholars (e.g., Berardo 2012; Jackson 2018a; LaBrack 2011; Ward 2015) argue that the curves of adjustment models lack sufficient empirical research and cannot accurately predict the degree of or even occurrence of culture shock. Questions have been raised about the applicability of the curved models of adjustment for all types of sojourners. LaBrack (2011), for example, points out that the W-curve model 'does not fit the global nomads and third culture kids (TCKs) very well, nor does it fit "heritage-seeking" students or education abroad populations from refugee/immigrant backgrounds' (p. 2). A **heritage study abroad student** is 'a student who studies abroad in a location that is linked in some way (for example, linguistically, culturally, historically) to his/her family or cultural background' (Forum on Education Abroad n.d.). For example, a Korean American student may join a semester-long international exchange program in Seoul.

In mixed-method investigations of study abroad sojourners (summer immersion, semester- and yearlong international exchange students), Jackson (2008, 2010, 2012, 2013, 2018a) found that some participants endure significant ups and downs while abroad whereas others do not. Some experience multiple, persistent symptoms of language and culture shock or confusion during their sojourn, while others claim their transition to the new culture was smooth and symptom free. A number suffer from identity confusion while abroad, whereas others do not. The amount and quality of contact with the host language and culture varies considerably among sojourners and this naturally affects their learning. Some study abroad students develop close bonds with host nationals and become more fluent in the host language whereas many others spend all of their free time with friends from their home country and do not enhance their linguistic or interpersonal skills.

The degree of reentry culture shock or confusion also varies. Some return home with higher levels of intercultural sensitivity, broadened self-identities, and a strong desire to use their second language in intercultural interactions. Along with a more open mindset, these returnees may feel that they have developed more cosmopolitan, multicultural identities while abroad. With heightened interest in international affairs they may continue to take steps to nurture a global mindset. In contrast, others are very negative about their international, inter-cultural experiences and have become even more ethnocentric and nationalistic after their stay abroad. Overwhelmed by cultural difference and ill-equipped to manage language and culture adjustment issues, some return home with reinforced stereotypes of host nationals, heightened xenophobia, and little interest in further developing the social dimension of their second lan-guage proficiency (Jackson 2008, 2010, 2012, 2018a).

A complicated mix of individual elements (e.g., education abroad aims, adaptive stress, personality, resilience, mindset, awareness of language, and culture learning strategies), level of intercultural competence, and external factors (e.g., degree of host receptivity, housing arrangement, exposure to host culture) account for differences in the developmental trajecto-ries of sojourners and significant variations in sojourn outcomes. As noted by Coleman (2009), Jackson (2012, 2018a), Kinginger (2009), and other language and education abroad research-ers, the experience of education abroad students is much more complex and variable than what is suggested by the curves of adjustment models. More longitudinal, mixed-method research or ethnographic studies are needed that capture the 'whole person' development of participants before, during, and after stays abroad.

Despite the limitations previously detailed, variations of the U- and W-curve adjustment models remain popular in pre-education abroad orientations, sojourn support programs, and reentry debriefings as they are simple to grasp and seem plausible. In light of recent research, more educators regard these models as 'useful heuristic devices to raise issues related to cul-tural adjustment but no longer present them as phases that everyone will automatically experi-ence' (Forum on Education Abroad 2009: 41). Although the curves models cannot accurately predict the developmental trajectories of individuals, they do raise awareness of the *potential* ups and downs that one might experience during acculturation and reentry.

AN INTEGRATIVE COMMUNICATION THEORY OF CROSS-CULTURAL ADAPTATION

In an effort to overcome the limitations of the curve models and incorporate common elements in long-term and short-term adaptation, Kim (2001, 2005, 2012, 2018) proposed the **integra-tive communication theory of cross-cultural adaptation** to depict an individual's gradual adaption to a new environment. Her model raises awareness of multiple individual and contex-tual elements that can influence the developmental trajectories.

To understand this theory, it is essential to have a basic understanding of key terms. For Kim (2012: 233), **cross-cultural adaptation** refers to 'the phenomenon in which individuals who, upon relocating to an unfamiliar cultural environment, strive to establish and maintain a relatively stable, reciprocal and functional relationship with the environment'. This process includes the individual and the environment as well as the process and outcomes of communication activities (e.g., intercultural interactions in the host culture). In the new environment, resocialization activities drive acculturation, that is, 'the change in individuals whose primary learning has been in one culture and who take over traits from another culture' (Marden & Meyer 1968: 36). New cultural understandings and behaviors are not just added to one's internal framework. Through the process of adaptive change, '**deculturation** (or unlearning) of some of the old cultural habits has to occur, at least in the sense that new responses are adopted in situations that previously would have evoked old, habitual ones' (Kim 2012: 233).

In her theory, Kim (2012: 233–4) addresses the following questions: (1) 'What is the essential nature of the adaptation process individual settlers undergo over time?' and (2) why are some settlers more successful than others in attaining a level of psychosocial fitness in the host environment?'. At the heart of her framework is the **stress-adaption-growth dynamic**, which is based on the notion that acculturative stress (e.g., language and culture shock) can gradually lead to adaptation. As newcomers grapple with challenges in the host environment, they become more attuned to culture difference and more adept at coping with the strain of living in the new culture. Over time, stress-adaptation experiences bring about new understandings and behavioral changes that enable the individual to more effectively manage challenges. Life in the new environment gradually becomes less stressful.

In Kim's model, **host communication competence** refers to 'the overall internal capacity of a stranger to decode and encode information in accordance with the host cultural communication practices' (ibid: 236). This includes **cognitive competence** ('knowledge of the host language and culture, history, social institutions, and rules of interpersonal conduct'), **affective competence** ('the emotional and motivational capacity to deal with the various challenges of living in the host environment'), and **operational competence** ('the capacity to express outwardly by choosing a "right" combination of verbal and nonverbal acts in specific social transactions of the host environment') (ibid: 236).

Environmental factors also play a role in the adaptation of newcomers. Kim's theory cites three elements in particular that can influence how a newcomer's adaptation proceeds: (1) **host receptivity** ('the degree to which the receiving environment welcomes and accepts strangers into its interpersonal networks and offers them various forms of informational, technical, material and emotional support'), (2) **host conformity pressure** ('the extent to which the host environment challenges them, implicitly or explicitly, to act in accordance with the normative patterns of the host culture', and (3) **ethnic group strength** ('the relative status or standing of a particular ethnic group in the context of the surrounding host society') (ibid: 237).

Individual differences among newcomers can also influence the adaption process, including: (1) **preparedness** ('the level of readiness to undertake the process of cross-cultural adaptation by developing host communication competence and participating in host social communication activities'), (2) **ethnic proximity/distance** ('the extent to which the ethnicity of an individual immigrant or sojourner plays a role in the cross-cultural adaptation process by serving either as a certain level of advantage or handicap', that is, whether it motivates or demotivates host nationals to welcome them into their social networks), and (3) **personality predisposition** ('three interrelated personality resources') (ibid: 237–8). With reference to the latter, Kim maintains that the following personality resources or traits facilitate adaptation: (1) **openness** ('an internal posture that is receptive to new information', (2) **strength** ('the quality of resilience, patience, hardiness and persistence', and (3) **positivity** ('an affirmative and optimistic outlook that enables the individual to better endure stressful events with a belief in the possibilities of life in general' (ibid: 238).

Kim's theory also identifies several potential benefits of adaptive change: (1) 'increased **functional fitness** in carrying out daily transactions' (e.g., knowing one's way around in the new environment, (2) 'improved **psychological health** in dealing with the environment' (a high level of host communication competence to be able to overcome culture shock and engage in social communication activities that reduce one's level of stress), and (3) the 'emergence of an **intercultural identity orientation**' ('an orientation towards self and others that is no longer rigidly defined by either the identity linked to the "home" culture or the identity of the host culture') (ibid: 238). Individuals who are genuinely open to this process of change may undergo **intercultural transformation**, that is, they may develop 'a new, alternative identity that is broader, more inclusive, more intercultural' (Kim 2001: 232–3). Thus, this model views culture shock or confusion as a potentially positive catalyst for personal growth and learning, including identity expansion.

OPTIMIZING INTERCULTURAL TRANSITIONS

If you decide to study, live, or work in an unfamiliar linguistic and cultural environment, there are steps you can take to ease your transition. Drawing primarily on research that has focused on short-term education abroad students (e.g., second language speakers), this section offers suggestions to make the most of international educational experience.

Prior to going abroad

Research your destination.
Set realistic goals and expectations.
Take a course in intercultural communication. (Make good use of the knowledge and skills you are developing in this course!)
Practice your second language.
Attend pre-sojourn orientations, when available.
Take advantage of online materials. (Consult the list at the end of this chapter.)

In the host environment

Familiarize yourself with the local context.
Be patient! Language and culture confusion are natural, and adjustment takes time.
Keep in touch with family and friends back home.
Develop a routine and take care of your health.
Take part in any orientation activities arranged by the host university.
Join extracurricular activities and have fun.
Be open to new experiences. Be adventurous!
Take the initiative to develop diverse social networks (e.g., form friendships with host nationals, international students, conationals).
Recognize hot button issues (e.g., culture differences that annoy you).

Find a cultural mentor and seek help when needed.

Revisit and revise the goals you set prior to the sojourn.

Enhance your second language skills (e.g., take the initiative to practice the language in informal situations, pay attention to sociopragmatic dimensions).

Recognize the limitations of your linguistic and cultural knowledge.

Limit negative thoughts and refrain from making snap judgments about cultural difference.

Anticipate setbacks and persevere when you experience setbacks.

Develop the habit of self-analysis and critical reflection.

Consult recommended online resources.

Prior to returning home

Begin your reentry preparations while abroad.

Say meaningful good-byes.

Take advantage of online materials that provide advice on reentry.

Reflect on what you have gained from your stay abroad.

Set concrete, manageable goals for your return home.

Back on home soil

Share your international stories in small doses and demonstrate interest in others (e.g., local happenings, the experiences of your friends and family members).

Participate in reentry debriefings or courses, when available.

Be patient. Refrain from making snap judgments about your home culture (or the host culture).

Avoid 'shoeboxing' your international experience (e.g., join international/second language organizations and study abroad alumni groups, share your experiences with a wider audience, e.g., local school children enter a study abroad writing contest).

Serve as a buddy for newcomers or volunteer to orientate students who will venture abroad.

Talk with people who understand your transition (e.g., other returning exchange students).

Stay in touch with friends abroad and continue to expand and diversify your social networks (e.g., make friends with incoming international exchange students).

Continue to practice your second language.

Take an intercultural (reentry) transitions course to 'unpack' your international experience.

Critically reflect on your international/reentry experience.

Consult online resources on reentry.

Make concrete plans for further intercultural/international experience.

SUMMARY

This chapter drew attention to the natural ups and downs of the process of adapting to an unfamiliar linguistic and cultural environment. While we cannot fully eliminate transition stress when we cross borders, there are steps we can take to reduce our stress level and optimize our stay in a new environment. Returning home also requires preparation and readjustment. It is also important to recognize the potential for growth in intercultural attitudes, skills, and knowledge by working through 'transition shock' in a constructive way. Crossing borders can lead to significant personal growth and the emergence of a more intercultural self *if* one is open to change. As noted by Maya Angelo, a celebrated author and civil rights activist in the U.S., 'Perhaps travel cannot prevent bigotry, but by demonstrating that all peoples cry, laugh, eat, worry, and die, it can introduce the idea that if we try and understand each other, we may even become friends'.

International experience, coupled with critical reflection, can lead to more linguistic and (inter)cultural awareness, identity expansion, the acquisition of new skills and understandings, and even suggest new possibilities for one's life. As noted by Dispenza (2002):

> [U]ndertaken with awareness, travel surely is one of the most available and most effective means to nourish, broaden, and quicken the soul. The destination does not matter as much as the attention we give to the understanding that all travel is inner travel.

(p. 5)

discussion questions

1 Explain what is meant by the following terms: sojourner, long-term expatriate, immigrant, refugee, and asylum seeker. How might their adaptation in a new land differ? Why? Discuss your ideas with a partner.
2 Why do some acculturation scholars prefer to use the term culture confusion instead of culture shock? What are your own views about this?
3 Explain how anxiety and a low tolerance of ambiguity can negatively affect one's second language socialization in a new environment.
4 Discuss the role that second language skills (e.g., fluency in the host language, sociopragmatic awareness) can play in the intercultural adjustment/adaptation process.
5 How have views about culture shock changed since Oberg's (1960) publication? What are the implications for border crossers (e.g., study abroad students, expatriates)?
6 What internal and external factors may affect a study abroad student's second language development, culture learning, and intercultural adjustment in the host environment?
7 Why do some sojourners develop a multicultural identity while others become more ethnocentric and nationalistic (e.g., develop stronger ties to their home country)?
8 Why might some expatriates or education abroad returnees experience more reentry culture shock (confusion) than others?

activities

1 Define the term acculturation and identify factors that can facilitate or hinder this process.

2 Describe the 'stress-adaptation-growth' dynamic. What factors can influence this process? Have you experienced this? Share your experiences with a classmate.

3 Define 'transition shock'. Identity three types that are especially relevant for sojourners and provide examples to illustrate each.

4 Have you ever experienced language and culture shock (confusion) in a foreign land? Describe your symptoms and coping strategies. Share your experiences with your classmates.

5 Imagine that you will soon join a semester-long international exchange program in a country that has a very different linguistic and cultural environment from your home country. How can you prepare for your stay abroad? What steps can you take after your arrival in the host country to ease your adjustment?

6 In small groups, discuss the following situation. Two South African university students of a similar age and background (e.g., same ethnic group, gender, education level, first language, grade point average, proficiency level in French) join a six-week French immersion program in France. Neither has previous travel experience. At the end of their sojourn one is delighted with her progress in French and feels at home in the host environment, whereas her classmate laments the fact that she did not have enough opportunity to use the language and believes that she gained little from her stay abroad. What might account for these disparate outcomes?

7 Imagine that you will soon join a year long international exchange program in a second language context that you have never visited. What would you do to prepare? What ideas did you learn from this chapter that you think would be most helpful to you? (If you have already participated in an education abroad program, share your insights and advice with a partner.)

8 Talk with international exchange students (or study abroad returnees) about their experiences with and reactions to unfamiliar learning and teaching practices (e.g., different roles and responsibilities for students and teachers). What adjustment strategies, if any, worked for them? Have you had similar experiences? If yes, how did you cope?

9 Define what is meant by reentry or reverse culture shock. In small groups, discuss strategies to ease the transition back home after a yearlong stay abroad. Also, identify ways the returnees might extend their language and intercultural learning on home soil.

further reading

Jackson, J. (2018) *Interculturality in International Education*, London and New York: Routledge.

This volume explores the multifarious individual and external elements that can influence the developmental trajectories of students who travel abroad to gain international educational experience.

Lantis, J.S. and DuPlaga, J. (2016) *The Global Classroom: An Essential Guide to Study Abroad*, Abingdon and New York: Routledge.

The authors offer practical suggestions for student sojourners to help optimize their stays abroad. This book encompasses three phases: pre-sojourn preparation, sojourn, and reentry.

Paige, R.M., Cohen, A.D., Kappler, B., Chi, J.C. and Lassegard, J.P. (2006) *Maximizing Study Abroad: A Student's Guide to Strategies for Language and Culture Learning and Use*, Minneapolis, MN: Center for Advanced Research on Language Acquisition, University of Minnesota.

This guide provides students with tools, creative activities, and advice to prepare for and enhance their culture and language learning while studying abroad. It can also help returnees adjust to life when they return home.

Slimbach, R. (2010) *Becoming World Wise: A Guide to Global Learning*, Sterling, VA: Stylus.

This book is designed to help sojourners optimize their stays abroad by cultivating mindfulness and a global perspective.

Video and online resources

Culture Shock: International Students in the United States (2006) CustomFlix.
This DVD addresses cross-cultural adaptation and culture shock issues. Focusing on the arrival and initial adjustment period, international students share their views about their experiences adjusting to life in the United States.

iStudent 101: Online learning for international students (This website offers free online resources for study abroad, primarily targeted international students in the United States. Materials cover all phases: pre-sojourn, sojourn, post-sojourn). (http://istudent101.com)

The Global Scholar. The 'Global Scholar Online Courses' website provides online curriculum to orient, train, and support students before, during, and after they study abroad. (http://globalscholar.us/)

What's Up with Culture? On-Line Cultural Training Resource for Study Abroad. In a project funded by FIPSE, the U.S. Department of Education, Bruce LaBrack (2003) and his team developed online modules to ease the cross-cultural preparation and reentry of study abroad students. (http://www2.pacific.edu/sis/culture/)

Companion Website: Continue your journey online

Visit the Companion Website for a variety of tools and resources to support and extend your intercultural learning. (Instructors who are qualified adopters of the text may access additional resources on this site.)

Note

1   This chapter draws on investigations of the acculturation and second language socialization of university students who took part in either a semester or year abroad international exchange program in one of 40 countries. This research was generously supported by funds from the Research Grants Council of the Hong Kong SAR (Project No. 2110167; RGC Ref Nos. CUHK444709, 445312) and a Teaching Development and Language Enhancement Grant from the Chinese University of Hong Kong (Ref. 4170510).

CHAPTER 8

Language and intercultural relationships

Because we live in a world in which there is increasing contact with diverse others, understanding how differences are bridged – regardless of which socially constructed boundary we happen to be speaking – is an important pursuit.

– (Vela-McConnell 2011: 3)

Communication between and among individuals is forever changed because of technology. People are now able to initiate, maintain, and terminate relationships through technological means. . . . The effects of technology on our interpersonal relationships are unprecedented, unpredictable, and unstoppable.

– (West & Turner 2011b: 379)

A key to maintaining an intercultural friendship lies in effective communication between members.

– (Lee 2008: 52)

learning objectives

By the end of this chapter, you should be able to:

1 Define what is meant by an intercultural relationship
2 Identify and describe ten categories of intercultural relationships
3 Explain the challenges and benefits of intercultural relationships
4 Identify internal and external factors that can facilitate or hinder intercultural relationships (friendship, romance, marriage), including computer-mediated unions
5 Identify constructive ways to nurture intercultural relationships

INTRODUCTION

Meaningful communication with other human beings is essential for our physical and mental health. No matter what part of the world we live in, forming intimate relationships is a vital element in life. This chapter begins by examining the connection between interpersonal communication and intercultural relationships. We then explore several categories of intercultural relationships (interethnic, interracial, international, interreligious) as well as ties between people who differ in terms of social class, language, age, ability (e.g., physical, mental), gender, and/or sexual orientation. Next, we discuss the numerous benefits of initiating and sustaining intercultural relationships in today's interconnected world.

We then turn our attention to issues related to intercultural friendships and social networks (e.g., differing cultural perceptions, cyber connections, the formation of intercultural friendships/networks, barriers to the development of friendships between people from different backgrounds). Next, we shift our focus to romantic intercultural relationships and briefly look at factors that can facilitate or hinder successful intercultural romance and marriage. Finally, drawing on recent research findings, this chapter concludes with suggestions for ways to enhance intercultural relationships.

INTERPERSONAL COMMUNICATION AND INTERCULTURAL RELATIONSHIPS

In addition to satisfying emotional and practical needs, interpersonal communication plays a major role in facilitating our social relationships and is a vital part of our life. **Interpersonal communication** refers to 'a distinctive, transactional form of human communication involving mutual influence, usually for the purpose of managing relationships' (Beebe *et al.* 2018: 30). This interaction, which may take place face to face, on the phone, or increasingly online, helps us to initiate and sustain personal bonds with other human beings.

While most of our encounters with people are fleeting and impersonal, for a variety of reasons, we crave a closer, unique connection with certain individuals (e.g., 'significant others', close friends, family members). Forging personal, intimate ties with fellow human beings is central to our socioemotional, mental health, and physical well-being. These bonds help us to define our personal and social identities and enable us to develop a sense of belonging in the complex, dynamic world in which we live.

To foster interdependence and camaraderie, we need to have well developed **interpersonal communication skills**, that is, communication strategies and techniques that can enhance relationships and be improved through knowledge, practice, feedback, and reflection (Beebe *et al.* 2018; Wood 2016). Successful interpersonal communication requires that we have confidence in ourselves as well as the ability to listen and understand. Language, culture, and context play a central role in determining how our social relationships are formed and maintained.

An **interpersonal relationship** refers to the connection or affiliation between two or more people, which fulfills physical, social, or emotional needs. This association may vary in many ways, including duration and intensity. **Short-term relationships** consist of interpersonal connections that are very brief (e.g., lasting a few weeks or months), whereas **long-term relationships** are characterized by an intimate interpersonal affiliation that lasts for many years and perhaps throughout one's lifetime. Interpersonal relationships may be intense or rather distant. The connection between individuals may be based on common interests or concerns, love, physical or sexual attraction ('chemistry'), religious beliefs, work, politics, social commitment, or other factors. Interpersonal relationships may form in educational or family settings, work, clubs or organizations, neighborhoods, places of worship, or elsewhere. All of our interpersonal relationships are developed within the context of particular social, cultural, linguistic, political, and environmental influences.

Relational bonds, that is, the interpersonal connection between individuals, serve as the basis of social groups and society as a whole. These ties may be guided by tradition, law, or mutual agreement between individuals. As we grow and mature, and possibly move to other parts of the world either temporarily or permanently, some of our affiliations fluctuate from

Plate 8.1   The number of intercultural (interfaith, interracial, interethnic) friendships is on the rise in most parts of the world. © Jane Jackson.

time to time, that is, they differ in intensity and degree of intimacy. Some relationships endure while others come to an end for a variety of reasons (e.g., faded chemistry, conflict, infidelity, different life paths, etc.).

Intercultural intimate relationships refers to 'unions between people who come from different sociocultural backgrounds, in ethnic, racial, religious, national, or class terms' (Wilczek-Watson 2018: 1339). Compared with previous decades, **intercultural relationships** (e.g., friendships, dating, cohabitation, marriages involving people with a different cultural or religious background) have become much more commonplace and accepted in many parts of the world. Despite this, communication difficulties and other threats to these relationships still exist. Developing satisfactory intercultural bonds is believed by many to be more challenging than **intracultural relationships (**interpersonal bonds that form between individuals who share the same linguistic and cultural background) or **intraracial relationships** (interpersonal relationships between individuals from the same socially constructed racial group). Not all societies are receptive to intercultural relationships, especially when they are of an intimate or romantic nature. Negative reactions can certainly hamper or even prohibit intercultural unions. In addition to individual characteristics and skills, societal norms and attitudes can play a significant role in determining whether intercultural connections flourish or falter.

CROSSING BOUNDARIES IN INTERCULTURAL RELATIONSHIPS

Intercultural relationships can take many forms and cross one or more socially and historically constructed boundary (e.g., class, race, language, religion). People may develop affiliations with individuals from different ethnic, linguistic, national, racial, and religious backgrounds or form bonds with those who differ in terms of such dimensions as age, ability (e.g., linguistic, physical, mental), gender, social class, and sexual orientation. The following section briefly describes various types of intercultural relationships and provides examples of each.

Interracial relationships

As noted in previous chapters, '**race**' is a culturally and historically transmitted concept. Orbe and Harris (2015: 9) define it as 'a largely social- yet powerful- construction of human difference that has been used to classify human beings into separate value-based categories'. As Goodman *et al.* (2012: 251) observe, '[a]mong humans there are no races except the human race'. Notions of race form the basis of racism and many interculturalists reject the use of the term. Nonetheless, perceptions and attitudes toward 'race' *can* still impact intercultural communication, and the formation of interracial relationships remains a sensitive issue in many parts of the world (Goodman *et al.* 2012; Orbe & Harris 2015).

Interracial communication refers to 'interactions between two individuals in a situational context where racial difference is a salient issue' (Orbe & Harris 2008: 268). The bond between individuals who are affiliated with a different race is referred to as an **interracial relationship**. An example would be a romance between a woman who is racially identified as Vietnamese and a man who is **biracial**, that is, he has both Hispanic and African roots. A friendship between a Black man and a White South African male would be another example. If an Australian Aborigine forms a romantic attachment with a White Australian, this, too, may be referred to as an interracial relationship.

Attitudes toward the crossing of racial boundaries have changed significantly in much of the world, due in large part to anti-racist/social justice education and legislation (Amico 2016; Plummer 2019). Despite this, as discussed in Chapter 6, racism persists and there are members of society who still view interracial relationships with suspicion, fear, and disdain. In some situations, people may tolerate **interracial friendships** (relationships between friends who are affiliated with a different race) but object to more intimate, romantic ties (e.g., dating, marriage).

Interethnic intercultural relationships

Different from race, **ethnicity** is defined by Orbe and Harris (2015: 327) as 'a cultural marker that indicates shared traditions, heritage, and ancestral origins'. An individual may be considered racially Asian but Japanese in terms of ethnicity. An African American from Puerto Rico may be regarded as Black in terms of race but be ethnically Hispanic.

The bond between individuals affiliated with different ethnic groups is referred to as an **interethnic relationship**. Friendship between a French Canadian and a Canadian with Irish-Scottish heritage or a romance between a Malaysian Singaporean and a Chinese Singaporean would be deemed interethnic. In both examples, the interethnic relationships are between individuals from the same racial group. Interethnic relationships may also develop between people who are categorized as belonging to differing races and ethnicities. For example, a friendship between an Indian Singaporean and a Chinese Singaporean, or a romance between a Latino American woman and an African American man, cross both ethnic and racial boundaries.

International intercultural relationships

Social ties that develop between individuals who are citizens of different countries may be defined as **international relationships**. On a university campus in Denmark, friendship between a Kenyan international exchange student and a Danish business major would be considered an international intercultural relationship. A romance that develops between a Syrian refugee and a Turkish citizen would also be an international union. Many relationships of this nature are interethnic, interracial, and, possibly, interreligious. In other words, international relationships often cross more than one social boundary.

Interfaith (interreligious) relationships

Increasingly, intercultural bonds between people involve multiple religions. **Interfaith (interreligious) relationships** consist of interpersonal connections between individuals or groups who are affiliated with a different religion such as ties between Buddhists, Christians, Hindus, Muslims, Jews, or other faiths (or nonbelievers). **Interfaith** or **interreligious friendship** is characterized as an interpersonal relationship or friendship bond between individuals who have a different religion.

The attitudes toward interreligious unions are viewed differently in different parts of the world, depending, in part, on the nature of the relationship (e.g., friendship, romance, marriage), the particular gender and religions involved, and the sociocultural, historical context (Cheetham *et al.* 2013; Goshen-Gottstein with Murray 2015). Further, within the same environment, perceptions of interfaith friendships and marriage may vary, especially among individuals from different generations.

A **pluralistic society** is comprised of people from numerous cultural and ethnic backgrounds, and cultural diversity among citizens is acknowledged and encouraged. In a **religious pluralistic society**, many different religious beliefs, concepts, and ideologies coexist. In such environments, individuals from different religious backgrounds may become friends or marry and live together in harmony. In contrast, contexts with strong social or religious sanctions or laws may discourage or even ban interfaith marriage.

Social class differences in intercultural relationships

Multiculturalism, globalization, immigration, the spread of democracy, ease of travel, and the internet are creating more possibilities for relationships to form between individuals who have a different social background and status. **Social class** refers to 'a social grouping of people based on common economic and other characteristics determined by society and reflecting a social hierarchy' (Goodman *et al.* 2012: 252). In different geographical locations at specific times in human history, individuals or groups have been divided into social classes that have been accorded different degrees of power, prestige, and influence. In industrial Britain, for example, people were recognized as belonging to one of the following classes: the upper class, middle class, working class, or under class (impoverished). In India, the Hindu caste system, a hereditary division of labor and status ascribed at birth, long dictated the kind of life people could lead. Those who were classified as 'untouchables' or 'Dalits' were at the bottom of the caste system and not allowed to freely associate with people from other castes. While this system is prohibited in modern, democratic India and the rigid class system that dictated everyday life in industrial Britain is no longer in force, differences in social classes and discrimination persist.

All over the world, groups of people are still distinguished by inequalities in such areas as authority, economic resources, power, education, working and living conditions, lifespan, religion, and culture. **Social markers** or indicators of class are still present and evolving. These context-depended markers may include one's cultural background, accent, proficiency in another language (bilingualism, fluency in an international, prestigious language), wealth and income (e.g., 'new' vs. 'old' money), material possessions (e.g., a fancy car, a large house), level and source of education, the prestige of one's occupation, racial or ethnic origin, the reputation of one's neighborhood, and so on (Block 2014; Holmes & Wilson 2017).

In many countries, it has become easier for relationships to form between individuals from different social classes; however, negative perceptions of these unions persist and can hamper their development. **Classism**, prejudice or discrimination on the basis of social class, encompasses individual attitudes and behaviors as well as policies and practices that privilege one class over another. Unfortunately, in many regions, **social class prejudice** still exists, that is, people harbor negative personal attitudes toward individuals of another class. As explained in Chapter 6, prejudice remains a powerful barrier to the formation of interpersonal relationships between individuals who display different social markers (e.g., accent, speech style) and have a different class culture and status.

Language differences in intercultural relationships

Language plays a significant role in the formation and maintenance of our intercultural relationships, whether our communication is primarily face to face, on the phone, or online (e.g., email, FaceTime, text messaging). In interpersonal situations, whether we realize it or not, our speech and nonverbal behaviors can convey information about our social status, personality, temperament, group affiliations, and so on. Our communication partners continuously form impressions of us based, in part, on our language use. As we speak, they are deciding how to respond or proceed (e.g., whether to share personal information, get to know us better, or discontinue the interaction, etc.). Our language and communication skills (both verbal and nonverbal) influence the quality and longevity of our interpersonal relationships, whether intracultural or intercultural.

In conversations, our speech can build and demonstrate solidarity with our communication partners, or it can lead to miscommunication, conflict, and separation. As discussed in Chapters 3 and 5, the **communication accommodation theory (CAT)** posits that individuals may adjust their language use or patterns (e.g., choice of accents or dialects, style of communication) to bring them closer to or further apart from their interlocutors (Giles *et al.* 2012). **Convergence** refers to the ways in which individuals adapt their communicative behaviors in order to reduce social differences between themselves and their conversation partners and facilitate relationship building. Individuals who become very close friends may even develop their own way of talking with each other that is unique to them. In contrast, **divergence** refers to the distancing of oneself from one's interlocutors by accentuating differences in one's speech (e.g., accent, communication style) or nonverbal behaviors (e.g., gestures, personal distance). Whether deliberate or not, acts of divergence have the potential to hamper the development of interpersonal relationships.

Nowadays, alliances frequently form between people who speak a different first language or dialect. In many parts of the world, English is the **lingua franca**, that is, the medium of communication between people who do not have the same first language. English is the most dominant language of international communication in both face-to-face interactions and online (Jenkins 2013, 2015).

When people from different linguistic and cultural backgrounds interact, the language that is used can be a powerful advantage for the most proficient speaker. For example, a native speaker of English who is communicating in the language with a less proficient speaker is privileged in this situation. The use of a second language in intercultural relationships also increases the likelihood of miscommunication, an issue that resurfaces when we discuss barriers to intercultural friendships and romance.

Age differences in intercultural relationships

Outside one's family circle, children tend to form close interpersonal bonds with peers, that is, those who are near in age, education, and social class since they spend much of their time together during their schooling. When people enter the workforce and gain more exposure to other social circles, either in face-to-face situations or online, friendships or romances may form with individuals who are from a different generation.

Attitudes toward age gaps in interpersonal relationships vary in different sociocultural contexts. The degree of acceptance or non-acceptance of the age difference may depend on the nature of the bond (e.g., friendship, romance) and the gender(s) involved, as well as many other dimensions (e.g., social, cultural, economic, political, historical).

In North America, it is not uncommon for wealthy older men to form intimate relationships (including marital unions) with considerably younger women. These so-called 'May-December' unions are generally accepted as normal; however, when older women form romantic attachments with younger men, they may be referred to as 'cougars', with their male partners dismissed as mere 'boy toys'. Among some elements of society, a double standard still exists. In Asia, as well as in Western nations, older, White males may marry considerably younger Asian women; however, it is less common for young White males to marry older Asian women. Societal norms and attitudes toward these age gaps are influenced by prevalent values and beliefs, which are conveyed by society, the mass media (e.g., television, films, the press), and social media (e.g., Facebook, Twitter).

Ability differences in intercultural relationships

The way society views people with disabilities (e.g., physical handicaps, cognitive impairment, mental illness) influences the interpersonal relationships that disabled individuals form with members of the community who are not disabled. Although the United Nations Convention on the Rights of Persons with Disabilities (United Nations – Disability n.d.) is bringing about positive changes in many countries, disability rights movements are at different stages across the globe. In some contexts, formal education emphasizes the acceptance of people who are disabled, and laws safeguard their rights, whereas in other cultures, the disabled are shunned and rarely seen in public.

Inclusiveness is defined by Orbe and Harris (2015) as 'general acceptance and appreciation of differences' within a community or society. **Social inclusion** refers to the act of giving all people in society an opportunity to participate irrespective of their background or characteristics (e.g., mental or physical disability, race, language, culture, gender, age, social status, etc.). **Social exclusion** refers to the opposite behavior (e.g., barring individuals or groups from participating in mainstream communal activities, strongly discouraging or preventing one's ingroup members from forming relationships with people who are disabled or from a different social class, religions, ethnicity, etc.).

Although the situation is improving in much of the world, segregation is still limiting interactions between disabled and able-bodied individuals. In some environments, people who are physically different or intellectually challenged are eyed with great suspicion. Considered a curse on the family or community, disabled individuals may be abandoned or kept hidden from the rest of society. Medical personnel may discourage parents from keeping babies with birth abnormalities and recommend that they be placed in a residential institution for the disabled.

In many countries, children with disabilities have no access to formal education or have limited opportunity to pursue higher education due to inadequate access and resources for the disabled and prejudicial attitudes. Cultural stigmas can significantly curtail opportunities for the development of interpersonal bonds between disabled people and other members of society (World Health Organization n.d).

In much of the world, attitudes toward physical disabilities differ from that of intellectual impairment or mental illness. Negative societal attitudes can make it particularly difficult for those with known mental illness (e.g., bipolarism, schizophrenia) or disability (e.g., autism, developmentally delayed) to develop relationships with other people. Prejudicial attitudes also make it more difficult for individuals with mental illness to seek professional help (Watson *et al.* 2012). In some societies, pejorative terms are still used to label individuals with mental or physical abilities, and they may be ostracized or excluded from mainstream society, which then limits opportunities for the formation of intercultural ties. (Chapter 6 discusses discrimination against people with disabilities.)

Gender differences in intercultural relationships

Gender can also play a role in intercultural relationships. Communication between boys and girls and men and women has been the subject of research for many decades (e.g., Fixmer-Oraiz & Wood 2019; Shi & Langman 2012; Tannen 2001). As noted in Chapters 3 and 5, differences in language patterns and use (e.g., word choice, communication style), self-identities, expectations, roles and responsibilities, privileges and constraints, status, power, and positioning can influence interpersonal alliances that form between men and women in a particular cultural context. Relationships between males and females in intra-cultural relationships are complicated and in intercultural or interracial unions. Partners who have been socialized in different linguistic and cultural environments may have divergent ideas about the roles, rights, and responsibilities of males and females (Fixmer-Oraiz & Wood 2019; Vela-McConnell 2011).

Sexual orientation and intercultural relationships

Intercultural relationships may also form between individuals who have a different sexual orientation. According to the American Psychiatric Association (2018),

> **Sexual orientation** refers to an enduring pattern of emotional, romantic and/or sexual attractions to men, women or both sexes. Sexual orientation also refers to a person's sense of identity based on those attractions, related behaviors and membership in a community of others who share those attractions . . . sexual orientation is usually discussed in terms of three categories: **heterosexual** (having emotional, romantic or sexual attractions

to members of the other sex), **gay/lesbian** (having emotional, romantic or sexual attractions to members of one's own sex) and **bisexual** (having emotional, romantic or sexual attractions to both men and women).

(*Bolding added to the original.)

Understandings of sexual orientation are shaped within particular cultural contexts and may be influenced by religious doctrine. Some groups, for example, maintain that sexual orientation is a matter of choice and can be changed (e.g., through sexual orientation conversion therapy, personal will); however, it is more widely accepted in academia and the medical community that sexual orientation is innate and develops as children mature. 'Individuals may become aware at different points in their lives that they are heterosexual, gay, lesbian, or bisexual'. (www.psychiatry.org/mental-health/people/lgbt-sexual-orientation)

Attitudes toward sexuality and sexual orientation are shaped within one's culture. Prevailing norms and perceptions can significantly affect the willingness to develop an interpersonal relationship with individuals who have a sexual orientation that differs from the majority. For example, if homosexuality is deemed socially unacceptable or even legally banned, gays are forced to hide their sexual orientation or risk harm. In hostile situations like this, it is very difficult or even impossible for individuals who are openly gay to form relationships with heterosexuals. Conversely, in inclusive societies heterosexual-homosexual friendships are more commonplace and widely accepted.

Multifaceted intercultural relationships

Intercultural relationships often involve multiple cultural differences and the crossing of more than one socially and historically constructed boundary (e.g., age, social class, language, ethnicity, nationality, race, region, religion, sexual orientation, etc.). In England, for example, a wealthy, middle-aged Muslim businessman from Pakistan may meet and develop a romantic relationship with an ethnic Chinese immigrant, a 30-year-old Christian woman from a lower middle-class family in Malaysia. As their relationship evolves through English, their lingua franca, at times, they may need to negotiate a language barrier as well as cultural differences in gender roles and expectations, communication styles, values, religious beliefs, and practices. If their romance becomes serious (e.g., they contemplate cohabitation or marriage), they would also likely need to deal with external pressures including the attitudes of their family members, friends, religious leaders (imam or minister), and the larger society toward such a union.

BENEFITS OF INTERCULTURAL RELATIONSHIPS

Developing connections with individuals who are different from oneself in terms of age, language, gender, ethnicity, race, ability, sexual orientation, religion, social class, and nationality can enrich one's life in multiple and often unexpected ways. Potential benefits include, but are not limited to, heightened self-awareness, more understanding of other ways of being, the breaking down of stereotypes, more sensitivity toward identity issues, the acquisition of new skills and pursuits, the refinement of one's intercultural communication skills, and more appreciation of diversity.

Heightened self-awareness

When you develop a relationship with someone from another cultural, linguistic, or religious background, you are apt to encounter different values, communication styles, cultural scripts, traditions, languages/dialects, or other ways of being. This can spur critical thinking about the messages you received from your **ingroup** (members of your culture) about **outgroups** (e.g., people who have a different religion, sexual orientation from your ingroup). Intercultural relationships can raise awareness of the many ways in which the socialization process has shaped your life (e.g., attitudes, values, beliefs) and self-identities. It can also enhance your awareness of your language use and communication style (verbal and nonverbal) and help you to identify aspects about yourself that are unique to you.

Sustained intercultural contact can prompt you to think more deeply about many aspects of your life (e.g., cultural heritage, language use, beliefs, daily rituals, etc.). While linguistic and cultural differences can be a source of irritation, they can also lead to heightened awareness of your attitudes, identities, and habits *if* you cultivate a **reflective mindset**, that is, the ability to revisit and make meaning from your experience. Critically reflecting on your intercultural interactions can raise awareness of how your habitual ways of thinking and behaving may be affecting your relationships.

Intercultural relationships can help you to recognize unique elements of your own culture and language. When questions are raised about your habitual ways of doing and saying things, you may find it difficult to explain communication styles, traditions, beliefs, and daily actions that you have long assumed were commonplace. You may be stumped by questions about the grammar, vocabulary, idiomatic expressions, and other features of the language you learned as a child. This can motivate you to seek more knowledge about your own culture, language, religion, education, personal history, and heritage, which can be a very positive outcome of intercultural relationships.

More understanding of different ways of being

When you develop a personal connection with someone who has a different linguistic and cultural background you are apt to gain exposure to some ways of thinking, acting, and communicating that are new to you. With some effort, you can deepen your knowledge and understanding of other ways of being (e.g., worldviews, values, beliefs, daily practices, linguistic expressions, communication styles). Over time, you may develop a deeper grasp of what it means to speak another language and be affiliated with other groups (e.g., linguistic, religious, ethnic, etc.).

The breaking down of stereotypes

Positive firsthand experience with individuals who have a different cultural, religious, or language background can challenge preconceived notions or stereotypes about the group(s) they are associated with. This is not always the case, however. Some people who develop intercultural relationships retain entrenched stereotypes and simply view their new friends or romantic partners as exceptions. In contrast, if you cultivate an open mindset, negative images and misperceptions are likely to dissipate as you gain a deeper understanding of differing practices and beliefs. Even if you disagree with certain cultural elements, making an effort to understand another perspective can enhance intercultural communication.

Intercultural relationships may compel you to critically reflect on how your home environment and personal experiences have influenced your perceptions and attitudes toward people who are different. Firsthand intercultural experience coupled with critical reflection can help you to break down stereotypes and become a more open, flexible intercultural communicator.

More sensitivity toward identity issues

Through sustained intercultural interactions, you can learn more about yourself and facets of your identity. If you are observant and employ active listening skills, you may also uncover clues about the preferred self-identities of your communication partners. A deeper understanding of how your intercultural friends or romantic partners regard themselves and their place in the world can help you to be a more sensitive, responsive intercultural communicator.

The acquisition of new skills and pursuits

Intercultural relationships can introduce you to clubs, organizations, and activities that might otherwise be unknown to you. Exposure to situations and practices that are unfamiliar to you offers the opportunity to acquire a new hobby or skills (e.g., Cajun cooking, cricket, sitar playing, mahjong, tai chi). Without your intercultural friends and/or romantic partners opening the door for you, you may miss out on these delights.

Hiroko, a Japanese international exchange student in Vienna, learned how to make mouth-watering apple strudel from her Austrian housemates. While working in Tokyo, Leo, an Australian English language teacher, discovered the art of karaoke singing when he became friends with some Japanese colleagues. Vincent, a university student in New Zealand, took

Plate 8.2   Intercultural friendships can expose you to new ideas and practices. A Cambodian chef is showing her Hong Kong friends how to make fresh spring rolls. © Jane Jackson

great pride in learning how to play the ruan, a traditional Chinese guitar, from Chen Peiyan, an immigrant from Xian, China, who had become a trusted friend.

Developing a relationship with someone from a different linguistic background also opens up the possibility of learning an additional language or dialect. The desire to deepen one's intercultural friendship or romance can be a powerful source of motivation for second language learning. For example, Elena, a Russian accountant, met and fell in love with Ahmed, a Jordanian law student, while doing an internship in the U.S. As their friendship blossomed into a romance, she became inspired to study Arabic, something she had never contemplated before. When she visited his family in Amman she was able to converse with his relatives. In some situations, like Elena's, new intercultural, international alliances can lead to the opportunity to get to know, and even visit or live in, another part of the world. Intercultural relationships can open your eyes to new worlds and vistas.

The refinement of intercultural communication skills

Interpersonal communication is the primary way in which humans build, nurture, and transform relationships. To create effective and meaningful interpersonal relationships, we need to develop **communication competence**, that is, 'the ability to achieve one's goals in a manner that is personally acceptable and, ideally, acceptable to others' (Adler *et al*. 2015: G-2). **Appropriate communication** refers to communication that enhances the relationship, while **effective communication** is associated with communication that achieves the desired results (Fantini 2019; Wiemann *et al*. 1997). Both dimensions can be improved through practice.

Developing interpersonal affiliations with people who have a different cultural background can also facilitate the enhancement of one's intercultural communication skills, which is vital in today's globalized world. Successful, meaningful relationships require effective interpersonal skills and when cultural differences are involved, it is imperative that we develop **intercultural communication competence**, a complex construct, which entails:

> impression management that allows members of different cultural systems to be aware of their cultural identity and cultural differences, and to interact effectively and appropriately with each other in diverse contexts by agreeing on the meaning of diverse symbol systems with the result of mutually satisfying relationships.
>
> (Kupka 2008: 16)

Through sustained intercultural interactions and reflection, you can learn to be sensitive to the preferred identities of others and discover how to mediate misunderstandings that naturally arise. Over time, as you hone your intercultural competence, you can become more 'Other-centered' ('partner-centered', 'audience-centered'), that is, aware of and sensitive to the needs and interests of your interlocutors. This, in turn, can help you to grow your interpersonal relationships.

If you are communicating in a second language with someone from another cultural background, it is vital to develop **intercultural communicative competence**, 'a complex of abilities needed to perform effectively and appropriately when interacting with others who are linguistically and culturally different from oneself' (Fantini & Tirmizi 2006: 12). Further, being able to communicate in multiple languages affords more possibilities for intercultural dialogue and friendship. (Chapter 11 explores intercultural [communicative] competence in more detail.)

Enhanced appreciation of diversity

With more exposure to people from different linguistic and cultural backgrounds and the cultivation of meaningful intercultural relationships whether in one's home environment or abroad, it is possible to acquire a deeper understanding and appreciation of diversity. This is significant as our world is becoming increasingly interconnected and multicultural. Accepting and embracing someone who is culturally and ethnically different from yourself sets a positive example for others (e.g., younger siblings, peers).

As you build intercultural relationships, develop more intercultural knowledge, and break down stereotypes, you can share your new understandings and attitudes with those around you. In this way, your more open mindset can have a positive impact on your friends, family, and colleagues who have not yet forged intercultural ties, perhaps due to fear or negative images of people who have a different cultural, linguistic, or religious background.

In contexts where intracultural ties are most prevalent, intercultural relationships can threaten 'the established and taken-for-granted order' of mainstream society and help move the society 'in the direction of increased egalitarianism' (Vela-McConnell 2011: 183). Individuals who dare to cross boundaries, whether in terms of language, race, sexual orientation, class, or other variables can inspire others to form similar unions. Gradually, relationships that were once seen as taboo may become accepted as normal.

INTERCULTURAL FRIENDSHIP AND DIVERSE SOCIAL NETWORKS

Increased migration, ease of travel, more ethnically diverse communities, and enhanced opportunities for computer-mediated communication (CMC) (e.g., Facebook, email, blogs, Myspace, Twitter, Internet relay chats, etc.) have made it more possible for intercultural friendships to form and this is leading to the diversification of social networks in one's home environment. Nowadays, both mobile and nonmobile individuals may enrich their lives through intercultural experience.

Intercultural friendship is a personal connection or affiliation forged between individuals who have a different cultural background. Increasingly, these interpersonal relationships entail the use of a second language (e.g., an international language or lingua franca) by one or more of the friendship partners (Jackson 2018c; Jenkins 2013). Rooted in anthropology, a **social network** refers to 'the multiple web of relationships an individual contracts in a society with other people who he or she is bound to directly or indirectly by ties of friendship, kinship or other social relationships' (Trudgill 2003: 121–2). Sociolinguist Miriam Meyerhoff (2010: 295) notes that in a social network 'not all members may know each other . . . and some members may know each other in a different capacity from others'. For example, a woman may form interpersonal relationships at work, have a different set of friends in her personal life, and yet another group of acquaintances in the sports club where she works out. Many of her contacts may never meet but they are still linked to each other by having a common friend. Their friends are also part of this woman's wider social network even if she does not interact with them. A **friendship network**, a type of social network, includes individuals who are very close personal friends, acquaintances (e.g., those who are more distant), and 'friends of friends'.

As more and more people are coming into contact with individuals who have a different background (e.g., cultural, linguistic, religious) or orientation (e.g., sexual), whether at home or abroad, researchers are beginning to take a closer look at the formation and quality of intercultural relationships. Questions such as the following are driving their studies: What factors facilitate or hinder the development of intercultural friendships and multicultural/multilingual social networks? How are the Internet, social media, and mass media affecting the development of intercultural alliances? What steps can be taken to nurture interpersonal relationships that cross linguistic and social boundaries? In what ways are diverse friendship alliances and networks impacting society?

As higher education campuses have become more diverse, researchers are paying more attention to the friendship patterns and social networks of local and international students (e.g., Green 2013; Mitchell *et al.* 2017). Many studies have found that study abroad students tend to maintain or develop friendship networks with individuals from their own country (**conationals** who speak the same first language) or individuals from other foreign countries (**multinationals**) (e.g., other international exchange students). While most express the desire to develop friendships with people from the host country (**host nationals**) prior to their sojourn, for a variety of reasons (e.g., culture shock, ethnocentrism, a language barrier, limited host receptivity, lack of intercultural competence, different understandings of friendship), many return home disappointed (Gareis 2012; Jackson 2018a).

In both domestic and international settings, researchers have also carried out investigations of intercultural and interracial friendships in the workplace (e.g., multinational firms) or community (e.g., expatriate or immigrant families and host nationals) (e.g., Chen & Nakazawa 2012). Their studies are deepening our awareness and understanding of potential barriers to successful intercultural relationships and the diversification of social networks. While individuals may face both internal and external challenges in forming and sustaining intercultural friendships, researchers also point to the numerous benefits of such unions (e.g., Marcoccia 2012; O'Dowd 2001, 2012, 2019). Additionally, contemporary investigations of diverse social networks are raising awareness of the most effective ways to nurture meaningful intercultural bonds.

Cultural perceptions of friendship

A life without a friend is a life without a sun.

(German proverb)

It is better to be in chains with friends than to be in a garden with strangers.

(Persian proverb)

Life without a friend is like death without a witness.

(Spanish proverb)

It is better in times of need to have a friend rather than money.

(Greek proverb)

Life without friends is not worth living.

(Turkish Proverb)

What do these proverbs from different lands have in common? All of them point to the pivotal role friends play in our lives irrespective of the language(s) we speak or our cultural background.

No matter where we reside in the world, friendship matters. It is through friendship that we gain much needed practical and socioemotional support and a sense of how we fit into society. Along with family relationships, friendship bonds help us to navigate the increasingly complex world in which we live. In situations where families are fragmented, close friendships can become even more crucial.

> Through friendship we gain practical and emotional support, and an important contribution to our personal identities. Friendship also helps to integrate us into the public realm and "act as a resource for managing some of the mundane and exceptional events" that confront us in our lives.
>
> (Allan 1989: 114)

Unlike relationships with family members or kinship bonds, friendship is more voluntary, although it is important to recognize that it is subject to the constraints of economic, political, linguistic, social, and cultural circumstances, and other factors (e.g., proximity or nearness). Within a particular cultural context, linguistic sanctions as well as social norms and expectations play a role in determining who we form friendships with and how.

To complicate matters, the meaning attached to the word 'friend' varies in different regions of the world. As noted by Badhwar (1993: 36), 'no account of friendship enjoys universal acceptance'. One's conception of what it means to be a 'friend' is culturally constructed and situated, and varies to some degree in different cultural contexts (Collier 2002; Jackson 2018c). In many cultures, specific linguistic terms or expressions are used to identify and distinguish between subcategories of friends.

> across all cultures and languages there is a word for a close relationship established outside the narrow family context. . . . We find indications that some languages, during some periods of their development, gave more emphasis to an objective or material reality, such as the importance of mutual help, in close relationships, whereas other languages stressed the affective union of friendship, referring to a subjective reality. . . . The scope of the connotations related to the words used for friendship seems to reflect the socio-historical circumstances under which the friendship was important. The horizon of these meanings includes family issues, ritual functions, mutual assistance, kindness, war comradeship, conflict solution, intimacy, and affection.
>
> (Krappman 1998: 24)

Since we live in a diverse, dynamic world, it is not surprising that differing understandings of friendship have formed in different regions. Even within the same sociocultural context, notions of friendship can differ among individuals due to such factors as age, class, religion, gender, and intercultural experience, among others (Adams *et al.* 2000, Chen & Nakazawa 2012).

In the United States, the term 'friend' can encompass casual acquaintances as well as lifelong, intimate companions (Gareis 2012). In this context, a **casual friend** or **acquaintance** refers to someone you have been introduced to but do not know very well. You might say hello when you meet and briefly engage in small talk (e.g., chat about the weather or an assignment) but not reveal many personal details about yourself. The connection with acquaintances tends to be friendly but rather superficial. In contrast, a **close friend** refers to someone you can rely on to provide emotional support and perhaps lend a hand when needed. As this relationship is more intimate, you are likely more willing to share very personal details about yourself (e.g., your family problems, love life) and engage in a much deeper level of conversation on a wider range of topics. Within this subcategory, U.S. Americans may also designate one or more individuals as their **best friends** to indicate that they are especially close to them.

In general, European Americans tend to have a large collection of 'friends' or acquaintances which changes over time and, in most cases, involves only very limited mutual obligations, if any. Although most are casual relationships, these individuals are often referred to as friends, which can confuse people who have divergent understandings of what friendship means (Gallois & Liu 2015). Collier (1996, 2002), for example, discovered that conceptions of friendship differed among ethnic groups in the U.S.: African Americans emphasize the importance of respect and acceptance, Latinos tend to value relational support, Asian Americans stress the positive sharing of ideas, and for European Americans, recognition of individual needs is paramount. Not surprisingly, these different understandings of friendships (e.g., expectations regarding obligations and trust) can cause misunderstandings and result in negative impressions.

In many cultural contexts, a clear distinction is made between friends and acquaintances. In China, the following proverb conveys the message that it is best to have a few close, lifelong friends rather than a large number of acquaintances who come and go: '*One's acquaintances may fill the world, but one's true friends can be but few*'. Another Chinese saying, '*Cooked at one stirring makes friends too easily*', underscores the need for adequate time and commitment to build up a genuine, long-lasting friendship. Researchers have found that friendship patterns among Chinese nationals are characterized by strong social bonds and obligations that develop over a long period of time. Li (2010: 15–16), for example, asserts that 'Chinese people make friends that tend to last longer, and each party expects full support of resources, time, and loyalty from the other instead of casual, short-term friendships'. In traditional Chinese culture, lifelong friends may be considered like family members.

In a review of cross-cultural studies of friendship, Cooper *et al.* (2007) identified a number of cultural variations in friendships, including: 'selection (who can be a friend), duration (how long the friendship lasts), the number of friends, the responsibilities and prerogatives of a friend, and how long a relationship exists before it can be considered a friendship' (p. 169). More research is needed to better understand the factors that impact notions of friendship (e.g., gender, culture, intercultural contact).

Language and intercultural cyber friendship

Technology and English, the primary lingua franca of the internet, are changing the nature of interpersonal communication in much of the world. West and Turner (2011b: 379) state that 'communication between and among individuals is forever changed because of technology. . . . The effects of technology on our interpersonal relationships are unprecedented, unpredictable, and unstoppable'. New communication technologies (e.g., the internet, email, iPads, smart phones) and social media (e.g., Facebook, Twitter, WeChat) are being introduced at a rapid pace. These innovations are expanding possibilities for the development and maintenance of both intracultural and intercultural relationships, especially among individuals who are able to converse in English or another international language.

Communication that is facilitated by computer technologies (e.g., the use of two or more networked computers) is referred to as **computer-mediated communication (CMC)**. Walther (1992: 52) defines it as 'synchronous or asynchronous electronic mail and computer conferencing, by which senders encode in text messages that are relayed from senders' computers as receivers'. In **synchronous communication** (e.g., Skype, chat rooms, Internet relay chat) all participants are online at the same time, whereas **asynchronous communication** (e.g., email) occurs with time constraints, that is, the receiver of an email message may not read it until several hours or days after it has been sent.

The rise of the internet has led to the development of a virtual community of **netizens**, that is, individuals who actively engage in online interactions. While English is the primary lingua franca in cyberspace, the speed and format of CMC is bringing about new language forms (e.g., abbreviations), symbols, and communication styles, which impact interpersonal relationships. To save time, netizens tend to communicate through **netspeak** (chatspeak or cyber-slang), 'an informal, concise and expressive style' (Marcoccia 2012). As CMC (email, chat rooms) is primarily text-based and dependent on verbal language, it has fewer nonverbal cues than in face-to-face interactions. To compensate for the lack of nonverbal information in text messages, graphic accents and symbols have become a regular feature in CMC (West & Turner 2011b). For example, emoticons (e.g., sad faces) and articons (e.g., pictures of objects) are frequently used to replace or enhance a verbal message.

In addition to email, the emergence of **social networking sites (SNSs)**, such as Facebook, Twitter, Myspace, and LinkedIn, is making it possible to initiate and maintain interpersonal relationships online, instead of relying solely on face-to-face communication or phone calls, as in years gone by. As long as they have access to the internet, people can now share personal information with friends and their wider social networks through Facebook, blogs, video chats, instant messaging, text messaging, FaceTime, and other media. Photos and video clips can be uploaded to one's Facebook account or circulated via email within a matter of minutes. Facebook allows us to 'friend' people we barely know. Skype, online video software, is now a widely used social tool that is connecting people around the world.

Intrigued by these innovations, researchers have been asking a number of key questions about the impact of the digital revolution on interpersonal communication and intercultural relations, such as: Are the internet and the proliferation of SNSs facilitating or hindering the formation of meaningful friendships and romantic connections between individuals from disparate linguistic and cultural backgrounds? How is the dominance of English in the internet affecting intercultural relations? In what ways does netspeak affect the interpersonal connections of netizens who have a different cultural background? What is the relationship between online interactions and face-to-face meetings within the context of intercultural friendship formation? Do they complement one another?

While researchers acknowledge that text-based CMC differs from face-to-face interaction, they disagree about its impact on interpersonal and intercultural relationships. Proponents maintain that the internet increases the possibility of contact between people from diverse backgrounds:

> The ability to reach so many different people from so many different places so quickly gives communication a new sense of power. Wherever we live, we can use the Internet to help bring diversity and new cultures into our lives, changing our social, political, and business lives.

> (Gamble & Gamble 2013: 37)

Individuals can now become acquainted with each other online without revealing many personal details (e.g., their ethnicity, first language, race, religion, nationality, etc.). Marcoccia (2012: 358) explain that 'some aspects of people's identity such as their ethnic group, gender, social class and accent are hidden in the text-based environment of Internet-mediated communication'. Netizens can freely express their views without revealing their real names and embarrassing themselves or their families. Advocates of internet-mediated communication maintain that this is a positive feature as it enhances free speech and reduces the negative impact of stereotypes and personal biases. They argue that people who might never have the opportunity to meet face to face can cross social and cultural boundaries (e.g., age, language, race, religion, sexual orientation) and form relationships online, which in turn can break down barriers and lead to enhanced intercultural understanding.

Critics, however, maintain that the use of technology does not necessarily lead to effective communication or the development of meaningful intercultural relationships. People may misrepresent themselves (e.g., lie about who they are) and, even if they are fully honest about their identities and what they stand for, the absence of personal information can limit the formation of meaningful intercultural friendships (Zimbler & Feldman 2011).

Compared with face-to-face interactions, emails, online discussion forums, and Internet relay chats (and many other internet tools) are characterized by fewer social cues (e.g., nonverbal signals, sociopragmatic information), and this can make it challenging to clearly convey one's ideas and emotions. Messages may not be interpreted as intended, especially when individuals from diverse linguistic and cultural backgrounds are interacting online in a second language.

While 'the informal and friendly style which characterizes much of the interaction on the internet' is familiar to people who have been socialized in the U.S. and other 'individualistic nations', O'Dowd (2001) contends that it can be confusing and unsettling for netizens who are used to a greater power distance and more formal discourse between people do not know each other well. Even if second language speakers of English have studied the language in school for many years, informal discourse and colloquialisms may be baffling at times and lead to miscommunication.

> Internet-mediated global English is the lingua franca of the internet. It is an opportunity for intercultural dialogue but also an obstacle in the sense that this 'cyberlingua franca' is not necessarily suited to any specific culture. CMC has a reduced social dimension. This characteristic aids intercultural communication because it reduces cultural differences, but, at the same time, it is an obstacle to intercultural communication because it increases misunderstandings or aggressiveness.
>
> (Marcoccia 2012: 366)

Much more research is needed to determine the potential of CMC and SNSs for the formation and maintenance of intercultural friendships, especially as new communication tools become available. While the internet, in theory, can reduce the perceived distance between individuals from different linguistic and cultural backgrounds, intercultural interactions can also be rife with misunderstandings. The dominance of English and American values may be barriers to the formation of equitable intercultural friendships in cyberspace.

Building intercultural friendships and social networks

Recent studies of intercultural friendship and social networks have identified a number of internal and external factors that facilitate the formation and maintenance of friendship bonds between individuals who are culturally different, including those who do not speak the same first language. While most investigations have focused on face-to-face interactions, in the past decade more attention is being paid to **cyber friendships** (e.g., email relationships) and ties formed through online social networking sites (SNS) (e.g., Facebook, Myspace, Skype). This is enriching our understanding of the nature, complexity, and variability of intercultural friendships.

A review of recent research on intercultural friendship reveals that multiple elements can impact the potential for these interpersonal relationships, including proximity, social networks, similarity-attraction, personality, willingness to communicate (WTC), empathy, identity recognition and validation, uncertainty reduction/anxiety management, disclosure and relational intimacy, shared identity and relational maintenance, intercultural communication competence, and social acceptance. Let's take a look at each of these variables.

Proximity

All intercultural relationships are affected by the affordances and constraints in one's environment. To develop intercultural friendships we first need to have the opportunity to come into close contact with people from different linguistic and cultural backgrounds. If you study, live, or work in a multicultural, multilingual environment, you are better positioned to initiate and develop intercultural friendships than if you are a member of the majority culture and live in a society which is much less diverse. In an environment where many people from different linguistic and cultural backgrounds intermingle in all aspects of life, it is easier to form intercultural relationships in both formal settings (e.g., at school, at work, in a place of worship) and informal situations (e.g., at a health club or social organization). Hence, proximity or nearness plays a role in the formation of intercultural alliances.

With an increase in CMC and SNSs (e.g., Facebook) it is becoming more possible to make connections with people who come from a different background (e.g., language, social class, race, culture). Marcoccia (2012: 353) asserts that the internet offers its users 'an unprecedented level of contact with people from other cultural and social groups'. As the internet reaches across national borders, proponents argue that it affords us more possibilities to develop intercultural ties, especially if we can communicate in an international language. 'By enabling us to join a wide range of online communities and interact with people who hold different worldviews, the internet enhances our ability to communicate within and across cultural boundaries' (Gamble & Gamble 2013: 40). For this to happen, at minimum, one needs to have access to this technology and proficiency in an international language. As discussed in Chapter 1, the disparity between rich and poor nations means that there is unequal access to the Internet, SNSs, and international language education. Not everyone has the opportunity to develop intercultural relationships online.

Social networks

The degree of diversity in one's social networks also influences one's opportunity to meet and interact with diverse individuals. If some of our family members, friends (acquaintances, close friends), or 'friends of friends' already have intercultural or interracial friendships, we are more likely to develop interpersonal relationships with people who are linguistically, racially, and culturally different (Vela-McConnell 2011). We are more likely to view these relationships as 'normal'.

Similarity-Attraction

The **Similarity-Attraction Hypothesis** posits that we are drawn to people we perceive to be similar to us (e.g., those who share our first language, race, ethnicity, beliefs, values, religion, worldview, group affiliations, etc.) (Adler *et al.* 2015; Byrne 1969). While there are naturally multiple differences in individuals who form intercultural friendships, there are also many similarities. In intercultural interactions, research suggests that we are attracted to what we have in common (e.g., similar personal characteristics, interests, values, experiences, life goals, etc.) (Osbeck *et al.* 1997; Vela-McConnell 2011).

In intercultural relationships, Chen (2002: 244) observes that '[g]reater perceived similarity facilitates a communicative relationship; interactions, once started, may lead to perception of greater similarity or convergence of partners' behavior, or both'. In a study of Japanese and U.S. American students, for example, Kito (2005) also found that individuals in both groups were attracted to their intercultural friends due to perceived similarity (e.g., shared interests, values, etc.). Let's look at some other examples that illustrate this theory.

While in Vancouver for a yearlong international exchange program, Irena, an avid tennis player from Mosco, was attracted to Parnchand, a Thai student who shared her love of the game as well as her passion for saving the environment. By the end of their sojourn they had spent a lot of time together and had become close friends. Juanita, a Brazilian exchange student, discovered that she and Amena, a Bahraini medical student were both interested in nature photography and this led to a meaningful friendship. Linguistic and cultural differences became less important as their connection deepened.

Personality

Intercultural friendship formation has also been linked to certain personality traits (e.g., extroversion, desire to help others, open-mindedness) (Gareis 2012; Peng 2011). In some studies, an extroverted personality has been found to enhance the likelihood of an individual to reach across social boundaries to initiate relationships with individuals from different backgrounds (Ying 2002).

While similarities in personality can facilitate the formation of friendships, differing personality traits may also work well if they complement one another, as in the following example. Nuran, an Egyptian American physiotherapist did not come from the same cultural or linguistic background as Meedy, an Indonesian doctor, but their religious affiliation brought them together. As their relationship grew they discovered that their temperaments made them very compatible. Nuran was outgoing and talkative, whereas her Indonesian friend was quiet and reserved. Meedy was happy to let Nuran take the lead. In this intercultural friendship, shared interests and beliefs drew them together and their different personalities complimented each other.

Willingness to communicate (WTC)

Another personality trait that is linked to interpersonal communication and intercultural friendship is **willingness to communicate (WTC)**. In first language contexts, McCrosky and Richmond (1987) characterize WTC as an individual's general personality orientation toward talking. Associated with 'a fairly stable personality trait', WTC is believed to develop as we mature, bringing about a 'global, personality-based orientation toward talking' (MacIntyre *et al.* 2003: 591). In second language interactions, the degree of fluency and confidence in one's second language ability influence the willingness to speak. Within the context of language learning, MacIntyre *et al.* (1998: 547) define WTC as an individual's 'readiness to enter into discourse at a particular time with a specific person or persons, using a L2'. **Language anxiety** (degree of nervousness when using the second language) and WTC affect an individual's desire to initiate and sustain intercultural friendships in a second language.

Empathy

Several studies of intercultural friendships have revealed that **empathy**, the ability to understand another person's feelings and point of view (Broome 2018; Cornes 2004), plays a vital role in determining the quality and longevity of both intracultural and intercultural friendships. Broome (2018) explains that 'intercultural empathy is created during interaction, and it emerges as we listen to one another respectively and engage in the process of exploring and learning together' (p. 1288). The ability to empathize with the perspective of someone from another cultural background is a key ingredient in successful intercultural relationships.

Identity recognition and validation

Understanding the personal meaning of one's self-identities and recognizing the preferred identities of one's communication partners are crucial elements in the formation of mutually satisfying intercultural friendships. Respecting the preferred self-identities of one's communication partners plays an important role in the development of trust in intercultural friendships (Ting-Toomey 2018). This, in turn, influences one's willingness to share personal information and spend time together.

Uncertainty reduction/anxiety management

One's ability to predict and explain behavior, especially in initial interactions, can lessen anxiety and influence the formation and quality of intercultural friendships. The **uncertainty reduction theory (URT)** posits that when individuals are anxious when communicating with people who are not affiliated with their ingroups (e.g., individuals who differ from them in terms of 'culture, ethnicity, gender, age, disability, social class, or other group memberships'), their apprehension hampers the development of constructive intercultural relations (Gudykunst 2004: 3). Accordingly, the greater our ability to predict and explain our communication partners' behavior, the greater the chance that our relationships will become more intimate (e.g., progress from stranger or acquaintance to close friend) (Berger & Calabrese 1975). As we become more familiar with our communication partners, we can develop more understanding of their communication style, values, and beliefs. This can then enhance our ability to predict their behavior and thereby lessen our communication anxiety.

The URT is linked to the **anxiety/uncertainty management (AUM) theory**, which suggests that increased knowledge and understanding of our communication partner reduces our level of stress or anxiety. As our sense of apprehension or fear diminishes, we can become more receptive to forming relationships with people who are different from us (Gao 2015; Gudykunst 2004; Plummer 2019).

Disclosure and relational intimacy

Researchers have also identified a linkage between self-disclosure and friendship development. **Self-disclosure** refers to the process of intentionally revealing details about oneself that are important and tend not to normally be known by others (Adler *et al.* 2015). Altman and Taylor's (1973) **social penetration theory (SPT)** suggests that as self-disclosure increases in depth (degree of intimacy on a particular topic), amount, and breadth (the number of topics about which one self-discloses to one's communication partner), our relationships become more intimate. While this theory assumes that self-disclosure leads to the development of positive impressions, cross-cultural studies have identified cultural variations in the topics, timing, amount of self-disclosure, and degree of relational intimacy in interpersonal relationships (e.g., Chen 2010, 2012). In a study of intercultural friendships, Chen and Nakazawa (2012: 146) discovered 'a complex interplay among cultural backgrounds, friendship types, and degrees of friendship in influencing patterns of self-disclosure'.

Linked to disclosure, is the notion of **relational intimacy**, which refers to 'the closeness one feels and/or enacts towards one's friend' (Chen & Nakazawa 2009: 83). In a survey of 252 ethnically diverse university students, Chen and Nakazawa (2012) discovered that cultural dissimilarities in disclosure had the most impact in the early stages of the relationship. In an earlier study, they found that, in general, as relationships grew, 'self-disclosure exchanges progressed from public-outer areas of the selves to all public, immediate, and private areas of the selves' (Chen & Nakazawa 2009: 93). The researchers concluded that 'communication in close intercultural friendship may not be as personalistic as that in close intracultural friendship and may be more complex' (Chen & Nakazawa 2012: 147).

Shared identity and relational maintenance

The formation and maintenance of successful intercultural relationships depends, in part, on the interpersonal communication skills of the interlocutors and their ability to establish a genuine connection with each other. Over time, as they get to know each other better, they may develop a **relational identity**, 'a privately transacted system of understandings that coordinates attitudes, actions, and identities of participants in a relationship' (Lee 2006: 6). The process of working together to develop a shared sense of identity in a relationship is referred to as **mutual facework** (Ting-Toomey 2015b, 2018). (See Chapter 9 for a more detailed discussion of face and facework in relation to conflict situations.)

As noted by Lee (2008), 'a key to maintaining an intercultural friendship lies in effective communication between members (p. 52). To develop and keep intercultural relationships working well, it is important for interlocutors to be attentive to their partners and use communication strategies that are appropriate to the situation and context. **Relational maintenance** requires the ability to read one's partner (e.g., recognize when he or she needs more personal space and privacy, or more support and closeness) (Adler *et al.* 2015). Individuals who are more skilled at reading their intercultural partners are better positioned to respond appropriately (e.g., provide reassurance when their partner is under stress, offer encouragement when their partner is worried or appears to lack self-confidence).

Intercultural communication competence

People have varying degrees of intercultural competence. Those who are interculturally sensitive and possess well developed intercultural communication skills are apt to be less fearful of interacting across social boundaries and more strongly motivated to establish friendships with people who differ from them in terms of first language, gender, ethnicity, religion, etc. Individuals who possess a high level of intercultural sensitivity and intercultural competence are also better positioned to nurture intercultural relationships and deal with misunderstandings that arise. Chen (1992) maintains that an individual's degree of 'other-orientation, sensitivity, and the ability to provide positive feelings predict success in initiating and managing intercultural friendships'.

The development and maintenance of intercultural friendship ties depends on effective communication. When interacting in a second language, fluency in the language *and* intercultural competence can greatly facilitate the formation of intercultural bonds. Individuals who are confident, fluent speakers of a second language are better positioned to use their second language to initiate interactions with potential intercultural friends than those who are excessively worried about making grammatical mistakes or saying the wrong word. This is linked to the notion of willingness to communicate (WTC) that was discussed earlier.

Social acceptance

Intercultural relationships do not form in a vacuum. Our perceptions of intercultural unions are shaped within our particular sociohistorical, political, and linguistic context. When we cross boundaries we are impacted to varying degrees by the beliefs and attitudes that are prevalent in our environment (e.g., the perceptions of our family members, community, religious figures, the mass media) and the degree of openness toward friendships and romance between people from different backgrounds. The attitudes toward intercultural relationships in one's social networks and community can affect our willingness to initiate interactions with people who are culturally different. In environments where anti-racist, multicultural education is a regular feature in classrooms and diverse social networks are commonplace, the atmosphere is likely to be much more conducive to the formation of intercultural friendships.

Barriers to intercultural friendships

Many scholars maintain that intercultural friendships are more difficult to initiate and sustain than intracultural relationships, that is, ties between individuals who share the same linguistic and cultural background. Chen and Nakazawa (2009: 77), for example, state that '[i]ntercultural and interracial relationships face barriers, tensions, and challenges that are absent from intracultural and intraracial relationships'. Researchers have identified a number of internal and external factors that can hamper the development of satisfying intercultural friendships (limited contact opportunities; differing motives; unmet expectations; anxiety and uncertainty; differences in communication styles; differing values, worldviews, and perceptions; stereotyping, prejudice, and discrimination; language barrier; miscommunication). Let's examine each in turn.

Limited contact opportunities

As noted in the previous section, demographic variables play an important role in the formation of intercultural friendships. For example, individuals from the majority culture who live in an area where there are few people with a different linguistic or cultural background (e.g., ethnic minorities, international students) have less opportunity to form intercultural friendships than those who reside in a multicultural, multilingual neighborhood.

While it is now possible to make intercultural connections online, in a review of recent research on social networking sites, Neuliep (2012: 338) observes that 'SNSs are used primarily for social interaction with friends with whom users have a preestablished relationship offline', adding that they primarily 'support preexisting social relations within geographically bound communities'. He concludes that 'SNSs such as Facebook are not the primary means by which people meet and initiate relationships with others from different cultures' (ibid: 338). More studies are needed that explore the connection between CMC, SNSs, and intercultural friendships.

Contact frequency, duration, and quality

As well as having sufficient opportunities for intercultural interactions, there must be adequate, quality time together to grow the relationship. For example, while **third culture kids** (TCKs) or global nomads are exposed to different language and cultures, if they move from place to place very frequently, there may not be sufficient time or they may be less motivated to develop deep interpersonal relationships, as noted by the following TCI:

> I have often been surrounded by people who don't fully understand me. In order for people to understand the many facets and undercurrents of my TCK traits, it takes time, and usually time is not on my side. Therefore I have often been misunderstood, and felt alone in a crowd and isolated. Just as you're allowing some of the walls to fall and getting closer to someone, it's time to move on. You begin to hold onto people and circumstances less and harden yourself a little in relationships.
>
> (Sand-Hart 2010: 137–8)

Unmet expectations

Ideas about what friends should and should not do are formed in our home environment during enculturation. When people from different cultural backgrounds interact, they may have different understandings of friendship. Conflicting cultural expectations of roles and obligations can lead to misunderstandings. DeCapua and Wintergerst (2004) and Gareis (2012) for example, observe that differing conceptions of friendship can result in unmet expectations, confusion, and hurt feelings between international students and their U.S. American hosts. In particular, the newcomers may feel let down by American students who are very friendly but less forthcoming with offers of help.

Disparate motives and degree of investment

If an intercultural relationship is to flourish, both parties must have a sufficient level of interest, motivation, time, energy, and commitment to interact and nurture the connection. Without this degree of investment, intercultural friendships may not move beyond the category of 'acquaintance' ('hi-bye' friend), as noted by the following TCK:

> The most important aspect in life is relationships, and my friends have been ripped away from me at every turn. It takes so much energy and effort to maintain hope in new friendships, when you keep losing them all the time. . . . Sometimes I don't see the potential of making a new friend; I see the work involved in getting to know them and quickly analyse whether it's worth it or not. This has been ingrained into my mentality from the routine of making and breaking friends so frequently. I am aware that it is a gamble, since you can miss out on a lot of friendships.
>
> (Sand-Hart 2010: 136)

Anxiety and uncertainty

Another challenge is the management of anxiety and uncertainty that naturally arises when one interacts with individuals who have a different linguistic and cultural background (e.g., different values, ways of being). This is linked to the AUM theory that was previously mentioned. If you have a high level of anxiety and lack confidence in your ability to come up with interesting talking points, or you worry excessively about making mistakes when communicating in a second language, inhibitions and lack of WTC can hold you back from initiating and developing intercultural friendships. For example, Mandy, a bright Taiwanese university student wished to join an international exchange program in Dublin. Her application was successful; however, as the departure date approached she grew increasingly nervous about what lay ahead.

> Because I'll be in a foreign country for such a long time, there'll be lots of problems. I really want to make friends with people from other cultures but I'm worried that I won't be able to get along well with the local students. I don't know what we can talk about and I've never used English much outside of class.

Lacking confidence in her interpersonal skills and informal English language skills, she withdrew. Her fears and low self-esteem also held her back from initiating conversations with international students on her home campus.

Cultural differences in communication styles

Differences in communication styles can also impede the development of intercultural friendships and lead to misunderstandings. In the U.K., for example, students are encouraged to express their opinions in class and to challenge the views of others – in ways that are deemed polite in their context. If they go to Japan, South Korea, or another East Asian country on exchange and continue to pose questions and openly disagree with the comments of their professor or another student, they may be considered loud and aggressive, and 'too proud' (arrogant). Local students who have been socialized to value the comments of their professors much more than their fellow students may resent the newcomers for speaking up and 'wasting valuable class time' (Jackson 2013, Jackson & Chen 2018; Ryan 2013).

In East Asian contexts, inbound international exchange students from the Netherlands and other countries that encourage direct discourse may attribute the reticence of local students to shyness, weak second language skills, insufficient knowledge, or lack of preparedness for class.

While some of their assumptions may be valid at times, the behavior may also be due to cultural differences in communication styles, learning strategies, teaching philosophies, 'cultures of learning', and social norms of discourse and demeanor in classroom settings (Cortazzi & Jin 2013; Jackson 2013, Jackson & Chen 2018). (See Chapter 7 for more on 'cultures of learning'.)

Differing values, perceptions, and worldviews

When individuals cross-cultural boundaries, they are exposed to differing values, perceptions, and worldviews. If one or more of the communicators has very limited intercultural experience, assumptions may be made that their ingroup's values, perceptions, and worldviews are shared by everyone. It can be quite a surprise to discover that this is not the case. When Larona, a university student from rural Botswana, traveled to San Francisco for a semester abroad, she found it difficult to accept some of the habits and values of her American roommate. She was especially shocked to discover that the young woman often spent the night with her boyfriend in his dorm room.

Stereotypes, prejudice, and discrimination

As noted in Chapter 6, ethnocentrism can lead to negative perceptions and attitudes toward individuals and groups who are different. When individuals first meet someone from another linguistic or cultural background, they may have already formed an impression of that person based on stereotypes or previous interactions with people they associate with the same group.

Within the context of race relations in the U.S., Gordon Allport (1954) proposed the '**contact hypothesis**', which suggests that increased contact between different cultural or ethnic groups can lead to mutual acceptance and reduced levels of tension and prejudice. Multiple studies have found that if intercultural relations are to be successful, certain conditions need to be met, such as social and institutional support, equal status between groups, intergroup cooperation, and the likelihood of meaningful interpersonal relationships (Joyce 2018; Lolliot 2018; Pettigrew & Tropp 2011). When these conditions are not in place, stereotypes may persist, and intercultural friendships do not materialize or progress. Therefore, simply increasing the number of international students on campus does not necessarily lead to meaningful intercultural dialogue.

Contested identities/identity misalignments

For intercultural friendships to flourish, the individuals involved must recognize and demonstrate respect for each other's preferred self-identities. As noted in Chapter 5, in intercultural interactions one's preferred identity may be misunderstood and contested. For example, while studying in France, it can be very upsetting for student sojourners who majored in French to be constantly reminded of their second language status by host nationals, especially when the newcomers see themselves as fluent speakers of the language.

When sojourners or immigrants cross-cultural and linguistic boundaries they may experience identity confusion, and this can negatively affect the development of intercultural friendship. If one feels insecure and confused about one's identities and positioning, it can be difficult to forge meaningful ties with people from other cultures. Feeling under threat, individuals may become defensive and cling more tightly to a national identity (Block 2007, 2014; Jackson 2018a). Ethnocentricism is not conducive to the formation of intercultural relationships. (See Chapter 6 for more discussion on ethnocentricism.)

Language and culture barrier

It is generally easier to explain your thoughts and feelings to individuals who share the same linguistic and cultural background. In many intercultural relationships, however, one or more of the friends may converse in a language or dialect that is not a first language. If not fully proficient in the language, it can be difficult to fully convey ideas and feelings. It can also be challenging to accurately interpret messages (verbal and nonverbal) that are being transmitted.

Many international students have learned formal English in classrooms in their home country; outside of academic situations, they may find idiomatic expressions and other forms of informal, social discourse confounding. In some intercultural relationships, people may attribute misunderstandings to cultural difference when a language barrier is to blame, and vice versa.

Expectancy violations

Through enculturation, the process of primary socialization in one's home environment, we learn to expect certain behaviors (verbal, nonverbal) in certain situations and when social norms are broken (e.g., cultural scripts for such speech acts as greetings, refusals, apologies, requests are not followed) we may be quite shocked. Individuals who break social norms of behavior (e.g., omit expressions of politeness) may be perceived as rude or ungrateful. A visibly negative reaction (e.g., puzzled look, frown, raised eyebrow, scowl) may then be taken personally, and, in some cases, wrongly interpreted as prejudice.

Not surprisingly, as suggested by the **expectancy violation theory** (Burgoon 1978) negative perceptions can curtail the cultivation of intercultural friendships. Insufficient cultural knowledge (e.g., lack of familiarity with linguistic and cultural norms in other cultures) can hamper intercultural relationships. (See Chapter 4 for more discussion of the expectancy violation theory in relation to nonverbal behavior.)

Humor

Cross-cultural differences in **humor styles** (the ways people use humor in everyday life) can also lead to interactional difficulties and negative reactions (e.g., Cortés 2015). The ability to recognize and create humor is vital in the development and maintenance of meaningful intercultural relationships. As noted by Matsumoto and Hwang (2012), and many other intercultural communication scholars, shared laughter binds people together.

While humor is a universal phenomenon, how, when, and why it is used can vary considerably among cultures. Very often, humor relies on shared understandings of culturally specific topics. People who share a common history and language are apt to use the same forms and styles of language or, at minimum, be familiar with them. This facilitates relationship development as they can understand each other's jokes and sense camaraderie between them. Individuals who have been socialized in a different environment, however, may fail to grasp what lies behind jokes. The stories and sarcastic remarks that send their intercultural friends into fits of laughter may be a complete mystery to them.

Individuals who do not share the same humor as their interlocutors may become quite irritated, especially if no attempt is made to help them understand the jokes. In some situations, this can be a significant barrier to the enhancement of cordial intercultural relationships. Lana, for example, found it challenging to build a warm relationship with her host family during her sojourn in England. Unable to grasp their humor, she felt like an outsider: 'I was so frustrated that I couldn't get their jokes. Everyone was laughing so happily at something which I could not understand!' In some situations, offensive humor (e.g., jokes about ethnic groups) may also serve as a barrier to the development of intercultural friendships. If one's communication partner remains silent when one's ethnic group (or other ingroup) is maligned, this can lead to the demise of the relationship.

Emotional display

Cultural variations in the display of feelings and emotions can also be a barrier to the development of satisfying intercultural friendships (Altarriba & Kazanas 2018; Matsumoto & Hwang 2012). **Emotion regulation** refers to the process of modifying one's emotions and expressions in particular situations (Gross 1998). Culturally shared norms influence 'how, when, and to whom people should express their emotional experiences' (Safdar *et al.* 2009). As people from different cultural backgrounds may have learned to express (or suppress) their emotions differently (verbally and nonverbally) in certain contexts, this can result in misunderstandings.

Limited emotional intelligence and sensitivity

Neuliep (2018d) defines **emotional intelligence** as 'one's ability to recognize one's own and other people's emotions, to discriminate between different feelings and label them appropriately, and to use emotional information to guide thinking and behavior' (p. 964). Individuals who have limited 'emotional intelligence' and intercultural sensitivity are apt to have a more difficult time building respectful, mutually satisfying intercultural friendships. They may be perceived as lacking empathy or viewed as too emotional and unstable. In some Asian countries, for example, people may smile when embarrassed or unsure how to respond and this can easily be misinterpreted as uncaring and insensitive by newcomers to the region. In contrast, individuals who possess high emotional intelligence tend to be 'team-oriented, cooperative, help each other learn together, and engage in overall enhanced social experiences' (ibid: 964).

Facework and conflict management

When people from different cultural or linguistic backgrounds interact, misunderstandings and conflicts are bound to occur from time to time (Ting-Toomey 2015b, 2018; van der Zee & Hofhuis 2018). Without **mutual facework**, the process of constructing a shared sense of identity, and effective conflict management skills and techniques, small problems may spiral into major disputes that can lead to permanent breakups. (See Chapter 9 for a more in-depth discussion of intercultural conflict, facework, and conflict mediation techniques.)

Social sanctions

Even if individuals who cross social boundaries (e.g., class, language, race, sexual orientation, religion) do not harbor negative sentiments about others, they may encounter a negative reaction from family members, ingroup friends, and the community in which they live. Hostile, racist contexts where segregation is the norm can certainly inhibit the formation and maintenance of intercultural friendships.

Despite these potential barriers, there is reason for optimism. With an open mindset and commitment, people can and do overcome obstacles and develop long-lasting friendships that cross linguistic and cultural boundaries. For example, in her investigation of intercultural friendships between Chinese and American students on a U.S. campus, Li (2010: 64) drew the following conclusion:

> Although intercultural friendships might seem challenging in the beginning stages, if the dyad is able to understand cultural influences on perceptions of self and others in the process of friendship and identify the factors that influence the formation and maintenance of intercultural friendships, intercultural friendships can be as strong and last as long as intracultural friendships.

INTERCULTURAL ROMANCE AND MARRIAGE

Where there is love there is no darkness.

(Burundi proverb)

The heart that loves is always young.

(Chinese proverb)

A life without love is like a year without summer.

(Lithuanian proverb)

It's better to have loved and lost, than to have never loved at all.

(Alfred Lord Tennyson, Britain)

Love is a flower which turns into fruit at marriage.

(Finnish proverb)

All of these international sayings clearly convey the notion that love and romance are important. While humans in all corners of the globe crave affection, there are differences in our perceptions of love and marriage. Just as views about intercultural friendship have evolved over time, attitudes toward intercultural and interracial romance are shifting in many parts of the world. These days, more people are dating and even marrying individuals who have a different cultural and linguistic background. The Internet (e.g., dating, matchmaking sites) and SNSs are playing a role in bringing people from different cultures together for romance and marriage, with English or another international language often serving as the lingua franca. According to the PEW Research Center, '[o]ne-in-six U.S. newlyweds (17%) were married to a person of a different race or ethnicity in 2015, a more than fivefold increase from 3% in 1967'

Plate 8.3 Romance and marriage between people who have a different linguistic and cultural background are becoming more common and accepted in many regions. © Jane Jackson

(Bialik 2017). In 2015, among all married people in the United States (11 million), 10% were intermarried. In many nations around the globe, it is now possible for people of the same sex to marry legally.

Terms associated with intercultural romantic relationships

Before we examine factors that facilitate or hinder intercultural romance, it is helpful to understand some of the many terms and issues that are associated with this complex topic. Many of the terms relate to the nature and quality of the relationship.

A **platonic intercultural relationship** refers to an affectionate friendship between individuals of the opposite sex who have a different cultural background; the connection does not involve sexual relations. A **casual intercultural relationship**, or **casual intercultural dating** are the terms used to describe a physical and emotional relationship between two people from different cultural backgrounds who may have a sexual relationship without necessarily expecting the commitments of a more formal romantic relationship. The term '**friends with benefits'** refers to a casual sexual relationship among friends who are not romantically or emotionally involved.

Intercultural romance is characterized as a close interpersonal relationship between individuals from diverse cultural backgrounds who share a romantic love for each other. An **intimate intercultural couple** refers to a romantic union between 'partners from different countries, nationalities, ethnicities, and religions who may possess quite divergent beliefs, assumptions, and values as a result of their socialization in different sociocultural spaces' (Killian 2009: xviii). **Intercultural gay (lesbian) romance** refers to a romantic relationship between two males or two females. **Intercultural cyber or online romance** is a romantic relationship that is primarily mediated through online or Internet contact. In net discourse, this contrasts with conventional **intercultural offline romantic relationships**, which are initiated and largely maintained through face-to-face interactions (Döring 2002).

Intercultural marriage entails a social union or legal contract between individuals from different cultural backgrounds who may possess differing values, worldviews, and personal philosophies (Renalds 2011; Romano 2008). This definition encompasses bonds between individuals who cross social and culturally constructed boundaries (e.g., linguistic, ethnic, racial, religious, social class, etc.). **Interfaith (interreligious) marriage** refers to marriage (a religious or civil union) between partners professing different religions, while **interracial marriage** refers to a union between individuals who are regarded as members of different races. A marriage between a Filipino Catholic woman and a Black Muslim man is an example of an interfaith, interracial marriage. **Interethnic marriage** refers to marriage between people with different ethnic backgrounds (e.g., bonds between a Welsh woman and a Scottish man). **Monogamy** refers to the practice of being married to only one woman at a time, whereas **polygamy** is the practice of having more than one spouse at a time. **Same sex marriage** or **gay marriage** denotes a union between members of the same sex (e.g., a marriage between two women or between two men). **Cohabitation** refers to living together in a sexual relationship without being legally married. Among individuals and cultural groups, reactions to cohabitation, same sex marriage, and multiple marital partners differ. Conventions and attitudes toward the dissolution of marriage (e.g., divorce) are also impacted by social and religious mores and laws, which vary significantly among cultures.

Factors that facilitate or hinder intercultural romantic relationships

Similar to intracultural unions, some intercultural romances and marriages are more successful than others. Even with an increase in global interconnectedness, significant cultural variations still exist in mating rituals and practices (courtship or dating behaviors) such as the age of sexual consent for males and females, parental involvement in matchmaking, and the degree of male-female contact permissible prior to marriage, etc. Differences in attitudes toward premarital sex may cause intergenerational and interethnic conflict especially among immigrants in Western countries (Lamanna *et al.* 2018); practices that differ from those of the majority culture (e.g., homosexual romance, arranged marriages) may be met with hostility in some quarters.

Based on interviews with intercultural couples, Romano (2008) identified the following factors or characteristics that contribute to successful marriages between people who have a different cultural background: commitment to the relationship, ability to communicate, sensitivity to each other's needs, a liking for the other's culture, flexibility, positive self-image, love as the main marital motive, common goals, spirit of adventure, and sense of humor.

Relational intimacy and the development of a relational identity also help determine the fate of these unions. Within the context of intercultural romance and marriage, **third culture building** refers to the melding of different cultural identities and practices to form an identity that is unique to the romantic partners or family unit (Barker 2018; Rosenblatt 2009). **Relational interdependence** (mutual dependence or reliance on each other) not only helps couples embrace and reconcile differences, it can help to cushion them from negative forces (e.g., hostile reactions from family members and religious figures who disapprove of the relationship). While intercultural couples may develop 'their own intricate, multilayered systems', they are impacted by 'the many other systems in which they are embedded, including their families and

cultures of origin and an assortment of other economic, legal, political, and social systems'
(Rosenblatt 2009: 3).

In addition to prejudice and racism, intercultural couples may face a number of other
obstacles, including: a language barrier, conflicting ideas about premarital sex, differing expectations and perceptions of roles and responsibilities (e.g., disparate views about appropriate
roles and duties for wives and husbands), differing ideas about acceptable displays of affection
in public and private domains, conflict management differences, a power imbalance, family
pressures and social constraints, differing perceptions of childrearing, and unfamiliar beliefs
and traditions (e.g., religious ceremonies and customs).

ENHANCING INTERCULTURAL RELATIONSHIPS

> There are those individuals from diverse backgrounds who have created a world, at least
> within their own private lives, that is not broken by the socially constructed boundaries
> of race, class, gender, sexual orientation, religion, ability, and age; people who have
> established deep, lasting relationships with others from very different backgrounds.
>
> (Vela-McConnell 2011: 3)

How have multicultural individuals been able to develop successful intercultural relationships?
How can you bridge linguistic and cultural barriers to initiate and maintain rewarding and
mutually satisfying relationships? Drawing on recent research on intercultural relationships
(friendships, romance, marriage), the following section offers practical suggestions to initiate
and optimize relationships with individuals who are linguistically and culturally different.

- If you do not have any intercultural relationships, reflect on the reasons why this is the
  case. Are your fears or attitudes (or those of your family/ social networks) holding you
  back from making intercultural connections? If yes, challenge yourself to leave your comfort zone and initiate communication with someone from a different linguistic and cultural
  background, whether face to face or online. Bear in mind that intercultural connections
  must be genuine and respectful if they are to be meaningful. They take time to develop.
- Perceptions of relationships differ across cultures. Consider your own views and expectations and how these ideas formed. How might these understandings differ from those of
  your intercultural partners?
- Do not assume that you or your intercultural friend or partner is an ambassador for a particular linguistic or cultural group. When you get to know someone from another linguistic or
  cultural background, you are developing an interpersonal relationship with an individual.
- Cultivate an open mindset. Refrain from forming expectations of behavior based solely on
  your own language and culture. For example, be attentive to differences in communication
  styles and recognize the validity of differing social norms (e.g., cultural scripts) and worldviews. Avoid making snap judgments about behaviors that puzzle or annoy you and make
  an effort to view the world from your partner's perspective.
- Engage in active listening and be mindful of the needs, identities, and interests of your
  communication partner;
- Be attentive to differences in disclosure norms, values, verbal behaviors, and nonverbal
  behaviors, and make an effort to develop relational intimacy.
- Work to eliminate any personal biases and prejudices that you may have that could negatively impact your intercultural relationships.

■ Recognize the importance of respect and genuine concern in intercultural friendships and romances. Are you attentive to the needs of your communication partners or overly focused on your own interests?

■ Assess your level of intercultural sensitivity and intercultural communication apprehension. Based on what you have learned in this book and elsewhere consider constructive ways to overcome impediments to the development of healthy intercultural relationships.

■ Make a personal commitment to devote the time necessary to enhance your intercultural communication skills to develop meaningful relationships (face to face and online).

As our world is becoming increasingly diverse and interdependent, it is vital for us to acquire the knowledge, skills, and mindset that can nurture meaningful connections with people who have a different cultural or linguistic background. While intercultural relationships (e.g., friendships, dating, marriage) can be more challenging than intracultural connections, they are well worth the extra time and effort involved. 'Because we live in a world in which there is increasing contact with diverse others, understanding how differences are bridged- regardless of which socially constructed boundary we happen to be speaking- is an important pursuit' (Vela-McConnell 2011: 3).

SUMMARY

In this chapter we reviewed various categories of intercultural relationships and discussed the many potential benefits of forming close interpersonal connections with people who have a different linguistic or cultural background, whether face-to-face or online. A number of internal and external factors can either facilitate or hinder intercultural friendships and the formation and maintenance of diverse social networks. Multiple complex variables can also lead to success or failure in intercultural romance and marriage. With an open mindset and the nurturing of our intercultural communication skills, all of us can optimize our intercultural relationships, which, in turn, can enrich our lives in multiple ways

discussion questions

1   Why do people tend to form most of their friendships with people who speak their first language and have a similar background?
2   Identify challenges people may experience in initiating and maintaining intercultural relationships. Discuss your ideas with a partner.
3   How can language affect intimate intercultural relationships?
4   What role can self-disclosure and relational maintenance play in intercultural relationships (e.g., platonic, romantic)? Provide examples and discuss your ideas with a partner.
5   Define the concept of 'face' and explain how facework can influence the quality of intercultural relationships.
6   In today's globalized world, how has technology changed the way intercultural friendships and romances are formed and maintained?
7   Intercultural marriages are on the rise in many parts of the world. With a partner, discuss the benefits and challenges of these unions.

activities

1   Define what friendship means to you. Identify categories of friends that are common in your current context and explain what you expect of each type of friend. In your first language, what terms are used for the types of friendship you have cited?

2   With a partner identify challenges that may arise in intercultural relationships when individuals have differing ideas about friendship. If possible, draw on your own experiences and discuss ways to build constructive relationships.

3   Define social networks. Draw diagrams to illustrate your own social networks. Do you have friends from other linguistic and cultural backgrounds? If not, why not?

4   In small groups, discuss the challenges bilingual intercultural couples might face, especially if they decide to make their relationships permanent and have children. Suggest ways to constructively deal with intercultural issues that may arise.

5   Interview local and international students about friendship and romance. Do they have different categories of friends (e.g., 'hi-bye' friends, close friends)? If yes, what are the terms they use (in their first language and English)? From their perspective, what are the challenges and benefits of close intercultural friendships? What factors do they believe facilitate or hinder the development of successful intercultural friendships/romance? Do you agree?

6   Drawing on your own intercultural experience and what you have read in this chapter and elsewhere, identify five strategies that might enhance intercultural relationships (e.g., friendship, platonic friendship, romance, marriage). Share your ideas with your classmates.

further reading

Acosta, H., Staller, M. and Hirayama, B. (2016) *Intercultural Communication: Building Relationships and Skills*, Dubuque, IA: Kendall Hunt Publishing.

This book explains communication theories and offers practical advice to enhance and maintain satisfying intercultural relationships.

Bystydzienski, J.M. (2011) *Intercultural Couples: Crossing Boundaries, Negotiating Difference*, New York: New York University Press.

The author examines the multidimensional experiences of intercultural couples who negotiate their identities, gender expectations, language use, family relations, childrearing, financial matters, and lifestyles.

Plummer, D. (2019) *Some of My Friends Are. . .: The Daunting Challenges and Untapped Benefits of Cross-Racial Friendships*, Boston: Beacon Press.

The author identifies and explores multiple factors that can influence the development and maintenance of 'cross-racial' friendships.

Vela-McConnell, J.A. (2011) *Unlikely Friends: Bridging Ties and Diverse Friendships*, Lanham, MD: Lexington Books.

This accessible book focuses on successful friendships that cross one or more social and cultural boundaries (e.g., age, race, gender, class, gender, sexual orientation, religious affiliation). The author raises awareness of techniques that can enhance intercultural friendships.

Companion Website: Continue your journey online

Visit the Companion Website for a variety of tools and resources to support and extend your intercultural learning. (Instructors who are qualified adopters of the text may access additional resources on this site.)

CHAPTER 9

Language and intercultural conflict

Intercultural conflict frustrations often arise because of our lack of necessary and sufficient knowledge to deal with culture-based conflict communication issues competently. When a second language is involved, the situation may be exacerbated. Our cultural ignorance or ineptness oftentimes clutters our ability to communicate appropriately, effectively, and adaptively across cultural and linguistic lines.

(Ting-Toomey 2012: 279)

Peace is not the absence of conflict but the presence of creative alternatives for responding to conflict.

(Dorothy Thompson 1893–1961, quoted in *Women's International League for Peace and Freedom*, n.d.)

In a few decades, the relationship between the environment, resources and conflict may seem almost as obvious as the connection we see today between human rights, democracy and peace.
(Wangari Maathai 1940–2011, quoted in Nobel Women's Initiative n.d.)

learning objectives

By the end of this chapter, you should be able to:

1 Identify and describe the nature and characteristics of conflict
2 Identify five types of conflict and provide examples of each
3 Explain the potential role(s) of face, language, and culture in conflict situations
4 Explain why it is important to consider the impact of social, political, and historical elements in intercultural conflicts
5 Identify strategies that might be used to deal effectively and appropriately with intercultural conflicts

INTRODUCTION

Today's globalized world is characterized by increasing contact between people with diverse backgrounds in all spheres of life (e.g., education, family, work, recreation, social, domestic and international politics, worship, etc.). While intercultural interactions have the potential to be very rewarding, they can also be challenging. Linguistic and cultural differences among individuals or group members, whether in a multicultural classroom, in linguistically and culturally diverse families, in multinational business teams, in international peace negotiations, or other domains, can be a source of misunderstanding and conflict (LeBaron & Pillay 2006;

Ting-Toomey 2012). 'Conflict breeds conflict, unless it is managed successfully' (Gudykunst 2004: 276). It is therefore imperative that we develop the knowledge and skills that can help us to resolve disagreements in a respectful, peaceful manner. It is not just world leaders who require intercultural conflict competence. In our progressively globalized society all of us need to hone the ability to deal appropriately and effectively with misunderstandings and conflict situations on an interpersonal level.

This chapter begins by describing the nature and characteristics of conflict. Next, we explore types of conflict, and the role(s) of language and culture in conflict situations, especially intercultural situations. We then turn our attention to intercultural conflict communication styles and the potential role(s) of face and facework in conflict situations. Finally, we discuss intercultural conflict competence and constructive ways to resolve language and intercultural misunderstandings and conflict situations.

THE NATURE AND CHARACTERISTICS OF CONFLICT

There are many definitions of conflict. One of the most widely quoted was put forward by Mortensen (1974: 93) who describes it as 'an expressed struggle over incompatible interests in the distribution of limited resources'. More recent conceptions tend to be variations of this. Folger *et al.* (2013), for example, refer to conflict as 'the interaction of interdependent parties who perceive incompatibility and the possibility of interference from others as a result of this incompatibility'. Adler *et al.* (2015) define conflict as 'an expressed struggle between at least two interdependent parties who perceive incompatible goals, scarce resources, and interference from the other party in achieving their goals'. Most conflict communication specialists also refer to conflict as 'an inevitable part of human experience'. Accordingly, Liu *et al.* (2019) observe that conflict 'permeates all social relationships'.

As these definitions suggest, scholars generally agree on the nature and characteristics of conflict and the relationship among those involved. Basically, **conflict** centers on 'incompatabilities, an expressed struggle, and interdependence among two or more parties' (Putnam 2013: 6). To gain a better understanding of how conflict impacts on everyday life, we now take a closer look at the common elements in these definitions.

Incompatibilities

In a conflict situation, it appears as if an individual or group's gain means another's loss. The parties involved may have incompatible goals or aspirations or they may favor seemingly irreconcilable means to achieve their goals (e.g., differing decision making techniques, conflicting communication styles). For example, an individual may employ aggressive tactics to dominate a situation, whereas the other party wishes to negotiate a settlement through lengthy, informal conversations. Accordingly, LeBaron (2015) describes conflict as 'a difference that matters, one that becomes a dividing line between "us" and "them" or between competing claims over fairness, law, or morality' (p. 495).

An expressed struggle

For conflict to develop, the parties involved must recognize that they disagree about something. You may be annoyed that someone keeps arriving late to meetings, but unless you convey your displeasure either verbally or nonverbally in such a way that this person is aware of your displeasure, there is no conflict (just resentment).

Scarce resources

Interpersonal conflicts can arise when people believe that there are insufficient resources (e.g., materials, food, time, wealth, quality education) for everyone. Many students may wish to join a second language immersion program but there are a limited number of places; conflict may develop if the selection criteria are not transparent or perceived as biased. In families, sibling rivalry may intensify if children believe that their parents are not distributing their time or attention evenly. Conflict may erupt if one child is given more allowance or privileges than another.

Scare resources can also lead to conflicts on a larger scale. In some parts of the world, limited natural resources (e.g., water, arable land) are leading to violent disputes as people struggle to survive. Wangari Maathai, the 2004 Nobel Peace Prize Laureate, warned that '[i]n a few decades, the relationship between the environment, resources and conflict may seem almost as obvious as the connection we see today between human rights, democracy and peace' (Nobel Women's Initiative n.d.). As the effects of global warming intensify (e.g., flooding, droughts, heat waves, cold snaps), crops will fail on land that used to be bountiful and with less food, prices will rise, spawning more conflicts as people struggle to feed their families.

Interdependence

Individuals or groups that are involved in a conflict are interdependent in some ways, even if they are not willing to acknowledge this. In interpersonal relationships, for example, parties depend on each other for psychological, emotional, and material resources (Folger *et al.* 2018). The well-being of one is affected by the behavior of the other party and vice versa. Resentment and hostility may cloud their judgment. A negative mindset may prevent people from recognizing that they need to accept their interdependence and work together in order to resolve their conflict.

Inevitability

Conflict is an inevitable fact of life and people routinely find themselves in conflict situations, whether in their home environment, in social or educational settings, or at work. Siblings may routinely come into conflict with each other and their parents about daily activities. At universities, students who work on projects together may differ about how they should proceed. Romantic partners may find themselves in conflict about whether they should have premarital sex or live together before marriage. When intercultural couples have children, they may find themselves in a conflict situation when they discover that they have very different views about childrearing practices and the role of religion and extended family members in their daily life. In the workplace, conflict about tasks and individual/group responsibilities may develop within work teams.

On the world stage, conflicts develop within regions and between nation-states as groups compete for limited resources (e.g., arable land, oil, water). This does not mean that violence is unavoidable. Later in this chapter we discuss peaceful ways to resolve conflict situations.

TYPES OF CONFLICT

Conflict can take many forms and cross one or more socially and historically constructed boundary (e.g., age, gender, ethnicity, race, language, religion, etc.). Let's take a look at various types of conflict and examples of each.

Intracultural conflict

A clash of opposing assumptions, beliefs, opinions, needs, and goals may occur whenever human beings come together, even if they have much in common (e.g., the same language, ethnicity). **Intracultural conflict** refers to a struggle between individuals with a similar linguistic and cultural background. For example, two Australian ESL teachers in Melbourne may become embroiled in a conflict situation when they vehemently disagree about the pedagogy that should be used in their language program. Malaysian parents who share the same first language and cultural background may find themselves in a highly emotional conflict situation when they have opposing views about what medium of instruction is best for primary children (e.g., a local language or English).

Interpersonal conflict

Interpersonal conflict basically refers to conflict or a struggle between two or more people who may or may not have a similar linguistic and cultural background. Describing interpersonal conflict as 'a problematic situation', Abigail and Cahn (2011: 4) associate it with the following characteristics:

1   The conflicting parties are interdependent.
2   They have the perception that they seek incompatible goals or outcomes, or they favor incompatible means to the same end.
3   The perceived incompatibility has the potential to adversely affect the relationship leaving emotional residues if not addressed.
4   There is a sense of urgency about the need to resolve the difference.

In an interpersonal conflict a struggle may occur when the communication partners cannot agree on how to meet their needs or goals. In this situation they may feel pulled in opposite directions. Sam may wish to join a German language immersion program in Berlin, but his parents insist that he work during the summer. Your partner wants to go to see a French movie with you, but you want to stay home and finish writing an essay that is due the following day. Different aims, expectations, and experiences can result in interpersonal conflict.

Intergroup conflict

Intergroup conflict refers to disputes that arise between two or more groups of people (e.g., different ethnic groups, work groups, study groups, sports teams, debate teams, choirs, etc.). Group conflict situations may develop 'when two work, cultural, or social groups seek to maximize their own goals without locating perceptual congruities' (Chen & Starosta 1998: 143).

Disparate objectives, values, communication styles, and a wide range of cultural differences may cause friction between groups. For example, business majors may come into conflict with English majors about the use of the same meeting space or other resources (e.g., funds, computers).

Organizational conflict

Organizational conflict refers to disputes that can arise within an organization (e.g., a business, educational institution, a department, political party, social club, etc.) as a result of competing needs, values, beliefs, and interests. Within organizations, conflict can assume many forms. There can be a clash among or between formal authority figures (e.g., senior administrators, executives, professors) and subordinates (individuals or groups with less power and status, such as office workers, junior staff, and students). Discord about a range of organizational or work-related issues may erupt between individuals, departments, unions, and management. Even among people who hold the same rank or status, disputes may arise about such aspects as the division of labor, the choice of language in meetings, the way duties or revenue should be divided, how tasks should be carried out, the hours of work, etc. Subtler forms of conflict (e.g., jealousies, rivalries, a clash of personalities) may also prevail as individuals and groups struggle to enhance their positioning and gain more power and privileges. Competing needs and demands may lead to protests and labor disputes (e.g., the refusal to use a particular language in meetings).

Within organizations, as well as in other contexts, conflicts may be either affective or cognitive in nature. **Affective conflict** refers to a type of conflict that centers on an emotional conflict between parties. Conflicts of this nature can be very destructive to companies (and interpersonal relationships) if left to fester and grow. A **cognitive conflict** centers on a dispute among individuals or groups about how to carry out and complete a task, which can arise due to differing beliefs, values, and/or work styles, for example. This type of conflict often points to serious problems or issues that a company or organization needs to address.

Intercultural conflict

Intercultural conflict refers to 'the experience of emotional frustration in conjunction with perceived incompatibility of values, norms, face orientations, goals, scarce resources, processes, and/or outcomes between a minimum of two parties from two different cultural communities in an interactive situation' (Ting-Toomey & Oetzel 2001: 17). Discord may arise due to 'the diverse cultural approaches people bring with them in expressing their different cultural or ethnic values, identity issues, interaction norms, face-saving orientations, power resource transactions, divergent goal emphasis, and contrastive conflict styles' (Oetzel & Ting-Toomey 2006: 545). **Conflict style** refers to a preferred way of behaving in conflict situations. 'It is a particular form of a person's more general patterns of communication behavior (Hammer 2015a: 493).

Intercultural conflict may materialize as '[o]ur cultural ignorance or ineptness oftentimes clutters our ability to communicate appropriately, effectively, and adaptively across cultural and linguistic lines' (Ting-Toomey 2012: 279). Limited second language proficiency may exacerbate conflict situations. In higher education, disparate views about what constitutes appropriate communication behaviors may lead to conflict between local and international students who have been socialized in different linguistic and cultural environments. In discussions, an international exchange student may frequently speak up and interrupt other speakers. While this may be quite normal (and expected) in her home environment, she may be perceived as overly direct and aggressive by local students and teachers who are not accustomed to this style of communication. Tension and discord (e.g., 'us' vs. 'them' discourse) may prevail. In another intercultural situation, an Algerian exchange student may find herself embroiled in a tense conflict with her Belgian professor who disapproves of her attending class wearing the hijab (headscarf worn by some Muslim women).

Intercultural conflicts may occur in group meetings or teams that involve students, workers, or professionals from diverse backgrounds. Differing ideas about how a task should be divided and accomplished may lead to disputes. If group members do not share the same linguistic and cultural norms of politeness tempers may flare. Lack of familiarity with **cultural scripts** (e.g., routines for requests, refusals, apologies) may result in miscommunication and **misattributions** (inaccurate assumptions), which may quickly spiral from a minor disagreement into a more serious conflict situation if not dealt with appropriately.

Interracial conflict

Under the broad category of intercultural conflict, there are many subcategories including interracial, interethnic, and interreligious conflict. **Interracial conflict** refers to a conflict situation whereby race or racial difference is an issue (Orbe & Harris 2015). For example, a dispute

Plate 9.1   The Israeli-Palestinian conflict, which began in the mid-20th century, is one of the world's longest-running and most controversial conflicts. © Jane Jackson

between an African American customer and an Asian American shopkeeper may escalate when claims of overcharging and racism are voiced.

Interethnic (ethnic) conflict

Interethnic (ethnic) conflict refers to a conflict situation between individuals or groups affiliated with different ethnic groups, whereby ethnicity is salient. A strong ethnic identity accompanied by ethnic hatred/distrust and inequalities (e.g., unequal financial resources) can lead to conflict situations that may escalate into violence. Conflict between Mexican Americans and European Americans may develop when different views are expressed about proposed changes to U.S. immigration laws and the building of a wall between Mexico and the U.S. In Cyprus, conflict between Greek and Turkish Cypriots may intensify when changes are proposed in educational language policies.

An extreme form of ethnic conflict may result in **ethnic cleansing** (the systematic and violent removal of an ethnic or religious group from a particular territory) and **genocide** (the widespread killing of a national, ethnic, racial, or religious group). In the 1990s, for example, in the former Yugoslavia, Bosnian Muslims and Bosnian Croats were forced to flee their homes by Serbs, and many were also raped and murdered.

In 1991, The United Nations Security Council established the **International Criminal Court (ICC)** in the Hague, the Netherlands to try '**crimes against humanity**', that is, the systemic practice of serious offenses against people that are either carried out or condoned by a government (e.g., widespread murder, religious persecution, rapes as a weapon of war, etc.). Many of these crimes involve atrocities that stem from ethnic conflicts, such as in Rwanda and Yugoslavia.

International conflict

International conflict has traditionally referred to disputes between different countries (e.g., the Iran-Iraq war) as well as conflict between people and organizations from different nation-states (e.g., trade disputes between China and the United States, disagreements between the governments of different nations). Nowadays, the term encompasses intergroup conflicts within a nation such as when one group is fighting for independence or for more political, social, or economic power (e.g., the war in Syria, the quest for independence from Spain in Catalonia). Some international conflicts (e.g., the Israeli-Palestinian conflict) are protracted and not easily solved.

Interfaith (interreligious) conflict

Interfaith (interreligious, religious) conflict refers to disputes or conflict situations between individuals or groups affiliated with different faiths, whereby religion is a salient issue. For example, in sub-Saharan Africa, with both Muslim and Christian populations growing rapidly, interfaith conflicts are increasing. In Egypt, India, and Nigeria interfaith conflict has led to sectarian violence and even murder. Religious disputes may also arise between individuals or groups affiliated with different sects or branches within the same religion. In Ireland, among

Christians, there have been long running tensions between Catholics and Protestants, and in Iraq, conflicts between Sunni and Shia Muslims. Intense passions and beliefs make interreligious conflicts difficult to resolve.

Intergenerational conflict

Intergenerational conflict refers to disputes between individuals or groups from different generations, whereby age and divergent life experiences are salient issues. For example, conflict between middle-aged immigrant parents and their children may arise due to differences in language practices, values, beliefs, and behaviors. A young female Muslim who was born and raised in Manchester, England, may insist on using English at all times and refuse to communicate with her immigrant parents in Urdu, their first language, especially in public. Her parents may forbid her from dating in secondary school and start the process of arranging a marriage for her with a cousin from their home village in Pakistan. In extreme cases, conflict can escalate and lead to an **honor killing**, whereby the young woman is murdered by relatives who believe that her actions (e.g., premarital sex, refusal to accept an arranged marriage) have brought dishonor on the family. Intergenerational conflict has been the subject of many films (e.g., *Bend it like Beckham*, *The Best Exotic Marigold Hotel*, *The Joy Luck Club*).

Gender conflict

Disputes may also occur between males and females in domestic, social, or work environments. **Gender conflict** refers to conflict situations in which gender is a key factor. In a work situation, for example, interpersonal conflict may take place between male and female coworkers as a consequence of differences in communication styles and role expectations, as well as a power imbalance (e.g., pay inequity).

Globally, more women are entering the work force and joining professions once reserved for males. In many regions, women are gaining more access to positions of power (e.g., leadership roles) in all sectors of society (e.g., education, government, work, the military, etc.). As they compete for jobs and better salaries and benefits, conflicts can arise when men (and some women) feel threatened by these changes. Females may experience discrimination and possible retribution (e.g., intimidation, violence). As they fight for their rights, they may come into direct conflict with males who are resistant to change and unwilling to share power and resources.

CULTURAL DIMENSIONS OF CONFLICT SITUATIONS

Culture plays a role in all conflict situations, whether intracultural or intercultural in nature. It can be a dominant factor, or it may influence the conflict in more subtle ways. Both personal characteristics and cultural dimensions may fuel disagreements and conflicts between individuals and groups. In particular, intercultural conflict situations may be exacerbated by a range of cultural elements, including mismatched expectations, higher levels of ambiguity and uncertainty, different values, language and nonverbal barriers, face and identity needs, and differing perceptions and understandings of conflict. Let's take a closer look at each of these factors.

Plate 9.2   Intercultural conflicts are exacerbated when individuals or groups have divergent ideas about conflict and ways to deal with discord. © Jane Jackson

Mismatched expectations

The **expectancy violation theory** posits that individuals have culturally based expectations about how people should behave in a communicative event (e.g., conversations, arguments) and when individuals or groups do not perform as expected, miscommunication and negative perceptions may develop (Burgoon 1995; Høgh-Olesen 2018). Expectations in conflict situations are influenced by the underlying values and norms (e.g., sociopragmatic rules of discourse) that are prevalent in a particular culture. Ideas about what is appropriate verbal and nonverbal behavior in conflicts are learned during the process of socialization and vary among cultures. Not surprisingly, intercultural conflict involves 'emotional frustrations or mismatched expectations that stem, in part, from cultural group membership differences' (Ting-Toomey & Oetzel 2001: 17). In intercultural disputes, negative emotional reactions to unexpected behaviors can lead to an escalation in the conflict.

During enculturation, we develop ideas about what is appropriate or inappropriate behavior by observing those around us. **Cultural norms** or rules serve as a guide for what we should or should not do in a conflict situation. A **conflict script** refers to 'the interaction placement and appropriate sequence of verbal and nonverbal message exchanges' (Ting-Toomey & Oetzel 2001: 11). Basically, this cognitive structure describes appropriate actions and sequences of events in a dispute (Folger *et al*. 2018; Roloff & Wright 2013). For example, a conflict script can signal who should speak first during the process of negotiation. It can also indicate how and when one should apologize and in what language, taking into account the nature of the conflict and the status of the individuals or groups involved.

Recent studies suggest that people have implicit culturally based scripts that shape their expectations about how a conflict should unfold and be resolved (Folger *et al*. 2018). To complicate matters, some researchers have also found variations in the conflict scripts of men and women in the same cultural context (Fehr *et al*. 1999). Difficulties may arise when individuals expect discussions to unfold in a different way.

Ambiguity and uncertainty

When people interact with individuals who have a different linguistic and cultural background, there is bound to be more ambiguity and uncertainty than in intracultural interactions. The parties involved may not know whether the conflict is seen in the same way and they may be unsure how to handle the dispute in a manner that is mutually acceptable. Sensitive intercultural communicators may be nervous about the possibility of offending others. There may be uncertainty in the meaning of verbal expressions when a second language is involved and some nonverbal dimensions (e.g., use of personal space) may be misinterpreted or simply overlooked. Individuals with a low tolerance for ambiguity are likely to find intercultural conflict situations more stressful than intracultural events. Heightened emotions and confusion can make it more difficult to resolve the conflict.

The **uncertainty reduction theory (URT)** (Berger & Calabrese 1975; Hogg & Wagoner 2018), which was introduced in Chapter 8, suggests that people are uncomfortable with ambiguity and strive to reduce uncertainty in communicative events (e.g., intercultural conflict situations). **Cognitive uncertainty** refers to uncertainty about the ways in which an individual's culturally influenced attitudes and beliefs impact on his or her way of thinking. Linked to the expectancy violation theory, **behavioral uncertainty** has to do with one's uncertainty about how the other person will behave in an intercultural conflict situation. The **anxiety/uncertainty management (AUM) theory** suggests that as we gain more knowledge and understanding of our communication partner, our level of stress or anxiety subsides. As our apprehension diminishes we can become more effective at resolving conflicts with individuals or groups who have been socialized in a different linguistic and cultural context (Gudykunst 2004; Neuliep 2018e).

Language and nonverbal barriers

Language is a key factor in all conflict situations, whether the parties involved share the same cultural background or not. In addition to word choice and verbal communication style (e.g., direct or indirect, emotionally expressive or restrained, formal or informal), our nonverbal behaviors (e.g., tone of voice, body language, gestures, posture, facial expressions, use of space) can affect the outcomes of both intracultural and intercultural interactions.

Whether intentional or not, intercultural conflict may escalate when a person employs verbal or nonverbal behavior that is considered rude or overly hostile to the receiver. For example, standing very close to someone you do not know well may be quite acceptable in one's home environment but may have a detrimental effect if one's communication partner is used to more personal distance. Feeling under threat, the person may respond negatively, and the conflict may escalate. Alternatively, the individual may withdraw with the situation left unresolved.

In intercultural interactions, it is common for one or more interactants to use a second language and if not fluent, the possibility of miscommunication and misunderstandings is greater. Even if the intercultural communicators speak the same first language, there may be differences in their preferred communication style, which can complicate the conflict situation. If a speaker insists on using a direct style of communication with someone who is much more at ease with subtle ways of communicating, a negative reaction may worsen the conflict situation. Direct communicators may be considered abrasive, rude, and confrontational, while those who favor an indirect style may be regarded as weak and indecisive. Misattributions and hurt feelings may make it more difficult to resolve conflicts. (See Chapter 3 for more on verbal communication styles.)

Although language can sometimes result in intercultural conflict or exacerbate conflict situations, it is also the primary vehicle for solving intercultural conflict. The ability to employ context-appropriate nonverbal behaviors and accurately read a range of nonverbal cues can facilitate the communication process and conflict resolutions.

Face and identity needs

In all cultures, people are concerned about how they are perceived by others and this also applies to conflict situations. Drawing on Goffman's (1969) notion of 'face' as a social phenomenon which is created through communication, Brown and Levinson (1978: 66) define **face** as 'the public self-image that every member wants to claim for himself, . . . something that is emotionally invested, and that can be lost, maintained, or enhanced, and must be constantly attended to in interaction'. It is generally viewed as 'how we want others to see us and treat us and how we actually treat others in association with their social self-concept expectations' (Ting-Toomey 2018: 775).

Besides our public image, face encompasses our identity, self-esteem, and honor. In intercultural conflict situations, our face is particularly vulnerable as we are often less certain about what will happen (e.g., how our partners will react to what we say and do). The concept of face is especially problematic in ambiguous situations when the identities of the parties are called into question. In intercultural interactions, conflict situations may arise when difficult, awkward, and unexpected requests are made. Individuals may be embarrassed and unsure how to respond.

Dimensions of face include positive and negative elements. **Positive face** refers to a person's desire to gain the approval of other people, whereas **negative face** is the desire to have autonomy and not be controlled by others. **Facework** denotes 'the communication strategies used to defend, challenge, support, or even upgrade self-face and other-face identity issues in an emotionally vulnerable encounter' (Ting-Toomey 2018: 776). While **positive facework** emphasizes the need for acceptance, respect, and inclusion, **negative facework** refers to the degree to which the disputants protect themselves from interference (Ting-Toomey 2015b, 2018). In conflict situations, individuals strive to protect and manage their self-image.

How people manage their self-image in conflict situations varies among cultures, as Ting-Toomey (2005) explains: 'While face and facework are universal phenomena, how we "frame" or interpret the situated meaning of face and how we enact facework differ from one cultural community to the next' (p. 73). Naturally, this can lead to misunderstandings and an escalation of disputes. (The importance of facework is explored further in this chapter when we examine the face negotiation theory.)

Differing perceptions and understandings of conflict

The way conflict is viewed and approached is influenced by our gender and cultural background. Through enculturation, we acquire the attitudes, knowledge structures, behaviors, and strategies that are most commonly used to define and respond to disagreements and conflict situations. From an early age, we learn how to deal with conflict by observing our parents and other members of our culture both in the community and through the mass media (e.g., television). We receive messages about what is appropriate for males and females in conflict situations. As our attitudes and perceptions of conflict are shaped within particular environments, it is not surprising that researchers have discovered individual and cultural differences in this domain.

In cultural contexts where **collectivism** is prevalent, the needs and wants of groups are given priority over individuals, and conflict tends to be viewed as destructive and harmful for relationships (e.g., China, Brazil, Japan) (Bhawuk 2018a; van Meurs & Spencer-Oatey 2010). To preserve relational harmony and one's public face, **pacifism** is generally favored, that is, individuals strive to avoid conflict situations. If conflicts do arise, people tend to restrain their emotions and try to manage disputes indirectly. Those who use this approach believe that relationships are made stronger and conflicts are lessened when emotions are kept in check. This perspective is clearly conveyed in the following Chinese proverb: 'The first person to raise his voice loses the argument'. It is also important to note, however, that contemporary researchers in East Asia have identified generational differences in people's perceptions of conflict. For example, young men and women in modern China increasingly prefer collaborative problem solving to resolve disputes, whereas their elders still favor avoiding conflict situation (Zhang et al. 2005).

In contexts which are more **individualistic** (self-reliance and personal independence are stressed) (e.g., Germany, the United States), people tend to perceive conflict (e.g., the open discussion of conflicting views) as potentially positive. Instead of shying away from conflict situations, individualists maintain that it is best to approach conflict directly (e.g., analyze the situation and take steps to find a solution). Persons who employ this style believe that it is better to show emotion during disagreements than to hide or suppress feelings. For these individuals, this outward display signals one's concern and commitment to resolving the conflict. Through enculturation, they have developed the belief that working through conflicts constructively can defuse more serious conflict situations and bring about stronger, healthier, and more mutually satisfying relationships (Bhawuk 2018a, Ting-Toomey 2012, 2017).

Gender also affects how conflict is defined and resolved. Although a direct approach to conflict resolution may be prevalent in some contexts, the type of dispute, the relationship of the disputants, and individual differences and personal preferences may lead to subtle differences in the way conflict situations unfold. This means that we cannot assume that people in a particular context will view and react to conflicts in the same way.

When individuals or groups from different cultural backgrounds engage in conflict, they may bring with them differing ideas about how disputes should be handled. As noted by Ting-Toomey and Oetzel (2001: 1), 'How we define the conflict problem, how we "punctuate" the differing triggering event that leads to the conflict problem, and how we view the goals for satisfactory conflict resolution are all likely to vary across cultures, situations, and individuals'. It is not difficult to imagine how misunderstandings and conflict situations can escalate when people have conflicting ideas about how their differences should be handled.

INTERCULTURAL CONFLICT STYLES

During the process of primary socialization, we become aware of particular ways to handle conflict situations. From our elders we learn when it is appropriate to display emotions and when it is not. We become attuned to subtle nuances that lead to variations in how we act and respond in a variety of conflict situations in different domains (e.g., family, workplace, etc.). Individuals gradually develop a particular orientation toward conflict through the influence of their cultural environment. Ting-Toomey and Oetzel (2001) refer to **conflict interaction style** as 'patterned responses to conflict in a variety of dissenting conflict situations' (p. 45).

A number of taxonomies have been developed to conceptualize conflict styles. Blake and Mouton (1964) and Hall (1969), for example, identified the following types of conflict behavior: a competing style (strategies are used to reach one's own goals at the cost of the other party's goals or feelings), an accommodating style (one's own goals are sacrificed for the sake of the other person/the relationship), an avoiding style (one either ignores or refuses to engage in the conflict), a collaborating style (parties work together cooperatively until a mutually agreeable solution is found), and a compromising style (there is a give and take of resources with no one achieving his or her original goal).

Rahim (1983) categorized and measured the following conflict styles based on the individual's concern for Self or Other: dominating style (high self/low other concern), obliging style (low self/high other concern), avoiding style (low self/other concern), integrating style (high self/other concern), and compromising style (moderate self/other concern). Rubin *et al.* (1994) view conflict styles in terms of withdrawing, yielding, problem solving, or inaction. More recently, Wilmot and Hocker (2017) identified the following five conflict styles: avoidance (lose-lose), accommodation (lose-win), competition (win-lose), passive aggression (indirect aggression or opposition), direct aggression (confrontation), compromise (negotiated lose-lose), and collaboration (win-win).

In Western contexts these typologies (or variations of them) are widely used by interpersonal and organizational communication specialists to help them make sense of differences in **conflict management** (the process by which individuals or groups try to find a satisfying outcome in conflict situations). To measure the conflict styles that feature in these taxonomies, a number of survey instruments have been developed (e.g., Hall's (1969) Conflict Management Survey; Rahim's (1983) Organizational Communication Conflict Instrument).

Most conceptualizations of conflict styles have been shaped within Western, individualistic cultural contexts, and questions have been raised about their applicability in other settings, especially in collectivist cultural contexts such as in Asia. Further, since the underlying conceptual frameworks of most of these taxonomies are not grounded in culturally based patterns of difference, Hammer (2005), for example, argues that they are not useful to identify and compare intercultural conflict styles.

With the limitations of previous taxonomies in view, Hammer (2005, 2015a) devised the **intercultural conflict style model** that is presented in Figure 9.1. This model is based on two core dimensions that he maintains are influenced by cultural values and beliefs: (1) the degree of directness when dealing with conflicts (**direct conflict styles** vs. **indirect conflict styles**) and (2) divergent ways of coping with the affective dimension of conflict interaction (**emotional expressive styles** vs. **emotionally restrained styles**). These responses are linked to individualism-collectivism and high-low-context communication patterns, which were discussed in Chapter 3.

As Figure 9.1 illustrates, Hammer's model identifies four basic conflict resolution styles that can be found in different cultural groups: (1) discussion (direct and emotionally restrained), (2) engagement (direct and emotionally expressive), (3) accommodation (indirect and emotionally restrained), and (4) dynamic (indirect and emotionally expressive). Let's take a brief look at each.

The **discussion style** emphasizes a verbally direct approach to conflict situations that is tempered by an emotionally restrained response. People who adopt this style generally follow

A Model of Intercultural Conflict Style

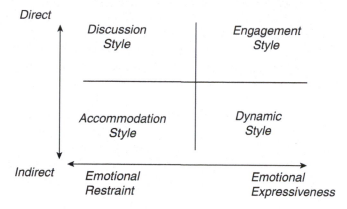

Figure 9.1 A model of intercultural conflict style (adapted from Hammer 2005).

the maxim, 'say what you mean and mean what you say'. They pay careful attention to their word choice so that their views are clearly conveyed. Intense expressions of emotion are avoided; instead people prefer to calmly discuss disagreements in a conversational, informal style, drawing on facts whenever possible rather than personal feelings. The discussion style is widely used by European Americans, Australians, and other people from individualistic nations.

The **engagement style** is characterized by a more verbally direct and confrontational or direct approach to dealing with conflict. The display of intense verbal and nonverbal expressions of emotion is considered an acceptable way to demonstrate one's sincerity, concern, and willingness to work hard to resolve conflict. Some studies have linked this style to African Americans, Southern Europeans, and some Russians (Martin & Nakayama 2018b).

The **accommodation style** emphasizes a more indirect and emotionally restrained approach to dealing with conflict. To prevent a dispute from escalating, people who use this style employ ambiguous language, silence, and avoidance. **Emotional restraint** (controlling the expression of one's emotions) is regarded as essential to maintain interpersonal harmony among the parties. Intermediaries (e.g., mutual friends, colleagues) or mediators may also be used to manage conflict. **Mediation** refers to the settlement or negotiation of a conflict or dispute by an independent person. **Negotiation** is a process by which the parties or group resolve a dispute by holding discussions and coming to an agreement that is mutually acceptable. **Mediators** or **intermediaries** are third parties that may facilitate negotiations and dialogue between the disputants. The accommodating style is often used by Latinos, American Indians, and Asians.

The **dynamic style** involves the use of indirect strategies and emotionally intense expression to deal with substantive disagreements. **Emotional expression** refers to observable verbal and nonverbal actions that convey emotions. People who adopt the dynamic style in conflict situations (e.g., Arabs) may use linguistic devices such as hyperbole and metaphors. They may also repeat their message, use ambiguous language, tell stories, or use third party intermediaries to try to resolve conflicts. Thus this style is characterized by emotionally confrontational discourse and expression. Hammer (2015a) asserts that the credibility and trustworthiness of each party is linked to the degree of emotional expressiveness.

For Hammer, 'the ability to recognize and respond appropriately to cultural differences in conflict style is critically important in effectively managing and resolving disagreements and conflict' (Intercultural Conflict Style, ICS n.d.). To facilitate this he devised the Intercultural

Conflict Style Inventory, a tool that is now widely used to measure preference for the cross-cultural conflict styles that feature in his model. As well as learning about their own conflict style, respondents are provided with information about the strengths and weaknesses of the other cross-cultural approaches to dealing with conflict. Hammer (2005, 2015a) posits that heightened awareness of culturally based styles can help resolve intercultural conflict.

While some cross-cultural studies indicate that people in different cultures tend to display consistent styles across a variety of conflict situations, it is important to recognize that individual level factors also influence actions and behaviors. For this reason we must be wary about making generalizations about cultures and conflict styles. Cultures are complex and dynamic. As conditions change, individuals and speech communities adapt their language use, nonverbal behaviors, communication strategies, and conflict styles. People may vary their responses to disagreements and conflicts depending on the setting and situation (e.g., the language being used, the status and power of the disputant, the degree of familiarity with the parties involved, the level of formality, etc.). Individual characteristics and preferences also influence the ways conflicts unfold. Taxonomies can lead to stereotyping if not verified by experience (LeBaron 2003). As noted by Folger *et al.* (2018), culture may influence one's conflict style, but many other elements may also play a role.

FACEWORK AND INTERCULTURAL CONFLICT RESOLUTION

Concerned about an overreliance on Western notions of conflict and conflict interaction styles, Ting-Toomey (2005, 2012, 2017, 2018) developed the **conflict face negotiation theory**, which addresses the ways face-losing and face-saving behaviors can influence intercultural conflict situations. In particular, her theory helps explain why individuals from high-context cultures (e.g., collectivist, Asian settings) tend to manage conflict differently than people who have been socialized in low-context cultures (e.g., individualistic, Western contexts). As you will see, in this framework identity is positioned as a major factor in intercultural conflict episodes.

Face is present in every culture on our planet although the ways individuals or groups interpret the meaning of face and enact facework varies. Within the context of the conflict face negotiation theory, the concept of **face** refers to 'an assessment of the "worthiness" of social image identity issues', while '**facework**' denotes the 'verbal and nonverbal behaviors that protect/save self-face, other-face, mutual-face, or communal-face within a sociocultural situation' (Ting-Toomey 2018: 775). Thus, face is linked to the 'emotional significance and estimated calculations that we attach to our own social self-worth and the social self-worth of others' (Ting-Toomey 2005: 73). It is 'a precious identity resource in communication because it can be threatened, enhanced, and undermined, and bargained over' (ibid: 73).

Within the face negotiation theory, there are many terms. **Self-face concern** refers to the 'protective concern for one's own identity image when one's own face is threatened in the conflict episode' (Ting-Toomey 2015b: 326). **Other-face concern** is 'the concern for accommodating the other conflict party's identity image in the conflict situation' (ibid, p. 326). **Mutual-face concern** refers to 'the concern for both parties' images and the image of the relationship' (ibid: 326). **Mutual facework** is the process of constructing a shared sense of identity (Ting-Toomey 2015b). Communicating respect and a positive regard for self and others is referred to as **face management**, while **facework** refers to 'the communication strategies used to defend, challenge, support, or even upgrade self-face and other-face identity issues in an emotionally vulnerable encounter' (Ting-Toomey 2018: 776). Cultural, relational, and situational factors affect the facework strategies that are used in conflict situations.

The conflict face negotiation theory stems from the following assumptions: (1) no matter their cultural background, people try to maintain and negotiate face in communicative events; (2) the concept of face is especially problematic in emotionally threatening or identity vulnerable situations when the situated identities of the communicators are challenged; (3) the cultural value scales of individualism-collectivism (Bhawuk 2018b) and small-large power distance (van der Zee & Hofhuis 2018) shape facework concerns and styles; (4) the value patterns inherent in individualism and collectivism shape members' preferences for self-oriented facework or other-oriented facework; (5) small and large power distance value patterns shape members' preferences for **horizontal-based facework** (informal-symmetrical strategies/equal treatment) vs. **vertical-based facework** (formal-asymmetrical strategies/deferential treatment); (6) the value dimensions, coupled with individual, relational, and situational factors, influence the use of specific facework behaviors in particular cultural scenes; and (7) **intercultural facework competence** is 'the optimal integration of knowledge, mindfulness, and communication skills in managing vulnerable identity-based conflict situations appropriately, effectively, and adaptively' (Ting-Toomey 2018: 776).

Intercultural conflict involves behaviors that can be both **face-threatening** (actions that cause someone to be humiliated) and **face-saving** or **face-giving** (actions that protect or support an individual's self-image or reputation). In an antagonistic conflict situation, individuals or groups may experience **face loss** when they are not treated in a way that respects their preferred self-identities (e.g., position, status, self-image). A **face-threatening act** involves a stressful episode in which one's identity is challenged or ignored. The conflict face negotiation theory posits that repeated face loss and face threat frequently result in an escalation in the conflict situation or a breakdown in negotiations.

In an intercultural conflict situation, individuals may have very different ideas about what language and communication styles are appropriate. **Face threats** (challenges to an individual's self-image) may intentionally or unintentionally occur due to **sociopragmatic expectancy violations** (e.g., nonverbal acts or language usage that is perceived to be inappropriate in relation to one's self-ascribed status or role identity) (Spencer-Oatey 2008b; Thomas 1995). People from different linguistic and cultural backgrounds may not share the same understandings about what discourse and nonverbal behaviors are appropriate in a particular setting or situation, and misunderstandings can escalate into conflict situations (Arundale 2006; Ting-Toomey 2012, 2015b, 2018). In a discourse community, individuals become familiar with specific face-related conflict behaviors and may be unsure how to respond when second language speakers do not speak or behave in the ways they expect (Arundale 2006; Spencer-Oatey 2005, 2008b). In intercultural interactions, individuals or groups may be surprised and even shocked when they are exposed to unfamiliar facework and **conflict management styles.** The latter refers to 'patterned responses to conflict across situations' (Zhang 2018: 1271) and may include behaviors such as animated displays of emotion, swearing, and avoidance, among others.

Spencer-Oatey (2008b) observes that people from different linguistic and cultural backgrounds may adopt different strategies to manage face and maintain **rapport** (mutual empathy and understanding) in interpersonal interactions and conflict situations: a **rapport-enhancement orientation** (a desire to strengthen or enhance harmonious relations between interlocutors), a **rapport maintenance orientation** (a desire to maintain or protect harmonious relations), a **rapport-neglect orientation** (a lack of concern for the quality of interpersonal relations perhaps because of a focus on the self), and a **rapport-challenge orientation** (a desire to challenge or impair harmonious relations between the interlocutors).

When a second language is involved in the conflict situation, various linguistic elements and paralanguage (e.g., the tone of voice, word choice) can result in a mismatch between **facework styles** (pattern of behaviors designed to manage face). Disparate conflict goals, assumptions, and **facework strategies** (steps taken to manage face) can further complicate the situation. Whether intended or not, both linguistic and nonlinguistic elements can hamper rapport between the interlocutors, derail the conflict management process, and lead to an escalation in the intercultural conflict.

INTERCULTURAL CONFLICT COMPETENCE

To prevent miscommunication and misattributions from continuously spiraling into major intercultural conflicts, it is essential to have an understanding of the components of intercultural conflict competence. While Chapter 11 broadly explores the construct of intercultural (communicative) competence, this section focuses on attributes and characteristics of individuals who skillfully manage intercultural conflict situations.

First, it is important to define what is meant by intercultural conflict competence. As noted in Chapter 1, Ting-Toomey (2012: 279–80) refers to it as 'the mindful management of emotional frustrations and conflict interaction struggles due primarily to cultural, linguistic, or ethnic group membership differences'. This term encompasses the use of effective and appropriate facework strategies in intercultural conflict situations (e.g., conflict facework competence as defined in the conflict face negotiation theory). **Conflict facework competence** entails 'the development of a deep knowledge structure of the cultural-framed social setting, the key conflict parties' sociocultural and personal identities, the conflict speech event, and the activation of culturally/linguistically appropriate and effective facework negotiation skills in respect to all the situational and multi-layered features' (ibid: 286).

Interculturalists (e.g., LeBaron 2003, Ting-Toomey 2004, 2012, 2017) have identified a number of core elements in intercultural conflict competence: culture-sensitive knowledge, mindfulness (mindful awareness, mindful fluency), constructive conflict communication skills (e.g., second language proficiency, sociopragmatic awareness, intercultural and interpersonal conflict management skills), and communication adaptability. Let's look at each in turn.

Culture-sensitive knowledge

Ting-Toomey (2004, 2009, 2012, 2015b, 2017) maintains that culturally based knowledge is the most vital ingredient in intercultural conflict competence. Without it, individuals may adhere to an ethnocentric stance and judge all unfamiliar conflict behaviors as weird or unsophisticated in comparison with their own (or their in-group's) ways of dealing with disputes. With more knowledge of diverse ways of handling conflicts (e.g., awareness of the conflict scripts and styles that are prevalent in other cultural settings), individuals can suspend negative valuations and reflect on what may lie behind unfamiliar or unexpected behaviors in misunderstandings and conflict episodes.

With adequate cultural knowledge one can learn to reframe one's interpretation of a conflict situation and take into account the other person's cultural frame of reference. At the same time it is essential to bear in mind that not all people from a particular linguistic, cultural, or ethnic background behave in the same way. Not all individuals who share a similar linguistic, cultural, or ethnic background adopt the same conflict style or view conflicts in the same way.

Mindfulness

To effectively manage intercultural conflicts it is essential to recognize the potential effect of one's personal and cultural communication expectations, conflict communication style, cognitions, and emotional display on the conflict situation. At the same time it is essential to become attuned to the other conflict party's communication assumptions, cognitions, language use, and emotions (Arasaratnam-Smith 2018; LeBaron & Pillay 2006; Ting-Toomey 2012, 2015b). For Ting-Toomey (2015b), **mindfulness**, within the context of conflict competence, means 'attending to one's internal assumptions, cognitions, and emotions and, at the same time, becoming attuned to the other's conflict assumptions, cognitions, and emotions' (p. 327).

Mindful awareness requires us to reflect on our own and other's cultural ways of knowing and being (LeBaron 2003; Ting-Toomey 2012). This process can draw our attention to the ways we frame conflict situations and make choices that ultimately either heighten tension or resolve intercultural conflicts. Recognition of face and identity needs (our own and those of the other person) is essential to resolve tense situations in a sensitive manner. **Mindful fluency** requires us to 'tune into our own cultural, linguistic, and personal habitual assumptions in scanning a problematic interaction scene' and 'the willingness to learn from the unfamiliar other' (Ting-Toomey 2012: 288). In other words, it is necessary to develop awareness of both self and other in conflict episodes. Closely related to this is **cultural intelligence**, that is, the ability and competence to use all the human senses to converse, empathize, function, and transact effectively with those of another cultural background' (Asser & Langbein-Park 2015: 165). In conflict situations, these skills are imperative.

It is also important to be open to learning other **conflict management practices** (ways to resolve disputes) from our communication partners (and through other means, such as this book). In order to accommodate intercultural differences, it is helpful to step back from the conflict situation to consider how your interlocutors may be viewing the dispute. Viewing intercultural conflict episodes from an ethnorelative orientation rather than a narrow, ethnocentric lens can reduce hostility and make it easier to negotiate a resolution. For example, if a second language speaker is using indirect responses or remaining silent in a conflict situation, instead of rushing to a negative valuation, a **mindful intercultural communicator** considers his or her emotional and cognitive reactions and reflects on why the individual may be behaving in this way. A flexible intercultural communicator may then consider modifying his or her own approach to the conflict and enact facework sensitive behaviors.

Constructive conflict communication skills

Language is a core element in intercultural conflict situations and if disagreements and disputes are to be resolved in a manner that is mutually satisfactory, interactants need well developed interpersonal communication skills and, in many cases, fluency in a second language. **Constructive conflict communication skills** refer to 'our operational abilities to manage a conflict situation appropriately and effectively via skillful language, verbal, and nonverbal behaviors, whether in a first or second language' (Ting-Toomey 2012: 288). In particular, skills such as deep listening, de-centering, face sensitive respectful dialogue skills, mindful reframing, comprehension checks, and collaborative conflict negotiation skills are essential for intercultural mediators, especially when a second language is involved (Putnam 2013; Ting-Toomey 2004, 2012).

Communication adaptability

In intercultural conflict episodes we must also be flexible and willing to modify our interaction behaviors and goals to meet the specific needs of the situation. Cognitive, affective, and behavioral adjustments can facilitate the resolution of intercultural conflict situations. For example, **dynamic conflict code-switching** (e.g., adapting our conflict style to meet the other conflict party's communication approach, using their first language) can signal our respect and desire to preserve the relationship and resolve the conflict in an amicable way. (This notion is similar to the act of convergence that is associated with the CAT, the communication accommodation theory that was introduced in Chapter 3.)

Individuals who develop the skills and attributes of intercultural conflict competence are in a much stronger and healthier position to deal with difficulties that arise when communicating with people who have been socialized in a different linguistic and cultural environment.

MANAGING LANGUAGE AND INTERCULTURAL CONFLICT SITUATIONS

The ability to thrive in a multicultural world is now central to our survival; it is a basic life-skill on our shrinking planet. In every land, people from around the world pass through, communicating, coupling, trading, and sometimes fighting. They make things together, share strategies and resources, draw on commonalities to build bridges, and

Plate 9.3 While conflict is a natural part of life, intercultural conflict competence can help people deal more constructively with conflicts that arise with individuals or groups who have a different linguistic and cultural background. © Jane Jackson

come into conflict over differences. . . . The need to summon creativity and exercise the choice to cooperate has never been more urgent.

– (Lebaron & Pillay 2006: 12)

While conflict is part of every culture and is unavoidable in human life, there are steps that all of us can take to enhance our intercultural conflict competence and prevent intercultural disagreements from escalating into destructive conflicts.

- In a conflict situation, be aware of your own goals and those of others. Look for common grounds or overlapping between your aims and those of the other person.
- Bear in mind that the way conflict is expressed, perceived, and dealt with varies among cultures. In intercultural interactions, your communication partner may not view the situation as you do and may try to manage the conflict in ways that are unfamiliar or uncomfortable for you. Make an effort to understand the situation from the other person's perspective and refrain from dismissing a different conflict style as simplistic and unworkable.
- Stay centered and push yourself to go beyond traditional stereotypes and dualistic ('us' vs. 'them') thinking, whereby 'us' is superior. While approaches to conflict vary across cultures, remember that not everyone who is affiliated with a particular cultural or ethnic group follows the styles identified in the taxonomies that have been discussed in this chapter. For example, don't automatically assume that your Japanese groupmate will be non-expressive and accommodating, or that your German friends will adopt an expressive, confrontational style in conflict situations. Observe and learn from experience.
- Listen attentively before responding. Conflicts can escalate when we do not listen to each other. Even if you feel that you are becoming emotional, try to be patient and attend to what others are saying. In second language situations be sensitive to the possibility that you are misunderstanding what is being said. It is also conceivable that you are not conveying your ideas or feelings in a way that is being understood as you would like. Lack of fluency in the language being used may serve as a barrier in conflict situations. Patience, careful listening, and explicit comprehension checks (e.g., asking questions to be sure one's message is clear) are essential in intercultural interactions, especially when a second language is involved. In a conflict situation, plan your message with care, especially when either you or your communication partner is using a second language.
- When misunderstandings and conflict arise, try to understand both sides of an issue, and be open to differing perspectives. Together, you and the other communicators may synthesize your ideas and come up with a creative third perspective or resolution that is mutually acceptable.
- If you are accustomed to verbally and nonverbally conveying your emotions, recognize that this may have negative consequences when the other person is used to a more indirect, restrained style of communication. Be careful of your word choice and monitor your nonverbal behaviors. Avoid actions which may appear threatening such as standing very close to the other person. While it is normal to become angry in some conflict situations, it is essential to move past the hostility and refrain from seeking retribution. Carefully observe the nonverbal behaviors of other people involved in your disagreement. Monitor and adapt your nonverbal behaviors in conflict situations.
- Be sensitive to face and identity needs (your own and those of the other party). In particular, make use of positive facework strategies and demonstrate respect for the other person's identities and position within a particular sociocultural context.

■ Avoid personal attacks, offensive or abusive language, profanity, name calling, and emotional overstatements in conflict situations. Disagreements may escalate if degrading or disrespectful comments are made about an individual's culture, language (e.g., accent, dialect), ethnicity, religion, or background. Also, remember that ignoring the discriminatory or racist behavior of others gives permission for these offenses to continue.

■ Even in difficult situations, try to retain your sense of humor, and be willing to let go of your hostility and feelings of revenge. Lessen your defensiveness in conflict situations. Be willing to admit mistakes, learn from them, and apply what you have learned in future intercultural interactions.

■ Be sensitive to the power dimension in all conflict situations. In conflict situations, some individuals may have more power or control. For example, if you are using your first language with someone who is not fully proficient in the language, remember that you are apt to be in a stronger position to convey your ideas in a persuasive manner.

■ Check your perceptions of an intercultural conflict with trusted friends or colleagues who are familiar with the linguistic and cultural background of the other party in the dispute. Intermediaries may be able to suggest more effective and appropriate ways to diffuse the situation. Their feedback may help you to better understand what lies behind unfamiliar actions. From trusted friends you may discover ways to adapt your verbal and nonverbal communication style to resolve the conflict in mutually acceptable ways.

■ Recognize that people have different conflict styles, which often have cultural origins as well as personal characteristics. Failure to recognize and respect individual and cultural differences can lead to negative evaluations of persons and an escalation of the dispute.

■ Generate possible solutions to the conflict instead of focusing on the difficulties. Be proactive. Work with your communication partner to try to negotiate a solution that is mutually acceptable.

■ Identify your preferred conflict management style. (You could use one of the taxonomies discussed in this chapter.) What language and communication style do you use in conflict situations? What nonverbal behaviors do you use to complement or substitute your verbal message? Even though we may modify our conflict strategies depending on the situation and the type of conflict, we are apt to rely on a similar style in most situations. When we interact with others we may find that some conflict situations are more challenging than others, since our preferred conflict style may not be compatible with the other person. As well as becoming more self-aware, be attentive to the behaviors and reactions of your communication partners. How do people respond to your verbal and nonverbal actions in a conflict situation?

■ Be creative and expand your repertoire of conflict management strategies. If a particular way of dealing with conflict is not working, be willing to experiment with a different style. For example, if you are used to using very direct discourse to get your point across, and this is negatively affecting your interactions with a Taiwanese friend, try to use more indirect expressions and a less expressive approach. Adaptability and flexibility are central in the enhancement of intercultural relations including conflict situations.

■ Recognize the importance of context in conflict situations. Conflicts within a multicultural family context are apt to have different dimensions and consequences in workplace environments or public settings.

■ Finally, recognize that disputes do not need to end a relationship. Instead of isolating yourself from or fighting with the other party, wait until tempers have cooled. Then try to start a dialogue to resolve your differences. Communication should be sincere, respectful, and not rushed. Be attentive and open to different ways of seeing the conflict. Dialogue can help you to reach a deeper understanding of diversity conflict experiences.

SUMMARY

It is essential that we enhance our understanding of conflict and its terrain so that we can navigate the physical, psychological, and spiritual chasms that threaten to swallow us, creative potential and all. Enhancing our understanding of conflict necessarily means building awareness of ourselves – the common sense we share in cultural groups – and coming to know something of those who are different from us by culture and worldview.

(Lebaron & Pillay 2006: 12)

Conflict between individuals and groups is a natural feature of the human condition. When we interact and form bonds with other individuals, groups, or entities (e.g., organizations, nations), disagreements inevitably arise from time to time. Doreen Thompson, a freelance journalist, observes that 'Peace is not the absence of conflict but the presence of creative alternatives for responding to conflict'.

How we perceive and manage conflict defines the quality of our interpersonal, intercultural, and international relationships. Our ability (or inability) to resolve conflicts can lead to either their enhancement or demise. Whether the conflict is at the individual level or on the national or world stage, it is incumbent on all of us to heed Lebaron and Pillay's advice and develop the knowledge, skills, and mindset that facilitate the resolution of disputes. As our world is becoming more interdependent, intercultural conflict competence is essential for all members of the human race.

discussion questions

1　As the world becomes more interconnected and nations more multicultural, why do we continue to witness intercultural conflicts across the globe? Are conflicts a natural consequence of the process of globalization?

2　What are the main sources of intercultural conflicts at the individual level? At the regional or national level? At the international level? Discuss your ideas with a partner.

3　Why is it important to understand the context in which intercultural conflict occurs?

4　To maintain constructive intercultural relationships, do you think it is helpful to have an understanding of intercultural conflict styles, as suggested by Hammer (2015a)?

5　How might power differentials come into play in intercultural conflicts which involve a second language? Provide examples to illustrate your points.

6　Explain and discuss how face-concerns can influence the ways we manage conflict in intercultural situations. Offer relevant examples.

7　What types of intercultural conflicts occur on your campus or community? What groups have frequent disputes? How do groups manage and address these conflicts?

8　What is intercultural conflict competence? Discuss how individuals can develop their intercultural conflict competence. Why does this entail lifelong learning? Share your ideas with a partner.

activities

1 Identify four types of intercultural conflict and provide examples of each.
2 Recall a conflict that you have experienced. Did your linguistic and cultural background affect how you handled the situation? If yes, how?
3 Describe the following intercultural conflict styles: discussion, engagement, accommodation, and dynamic. Provide examples of each.
4 In small groups discuss your personal conflict style. What style do you use most often? How have your family, friends, educational, religious, and political institutions influenced this style? How does your personal conflict style affect your intercultural relationships? Discuss whether a different approach in some situations might lead to different outcomes.
5 With a partner, identify and agree on the requisite traits, skills, and knowledge of an effective intercultural conflict mediator.
6 Identify five ways in which face can play a role in the way conflict situations unfold.
7 In this chapter a number of suggestions have been offered to help manage language and intercultural conflict situations. Which ideas do you think are the most useful? In a small group discuss other constructive ways to resolve intercultural conflicts, especially ones that involve a second language.

further reading

Cahn, D.D. and Abigail, R.A. (2013) *Managing Conflict Through Communication*, 5th edn, Harlow: Pearson.

This text introduces the study of conflict and covers such topics as anger management and facework in relation to interpersonal conflict, group conflict, organizational conflict, and social conflict.

Cupach, W.R., Canary, D.J. and Spitzberg, B.H. (2009) *Competence in Interpersonal Conflict*, 2nd edn, Long Grove, IL: Waveland Press, Inc.

This text presents a conceptual framework to explain why communication competence is central to conflict management. The authors offer constructive guidelines that provide a basis for dealing with conflicts in five settings: intercultural, organizational, familial, mediation, and violence in intimate relationships.

Dai, X. and Chen, G-M. (eds.) (2017) *Conflict Management and Intercultural Communication: The Art of Intercultural Harmony*, London and New York: Routledge.

Adopting an interdisciplinary approach, this edited collection presents diverse views about ways to handle intercultural conflicts in a constructive manner in various cultural contexts.

Folger, J.P., Poole, M.S. and Stutman, R.K. (2013) *Working Through Conflict: Strategies for Relationships, Groups and Organizations*, 7th edn, Boston: Pearson.

This accessible text provides an introduction to conflict and conflict management that is grounded in theory, research, and practice. It includes a chapter on face-saving.

Companion Website: Continue your journey online

Visit the Companion Website for a variety of rich tools and resources to support and extend your intercultural learning. (Instructors who are qualified adopters of the text may access additional resources on this site.)

CHAPTER 10

Language and intercultural communication in the global workplace

Organizations face unprecedented challenges and opportunities driven largely by civilization's evolution into being more of a global, interconnected multiracial, multiethnic, and multicultural hybrid village.

(Tapia & Gisbert 2018: 485)

The increasing expansion of business activities into the international market and international recruitment have made linguistic and cultural diversity common attributes of a majority of workplaces in the world today, where most of the daily interaction among people inevitably involves intercultural communication.

(Sharifian & Jamarani 2013: 13)

As commerce continues to become more globalized and many countries become more linguistically diverse, the demand for multilingual communicators continues to grow as well. The ability to communicate in more than one language can make you a more competitive job candidate and open up a wider variety of career opportunities.

(Thill & Bovée 2015: 78)

learning objectives

By the end of this chapter, you should be able to:

1   Discuss the impact of globalization on today's workforce
2   Identify the benefits and challenges of diversity for the global workplace
3   Explain the role of language, culture, and power in the global workplace
4   Identify and explain key elements in cultural difference frameworks
5   Identify the benefits, limitations, and potential dangers of using the cultural difference frameworks for intercultural business education and diversity training
6   Identify constructive ways to enhance language and intercultural communication in the global workplace

INTRODUCTION

Today's interconnected world economy has had a profound effect on the global workplace. Large corporations and even small businesses have become increasingly multicultural and multilingual. Migration and global workforce mobility are bringing about more intercultural contact as temporary workers and long-term expatriates intermingle with people from many parts of the world. In organizations, individuals routinely work on teams or projects with colleagues or coworkers who have different linguistic, religious, and cultural backgrounds or disabilities.

This chapter begins by exploring the impact of globalization on the workplace and the dominant role of international English as the de facto language or lingua franca of global business. Next, we discuss the benefits of diversity in the global workforce and identify potential barriers to successful intercultural communication and integration in global organizations and work environments. We then review and critique five cultural difference frameworks that have been widely applied to business and management contexts. Attention then shifts to alternative, less essentialist approaches to understanding intercultural interactions in the global workplace. New understandings have implications for the preparation and support of workers and leaders in diverse organizations. Finally, the chapter concludes with some practical suggestions to enhance intercultural communication in the increasingly multicultural, multilingual workplace.

GLOBALIZATION AND DIVERSITY IN THE WORKPLACE

In a global environment characterised by complexity and ambiguity, one certainty about the future of organisations is that they are becoming increasingly multicultural and people will need to know more about culture and cultural differences to be effective in their everyday working lives. . . . The social context in which we live makes the understanding of intercultural interaction a prerequisite for those who aspire to successful careers.

(Mughan & O'Shea 2010: 109)

Globalization is not new; the exchange of ideas, goods, and people has long been a part of human history. As explained in Chapter 1, what is different today is the significant increase in the speed and volume of this contact due, in part, to advances in information and communication technologies, as well as modes of transportation. The modern world is experiencing much greater cultural, economic, political, and social interconnectedness (Sharifian & Jamarani 2013; Steger 2017). Nowadays, communication and organizational operations increasingly cross national boundaries and involve global business operations.

One of the consequences of globalization is increasing diversity in the workplace, which is profoundly changing the nature of organizations (Barak 2017; Cardon 2018). **Diversity** encompasses differences among humans with regard to culture, language, race, ethnicity, nationality, regional identification, gender, socioeconomic status, age, physical abilities and attributes, religious beliefs, sexual orientation, and political beliefs or other ideologies. **Surface-level diversity** refers to 'differences that are easily seen and generally verifiable via a quick assessment of physical characteristics, including gender, age, race, and national origin/ethnicity' (Baldwin *et al.* 2013: 471), whereas **deep level diversity** relates to differences that lie below the surface and are not so easily observable such as attitudes, beliefs, knowledge, skills, and values or worldviews. Later in the chapter we take a closer look at the benefits and challenges posed by increasing diversity in the global workplace. Before we do, let's turn our attention to the linguistic dimension of intercultural business interactions and consider the dominance of English in the global workplace.

ENGLISHIZATION, IDENTITY, AND THE GLOBAL WORKFORCE

Due, in part, to globalizing forces, the use of English in business and other sectors has strengthened significantly in recent decades. 'English is not only a language of wider communication in the modern world, it is far more than that— it is, in a singularly powerful sense, *the* "global language" of commerce, trade, culture, and research in the contemporary world' (Reagan & Schreffler 2005: 116). With the emergence of the 'knowledge society' or 'knowledge economy', English has become the lingua franca for business negotiations, multinational organizations, scientific communication, diplomacy, academic conferences, and international education in many nations on all continents (Jenkins 2013, 2015; Steger 2017). In many transnational corporations and outsourcing jobs, English has become a requirement for employment or promotion. By transforming English language learning and use into commodities for the global marketplace, the linguistic and cultural capital or value of English (Bourdieu 1986, 1991) has increased markedly in recent decades.

Reactions to the spread of English in the global workforce vary. In some regions, the language is considered a homogenizing, Western vehicle of **power** (authority or strength), domination, and privilege and is met with resistance and suspicion. The rise of English as the primary language of global business can have negative consequences for individuals and groups who do not have access to quality education in the language. As Krizan *et al.* (2011: 50) explain, '[t]he extensive use of English as the primary business language is fortunate for English-speaking citizens; however, recognize that for most people in the world English is a second language'. Critics of globalization warn that lack of proficiency in English and the skills prized by today's knowledge industries (e.g., advanced technological skills) can disadvantage individuals and organizations by denying them access to resources and global markets (e.g., lucrative deals, intercultural/international contracts). This results in a **power imbalance**, that is, an unequal distribution of influence and control with certain individuals, groups, or nations dominating others. This imbalance perpetuates economic disparity, often privileging Western citizens, nations, and corporations (Sorrells 2012, 2016). The term '**English hegemony**' refers to 'the situation in which English is so dominant that various forms of inequality and discrimination take place in communication all around the world' (Tsuda 2018: 720). For example, in some contexts minority languages have been displaced by English, as organizations and communities struggle to compete in the global arena.

In today's global marketplace business professionals who speak English as an additional language routinely communicate in the language with professionals who have another first language. In these situations they may speak a localized variety of English rather than a 'native speaker, standard' form of the language (e.g., received pronunciation). This phenomenon is prevalent in business interactions in a growing number of postcolonial contexts (e.g., Singapore, Ghana, Hong Kong, Indonesia Liberia).

The spread of English or **Englishization** in organizations and businesses in many regions has also brought about an increase in the mixing of a local language or dialect with English among bilingual or emerging bilingual employees (e.g., code-mixing, code-switching) (Coulmas 2005; Holmes & Wilson 2017). Globally, English has become the most widely used language in both code-mixing and code-switching styles of communication.

In India, South Asian professionals routinely mix English with their mother tongue in oral and written discourse in both business and social contexts. Kachru (2005) attributes this practice to a complex mix of motives (e.g., sociolinguistic, psycholinguistic, situational, instrumental, identity).

It is not necessarily for lack of competency that speakers switch from one language to another, and the choices they make are not fortuitous. Rather, just like socially motivated choices of varieties of one language, choices across language boundaries are imbued with social meaning.

(Coulmas 2005: 109)

Kachru (2005: 114) concurs, adding that, 'the social value attached to the knowledge of English' in many situations, including intercultural business interactions, may be even more important than instrumental motives.

When English serves as 'an indicator of status, modernization, mobility and "outward-looking" attitude', business professionals in South Asia and other parts of the world may seek to enhance their social positioning and work status by incorporating it into their discourse (Kachru 2005: 114). Code-mixing then functions as 'an index of social identity' (Myers-Scotton 2006: 406) and workplace prestige (McKay & Bokhorst-Heng 2008). In Nigeria and Sri Lanka, for example, the desire for an elevated social status can motivate educated elites (e.g., business executives, team leaders) to use a mixture of English and the vernacular in social and workplace contexts. As Trudgill (2003: 23) explain, code-mixing may serve as a strategy to project a **dual identity**: 'that of a modern, sophisticated, educated person *and* that of a loyal, local patriot'. Language usage in the bilingual or multilingual workplace can be complicated and more strategic than it first appears.

As explained in Chapter 5, it is important to remember that there is a close connection between language, culture, and identity. The choice of the language and variety one uses (e.g., regional dialect, accent, code-mixing) can affect one's status and positioning within organizations. Both linguistic and social restrictions influence code choices and attitudes in the bilingual or multilingual workplace (Coulmas 2005; Holmes & Wilson 2017). In some contexts or situations, for instance, employees who are non-native speakers of English may switch less frequently to English or even shun code-mixing completely to maintain ingroup ties (e.g., fit in with their work team). Cliques may also form among speakers who use a particular variety of the language. (This issue is explored further when we discuss challenges in the diverse workplace.) Second language speakers may also use particular codes to 'renegotiate and perhaps resist the established identities, group loyalties, and power relations' (Canagarajah 1999: 73). The relationship between code choice, identity, and culture in the global workplace as well as in the wider society is dynamic, complex, context-dependent, and power-laden.

THE BENEFITS OF DIVERSITY IN THE WORKPLACE

Differences in everything from age and gender to religion and ethnic heritage to geography and military experience enrich the workplace. . . . Immigration and workforce diversity both create advantages – and challenges – for business communicators throughout the world.

(Thill & Bovée 2015: 67)

In today's globalized world an organization's success increasingly depends on its ability to embrace and manage diversity (Tapia & Gisbert 2018; Thill & Bovée 2015). A multicultural and multilingual workforce can be beneficial in a number of ways. It can add value to businesses and organizations by helping them to become more adaptable, flexible, and productive.

Synergy and enhanced creativity can lead to innovations, more effective problem solving, and better relations with diverse customers or clients both in their home environment and abroad. Diversity in the workplace can help organizations and businesses to extend into the global marketplace and, ultimately, enhance their reputation and competitive advantage. As well as bolstering organizations, diversity has the potential to strengthen the personal growth and intercultural sensitivity of staff. This, in turn, can lead to positive intercultural interactions in other life domains. Let's take a closer look at potential benefits.

Increased adaptability and productivity

When managed well, diversity can help organizations become more adaptable to the increasingly complex, dynamic, and interconnected world in which we live and work. Besides unique individual characteristics, employees possess strengths derived from their linguistic, gender, and cultural socialization. Coworkers with diverse backgrounds, ages, religions, and attributes bring unique experiences, ideas, and perceptions to groups and work teams. Pooling their

Plate 10.1 Diversity can enrich the global workplace and also benefit one's social life, potentially bringing about significant personal growth and intercultural sensitivity. © Jane Jackson

varied skills and knowledge can strengthen the team's productivity and responsiveness to the changes being brought about by globalization. Diverse employees can help companies to adapt to demographic changes in their physical location as well as fluctuating markets and customer demands. When handled properly, diversity in the workplace can leverage the strengths and talents of each worker to enhance the adaptability, flexibility, productivity, and overall performance of organizations. This can provide a competitive advantage.

Organizations that embrace diversity in the workplace can inspire employees to perform to their highest ability. Company-wide strategies can be implemented to optimize the potential of all members. Individual or group contributions may be recognized and rewarded, taking into account what is appropriate in that context. When employees from diverse backgrounds feel valued and included in decision making, they are likely to be more invested in the success of the organization. All of these steps can lead to higher levels of satisfaction, a greater sense of belonging in the organization, and, ultimately, more productivity, profit, and return on investment.

Synergy and enhanced creativity

Businesses and organizations that employ a diverse workforce can generate a greater variety of solutions to a wide range of issues (e.g., problems in service, sourcing, allocation of resources, labor disputes, the pressure to expand in the global marketplace). The sharing of diverse experiences can inspire idea creation and increase innovation. For this to materialize, leaders (e.g., administrators, team leaders, unit managers) must take steps to cultivate an open, responsive atmosphere in teams and other workplace domains or activities.

Fluency in more than one language, exposure to diverse cultures (e.g., international internships or work placements, service learning, study abroad), previous work experience (e.g., diverse group or teamwork), and intercultural competence are assets for the modern workplace. With support and encouragement, the sharing of diverse perspectives can generate novel ideas for products, customer interaction strategies, and advertising methods, among others. In a receptive atmosphere, creativity and idea generation can flourish.

When employees from different backgrounds are encouraged to express their views in ways that are comfortable for them, they are more likely to contribute. Workers who are at ease expressing viewpoints that differ from the majority can generate a much larger and more varied pool of innovative ideas and proposals. **Cultural synergy** refers to the combined power of different cultural elements (e.g., people from diverse backgrounds) working together to create a greater, stronger effect than if they were separate. In the global workplace this collaboration can be a positive force for creativity and change. Clever, forward thinking organizations that draw on the ideas of diverse employees to develop business plans and strategies are better positioned to meet the needs of diverse customers and clients.

Enhanced relations with diverse customers/clients

With increasing global mobility, a company's current and potential customers or clients are likely to come from a variety of linguistic and cultural backgrounds. A diverse workforce can strengthen the organization's relations with multicultural and multilingual populations and better meet the needs of specific customer groups (e.g., minorities who are not fluent in the primary language of the community, members of a particular religion). Ideally, the cultural and linguistic diversity of the staff base reflects the community that the organization serves.

Employing staff from diverse backgrounds can increase the overall responsiveness of service and enhance worker-customer relations. Employees that resemble the natural diversity in society can help a company to improve and increase customer relationship connections. Shared visions and understandings can allow employees to reach out to customers in more appropriate and effective ways. When customers feel that their needs and concerns have been properly addressed, they are liable to be more satisfied. Customers who feel heard and understood are more likely to become repeat customers.

If customers or clients can use their first language when interacting with customer service representatives, they may have a better impression of both the representative and the company. In Brussels, for example, multilingual customer service representatives may interact with French-speaking, Dutch-speaking, German-speaking, or English-speaking customers in their first language. As noted by Thill and Bovée (2015), proficiency in more than one language can be a great asset in organizations. With the intensification of globalization and migration, one can expect the demand for bilingual or multilingual communicators to grow.

International reach

Diversity in terms of language competency and ethnic affiliations can also benefit a company that has global aspirations or ties. In addition to interacting with local minorities, bilingual or multilingual employees can help a business to explore and penetrate new global markets and cope with the challenges of international partnerships. Administrators and other employees with international experience and effective intercultural communication skills can assist a company to provide customers with culturally and linguistically appropriate products to customers both locally and abroad.

Globally minded individuals who have well developed second language skills, intercultural sensitivity, and business acumen can help an organization to expand its reach and offer culturally and linguistically appropriate services to foreign clients. **Business acumen** refers to one's ability to understand business situations and make appropriate decisions in a short amount of time. Skilled, global-ready employees can help small businesses to better understand the needs of diverse customers, broaden their range of services or products, and widen the international scope of their operation.

Enhanced reputation and competitive advantage

Organizations that promote diversity and inclusion are much more likely to be viewed favorably by multicultural customers, local and global business partners, and the media. When a business develops a reputation as an open, inclusive workplace, it also has a greater chance of recruiting and retaining talented individuals from diverse backgrounds, including skilled individuals with disabilities. Positive, multicultural environments can attract the best and brightest from all backgrounds. With a capable, diverse workforce, companies are better positioned for success in the competitive marketplace.

Personal growth and intercultural development

In addition to enhancing the competitiveness of organizations, workplace diversity has the potential to stimulate personal growth in employees and their leaders. Exposure to new languages, perspectives (e.g., different worldviews), values, and behaviors (e.g., communication styles) can help individuals develop intellectually, psychologically, and socially. Through sustained intercultural contact and interactions, employees may begin to see their work and surroundings in a new light. If observant and open to novel ideas and ways of being, over time, they can enhance their intercultural awareness and sensitivity. Workers may also become motivated to learn another language and venture abroad. Their horizons may be further broadened as friendships form with coworkers from diverse backgrounds.

As they become more receptive to diversity, individuals can acquire the habit of reflecting on issues and situations from multiple perspectives instead of relying on a monocultural lens and familiar ways of doing things. Gradually, they may shift from an ethnocentric to an ethnorelative orientation and develop more effective and appropriate ways to communicate with people (e.g., colleagues, customers) who have a different linguistic and cultural background. They may also become more at ease when interacting with people who have disabilities. Interacting with culturally diverse coworkers and customers/clients has the potential to gradually break down the subconscious barriers of ethnocentrism and xenophobia that were discussed in Chapter 6. This can have benefits that extend well beyond the workplace. Along with adding value to organizations, it can help employees to become more responsible citizens and mindful, ethical members of society.

THE CHALLENGES OF DIVERSITY IN THE WORKPLACE

> No one can be exempted from dealing with issues related to cultural diversity. . . . Establishing common ground with others and developing the necessary empathy and degree of intercultural awareness, while constantly challenging one's own perspectives, has therefore become almost a daily obligation for all those involved in the work process.
>
> (Guilherme *et al.* 2010: 243)

Although there are many rewards to be gained from workplace diversity, it can also pose challenges for both frontline employees (e.g., blue collar workers) and administrators (e.g., managers, team leaders, supervisors). To reap the benefits of diversity, it is essential for organizations to recognize potential difficulties and know how to deal with them in an effective, ethical manner. Some of the most common challenges of workplace diversity are: a language barrier (e.g., a power imbalance), translating/interpreting limitations, conflicting communication styles (both verbal and nonverbal), variations in emotional display, a clash in values, conflict (interpersonal, intercultural, and organizational), opposition to change, resistance to integration, gender differences, religious differences, sociocultural differences, ethnocentricism and assumptions of similarities, prejudicial attitudes, discrimination, and racism. Let's examine each in more detail.

A language barrier

In a diverse workplace, individuals who are not fluent in the primary language of communication are disadvantaged. It can also be challenging for proficient speakers to explain ideas and procedures to second language workers or colleagues who are not following the discourse. Communication difficulties are compounded when jargon, slang, and special codes are used in business contexts. Ineffective communication can result in confusion, frustration, misunderstandings, lack of teamwork, conflict, anger, and low morale. In worst case scenarios it can also result in accidents and injuries in the workplace.

When workers find directions confusing and do not understand what is expected of them, naturally, it is difficult for them to carry out tasks. This can lead to a decrease in productivity and frustration for all involved. For example, if a manager gives instructions about completing a report and the employee cannot fully comprehend what has been said, errors may ensue. Tasks may not be carried out in a satisfactory manner, especially if managers do not use explicit comprehension checks to ensure that the directions have been fully understood.

Communication problems may also arise among individuals who speak different varieties of the same language. For example, using the same terms and expressions in Britain and Australia may lead to misunderstandings when the meanings differ. In the workplace it is also essential to bear in mind that language barriers may be misinterpreted as cultural misunderstandings, and vice versa.

When many employees are not fully proficient in the primary language of the workplace, companies may organize language for specific purposes courses that are tailor-made for them. For example, a branch of a global company may arrange language enhancement courses for employees that are directly related to the language needs of their specific jobs (e.g., separate classes for secretarial staff, managers, phone operators, etc.).

Outsourcing, the contracting out of an internal business process to a third party organization, often requires workers to perform tasks in a second language. At call centers in Egypt, India, and the Philippines, for example, employees learn English expressions (e.g., colloquialisms) and master accents that can be understood by the international customers they serve.

For diversity to benefit a workplace, language barriers must be overcome in ways that are constructive and culturally sensitive. In addition to targeted business language lessons for second language speakers, it is helpful for those who speak the primary language of the workplace to learn at least basic expressions in the languages of their minority colleagues. For example, in a workplace situation in Vancouver where many of the employees are from Mainland China it can be conducive to positive working relations if local English-speaking employees learn to say at least some phrases in Mandarin. For diversity to succeed in the workplace, language barriers need to be overcome in creative and sensitive ways.

Translation/interpreting limitations

To deal with a language barrier in intercultural interactions, companies often seek help from bilingual speakers (e.g., their employees) who do not have special training in translating/interpreting. Recognizing the difficult, sensitive nature of this work, corporations may elect to hire professional translators and interpreters. **Translation** refers to the written form of mediation (e.g., translation of written business documents and texts), while **interpreting** the oral form (e.g., the interpreter translates spoken communication). **Simultaneous interpreting** refers to the act of interpreting while the speaker is talking (e.g., at international business conference or meeting); **consecutive interpreting** takes place after the speaker has finished. As different skills are required, translators and interpreters usually receive different, specialized training.

In the global workplace, both translation and interpreting are challenging endeavors, and hiring bilingual speakers who are not professionally trained can easily lead to miscommunication. At minimum, professional interpreters need to possess the following knowledge and skills: adequate understanding of the subject to be interpreted, familiarity with both cultures, extensive vocabulary in both languages, and the ability to express thoughts clearly in both languages. Expressions in one language do not necessarily have an equivalent meaning in other languages, and concepts may be difficult to describe or explain in another language, especially for nonprofessionals (House 2012, 2018). Complications may then arise when the meaning in the translation is inaccurate.

Culture brokers or intermediaries may also be employed to bridge cultural differences in the workplace (e.g., facilitate the negotiation of international contracts, mediate intercultural conflicts, help immigrant workers adjust to the workplace). **Culture brokering** refers to the act of bridging or mediating between groups or people who have a different cultural backgrounds in order to reduce conflict or bring about change (Jezewski & Sotnik 2001; Michie 2014). A cultural broker or 'go-between' may advocate on behalf of individuals or groups (e.g., second language workers in a factory) to enhance working conditions and benefits.

Conflicting communication styles

Workplace settings typically involve both individual and group tasks. When people differ in terms of age, gender, language, culture, ethnicity, and many other aspects, it can be challenging for them to work together in a productive way, especially if they have divergent work styles and are unwilling to adapt. Instead of synergy, negative attitudes and lack of acceptance of differing verbal and nonverbal communication styles and degrees of formality can impede intercultural interactions, productivity, and camaraderie in the workplace. In some contexts, for example, business executives are accustomed to a formal style of communication and may feel ill at ease when their communication partners dispense with formalities (e.g., the use of formal titles and other honorifics) and interact in a relaxed, informal style. The use of first names may be considered too personal and this may impede business relationships. A mismatch of communication styles may also result in poor outcomes in intercultural job interviews as illustrated in *Cross-Talk*, a video produced by Gumperz (1979/1990) to draw attention to sources of miscommunication in intercultural organizational settings.

An employee who is used to **direct language** and a more forthright style of communication (e.g., giving explicit directions, clearly expressing likes and dislikes) may become easily frustrated, irritated, and confused when interacting with a coworker or supervisor who employs a more indirect style of communication (e.g., infers, suggests, implies views, or changes the subject rather than stating opinions directly). Examples of **indirect language** include: 'I have one small suggestion', 'I'm not sure if this is relevant but'. In both written communication (e.g., emails, letters) and oral discourse (e.g., conversations, meetings), **hedging**, the use of cautious of vague language, may be employed by indirect communicators (e.g., 'It may be that. . .', 'Perhaps, that might work. . .', 'It appears that. . .').

More used to 'telling it like it is', a direct communicator may mistakenly assume that the less direct speaker does not have a strong opinion about an issue and is rather indecisive or weak. In a business meeting, if an employee remains silent the direct communicator may incorrectly assume that the individual has understood, agreed, approved, or accepted what has been proposed. When suggestions are put forward in an indirect way, they may easily be overlooked by employees or managers who are more accustomed to people explicitly stating what is on their minds. Conversely, individuals who are more familiar with a less direct style of communication may perceive direct communicators as rude and aggressive.

Intercultural communication differences may also arise with regard to what is considered important or appropriate to share or communicate in a meeting or other business event. Views about how and when ideas should be introduced and expressed may differ. Expectations about when and how feedback (including reprimands) should be given or received can also vary among individuals from different cultural backgrounds. Communication style differences between male and female employees may further complicate workplace interactions. (See Chapter 3 for a discussion of verbal communication styles.)

Variations in emotional display/nonverbal codes

Workers may find some of the affective verbal and nonverbal behavior (e.g., emotional displays) of their colleagues baffling and annoying. In particular, the ways individuals from different cultural backgrounds respond to reprimands and requests may differ and this can lead to misattributions and misunderstandings. When a boss publicly reprimands an employee for failing to carry out a task in a satisfactory manner, the response may not be as expected and this can easily lead to more anger and mistrust. In some Asian contexts, for example, individuals who are reprimanded in the workplace may smile and look away. Rather than amusement, this nonverbal behavior is a sign of embarrassment as the person is losing face in front of others. Individuals who are not familiar with the local culture, however, can misinterpret this response as uncaring or defiant. Not surprisingly, negative perceptions and reactions can hinder intercultural communication and trust in the workplace. (See Chapter 4 for a discussion of nonverbal communication styles.)

A clash in values

Values are judgments about what is considered good and bad, important and unimportant in a particular culture. During enculturation, as children we learn what is acceptable and unacceptable behavior in particular contexts and situations. As we develop **sociopragmatic competence**, the ability to communicate appropriately in social situations in a particular cultural context, we learn to consider the status of our communication partners when we speak and express ourselves both verbally and nonverbally. For example, we may use different gestures and style of speech when interacting with our grandparents and peers. This learning continues when we enter the workforce and gain exposure to different situations and settings.

Even if we are working in our home environment and are members of the majority culture, we still need to learn new cultural rules within an organization or corporation. The term **corporate culture** refers to the culture of a particular business. In the workforce, we learn appropriate ways to represent our employer and interact with supervisors, coworkers, and clients. We learn what level of formality is appropriate in particular situations (e.g., dress, linguistic expressions, verbal and nonverbal communication styles). These organizational behaviors are guided by the prevalent values of the company and the wider community. Therefore individuals who come from a different cultural background may face more value conflicts than those from the majority culture. Cross-cultural psychologists have raised awareness of the challenges and consequences of conflicting values and expectations in the workplace. (Later in this chapter we examine and critique Hofstede's (2001, 2003) influential international study of cultural values in the workplace as well as other cultural difference frameworks.)

Conflict (interpersonal, intercultural, organizational, gender, etc.)

Just as in other domains of life, conflicts and disputes may occur in workplace situations. When employees from diverse backgrounds interact they bring with them ideas, values, and expectations that have been influenced by their upbringing and life experiences. From an early age, within a particular cultural context, males and females learn strategies to employ to avoid or cope with confrontations within particular cultural contexts. Some approaches work well in some business settings but are less effective in others. Well-intended conflict management techniques may backfire, and disputes may escalate.

Intercultural conflicts in organizations may stem from a range of factors, including differences in communication or work styles among team members, divergent views about the best ways to achieve company goals, disparate values, disagreements about policies and procedures, perceptions of discrimination (e.g., ethnic, gender, religious), and miscommunication due to a language barrier, among others. When individuals have a different **work ethic** (set of values based on hard work and discipline) this can cause friction.

Conflicts that are repressed or denied may fester and build resentment and frustration, creating additional problems for the organization. If managers and employees are not skillful in managing disagreements in the workplace, they may spiral into conflicts that are more difficult to resolve. (See Chapter 9 for more discussion on intercultural conflict and conflict resolution.)

Opposition to change

In any work situation, employees may refuse to accept that the social, linguistic, and cultural makeup of their workplace has become or is becoming more diverse. Some may be uncomfortable working alongside people with disabilities or individuals who speak a different language, have a different skin color, or belong to another religion. Individuals may reject the notion that change is inevitable. The 'we've always done it this way' mentality can curtail new ideas and inhibit growth in a company. Those who vehemently oppose workforce diversity may reject diversity initiatives and make the work environment unpleasant and less productive. Negative attitudes and a lack of willingness 'to bend' can destroy creativity, synergy, and harmony in the workplace. Intentionally or unintentionally, local or long-serving staff may make newcomers (and their ideas) feel unwanted. If opposition is not handled well, diversity may not provide the intended benefits to the organization. Moreover, highly qualified individuals (e.g., second language speakers from minority backgrounds) who do not feel valued or respected may seek posts in more welcoming, multicultural environments.

To deal with resistant employees, through workshops and other interventions, companies need to clearly explain the reasons for diversity and identify the many benefits that diversity brings to both management and employees. Alleviating fears about workplace diversity (e.g., anxiety about the loss of jobs) may reduce much of the opposition.

Resistance to integration

In workplace settings it is not unusual for exclusive social groups or cliques to form. Newcomers who differ from the majority in terms of language, ethnicity, age, physical ability, gender, etc. may find social integration at work very challenging. Informal divisions may exist among staff which are difficult to penetrate. For example, people who are affiliated with the same ethnic group may cluster together and avoid social interactions with 'outsiders' during breaks and lunches. Some employees may socialize outside of work and avoid interactions with those who are not part of their clique. Lack of social integration among diverse employees can hinder interpersonal relations and limit the sharing of knowledge, ideas, skills, and experience. It can also inhibit the development of a sense of belonging within the organization. This, in turn, can curb productivity growth and limit the effectiveness of teams.

Gender differences

Attitudes toward men and women in the workplace vary in different parts of the world, and these differences can affect intercultural communication in businesses. In some cultural contexts, males hold all or nearly all of the positions of power, and women, if employed at all, are assigned subservient or supportive roles. Even in organizations which have long been open to females, the number of female executives may still be small. Gender inequality in the global workplace remains a contentious issue in much of the world.

Females who have risen to senior posts in companies that are open to gender diversity may find it challenging to communicate with officials or representatives from male-dominated environments. Males (and some women) who find themselves in situations where they need to report to a female supervisor for the first time in their life may initially react in negative, hostile ways. As more females assume leadership roles and participate in all levels of an organization, males and females need to learn how to work together effectively and demonstrate genuine respect for each other.

Religious differences

In many cultures, religion plays a dominant role in daily life, including the workplace. When employees from different faiths interact at work, in some contexts this may pose communication challenges. Immigrants from nations where breaks are routinely given for prayers, for example, may find it difficult to adjust to a secular work environment where employees are discouraged from openly expressing their religious beliefs. Some international companies permit employees to form faith-based support groups and arrange religious activities, while others do not. In some contexts, minority employees may be permitted to observe religious holidays that are not officially sanctioned, nationwide events. Attitudes toward religion in the workforce vary significantly and can affect workforce relations.

Sociocultural differences

Socialization influences understandings of what social behaviors are considered appropriate in particular settings and situations, including business contexts. **Business protocol** is a general term that encompasses the discourse, nonverbal behavior, dress, procedures, and social conventions that are expected within a particular company or organization. **Business etiquette** denotes rules that guide social behavior in workplace situations (e.g., greetings in business meetings, the exchanging of business cards, seating arrangements in business meetings/dinners, table manners at business lunches and formal dinners). **Business netiquette** refers to guidelines for courtesy in the use of email and the Internet for communication purposes.

Among individuals from different linguistic and cultural backgrounds, sociocultural norms and values in business situations can vary in a number of key areas (e.g., roles and attitudes toward work, responsibilities, and definitions of success, manners, concepts of time, degree of openness to people from outgroups, gift giving, level of formality in emails/face-to-face meetings, etc.). Contrasting work ethics among team members can be a major source of irritation and miscommunication in the workplace.

Gift giving refers to the ritual of providing gifts to business clients. In international business, gift giving etiquette varies from one culture to another (when to present a gift, how to present it, what to present). The type of gift is often linked to rank and seniority. When individuals do not follow the expected rules (e.g., consider the status of individuals when giving gifts, offer name cards in expected ways), misunderstandings and controversy may ensue. This can hamper relationship building and hamper business negotiations.

Ethnocentricism and assumptions of similarities

As explained in Chapter 6, **ethnocentricism** is the tendency to judge people from other cultures according to the standards, behaviors, and customs of one's own culture. Typically, ethnocentric individuals elevate their own culture or group to a status or position above all other cultures or groups. Problems can occur between employees from different cultural backgrounds when individuals assume that their own cultural norms are the right way and only way to accomplish tasks. Ethnocentric individuals may also wrongly believe that the patterns of behavior that they are accustomed to in their own cultural environment are universal (e.g., what they say or do, think or believe is shared by everyone). People in the workplace who have an ethnocentric mindset are not likely to communicate successfully with individuals or groups from other cultural backgrounds. Not surprisingly, their sense of superiority and entitlement can lead to resentment, hostility, and anger.

Distorted images and perceptions of people who are different from us in some ways (e.g., age, gender, race, accent, dialect, physical ability, religion, etc.) can also have a negative impact on the work environment. Assigning a broad range of characteristics or attributes to an individual on the basis of perceived membership in a particular cultural or social group is referred to as **stereotyping**. Stereotypes are often based on false assumptions and anecdotes. Characteristics thought to be common to a group are then applied to every person perceived to be affiliated with that group. Whether the values or attributes that are assigned are positive or negative, stereotyping can be harmful. Assuming that an immigrant worker from Bangladesh will be computer illiterate and speak little English, or that a Chinese manager will be a whiz in math, or that an older employee will not be able to master new technology are all examples of stereotyping in the workplace. (See Chapter 6 for more on stereotyping.)

Prejudicial attitudes, discrimination, harassment, and racism

In the workplace, employees may harbor negative attitudes toward people who differ from them in terms of religion, age, language, gender, or other attributes. This can lead to a lack of tolerance, bias, and unfairness. Prejudice and acts of discrimination and racism can extend beyond individuals. **Workplace discrimination (employment discrimination)** refers to unfair practices in hiring, promotion, job assignment, termination, and compensation. It also includes various types of **harassment**, that is, behaviors of an offensive or threatening nature. **Sexual harassment** in the workplace refers to repetitive and unwanted sexual advances, where the consequences of refusing could be very disadvantageous to the victim. For example, a female secretary who is propositioned by her manager may be directly or indirectly threatened with the loss of her job if she does not comply. Unless the organization has created a climate that condemns sexual harassment and put in place mechanisms to report and respond seriously to offenses, she may be too afraid of retribution to speak up.

Organizational policies, social attitudes, and individual beliefs can all be imbued with prejudice. Women and minorities may be passed over for promotion; second language speakers or people from a particular religion or race may be excluded from positions of power. Due to prejudice, they may find it difficult to break through the **glass ceiling**, 'the unseen, yet unbreachable barrier that keeps minorities and women from rising to the upper rungs of the corporate ladder, regardless of their qualifications or achievements' (Federal Glass Ceiling Commission 1995).

CULTURAL DIFFERENCE FRAMEWORKS AND THE GLOBAL WORKPLACE

In the last few decades a number of scholars from diverse areas of study (e.g., anthropology, cross-cultural communication, psychology, international business/management) have tried to account for the influence of cultural difference in organizations. Much of their research draws on notions of culture as learned patterns of behavior that are developed within groups through interaction in a shared social space. It is through enculturation that values (attitudes and beliefs), work ethics, and worldviews are thought to be transmitted from one generation to another. Thus, at the heart of most cultural difference research is the conviction that we need to identify core values or 'shared value orientations' within cultural groups in order to understand why people from different cultural backgrounds behave differently in similar situations (e.g., display a different work ethic). Most cultural difference frameworks aim to identify culture-specific rules, goals, and values that influence the ways people communicate and behave in particular societies and cultures.

This section reviews five models that have influenced the way intercultural communication is viewed in the global workplace: Hall's (1959, 1966, 1968, 1976) dimensions of culture difference (monochromic vs. polychromic communication, high-/low-context communication, use of personal space), Kluckholn and Strodtbeck's (1961) cultural orientation frameworks, Hampden-Turner and Trompenaars' (1998) seven value dimensions, Hofstede's (1984) value-orientations framework, and the GLOBE cultural framework (House *et al.* 2004).

Hall's dimensions of cultural difference

Many of anthropologist E.T. Hall's (1959, 1966, 1968, 1976, 1983, 1998) publications center on dimensions of cultural difference, including the monochronic-polychronic time system (See Chapter 4), use of personal space (Chapter 4), and low-context vs. high-context communication (Chapter 3). Based on his observations, he classified cultures according to differences in these dimensions. As elements of his cultural difference framework have broadly been discussed in previous chapters, this section briefly explains how his understandings of culture and communication styles shaped his views about intercultural interactions in business contexts.

When describing the relationship between culture and communication, Hall (1998) distinguishes between **'high-context' communication** and **'low-context' communication**. He suggests that in high-context cultures, the majority of information in communicative events is conveyed indirectly through nonverbal cues (e.g., gestures, eye contact, facial expressions, differences in time orientation, use of personal space, silence) and other implicit messages that are embedded in the discourse (e.g., indirect speech) and context. As most information tends to be located in the physical context or internalized within an individual, few details are provided in the coded, explicit part of the message. Hall's framework suggests that business professionals in a high-context environment (e.g., China, Japan) tend to communicate verbally and nonverbally in ways that assume that others know much of what they know (e.g., cultural scripts, historical background, social conventions). Further, high-context communicators place a great deal of emphasis on *how* they convey their ideas and feelings (Hall 1976; Nam 2015) to maintain face and harmony in business relations (Ting-Toomey 2012).

In contrast, in low-context cultures (e.g., Germany, the United States, the United Kingdom), most of the meaning is conveyed in the verbal code (Hall 1976; Nam 2015). In business meetings, the aim is to be explicit so that one's message is unambiguous and well understood by one's interlocutors. Business professionals who employ a low-context style of communication do not make assumptions about their communication partner's knowledge and typically provide detailed information in their verbal message, whether oral or written (e.g., conversations, memos, letters, official documents, business contracts) (McKay-Semmler 2018; Nam 2015).

For Hall (1976), there is a strong correlation between high-context and low-context cultures and collectivism-individualism, a dimension that features in Hofstede's (2001, 2003) framework. He posits that membership in a collectivist or individualistic culture influences how business professionals relate to co-nationals and plays a role in determining how much information is provided in intercultural interactions. It is also important to note that Hall and Hall (2002) recognize that within each culture there are 'individual differences in the need for contexting' (p. 201).

Kluckhohn and Strodtbeck's cultural orientation framework

Based on a review of hundreds of ethnographic investigations of ethnic groups in different parts of the world, anthropologists Kluckholn and Strodtbeck (1961) developed the *Cultural Orientation Framework*, which identifies five problems or challenges that all cultures face.

1   What is the character of innate human nature? (the human nature orientation)
2   What is the relationship of people to nature? (the human nature orientation)
3   What is the temporal focus of human life? (the time orientation, e.g., future, present, or past oriented ways of thinking and acting)
4   What is the modality of human activity? (the activity orientation, e.g., 'doing' or action oriented as opposed to 'being', which is person oriented)
5   What is the modality of an individual's relationship to other people? (the relational orientation)

Kluckholn and Strodtbeck (1961) also identified three possible ways in which cultures typically respond to each of these universal problems (e.g., a view of the character of human nature as evil, a mixture of good and evil, or good; a past, present, or future time orientation). Their framework has been used by business professionals and other border crossers to develop an understanding of broad differences in values among various cultural groups.

Hampden-Turner and Trompenaars' value dimensions

Another value orientation framework that is used in business and management research and practice was developed by Hampden-Turner and Trompenaars (1998). Drawing on the work of anthropologists and sociologists, these management philosophers identified seven dimensions of cultural variability:

1   Universalism vs. particularism (What is most important – rules or relationships?) (**Universalism** refers to the application of the same rules for everyone regardless of their status

or relationship. Universalists try to treat people fairly based on certain standards or rules, whereas in **particularism,** individuals may be treated differently depending on interpersonal relationships and obligations. For particularists, relationships come before rules. Cultures will have elements of both universalism and particularism but tend to be more one than the other.)

2   Individualism vs. collectivism (Do we function in a group or as individuals?)

3   Neutral vs. emotional (Do we display our emotions, or do we hide them?)

4   Specific vs. diffuse (Do we handle our relationships in specific and predetermined ways, or do we see our relationships as changing and related to contextual settings?)

5   Achievement vs. ascription (Do we have to prove ourselves to receive status, or is status given to us?)

6   Sequential vs. synchronic (Do we do things one at a time or several things at once?)

7   Internal vs. external control (Do we believe that we can control our environment, or do we believe that the environment controls us?)

To determine the impact of culture on people's behavioral choices, Hampden-Turner and Trompenaars (1998) devised scenarios of everyday dilemmas with a limited number of possible resolutions. Each option was linked to one of the seven dimensions they had identified. Approximately 15,000 respondents in 50 countries took part in their study. The researchers then calculated the percentage of individuals per country who selected a particular response. These statistics were then used to formulate generalizations about how people in a particular culture are most apt to respond to everyday dilemmas and interactions with people. Hampden-Turner and Trompenaars (1998) maintain that participants' responses revealed the values that are deeply entrenched in their national culture. The results of this study have been employed in business contexts to understand intercultural interactions and provide expatriates with guidance on how to perform tasks and communicate with people in different cultures.

Hofstede's value-orientations framework

The most widely cited value-orientations framework today is that of Geert Hofstede (1984), a Dutch social psychologist, who published his classic volume, *Culture's Consequences*, in 1980. Characterizing culture as 'software of the mind', he believes that cultural patterns program people to behave in particular ways. Much of his work has centered on how values in the workplace are influenced by our cultural programing. For the last few decades, his framework has served as a theoretical model for cross-cultural studies and training in management/business.

Drawing on surveys administered to more than 100,000 IBM employees in 40 countries, Hofstede (1980, 1981) examined the ways in which people from diverse 'national cultures' viewed and interpreted work and approached their social relationships in a work environment. He categorized their responses into the following four dimensions or value orientations of cultural difference: power distance, femininity/masculinity, uncertainty avoidance, and individualism-collectivism (a binary first proposed by Kluckholn and Strodtbeck 1961). Later, he added Confucian dynamism as a fifth value orientation. Let's take a closer look at each dimension.

Power distance

Power distance refers to the degree to which less powerful members of a society or organization expect and accept the unequal distribution of power among members. Small or low power distance cultures have a tendency to stress equality, self-initiative, and collaborative problem solving with supervisors and employees. Punishment and rewards tend to be distributed based on individual performance. In small power distance cultures, it may be normal for a president of a company and a construction worker to be on a first name basis, whereas in high power distance cultures this would be unthinkable. Austria, New Zealand, Denmark, and Israel value low power distance, minimizing hierarchies of power. By contrast, countries such as Venezuela, India, China, and Mexico are high in power distance; unequal status among members of an organization is accepted, and authority figures are expected to make decisions. Relationships between managers and their subordinates are formalized and more distant. High power distance cultures reward rank, status, and years of service.

Femininity/masculinity

Femininity/masculinity refers to the extent to which gender roles are valued, and attitudes toward ascribed masculine values (e.g., achievement, ambition). According to Hofstede (2001), **feminine cultures** promote gender equality, interpersonal contact, flexible balancing of life and work, and group decision making, whereas **masculine cultures** stress distinct differences in gender roles between men and women in the workplace. Gardiner (2017) characterizes this dimension as 'working to live' vs. 'living to work'. Northern European countries (Sweden, Denmark, Norway) demonstrate a tendency to value the feminine orientation, while Italy, Switzerland, Austria, and Japan have a tendency to promote masculine values in the workplace.

Uncertainty avoidance

Uncertainty avoidance refers to the tendency of people to feel threatened by ambiguous situations and to strive to avoid uncertainty. Countries with low or weak uncertainty avoidance (e.g., Denmark, Singapore, Sweden) tend to be more risk taking, less rule-governed, and more accepting of dissent. Countries with strong uncertainty avoidance (e.g., Japan, Portugal, Greece, Belgium) are more averse to risk taking; they tend to favor rules and regulations and seek consensus about goals.

Individualism-collectivism

Individualism/collectivism is concerned with individual vs. group orientations. **Individualism** refers to the broad value tendencies of a culture to stress personal over group goals, and they tend to have weaker group and organizational loyalty. In New Zealand, Australia, and the United States, for example, personal autonomy and individual identities, rights, and responsibilities tend to be emphasized. In contrast, **collectivism** refers to the broad value tendencies of a culture to focus on collaboration, shared interests, long-term relationships, traditions, harmony, and maintaining face (Bhawuk 2018b). According to Hofstede's (2001) findings, Arab and Asian countries, Brazil, and India tend to be collectivist, that is, emphasis in organizations is placed on the common good (e.g., the needs, interests, and goals of the group).

A fifth dimension: Confucian dynamism

Drawing on the work of cross-cultural psychologist Michael Bond and his colleagues in Hong Kong (Chinese Culture Connection 1987), Hofstede (2001) added a fifth dimension to his model to account for the particular cultural characteristics and behaviors that are prevalent in East Asian nations (Bhawuk 2018b; Taras 2018). The primary values in **Confucian dynamism** are associated with the philosophy and teachings of Confucius (551 to 479 BC, Lu, a Chinese philosopher and educator who espoused a practical code of conduct for people in daily life.

The Confucian dynamism orientation emphasizes persistence, personal stability, traditions, frugality, respect for elders, status-oriented relationships, a long-term orientation to time, hard work, a sense of shame, and collective face-saving. These Confucian values are often credited with the dramatic economic growth in the Five Dragons (Hong Kong, Taiwan, Japan, Singapore, and South Korea). In these work environments, Hofstede (2001) maintains that employees demonstrate respect for status differences and tend to possess a long-term orientation toward work as well as a strong work ethic. In contrast, a short-term orientation to work is more common in the United States, the United Kingdom, and Canada, where the focus is on hard work to gain immediate results and there is less concern about status.

The GLOBE cultural framework

Building on Hofstede's work, researchers in the GLOBE (Global Leadership and Organizational Behavior Effectiveness) project developed surveys to measure the relationship between societal culture, organizational culture, and leadership (House *et al.* 2004). Approximately 17,000 middle managers in finance, food processing, and telecommunication in more than 60 countries responded to survey items that are designed to assess their cultural values and practices based on nine cultural dimensions. Six of the nine **GLOBE dimensions** resemble those put forward by Hofstede (2001) to address institutional and group collectivism, gender egalitarianism, power distance, uncertainty avoidance, and future orientation. The other dimensions that have been added include: assertiveness (the extent to which people in organizations are strong-willed and confrontational), performance orientation (the degree to which an organization rewards members for their participation and quality of work), and humane orientation (the extent to which an organization rewards members for being kind and fair to others) (House *et al.* 2004).

Researchers used the statistical results of the survey analysis to group countries together based on levels of similarity and difference. Higher levels of cultural similarity were found among the following country clusters: Confucian Asia (e.g., Hong Kong, Singapore, Taiwan, China), Southern Asia (e.g., Indonesia, India, Malaysia, Iran), Latin America (e.g., Ecuador, Bolivia, Brazil), Nordic Europe (e.g., Denmark, Finland, Sweden), Anglo nations (e.g., Australia, Canada, the U.S.), Germanic Europe (e.g., Austria, the Netherlands, Germany), Latin Europe (e.g., Israel, Italy, Spain, Portugal), Sub-Sahara Africa (e.g., Zimbabwe, Namibia, Nigeria), Eastern Europe (e.g., Greece, Hungary, Poland, Russia), and the Middle East (e.g., Egypt, Morocco, Qatar).

When presenting their findings the researchers drew attention to the degree of cultural difference between clusters. For example, they maintain that there is a greater cultural difference between Southern Asia and Germanic Europe than between Southern Asia and Confucian Asia. Similar to Hofstede's (2001) cultural dimensions framework, the GLOBE dimensions are used by business professionals to compare home and host cultures and to predict cultural challenges and potential commonalities.

The impact of the frameworks on global business research, education, and practice

Business students and professionals across the globe are still using cultural difference frameworks to identify the core values and assumptions of their own culture as well as the target or host culture (e.g., international clients from a particular nation). Armed with this awareness of cultural difference, in theory, business professionals are better positioned to predict difficulties that might arise when they interact with colleagues and clients from the other culture. It is believed that this knowledge can help them avoid intercultural misunderstandings (e.g., by using culture-specific strategies, adjusting their communication style) and more effectively resolve difficulties or conflicts when they arise.

Among the cultural difference or values frameworks previously described, Hofstede's model (2001) (or variations of it) remains particularly influential in intercultural business and cultural diversity training in organizations (Holmes 2012). Additionally, the values frameworks continue to impact communication research in business and management studies (e.g., cross-cultural marketing surveys of potential customer values, investigations of values impacting on business negotiations in different countries).

Limitations and dangers of the cultural difference frameworks

Although still widely used in intercultural business education (training) and research, culture difference frameworks are not without critics. The emergence of critical notions of culture, questions about the methodologies employed in taxonomy studies, perceptions of Western or Eurocentric bias, and the potential for overgeneralizations have resulted in many publications that rally against their use or, at minimum, recommend that users exercise caution when interpreting and applying the findings. Let's take a closer look at these concerns.

Increasingly, interculturalists are questioning views of culture as static and shared by all members of a particular nation. For example, as explained in Chapter 2, Holliday (1999, 2012, 2019) distinguishes between the notion of **'large culture'** and **'small culture'**. He warns that the former can lead to 'culturist ethnic, national or international stereotyping' (1999: 237), whereas the latter recognizes 'small social groupings or activities wherever there is cohesive behaviour' (ibid: 237). Within a 'large culture' or nation, he explains that there are actually many 'small cultures' (e.g., subcultures, discourse communities), which can easily be overlooked if solely focused on the broad picture.

Taxonomies of cultural difference are designed to identify the main components of 'national culture', that is, they attempt to describe 'large cultures' across a range of behaviors and values. Dervin (2016), Holliday (1999, 2012, 2019), Holmes (2012, 2018), Piller (2009, 2012, 2017), and many other critics argue that this approach is outdated. In our increasingly globalized world, nations have become much more multicultural and cosmopolitan, and this diversity is often ignored in discussions of national cultural difference. As geographical boundaries become less and less relevant, the notion of 'culture as nation' becomes less plausible. The idea that all people from a particular nation belong to the same culture (e.g., possess the same values and perspectives) does not resonate with societies today. Within any nation there is diversity in terms of social class, accent, age, ethnicity, religion, gender, profession, physical ability, and so on. There is also increasing diversity within organizations.

Frameworks of cultural difference have also been strongly criticized for their Western bias and methodological limitations (e.g., reliance on surveys with a limited number of respondents and no triangulation, that is, no data from other sources or types of data). When describing national cultural characteristics based solely on closed surveys, there is always the risk of over-generalizations and stereotyping. Consequently, many critics characterize this work as essentialist and reductionist. As has been noted in earlier chapters, **essentialism** denotes an approach in which certain characteristics are linked to a particular cultural group, and all individuals categorized as members of this group are assumed to possess these attributes and adhere to similar patterns of behavior (Holliday 2012; Martinez 2018; Strauss 2018). In other words they are reduced to a single representation or image. When culture is viewed as a stable feature of an individual or group, multifaceted cultural identities and the dynamic nature of culture are largely ignored. The results of surveys that were administered decades ago are also unlikely to accurately and fully portray the current situation.

ALTERNATIVE APPROACHES TO INTERCULTURAL BUSINESS RESEARCH, EDUCATION, AND PRACTICE

Noting the limitations and dangers of cultural difference frameworks, more scholars (e.g., Holmes 2012, 2018; Scollon *et al.* 2012, Ting-Toomey 2010) call for context-specific analyses of intercultural communication in business contexts (e.g., interpretive, experiential, and critical approaches to understanding how language and nonverbal communication are used in intercultural interactions in the global workplace). In particular, more ethnographic studies, interactional sociolinguistic explorations, and critical studies of intercultural business interactions (e.g., critical discourse analyses) should inform practice (e.g., the design and delivery of business intercultural education workshops and courses). Intercultural communication in organizations and businesses does not take place in a power vacuum. Nor does it typically involve equal power relations. More contextualized studies are therefore needed that take into account the power dimension in intercultural interactions whether in domestic or international settings.

Critical intercultural communication scholars recommend the use of locally relevant methods and tools instead of relying on large-scale surveys developed in Western contexts. More ethnographic studies and discourse analyses are needed that examine the actual use of language and nonverbal codes in intercultural business interactions (e.g., team meetings, supervisor-employee conversations, employee-customer encounters). Building on the earlier work of Gumperz (1979/1990), Newton and Kusmierczyk (2011) advocate the careful examination of recordings of authentic workplace interactions in work-related language programs (e.g., job-specific English language modules for workers). These theoretical and methodological developments shift the focus away from 'differences between national cultures and the development of universalized competences within international groups, toward multiple identities and particular competences within local groups' (Lund & O'Reagan 2010: 56).

In business education contexts, instead of relying on cultural difference frameworks that can potentially foster stereotyping and Othering, critical intercultural educators prompt the examination of 'real world' intercultural interactions (e.g., an examination of transcripts of business meetings or conversations between clients and managers) and experiential modes of learning (e.g., internships in the linguistically and culturally diverse workplace). Through first-hand intercultural experience and guided reflection, students can gain exposure to 'emotional and communication challenges and practice context-pertinent communication skills' (Ting-Toomey 2010: 21). This approach contrasts sharply with intercultural training sessions for business students that focus on a list of cultural differences.

ENHANCING INTERCULTURAL COMMUNICATION IN TODAY'S GLOBAL WORKPLACE

> Effective global communication requires flexibility, a desire to learn, sensitivity to culture and traditions in a foreign setting, and the ability to apply what you have learned to interactions with others in overseas locations. In addition, combine professionalism, firmness, and business savvy with grace, respect, and kindness. Build appropriate relationships and friendships, and network through international societies and trade groups.
>
> (Krizan *et al*. 2011: 51)

As our workplaces and communities become increasingly diverse and globally oriented, intercultural competence is becoming more imperative. Mughan and O'Shea (2010) argue that 'the social context in which we live makes the understanding of intercultural interaction a prerequisite for those who aspire to successful careers' (p. 109). To work more effectively in the multicultural workplace, there are a number of general guidelines that individuals can follow.

Acknowledge diversity in the workplace

First, it is important to recognize and acknowledge the wealth of diversity that exists in work environments today. As explained in this chapter, diversity can take many forms (e.g.,

Plate 10.2 Efforts to enhance one's intercultural communication skills and develop an open mindset can help to cultivate and maintain good working relationships in multicultural organizations.
© Jane Jackson

differences in age, language, gender, race, ethnicity, physical ability, religion, sexual orientation, social class, etc.). All workplaces are diverse in multiple ways. You do not need to go to a
foreign country to experience diversity.

Becoming more knowledgeable about linguistic and cultural dimensions

In today's global workplace employees must build strong linguistic and cultural awareness
in order to enhance their intercultural communication skills and effectiveness at work. It is
useful to learn how enculturation influences attitudes, language use, beliefs, **business ethics**
(the principles that guide behavior in business), one's work ethic, and style of communication
(verbal and nonverbal). It is also vital to recognize that not everyone from a particular cultural
background follows the same patterns of behavior or shares a similar worldview or work ethic.
There is diversity *within* cultures. Instead of rigidly sticking to preconceived ideas (e.g., stereotypes), we can observe and learn from our intercultural experience.

Demonstrate second language sensitivity

If you are using your first language with coworkers or customers who are not fully fluent in the
language, recognize the advantage you have, especially if you are communicating on the phone
or online (e.g., Skype). Demonstrate appreciation for the efforts they are making and provide
assistance, when necessary. Use explicit comprehension, whenever appropriate, to gauge how
your message is being interpreted. You could also learn basic expressions in your coworkers'
or clients' first language to make them feel more welcome in the workplace. Becoming aware
of how power imbalances may affect interactions can help you become a more competent intercultural communicator in the workplace. With enhanced linguistic and cultural sensitivity you
are better positioned to engage diversity with more ease and confidence.

Become more self-aware

In addition to learning more about other ways of being, it is essential to develop **mindful
awareness** (recognition of our own cultural ways of knowing and being and their impact on
our intercultural communication) (LeBaron 2003). Enculturation affects how we perceive
and interact with people from other cultural backgrounds both in our social life as well as at
work. Be mindful of how your own linguistic and cultural socialization and life experiences
have shaped your attitudes, perceptions, values, identities, and communication styles (verbal
and nonverbal). To become more interculturally sensitive, it is vital to recognize attitudes and
behaviors that are holding you back from adopting a more ethnorelative, inclusive perspective.

Recognize one's biases

The ability to communicate effectively with coworkers or clients who have a different linguistic or cultural background or who differ from you in other ways (e.g., gender, age, physical

disability) requires awareness of your personal biases and expectations. For example, realizing that you have learned to value independence and individual responsibility can raise your awareness of the need to be patient in situations where it is considered more important to work cooperatively and not stand out. Recognizing that you have a bias against second language speakers can push you to question the source of your beliefs and make more of an effort to be more understanding of the challenges people face when communicating in a second language. Heightened awareness of your stereotypes and biases can pinpoint aspects that you need to work on in order to become more interculturally competent.

Be flexible

In the global workplace, you are bound to encounter different ways of speaking and doing things. Insisting that your way is the only way is not conducive to harmony or productivity. Flexible individuals who demonstrate interest in and respect for other ways of being are far more likely to encourage colleagues from diverse backgrounds to voice their ideas, opinions, and concerns in the workplace. Acceptance of new ideas is a characteristic of effective intercultural communicators. Enhance your ability to encourage collaboration and help your organizations and communities leverage the many opportunities that diversity presents.

Expand repertoire of communication/conflict management styles

In today's workforce it is natural to come across unfamiliar styles of communication (verbal and nonverbal) and conflict management. Instead of rigidly sticking to familiar habits (e.g., communication patterns), as an employee you can make an effort to develop a range of communication strategies and tools that can help you to become a more effective and appropriate communicator in intercultural situations. You will then be better positioned to mediate and resolve intercultural conflict situations in ways that are mutually acceptable. For example, learning face negotiation strategies that respect the self-identities and dignity of others can enhance interpersonal communication in the workplace.

Be patient and humble

It is natural to commit faux pas (e.g., unintentionally violate social norms) when interacting with people from a different linguistic and cultural background in the workplace. Admitting mistakes and showing humility can create goodwill. Being able to laugh at yourself and learn from mistakes are vital characteristics of sensitive intercultural communicators.

Keep an open mind and respect diversity

Learn about other ways of being, beliefs, and customs and resist the temptation to judge them by your own cultural standards and habits. In other words, make an effort to move beyond an ethnocentric perspective and try to see situations through the eyes of your coworkers or clients who have a different background from you.

Advocate equity in the workplace

Valuing diversity in the workplace means recognizing and respecting the unique characteristics and contributions of *all* employees. Strengthen inclusive practices and be an advocate for coworkers or customers who are not treated fairly. Remaining silent signals support for inequity and injustice. (Chapter 11 explores the responsibilities of ethical global citizens.)

SUMMARY

> The need for cultural reflection and the building of intercultural competence are increasingly pervasive in our daily professional and private lives, as we are more and more likely to interact and cooperate with people from very different cultural backgrounds.
>
> (Guilherme *et al*. 2010: 243)

This chapter began by discussing the impact of globalization and Englishization on today's workplace. As Tapia and Gisbert (2018) explain, '[O]rganizations face unprecedented challenges and opportunities driven largely by civilization's evolution into being more of a global, interconnected multiracial, multiethnic, and multicultural hybrid village' (p. 485). Increasing diversity in the workforce and wider society has profound implications for the ways that organizations should function both internally and externally (e.g., with clients or customers). Business professionals and organizations must make changes in order to remain current and competitive (Guilherme *et al*.2010; Tapia & Gisbert 2018). The need has never been greater for employees to possess intercultural competence and bilingual (multilingual) ability, or, at minimum, knowledge of an international language.

discussion questions

1   In what ways has globalization influenced intercultural communication and language use in the workplace? Discuss your views with a partner.
2   Do you agree that English is the de facto language of global business today? Why or why not? Do you think there will be a dominant global language of business in 20 years? Fifty years? If yes, what language will it be?
3   Offer your understanding of cultural synergy. Discuss ways that companies can promote synergy in work teams.
4   How might different verbal communication styles and degrees of formality lead to miscommunication at work? Provide examples and discuss your ideas with a partner.
5   How can attitudes toward women affect the intercultural workplace? In your home country, how are gender and age related to position, status, and power? Identify other cultural contexts where the situation differs.
6   What role, if any, does religion play in the workplace in your country? Identify another country where religion is viewed differently in the world of business. How

does this affect the way business is conducted? What are the implications for inter-cultural communication?

7   How do business introductions vary in different parts of the world? Describe and discuss cultural variations in the exchange of business cards and the potential consequences if protocol is not followed.

8   What are some of the established communication protocols that govern business interactions in your environment? How might some of these protocols create a problem when dealing with business representatives from other linguistic and cultural backgrounds? What recommendations would you offer to deal with these issues? Discuss your ideas with a partner.

activities

1   Identify four benefits of diversity in the global workplace. Provide examples to illustrate your ideas.

2   In small groups, identity five challenges that diversity can pose in the global workplace and offer concrete suggestions to overcome them.

3   You are responsible for creating an inclusive organizational climate that values and embraces diversity. How would you accomplish this?

4   Working with a partner, identify and come to an agreement on the attitudes, skills, and knowledge that you think are essential for the following:

    a   A competent intercultural communicator in an organization
    b   An effective multicultural team
    c   An effective global organization

5   Identify actions that people can take to become more interculturally and linguistically competent in the workplace.

6   With a partner discuss how your ability to switch communication styles (e.g., use indirect discourse in situations that favor face-saving and harmony; use more direct expressions in situations which favor a more forthright stance) might enhance your communication in the multicultural workplace.

7   In high-context communication, individuals tend to avoid negative or confrontational verbal messages like this: 'I completely disagree with your proposal. It just won't work!' Instead of overtly disagreeing with the ideas that have been presented, indirect communicators may remain silent, nod their head, or simply say that they understand the proposal so that the presenter will not be embarrassed and lose face. Not surprisingly, indirect expressions can easily be misinterpreted by individuals who are used to more direct, low-context communication. What would you suggest to improve the communication between employees who have very different styles of communication?

further reading

Guilherme, M. *et al.* (eds.) (2010) *The Intercultural Dynamics of Multicultural Working*, Bristol: Multilingual Matters.

From theoretical and interdisciplinary perspectives, the chapters in this volume examine intercultural communication in various types of work environments and contexts (e.g., multicultural work teams).

Lauring, J. and Jonasson, C. (2010) *Group Processes in Ethnically Diverse Organizations: Language and Intercultural Learning*, Hauppauge, NY: Nova Science Pub Inc.

This book explores the complex relationship between language, identity, and intercultural communication in diverse organizations.

Nardon, L. (2017) *Working in a Multicultural World: A Guide to Developing Intercultural Competence*, Toronto: University of Toronto Press.

This practical book suggests ways to enhance intercultural communication in today's multicultural and globalized workforce.

Rabotin, M. (2011) *Culture Savvy: Working and Collaborating Across the Globe*, Alexandria, VA: ASTD Press.

The author draws attention to how fear, stereotypes, and misunderstandings negatively impact intercultural relations. Suggestions are offered to develop respectful, rewarding relationships with individuals who have been socialized in a different cultural and linguistic background.

Schmidt, W.V., Conaway, R.N., Easton, S.S. and Wardrope, W.J. (2007) *Communicating Globally: Intercultural Communication and International Business*, Thousand Oaks, CA: Sage.

Integrating intercultural communication theory with the practices of multinational organizations, the authors raise awareness of the potential impact of diverse worldviews in intercultural interactions and suggest ways to enhance intercultural communication in the workplace.

Scollon, R., Wong Scollon, S. and Jones, R.H. (2012) *Intercultural Communication: A Discourse Approach*, 3rd edn, London: Blackwell.

Grounded in interactional sociolinguistics and discourse analysis, this book explores key concepts in intercultural communication with multiple examples of corporate and professional discourse.

Weaver, G. (2014) *Intercultural Relations: Communication, Identity, and Conflict*, Boston: Pearson.

This book explores ways in which organizations can enhance intercultural relations and more successfully mediate conflict situations.

Companion Website: Continue your journey online

Visit the Companion Website for a variety of rich tools and resources to support and extend your intercultural learning. (Instructors who are qualified adopters of the text may access additional resources on this site.)

CHAPTER 11

Language, interculturality, and global citizenship

To shift our level of awareness from the ethnocentric to the geocentric, we must challenge ourselves to leave our comfort zone. Whatever narrow identity we were born into, it is time to step out of it and into the larger world. We can still cherish our own heritage, lineage, and culture, but we must liberate ourselves from the illusion that they are separate from everyone else's.

– (Gerzon 2010: xxi)

Language clearly plays an important role in the process of developing intercultural competence. Through the study of a foreign language, it becomes easier to enter the cognitive concepts of another culture. However, language learning alone is not sufficient to grasp the complexities of another culture. . . . Becoming interculturally competent is a process of changing one's mindset. . . . It is a process of continuous transformation that, ideally, never ends.

– (Guilherme *et al.* 2010: 243–4)

As individuals increase their awareness of the ways people, throughout their lives, learn to operate in multiple communities, cross boundaries, and shift the ways they interact and use language to fit those different communities, it becomes clear that developing intercultural competence is an extension of a lifelong identity construction process.

– (Temples 2015: 576–7)

learning objectives

By the end of this chapter, you should be able to:

1 Define global citizenship and identify the traits, characteristics, and ethical obligations of global citizens
2 Define intercultural (communication/communicative) competence and identify fundamental components
3 Define what is meant by 'the intercultural speaker' or 'intercultural mediator'
4 Describe four models of intercultural competence/sensitivity
5 Discuss the relationship between second language proficiency and intercultural competence
6 Describe ways to enhance one's intercultural competence and intercultural/global citizenry
7 Explain why intercultural competence is best viewed as a lifelong process

INTRODUCTION

Previous chapters discussed the many ways in which our world has become globally interdependent and interculturally complex, due, in part, to accelerating globalization, migration, and rapid advances in transportation and telecommunications. These changes have affected our self-identities and attitudes toward diversity. With more and more intercultural interactions in our home environment and beyond, the potential for miscommunication and conflict is also on the rise, both among individuals and groups. Hence the need for global, bi(multi)lingual, and intercultural competency has never been greater.

As the gap between the rich and poor widens and we compete for limited resources (e.g., food, water, land, wealth, shelter, power, etc.), the importance of global perspectives and peaceful, equitable solutions deepens. The development of a global mindset and the mastery of intercultural communication knowledge and skills are a matter of urgency for both individuals and societies worldwide. It is imperative for all of us to become responsible, ethical members of the global village that we share.

This concluding chapter begins by exploring what is meant by global citizenship, global competency, intercultural competency, and intercultural citizenship. We then examine several models of intercultural (communication/communicative) competence and discuss the construct of the 'intercultural speaker' in relation to second language speakers. Attention is drawn to the vital role of language in intercultural competency. We then review the global, linguistic, and intercultural competencies that are needed in today's complex world. Finally, suggestions are offered to enhance one's intercultural (communicative) competency and take steps toward ethical, global citizenship.

GLOBAL CITIZENSHIP

What is global citizenship and what does it mean to be a global citizen in today's increasingly complex world? What are the qualities and duties of global citizens? What is the relationship between identity, language, global citizenship, and ethics? How can one acquire the dimensions of global citizenship? In the new millennium, why is it essential to take steps in this direction? These are just a few of the many questions that preoccupy philosophers, educators, interculturalists, social justice activists, and students in modern times.

Citizenship

Before we look at definitions of global citizenship, it is necessary to have an understanding of what is meant by citizenship. Throughout the history of humankind, **citizenship** has been linked to an individual's conduct, rights, and obligations within a particular society or nation. Most definitions of citizenship focus on people's affiliation with the state and their behaviors or duties in relation to it. In political philosophy, for example, citizenship is generally viewed as a series of rights and responsibilities associated with the individual as a member of a political community. Typically, this includes such aspects as civic, economic, linguistic, political, and social rights as well as duties or obligations. Basically, citizenship describes the relationship between the individual and the state, and the need for citizens to understand the economic and political processes, structures, institutions, laws, rights, and responsibilities within the system that governs the state (e.g., democracy, communism, socialism, monarchy).

Citizenship and sense of belonging

The mode of governance affects perceptions of citizenship as well as an individual's status, duties, rights, and freedoms. It influences dimensions of one's identity and sense of belonging within the state (e.g., the strength of one's national identity or affiliation with the state). Within the context of democratic societies, Osler (2005: 12–13) maintains that citizenship involves:

1   *A status* (which confers on the individual the rights to residence, vote, and employment)
2   *A feeling* (sense of belonging to a community)
3   *Practice* (active participation in the building of democratic societies)

Citizens who feel a deep attachment or connection to their nation are apt to possess a strong national identity, whereas those who are more ambivalent about this bond may have a weak national identity. Increasingly, individuals are developing multiple identities and affiliations that go beyond the local. Second language speakers who master English, for example, may feel connected to people in other parts of the world who speak this global language. Through this international language, they may forge a **global identity** (an identity that affords a sense of belonging to an imagined worldwide culture), while maintaining a **local self** (e.g., a regional or national identity). They may also develop a sense of inbetweenness or hybridity (Jackson 2018b; Uryu 2018). (Chapter 6 discusses local, global, national, and hybrid identifications and the complex connection between language, identity, and culture). We now take a closer look at the relationship between citizenship and the wider, global community.

Plate 11.1   As a consequence of war, famine, and persecution, individuals and groups may be compelled to flee their home country and be afraid to return. In their new environment, how can global citizens help refugees feel safe and at home? © Jane Jackson

Conceptions of global citizenship

There are many definitions of global citizenship. Most stress common values and concerns that unite people who care deeply about the current state of our planet and the quality of life of future generations. As all of us inhabit the same universe, advocates of global citizenry argue that all human beings and communities should work together to solve the major problems facing humanity (e.g., global warming, armed conflicts, border disputes, the migrant or refugee crisis, unequal distribution of wealth and natural resources, natural catastrophes like earthquakes and tsunamis).

For Toh (1996: 185), **global citizenship** entails 'awareness of and commitment to societal justice for marginalized groups, grassroots environment, nonviolent and authentic democracy, environmental care, and North-South relations based on principles of equity, respect, and sharing'. Based on a review of definitions put forward by global scholars from around the world (e.g., Deardorff 2006, 2009; Hunter *et al.* 2006), Morais and Ogden (2011) devised a conceptual model of global citizenship that is depicted in Figure 11.1.

The core elements in this framework are: **social responsibility** (the perceived level of interdependence and social concern for others, the society, and the environment), **global competence** ('having an open mind while actively seeking to understand others' cultural norms and expectations and leveraging this knowledge to interact, communicate, and work effectively outside one's environment', and **global civic engagement** ('the demonstration of action and/or predisposition toward recognizing local, state, national, and global community issues and responding through actions such as volunteerism, political activism, and community participation (Andrzejewski & Alessio 1999; Paige *et al.* 2008)' (Morais & Ogden 2011: 448).

Figure 11.1 Global citizenship conceptual model
Source: Morais and Ogden (2011: 447). Reproduced with permission.

Unlike national citizenship, there is no world state or governing body that can grant global citizenship (e.g., global rights, status, responsibilities). Further, individuals may possess a strong sense of **global consciousness** (concern about the welfare of our planet) and still declare allegiance to the state or region where they have legal citizenship. Put another way, a global identity may coexist with a regional, national, or local identity. Tensions may surface, however, when local needs (e.g., deforestation to provide land for an increasing population, expansion of industries that burn fossil fuels) conflict with global concerns (e.g., protection of the environment, climate warming).

What is a global citizen?

For Israel (2012: 79), a **global citizen** is 'someone who identifies with being part of an emerging world community and whose actions contribute to building this community's values and practices'. Instead of seeing oneself as only narrowly connected to a particular region or nation, individuals who identify themselves as global citizens possess a sense of belonging to a world community. As Gerzon (2010: xxi) explains, global citizens may still have fond feelings for their 'heritage, lineage, and culture' but are free of the 'illusion' that their identities are 'separate from everyone else's'. Their sense of self embraces a concern for all humankind and the future of the planet. People with a global identity may also be referred to as **international, transnational,** or **world citizens.**

The traits and actions of global citizens

A number of traits and behaviors are associated with global citizens. For Daisaku Ikeda, a Buddhist philosopher, peace builder, and educator, the following are essential:

- The wisdom to perceive the interconnectedness of all life and living.
- The courage not to fear or deny difference; but to respect and strive to understand people of different cultures, and to grow from encounters with them.
- The compassion to maintain an imaginative empathy that reaches beyond one's immediate surroundings and extends to those suffering in distant places.

(Ikeda n.d.)

Oxfam, a development and relief organization that strives to find solutions to poverty and end suffering around the world, maintains that a global citizen is someone who:

- Is aware of the wider world and has a sense of his or her own role as a world citizen
- Respects and values diversity
- Has an understanding of how the world works
- Is troubled by social injustice
- Participates in the community at a range of levels, from the local to the global
- Is willing to act to make the world a more equitable and sustainable place
- Takes responsibility for her or his actions
- Feels an ethical responsibility to others around the globe.

(adapted from Oxfam 2015: 5)

Plate 11.2 Global citizens are troubled by social injustice and inequality and take steps to make the world a more equitable and sustainable place. © Jane Jackson

Our ethical responsibility

Most scholars emphasize that global citizenship entails a commitment to live responsibly by taking care of the earth and its inhabitants (e.g., protecting the environment, safeguarding the rights of other human beings). A global citizen is concerned about the welfare of *all* human beings, not just his or her own ethnic, linguistic, or national group. Instead of seeking the betterment of one's community or ingroup at the expense of others, global citizens recognize the dignity of every human being and proactively seek the common good for society and the environment. With this orientation in view, Patel *et al.* (2011) recommend that all of us resolve to:

1 Develop an understanding of global interrelatedness and interdependence
2 Respect cultural diversity

3   Fight racial discrimination
4   Protect the global environment
5   Understand human rights
6   Accept basic social values.

(Adapted from Patel *et al*. 2011: 79)

Martin and Nakayama (2008) argue that all of us have an ethical responsibility to enhance our intercultural knowledge and develop a sense of social justice:

> as members of an increasingly interdependent global community, intercultural communication students have a responsibility to educate themselves, not just about interesting cultural differences, but also about intercultural conflicts, the impacts of stereotyping and prejudice, and the larger systems that can oppress and deny basic human rights – and to apply this knowledge to the communities in which they live and interact.
>
> (Martin & Nakayama 2008: 22)

Genuine global citizens are dedicated to fostering a sustainable, inclusive world, which offers promise for all inhabitants. Recognizing the interdependence of communities, global citizens are passionate about **social justice** (the fair administration of laws to treat all people as equal regardless of ethnicity, religion, race, language, gender, origin, etc.), **economic justice** (economic policies that distribute benefits equally to all), **human rights** (the fundamental rights and freedoms to which all humans are entitled, such as the right to life and liberty, freedom of thought and expression, and equality before the law), **language (linguistic) rights** (the right to choose the language(s) for communication in private and public places; the right to one's own language in legal, administrative, and judicial acts, language education, and the media), and **global ethics** (basic shared ethical values, criteria, and attitudes for peaceful coexistence among humans). Becoming a global citizen involves much more than traveling to many different countries and speaking multiple languages. It requires a commitment to bettering our planet. (Later in this chapter we explore the related construct of 'intercultural citizenship'.)

Global citizenship activism

To build and nurture our emerging world community, global citizens may assume activist roles, which cultivate ethical values, principles, and practices. **Global citizenship activism** can take many forms. For example, individuals or groups may lobby for changes in local, national, and international policies and practices that affect the environment. They may initiate or join activities designed to curb global warming and protect the earth's ozone level. Activists may also join organizations that aim to solve pressing global problems (e.g., famine, regional conflicts, pollution, economic disparity, unequal opportunities to learn international languages). Besides contributing to worldwide humanitarian relief efforts, individuals may organize and actively participate in activities and events that celebrate global **diversity** (e.g., rich variations in art, language, culture, religion, music, cuisine) and promote equitable, harmonious intercultural interactions. Global citizens may also take an active role in the decision making processes of global governing bodies and international agencies that strive to make the world a better place, such as the United Nations Educational, Scientific, and Cultural Organization (UNESCO), Oxfam (a developmental organization), the Global Relief Agency, and Medics without Borders, to name a few.

Advocates of global citizenship warn that we need to work together to deal with the many challenges facing our planet. Israel (2012: 79) argues that all citizens should be concerned about 'human rights, environmental protection, religious pluralism, gender equity, sustainable worldwide economic growth, poverty alleviation, prevention of conflicts between countries, elimination of weapons of mass destruction, humanitarian assistance and preservation of cultural diversity'. Linguists also point out that care should be taken to prevent **language death** (language extinction, linguistic extinction or linguicide), a process whereby a language that has been used in a speech community gradually dies out (Tsuda 2018). In this scenario, the level of linguistic competence that speakers possess in a particular language variety decreases to the extent that eventually there are no fluent speakers of that variety left. Linguists caution that the dominance of global English is leading to the loss of minority languages and linguistic diversity in some parts of the world (Tsuda 2018). The concerns of global citizens are many and varied.

GLOBAL COMPETENCY

There are many definitions of global competence (sometimes referred to as '**transnational competence**') besides the one offered by Morais and Ogden (2011) in relation to their global citizenship conceptual model (see Figure 11.1). Lambert (1996), for example, defines a **globally competent person** as an individual who has knowledge of current events, the capacity to empathize with others, the ability to maintain a positive attitude, second language competence, and an appreciation of foreign ways of doing things. Olson and Kroeger (2001) maintain that a globally competent individual possesses sufficient substantive **global knowledge** (e.g., understanding of cultures, languages, global events and concerns), **perceptual understanding** (e.g., open-mindedness, sophisticated cognitive processing, resistance to stereotyping), and **intercultural communication skills** (e.g., adaptability, **empathy** (concern for others), cross-cultural awareness, intercultural mediation, intercultural sensitivity) to interact appropriately and effectively in our globally interconnected world.

The Stanley Foundation (2003), a U.S.-based organization that funds research on global education, defines global competency as 'an appreciation of complexity, conflict management, the inevitability of change, and the interconnectedness between and among humans and their environment'. The Foundation emphasizes that, 'globally competent citizens know they have an impact on the world and that the world influences them. They recognize their ability and responsibility to make choices that affect the future'.

International educators Donatelli *et al.* (2005: 134) cite the following as common traits of global competence:

- General knowledge of one's own culture, history, and people
- General knowledge of cultures, histories, and peoples other than one's own
- Fluency in a world language other than one's native tongue
- Cross-cultural empathy
- Openness and cognitive flexibility
- Tolerance for ambiguity, perceptual acuity, and attentiveness to nonverbal messages
- Awareness of issues facing the global community

Hunter (2004) surveyed senior international educators, transnational corporation human resource managers, and United Nations officials to ascertain their perception of the knowledge, skills, attitudes, and experiences necessary to become globally competent. For these individuals, a globally competent person is someone who is 'able to identify cultural differences to compete globally, collaborate across cultures, and effectively participate in both social and business settings in other countries' (Deardorff & Hunter 2006: 77). **Global competence** means 'having an open mind while actively seeking to understand cultural norms and expectations of others, leveraging this gained knowledge to interact, communicate and work effectively outside one's environment' (Hunter 2004: 74).

Based on the findings of his study, Hunter (2004) developed the **global competence model** to provide a framework for international educators to prepare '**global-ready graduates**' (individuals who are adequately prepared for a diverse workforce and society that necessitates intercultural and global competencies). Central to his model is the conviction that if one is to achieve global competency, one must recognize that one's own worldview is not universal. In other words, it is vital to move away from an ethnocentric perspective toward a more open, inclusive stance. His framework emphasizes that '[a]ttitudes of openness, curiosity, and respect are key starting points upon which to build the requisite knowledge and skills' (Deardorff & Hunter 2006: 79). While second language proficiency is not cited in the graphic illustration, it is referred to in publications that explain the model.

INTERCULTURAL COMPETENCY

Many definitions of intercultural competence (e.g., **intercultural effectiveness**) have been put forward in the last few decades by speech communication specialists and general education scholars as well as by applied linguists who have a particular interest in the cultural dimension of language learning and use. The former have long criticized applied linguists for not paying sufficient attention to the cultural component in language education teaching and research; conversely, second language specialists have rebuked communication specialists for largely ignoring the language component in their studies and theories of intercultural communication.

Many cross-cultural psychologists, anthropologists, international educators, language and social psychologists, and scholars from other disciplines have focused their attention on the traits, skills, and behaviors of interculturally competent individuals who reside temporarily or permanently in a new culture. Consequently, many understandings of intercultural competence have centered on adaptability and effectiveness in unfamiliar cultural contexts (e.g., intercultural adjustment and adaptation while studying abroad). Other broader, more general conceptions of **intercultural competence** refer to intercultural traits, knowledge, and behaviors related to one's interactions in any intercultural situation or context (e.g., in one's home environment or in international settings). (See Chapter 7 for a discussion of intercultural effectiveness in relation to intercultural transitions.)

Much can be learned by examining the perspectives of scholars and practitioners from diverse areas of specialization. In today's complex, globalizing world, whenever feasible, an interdisciplinary approach to intercultural communication is imperative to integrate and build on the strengths of different theories and modes of research. This can help us to better understand the concept of intercultural competency and identify the most effective ways to enhance our intercultural communication knowledge and skills. It is also important to bear in mind that this process entails lifelong learning. Let's take a look at various conceptions of intercultural (communication/communicative) competence that have been formulated by scholars from diverse disciplines.

Intercultural (communication) competence

Influenced by their discipline, research, and life experience, scholars have used a variety of terms to refer to the competence of individuals in intercultural interactions, including inter-cultural competence, intercultural communication competence, intercultural communicative competence, cross-cultural competence, multicultural competence, cultural fluency, intercul-tural sensitivity, cultural intelligence, and so on. (See Fantini 2012b for a longer list of terms.)

In relation to sojourners and longer-term migrants, Taylor (1994: 154), an adult education specialist, defines **intercultural competence** as 'an adaptive capacity based on an inclusive and integrative world view which allows participants to effectively accommodate the demands of living in a host culture'. 'Interculturally competent persons', according to Chen and Starosta (2006: 357), 'know how to elicit a desired response in interactions and to fulfill their own communication goals by respecting and affirming the worldview and cultural identities of the interactants'. For these communication scholars, **intercultural communication competence** is 'the ability to acknowledge, respect, tolerate, and integrate cultural differences that qualifies one for enlightened global citizenship' (*ibid.*: 357). Among many communication scholars, intercultural communication competence generally refers to 'effective and appropriate com-munication between persons of different cultural worldviews' (Arasaratnam-Smith 2018: 977).

Further, in Jandt's (2007: 48) view, '[g]ood intercultural communicators have **personality strength** (with a strong sense of self and are socially relaxed), communication skills (verbal and nonverbal), **psychological adjustment** (ability to adapt to new situations), and **cultural awareness** (understanding of how people of different cultures think and act)'. For this commu-nication specialist, intercultural communication competence requires 'understanding dominant cultural values' and the ways in which our own cultural values influence our perceptions of ourselves and others (Jandt 2018). None of these conceptions of intercultural competence deals explicitly with the use of a second language in intercultural interactions.

Intercultural communicative competence

Michael Byram, a foreign language education specialist, observed that many understandings of intercultural competency largely ignore the language component even though language is a core element in intercultural communication and most interactions of this nature involve a second language. Accordingly, he distinguishes between intercultural competence and intercul-tural communicative competence. For Byram (1997, 2012), the former refers to the skills and ability that individuals draw on to interact in their native language with people from another culture (e.g., a first language speaker of English from New Zealand interacting with a Cana-dian first language speaker of English). By contrast, the latter refers to 'the ability of second language speakers to mediate/interpret the values, beliefs and behaviors (the "cultures") of themselves and of others and to "stand on the bridge" or indeed "be the bridge" between peo-ple of different languages and cultures' (Byram 2006: 12). More simply put, it is the ability of individuals to interact successfully across cultures while using a second language (e.g., com-munication between a Taiwanese second language speaker of English and a Malaysian second language speaker of English or a first language speaker of English from Australia).

Plate 11.3 Learning another language and improving one's intercultural communication skills can lead to a broadening of one's sense of self. © Jane Jackson

Intercultural communicative competence focuses on 'establishing and maintaining relationships' instead of merely communicating messages or exchanging information (Byram 1997: 3) This involves 'accomplishing a negotiation between people based on both culture-specific and culture-general features that is on the whole respectful of and favorable to each' (Guilherme 2004: 297). Within the context of intercultural education, programs may involve culture-specific or culture-general approaches (Bhawuk 2018c).

Culture-specific intercultural education primarily aims at the achievement of cultural competence in a particular cultural context. For example, Danish students may prepare for a year abroad program in Barcelona by taking Spanish language lessons, reading about Spanish culture, and participating in a pre-sojourn course that centers on how to communicate effectively and appropriately in various contexts and situations in Spain.

Instead of focusing on a particular culture, **culture-general intercultural education** centers on the development of the knowledge, skills, and mindset that can help individuals analyze their linguistic and cultural context and engage in successful intercultural interactions, no matter where they are in the world. For example, this intercultural communication text provides examples from many different cultural contexts and is designed to raise awareness of core issues in intercultural relations (e.g., ethnocentrism, intercultural sensitivity, cultural self-awareness). As broad intercultural competence cannot be achieved by focusing on the ability to behave properly in a particular culture, intercultural learning should involve a mix of 'culture-specific' and 'culture-general' approaches.

Intercultural communicative competence and the intercultural speaker

The close relationship between language, culture, and intercultural competence is conveyed in the notion of the **intercultural speaker**, a term coined by Byram (see Byram & Zarate 1997)

to describe foreign language/culture learners who successfully establish intercultural relationships while using their second language. Intercultural speakers

> operate their linguistic competence and their sociolinguistic awareness . . . in order to
> manage interaction across cultural boundaries, to anticipate misunderstandings caused by
> difference in values, meanings and beliefs, and . . . to cope with the affective as well as
> cognitive demands of engagement with otherness.
>
> (*ibid.*: 25)

Intercultural speakers are depicted as competent, flexible communicators (Byram 2012;
Byram & Zarate 1997; Wilkinson 2012) who 'engage with complexity and multiple identities' and 'avoid stereotyping which accompanies perceiving someone through a single identity'
(Byram *et al.* 2002: 5). For Guilherme (2004: 298), *critical* **intercultural speakers** are able
to 'negotiate between their own cultural, social, and political identifications and representations with those of the other', and in the process, become aware of 'the multiple, ambivalent,
resourceful, and elastic nature of cultural identities in an intercultural encounter' (*ibid.*: 125).
The term 'intercultural speaker' is still widely used today, although some scholars prefer the
term **'intercultural mediator'** to emphasize 'the individual's potential for social action rather
than the competencies acquired as a consequence of teaching' (Alred & Byram 2002: 341).
Later in this chapter, when we discuss Byram's model of intercultural communicative competence, we revisit notions of the intercultural speaker.

Intercultural communicative competence and intercultural citizenship

Byram (2008, 2011a, 2012) and his associates (e.g., Byram *et al.* 2017; Byram & Parmenter
2015; Wagner & Byram 2018) have linked the notion of intercultural communicative competence with citizenship education. In recent publications Byram defines the competencies that
enable intercultural speakers to engage in community activities with people from another country who speak a different first language. To foster the development of '**intercultural political
competence**', Byram (2011b: 17) advocates for 'the enrichment of citizenship education with
an international dimension' coupled with the infusion of a 'political/citizenship dimension'
in second or foreign language education. This approach to **intercultural citizenship** brings
together 'the general dimensions of attitudes, knowledge and behaviour' common to both citizenship and language education.

> In intercultural citizenship, the question of national or cosmopolitan allegiances is not
> important; intercultural citizenship is not a matter of creating identifications with state
> or any other entity. It is rather, the development of competencies to engage with oth-
> ers in political activity across linguistic and cultural boundaries both within and across
> state frontiers. International 'bonds' – and the reduction of prejudice – are the intended
> outcomes.
>
> (Byram 2011b: 19)

Intercultural citizenship, which favors multiculturalism and equality, requires awareness and
respect of self and other, the desire to interact across cultures, and the acquisition of the knowledge

and skills that facilitate constructive, active participation in today's complex, globalized society. For Guilherme (2007: 87), this entails 'the control of the fear of the unknown (at the emotional level), the promotion of a critical outlook (at the cognitive level), as well as the enhancement of self-development (at the experiential level)'. Through education and international experience, many interculturalists (e.g., Alred *et al.* 2003; Guilherme 2002, 2007; Wagner & Byram 2018) maintain that it is possible to cultivate the understanding (e.g., cultural knowledge, open mindset) and skills (e.g., culture-sensitive behaviors, culture learning strategies) that characterize intercultural communicative competence and cosmopolitan, intercultural citizenship.

'Effective' and 'appropriate' intercultural communication

Alvino Fantini (e.g., 2012a, 2012b, 2019) has also written extensively about intercultural communication in second language situations. For this applied linguist, intercultural communicative competence is 'a complex of abilities needed to perform *effectively* and *appropriately* when interacting with others who are linguistically and culturally different from oneself' (Fantini & Tirmizi 2006: 12). Implicit in this definition are individual traits and characteristics (e.g., personality); the domains of relationships, communication, and collaboration; the dimensions of knowledge, **attitude** (emotional response to people/things), skills, and awareness; proficiency in the host language; and a developmental process.

In Fantini's definition, *effective* **intercultural communication** relates to one's perception of one's performance in intercultural encounters, drawing on an 'etic' or outsider's view of the host/second language culture. By contrast, the notion of *appropriate* **intercultural communication** is linked to how one's behavior is perceived by one's hosts (i.e., an 'emic' or insider's understanding of what is acceptable in the host/second language culture). This conceptualization of intercultural communicative competence acknowledges the importance of the views of *both* interactants (the sender and receiver) in terms of outcomes. In other words, for the communication to be successful, the message must also be received as interculturally sensitive and appropriate, and the meaning should generally be interpreted as intended.

Critical applied linguists Dervin and Dirba (2006) maintain that second language speakers possess intercultural competence 'when they are able/ willing to communicate effectively with others, accept their position as "strangers" when meeting others, and realize that all individuals, including themselves, are multicultural and complex (sex, age, religion, status in society, etc.)' (p. 257). For Sercu (2005: 2), an applied linguist, an interculturally competent individual possesses the following traits and skills:

> the willingness to engage with the foreign culture, self-awareness and the ability to look upon oneself from the outside, the ability to see the world through the others' eyes, the ability to cope with uncertainty, the ability to act as a cultural mediator, the ability to evaluate others' points of view, the ability to consciously use culture learning skills and to read the cultural context, and the understanding that individuals cannot be reduced to their collective identities.

A common definition of intercultural competence

Deardorff (2004) surveyed 23 leading intercultural communication experts (e.g., Michael Byram, Janet Bennett, Guo-Ming Chen) with the aim of arriving at a common understanding of intercultural competence. The top three elements that the respondents associated with this construct were: 'awareness, valuing, and understanding of cultural differences; experiencing other cultures; and self-awareness of one's own culture' (*ibid.*: 247). After reviewing nine definitions of intercultural competence, the scholars considered the following one as most relevant to their institution's internationalization strategies: 'Knowledge of others, knowledge of self; skills to interpret and relate; skills to discover and/ or to interact; valuing others' values, beliefs, and behaviors; and relativizing one's self. Linguistic competence plays a key role' (Byram 1997: 34). Although the majority of the experts surveyed were not language educators, they appeared to recognize the importance of language in intercultural encounters as they gave the highest rating to Byram's (1997) definition, which drew attention to the linguistic dimension.

After analyzing the input of the survey respondents, Deardorff (2004: 194) concluded her study by formulating the following broad definition of intercultural competence: 'the ability to communicate effectively and appropriately in intercultural situations based on one's intercultural knowledge, skills and attitudes'. Although the language dimension (e.g., use of a second language) was not made explicit, it is mentioned in related publications.

MODELS OF INTERCULTURAL COMPETENCE

Building on their understandings of intercultural communication and intercultural effectiveness, numerous scholars (e.g., speech communication specialists, applied linguists, interculturalists, international educators) have devised models of intercultural competence. Let's take a look at some of the most widely known frameworks: Byram's (1997) model of intercultural communicative competence, Chen and Starosta's (2008) model of intercultural communication competence, M.J. Bennett's (1993) Developmental model of Intercultural sensitivity, and Deardorff's (2004) process model of intercultural competence.

Byram's model of intercultural communicative competence

Byram's (1997) model of intercultural communicative competence has had a profound effect on the teaching of second or foreign languages, especially in European contexts. His conceptual framework draws attention to the need to integrate culture into second language teaching and learning. As illustrated in Figure 11.2, Byram's work builds on notions of communicative competence put forward by Hymes (1966, 1972) and expanded on by other applied linguists in relation to the teaching and learning of foreign languages (e.g., Bachman 1990; Canale and Swain 1980). **Communicative competence** refers to 'what a speaker needs to know, and what a child needs to learn, to be able to use language appropriately in specific social/cultural settings' (Swann *et al.* 2004: 42). Thus it is linked to notions of first and second language socialization that were discussed in earlier chapters.

In the first part of his model, Byram (1997: 48) cites the following *linguistic* elements as characteristic of an interculturally competent second language speaker (the intercultural speaker or mediator):

- **Linguistic competence**: the ability to apply knowledge of the rules of a standard version of the language to produce and interpret spoken and written language
- **Sociolinguistic competence**: the ability to give to the language produced by an interlocutor — whether native speaker or not — meanings that are taken for granted by the interlocutor or negotiated and made explicit with the interlocutor

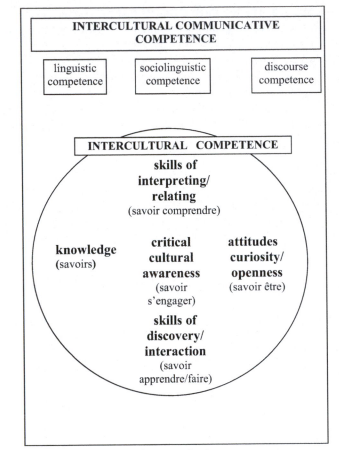

Figure 11.2 The components of intercultural communicative competence

Source: Michael Byram. Reproduced with permission. (An earlier version appeared in Byram, M. (1997) *Teaching and Assessing Intercultural Communicative Competence,* Clevedon, U.K.: Multilingual Matters.)

■ **Discourse competence**: the ability to use, discover, and negotiate strategies for the production and interpretation of monologue or dialogue texts which follow the conventions of the culture of an interlocutor or are negotiated as intercultural texts for particular purposes.

The second part of this framework identifies five *savoirs* or components that are linked to the *cultural* dimension of the intercultural speaker's competence (ibid: 12–13). The first two are considered prerequisites for successful intercultural/interlingual communication:

■ **Intercultural attitudes (*savoir être*)** – curiosity and openness, readiness to suspend disbelief about other cultures and belief about one's own intercultural attitudes
■ **Knowledge (*savoirs*)** – of social groups and their products and practices in one's own and interlocutor's country

Finally, the next three components feature the skills deemed necessary for successful communication across cultures and languages:

- **Skills of interpreting and relating (*savoir comprendre*):** the ability to interpret a document or event from another culture, to explain it and relate it to documents or events from one's own
- **Skills of discovery and interaction (*savoir apprendre/faire*):** the ability to acquire new knowledge of a culture and to operate this knowledge in real time communication
- **Critical cultural awareness (*savoir s'engager*):** the ability to evaluate critically and on the basis of explicit criteria, perspectives, practices and products in one's own and other cultures and countries

This model draws attention to the need for language teachers to integrate a cultural component into their language teaching. With this in view, Byram *et al.* (2002: 6) offer the following advice:

> developing the intercultural dimension in language teaching involves recognizing that the aims are: to give learners intercultural competence as well as linguistic competence; to prepare them for interaction with people of other cultures; to enable them to understand and accept people from other cultures as individuals with other distinctive perspectives, values and behaviours; and to help them to see that such interaction is an enriching experience.

Knowing grammar rules and vocabulary in a second language is not sufficient for one to be interculturally competent. Byram's model of intercultural communicative competence raises awareness of the importance of culture learning for second language learners (e.g., learning about the values and practices of their own and other cultures). After examining the Developmental Model of Intercultural Sensitivity (DMIS), we delve further into the relationship between second language proficiency and intercultural competence.

Chen and Starosta's model of intercultural communication competence

Speech communication specialists Chen and Starosta (2008) have developed and refined their own model of intercultural communication competence, which emphasizes a 'transformational process of symmetrical interdependence'. Their conceptual framework consists of three 'equally important', interrelated dimensions that work together to create 'a holistic picture of intercultural communication competence': (1) affective or intercultural sensitivity; (2) cognitive or intercultural awareness, and (3) behavioral or intercultural adroitness. This model does not, however, deal explicitly with intercultural interactions in a second language.

Intercultural communication competence, in Chen and Starosta's (2008: 223) view, requires **affective** or **intercultural sensitivity**, that is, 'positive emotion that enables individuals to be sensitive enough to acknowledge and respect cultural differences'. This affective process is linked to the following personal elements or characteristics: 'self-concept, open-mindedness, nonjudgmental attitudes, and social relaxation' (*ibid.*: 223). Similar to Byram (1997), these scholars have found that people who are competent intercultural communicators possess higher levels of **cognitive** or **intercultural awareness**, that is, **self-awareness** (e.g., knowledge of one's own personal identities/cultures) and **cultural awareness** (e.g., understanding of how cultures differ).

To be competent intercultural communicators, Chen and Starosta (2008: 227) maintain that individuals must also enhance their **behavioral** or **intercultural adroitness** ('message skills, knowledge regarding appropriate self-disclosure, behavioral flexibility, interaction management, and social skills'). These skills and actions, in their view, are vital for world citizens to act effectively in intercultural encounters and 'achieve the goal of multicultural interdependence and interconnectedness in the global village' (*ibid.*: 227).

Recognizing 'the complex multicultural dynamics' of 'our current global society', Chen and Starosta (2008: 227) recommend that measures of intercultural communication competence take into account the multiple perspectives and identities that are now a common feature within communities and cultures:

> The trends of technology development, globalization of the economy, widespread population migration, development of multiculturalism, and the demise of the nation-state in favor of sub- and supranational identifications have shrunk and multiculturalized the world, and traditional perceptions of *self* and *other* must be redefined. The global context of human communication and the need to pursue a state of multicultural coexistence require that we abolish the boundaries separating *me* and *you*, *us* and *them*, and develop a theory of communication competence that takes into account individuals' multiple identities.

Challenging traditional notions of Self and Other, their recommendation is in line with critical theorists (e.g., Dervin 2012; Holliday 2019; Kramsch & Uryu 2012) who rally against homogenizing, static perspectives of culture that adopt a 'culture as nation' perspective and fail to acknowledge the dynamic nature of identities, hybridity within individuals, and diversity within groups.

The Developmental Model of Intercultural Sensitivity (DMIS)

While some theorists have focused on describing the behaviors and traits associated with intercultural competence, others have proposed models that aim to depict the *process* of becoming interculturally competent. One such framework is the **Developmental Model of Intercultural Sensitivity (DMIS)**. The DMIS is widely used in intercultural communication research (e.g., education abroad) and practice (e.g., diversity training programs). In relation to this model, Bennett and Bennett (2004) define **intercultural competence** as 'the ability to communicate effectively in cross-cultural situations and to relate appropriately in a variety of cultural contexts' (p. 149), while **intercultural sensitivity** refers to the developmental process that impacts an individual's psychological ability to deal with cultural differences.

Phenomenological in nature, this theoretical framework was developed by Milton Bennett (1993) to explain the observed and reported experiences of individuals in intercultural encounters. 'The underlying assumption of the model is that as one's *experiences of cultural difference* becomes more sophisticated, one's competence in intercultural relations increases' (Bennett & Bennett 2004: 152). The DMIS centers on the constructs of **ethnocentrism** and **ethnorelativism** (Bennett 2009, 2018). In the former, 'the worldview of one's own culture is central to all reality' (Bennett 1993: 30), whereas the latter is linked to 'being comfortable with many standards and customs and to having an ability to adapt behavior and judgments to a variety of interpersonal settings' (*ibid.*: 26).

In this theory, intercultural sensitivity is associated with personal growth and the development of an **intercultural mind**, 'a mindset capable of understanding from within and from without both one's own culture and other cultures' (Bennett *et al*. 2003: 252). Bennett (1993, 2012, 2018) suggests that the development of intercultural sensitivity occurs as the constructs and experiences of cultural differences evolve toward an increased awareness and acceptance of those differences. Specifically, the DMIS theorizes that individuals move from ethnocentric stages where one's culture is experienced as 'central to reality' (denial, defense, minimization), through ethnorelative stages of greater recognition and acceptance of difference (acceptance, adaptation, and integration). People, however, do not necessarily follow a linear progression (e.g., advancing to the next stage in sequence). Due to unpleasant intercultural experiences or acute culture shock, for example, they may retreat to a lower level of sensitivity.

Denial of difference measures a worldview that ignores or simplifies cultural difference. In this stage, one's own culture is experienced as the only real one. *Polarization*: *defense/ reversal* measures a judgmental orientation that views cultural differences in terms of 'us' and 'them', whereby one's own culture (or an adopted one) is experienced as the best way of doing things. *Minimization* (M) measures a transitional worldview that emphasizes cultural commonality and universal values. With limited cultural self-awareness, individuals in this phase are still ethnocentric and may not pay sufficient attention to cultural differences, assuming that other cultures are similar to one's own. *Acceptance of difference* measures a worldview that can comprehend and appreciate complex cultural differences, while *adaptation to difference* identifies the capacity to alter one's cultural perspective and adapt one's behavior so that it is appropriate in a particular cultural context. The DMIS posits that ethnorelative worldviews (*acceptance, adaptation, integration*) have more potential to generate the attitudes, knowledge, and behavior that constitute intercultural competence and facilitate adjustment in a new milieu.

Describing individuals in *integration* as 'cultural bridge builders', Paige and Bennett (2015) posit that people in this ethnorelative stage have 'transcended the primary cultural affiliations and identities. Cultural identity is now an ongoing process of integrating, reintegrating, and bridging different cultural perspectives' (p. 523). Hammer (2015b) asserts that 'the integration stage is focused more on identity reformulation than on intercultural competence' (p. 483). (See Chapters 5 and 7 for more discussion on cultural marginality and feelings of inbetweenness).

In the DMIS, intercultural competence is viewed as a developmental phenomenon, in harmony with Mezirow's (1994, 2000) **transformational learning theory** in adult education. The latter posits that adults who engage in critical reflection and self-examination may experience a dramatic **transformation** (the act or process of change) in response to significant events or difficult stages in their lives (e.g., relocating to another linguistic and cultural environment, taking part in a global internship in a foreign land, moving from secondary school to university).

Within the context of intercultural communication, **critical (deep) reflection** is the process of analyzing, reconsidering, and questioning intercultural experiences with the aim of developing a better understanding of internal and external factors that influenced the outcome. From a transformational learning perspective, intercultural competence involves a continuous learning process with 'new or revised interpretations of the meaning of one's experience' (Mezirow 1994: 222). Through intercultural contact, individuals encounter cultural differences (and similarities) and face challenges that may cause them to question their usual ways of doing things. As they deepen their awareness and understanding of these differences, they may adjust their attitudes and mindset (e.g., develop an ethnorelative perspective) and gradually employ new behaviors that help them communicate more effectively and appropriately in intercultural interactions. Mezirow (1994, 2000) suggests that this process has the potential to lead to a life-altering transformation and restructuring of one's sense of self (e.g., identity expansion, identity reconstruction) in some individuals. (See Chapter 5 for a discussion of this phenomenon.)

The DMIS assumes a social construction of identity, positioning it as relational and subject to change. This perspective is aligned with contemporary critical and poststructuralist notions of identity (e.g., Baxter 2016; Noels *et al.* 2012; Norton 2000) that recognize the fluid, contradictory nature of this construct. In contrast with traditional views of identity as fixed, static, and unitary, this perspective allows for the impact of globalization and intercultural contact and the evolution of hybrid, global identities.

In sum, the DMIS offers a theory-based explanation of individual effectiveness in intercultural encounters, capturing the elements that Bhawuk and Brislin (1992: 416) argue are key predictors of success in intercultural contexts: 'To be effective in another culture, people must be interested in other cultures, be sensitive enough to notice cultural differences, and then also be willing to modify their behavior as an indication of respect for the people of other cultures'.

The process model of intercultural competence

Drawing on the input of 23 leading interculturalists, Deardorff (2004: 194), an international educator, also devised a process model. Her graphic representation of intercultural competence, which is presented in Figure 11.3, depicts movement from 'the individual level of attitudes/ personal attributes to the interactive cultural level in regard to the outcomes'. It draws attention to the internal shift in frame of reference that is essential for effective and appropriate behavior in intercultural encounters.

A strength of this process model is that it recognizes the *ongoing* complexity of the development of intercultural competence and the importance of reflection in the lifelong journey toward interculturality. Leclercq (2003: 9) defines **interculturality** as 'the set of processes through which relations between different cultures are constructed', whereby '[t]he aim is to enable groups and individuals who belong to such cultures within a single society or geopolitical entity to forge links based on equity and mutual respect'.

Similar to the models developed by Chen and Starosta (2008) and Byram (1997, 2006), Deardorff's (2004) conceptual framework accentuates the vital role that attitude plays in intercultural learning. Significantly, the intercultural experts she surveyed stress that 'the attitudes of openness, respect (valuing all cultures), curiosity and discovery (tolerating ambiguity)' are essential for one to become interculturally competent (Deardorff 2004: 193). Further, in accord with Byram's (1997) '*savoirs*', her model recognizes that intercultural competence necessitates knowledge and understanding of 'one's own cultural norms and sensitivity to those of other cultures' (Deardorff 2008: 37).

Deardorff's process model (2004, 2006, 2008) identifies key internal outcomes that may occur as a result of 'an informed frame of reference shift', namely, adaptability, an ethnorelative perspective, empathy, and a flexible mindset. Her graphic also specifies desired external outcomes that can be assessed (e.g., 'behaving and communicating appropriately and effectively' in intercultural situations). In Deardorff's (2008: 42) words, her model provides 'a holistic framework for intercultural competence development and assessment'.

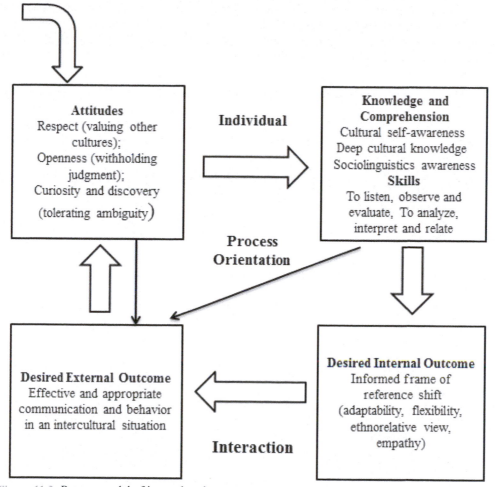

Figure 11.3 Process model of intercultural competence

Source: Deardorff (2004: 198). Reproduced with permission.

NOTES:

- Begin with attitudes, move from individual level (attitudes) to interaction level (outcomes)
- Degree of intercultural competence depends on degree of attitudes, knowledge/ comprehension and skills achieved

All of these models have contributed to our understanding of the multiple factors involved in intercultural competence and the process of gradually moving from an ethnocentric (mono-cultural) perspective to an ethnorelative or **intercultural mindset**.

SECOND LANGUAGE PROFICIENCY AND INTERCULTURAL COMPETENCE

Recently, scholars have attempted to link levels of intercultural competence with proficiency in the second or foreign language (e.g., language of the host community). The development of 'an intercultural mindset', according to Bennett *et al.* (2003: 252), 'resonates positively with communicative competence and proficiency-related theories of language learning'. They hypothesize that there is a 'typical fit between language proficiency levels and developmental levels of intercultural sensitivity' (*ibid.*: 255).

> Although language proficiency is not a specific element of the DMIS, the model nevertheless supports the view of language learning as a communication endeavor and as a humanistic enterprise. As a communication endeavor, language competence is defined as the ability to use the language as an *insider*. The DMIS creates a parallel to language competence by defining cultural competence as the ability to interpret and behave within culture as an *insider*. As a humanistic enterprise, language learning creates an awareness and appreciation of language itself. The DMIS parallel is that intercultural sensitivity involves an awareness and appreciation of culture itself.
>
> (Bennett *et al.* 2003: 253)

More specifically, they suggest that progression through the stages of the DMIS correlates with advances in one's second language proficiency. In particular, they speculate that learners who have an advanced level of proficiency are apt to be in an ethnorelative stage of cultural development (e.g., adaptation/integration). Conversely, those who are novice learners of the language are likely to be in an ethnocentric stage of development (e.g., denial/defense). But are intercultural development and second language proficiency necessarily parallel? What evidence supports or refutes this hypothesis?

Thus far, only a few studies have explored this question. In South Korea, Park (2006) examined the relationship between intercultural sensitivity and linguistic competence in 104 pre-service EFL (English as a foreign language) teachers. The Intercultural Development Inventory (a cross-culturally validated psychometric instrument) to measure the participants' level of intercultural sensitivity as outlined in the DMIS. The Michigan English Language Assessment Battery (MELAB) was used to assess their level of language competence. Park (2006) found little correlation between the participants' level of intercultural sensitivity and linguistic competence; those with advanced proficiency in English did not necessarily possess a higher level of intercultural sensitivity. The findings suggest that 'intercultural competence might not naturally grow with the development of linguistic competence'; in fact, it may progress at a much slower rate than proficiency in a second language. Park (2006) recommends that intercultural competence be taught explicitly, as is the case with second or foreign (international) languages (e.g., formal classroom-based instruction).

To better understand the link between linguistic and intercultural development, Edstrom (2005) interviewed 13 American women (second language users of Spanish) living in Venezuela. Employing the DMIS as a theoretical framework, she discovered that the following factors influenced the women's participation in second language conversation: their knowledge of second language (L2) conversational styles, their willingness to accept differences in communication styles, and their interest in the topics of conversation. '[A]lthough an appreciation for the complexity of language and an understanding of the relationship between language and culture do not produce proficient, bilingual learners', Edstrom (2005: 32) notes that, 'these concepts may contribute to the formation of informed, tolerant learners who appreciate the difficulty of mastering an L2'.

Similar to Park (2006), Edstrom (2005) recommends that intercultural communication theories and strategies be made explicit in second language education. In particular, she suggests that awareness of cross-cultural differences in conversational styles be incorporated into language teaching along with tasks designed to increase intercultural sensitivity. In her view,

> exploring the role of personal background and intercultural sensitivity in the language learning process does not ensure learners' successful participation in L2 conversation but it does expose them to the complex relationship between language and its users . . . and this awareness may serve them longer than their L2 skills.
>
> (p. 32)

In separate surveys of interculturalists and global education experts, Deardorff and Hunter (2006: 81) found a consensus that 'neither language nor education abroad alone makes someone interculturally or globally competent'. In both studies the participants argued that 'more language course offerings must include key cultural knowledge that goes beyond the "tip of the iceberg" of food, music, and holidays to explore and understand the deep cultural knowledge of underlying values, norms, and worldviews' (*ibid*.: 81). Consistent with Deardorff's (2004) study, Hunter's (2004) respondents maintain that 'simply studying abroad, learning a L2, or majoring in international relations is no longer enough to prepare students for the global workforce. The approach to preparedness must be comprehensive' (Deardorff & Hunter 2006: 79).

Further, a growing number of study abroad researchers and specialists in intercultural/second language pedagogy (e.g., Fantini 2019; Jackson 2018a; Vande Berg *et al*. 2012) concur with Ryan's (2003: 132) observation that, '[r]esidence in another country does not automatically produce interculturality'. Simply put, intercultural contact and international travel do not necessarily lead to intercultural communicative competence. Guilherme *et al*. (2010: 243–4) note that, 'language learning alone is not sufficient to grasp the complexities of another culture and to finally achieve intercultural competence'. Knowing the grammar and vocabulary of another language does not ensure that people will be able to communicate successfully across cultures in that language. With this in mind, Bennett (1997: 16–21) offers the following description of 'a fluent fool':

> A fluent fool is someone who speaks a foreign language well but doesn't understand the social or philosophical content of that language. Such people are likely to get into all sorts of trouble because both they themselves and others overestimate their ability. They may be invited into complicated social situations where they cannot understand the events deeply enough to avoid giving or taking offense. Eventually, fluent fools may develop negative opinions of the native speakers whose language they understand but whose basic beliefs and values continue to elude them. . . . To avoid becoming a fluent fool, we need to understand more completely the cultural dimension of language.

While the label 'fluent fool' is rather jarring, Bennett's (1997) admonition does raise our awareness of the need to develop intercultural competence along with proficiency in a second or foreign language.

REQUISITE COMPETENCIES FOR TODAY'S GLOBAL SOCIETY

What competencies are necessary for individuals to become responsible, ethical global citizens in today's diverse world? What knowledge, attitudes, and skills are vital for success in today's global workforce and society? International educators and scholars from various disciplines

Knowledge

- Knowledge of world geography, conditions, languages, issues, and events
- Awareness of the complexity and interdependency of world events and issues
- Understanding of historical forces that have shaped the current world system
- Knowledge of one's own culture, language, and history
- Knowledge of effective communication, including knowledge of a foreign language, intercultural communication concepts, international business etiquette, and netiquette
- Sociopragmatic knowledge of a foreign language (e.g., awareness of cultural scripts)
- Understanding of the diversity found in the world in terms of values, beliefs, ideas, languages, and worldviews
- Civic knowledge and engagement- local and global

Attitudes: Personal and social responsibility

- Openness to learning and a positive orientation to new opportunities, ideas, languages, and ways of thinking
- Tolerance for ambiguity and unfamiliarity
- Sensitivity and respect for personal, linguistic, and cultural differences
- Empathy or the ability to take multiple perspectives
- Self-awareness and self-esteem about one's own identity, language, and culture
- Appreciation of other ways of being (e.g., diverse communication styles, worldviews)
- Ethical reasoning and action

Skills

- Technical skills to enhance one's ability to learn about the world (i.e., research skills, computer literacy)
- Critical and comparative thinking skills, including the ability to think creatively and integrate knowledge rather than uncritical acceptance of knowledge
- Communication skills, including the ability to use another language effectively and interact *effectively and appropriately* with people who have a different cultural background (e.g., well developed sociopragmatic awareness and communication skills)
- Teamwork and problem solving
- Coping and resiliency skills in unfamiliar and challenging intercultural situations

Figure 11.4 Requisite competencies for today's global citizens

Source: Adapted from Association of American Colleges and Universities (AAC & U) 2007; Green & Olson 2003: 106–7; Olson *et al.* 2007.

have identified a number of requisite competencies of world citizens, which are presented in Figure 11.4.

While this list includes many international/intercultural competencies, it is not exhaustive. Can you identify other items that should be included?

ENHANCING INTERCULTURAL (COMMUNICATIVE) COMPETENCE AND GLOBAL CITIZENSHIP

History shows that we human beings have both the capacity to open our eyes, minds, hearts, and hands – and to close them. We have the capacity to build an interdependent, peaceful global civilization and to splinter and fragment into endless conflict.

We can see the world narrowly, or broadly, depending on which parts of ourselves we are able to develop. Indeed, wherever we may live, the drama of the Earth itself is occurring within each of us.

If we are willing to open our eyes, minds, hearts, and hands, then every one of us can become a global citizen.

Yes, *everyone*.

(Gerzon 2010: xxiv)

How can each of us develop ourselves as global and intercultural citizens? What actions can we take to overcome ethnocentric tendencies and become more sensitive, effective intercultural communicators? In this chapter, we have reviewed the traits and actions of people who are

Plate 11.4 What knowledge, skills, and attributes are essential for today's graduates to be 'global-ready'?
© Jane Jackson

considered interculturally competent, global citizens. We have examined theories and models of both intercultural competence and global competence. Let's now take a look at some practical steps that you can take to become more globally minded and intercultural.

Become more self-aware

Throughout this book, the importance of becoming more self-aware has been emphasized. To become an effective intercultural communicator and global citizen, it is imperative to recognize one's strengths and weaknesses; this can help to set realistic learning targets. For example, if you have a low tolerance for ambiguity, you can make a concerted effort to reduce your anxiety in unfamiliar or unclear situations. Recognizing your tendency to become quickly frustrated and overwhelmed is the first step to identifying effective coping strategies. If you make snap judgments when meeting people for the first time, you can try to curb this tendency by focusing on the positive. If you discover that you have very little knowledge about your cultural/linguistic background and find it difficult to respond to related questions in intercultural interactions, you can do research in this area. If you feel out of your depth when people are talking about global issues, you can resolve to enhance your knowledge of international affairs.

Become more aware of your preferred self-identities and communication styles and identify the cultural behaviors that seem to annoy or disturb you the most. Then make an effort to change your attitude so that you approach intercultural situations with a more positive mindset. By developing the habit of critical self-reflection, you can gain a better understanding of what you need to improve. It is important for this process of discovery, reflection, and growth to be ongoing throughout your life.

Demonstrate mindfulness and flexibility

In intercultural interactions, in addition to being self-aware, pay close attention to the intercultural attitudes, perspectives, emotions, and communication styles of your interlocutors as well as the context or situation in which the interaction is taking place (e.g., social, linguistic, political, historical dimensions). **Mindfulness** (being aware of our own assumptions, ideas, and emotions and those of our communication partners) can affect the way intercultural encounters unfold. For Ting-Toomey (2015c), 'a mindful intercultural communicator is an adaptive individual who has a strong present-in-the-moment orientation with cognitive, affective, and behavioral flexibility' (p. 625). This perspective fits with Chen and Starosta's (2008) model of intercultural communication competence that was described earlier in this chapter.

Observe and actively listen

In an unfamiliar cultural context or in intercultural situations in your home environment, carefully observe the verbal and nonverbal behaviors of your communication partners who have a different linguistic and cultural background. Be an active listener. As well as paying attention to what is being said, **active listening** means noticing how and when ideas are conveyed, as well as what is *not* being said. In intercultural interactions, also keep in mind that you may not be interpreting messages in the way that the speaker intended. Consider the possibility of other perspectives and resist the temptation to make quick, negative assumptions about the speaker and his or her linguistic or cultural background. Strive to avoid stereotyping. If you have a negative encounter with someone from a particular background that does not mean that all people who are associated with this language or culture will act or think in the same way.

Cultivate openness

Overcoming ethnocentric tendencies and developing an intercultural or ethnorelative mindset is a critical goal for all citizens. **Ethnocentricism** refers to an attitude that one's ways of being are superior to others. Whereas an ethnocentric individual may regard cultural difference as inferior and unacceptable, an open-minded person is receptive to new ideas and behaviors.

Effective intercultural communicators strive to understand what lies behind unfamiliar practices and worldviews instead of making quick value judgments. In international intercultural situations, for example, you can demonstrate a willingness to try new things (e.g., local cuisine, different communication styles), make an effort to learn the host language, and broaden your repertoire of verbal and nonverbal behaviors so that your actions are effective and appropriate for the cultural context. Being intercultural, however, does not mean that you must accept social or culture practices that demean or degrade others (e.g., female mutilation, slavery). As ethical, intercultural, and global citizens we should all be concerned about social justice and human rights that affect outgroup members as well as people from our own ingroups, however we define them.

Display respect

There is a fundamental difference between respect and tolerance. The Latin origin of 'tolerance' refers to enduring something and does not convey affirmation or support. Being tolerant suggests an imbalance of power in the relationship, whereby an individual is in the position to grant or refuse permission for the other person to behave in certain ways. In contrast, the Latin word for respect conveys the idea that individuals are equally deserving of honor and mutual regard. Within the context of intercultural communication, **respect** signifies positive regard for an individual from a different cultural background, whereas **tolerance** implies going along with behaviors that one does not necessarily respect or accept. In this regard, tolerance can be viewed as patronizing. For example, tolerating religious diversity suggests that one feels superior to people from other faiths.

Being intercultural also means recognition that the ways in which we express respect for others varies depending on the cultural context. Verbal and nonverbal expressions of respect may work well in one context and be perceived as insincere and inappropriate in another. Cultural knowledge and sensitivity also influence the effectiveness of your communication in intercultural situations.

Be empathetic

Empathy refers to an individual's ability to convey awareness of another person's feelings, circumstances, and experiences. In intercultural interactions, instead of focusing solely on your own message and goals, be aware of and sensitive to your communication partner's needs and feelings. Consider how your message is being received. Effective intercultural communicators have the ability to empathize with the worldviews and situations of people who have a different linguistic and cultural background. **Empathetic behaviors** include nonverbal actions that indicate you are attending to the messages of others (e.g., facial expressions of concern) as well as verbal expressions (e.g., words that convey solidarity).

Learn another language

Mastering another language can enable you to interact with people who do not speak your first language without relying on an interpreter. When studying a second language, it is essential to enhance your cultural knowledge and intercultural communication skills as you develop awareness of grammatical structures and expand your vocabulary. Remember that advanced second language proficiency does not necessarily mean a high level of intercultural competence. Knowledge of grammar does not indicate that you have a high level of **sociopragmatic competence** (the ability to communicate appropriately in social situations in another cultural context). One can be **bilingual** (speak two languages) or **multilingual** (speak more than two languages) and not be **bicultural** (interculturally competent in two cultural contexts) or **multicultural** (interculturally competent in multiple cultural contexts). Just as you need to devote time and attention to language elements, intercultural communication knowledge and skills merit attention.

Intercultural speakers take advantage of opportunities to use their second language. Instead of waiting for people to approach them; they initiate intercultural interactions and demonstrate a high level of willingness to communicate in their second language and enhance their intercultural competence. They make an effort to share their feelings and ideas with people from diverse backgrounds. Bilingualism and biculturalism can both be great assets in today's globalized world.

Seek feedback

Intercultural competence implies effective and appropriate communication with individuals who have a different cultural background. This depends not only on your impression of communicative events, but the perceptions of your communication partners. In intercultural interactions you can get a sense of how effective and appropriate your verbal and nonverbal actions are by paying close attention to their reactions. Of course, it is also possible to misread signals or be unsure of their response so it can be very helpful to get honest and frank feedback from intercultural friends. As well as demonstrating your commitment to becoming a better intercultural communicator, their input can identify areas which you need to improve (e.g., the use of less direct phrases, more appropriate nonverbal behaviors in certain situations, allowing additional time for second language speakers to process your speech and respond).

Be engaged in the world

As well as developing intercultural competency and fluency in another language, global citizens take an interest in world affairs. Instead of restricting yourself to local news and events, develop the habit of watching global newscasts (on television or online) on a regular basis or access international reports in newspapers (hard copies or online) in your first or second language. On campus, talk with international students or professors about issues and life in other parts of the world. You could also join a study abroad program, volunteer abroad, participate in a global internship, or undertake service learning in another linguistic/cultural setting. Participate in international associations which aim to make the world a better place (e.g., improve the environment, foster intercultural interactions, celebrate diversity) or campaign for human rights and social justice. Explore opportunities for involvement in your community and beyond. Don't wait for others to come to you with ideas about what you can do. Be proactive! Become interested, informed, and involved in local and global issues. Working cooperatively with others you can make a valuable contribution to your community and our global society and become a more effective intercultural and global citizen. As well as helping others, your involvement can enrich your life by adding meaning, purpose, and diversity.

Be patient

Finally, bear in mind that developing global and intercultural competencies takes time, commitment, and energy. Learning a foreign language also requires perseverance and investment. Second language socialization and the acquisition of a global mindset do not happen overnight. Be patient and keep yourself motivated by setting realistic, focused targets. Recognize improvements. Developing intercultural communicative competence is a process of long duration. As noted by Guilherme *et al.* (2010: 244), 'Becoming interculturally competent is a process of changing one's mindset. . . . It is a process of continuous transformation that, ideally, never ends'. Changing habits and opening yourself up to other ways of being involve emotions, attitudes, and knowledge. A deep level of engagement is required. Change takes time, but the rewards are many.

Developing oneself as a globally minded, intercultural communicator is best viewed as a lifelong process rather as something that can quickly be accomplished in an intercultural communication course, for example. As Temples (2105) explains, 'developing intercultural competence is an extension of a lifelong identity construction process' (p. 577). When you are open to new ideas and experiences you will continue to grow and evolve throughout your life. With an intercultural, global mindset we can contribute to making the world a better, more humane place. Each of us has the capacity to make a difference.

SUMMARY

In the 21st century it is imperative that all of us develop intercultural competence and become responsible intercultural, global citizens. Becoming proficient in two or more languages is also important in today's diverse world. Our personal well-being and the future of our communities, and indeed our planet, depend on our ability to meet the challenges of modern life (e.g., linguistic and cultural diversity, intercultural conflicts, pollution, the widening gap between the rich and poor, limited resources, etc.). As our world has become more diverse and interconnected it is vital for *all* humans to make an effort to respect one another and live in harmony. For life on our planet to flourish, we must transcend regional and national boundaries and reach out to people from different linguistic and cultural backgrounds within our communities and beyond. The future of humankind and the quality of our environment depend on the choices we make. Each of us can and must make a difference. It is also essential to view intercultural competence as a lifelong process.

discussion questions

1 Why does Byram (1997, 2009) distinguish between intercultural competence and intercultural communicative competence? Do you think this distinction is useful or necessary? Why or why not?
2 What does it mean to be an 'intercultural speaker'? An 'intercultural mediator'? Discuss and provide examples to illustrate your ideas.
3 Describe the complex relationship between language, culture, and intercultural competence and share your ideas with a partner.
4 How do you know if you have communicated 'effectively' and 'appropriately' in intercultural interactions?
5 How would you define 'social justice'? How is this concept linked to global citizenship?
6 How can interculturally sensitive and globally minded individuals benefit the community on local, national, and international levels?
7 What is the relationship between second language proficiency and intercultural competence? Discuss your ideas with a partner.
8 Reflect on why intercultural competence is best viewed as a lifelong process. Share your views about this in a small group.

activities

1 Offer your own definition of global citizenship. In small groups, share your views. How do your ideas differ?
2 Think back to your understanding of intercultural communication and global citizenship before you read Chapter 1. How have your ideas changed? Can you identify more imperatives to develop global-mindedness and intercultural communicative competence today? What are the benefits of becoming bi(multi)lingual and globally competent?
3 Identify a well-known bilingual person whom you consider highly intercultural. What characteristics qualify him or her as an intercultural person?
4 Identify the ethical obligations of global citizens today. Compare your views with the ideas presented in this chapter.
5 Individually or with a partner, use your smartphone to conduct a videotaped interview with people who have a different linguistic and cultural background from you and your partner. With the consent of your interviewees, solicit their understanding of intercultural competence and global citizenship and the importance of these dimensions in today's world. Share a hyperlink to your edited recording (approx. five minutes long) with your classmates. How do your own views converge or differ with those of your interviewees?
6 With a partner discuss the meaning of the following quote: 'Being "global souls" – seeing ourselves as members of a world community, knowing that we share the

future with others – requires not only intercultural experience but also the capacity to engage that experience transformatively' (Bennett 2008: 13). Do you share the author's views? Please explain.

7 'You must be the change you wish to see in the world'. This appeal was made by Mahatma Gandhi, the nonviolent activist who led India to independence and inspired peace movements around the world. Reflect on the meaning of Gandhi's words and identify steps that you can take in your own environment to make a positive difference in the world around you. Link your actions with what you have learned about intercultural competence and citizenship.

8 Review the list of global, linguistic, and intercultural competencies provided in this chapter and identify the ones that you possess. What aspects do you need to work on? Identify concrete strategies to use to accomplish your learning targets.

further reading

Byram, M., Golubeva, I., Hui, H. and Wagner, M. (eds.) (2017) *From Principles to Practice in Education for Intercultural Citizenship*, Bristol: Multilingual Matters.

The contributors offer their views about ways to promote competencies in intercultural communication and citizenship in foreign language education.

Davies, I., Sant, E., Schultz, L. and Pashby, K. (2018) *Global Citizenship Education: A Critical Introduction to Key Concepts and Debates*, London and New York: Bloomsbury.

In this volume global citizenship education is discussed in relation to citizenship education, global education, development education, and peace education.

Deardorff, D. (ed.) (2009) *The Sage Handbook of Intercultural Competence*, Thousand Oaks, CA: Sage.

Linking theory with research and practice, this handbook raises awareness of the complexity of intercultural communication and draws attention to evolving understandings of what it means to be interculturally competent.

Gerzon, M. (2010) *Global Citizens*, London: Rider.

The author draws attention to the major problems facing the world today and stresses the need for individuals to become responsible global citizens to improve the world.

Harden, A. and Witte, T. (ed.) (2011) *Intercultural Competence: Concepts, Challenges, Evaluations*, Berlin: Peter Lang.

The essays in this volume explore a broad range of perspectives on intercultural competence, including theories and applications in the teaching and learning of foreign languages.

Companion Website: Continue your journey online

Visit the Companion Website for a variety of tools and resources to support and extend your intercultural learning. (Instructors who are qualified adopters of the text may access additional resources on this site.)

References

Abdallah-Pretceille, M. (2003) *Former en Contexte Hétérogène. pour un Humanisme du Divers*, Paris: Anthropos.

Abigail, R.A. and Cahn, D.D. (2011) *Managing Conflict Through Communication*, 4th edn, Boston: Pearson.

Adams, R.J., Blieszner, R. and de Vries, B. (2000) 'Definitions of friendship in the third age: Age, gender, and study location effects', *Journal of Aging Studies*, 14: 117–33.

Adler, P. (1975) 'The transitional experience: An alternative view of culture shock', *Journal of Humanistic Psychology*, 15: 13–23.

Adler, R.B., Rosenfeld, L.B. and Proctor II, R.F. (2015) *Interplay: The Process of Interpersonal Communication*, 13th edn, Oxford: Oxford University Press.

Agar, M. (2006) 'Culture: Can you take it anywhere?' *International Journal of Qualitative Methods*, 5(2): 1–12.

Allan, G. (1989) *Friendship: Developing a Sociological Perspective*, London: Simon and Schuster.

Allport, G.W. (1954) *The Nature of Prejudice*, Cambridge, MA: Addison-Wesley.

Alred, G. and Byram, M. (2002) 'Becoming an intercultural mediator: A longitudinal study of residence abroad', *Journal of Multilingual and Multicultural Development*, 23(5): 339–52.

Alred, G., Byram, M. and Fleming, M. (2003) *Intercultural Experience and Education*, Clevedon: Multilingual Matters.

Altarriba, J. and Kazanas, S.A. (2018) 'Emotions and expressions across cultures', in Y.Y. Kim (ed.) *The International Encyclopedia of Intercultural Communication, Volume 1*, Hoboken, NJ: John Wiley & Sons, Inc., pp. 711–20.

Altman, I. and Taylor, D. (1973) *Social Penetration: The Development of Interpersonal Relationships*, New York: Holt.

American Psychiatric Association (2018) 'Sexual orientation & homosexuality', Online. Available: www.apa.org/topics/lgbt/orientation.aspx (accessed 27 January 2019).

Amico, R.P. (2016) *Anti-Racist Teaching*, London and New York: Routledge.

Anderson, B. (1983) *Imagined Communities: Reflections on the Origin and Spread of Nationalism*, London: Verso.

Anderson, B. (1991) *Imagined Communities: Reflections on the Origin and Spread of Nationalism*, 2nd edn, London and New York: Verso.

Anderson, B. (2006) *Imagined Communities*, London: Verso.

Anderson, M. (1959) 'What is communication?' *Journal of Communication*, 9: 5.

Anderson, P.A., Hecht, M.L., Hoobler, G.D. and Smallwood, M. (2003) 'Nonverbal communication across cultures', in W.B. Gudykunst (ed.) *Cross-Cultural and Intercultural Communication*, Thousand Oaks, CA: Sage, pp. 73–90.

Andrew, P. (2016) 'Constructing age identity: The case of Mexican EFL learners', in S. Preece (ed.) *The Routledge Handbook of Language and Identity*, London and New York: Routledge, pp. 337–50.

Andrzejewski, J. and Alessio, J. (1999) 'Education for global citizenship and social responsibility', *Progressive Perspectives*, 1(2): 2–17.

Appadurai, A. (1990) 'Disjuncture and difference in the global cultural economy', in M. Featherstone (ed.) *Global Culture: Nationalism, Globalization and Modernity*, London: Sage, pp. 295–310.

Arasaratnam-Smith, L.A. (2018) 'Intercultural communication competence', in Y.Y. Kim (ed.) *The International Encyclopedia of Intercultural Communication, Volume 2*, Hoboken, NJ: John Wiley & Sons, Inc., pp. 977–89.

Argyle, M. and Cook, M. (1976) *Gaze and Mutual Gaze*, New York: Cambridge University Press.

Argyle, M. and Trower, P. (1979) *Person to Person: Ways of Communicating*, New York: HarperCollins Publishers.

Arkoudis, S. and Baik, C. (2014) 'Crossing the interaction divide between international and domestic students in higher education', *HERDSA Review of Higher Education*, 1: 47–62.

Arkoudis, S., Dollinger, M., Baik, C. and Patience, A. (2018) 'International students' experience in Australian higher education: Can we do better?' *Higher Education*, Online. Available: https://link.springer.com/article/10.1007%2Fs10734-018-0302-x (accessed 3 March 2019).

Arnett, J.J. (2002) 'The psychology of globalization', *American Psychologist*, 57: 774–83.

Arnold, M. (1869) *Culture and Anarchy*, New York: Macmillan.

Arthur, N. (2004) *Counseling International Students: Clients from Around the World*, New York: Springer.

Arundale, R. (2006) 'Face as relational and interactional: A communication framework for research on face, facework, and politeness', *Journal of Politeness Research*, 2: 193–216.

Asante, M., Miike, Y. and Yin, J. (2014) 'Introduction: New directions for intercultural communication research', in M.K. Asante, Y. Miike and J. Yin (eds.) *The Global Intercultural Communication Reader*, 2nd edn, London and New York: Routledge, pp. 1–16.

Asser, M. and Langbein-Park, A. (2015) 'Cultural intelligence', in J.M. Bennett (ed.) *The Sage Encyclopedia of Intercultural Competence, Volume 1*, Los Angeles: Sage, pp. 164–9.

Association of American Colleges and Universities (AAC&U) (2007) *College Learning for the New Global Century: A Report from the National Leadership Council for Liberal Education and America's Promise*, Washington, DC: Association of American Colleges and Universities.

Awad, G.H. and Rackley, K.R. (2018) 'Prejudice and discrimination', in Y.Y. Kim (ed.) *The International Encyclopedia of Intercultural Communication, Volume 3*, Hoboken, NJ: John Wiley & Sons, Inc., pp. 1715–23.

Bachman, L. (1990) *Fundamental Considerations in Language Testing*, Oxford: Oxford University Press.

Badhwar, N.K. (1993) 'Introduction: The nature and significance of friendship', in N.K. Badhwar (ed.) *Friendship: A Philosophical Reader*, New York: Cornell University, pp. 1–38.

Baldwin, J.R., Faulkner, S.L. and Hecht, M.L. (2006) 'A moving target: The elusive definition of culture', in J.R. Baldwin, S.L. Faulkner, M.L. Hecht and S.L. Lindsley (eds.) *Redefining Culture: Perspectives Across the Disciplines*, New York and London: Routledge, pp. 3–26.

Baldwin, T.T., Bommer, W.H. and Rubin, R.S. (2013) *Managing Organizational Behavior: What Great Managers Know and Do*, 2nd edn, New York: McGraw-Hill Irwin.

Barak, M.E.M. (2017) *Managing Diversity: Toward a Globally Inclusive Workplace*, 4th edn, Los Angeles: Sage.

Barker, G. (2018) 'Third-culture individuals', in Y.Y. Kim (ed.) *The International Encyclopedia of Intercultural Communication, Volume 3*, Hoboken, NJ: John Wiley & Sons, Inc., pp. 1904–12.

Barker, L.L. and Barker, D.L. (1993) *Communication*, Englewood Cliffs, NJ: Prentice Hall.

Barnlund, D.C. (1975) *Public and Private Self in Japan and the United States: Communication Styles of Two Cultures*, Tokyo: Simile Press.

Baxter, J. (2016) 'Positioning language and identity: Poststructuralist perspectives', in S. Preece (ed.) *The Routledge Handbook of Language and Identity*, London and New York: Routledge, pp. 34–49.

Beebe, S.A., Beebe, S.J., Redmond, M.V. and Salem-Wiseman, L. (2018) *Interpersonal Communication: Relating to Others*, 7th Canadian edn, Don Mills, ON: Pearson Canada.

Beelen, J. and Jones, E. (2015) 'Redefining internationalization at home', in A. Curaj, L. Matei, R. Pricopie, J. Salmi and P. Scott (eds.) *The European Higher Education Area: Between Critical Reflections and Future Policies*, New York: Springer, pp. 59–72.

Begley, P.A. (2009) 'Dismantling misconceptions about Islam in Egypt', in L.A. Samovar, R.E. Porter and E.R. McDaniel (eds.) *Intercultural Communication: A Reader*, Boston: Wadsworth Cengage Learning, pp. 162–71.

Beijaard, D., Meijer, P.C. and Verloop, N. (2004) 'Reconsidering research on teachers' professional identity', *Teaching and Teacher Education*, 20: 107–28.

Beinhoff, B. and Rasinger, S.M. (2016) 'The future of identity research: Impact and new developments in sociolinguistics', in S. Preece (ed.) *The Routledge Handbook of Language and Identity*, London and New York: Routledge, pp. 572–85.

Bell, A. (2007) 'Style and the linguistic repertoire', in C. Llamas, L. Mullany and P. Stockwell (eds.) *The Routledge Companion to Sociolinguistics*, London and New York: Routledge, pp. 95–100.

Bennett, J.M. (1998) 'Transition shock: Putting culture shock in perspective', in M.J. Bennett (ed.) *Basic Concepts of Intercultural Communication*, Yarmouth, ME: Intercultural Press.

Bennett, J.M. (2008) 'On becoming a global soul: A path to engagement during study abroad,' in V. Savicki (ed.) *Developing Intercultural Competence and Transformation: Theory, Research, and Application in International Education*, Sterling, VA: Stylus, pp. 13–31.

Bennett, J.M. (2009) 'Cultivating intercultural competence: A process perspective', in D. Deardorff (ed.) *The Sage Handbook of Intercultural Competence*, Thousand Oaks, CA: Sage, pp. 121–40.

Bennett, J.M. and Bennett, M.J. (2004) 'Developing intercultural sensitivity: An integrative approach to global and domestic diversity', in D. Landis, J.M. Bennett and M.J. Bennett (eds.) *Handbook of Intercultural Training*, 3rd edn, Thousand Oaks, CA: Sage, pp. 145–67.

Bennett, J.M., Bennett, M.J. and Allen, W. (2003) 'Developing intercultural competence in the language classroom', in D. Lange and M. Paige (eds.) *Culture as the Core: Perspectives on Culture in Second Language Learning*, Greenwich, CT: Information Age Publishing, pp. 237–70.

Bennett, M.J. (1993) 'Towards a developmental model of intercultural sensitivity', in R. Michael Paige (ed.) *Education for the Intercultural Experience*, Yarmouth, ME: Intercultural Press, pp. 21–71.

Bennett, M.J. (1997) 'How not to be a fluent fool: Understanding the cultural dimensions of language', in A.E. Fantini (ed.) *New Ways in Teaching Culture. New Ways in TESOL Series II: Innovative Classroom Techniques*, Alexandria, VA: TESOL, pp. 16–21.

Bennett, M.J. (2012) 'Paradigmatic assumptions and a developmental approach to intercultural learning', in M. Vande Berg, R.M. Paige and K.H. Lou (eds.) *Student Learning Abroad: What Our Students Are Learning, What They're Not, and What We Can Do About It*, Sterling, VA: Stylus, pp. 90–114.

Bennett, M.J. (2018) 'Developmental model of intercultural sensitivity', in Y.Y. Kim (ed.) *The International Encyclopedia of Intercultural Communication, Volume 1*, Hoboken, NJ: John Wiley & Sons, Inc., pp. 643–52.

Berardo, K. (2012) 'Manage cultural transitions', in K. Berardo and D.K. Deardorff (eds.) *Building Cultural Competence: Innovative Activities and Models*, Sterling, VA: Stylus, pp. 183–9.

Berelson, B. and Steiner, G.A. (1964) *Human Behavior; An Inventory of Scientific Findings*, New York: Harcourt, Brace & World.

Berger, C.R. and Calabrese, R.J. (1975) 'Some exploration in initial interaction and beyond: Toward a developmental theory of communication', *Human Communication Research*, 1: 99–112.

Berger, P.L. (1969) *The Sacred Canopy: Elements of a Sociological Theory of Religion*, New York: Anchor Books.

Berglund, J. (2015) 'Time (Chronemics)', in J.M. Bennett (ed.) *The Sage Encyclopedia of Intercultural Competence, Volume 2*, Los Angeles: Sage, pp. 800–2.

Berry, J.W. (1974) 'Psychological aspects of cultural pluralism', *Topics in Culture Learning*, 2: 17–22.

Berry, J.W. (1997) 'Immigration, acculturation, and adaptation', *Applied Psychology: An International Review*, 46(1): 5–34.

Berry, J.W. (2003) 'Conceptual approaches to acculturation', in K. Chun, P. Balls Organista and G. Marin (eds.) *Acculturation: Advances in Theory, Measurement and Applied Research*, Washington, DC: APA Press, pp. 17–37.

Berry, J.W. (2006) 'Contexts of acculturation', in D.L. Sam and J.W. Berry (eds.) *The Cambridge Handbook of Acculturation Psychology*, Cambridge: Cambridge University Press, pp. 27–42.

Berry, J.W. (2015) 'Acculturation', in J.M. Bennett (ed.) *The Sage Encyclopedia of Intercultural Competence, Volume 1*, Los Angeles: Sage, pp. 1–4.

Berry, J.W., Poortinga, Y.H., Breugelmans, S.M., Chasiotis, A. and Sam, D.L. (2011) *Cross-Cultural Psychology: Research and Applications*, 3rd edn, Cambridge: Cambridge University Press.

Bhawuk, D.P.S. (2015) 'Beliefs, values, norms, customs (definitions)', in J.M. Bennett (ed.) *The Sage Encyclopedia of Intercultural Competence, Volume 1*, Los Angeles: Sage, pp. 29–30.

Bhawuk, D.P.S. (2018a) 'Individualism and collectivism', in Y.Y. Kim (ed.) *The International Encyclopedia of Intercultural Communication, Volume 2*, Hoboken, NJ: John Wiley & Sons, Inc., pp. 920–9.

Bhawuk, D.P.S. (2018b) 'Cultural value dimensions', in Y.Y. Kim (ed.) *The International Encyclopedia of Intercultural Communication, Volume 1*, Hoboken, NJ: John Wiley & Sons, Inc., pp. 580–96.

Bhawuk, D.P.S. (2018c) 'Culture-specific and culture-general training', in Y.Y. Kim (ed.) *The International Encyclopedia of Intercultural Communication, Volume 1*, Hoboken, NJ: John Wiley & Sons, Inc., pp. 636–42.

Bhawuk, D.P.S. and Brislin, R.W. (1992) 'The measurement of cultural sensitivity using the concepts of individualism and collectivism', *International Journal of Intercultural Relations*, 16: 413–36.

Bialik, K. (2017) 'Key facts about race and marriage, 50 years after loving v. Virginia', *FactTank News in the Numbers, Pew Research Center, 12 June 2017*, Online. Available: www.pewresearch.org/fact-tank/2017/06/12/key-facts-about-race-and-marriage-50-years-after-loving-v-virginia/ (accessed 7 February 2019).

Blackburn, S. (2009) *Ethics: A Very Short Introduction*, Oxford: Oxford University Press.

Blake, R.R. and Mouton, J.S. (1964) *The Managerial Grid*, Houston: Gulf Publishing.

Block, D. (2007) *Second Language Identities*, London: Continuum.

Block, D. (2014) *Social Class in Applied Linguistics*, London: Routledge.

Bourdieu, P. (1986) 'The forms of capital', in J. Richardson (ed.) *The Handbook of Theory and Research in the Sociology of Education*, New York: Greenwood Press, pp. 241–58.

Bourdieu, P. (1991) *Language and Symbolic Power*, Boston: Harvard University Press.

Boyett, J. (2016) *12 Major World Religions: The Beliefs, Rituals, and Traditions of Humanity's Most Influential Faiths*, Berkeley, CA: Zephyros Press.

Bradford, L., Burrell, N.A. and Mabry, E.A. (2004) 'Negotiating cultural identity: Strategies for belonging', in M. Fong and R. Chuang (eds.) *Communicating Ethnic and Cultural Identity*, Oxford: Rowman and Littlefield, pp. 313–28.

Bremmer, I. (2018) *Us vs. Them: The Failure of Globalism*, New York: Portfolio, Penguin.

Brooker, P. (2003) *A Glossary of Cultural Theory*, London: Arnold.

Broome, B.J. (2018) 'Intercultural empathy', in Y.Y. Kim (ed.) *The International Encyclopedia of Intercultural Communication, Volume 2*, Hoboken, NJ: John Wiley & Sons, Inc., pp. 1284–9.

Brown, P. and Levinson, S.C. (1978) 'Universals in language usage: Politeness phenomena', in E.N. Goody (ed.) *Questions and Politeness: Strategies in Social Interaction*, Cambridge: Cambridge University Press, pp. 56–311.

Brown, S. and Eisterhold, J. (2004) *Topics in Language and Culture for Teachers*, Ann Arbor, MI: University of Michigan Press.

Bucholtz, M. (2003) 'Sociolinguistic nostalgia and the authentication of identity', *Journal of Sociolinguistics*, 7(3): 398–416.

Burgoon, J.K. (1978) 'A communication model of personal space violation: Explication and an initial test', *Human Communication Research*, 4: 129–42.

Burgoon, M. (1995) 'Language expectancy theory: Elaboration, explication and extension', in C.R. Berger and M. Burgoon (eds.) *Communication and Social Influence Processes*, East Lansing, MI: Michigan State University Press, pp. 29–51.

Butler, J. (1990) *Gender Trouble: Feminism and the Subversion of Identity*, New York: Routledge.

Byram, M. (1997) *Teaching and Assessing Intercultural Communicative Competence*, Clevedon: Multilingual Matters.

Byram, M. (2006, July) 'Language teaching for intercultural citizenship: The European situation', paper presented at the New Zealand Association of Language Teachers (NZALT) conference, University of Auckland.

Byram, M. (2008) *From Foreign Language Education to Education for Intercultural Citizenship: Essays and Reflection*, Clevedon: Multilingual Matters.

Byram, M. (2009) 'Intercultural competence in foreign languages – The intercultural speaker and the pedagogy of foreign language education', in D.K. Deardorff (ed.) *The Sage Handbook of Intercultural Competence*, Thousand Oaks, CA: Sage, pp. 304–20.

Byram, M. (2011a) 'From Foreign language education to education for intercultural citizenship', *Intercultural Communication Review*, 9: 17–36.

Byram, M. (2011b) 'Intercultural citizenship from an internationalist perspective', *Journal of the NUS Teaching Academy*, 1(1): 10–20.

Byram, M. (2012) 'Conceptualizing intercultural (communicative) competence and intercultural citizenship', in J. Jackson (ed.) *Routledge Handbook of Language and Intercultural Communication*, London and New York: Routledge, pp. 85–97.

Byram, M., Golubeva, I., Hui, H. and Wagner, M. (2017) 'Reflections: Learning from the challenges and seeking the way forward', in M. Byram, I. Golubeva, H. Hui and M. Wagner (eds.) *From Principles to Practice in Education for Intercultural Citizenship*, Bristol: Multilingual Matters, pp. 251–9.

Byram, M., Gribkova, B. and Starkey, H. (2002) *Developing the Intercultural Dimension in Language Teaching: A Practical Introduction for Teachers*, Strasbourg: Council of Europe.

Byram, M. and Parmenter, L. (2015) 'Global citizenship', in J.M. Bennett (ed.) *The Sage Encyclopedia of Intercultural Competence, Volume 1*, Los Angeles: Sage, pp. 346–8.

Byram, M. and Zarate, G. (1997) 'Defining and assessing intercultural competence: Some principles and proposals for the European context', *Language Teaching*, 29: 14–18.

Byrne, D. (1969) 'Attitudes and attraction', in L. Berkowitz (ed.) *Advances in Experimental Social Psychology, Volume 4*, New York: Academic Press, pp. 36–89.

Byrnes, F.C. (1966) 'Role shock: An occupational hazard of American technical assistants abroad', *The Annals*, 368: 95–108.

Campbell, R., Martin, C.R. and Fabos, B. (2017) *Media and Culture: Mass Communication in a Digital Age*, 11th edn, Boston: Bedford, St. Martin's.

Canagarajah, A.S. (1999) *Resisting Linguistic Imperialism in English Language Teaching*, Oxford: Oxford University Press.

Canale, M. and Swain, M. (1980) 'Theoretical bases of communicative approaches to second language teaching and testing', *Applied Linguistics*, 1: 1–47.

Cardon, P.W. (2018) *Business Communication: Developing Leaders for a Networked World*, 3rd edn, New York: McGraw-Hill Education.

Carey, J. (1989) *A Cultural Approach to Communication*, New York: Routledge.

Center for Advanced Research on Language Acquisition (CARLA), University of Minnesota, (n.d.) 'What is culture?' Online. Available: www.carla.umn.edu/culture/definitions.html (accessed 5 February 2019).

Chawla, D. (2018) 'Othering and otherness', in Y.Y. Kim (ed.) *The International Encyclopedia of Intercultural Communication, Volume 3*, Hoboken, NJ: John Wiley & Sons, Inc.

Cheetham, D., Pratt, D. and Thomas, D. (2013) 'Introduction', in D. Cheetham, D. Pratt and D. Thomas (eds.) *Understanding Interreligious Relationships*, Oxford: Oxford University Press, pp. 1–11.

Chen, G.M. (1992) 'Communication adaptability and interaction involvement as predictors of cross-cultural adjustment', *Communication Research Reports*, 9(1): 33–41.

Chen, G.M. (2010) 'Relational mobility explains between- and within-culture differences in self-disclosure to close friends', *Psychological Science*, 21: 1471–8.

Chen, G.M. (2012) 'A cross-cultural test of the relational turbulence model: Relationship characteristics that predict turmoil and topic avoidance for Koreans and Americans', *Journal of Social and Personal Relationships*, 29: 545–65.

Chen, G.M. and Starosta, W.J. (1998) *Foundations of Intercultural Communication*, Needham Height, MA: Allyn and Bacon.

Chen, G.M. and Starosta, W.J. (2005) *Foundations of Intercultural Communication*, 2nd edn, Lanham, MD: UPA.

Chen, G.M. and Starosta, W.J. (2006) 'Intercultural awareness', in L.A. Samovar, R.E. Porter and E.R. McDaniel (eds.) *Intercultural Communication: A Reader*, Belmont, CA: Wadsworth Cengage Learning, pp. 357–66.

Chen, G.M. and Starosta, W.J. (2008) 'Intercultural communication competence: A synthesis', in M.K. Asante, Y. Miike and J. Yin (eds.) *The Global Intercultural Communication Reader*, New York: Routledge, pp. 215–37.

Chen, L. (2002) 'Communication in intercultural relationships', in W. Gudykunst and B. Mody (eds.) *Handbook of International and Intercultural Communication*, 2nd edn, Thousand Oaks, CA: Sage, pp. 241–57.

Chen, Y.W. and Nakazawa, M. (2009) 'Influences of culture on self-disclosure as relationally situated in intercultural and interracial friendships from a social penetration perspective', *Journal of Intercultural Communication Research*, 38(2): 77–98.

Chen, Y.W. and Nakazawa, M. (2012) 'Measuring patterns of self-disclosure in intercultural friendship: Adjusting differential item functioning using multiple-indicators, multiple-causes models', *Journal of Intercultural Communication, Research*, 41(2): 131–51.

Chicago Tribune Staff and Hawbaker, K.T. (2019) '#MeToo: A timeline of events', *Chicago Tribune*, Online. Available: www.chicagotribune.com/lifestyles/ct-me-too-timeline-20171208-htmlstory.html (accessed 2 February 2019).

Chinese Culture Connection. (1987) 'Chinese values and the search for culture-free dimensions of culture', *Journal of Cross-Cultural Psychology*, 18(2): 143–64.

Chowdhury, Q.H. (2016) 'Construction of heritage language and cultural identities: A case study of two young British-Bangladeshis in London', in S. Preece (ed.) *The Routledge Handbook of Language and Identity*, London and New York: Routledge, pp. 476–91.

Chung, L. (2015) 'Ethnic cultural identity model', in J.M. Bennett (ed.) *The Sage Encyclopedia of Intercultural Competence, Volume 1*, Los Angeles: Sage, pp. 305–8.

Clyne, M. (1994) *Inter-Cultural Communication at Work*, Cambridge: Cambridge University Press.

Coates, J. (2016) *Women, Men, and Language: A Sociolinguistic Account of Differences in Language*, 3rd edn, London and New York: Routledge.

Cole, P.M. (1986) 'Children's spontaneous control of facial expression,'*Child Development*, 57: 1309–321.

Coleman, J.A. (2009) 'Study abroad and SLA: Defining goals and variables', in A. Berndt and K. Kleppin (eds.) *Sprachlehrforschung: Theorie und Empire, Festschrift fur Rudiger Grotjahn*, Frankfurt am Main: Peter Lang, pp. 181–96.

Collier, M.J. (1994) 'Cultural identity and intercultural communication', in L.A. Samovar and R.E. Porter (eds.) *Intercultural Communication: A Reader*, 10th edn, Belmont, CA: Wadsworth Cengage Learning, pp. 412–29.

Collier, M.J. (1996) 'Communication competence problematics in ethnic friendships', *Communication Monographs*, 63: 314–16.

Collier, M.J. (2002) 'Intercultural friendships as interpersonal alliances', in J.N. Martin, T.K. Nakayama and L.A. Flores (eds.) *Readings in Intercultural Communication: Experiences and Contexts*, 2nd edn, Boston: McGraw-Hill.

Cooper, P.J., Calloway-Thomas, C. and Simonds, C.J. (2007) *Intercultural Communication: A Text with Readings*, Boston: Pearson.

Cornes, A. (2004) *Culture from the Inside Out: Travel and Meet Yourself*, Yarmouth, ME: Intercultural Press.

Cortazzi, M. and Jin, L. (1997) 'Communication for learning across cultures', in D. McNamara and R. Harris (eds.) *Overseas Students in Higher Education*, London: Routledge, pp. 76–90.

Cortazzi, M. and Jin, L. (eds.) (2013) *Researching Cultures of Learning*, Basingstoke: Palgrave Macmillan.

Cortés, C.E. (2015) 'Intercultural humor', in J.M. Bennett (ed.) *The Sage Encyclopedia of Intercultural Competence, Volume 2*, Los Angeles: Sage, pp. 502–5.

Coulmas, F. (2005) *Sociolinguistics: The Study of Speakers' Choices*, Cambridge: Cambridge University Press.

Cruse, D.A. (2006) *A Glossary of Semantics and Pragmatics*, Edinburgh: Edinburgh University Press.

Crystal, D. (2010) *The Cambridge Encyclopedia of Language*, Cambridge: Cambridge University Press.

Culkin, N. and Simmons, R. (2019) *Tales of Brexits Past and Present*, Bingley: Emerald Publishing.

Cummins, J. (1994) 'The acquisition of English as a second language', in K. Spangenberg-Urbschat and R. Pritchard (eds.) *Reading Instruction for ESL Students*, Delaware: International Reading Association, pp. 36–62.

Cushner, K. and Brislin, R. (1996) *Intercultural Interactions: A Practical Guide*, 2nd edn, Thousand Oaks, CA: Sage.

Darvin, R. (2016) 'Language and identity in the digital age', in S. Preece (ed.) *The Routledge Handbook of Language and Identity*, London and New York: Routledge, pp. 523–40.

Darwin, C. (1872) *The Expression of Emotion in Man and Animals*, New York: Oxford University Press.

Davies, A. (2005) *A Glossary of Applied Linguistics*, Edinburgh: Edinburgh University Press.

Deardorff, D.K. (2004) 'The identification and assessment of intercultural competence as a student outcome of internationalization at institutions of higher education in the United States', unpublished dissertation, North Carolina State University, Raleigh, NC, Online. Available: https://repository.lib.ncsu.edu/bitstream/handle/1840.16/5733/etd.pdf?sequence=1&isAllowed=y (accessed 18 March 2019).

Deardorff, D.K. (2006) 'Identification and assessment of intercultural competence as a student outcome of internationalization', *Journal of Studies in International Education*, 10(3): 241–66.

Deardorff, D.K. (2008) 'Intercultural competence: A definition, model, and implications for education abroad', in V. Savicki (ed.) *Developing Intercultural Competence and Transformation: Theory, Research, and Application in International Education*, Sterling, VA: Stylus, pp. 32–52.

Deardorff, D.K. (2009) 'Synthesizing conceptualizations of intercultural competence: A summary and emerging themes', in D.K. Deardorff (ed.) *The Sage Handbook of Intercultural Competence*, Thousand Oaks, CA: Sage, pp. 264–70.

Deardorff, D.K. and Hunter, W.D. (2006) 'Educating global-ready graduates', *International Educator*, 72–83.

Deaux, K. (2001) 'Social identity', in J. Worrell (ed.) *Encyclopedia of Women and Gender, Volume 2*, San Diego, CA: Academic Press, pp. 1059–67.

DeCapua, A. and Wintergerst, A.C. (2004) *Crossing Cultures in the Language Classroom*, Ann Arbor, MI: University of Michigan Press.

De Fina, A. (2016) 'Linguistic practices and transnational identities', in S. Preece (ed.) *The Routledge Handbook of Language and Identity*, London and New York: Routledge, pp. 163–78.

de Groot, A.M.B. (2018) 'Bi- and multilingualism', in Y.Y. Kim (ed.) *The International Encyclopedia of Intercultural Communication, Volume 1*, Hoboken, NJ: John Wiley & Sons, Inc., pp. 47–56.

Dervin, F. (2012) 'Cultural identity, representation and othering', in J. Jackson (ed.) *Routledge Handbook of Language and Intercultural* Communication, London and New York: Routledge, pp. 181–94.

Dervin, F. (2016) *Interculturality in Education: A Theoretical and Methodological Toolbox*, Basingstoke: Palgrave Macmillan.

Dervin, F. and Dirba, M. (2006) 'On liquid interculturality: Finnish and Latvian student teachers' perceptions of intercultural competence', in P. Pietilä, P. Lintunen and H-M. Järvinen (eds.) *Language Learners of Today, Volume 64*, Jyväskylä: Suomen soveltavan kielitieteen yhdistyksen (AFinLA) julkaisuja, pp. 257–73.

de Wit, H. and Hunter, F. (2015) 'The future of internationalization of higher education in Europe', *International Higher Education*, 83(Special Issue), 2–3.

Discovery Education (n.d.) 'Web 2.0 tools', Online. Available: https://blog.discoveryeducation.com/?s=Web+2.0 (accessed 5 February 2019).

Dispenza, J. (2002) *The Way of the Traveler: Making Every Trip a Journey of Self-Discovery*, 2nd edn, Emeryville, CA: Avalon Travel Publishing.

Dodd, C.H. (2018) 'Worldview in intercultural communication', in Y.Y. Kim (ed.) *The International Encyclopedia of Intercultural Communication, Volume 3*, Hoboken, NJ: John Wiley & Sons, Inc., pp. 2002–10.

Donatelli, L., Yngve, K., Miller, M. and Ellis, J. (2005) 'Technology and education abroad', in J.L. Brockington, W.W. Hoffa and P.C. Martin (eds.) *NAFSA's Guide to Education Abroad for Advisors and Administrators*, Washington, DC: NAFSA, Association of International Educators, pp. 129–50.

Döring, N. (2002) 'Studying online-love and cyber-romance', in B. Batinic, U-D. Reips and M. Bosnjak (eds.) *Online Social Sciences*, Seattle: Hogrefe and Huber Publishers, pp. 333–56.

Duff, P.A. (2010) 'Language socialization', in N.H. Hornberger and S.L. McKay (eds.) *Sociolinguistics and Language Education*, Bristol: Multilingual Matters, pp. 427–52.

Eaves, M.H. and Leathers, D. (2018) *Successful Nonverbal Communication: Principles and Applications*, 5th edn, New York: Routledge.

Eckert, P. and McConnell-Ginet, S. (1992) 'Think practically and look locally: Language and gender as community – based practice', *Annual Review of Anthropology*, 21: 461–90.

Eckert, P. and Rickford, J. (2001) *Style and Sociolinguistic Variation*, Cambridge: Cambridge University Press.

Edstrom, A.M. (2005) 'Female, nonnative perspectives on second language conversation: Connecting participation with intercultural sensitivity', *Foreign Language Annals*, 38(1): 25–34.

Efron, D. (1968) *Gesture and Environment*, New York: King's Crown Press.

Ekman, P. (1972) 'Universal and cultural differences in facial expression of emotion', in J.R. Cole (ed.) *Nebraska Symposium on Motivation 1971, Volume 19*, Lincoln, NE: Nebraska University Press, pp. 207–83.

Ekman, P. (ed.) (1973) *Darwin and Facial Expression: A Century of Research in Review*, New York: Academic Press.

Ekman, P. (2004) 'Emotional and conversational nonverbal signals', in J.M. Larrazabal and L.A. Pérez Miranda (eds.) *Language, Knowledge, and Representation*, Amsterdam: Kluwer Academic Publishers, pp. 39–50.

Ekman, P. (2009) 'Become versed in reading faces', *Entrepreneur Media*, Online. Available: www.entre preneur.com/article/200934 (accessed 3 March 2019).

Ekman, P. and Friesen, W.V. (1969) 'The repertoire of nonverbal behavior: Categories, origins, usage, and coding', *Semiotica*, 1: 49–98.

Ekman, P. and Friesen, W.V. (1971) 'Constants across culture in the face and emotion', *Journal of Personality and Social Psychology*, 17: 124–9.

Ekman, P. and Heider, K.G. (1988) 'The universality of a contempt expression: A replication', *Motivation and Emotion*, 12(3): 303–8.

Ekman, P. and Rosenberg, E.L. (eds.) (1998) *What the Face Reveals: Basic and applied Studies of Spontaneous Expression Using the Facial Action Coding System (FACS)*, New York: Oxford University Press.

Emerson, R.W. (1930) *Essays and Lectures: Conduct of Life, Solitude and Society and Other Essays and Addresses*, New York: Three Sirens Press.

Encyclopedia Britannica (n.d.) 'Superstition', Online. Available: www.britannica.com/EBchecked/topic/574567/superstition (accessed 5 March 2019).

Erikson, E.H. (1968) *Identity: Youth and Crisis*, New York: Norton.

Equal Opportunity Unit (2005) *Watch Your Language: Guidelines for Non-Discriminatory Language*, Melbourne: University of Melbourne.

Fairclough, N. (2006) *Language and Globalization*, London and New York: Routledge.

Fairclough, N. (2010) *Critical Discourse Analysis: The Critical Study of Language*, London and New York: Routledge.

Fantini, A.E. (2012a) 'Language: An essential component of intercultural communicative competence', in J. Jackson (ed.) *Routledge Handbook of Language and Intercultural Communication*, London and New York: Routledge, pp. 263–78.

Fantini, A.E. (2012b) 'Multiple strategies for assessing intercultural communicative competence', in J. Jackson (ed.) *Routledge Handbook of Language and Intercultural Communication*, London and New York: Routledge, pp. 390–405.

Fantini, A.E. (2019) *Intercultural Communicative Competence in Educational Exchange: A Multinational Perspective*, New York and London: Routledge.

Fantini, A.E. and Tirmizi, A. (2006) *Exploring and Assessing Intercultural Competence*, Brattleboro, VT: Federation of the Experiment in International Living.

Fasching, D., deChant, D. and Lantigua, D.M. (2011) *Comparative Religious Ethics: A Narrative Approach to Global Ethics*, Oxford: Wiley-Blackwell.

Federal Glass Ceiling Commission (1995) *Solid Investments: Making Full Use of the Nation's Human Capital*, Washington, DC: U.S. Department of Labor.

Fehr, B.J., Baldwin, M., Collins, L., Patterson, S. and Benditt, R. (1999) 'Anger in close relationships: An interpersonal script analysis', *Personality and Social Psychology*, 25: 299–312.

Fehr, B.J. and Exline, R.V. (1987) 'Social visual interactions: A conceptual and literature review', in A.W. Siegman and S. Feldstein (eds.) *Nonverbal Behavior and Communication, Volume 2*, Hillsdale, NJ: Lawrence Erlbaum, pp. 225–326.

Fieber, P. (2013, March 28) 'Q&A Maya Angelou: Marking national poetry month with a literary icon', *Westjet Magazine*, Online. Available: www.westjetmagazine.com/story/article/qa-maya-angelou (accessed 8 March 2019).

Fixmer-Oraiz, N. and Wood, J. (2019) *Gendered Lives: Communication, Gender, and Culture*, 13th edn, Boston: Cengage Learning.

Floyd, K., Ramirez, A. and Burgoon, J.K. (2008) 'Expectancy violations theory', in L.K. Guerrero, J.A. DeVito and M.L. Hecht (eds.) *The Nonverbal Communication Reader: Classic and Contemporary Readings*, 3rd edn, Prospect Heights, IL: Waveland, pp. 503–10.

Folger, J.P., Poole, M.S. and Stutman, R.K. (2013) *Working Through Conflict: Strategies for Relationships, Groups and Organizations*, 7th edn, Boston: Pearson.

Folger, J.P., Poole, M.S. and Stutman, R.K. (2018) *Working Through Conflict: Strategies for Relationships, Groups and Organizations*, 8th edn, London and New York: Routledge.

Fong, M. (2004) 'Identity and the speech community', in M. Fong and R. Chuang (eds.) *Communicating Ethnic and Cultural Identity*, Oxford: Rowman & Littlefield, pp. 1–3.

Fong, M. and McEwen, K.D. (2004) 'Cultural and intercultural speech uses and meanings of the term *nigga*', in M. Fong and R. Chuang (eds.) *Communicating Ethnic and Cultural Identity*, Oxford: Rowman and Littlefield, pp. 165–78.

Fortman, J. and Giles, H. (2006) 'Communicating culture', in J.R. Baldwin, S.L. Faulkner, M.L. Hecht and S.L. Lindsley (eds.) *Redefining Culture: Perspectives Across the Disciplines*, Mahwah, NJ: Lawrence Erlbaum Associates, pp. 91–102.

Forum on Education Abroad (FEA) (2009) *Education Abroad Glossary*, Carlisle, PA: Forum on Education Abroad.

Forum on Education Abroad (FEA) (2011) *Education Abroad Glossary*, 2nd edn, Carlisle, PA: Forum on Education Abroad.

Forum on Education Abroad (FEA) (n.d.) *Education Abroad Glossary*, Carlisle, PA: Forum on Education Abroad, Online. Available: https://forumea.org/resources/glossary/ (accessed 23 January 2019).

Freadman, A. (2004, November 23) 'When the king and queen of England came to town: Popular entertainment, everyday life, and the teaching of "culture"', inaugural lecture in the University of Melbourne, Melbourne.

Frick, E. (2017) *Information Technology Essentials: An Introduction to Communication Technologies*, Amazon Digital Services LLC.

Furnham, A. (2015) 'Mobility in a global era', in J.M. Bennett (ed.) *The Sage Encyclopedia of Intercultural Competence, Volume 2*, Los Angeles: Sage, pp. 630–4.

Furnham, A. and Bochner, S. (1986) *Culture Shock: Psychological Reactions to Unfamiliar Environments*, New York: Methuen.

Furstenberg, G., Levet, S., English, K. and Maillet, K. (2001) 'Giving a voice to the silent language of culture: The *Cultura* project', *Language Learning and Technology*, 5(1): 55–102.

Galanti, G.A. (2000) 'An introduction to cultural differences', *Western Journal of Medicine*, 172(5): 335–6.

Gallois, C. and Liu, S. (2015) 'Intercultural relations and globalization', in J.M. Bennett (ed.) *The Sage Encyclopedia of Intercultural Competence, Volume 2*, Los Angeles: Sage, pp. 516–19.

Gamble, T.K. and Gamble, M. (2013) *Communication Works*, 11th edn, Boston: McGraw Hill.

Gao, G. (2015) 'Anxiety and uncertainty management', in J.M. Bennett (ed.) *The Sage Encyclopedia of Intercultural Competence, Volume 1*, Los Angeles: Sage, pp. 5–8.

Gardiner, H.W. (2017) *Lives Across Cultures: Cross-Cultural Human Development*, 6th edn, New York: Pearson.

Gareis, E. (2012) 'Intercultural friendship: Effects of home and host region', *Journal of International and Intercultural Communication*, 5(4): 309–28.

Gaw, K.F. (2000) 'Reverse culture shock in students returning from overseas', *International Journal of Intercultural Relations*, 24: 83–104.

Geertz, H. (1973) *The Interpretation of Cultures*, New York: Basic Books.

Gerzon, M. (2010) *Global Citizens: How Our Vision of the World Is Outdated, and What We Can Do About It*, London: Rider.

Giddens, A. (1990) *The Consequences of Modernity*, Stanford: Stanford University Press.

Giles, H., Bonilla, D. and Speer, R.B. (2012) 'Acculturating intergroup vitalities, accommodation and contact', in J. Jackson (ed.) *Routledge Handbook of Language and Intercultural Communication*, London and New York: Routledge, pp. 244–59.

Giroux, H.A. (1988) *Teachers as Intellectuals: Towards a Critical Pedagogy of Learning*, Granby, MA: Bergin and Garvey.

Goddard, C. (2004) 'Speech-acts, values and cultural scripts: A study in Malay ethnopragmatics', paper presented at the 15th Biennial conference of the Asian Studies Association of Australia, Canberra, Australia.

Goddard, V. (2006) 'Ethnopragmatics: A new paradigm', in C. Goddard (ed.) *Ethnopragmatics: Understanding Discourse in Cultural Context*, Cambridge: Cambridge University Press, pp. 1–30.

Goffman, E. (1969) *Strategic Interaction*, Philadelphia: University of Pennsylvania Press.

Golash-Boza, T-M. (2018) *Race and Racisms: A Critical Approach*, 2nd edn, Oxford: Oxford University Press.

Goodman, A.H., Moses, Y.T. and Jones, J.L. (2012) *Race: Are We so Different?* Malden, MA: Wiley-Blackwell.

Goshen-Gottstein, A. and Murray, S.B. (2015) 'Introduction', in A. Goshen-Gottstein (ed.) *Friendship Across Religions: Theological Perspectives on Interreligious Friendship*, New York: Lexington Books, pp. xi–lii.

Green, M.F. and Olson, C.L. (2003) *Internationalizing the Campus: A User's Guide*, Washington, DC: American Council on Education, Center for Institutional and International Initiatives.

Green, W. (2013) 'Great expectations: The impact of friendship groups on the intercultural learning of Australian students abroad', in S. Dovic and M. Blythman (eds.) *International Students Negotiating Higher Education*, London: Routledge, pp. 211–25.

Gross, J.J. (1998) 'The emerging field of emotion regulation: An integrative review', *Review of General Psychology*, 2: 271–99.

Gudorf, C.E. (2013) *Comparative Religious Ethics: Everyday Decisions for Our Everyday Lives*, Minneapolis: Fortress Press.

Gudykunst, W.B. (2003) 'Introduction to cross-cultural communication', in W.B. Gudykunst (ed.) *Cross-Cultural and Intercultural Communication*, 2nd edn, Thousand Oaks, CA: Sage, pp. 163–6.

Gudykunst, W.B. (2004) *Bridging Differences: Effective Intergroup Communication*, 4th edn, Thousand Oaks, CA: Sage.

Guilherme, M. (2002) *Critical Citizens for an Intercultural World: Foreign Language Education as Cultural Politics*, Clevedon: Multilingual Matters.

Guilherme, M. (2004) 'Intercultural competence', in M. Byram (ed.) *Routledge Encyclopedia of Language Teaching and Learning*, London: Routledge, pp. 297–300.

Guilherme, M. (2007) 'English as a global language and education for cosmopolitan citizenship', *Language and Intercultural Communication*, 7(1): 72–90.

Guilherme, M., Glaser, E. and Méndez-García, M.C. (2010) 'Conclusion: Intercultural competence for professional mobility', in M. Guilherme, E. Glaser and M.C. Méndez-García (eds.) *The Intercultural Dynamics of Multicultural Working*, Bristol: Multilingual Matters, pp. 241–5.

Guirdham, M. (2011) *Communication Across Cultures at Work*, Basingstoke: Palgrave Macmillan.

Gullahorn, J.T. and Gullahorn, J.E. (1963) 'An extension of the U-curve hypothesis', *Journal of Social Issues*, 19: 33–47.

Gumperz, J.J. (1979/1990) *Crosstalk* (BBC film). London: National Centre for Industrial Language Training, Online. Video segment available: www.lib.berkeley.edu/ANTH/emeritus/gumperz/gumptalk.html (accessed 1 February 2019).

Gumperz, J.J. and Cook-Gumperz, J. (2012) 'Interactional sociolinguistics: Perspectives on intercultural communication', in C.B. Paulston, S.F. Kiesling and E.S. Rangel (eds.) *The Handbook of Intercultural Discourse and Communication*, Malden, MA: Wiley-Blackwell, pp. 63–76.

Hall, B.J., Covarrubias, P.O. and Kirschbaum, K.A. (2018) *Among Cultures: The Challenge of Communication*, 3rd edn, London and New York: Routledge.

Hall, E.T. (1959) *The Silent Language*, New York: Doubleday.

Hall, E.T. (1963) 'A system for the notation of proxemic behaviors', *American Anthropologist*, 65: 1003–26.

Hall, E.T. (1966) *The Hidden Dimension*, New York: Doubleday.

Hall, E.T. (1968) 'Proxemics', *Current Anthropology*, 9: 83–108.

Hall, E.T. (1976) *Beyond Culture*, 1st edn, New York: Doubleday.

Hall, E.T. (1983) *The Dance of Life: The Other Dimension of Time*, New York: Doubleday, Anchor.

Hall, E.T. (1998) 'The power of hidden differences', in M. J. Bennett (ed.) *Basic Concepts of Intercultural Communication: Selected Readings*, Yarmouth, ME: Intercultural Press, pp. 53–68.

Hall, E.T. and Hall, M.R. (1990) *Understanding Cultural Differences: Germans, French, and Americans*, Boston: Intercultural Press.

Hall, E.T. and Hall, M.R. (2002) 'Key concepts: Underlying structures of culture', in J.N. Martin, T.K. Nakayama and L. Flores (eds.) *Readings in Intercultural Communication: Experiences and Contexts*, 2nd edn, Boston: McGraw Hill, pp. 165–74.

Hall, J. (1969) *Conflict Management Survey: A Survey on One's Characteristic Reaction to and Handling of Conflicts Between Himself and Others*, Monroe, TX: Teleometrics International.

Hall, S. (1990) 'Cultural identity and diaspora', in J. Rutherford (ed.) *Identity, Community, Culture, Difference*, London: Lawrence and Wishart, pp. 222–37.

Halualani, R.T. and Nakayama, T.K. (2010) 'Critical intercultural communication studies: At a crossroads', in T.K. Nakayama and R.T. Halualani (eds.) *Handbook of Critical Intercultural Communication*, Oxford: Blackwell, pp. 1–16.

Hammer, M.R. (2005) 'The intercultural conflict style inventory: A conceptual framework and measure of intercultural conflict resolution approaches', *International Journal of Intercultural Relations*, 29: 675–95.

Hammer, M.R. (2015a) 'Intercultural conflict styles', in J.M. Bennett (ed.) *The Sage Encyclopedia of Intercultural Competence, Volume 2*, Los Angeles: Sage, pp. 492–5.

Hammer, M.R. (2015b) 'Intercultural competence development', in J.M. Bennett (ed.) *The Sage Encyclopedia of Intercultural Competence, Volume 2*, Los Angeles: Sage, pp. 483–6.

Hampden-Turner, C. and Trompenaars, F. (1998) *Riding the Waves of Culture: Understanding Diversity in Global Business*, New York: McGraw-Hill.

Hannerz, U. (1996) *Transnational Connections: Culture, People, Places*, London: Routledge.

Harlow, L.L. (1990) 'Do they mean what they say? Sociopragmatic competence and second language learners', *The Modern Language Journal*, 74(3): 328–51.

Hayles, R. (2015) 'Racism, institutional', in J.M. Bennett (ed.) *The Sage Encyclopedia of Intercultural Competence, Volume 2*, Los Angeles: Sage, pp. 716–20.

Hecht, M.L., Baldwin, J.R. and Faulkner, S.L. (2006) 'The (in)conclusion of the matter: Shifting signs and models of culture', in J.R. Baldwin, S.L. Faulkner, M.L. Hecht and S.L. Lindsley (eds.) *Redefining Culture: Perspectives Across the Disciplines*, Mahwah, NJ: Lawrence Erlbaum, pp. 53–73.

Hecht, M.L., Jackson, R.J., II and Pitts, M.J. (2005) 'Culture', in J. Harwood and H. Giles (eds.) *Intergroup Communication: Multiple Perspectives*, New York: Peter Lang, pp. 21–42.

Hertenstein, M.J., Holmes, R., McCullough, M. and Keltner, D. (2009) 'The communication of emotion via touch', *Emotion*, 9(4): 566–73.

Hewings, A. and Hewings, M. (2005) *Grammar and Context*, London and New York: Routledge.

Hewstone, M. and Brown, R.J. (1986) 'Contact is not enough: An intergroup perspective on the "contact hypothesis"', in M. Hewstone and R. Brown (eds.) *Contact and Conflict in Intergroup Encounters*, Oxford: Blackwell, pp. 1–44.

Hickson, M., Stacks, D.W. and Moore, N.J. (2004) *Nonverbal Communication: Studies and Applications*, Los Angeles: Roxbury Publishing Co.

Hile, P. (1979) *Language Shock, Culture Shock and How to Cope*, Abilene Christian University Mission Strategy Bulletin 7.2.

Hofstede, G.H. (1980) *Culture's Consequences: International Differences in Work-Related Values*, Beverly Hill, CA: Sage.

Hofstede, G.H. (1981) 'Culture and organizations', *International Studies of Management and Organization*, 10(4): 15–41.

Hofstede, G.H. (1984) *Culture's Consequences*, Beverly Hills, CA: Sage.

Hofstede, G.H. (1991) *Cultures and Organizations: Software of the Mind*, London: McGraw-Hill.

Hofstede, G.H. (2001) *Culture's Consequences: Comparing Values, Behaviors, Institutions, and Organizations Across Nations*, Thousand Oaks, CA: Sage.

Hofstede, G.H. (2003) *Culture's Consequences: Comparing Values, Behaviors, Institutions, and Organizations Across Nations*, 2nd edn, Thousand Oaks, CA: Sage.

Hofstede, G.J. (n.d.) 'What is culture?' Online. Available: https://geerthofstede.com/culture-geert-hofstede-gert-jan-hofstede/definition-culture/ (accessed 10 February 2019).

Hogg, M.A. and Wagoner, J.A. (2018) 'Uncertainty-identity theory', in Y.Y. Kim (ed.) *The International Encyclopedia of Intercultural Communication, Volume 3*, Hoboken, NJ: John Wiley & Sons, Inc., pp. 1971–9.

Høgh-Olesen, H. (2018) 'Personal space across cultures', in Y.Y. Kim (ed.) *The International Encyclopedia of Intercultural Communication, Volume 3*, Hoboken, NJ: John Wiley & Sons, Inc., pp. 1668–77.

Holliday, A.R. (1999) 'Small cultures', *Applied Linguistics*, 20(2): 237–64.

Holliday, A.R. (2010) 'Interrogating the concept of stereotypes in intercultural communication', in S. Hunston and D. Oakey (eds.) *Introducing Applied Linguistics: Concepts and Skills*, London and New York: Routledge, pp. 134–9.

Holliday, A.R. (2011) *Intercultural Communication and Ideology*, London: Sage.

Holliday, A.R. (2012) 'Culture, communication, context and power', in J. Jackson (ed.) *The Routledge Handbook of Language and Intercultural Communication*, London and New York: Routledge, pp. 37–51.

Holliday, A.R. (2016) 'Revisiting intercultural competence: small culture formation on the go through threads of experience', *International Journal of Bias, Identity and Diversities in Education*, 1(2): 1–13.

Holliday, A.R. (2019) *Understanding Intercultural Communication: Negotiating a Grammar of Culture*, 2nd edn, New York: Routledge.

Holmes, J. and Wilson, N. (2017) *An Introduction to Sociolinguistics*, 5th edn, London and New York: Routledge.

Holmes, P. (2012) 'Business and management education', in J. Jackson (ed.) *Routledge Handbook of Language and Intercultural Communication*, London and New York: Routledge, pp. 464–80.

Holmes, P. (2018) 'Intercultural communication in the global workplace, critical approaches', in Y.Y. Kim (ed.) *The International Encyclopedia of Intercultural Communication, Volume 2*, Hoboken, NJ: John Wiley & Sons, Inc., pp. 1001–16.

Hopkins, P.E. (2010) *Young People, Place and Identity*, London: Routledge.

Hottola, P. (2004) 'Culture confusion: Intercultural adaptation in tourism', *Annals of Tourism Research*, 31(2): 447466. DOI:10.1016/j.annals.2004.01.003.

House, J. (2012) 'Translation, interpreting and intercultural communication', in J. Jackson (ed.) *Routledge Handbook of Language and Intercultural Communication*, London and New York: Routledge, pp. 495–509.

House, J. (2018) 'Intercultural communication and translation', in Y.Y. Kim (ed.) *The International Encyclopedia of Intercultural Communication, Volume 2*, Hoboken, NJ: John Wiley & Sons, Inc., pp. 1249–62.

House, R.J., Hanges, P.J., Javidan, M., Dorfman, P.W. and Gupta, V. (eds.) (2004) *Culture, Leadership, and Organizations: The Globe Study of 62 Societies*, Thousand Oaks, CA: Sage.

Hummert, M.L. (2018) 'Stereotypes', in Y.Y. Kim (ed.) *The International Encyclopedia of Intercultural Communication, Volume 3*, Hoboken, NJ: John Wiley & Sons, Inc., pp. 1852–60.

Hunter, B., Godbey, G. and White, G.P. (2006) 'What does it mean to be globally competent?' *Journal of Studies in International Education*, 10(3): 267–85.

Hunter, W.D. (2004) 'Knowledge, skills, attitudes, and experience necessary to become globally competent', unpublished Ph.D. dissertation, Lehigh University, Bethlehem, PA.

Hwang, H.S., Matsumoto, D., LeRoux, J.A., Yager, M. and Ruark, G.A. (2010, July) 'Cross-cultural similarities and differences in emblematic gestures', paper presented at the Biannual Conference of the International Association for Cross-Cultural Psychology, Melbourne.

Hymes, D.H. (1966) 'Two types of linguistic relativity', in W. Bright (ed.) *Sociolinguistics*, The Hague: Mouton. pp. 114–58.

Hymes, D.H. (1972) 'On communicative competence', in J. Pride and J. Holmes (eds.) *Sociolinguistics*, Harmondsworth: Penguin, pp. 269–93.

Ikeda, D. (n.d.) 'Thoughts on education for global citizenship', Online. Available: www.daisakuikeda.org/sub/resources/works/lect/lect-08.html (accessed 13 February 2019).

Inda, J.X. and Rosaldo, R. (2006) 'Introduction: A world in motion', in J.X. Inda and R. Rosaldo (eds.) *The Anthropology of Globalization*, Oxford: Blackwell, pp. 1–34.

Intercultural Conflict Style (ICS) (n.d.) 'Resolving conflict across cultural boundaries: Using the intercultural conflict style inventory (ICS)', Online. Available: https://icsinventory.com/ics-inventory (accessed 7 January 2019).

International Organization for Migration (IOM) (2019) 'World migration report 2018', Online. Available: www.iom.int/wmr/world-migration-report-2018 (accessed 16 February 2019).

International Phonetic Association (IPA) (n.d.) 'Full IPA chart', Online. Available: www.international phoneticassociation.org/content/full-ipa-chart (accessed 8 March 2019).

Internet World Stats – Usage and Populations Statistics (n.d.) 'Internet users in the world: Distribution by world regions', Online. Available: www.internetworldstats.com/stats.htm (accessed 16 January 2019).

Israel, R.C. (2012) 'What does it mean to be a global citizen?' *Cosmos*, Online. Available: www.kosmos journal.org/articles/what-does-it-mean-to-be-a-global-citizen (accessed 20 February 2019).

Izard, C.E. (1971) *The Face of Emotion*, East Norwalk, CT: Appleton-Century-Crofts.

Jacks, G. and Phipps, A. (2005) *Tourism and Intercultural Exchange: Why Tourism Matters*, Clevedon: Channel View Publications.

Jackson, J. (2008) *Language, Identity, and Study Abroad*, London: Equinox.

Jackson, J. (2010) *Intercultural Journeys: From Study to Residence Abroad*, Hampshire: Palgrave Macmillan.

Jackson, J. (2012) 'Education abroad', in J. Jackson (ed.) *Routledge Handbook of Language and Intercultural Communication*, London and New York: Routledge, pp. 449–63.

Jackson, J. (2013) 'Adjusting to differing cultures of learning: The experience of semester-long exchange students from Hong Kong', in L. Jin and M. Cortazzi (eds.) *Researching Intercultural Learning*, Basingstoke: Palgrave Macmillan, pp. 235–52.

Jackson, J. (2018a) *Interculturality in International Education*, London and New York: Routledge.

Jackson, J. (2018b) 'Identity, bilingual and multilingual', in Y.Y. Kim (ed.) *The International Encyclopedia of Intercultural Communication, Volume 2*, Hoboken, NJ: John Wiley & Sons, Inc., pp. 831–9.

Jackson, J. (2018c) 'Intercultural friendship', in Y.Y. Kim (ed.) *The International Encyclopedia of Intercultural Communication, Volume 2*, Hoboken, NJ: John Wiley & Sons, Inc., pp. 1319–28.

Jackson, J. and Chen, X. (2018) 'Discussion-based pedagogy through the eyes of Chinese international exchange students', *Pedagogies: An International Journal*, 13(4): 289–307. DOI:10.1080/15544 80X.2017.1411263

Jackson, J. and Oguro, S. (2018) 'Introduction: Enhancing and extending study abroad learning through intercultural interventions', in J. Jackson and S. Oguro (eds.) *Intercultural Interventions in Study Abroad*, London and New York: Routledge, pp. 1–17.

Jacoby, B. (2015) *Service-Learning Essentials: Questions, Answers, and Lessons Learned*, San Francisco: Jossey Bass.

James, C.E. (2001) 'Introduction: Encounters in race, ethnicity, and language', in A. Shadd (ed.) *Talking About Identity: Encounters in Race, Ethnicity, and Language*, Toronto: Between the Lines, pp. 1–7.

Jandt, F. (2007) *An Introduction to Intercultural Communication: Identities in a Global Community*, 5th edn, Thousand Oaks, CA: Sage.

Jandt, F. (2018) *An Introduction to Intercultural Communication: Identities in a Global Community*, 9th edn, Thousand Oaks, CA: Sage.

Jenkins, J. (2013) *English as a Lingua Franca in the International University*, London: Routledge.

Jenkins, J. (2015) *Global Englishes: A Resource Book for Students*, 3rd edn, London and New York: Routledge.

Jezewski, M.A. and Sotnik, P. (2001) *Culture Brokering: Providing Culturally Competent Rehabilitation Services to Foreign-Born Persons*. Center for International Rehabilitation Research Information and Exchange. CIRRIE Monograph Series, John Stone, Ed. Buffalo, NY: CIRRIE.

Jones, A. (2017) *Genocide: A Comprehensive Introduction*, 3rd edn, London and New York: Routledge.

Jones, L. (2016) 'Language and gender identities', in S. Preece (ed.) *The Routledge Handbook of Language and Identity*, London and New York: Routledge, pp. 210–24.

Joyce, N. (2018) 'Intergroup contact theory', in Y.Y. Kim (ed.) *The International Encyclopedia of Intercultural Communication, Volume 2*, Hoboken, NJ: John Wiley & Sons, Inc., pp. 1472–80.

Kachru, B.B. (2005) *Asian Englishes: Beyond the Canon*, Hong Kong: Hong Kong University Press.

Kälvermark, T. and van der Wende, M.C. (1997) *National Policies for Internationalization of Higher Education in Europe*, Stockholm: National Agency for Higher Education.

Kaplan, A.M. and Haenlien, M. (2010) 'Users of the world unite! The challenges and opportunities of social media', *Business Horizons*, 53(1): 59–68.

Katz, B. and Nowak, J. (2018) *The New Localism: How Cities Can Thrive in the Age of Populism*, Washington, DC: The Brookings Institute.

Kaufman-Scarborough, C. (2018) 'Monochronic and polychronic', in Y.Y. Kim (ed.) *The International Encyclopedia of Intercultural Communication, Volume 3*, Hoboken, NJ: John Wiley & Sons, Inc., pp. 1581–6.

Keltner, D. and Ekman, P. (2003) 'Introduction: Expression of emotion', in R.J. Davidson, K.R. Scherer and H.H. Goldsmith (eds.) *Handbook of Affective Sciences*, New York: Oxford University Press, pp. 411–14.

Kiesling, S.F. (2012) 'Ethnography of speaking', in C.B. Paulston, S.F. Kiesling and E.S. Rangel (eds.) *The Handbook of Intercultural Discourse and Communication*, Malden, MA: Wiley-Blackwell, pp. 77–89.

Killian, K.D. (2009) 'Introduction', in T.A. Karis and K.D. Killian (eds.) *Intercultural Couples: Exploring Diversity in Intimate Relationships*, New York: Routledge, pp. xvii–xxv.

Kim, M.S. (2010) 'Intercultural communication in Asia: Current state and future prospects', *Asian Journal of Communication*, 20(2): 166–80.

Kim, M.S. and Ebesu Hubbard, A.S. (2007) 'Intercultural communication in the global village: How to understand "the Other" ', *Journal of Intercultural Communication Research*, 36(3): 223–35.

Kim, Y.Y. (2001) *Becoming Intercultural: An Integrative Theory of Communication and Cross-Cultural Adaptation*, Thousand Oaks, CA: Sage.

Kim, Y.Y. (2005) 'Inquiry in intercultural and development communication', *Journal of Communication*, 55(3): 554–77.

Kim, Y.Y. (2012) 'Beyond cultural categories: Communication adaptation and transformation', in J. Jackson (ed.) *Routledge Handbook of Language and Intercultural Communication*, London and New York: Routledge, pp. 229–43.

Kim, Y.Y. (2015) 'Theory of acculturation', in J.M. Bennett (ed.) *The Sage Encyclopedia of Intercultural Competence, Volume 2*, Los Angeles: Sage, pp. 792–7.

Kim, Y.Y. (2018) 'Integrative communication theory of cross-cultural adaptation', in Y.Y. Kim (ed.) *The International Encyclopedia of Intercultural Communication, Volume 2*, Hoboken, NJ: John Wiley & Sons, Inc., pp. 929–41.

Kinginger, C. (2009) *Language Learning and Study Abroad: A Critical Reading of Research*, Basingstoke: Palgrave Macmillan.

Kinginger, C. (2017) 'Language socialization in study abroad', in P.A. Duff and S. May (eds.) *Language Socialization, Encyclopedia of Language and Education*, 3rd edn, New York: Springer, pp. 227–38.

Kito, M. (2005) 'Self-disclosure in romantic relationships and friendships among American and Japanese college students', *Journal of Social Psychology*, 145(2): 127–40.

Kluckholn, C. and Strodtbeck, F. (1961) *Variations in Value Orientations*, Evanston, IL: Row, Peterson.

Knapp, M.L., Hal, J.A. and Horgan, T.G. (2014) *Nonverbal Communication in Human Interaction*, 8th edn, Boston: Wadsworth Cengage Learning.

Knight, J. (1997) 'Internationalization of higher education: A conceptual framework', in J. Knight and H. de Wit (eds.) *Internationalization of Higher Education in Asia Pacific Countries*, Amsterdam: European Association for International Education, pp. 5–19.

Knight, J. and de Wit, H. (2018) 'Preface: Internationalization of higher education: Where have we come from and where are we going?' in D. Proctor and L.E. Rumbley (eds.) *The Future Agenda for Internationalization in Higher Education: Next Generation Insights into Research, Policy, and Practice*, London and New York: Routledge, pp. xix–xxiv.

Kochman, T. and Mavrelis, J. (2015) 'Stereotypes and generalizations', in J.M. Bennett (ed.) *The Sage Encyclopedia of Intercultural Competence, Volume 2*, Los Angeles: Sage, pp. 774–6.

Komisarof, A. and Hua, Z. (2016) 'Making sense of transnational academics' experiences: Constructive marginality in liminal spaces', in A. Komisarof and Z. Hua (eds.) *Crossing Boundaries and Weaving Intercultural Work, Life, and Scholarship in Globalizing Universities*, London and New York: Routledge, pp. 174–200.

Kraidy, M.M. (2005) *Hybridity, or the Cultural Logic of Globalization*, Philadelphia: Temple University Press.

Kramsch, C. (1993) *Context and Culture in Language Teaching*, Oxford: Oxford University Press.

Kramsch, C. (1998) *Language and Culture*, Oxford: Oxford University Press.

Kramsch, C. (2009) *The Multilingual Subject*, New York: Oxford University Press.

Kramsch, C. and Uryu, M. (2012) 'Intercultural contact, hybridity, and third space', in J. Jackson (ed.) *Routledge Handbook of Language and Intercultural Communication*, London and New York: Routledge, pp. 211–26.

Krappman, L. (1998) 'Amicita, drujba, shin-yu, philia, freudschaft, friendship: On the cultural diversity of a human relationship', in W.M. Bukowski, A.F. Newcomb and W.W. Hartup (eds.) *The Company They Keep: Friendships in Childhood and Adolescence*, Cambridge: Cambridge University Press, pp. 19–40.

Kress, G. (1988) 'Glossary of terms', in G. Kress (ed.) *Communication and Culture*, Kensington, NSW: New South Wales University Press.

Krizan, A.C., Merrier, P., Logan, J. and Williams, K. (2011) *Business Communication*, 8th edn, Mason, OH: South-Western Cengage Learning.

Kroeber, A.L. and Kluckhohn, C. (1952) *Culture: A Critical Review of Concepts and Definitions*, Cambridge, MA: The Museum.

Kubota, R. (2014) 'Critical approaches to intercultural discourse and communication', in C.B. Paulston, S.F. Kiesling and E.S. Rangel (eds.) *The Handbook of Intercultural Discourse and Communication*, Malden, MA: Wiley-Blackwell, pp. 90–109.

Kupka, B. (2008) 'Creation of an instrument to assess intercultural communication competence for strategic international human resource management', unpublished doctoral dissertation, University of Otago, Otago, New Zealand.

LaBrack, B. (2003) 'What's up with culture?' Online. Available: http://www2.pacific.edu/sis/culture/index.htm (accessed 5 January 2019).

LaBrack, B. (2011) 'Theory connections, reflections, and applications for international educators', paper presented at the 63rd Annual NAFSA: Association of International Educators conference, Vancouver, BC, Canada.

LaBrack, B. (2015) 'Reentry', in J.M. Bennett (ed.) *The Sage Encyclopedia of Intercultural Competence, Volume 2*, Los Angeles: Sage, pp. 723–7.

LaBrack, B. and Berardo, K. (2007) 'Is it time to retire the U- and W-curves of adjustment?' paper presented at the Forum on Education Abroad conference, Austin, TX.

Lam, Q.K.H. and Wächter, B. (2014) 'Executive summary', in B. Wächter and F. Maiworm (eds.) *English-Taught Programmes in European Higher Education: The State of Play in 2014* (ACA Papers on International Cooperation in Education), Bonn: Lemmens, pp. 15–24.

Lamanna, M.A., Reidmann, A. and Stewart, S. (2018) *Marriages, Families, and Relationships: Making Choices in a Diverse Society*, 13th edn, Boston: Cengage Learning.

Lambert, R.D. (1996) 'Parsing the concept of global competence', in R.D. Lambert (ed.) *Educational Exchange and Global Competence*, New York: Council on International Educational Exchange, pp. 11–23.

Landis, D. (2018) 'Interethnic conflict theories and models', in Y.Y. Kim (ed.) *The International Encyclopedia of Intercultural Communication, Volume 2*, Hoboken, NJ: John Wiley & Sons, Inc., pp. 1420–33.

Lantis J.S. and DuPlaga, J. (2010) *The Global Classroom: An Essential Guide to Study Abroad*, Boulder, CO: Paradigm Press.

Lave, J. and Wenger, E. (1991) *Situated Learning: Legitimate Peripheral Participation*, Cambridge: Cambridge University Press.

LeBaron, M. (2003) *Bridging Cultural Conflicts: A New Approach for a Changing World*, San Francisco: Jossey-Bass.

LeBaron, M. (2015) 'Intercultural conflict transformation', in J.M. Bennett (ed.) *The Sage Encyclopedia of Intercultural Competence, Volume 2*, Los Angeles: Sage, pp. 495–9.

LeBaron, M. and Pillay, V. (2006) *Conflict Across Cultures: A Unique Experience of Bridging Differences*, Boston: Intercultural Press.

Leclercq, J.M. (2003) *Facets of Interculturality in Education*, Strasbourg: Council of Europe Publishing.

Lee, P.W. (2006) 'Bridging cultures: Understanding the construction of relational identity in intercultural friendship', *Journal of Intercultural Communication Research*, 35(1): 3–22.

Lee, P.W. (2008) 'Stages and transitions of relational identity formation in intercultural friendship: Implications for identity management theory', *Journal of International and Intercultural Communication*, 1(1): 51–69.

Le Page, R.B. and Tabouret-Keller, A. (1985) *Acts of Identity: Creole-Based Approaches to Language and Ethnicity*, Cambridge: Cambridge University Press.

Levine, D.N. (1971) 'Introduction', in D.N. Levine (ed.) *Georg Simmel: On Individuality and Social Forms Selected Writings*, Chicago: Chicago University Press, pp. ix–lxv.

Li, Z.F. (2010) 'Bridging the gap: Intercultural friendship between Chinese and American students', unpublished M.A. thesis, Liberty University, Lynchburg, VA.

Lindsay, R.B., Robins, K.N. and Terrell, R.D. (1999) *Cultural Literacy: A Manual for School Leaders*, Thousand Oaks, CA: Corwin.

Liu, S. (2018) 'Identity, bicultural and multicultural', in Y.Y. Kim (ed.) *The International Encyclopedia of Intercultural Communication, Volume 2*, Hoboken, NJ: John Wiley & Sons, Inc., pp. 823–31.

Liu, S., Volčič, Z. and Gallois, C. (2011) *Introducing Intercultural Communication: Global Cultures and Contexts*, London: Sage.

Liu, S., Volčič, Z. and Gallois, C. (2019) *Introducing Intercultural Communication: Global Cultures and Contexts*, 3rd edn, London: Sage.

Llamas, C., Mullany L. and Stockwell, P. (2007) 'Glossary', in C. Llamas, L. Mullany and P. Stockwell (eds.) *The Routledge Companion to Sociolinguistics*, London: Routledge, pp. 205–34.

LoCastro, V. (2003) *An Introduction to Pragmatics: Social Action for Language Teachers*, Ann Arbor, MI: University of Michigan Press.

Lolliot, S. (2018) 'Secondary transfer effect of intergroup contact', in Y.Y. Kim (ed.) *The International Encyclopedia of Intercultural Communication, Volume 3*, Hoboken, NJ: John Wiley & Sons, Inc., pp. 1757–62.

Lorde, A. (1986) *Our Dead Behind Us: Poems*, New York: W.W. Norton.

Lund, A. and O'Reagan, J. (2010) 'National occupational standards in intercultural working: models of theory and assessment', in M. Guilherme, E. Glaser and M.C. Méndez-García (eds.) *The Intercultural Dynamics of Multicultural Working*, Clevedon: Multilingual Matters, pp. 41–58.

Lysgaard, S. (1955) 'Adjustment in a foreign society: Norwegian Fulbright grantees visiting the United States', *International Social Science Bulletin*, 7: 45–51.

MacIntyre, P.D., Baker, S., Clément, R. and Donovan, L.A. (2003) 'Talking in order to learn: Willingness to communicate and intensive language programs', *Canadian Modern Language Review*, 59: 589–607.

MacIntyre, P.D., Dörnyei, Z., Clément, R. and Noels, K. (1998) 'Conceptualising willingness to communicate in a L2: A situational model of L2 confidence and affiliation', *The Modern Language Journal*, 82(4): 545–62.

Marcoccia, M. (2012) 'The internet, intercultural communication and cultural variation', *Language and Intercultural Communication*, 12(4): 353–68.

Marden, C. and Meyer, G. (1968) *Minorities in America*, 3rd edn, New York: Van Nostrand Reinhold.

Markus, H.R., Kitayama, S. and Heiman, R.J. (1996) 'Culture and "basic" psychological principles', in E.T. Higgins and A.W. Kruglanski (eds.) *Social Psychology: Handbook of Basic Principles*, New York: Guilford, pp. 857–913.

Martin, J.N. and Harrell, T. (2004) 'Intercultural reentry of students and professionals: Theory and practice', in D. Landis, J.M. Bennett and M.J. Bennett (eds.) *Handbook of Intercultural Training*, 3rd edn, Thousand Oaks, CA: Sage, pp. 309–36.

Martin, J.N. and Nakayama, T.K. (2000) *Intercultural Communication in Contexts*, 2nd edn, Mountain View, CA: Mayfield.

Martin, J.N. and Nakayama, T.K. (2008) *Experiencing Intercultural Communication: An Introduction*, 3rd edn, New York: McGraw Hill.

Martin, J.N. and Nakayama, T.K. (2018a) *Experiencing Intercultural Communication: An Introduction*, 6th edn, New York: McGraw Hill.

Martin, J.N. and Nakayama, T.K. (2018b) *Intercultural Communication in Contexts*, 7th edn, New York: McGraw Hill.

Martin, J.N., Nakayama, T.K. and Carbaugh, D. (2012) 'The history and development of the study of intercultural communication and applied linguistics', in J. Jackson (ed.) *The Routledge Handbook of Language and Intercultural Communication*, London and New York: Routledge, pp. 17–36.

Martinez, J.M. (2018) 'Cultural essentialism and neo-essentialism', in Y.Y. Kim (ed.) *The International Encyclopedia of Intercultural Communication, Volume 1*, Hoboken, NJ: John Wiley & Sons, Inc., pp. 514–22.

Matsumoto, D. (1992) 'More evidence for the universality of a contempt expression', *Motivation and Emotion*, 16(4): 363–8.

Matsumoto, D. and Hwang, H.S. (2012) 'Nonverbal communication: The messages of emotion, action, space and silence', in J. Jackson (ed.) *Routledge Handbook of Language and Intercultural Communication*, London and New York: Routledge, pp. 130–47.

Matsumoto, D. and Hwang, H.S. (2015) 'Intercultural nonverbal communication', in in J.M. Bennett (ed.) *The Sage Encyclopedia of Intercultural Competence, Volume 2*, Los Angeles: Sage, pp. 509–13.

Matsumoto, D. and Hwang, H.S. (2016) 'The cultural bases of nonverbal communication', in D. Matsumoto, H.S. Hwang and M.G. Frank (eds.) *APA Handbook of Intercultural Communication*, Washington, DC: American Psychological Association, pp. 45–76.

Matsumoto, D., Keltner, D., Shiota, M.N., Frank, M.G. and O'Sullivan, M. (2008) 'What's in a face? Facial expressions as signals of discrete emotions', in M. Lewis, J.M. Haviland and L. Feldman Barrett (eds.) *Handbook of Emotions*, New York: Guilford Press, pp. 211–34.

McCrosky, J.C. and Richmond, V.P. (1987) 'Willingness to communicate', in J.C. McCroskey and J.A. Daly (eds.) *Personality and Interpersonal Communication*, Newbury Park, CA: Sage, pp. 129–56.

McDaniel, E.R. and Samovar, L.A. (2015) 'Understanding and applying intercultural communication in the global community: The fundamentals', in A. Samovar, R.E. Porter E.R. McDaniel and C. Roy (eds.) *Intercultural Communication: A Reader*, 14th edn, Boston: Wadsworth, Cengage Learning, pp. 5–16.

McGrew, A. (1992) 'A global society?' in S. Hall, D. Held and A. McGrew (eds.) *Modernity and Its Futures*, Cambridge: Polity, pp. 61–102.

McKay, S.L. and Bokhorst-Heng, W.D. (2008) *International English in Its Sociolinguistic Contexts: Towards a Socially Sensitive EIL Pedagogy*, New York: Routledge.

McKay-Semmler, K.L. (2018) 'High- and low-context cultures', in Y.Y. Kim (ed.) *The International Encyclopedia of Intercultural Communication, Volume 2*, Hoboken, NJ: John Wiley & Sons, Inc., pp. 809–14.

McLoud-Schingen, K. (2015) 'Prejudice, bias, discrimination', in J.M. Bennett (ed.) *The Sage Encyclopedia of Intercultural Competence, Volume 2*, Los Angeles: Sage, pp. 690–3.

McLuhan, M. (1962) *The Gutenberg Galaxy: The Making of Typographic Man*, Toronto: University of Toronto Press.

Mead, M. (1930) *Growing Up in New Guinea: A Comparative Study of Primitive Education*, New York: Harper.

Mehrabian, A. (1969) 'Significance of posture and position in the communication of attitude and status relationships', *Psychological Bulletin*, 71(5): 359–72.

Mehrabian, A. (1982) *Nonverbal Communication*, Chicago: Aldine.

Meier, L. (2015) 'Migration studies', in J.M. Bennett (ed.) *The Sage Encyclopedia of Intercultural Competence, Volume 2*, Los Angeles: Sage, pp. 615–17.

Merrian-Webster Online (n.d., a) 'Dictionary: Artifact', Online. Available: www.merriam-webster.com/dictionary/artifact (accessed 5 February 2019).

Merriam-Webster Online (n.d., b) 'Dictionary: House', Online: Available: www.merriam-webster.com/dictionary/house (accessed 3 February 2019).

Meyerhoff, M. (2010) *Introducing Sociolinguistics*, 2nd edn, London and New York: Routledge.

Mezirow, J. (1994) 'Understanding transformative theory', *Adult Education Quarterly*, 44: 222–32.

Mezirow, J. (2000) 'Learning to think like an adult', in J. Mezirow and Associates (eds.) *Learning as Transformation: Critical Perspectives on a Theory in Progress*, San Francisco: Jossey-Bass, pp. 3–33.

Michie, M. (2014) *Working Cross-Culturally: Identity Learning, Border Crossing and Culture Brokering*, Rotterdam: Sense Publishers.

Miller, G.R. (1966) 'On defining communication: Another stab', *Journal of Communication*, 16: 88–98.

Mitchell, R., Tracy-Ventura, N. and McManus, K. (2017) *Anglophone Students Abroad: Identity, Social Relationships and Language Learning*, London and New York: Routledge.

Moffitt, B. (2016) *The Global Rise of Populism: Performance, Political Style, and Representation*, Stanford: Stanford University Press.

Moon, D.G. (2002) 'Thinking about "culture" in intercultural communication', in J.N. Martin, T.K. Nakayama and L.A. Flores (eds.) *Readings in Intercultural Communication: Experiences and Contexts*, 2nd edn, Boston: McGraw-Hill, pp. 13–21.

Moon, D.G. (2008) 'Concepts of "culture": Implications for intercultural communication research', in M.K. Asante, Y. Miike and J. Yin (eds.) *The Global Intercultural Communication Reader*, New York: Routledge, pp. 11–26.

Moon, D. (2010) 'Critical reflections on culture and critical intercultural communication', in T.K. Nakayama and R.T. Halualani (eds.) *The Handbook of Critical Intercultural Communication*, Oxford: Blackwell Publishing Ltd., pp. 34–52.

Moore, N.J., Hickson, M. and Stacks, D.W. (2014) *Nonverbal Communication: Studies and Applications*, 6th edn, Oxford: Oxford University Press.

Morais, D.B. and Ogden, A.C. (2011) 'Initial development and validation of the global citizenship scale', *Journal of Studies in International Education*, 15: 445–66.

Morgan, M. (2002) *Language, Discourse and Power in African American Culture*, Cambridge: Cambridge University Press.

Morgan, M. (2006) 'Speech community', in A. Duranti (ed.) *A Companion to Linguistic Anthropology*, Malden, MA: Wiley-Blackwell, pp. 450–64.

Mort, F. (1989) 'The politics of consumption', in S. Hall and M. Jacques (eds.) *New Times: The Changing Face of Politics in the 1990's*, London: Lawrence and Wishart, pp. 160–72.

Mortensen, C.D. (1974) 'A transactional paradigm of social conflict', in G.R. Miller and H.W. Simons (eds.) *Perspectives on Communication in Social Conflict*, Englewood Cliffs, NJ: Prentice Hall, pp. 90–124.

Mosby (2009) 'Social sanctions', in *Mosby's Medical Dictionary*, 8th edn, St. Louis, MI: Elsevier.

Mudde, C. and Kaltwasser, C.R. (2017) *Populism: A Very Short Introduction*, Oxford: Oxford University Press.

Mughan, T. and O'Shea, G. (2010) 'Intercultural interaction: A sense-making approach', in M. Guilherme, E. Glaser and M. del Carmen Méndez-García (eds.) *The Intercultural Dynamics of Multicultural Working*, Bristol: Multilingual Matters, pp. 109–20.

Müller-Jacquier, B. (2004) 'Intercultural communication', in M. Byram (ed.) *Routledge Encyclopedia of Language Teaching and Learning*, London: Routledge, pp. 295–7.

Myers-Scotton, C. (2006) *Multiple Voices: An Introduction to Bilingualism*, Oxford: Blackwell Publishing.

Nakayama, T.K. and Martin, J.N. (2018) 'Critical intercultural communication, overview', in Y.Y. Kim (ed.) *The International Encyclopedia of Intercultural Communication, Volume 1*, Hoboken, NJ: John Wiley & Sons, Inc., pp. 366–78.

Nam, K-A. (2015) 'High-context and low-context communication', in J.M. Bennett (ed.) *The Sage Encyclopedia of Intercultural Competence, Volume 1*, Los Angeles: Sage, pp. 377–81.

NASA (n.d.) 'Global climate change: Vital signs of the planet', Online. Available: https://climate. nasa.gov/faq/12/whats-the-difference-between-climate-change-and-global-warming/ (accessed 24 February 2019).

National Council for Curriculum and Assessment (NCCA) (2005) *Intercultural Education in the Primary School: Guidelines for Schools*, Dublin: Government Stationery Office.

Neuliep, J.W. (2012) *Intercultural Communication: A Contextual Approach*, 5th edn, Thousand Oaks, CA: Sage.

Neuliep, J.W. (2018a) 'Ethnocentricism', in Y.Y. Kim (ed.) *The International Encyclopedia of Intercultural Communication, Volume 1*, Hoboken, NJ: John Wiley & Sons, Inc., pp. 752–6.

Neuliep, J.W. (2018b) 'Sapir-Whorf hypothesis', in Y.Y. Kim (ed.) *The International Encyclopedia of Intercultural Communication, Volume 3*, Hoboken, NJ: John Wiley & Sons, Inc., pp. 1749–53.

Neuliep, J.W. (2018c) 'Culture shock and reentry shock', in Y.Y. Kim (ed.) *The International Encyclopedia of Intercultural Communication, Volume 1*, Hoboken, NJ: John Wiley & Sons, Inc., pp. 618–26.

Neuliep, J.W. (2018d) 'Intercultural communication apprehension', in Y.Y. Kim (ed.) *The International Encyclopedia of Intercultural Communication, Volume 2*, Hoboken, NJ: John Wiley & Sons, Inc., pp. 960–5.

Neuliep, J.W. (2018e) 'Anxiety/uncertainty management (AUM) theory', in Y.Y. Kim (ed.) *The International Encyclopedia of Intercultural Communication, Volume 1*, Hoboken, NJ: John Wiley & Sons, Inc., pp. 25–33.

Newton, J. and Kusmierczyk, E. (2011) 'Teaching second languages for the workplace', *Annual Review of Applied Linguistics*, 31: 1–19.

Nguyen, A.M.D. and Benet-Martínez, V. (2010) 'Multicultural identity: What it is and why it matters', in R. Crisp (ed.) *The Psychology of Social and Cultural Diversity*, Hoboken, NJ: Wiley-Blackwell, pp. 87–114.

Nobel Women's Initiative (n.d.) 'Meet the laureates', Online. Available: http://nobelwomensinitiative. org/meet-the-laureates/wangari-maathai/ (accessed 13 January 2019).

Noels, K.A., Yashima, T. and Zhang, R. (2012) 'Language, identity and intercultural communication', in J. Jackson (ed.) *Routledge Handbook of Language and Intercultural Communication*, London and New York: Routledge, pp. 52–66.

Nolan, R.W. (1999) *Communicating and Adapting Across Cultures: Living and Working in the Global Culture*, Westport, CT: Greenwood Publishing Group.

Norton, B. (2000) *Identity and Language Learning: Gender, Ethnicity and Educational Change*, Harlow, England: Pearson Education Ltd.

OABITAR (Objectivity, Accuracy, and Balance in Teaching About Religion (n.d.) 'Rites of birth and death', *Teaching About Religion: In Support of Civic Pluralism*, Online. Available: www.teaching aboutreligion.org/comparerites.html (accessed 5 January 2019).

Oberg, K. (1960) 'Cultural shock: Adjustment to new cultural environments', *Practical Anthropology*, 7: 177–82.

Ochs, E. and Schieffelin, B.B. (1984) 'Language acquisition and socialization: Three developmental stories and their implications', in R. Shweder and R.A. LeVine (eds.) *Culture Theory: Essays on Mind, Self, and Emotion*, New York: Cambridge University, pp. 276–320.

Ochs, E. and Schieffelin, B.B. (2014) 'The theory of language socialization', in A. Duranti, E. Ochs and B.B. Schieffelin (eds.) *The Handbook of Language Socialization*, Chichester: Wiley Blackwell, pp. 1–22.

O'Dowd, R. (2001) 'In search of a truly global network: The opportunities and challenges of on-line intercultural communication', *CALL-EJ Online*, 3(1).

O'Dowd, R. (2012) 'Intercultural communicative competence through telecollaboration', in J. Jackson (ed.) *The Routledge Handbook of Language and Intercultural Communication*, London and New York: Routledge, pp. 340–56.

O'Dowd, R. (2019) *Internationalising Higher Education and the Role of Virtual Exchange*, London and New York: Routledge.

Oetzel, J.G. (2009) *Intercultural Communication: A Layered Approach*, international edn, New York: Vango Books.

Oetzel, J.G. and Ting-Toomey, S. (2006) 'Part IV: Intercultural/international conflict', in J.G. Oetzel and S. Ting-Toomey (eds.) *The Sage Handbook of Conflict Communication: Integrating Theory, Research, and Practice*, Thousand Oaks, CA: Sage, pp. 545–8.

Olson, C.L., Evans, R. and Schoenberg, R.F. (2007) *At Home in the World: Bridging the Gap Between Internationalization and Multicultural Education*, Washington, DC: American Council on Education.

Olson, C.L. and Kroeger, K.R. (2001) 'Global competency and intercultural sensitivity', *Journal of Studies in International Education*, 5(2): 116–37.

Orbe, M.P. and Harris, T.M. (2008) *Interracial Communication: Theory into Practice*, Thousand Oaks, CA: Sage.

Orbe, M.P. and Harris, T.M. (2015) *Interracial Communication: Theory into Practice*, 3rd edn, Thousand Oaks, CA: Sage.

Organization for Economic Cooperation and Development (OECD) (2015) 'Education at a glance 2015: OECD indicators', Online. Available: www.oecd.org/education/education-at-a-glance-2015.htm (accessed 2 February 2019).

Osbeck, L.M., Moghaddam, F.M. and Perreault, S. (1997) 'Similarity and attraction among majority and minority groups in a multicultural environment', *International Journal of Intercultural Relations*, 21(1): 113–23.

Osler, A. (2005) 'Education for democratic citizenship: New challenges in a globalised world', in A. Osler and H. Starkey (eds.) *Citizenship and Language Learning: International Perspectives*, Stoke-on-Trent and Sterling: Trenthamp in Partnership with the British Council, pp. 3–22.

Ota, H. and Horicuhi, K. (2018) 'Internationalization through English-medium instruction in Japan', in D. Proctor and L.E. Rumbley (eds.) *The Future Agenda for Internationalization in Higher Education: Next Generation Insights into Research, Policy, and Practice*, London and New York: Routledge, pp. 15–27.

Ottenheimer, H.J. and Pine, J.M.S. (2019) *The Anthropology of Language: An Introduction to Linguistic Anthropology*, Boston: Cengage.

Oxfam (2015) 'Education for global citizenship: A guide for schools', Online. Available: www.oxfam.org.uk/education/resources/education-for-global-citizenship-a-guide-for-schools (accessed 24 February 2019).

Pacansky-Brock, M. (2017) *Best Practices for Teaching with Emerging Technologies*, 2nd edn, New York and London: Routledge.

Paige, R.M. and Bennett, J.M. (2015) 'Intercultural sensitivity', in J.M. Bennett (ed.) *The Sage Encyclopedia of Intercultural Competence, Volume 2*, Los Angeles: Sage, pp. 519–25.

Paige, R.M., Stallman, E. and Josić, J. (2008, May) 'Study abroad for global engagement: A preliminary report on the Study Abroad Global Engagement (SAGE) research project', Presentation at SAGE annual conference, Washington, DC.

Paltridge, B. (2012) *Discourse Analysis: An Introduction*, 2nd edn, London: Bloomsbury.

Park, M. (2006) 'A relational study of intercultural sensitivity with linguistic competence in English-as-a-foreign-language (EFL) pre-service teachers in Korea', unpublished Ph.D. thesis, The University of Mississippi, Oxford.

Parker, P.S. and Mease, J. (2009) 'Beyond the knapsack: Disrupting the production of White racial privilege through organizational practices', in L.A. Samavor, R.E. Porter and E.R. McDaniel (eds.)

Intercultural Communication: A Reader, 12th edn, Belmont, CA: Wadsworth Cengage Learning, pp. 313–24.

Patel, F., Li, M. and Sooknanan, P. (2011) *Intercultural Communication: Building a Global Community*, New Delhi: Sage.

Pauwels, A. (1991) *Non-Discriminatory Language*, Canberra: AGPS.

Peale, N.V. (2007) *A Guide to Confident Living*, New York: Simon and Schuster.

Peck, M.S. (1978) *The Road Less Travelled*, New York: Simon and Schuster.

Peng, F. (2011) 'Intercultural friendship development between Finnish and international students', unpublished M.A. thesis, University of Jyväskylä, Finland.

Pennycook, A. (1995) *The Cultural Politics of English as an International Language*, New York: Longman.

Pettigrew, T.F. and Tropp, L.R. (2011) *When Groups Meet: The Dynamics of Intergroup Contact*, New York and Hove: Psychology Press.

Pilkington, A. (2003) *Racial Disadvantage and Ethnic Diversity in Britain*, Basingstoke: Palgrave Macmillan.

Piller, I. (2009) 'Intercultural Communication', in F. Bargiela-Chiappini (ed.) *The Handbook of Business Discourse*, Edinburgh: Edinburgh University Press, pp. 317–29.

Piller, I. (2012) 'Intercultural communication: An overview', in C.B. Paulston, S.F. Kiesling and E.S. Rangel (eds.) *The Handbook of Intercultural Discourse and Communication*, Malden, MA: Wiley-Blackwell, pp. 3–18.

Piller, I. (2017) *Intercultural Communication: A Critical Introduction*, 2nd edn, Edinburgh: Edinburgh University Press.

Plummer, D. (2019) *Some of My Friends Are . . . the Daunting Challenges and Untapped Benefits of Cross-Racial Friendships*, Boston: Beacon Press.

Proctor, D. and Rumbley, L.E. (2018) 'New voices, new ideas, and new approaches in the internationalization of higher education', in D. Proctor and L.E. Rumbley (eds.) *The Future Agenda for Internationalization in Higher Education: Next Generation Insights into Research, Policy, and Practice*, London and New York: Routledge, pp. 3–12.

Prosser, M. (1976) 'The cultural communicator', in H.D. Fischer and J.C. Merrill (eds.) *International and Intercultural Communication*, New York: Hastings House Publishers, pp. 417–23.

Puri, J. (2004) *Encountering Nationalism*, Malden, MA: Blackwell.

Putnam, L.L. (2013) 'Definitions and approaches to conflict and communication', in J.G. Oetzel and S. Ting-Toomey (eds.) *The Sage Handbook of Conflict Communication: Integrating Theory, Research, and Practice*, 2nd edn, Thousand Oaks, CA: Sage, pp. 1–40.

Rahim, M.A. (1983) 'A measure of styles of handling interpersonal conflict', *Academy of Management Journal*, 26: 369–76.

Reagan, T. and Schreffler, S. (2005) 'Higher education language policy and the challenge of linguistic imperialism: A Turkish case study', in A.M.Y. Lin and P.W. Martin (eds.) *Decolonisation, Globalisation: Language-in-Education Policy and Practice*, Clevedon: Multilingual Matters, pp. 115–30.

Renalds, T. (2011) 'Communication in intercultural marriages: Managing cultural differences and conflict for marital satisfaction', unpublished M.A. thesis, Liberty University, Lynchburg, VA.

Rogers, E.M. and Hart, W.B. (2002) 'The histories of intercultural, international, and development communication', in W.B. Gudykunst and B. Mody (eds.) *The Handbook of International and Intercultural Communication*, Thousand Oaks, CA: Sage, pp. 1–18.

Rogers, E.M. and Steinfatt, T.M. (1999) *Intercultural Communication*, Prospect Heights, IL: Waveland Press.

Roloff, M.E. and Wright, C.N. (2013). 'Social cognition and conflict', in in J.G. Oetzel and S. Ting-Toomey (eds.) *The Sage Handbook of Conflict Communication*, Thousand Oaks, CA: Sage, pp. 133–60.

Romano, D. (2008) *Intercultural Marriage: Promises and Pitfalls*, 3rd edn, Yarmouth, ME: Intercultural Press.

Rosenblatt, P.C. (2009) 'A systems theory analysis of intercultural couple relationships', in T.A. Karis and K.D. Killiam (eds.) *Intercultural Couples: Explaining Diversity in Intimate Relationships*, New York: Routledge, pp. 3–20.

Rothman, J.C. (2008) *Cultural Competence in Process and Practice*, Boston: Pearson, Allyn and Bacon.

Rubin, J.Z., Pruitt, D.G. and Kim, S.H. (1994) *Social Conflict: Escalation, Stalemate, and Settlement*, 2nd edn, Columbus, OH: McGraw-Hill.

Rumbley, L.E., Altbach, P.G. and Reisberg, L. (2012) 'Internationalization within the higher education context', in D.K. Deardorff, H. de Wit, J.D. Heyl and T. Adams (eds.) *The Sage Handbook of International Higher Education*, Thousand Oaks, CA: Sage, pp. 3–26.

Ryan, J. (2013) 'Comparing learning characteristics in Chinese and anglophone cultures: Pitfalls and insights', in L. Jin and M. Cortazzi (eds.) *Researching Intercultural Learning*, Basingstoke: Palgrave Macmillan, pp. 41–60.

Ryan, P. (2003) 'Searching for the intercultural person', in G. Alred, M. Byram and M. Fleming (eds.) *Intercultural Experience and Education*, Clevedon: Multilingual Matters, pp. 131–54.

Ryan, S. (2006) 'Language learning motivation within the context of globalization: An L2 self within an imagined global community', *Critical Inquiry in Language Studies: An International Journal*, 3(1): 23–45.

Safdar, S., Friedlmeier, W., Matsumoto, D., Yoo, S.H., Kwantes, C.T. and Kakai, H. *et al.* (2009) 'Variations of emotional display rules within and across cultures: A comparison between Canada, USA, and Japan', *Canadian Journal of Behavioral Science*, 41(1): 1–10.

Samovar, L.A., Porter, R.E. and McDaniel, E.R. (2010) *Communication Between Cultures*, 7th edn, Boston: Wadsworth Cengage Learning.

Samovar, L.A., Porter, R.E., McDaniel, E.R. and Roy, C.S. (2012) *Communication Between Cultures*, 8th edn, Boston: Wadsworth Cengage Learning.

Samovar, L.A., Porter, R.E., McDaniel, E.R. and Roy, C.S. (2017) *Communication Between Cultures*, 9th edn, Boston: Wadsworth Cengage Learning.

Sand-Hart, H. (2010) *Home Keeps Moving: A Glimpse into the Extraordinary Life of a 'Third Culture Kid'*, Hagerstown, MD: McDougal Publishing.

Saphiere, D.H., Mikk, B.K. and Devries, B.I. (2005) *Communication Highwire: Leveraging the Power of Diverse Communication Styles*, Yarmouth, ME: Intercultural Press.

Sapir, E. (1921) *Language*, New York: Harcourt.

Savicki, V., Cooley, E. and Donnelly, R. (2008) 'Acculturative stress, appraisal, coping, and intercultural adjustment', in V. Savicki (ed.) *Developing Intercultural Competence and Transformation: Theory, Research, and Application in International Education*, Sterling, VA: Stylus, pp. 173–92.

Schacter, S. (1951) 'Deviation, rejection, and communication', *Journal of Abnormal and Social Psychology*, 46: 190–207.

Schaetti, B.F. (2015a) 'Identity', in J.M. Bennett (ed.) *The Sage Encyclopedia of Intercultural Competence, Volume 1*, Los Angeles: Sage, pp. 405–10.

Schaetti, B.F. (2015b) 'Third-culture kids/global nomads', in J.M. Bennett (ed.) *The Sage Encyclopedia of Intercultural Competence, Volume 2*, Los Angeles: Sage, pp. 797–800.

Schecter, S.R. and Bayley, R. (2002) *Language as Cultural Practice: Mexicanos en el Norte*, Mahwah, NJ: Lawrence Erlbaum.

Schirato, T. and Yell, S. (2000) *Communication and Culture: An Introduction*, London: Sage.

Schmid, K. (2018) 'Social identity theory', in Y.Y. Kim (ed.) *The International Encyclopedia of Intercultural Communication, Volume 3*, Hoboken, NJ: John Wiley & Sons, Inc., pp. 1797–804.

Schmidt, W.V., Conaway, R.N., Easton, S.S. and Wardrope, W.J. (2007) *Communicating Globally: Intercultural Communication and International Business*, Thousand Oaks, CA: Sage.

Scholte, J.A. (2000) *Globalization: A Critical Introduction*, London: Palgrave Macmillan.

Scollon, R., Wong Scollon, S. and Jones, R.H. (2012) *Intercultural Communication: A Discourse Approach*, 3rd edn, London: Blackwell.

Scovel, T. (1994) 'The role of culture in second language pedagogy', *System*, 22(2): 205–19.

Senft, G. (2009) 'Introduction', in G. Senft, J-O. Östman and J. Verschueren (eds.) *Culture and Language Use*, Amsterdam: John Benjamins, pp. 1–17.

Sercu, L. (2005) 'Teaching foreign languages in an intercultural world', in L. Sercu, E. Bandura, P. Castro, L. Davcheva, C. Laskaridou, U. Lundgren, M. del Carmen, M. García and P. M. Ryan (eds.) *Foreign Language Teachers and Intercultural Competence: An International Investigation*, Clevedon: Multilingual Matters, pp. 1–18.

Shahghasemi, E. (2018) 'Cultural schema theory', in Y.Y. Kim (ed.) *The International Encyclopedia of Intercultural Communication, Volume 1*, Hoboken, NJ: John Wiley & Sons, Inc., pp. 567–75.

Shakespeare, W. (1914) 'Troilus and Cressida' (Folger Shakespeare Library), Online: www.folgerdigital texts.org/html/Tro.html (accessed 3 May 2019).

Sharifian, F. (2012) 'World Englishes, intercultural communication and requisite competences', in J. Jackson (ed.) *Routledge Handbook of Language and Intercultural Communication*, London and New York: Routledge, pp. 310–22.

Sharifian, F. and Jamarani, M. (2013) 'Language and intercultural communication: From the old era to the new one', in F. Sharifian and M. Jamarani (eds.) *Language and Intercultural Communication in the New Era*, New York and London: Routledge, pp. 1–19.

Shi, X. and Langman, J. (2012) 'Gender, language, identity, and intercultural communication', in J. Jackson (ed.) *Routledge Handbook of Language and Intercultural Communication*, London and New York: Routledge, pp. 167–80.

Singh, N.G.K. (2011) *Sikhism: An Introduction*, Cornwall: I.B. Taurus.

Skelton, T. and Allen, T. (1999) 'Introduction', in T. Skelton and T. Allen (eds.) *Culture and Global Change*, London: Routledge, pp. 1–10.

Smalley, W. (1963) 'Culture shock, language shock, and the shock of self-discovery', *Practical Anthropology*, 10: 49–56.

Smith, A.G. (1966) *Communication and Culture*, New York: Holt, Rinehart and Winston.

Smith, H. (2009) *The World's Religions*, New York: HarperOne.

Smith, P.B., Bond, M.H. and Kağitçibaşi, Ç. (2006) *Understanding Social Psychology Across Cultures: Living and Working in a Changing World*, London: Sage.

Smith, P.B., Fischer, R., Vignoles, V.L. and Bond, M.H. (2013) *Understanding Social Psychology Across Cultures: Engaging with Others in a Changing World*, 2nd edn, Los Angeles: Sage.

Sorrells, K. (2012) 'Intercultural training in the global context', in J. Jackson (ed.) *Routledge Handbook of Language and Intercultural Communication*, London and New York: Routledge, pp. 372–89.

Sorrells, K. (2013) *Intercultural Communication: Globalization and Social Justice*, Thousand Oaks, CA: Sage.

Sorrells, K. (2015) 'Essentialism', in J.M. Bennett (ed.) *The Sage Encyclopedia of Intercultural Competence, Volume 1*, Los Angeles: Sage, pp. 297–9.

Sorrells, K. (2016) *Intercultural Communication: Globalization and Social Justice*, 2nd edn, Thousand Oaks, CA: Sage.

Sparrow, L. (2000) 'Beyond multicultural man: Complexities of identity', *International Journal of Intercultural Relations*, 24(2): 173–201.

Spencer-Oatey, H. (2005) '(Im)politeness, face and perceptions of rapport: Unpacking their bases and interrelationships', *Journal of Politeness Research*, 1: 95–119.

Spencer-Oatey, H. (2008a) 'Glossary', in H. Spencer-Oatey (ed.) *Culturally Speaking: Culture, Communication, and Politeness Theory*, 2nd edn, London: Continuum, pp. 326–37.

Spencer-Oatey, H, (2008b) 'Face, (im)politeness and rapport', in H. Spencer-Oatey (ed.) *Culturally Speaking: Culture, Communication, and Politeness Theory*, 2nd edn, London: Continuum, pp. 11–47.

Stanlaw, J., Adachi, N. and Salzmann, Z. (2018) *Language, Culture, and Society: An Introduction to Linguistic Anthropology*, 7th edn, New York: Routledge.

Stanley Foundation (2003) 'Educator support programs', Online. Available: http://vps.stanleyfoundation.org/programs/esp/gtn.html (accessed 3 March 2019).

Steger, M.B. (2017) *Globalization: A Very Short Introduction*, 4th edn, Oxford: Oxford University Press.

Stephan, W.G. and Stephan, C.W. (2015) 'Ingroup/outgroup', in J.M. Bennett (ed.) *The Sage Encyclopedia of Intercultural Competence, Volume 1*, Los Angeles: Sage, pp. 429–35.

Stiglitz, J.E. (2018) *Globalization and Its Discontents Revisited: Anti-Globalization in the Era of Trump*, New York and London: W.W. Norton & Co.

Strauss, R. (2018) 'Essentialism and universalism', in Y.Y. Kim (ed.) *The International Encyclopedia of Intercultural Communication, Volume 1*, Hoboken, NJ: John Wiley & Sons, Inc., pp. 730–8.

Street, B. (1993) 'Culture is a verb: Anthropological aspects of language and cultural process', in D. Graddol, L. Thompson and M. Byram (eds.) *Language and Culture*, Clevedon: Multilingual Matters and BAAL, pp. 23–43.

Suler, J.R. (2002) 'Identity management in cyberspace', *Journal of Applied Psychoanalytic Studies*, 4: 455–60.

Sumner, W.J. (1911) *War and Other Essays*, New Haven, CT: Yale University Press.

Swallow, D. (2010) 'The stages of adjusting to a new culture', Online. Available: www.deborahswallow.com/2010/05/14/the-stages-of-adjusting-to-a-new-culture/ (accessed 1 March 2019).

Swann, J., Deumert, A., Lillis, T. and Mesthrie, R. (2004) *A Dictionary of Sociolinguistics*, Edinburgh: Edinburgh University Press.

Synnott, A. (1993) *The Body Social: Symbolism, Self, and Society*, London: Routledge.

Szkudlarek, B. (2010) 'Reentry: A review of the literature', *International Journal of Intercultural Relations*, 34(1): 1–21.

Tajfel, H. (1981) *Human Groups and Social Categories*, Cambridge: Cambridge University Press.

Tajfel, H. (1982) 'Social psychology of intergroup relations', *Annual Review of Psychology*, 33: 1–39.

Tajfel, H. and Turner, J.C. (1979) 'An integrative theory of intergroup conflict', in W.G. Austin and S. Worchel (eds.) *The Social Psychology of Intergroup Relations*, Belmont, CA: Wadsworth Cengage Learning, pp. 33–53.

Tajfel, H. and Turner, J.C. (1986) 'An integrative theory of intergroup conflict', in S. Worchel and W.G. Austin (eds.) *Psychology of Intergroup Relations*, Chicago, IL: Nelson-Hall, pp. 2–24.

Tannen, D. (1995, September–October) 'The power of talk: Who gets heard and why', *Harvard Business Review*, 73(5): 138–48.

Tannen, D. (1996) *Gender and Discourse*, Oxford: Oxford University Press.

Tannen, D. (2001) *You Just Don't Understand: Women and Men in Conversation*, New York: William Morrow.

Tapia, A.T. and Gisbert, G. (2018) 'Cultural diversity in organizations', in Y.Y. Kim (ed.) *The International Encyclopedia of Intercultural Communication, Volume 1*, Hoboken, NJ: John Wiley & Sons, Inc., pp. 485–502.

Taras, V. (2018) 'Cultural dimensions, Hofstede', in Y.Y. Kim (ed.) *The International Encyclopedia of Intercultural Communication, Volume 1*, Hoboken, NJ: John Wiley & Sons, Inc., pp. 472–7.

Taylor, E.W. (1994) 'Intercultural competency: A transformative learning process', *Adult Education Quarterly*, 44(3): 154–74.

Taylor, S. (2001) 'Locating and conducting discourse analytic research', in M. Wetherell, S. Taylor and S.J. Yates (eds.) *Discourse as a Data: A Guide for Analysis*, London: Sage, pp. 5–48.

Temples, A.L. (2015) 'Language and identity', in J.M. Bennett (ed.) *The Sage Encyclopedia of Intercultural Competence, Volume 2*, Los Angeles: Sage, pp. 573–7.

Thill, J.V. and Bovée, C.L. (2015) *Excellence in Business Communication*, 11th edn, Boston: Pearson.

Thomas, J. (1995) *Meaning in Interaction: An Introduction to Pragmatics*, London: Longman.

Ting-Toomey, S. (2004) 'Translating conflict face-negotiation theory into practice', in D. Landis, J.M. Bennett and M.J. Bennett (eds.) *Handbook of Intercultural Training*, Thousand Oaks, CA: Sage, pp. 217–48.

Ting-Toomey, S. (2005) 'The matrix of face: An updated face-negotiation theory', in W.B. Gudykunst (ed.) *Theorizing About Intercultural Communication*, Thousand Oaks, CA: Sage, pp. 71–92.

Ting-Toomey, S. (2009) 'Intercultural conflict competence as a facet of intercultural competence development: Multiple conceptual approaches', in D.K. Deardorff (ed.) *The Sage Handbook of Intercultural Competence*, Thousand Oaks, CA: Sage, pp. 100–20.

Ting-Toomey, S. (2010) 'Intercultural conflict interaction competence: From theory to practice', in M. Guilherme, E. Glaser and M.C. Méndez-García (eds.) *The Intercultural Dynamics of Multicultural Working*, Bristol: Multilingual Matters, pp. 21–40.

Ting-Toomey, S. (2012) 'Understanding conflict competence: Multiple theoretical insights', in J. Jackson (ed.) *Routledge Handbook of Language and Intercultural Communication*, London and New York: Routledge, pp. 279–95.

Ting-Toomey, S. (2015a) 'Identity negotiation theory', in J.M. Bennett (ed.) *The Sage Encyclopedia of Intercultural Competence, Volume 1*, Los Angeles: Sage, pp. 418–23.

Ting-Toomey, S. (2015b) 'Facework/facework negotiation theory', in J.M. Bennett (ed.) *The Sage Encyclopedia of Intercultural Competence, Volume 1*, Los Angeles: Sage, pp. 325–30.

Ting-Toomey, S. (2015c) 'Mindfulness', in J.M. Bennett (ed.) *The Sage Encyclopedia of Intercultural Competence, Volume 2*, Los Angeles: Sage, pp. 620–6.

Ting-Toomey, S. (2017) 'Conflict face-negotiation theory: Tracking its evolutionary trajectory', in X. Dai and G-M Chen (eds.) *Conflict Management and Intercultural Communication: The Art of Intercultural Harmony*, London and New York: Routledge, pp. 123–43.

Ting-Toomey, S. (2018) 'Facework and face negotiation theory', in Y.Y. Kim (ed.) *The International Encyclopedia of Intercultural Communication, Volume 2*, Hoboken, NJ: John Wiley & Sons, Inc., pp. 775–9.

Ting-Toomey, S. and Chung, L.C. (2012) *Understanding Intercultural Communication*, 2nd edn, Oxford: Oxford University Press.

Ting-Toomey, S. and Dorjee, T. (2019) *Communicating Across Cultures*, 2nd edn, New York: Guilford Press.

Ting-Toomey, S. and Oetzel, J.G. (2001) *Managing Intercultural Conflict Effectively*, Thousand Oaks, CA: Sage.

Toh, S.H. (1996) 'Partnerships as solidarity: Crossing North-South boundaries', *The Alberta Journal of Educational Research*, XLII(2): 178–91.

Tompkins, P.S. (2019) *Practicing Communication Ethics: Development, Discernment, and Decision Making*, 2nd edn, New York and London: Routledge.

Triandis, H.C. (1995) *Individualism and Collectivism*, Boulder, CO: Westview Press.

Trudgill, P. (2003) *A Glossary of Sociolinguistics*, Edinburgh: Edinburgh University Press.

Tsuda, Y. (2018) 'English hegemony', in Y.Y. Kim (ed.) *The International Encyclopedia of Intercultural Communication, Volume 1*, Hoboken, NJ: John Wiley & Sons, Inc., pp. 720–5.

Tubbs, S. (2009) *Human Communication: Principles and Contexts*, Boston: McGraw-Hill.

Tylor, E.B. (1871) *Primitive Culture: Researches into the Development of Mythology, Philosophy, Religion, Art, and Custom*, New York: Gordon Press.

UNESCO (2018) 'Global flow of tertiary-level students', UNESCO Institute for Statistics, Online. Available: http://uis.unesco.org/en/uis-student-flow (accessed 1 January 2019).

United Nations – Disability (n.d.) *United Nations Convention on the Rights of Persons with Disabilities*. New York: United Nations, Online. Available: www.un.org/development/desa/disabilities/convention-on-the-rights-of-persons-with-disabilities.html (accessed 24 February 2019).

United Nations High Commissioner for Refugees (UNHCR) (2011) 'Handbook and guidelines on procedures and criteria for determining refugee status under the 1951 convention and the 1967 protocol relating to the status of refugees', Online. Available: www.unhcr.org/publ/PUBL/3d58e13b4.pdf (accessed 4 January 2019).

United Nations High Commissioner for Refugees (UNHCR) (2018) 'Figures at a glance', Online. Available: www.unhcr.org/figures-at-a-glance.html (accessed 23 February 2019).

United Nations International Convention on the Elimination of All Forms of Racial Discrimination (ICERD) (1989) *CCPR General Comment No. 18*, New York: Office of the High Commissioner for Human Rights, Online. Available: www.unhchr.ch/tbs/doc.nsf/0/3888b0541f8501c9c12563ed004b8d0e (accessed 22 February 2019).

United Nations World Tourism Organization (UNWTO) (2018) 'Understanding tourism; Basic glossary', Online. Available: http://cf.cdn.unwto.org/sites/all/files/docpdf/glossaryenrev.pdf (accessed 8 March 2019).

United States Department of Health and Human Services (2001) *Mental Health: Culture, Race, and Ethnicity – A Supplement to Mental Health: A Report of the Surgeon General*, Rockville, MD: U.S. Department of Health and Human Services, Substance Abuse and Mental Health Services Administration, Center for Mental Health Services, Online. Available: www.surgeongeneral.gov/library/mentalhealth/cre/sma-01-3613.pdf (accessed 1 February 2019).

Uryu, M. (2018) 'Hybridity, theories of', in Y.Y. Kim (ed.) *The International Encyclopedia of Intercultural Communication, Volume 2*, Hoboken, NJ: John Wiley & Sons, Inc., pp. 814–22.

van de Vijver, F. (2018a) 'Ethnicity, definitions of', in Y.Y. Kim (ed.) *The International Encyclopedia of Intercultural Communication, Volume 1*, Hoboken, NJ: John Wiley & Sons, Inc., pp. 748–52.

van de Vijver, F. (2018b) 'Nonverbal communication across cultures', in Y.Y. Kim (ed.) *The International Encyclopedia of Intercultural Communication, Volume 3*, Hoboken, NJ: John Wiley & Sons, Inc., pp. 1617–26.

van der Zee, K. and Hofhuis, J. (2018) 'Conflict management styles across cultures', in Y.Y. Kim (ed.) *The International Encyclopedia of Intercultural Communication, Volume 1*, Hoboken, NJ: John Wiley & Sons, Inc., pp. 302–10.

van Meurs, N. and Spencer-Oatey, H. (2010) 'Multidisciplinary perspectives on intercultural conflict: The "Bermuda triangle" of conflict, culture, and communication', in D. Matsumoto (ed.) *APA Handbook of Intercultural Communication*, Washington, DC: American Psychological Association and New York: Walter de Gruyter, Inc. pp. 59–77.

Vande Berg, M., Paige, R.M. and Lou, K.H. (2012) 'Student learning abroad: Paradigms and assumptions', in M. Vande Berg, R.M. Paige and K.H. Lou (eds.), *Student Learning Abroad: What Our Students Are Learning, What They're Not, and What We Can Do About It*, Sterling, VA: Stylus, pp. 3–28.

Vela-McConnell, J.A. (2011) *Unlikely Friends: Bridging Ties and Diverse Friendships*, Plymouth: Lexington Books.

Vygotsky, L.S. (1997) 'Genesis of higher mental functions', in R.W. Rieber (ed.) *The Collected Works of L.S. Vygotsky, Volume 4: The History of the Development of Higher Mental Functions*, New York and London: Plenum Press, pp. 97–120.

Wagner, M. and Byram, M. (2018) 'Intercultural citizenship', in Y.Y. Kim (ed.) *The International Encyclopedia of Intercultural Communication, Volume 2*, Hoboken, NJ: John Wiley & Sons, Inc., pp. 955–60.

Walther, J.B. (1992) 'Interpersonal effects in computer-mediated interaction: A relational perspective', *Communication Research*, 19: 52–90.

Ward, C.A. (2015) 'Culture shock', in J.M. Bennett (ed.) *The Sage Encyclopedia of Intercultural Competence, Volume 1*, Los Angeles: Sage, pp. 207–10.

Ward, C.A., Bochner, S. and Furnham, A. (2001) *The Psychology of Culture Shock*, London: Routledge.

Wardaugh, R. and Fuller, J.M. (2015) *An Introduction to Sociolinguistic'*, 7th edn, Chichester, West Sussex: Wiley-Blackwell.

Watson, B., Gallois, C., Hewett, D.G. and Jones, L. (2012) 'Culture and health care: Intergroup communication and its consequences', in J. Jackson (ed.) *The Routledge Handbook of Language and Intercultural* Communication, London and New York: Routledge, pp. 510–22.

Watzlawick, P., Beavin, J. and Jackson, D. (1967) *The Pragmatics of Human Communication*, New York: Norton.

Wellman, C. (1988) *Morals and Ethics*, 2nd edn, Englewood Cliffs, NJ: Prentice Hall.

Wenger-Trayner, E. and Wenger-Trayner, B. (2015) 'Communities of practice: A brief introduction', Online. Available: http://wenger-trayner.com/wp-content/uploads/2015/04/07-Brief-introduction-to-communities-of-practice.pdf (accessed 23 March 2019).

West, B. (2015) 'Internet identity', in J.M. Bennett (ed.) *The Sage Encyclopedia of Intercultural Competence, Volume 2*, Los Angeles: Sage, pp. 557–60.

West, R. and Turner, L.H. (2011a) *Understanding Interpersonal Communication: Making Choices in Changing Times*, 2nd edn, Boston: Wadsworth Cengage Learning.

West, R. and Turner, L.H. (2011b) 'Technology and interpersonal communication', in K.M. Galvin (ed.) *Making Connections: Readings in Relational Communication*, Oxford: Oxford University Press, pp. 379–86.

Westerhof, G.J. (2008) 'Age identity', in D. Carr (ed.) *Encyclopedia of the Life Course and Human Development*, Farmington Hills, MI: Palgrave Macmillan, pp. 10–14.

Wetherell, M. and Potter, J. (1992) *Mapping the Language of Racism*, London: Sage.

Whorf, B.L. (1956) 'The relation of habitual thought and behavior to language', in J.B. Carroll (ed.) *Language, Thought, and Reality: Selected Writings of Benjamin Lee Whorf*, Cambridge: MIT Press, pp. 134–59.

Wiemann, J.M., Takai, J., Ota, H. and Wiemann, M.O. (1997) 'A relational model of communication competence', in B. Kovacic (ed.) *Emerging Theories of Human Communication*, Albany, NY: State University of New York Press, pp. 25–44.

Wierzbicka, A. (2006) *English: Meaning and Culture*, Beijing: Foreign Language Teaching and Research Press, Oxford University Press.

Wilczek-Watson, M. (2018) 'Intercultural intimate relationships', in Y.Y. Kim (ed.) *The International Encyclopedia of Intercultural Communication, Volume 2*, Hoboken, NJ: John Wiley & Sons, Inc., pp. 1339–47.

Wilkinson, J. (2012) 'The intercultural speaker and the acquisition of intercultural/global competence', in J. Jackson (ed.) *The Routledge Handbook of Language and Intercultural Communication*, London and New York: Routledge, pp. 296–309.

Williams, R. (1981) *Culture*, London: Fontana.

Wilmot, W. and Hocker, J. (2017) *Interpersonal Conflict*, 10th edn, Boston: McGraw-Hill.

Wintergerst, A. and McVeigh, J. (2011) *Tips for Teaching Culture: Practical Approaches to Intercultural Communication*, White Plains, NY: Pearson ESL.

Wodak, R. (2008) '"Us and them": Inclusion and exclusion', in G. Delanty, R. Wodak and P. Jones (eds.) *Identity, Belonging and Migration*, Liverpool: Liverpool University Press, pp. 54–77.

Wodak, R. (2015) *The Politics of Fear: What Right-Wing Populist Discourses Mean*, London: Sage.

Women's International League for Peace and Freedom (n.d.) 'Peace quotes', Online. Available: https://wilpf.org/peace-quotes/ (Accessed 28 February 2019).

Wood, J.T. (2005) *Gendered Lives: Communication, Gender, and Culture*, 7th edn, Belmont, CA: Wadsworth.

Wood, J.T. (2016) *Interpersonal Communication: Everyday Encounters*, 8th edn, Boston: Wadsworth Cengage Learning.

Wood, P. and Landry, C. (2010) *The Intercultural City: Planning for Diversity Advantage*, London: Earthscan.

World Health Organization (WHO) (n.d.) 'Gender, equity, and human rights', Online. Available: www.who.int/gender-equity-rights/understanding/gender-definition/en/ (accessed 25 February 2019).

Xinhua (2017) 'Over 500 Confucius institutes founded in 142 countries, regions', Online. Available: www.chinadaily.com.cn/china/2017-10/07/content_32950016.htm (accessed 28 February 2019).

Ying, Y.W. (2002) 'Formation of cross-cultural relationships of Taiwanese international students in the U.S.', *Journal of Community Psychology*, 30(1): 45–55.

Yule, G. (2008) *Pragmatics*, Oxford: Oxford University Press.

Yule, G. (2017) *The Study of Language*, 6th edn, Cambridge: Cambridge University Press.

Zaharna, R.S. (1989) 'Self-shock: The double-binding challenge of identity', *International Journal of Intercultural Relations*, 13: 501–26.

Zenner, W. (1996) 'Ethnicity', in D. Levinson and M. Ember (eds.) *Encyclopedia of Cultural Anthropology*, New York: Holt, pp. 393–5.

Zhang, Q. (2018) 'Intercultural conflict and conflict management', in Y.Y. Kim (ed.) *The International Encyclopedia of Intercultural Communication, Volume 2*, Hoboken, NJ: John Wiley & Sons, Inc., pp. 1270–9.

Zhang, Y.B. and Giles, H. (2018) 'Communication accommodation theory', in Y.Y. Kim (ed.) *The International Encyclopedia of Intercultural Communication, Volume 1*, Hoboken, NJ: John Wiley & Sons, Inc., pp. 95–108.

Zhang, Y.B., Harwood, J. and Hummert, M.L. (2005) 'Perceptions of conflict management styles in Chinese intergenerational dyads', *Communication Monographs*, 72: 71–91.

Zhu, H. (2011) 'Glossary', in H. Zhu (ed.) *The Language and Intercultural Communication Reader*, London and New York: Routledge, pp. 418–25.

Zimbler, M. and Feldman, R.S. (2011) 'Liar, liar, hard drive on fire: How media context affects lying behavior', *Journal of Applied Social Psychology*, 41(10): 2492–507. DOI: https://doi.org/10.1111/j.1559-1816.2011.00827.x

Glossary

accent A distinctive way of pronouncing a language, e.g., a way of speaking typical of a particular group of residents in a region

acceptance of difference According to the developmental model of intercultural sensitivity (DMIS), individuals in this phase accept the existence of culturally different ways of organizing human existence, although they may not like or agree with them

accommodation (conflict) style This communication style emphasizes an indirect and emotionally restrained approach to dealing with conflict

acculturation The process through which an individual is socialized into a new cultural environment

acculturation strategies The ways that individuals and ethnocultural groups respond to the process of acculturation adjust to a new environment

acculturative stress A negative psychological reaction to the experiences of acculturation, often characterized by anxiety, depression, and a variety of psychosomatic problems

acquaintance *See* casual friend

active listening Noticing how and when ideas are conveyed as well as what is *not* being said

'acts of identity' Dimensions of oneself (e.g., age, gender, class, nationality, ethnicity, personality) and the degree of social or ethnic solidarity with one's communication partner are conveyed through language choice and use

adaptation The act or process of adjusting or adapting to a new cultural environment

adaptation to difference According to the developmental model of intercultural sensitivity (DMIS), individuals in this phase can expand their own worldviews to understand other ways of being and behave in culturally appropriate ways

adaptors Gestures or movements that satisfy personal or bodily needs (e.g., scratching, yawning)

additive bilingualism A process whereby one's first language and culture continue to be nurtured as one's second language develops

affect display The use of physical movement (e.g., facial expressions, posture) to convey the strength of one's feelings or emotions

affective competence The emotional and motivational capacity to cope with the challenges of living in a new environment

affective conflict A type of conflict that centers on an emotional conflict between parties

affective sensitivity *See* intercultural sensitivity

affirmative action Education, business, or employment policies that aim to redress the negative, historical impact of discrimination by taking factors such as race, sex, religion, gender, or national origin into consideration in hiring/promotion situations

age identity How people feel and think about themselves and others in relation to age

ageism The stereotyping or discrimination of a person or group of people based on their age

ageist language Language that is used to convey stereotypes of people based on their age

ageist stereotyping The categorizing of individuals into groups according to their age and then ascribing certain characteristics and behaviors to all people of that age group (e.g., teenagers, Generation X, old folks)

anti-Christian sentiments Opposition to or objection to Christians and the practice of Christianity, which can lead to prejudice, discrimination, racism, and/or acts of violence against Christians

anti-discrimination legislation A set of laws that exists to protect the rights of individuals and promote equality among people regardless of their differences (e.g., sex, gender, religion, ethnicity, social class, physical ability)

anti-racist legislation Regulations or laws protecting human rights in certain sectors of society

anti-Semitism Hostility to, prejudice, discrimination or racist acts against Jews

anxiety/uncertainty management (AUM) theory A theory developed by W. Gudykunst (1985) which suggests that one's level of stress or anxiety subsides as one gains more knowledge and understanding of one's communication partner(s)

appearance message The nonverbal signals (e.g., clothing, mannerisms) that facilitate judgments about an individual's personality, abilities, and other attributes

appropriate communication Communication that enhances a relationship

appropriate intercultural communication Communication that enhances intercultural relationships from the perspective of both interactants

artifact An object created or shaped by humans, usually for a practical purpose

ascribed identity The identity that others assign to us (or we give to someone else)

ascription The process of ascribing or assigning an identity to someone else

assimilation The process whereby immigrants do not retain their original cultural identity and link to their heritage/culture; instead, they seek close interaction with the host culture and adopt the cultural values, norms, and traditions of the new society

asylum seeker An individual who is seeking protection as a refugee and is waiting for his or her claim to be assessed by a country that has signed the Geneva Convention on Refugees

asynchronous communication A type of e-communication that occurs without the need for individuals to be online at the same time, e.g., the receiver of an email message may not read it until several hours or days after it has been sent

attitude An emotional (positive or negative) response to people, ideas, and objects

audience design framework A scheme developed by Allan Bell (1984) to explain observed variations in speech styles

avoidance strategy Deliberate steps taken to avoid an uncomfortable situation

avowal The process of conveying what self-identity(ies) one wishes others to acknowledge

avowed identity The identity that an individual wishes to present or claim in an interaction

behavioral (intercultural) adroitness Skills that are needed for one to be interculturally competent, e.g., message skills, knowledge regarding appropriate self-disclosure, behavioral flexibility, interaction management, social skills

behavioral uncertainty One's uncertainty about how one's communication partner will behave or act

beliefs Learned assumptions and convictions about concepts, events, people, and ways of being that are held to be true by an individual or a group

best friend Someone who is especially close to you

bias A personal preference, like or dislike, which can interfere with one's ability to be objective, impartial, and without prejudice

bicultural An individual who is culturally competent in two cultural contexts (e.g., his or her original home environment and the host environment)

bilingual Using or able to use two languages with equal or nearly equal fluency

bilingual identity A hybrid sense of self linked to the use of two languages

biracial Having parents of two different races

bisexual Having emotional, romantic or sexual attractions to individuals who are not from one particular sex

body language A form of human nonverbal communication consisting of body posture, gestures, facial expressions, and eye movements (*See also* kinesics)

business acumen One's ability to understand business situations and make appropriate decisions in a short amount of time

business ethics Principles that guide behavior in business

business etiquette Rules that guide social behavior in workplace situations

business netiquette Guidelines for courtesy in the use of email and the Internet for communication purposes in business

business protocol The discourse, nonverbal behavior, dress, procedures, and social conventions that are expected within a particular company or organization

casual friend A person you see from time to time who is not a particularly close friend

casual intercultural dating Individuals from different cultural backgrounds who spend some time with each other socially and perhaps have sex without necessarily expecting the commitments of a more serious romantic relationship

casual intercultural relationship A physical and emotional relationship between two people from different cultural backgrounds who may have a sexual relationship without necessarily expecting the commitments of a more serious romantic relationship

channel The way in which a message is conveyed from one person to another, e.g., through speech, writing, and nonverbal signals

chronemics The study of how people use and structure time

citizenship The relationship between the individual and the state and the need for citizens to understand the economic and political processes, structures, institutions, laws, rights, and responsibilities within the system that governs the state

class identity A sense of belonging or attachment to a group that shares similar economic, occupational, or social status

classism Prejudice or discrimination on the basis of social class

climate 'The long-term regional or even global average of temperature, humidity and rainfall patterns over seasons, years or decades' (NASA n.d.)

climate change A broad range of changes in global weather patterns created predominantly by burning fossil fuels

close friend Someone who can be relied on to provide emotional support and perhaps lend a hand when needed

co-culture Smaller, coherent collective groups that exist within a larger dominant culture and which are often distinctive because of race, social class, gender, etc.

cohabitation Living together in a sexual relationship without being legally married

conational An individual from one's home nation

code of ethics Guidelines that spell out what is 'right' or 'wrong' behavior in everyday life as well as in professional contexts

code-mixing The mixing of two or more languages or language varieties in speech

code-switching Changing between different languages when communicating

cognitive (intercultural) awareness Knowledge of one's own personal identities/cultures and understanding of how cultures differ

cognitive competence Knowledge of the host language and culture, history, social institutions, and rules or norms of interpersonal conduct in specific situations

cognitive conflict A type of conflict that centers on the completion of a task

cognitive uncertainty Uncertainty about the ways in which an individual's culturally influenced attitudes and beliefs affect his or her way of thinking

collectivism Interdependence and social cohesion are emphasized so that the needs and wants of groups are given priority over individuals

communication A symbolic, dynamic process by which we create and share meaning with others

communication accommodation theory (CAT) A theory developed by Howard Giles and his colleagues that posits that people in intercultural interactions adjust their communication toward or away from their communication partner, conveying different aspects of their identities

communication adaptability The ability to modify one's interaction behaviors and goals to meet the specific needs of the situation

communication competence The ability to achieve one's goals in a way that is acceptable to both communication partners

communication style The way individuals or a group of individuals prefer to communicate with others

communicative competence What a speaker needs to know to be able to use language appropriately and effectively in specific social/cultural settings

community of practice (CoP) A group of people who share a concern or passion for something they do and gradually learn how to do it better through interaction with more experienced individuals on a regular basis

computer-mediated communication (CMC) Communication that is facilitated by computer technologies (e.g., the use of two or more networked computers)

conational A member of the same nation

conflict An expressed struggle between interdependent individuals or groups over perceived incompatible interests, goals, values, and resources

conflict face negotiation theory A theory developed by Stella Ting-Toomey which addresses the ways face-losing and face-saving behaviors influence intercultural conflict situations

conflict facework competence The use of culturally/linguistically appropriate and effective facework negotiation skills in conflict situations

conflict interaction style Patterned responses to conflict situations

conflict management The process by which individuals or groups try to find a satisfying outcome in conflict situations

conflict management practices Steps that individuals or groups adopt to resolve conflicts

conflict management style Preferred ways of dealing with conflict situations

conflict negotiation strategies Preferred strategies for negotiating conflicts

conflict script A routinized sequence of verbal and nonverbal actions in a dispute

conflict style A preferred way of behaving in conflict situations

Confucian dynamism A value dimension that aims to account for particular cultural characteristics and behaviors (Confucian values) that are prevalent in East Asian nations, e.g., persistence, a long-term orientation to time (*See also* Hofstede's value-orientations framework)

consecutive interpreting Interpreting that takes place after the speaker has finished

constructive conflict communication skills The ability to manage a conflict situation appropriately and effectively by way of skillful interpersonal conflict management skills and verbal and nonverbal communication, whether in a first or second language

contact hypothesis George Allport's notion that increased contact between different cultural or ethnic groups can lead to mutual acceptance and reduced levels of tension/prejudice provided that certain conditions are met

contested identity Facets or elements of one's identity that are not recognized or accepted by the people one is in contact with

context The overall environment in which communication occurs (e.g., physical, psychological, sociocultural, political, sociorelational)

convergence The act of adjusting one's communication (e.g., verbal, nonverbal) and stressing particular identities to become more aligned with one's addressees to convey solidarity and reduce social distance

corporate culture The culture of a particular business or organization

crimes against humanity The systemic practice of serious offenses against people that are either carried out or condoned by a government (e.g., widespread murder, religious persecution, rapes as a weapon of war)

critical cultural awareness/political education (*savoir s'engager*) The ability to critically evaluate perspectives, practices, and products in one's own and other cultures

critical discourse analysis A form of discourse analysis which aims to bring about social change by disclosing connections of hidden relationships encoded in language that may not be immediately evident

critical intercultural communication studies Research that critically examines the role of power and positioning in language and intercultural communication within a particular context

critical intercultural speaker An individual (second language speaker) who is able to negotiate between his or her own cultural, social, and political identifications and representations with those of the other', and in the process, become critically aware of the complex nature of cultural identities in an intercultural encounter (*See also* intercultural speaker)

critical (deep) reflection The process of analyzing, reconsidering, and questioning intercultural experiences with the aim of developing a more in-depth understanding of internal and external factors that influenced the outcome

cross-cultural adaptation The process whereby individuals from one cultural context move to a different cultural context and strive to learn the societal norms, customs, and language of the host culture in order to function in the new environment

cross-cultural communication research Investigations that compare and contrast native discourse and ways of being (e.g., communication styles) in different cultures

cultural awareness An understanding of how an individual's cultural background may inform his or her values, behavior, beliefs, and basic assumptions

cultural display rules Cultural rules that influence whether and how to express one's emotions in a particular situation

cultural distance The gap between the ways of being of two different cultural groups

cultural fluency Recognition that culture profoundly shapes who we are and how we cooperate and engage conflict

cultural identity A social identity that is influenced by one's membership or affiliation with particular cultural groups

cultural identity formation The formation of a sense of belonging or attachment to a particular cultural group that develops through shared experiences and the teachings of other members of the group

cultural intelligence The ability and competence to use all of the human senses to empathize and communicate effectively and appropriately with people who have a different cultural background

cultural maintenance The effort of immigrants or minorities to sustain elements of their home culture or heritage (e.g., preserve core values, traditions, language(s), and other ways of being) especially when faced with pressure to adopt the customs of the new, dominant culture (e.g., the majority group)

cultural membership One's affiliation or sense of belonging with a particular cultural group

cultural norms Shared expectations of appropriate behaviors in certain situations and contexts

cultural relativism The view that beliefs, value systems, and social practices are culturally relative, that is, no culture is inherently superior to another

cultural schema A mental structure in which our knowledge and understanding of the world is organized to facilitate our thinking, communication, etc.

cultural script Representations of cultural norms which are widely held in a given society and which are reflected in verbal and nonverbal acts (e.g., a sequence of expressions and behaviors in certain situations)

cultural similarity The degree of dissimilarity between one's home culture and the host culture in terms of language, values, beliefs, diet, nonverbal behaviors, customs, 'cultures of learning', religion, etc.

cultural socialization *See* enculturation

cultural space A physical or virtual place where individuals have a sense of community and culture, e.g., a neighborhood, region, virtual space

cultural synergy The combined power of people from diverse cultural backgrounds working together to create a greater, stronger effect than if they were separate

culture A community or group that shares a common history, traditions, norms, and imaginings in a particular cultural space (e.g., a neighborhood, region, virtual space)

'culture as nation' perspective An orientation toward culture in which nations or large communities are viewed as homogeneous and the diversity within is largely ignored

culture broker (intermediary) An individual who is tasked with bridging cultural differences

culture brokering The act of bridging or mediating between groups or people who have a different cultural background in order to facilitate communication and reduce conflict

culture-general intercultural education A form of intercultural education that broadly centers on the development of the knowledge, skills, and mindset that can help individuals become more attuned to their linguistic and cultural environment and engage in constructive intercultural interactions, no matter where they are in the world

culture-sensitive knowledge Awareness of the conceptions, beliefs, values, and ways of being associated with a culture

culture shock (confusion) Disorientation and discomfort that an individual may experience when entering an unfamiliar cultural environment

culture-specific intercultural education A form of intercultural education that primarily aims at helping individuals learn to communicate effectively and appropriately in a particular target culture

'cultures of learning' The norms, values, and expectations of teachers and learners that influence classroom activities in a particular cultural setting

cyber friendship A personal connection or affiliation forged between people online

cyber identity *See* internet identity

cyberculture The culture that develops through the use of computer networks for communication, business, and entertainment

decoding The process by which the receiver tries to understand the meaning of a message that is being sent

decorative ornamentation Accessories or materials used for decoration

deculturation The unlearning of cultural habits

deep level diversity Differences among individuals and groups that are not easily observable such as attitudes, beliefs, knowledge, skills, and values or worldviews

defense against difference According to the developmental model of intercultural sensitivity (DMIS), individuals in this ethnocentric phase view their own culture/way of life uncritically as the best; overt negative stereotyping of others is common

defense/reversal According to the developmental model of intercultural sensitivity (DMIS), in this ethnocentric phase one's own culture is devalued, and another culture or way of life is romanticized as superior

denial of difference According to the developmental model of intercultural sensitivity (DMIS), individuals in this ethnocentric phase experience their own culture as the only 'real' one and other cultures are either not noticed or are understood in a simplistic way

developmental model of intercultural sensitivity (DMIS) A framework developed by Milton Bennett to depict the process of becoming interculturally sensitive; it describes various ways that individuals perceive and react to cultural difference

dialect A variety of language used in a specific region

direct communication The speaker's intentions and views are made clear by the use of explicit verbal messages and a forthright tone of voice

direct conflict style A verbally direct and confrontational approach to dealing with conflict

direct eye contact Looking into the eyes of one's communication partner

direct language The use of precise, explicit discourse

discourse Written or spoken communication

discourse analysis Investigations of spoken or written language in use

discourse community A group of people who share common social space and history as well as ways of communicating their values and goals

discourse competence The ability to understand and produce the range of spoken, written, and visual texts that are characteristics of a language

discrimination The prejudicial or unequal treatment of individuals based on their membership, or perceived membership, in a particular group or category

discriminatory language Derogatory terms, stereotypes, or generalizations about an individual or group (e.g., ethnic, gender, minority, religious)

discussion (conflict) style A verbally direct approach to conflict situations that is tempered by an emotionally restrained response

divergence The distancing of oneself from one's interlocutors by accentuating differences in one's speech (e.g., accent, communication style), identities, or nonverbal behaviors (e.g., gestures, personal distance)

diversity Differences among humans in terms of such aspects as culture, language, race, ethnicity, gender, socioeconomic status, age, physical/cognitive abilities, national origin, physical attributes, sexual orientation, ethnic affiliation, regional differences, religious beliefs, political beliefs, or other ideologies.

dual identity Possessing two identities (e.g., a local and global self)

dynamic conflict code-switching Adopting one's conflict style to meet the other conflict party's communication approach

dynamic (conflict) style The use of indirect strategies and emotionally intense expression to deal with major disagreements or conflicts

economic justice Economic policies that distribute benefits equally to all

education abroad Education outside one's home country (e.g., study abroad, internships, volunteering, directed travel with learning goals)

e-identity *See* internet identity

effective communication Communication that achieves the desired results from the perspective of both the sender and receiver

effective intercultural communication Intercultural communication that achieves the desired results from the perspective of both the sender and receiver

emblem (emblematic gesture) Direct nonverbal replacement for word(s) (e.g., OK signal in U.S.)

emblem of identity Markers of affiliation with a particular group (e.g., clothing, language, communication style, tattoos, flags)

emoticon Pictorial representations of facial expressions and other symbols that are meant to convey particular emotions

emotion regulation The culturally influenced process of modifying one's emotions and expressions in certain situations and contexts

emotional display The expression of one's emotions

emotional expression Observable verbal and nonverbal actions that convey emotions

emotional intelligence The ability to understand and manage one's own emotions and display sensitivity to others' feelings

emotional restraint Controlling the expression of one's emotions

emotionally expressive (conflict) style A conflict style that is characterized by emotionally confrontational discourse and expression

emotionally restrained style A conflict style that is characterized by emotional restraint and careful word choice

empathetic behavior Verbal and nonverbal actions that indicate that one is attending to the messages of others

empathy The ability to understand another person's feelings and point of view

employment discrimination *See* workplace discrimination

encoding The process of putting an idea or message into a set of symbols (e.g., words, gestures)

enculturation The learning of social norms, values, and practices in one's home environment from an early age

engagement (conflict) style A conflict style characterized by a more verbally direct and confrontational or direct approach

English hegemony The power and domination of English so that it brings about inequality and discrimination

Englishization The spread of English throughout the world

essentialism The belief that the attributes and behavior of socially defined groups can be explained by reference to cultural and/or biological characteristics believed to be inherent to the group (*See also* 'culture as nation' perspective, reductionism)

ethics Principles of conduct that help govern the behavior of individuals and groups

ethnic cleansing The systematic and violent removal of an ethnic or religious group from a particular territory

ethnic group A group of people who share a common cultural background and heritage

ethnic group strength The relative status or standing of a particular ethnic group within the context of the dominant society

ethnic identity An identity linked to one's perceptions and emotions regarding one's affiliation with one's own ethnic group(s)

ethnic proximity/distance The gap or degree of closeness between ethnic groups

ethnicity A socially defined category based on such aspects as common ancestry, cuisine, dressing style, heritage, history, language or dialect, physical appearance, religion, symbols, traditions, or other cultural factors

ethnocentric mindset A way of thinking which holds that one's cultural worldview and way of life are superior to all others

ethnocentricism A point of view that views one's group's standards as the best and judges all other groups in relation to them

ethnorelative mindset A way of thinking which is able to view another person's cultural worldview and way of life from that person's perspective

ethnorelativism The ability to understand a communication practice or worldview from another person's cultural frame of reference

expatriate An individual who lives and/or works outside their country of origin

expectancy violation theory A theory developed by Judee Burgoon that posits that individuals have culturally based expectations about how people should behave in a communicative event and when they do not perform as expected, miscommunication and negative perceptions may develop

extremism The holding of extreme or fanatical political, racial, or religious views

eye contact Direct visual contact with another person's eyes

eye movement The movement of the eye(s) that conveys meaning (e.g., rolling the eyes to convey contempt, direct gaze to convey interest)

face The public self-image that one wants others to recognize and support

face-giving *See* face-saving

face loss Experienced by individuals when they are not treated in a way that respects their preferred self-identities (e.g., position, status, self-image)

face maintenance The desire to project a positive image and avoid appearing weak or foolish

face management Communicating respect and a positive regard for self and others

face-saving Actions that protect or support an individual's self-image or reputation

face threat Challenges to an individual's self-image

face-threatening act Actions that cause someone to be humiliated

facework Verbal and nonverbal actions that individuals use to maintain or restore face loss and to uphold and honor face gain

facework strategies Steps taken to manage face

facework style Pattern of behaviors designed to manage face

facial expressions Facial movements that convey one's emotional state

fantasy identity A sense of belonging which centers on characters from science fiction movies, comic books, and anime

feedback Intentional or unintentional verbal or nonverbal signals which receivers give to a speaker to indicate they have processed what the speaker has said

feminine culture A culture that promotes gender equality, interpersonal contact, flexible balancing of life and work, and group decisions

femininity Gender roles that dictate certain roles and behaviors for women (e.g., modesty, tenderness, group decision making)

'friends with benefits' A casual sexual relationship among friends who are not romantically or emotionally involved

friendship A personal connection or affiliation forged between individuals

friendship network A type of social network, includes individuals who are very close personal friends, acquaintances (e.g., those who are more distant), and 'friends of friends'

functional fitness Knowing one's way around in the new environment

gay A person attracted to another person of the same sex (homosexual)

gay marriage *See* same sex marriage

gaze That act of looking at someone or something

gender One's identification as male, female, both male and female, or neither

gender conflict Conflict situations in which gender is a key factor

gender-crossing Beginning life as a male and assuming female behaviors and characteristics (or vice versa)

gender identity The meanings and interpretations individuals hold about their self-images and expected other-images of femaleness and maleness

gender socialization The process of developing gender identities in particular social and cultural contexts

gender stereotyping Simplistic overgeneralizations about the gender characteristics, differences, and roles of males and females

gendered identities An acknowledgment that multiple identities are shaped by one's gender and that social identities overlap

generalization A statement about common trends or elements in a group coupled with an understanding that more information is required to determine whether the generalization applies to a particular individual

genocide The targeted killing of a particular ethnic, religious group

gesture A movement or position of the hand, arm, body, head, or face that conveys an idea, opinion, or emotion

gift giving The ritual of providing gifts to business clients

glass ceiling An unseen barrier that keeps minorities and women from rising to more senior positions in organizations, regardless of their qualifications or achievements

global citizen An individual who identifies with being part of an emerging world community and whose actions contribute to building this community's values and practices

global citizenship Awareness of and commitment to societal justice for marginalized groups and care for the environment based on principles of equity, respect, and sharing

global citizenship activism Assuming an activist role to cultivate ethical values, principles, and practices characteristic of global citizenship

global civic engagement Recognition of local, state, national, and global community issues and response through actions such as volunteerism, political activism, and community participation

global competence Possessing an open mind while actively seeking to understand different cultural norms and expectations, and using this knowledge to interact, communicate, and work effectively outside one's environment

global competence model A framework developed by W. Hunter (2004) to help international educators prepare individuals for a diverse workforce and society that necessitates intercultural and global competencies

global consciousness Concern about the welfare of our planet

global English English as the international language for business negotiations, multinational organizations, scientific communication, diplomacy, tourism, e-communication, academic conferences, and international education, etc.

global ethics Basic shared ethical values, criteria, and attitudes for peaceful coexistence among humans

global identity An identity which affords an individual a sense of belonging or attachment to a worldwide culture and is often associated with the use of an international language

global knowledge An understanding of diverse cultures, languages, global events and concerns

global nomad An individual who has an international lifestyle (e.g., lives and works in more than one country for a long period of time), includes someone who has grown up in many different cultural contexts because his/her parents have frequently relocated (*See also* third culture individuals (TCIs), third culture kids (TCKs))

global-ready graduate An individual who is adequately prepared for a diverse workforce and society that necessitates intercultural and global competencies

global village The term coined by Marshall McLuhan in the 1960s to refer to the way the world is 'shrinking' as people become increasingly interconnected through media and other communication advances

global warming The long-term rising of the earth's atmosphere and oceans that is bringing about droughts and floods

globalization The growing tendency toward international interdependence in business, media, and culture.

globally competent person An individual who has knowledge of current events, the capacity to empathize with others, the ability to maintain a positive attitude, second language competence, and an appreciation of foreign ways of doing things

GLOBE cultural framework A framework developed by the Global Leadership and Organizational Behavior Effectiveness (GLOBE) project to measure the relationship between societal culture, organizational culture, and leadership

GLOBE dimensions Cultural differences in societal values and practices identified by the GLOBE project: institutional and group collectivism, gender egalitarianism, power distance, uncertainty avoidance, future orientation, assertiveness, performance orientation, and humane orientation

haptics The use of touch in communication, including the type of contact as well as its frequency and intensity

harassment Behaviors of an offensive or threatening nature

hedging The use of cautious or vague language

hegemony Domination through consent whereby the aims, ideas, and interests of the dominant class are so engrained that minorities go along with their own subordination and exploitation

heritage Aspects that are inherited or linked to the past (e.g., language, rituals, preferences for music, certain foods, dress)

heritage language learning The acquisition of a minority or indigenous language at home that typically is incomplete

heritage study abroad student A student who studies abroad in a location that is linked in some way (e.g., linguistically, culturally, historically) to his/her family or cultural background

heterosexuality Sexual attraction to members of the opposite sex

high-contact culture A kind of culture in which people display considerable interpersonal closeness or immediacy

high-context communication A style of communication in which most information is implicitly communicated through indirect, nonverbal, and mutually shared knowledge rather than expressed explicitly in words

high culture Culture that is linked to the arts (e.g., fine paintings, classical music, literature)

Hofstede's value-orientations framework The identification of systematic differences in national cultures by Geert Hofstede: power distance (PDI), individualism (IDV), uncertainty avoidance (UAI) and masculinity (MAS), with Confucian dynamism added later

Holocaust The mass slaughter of Jews and Gypsies by the Nazis during WWII

homogenization The loss of linguistic and cultural distinctiveness through the process of globalization

homosexuality Sexual attraction to members of the same sex

honor killing The murder of a young woman by relatives who believe that her actions (e.g., premarital sex, refusal to accept an arranged marriage) have brought dishonor on the family

honorifics Words (e.g., titles) or expressions in some languages that convey respect toward a social superior

horizontal-based facework Informal-symmetrical strategies/equal treatment

host communication competence The ability of a newcomer to decode and encode information in accordance with host cultural communication practices

host conformity pressure The extent to which the host environment challenges newcomers, implicitly or explicitly, to adopt local norms of behavior

host national A person from the host country

host receptivity The degree to which the host environment welcomes newcomers into its interpersonal networks and offers them support

human migration Physical movement by people from one place to another, sometimes over long distances

human rights The basic rights and freedoms to which all humans are entitled, e.g., the right to life and liberty, freedom of thought and expression, and equality before the law

human trafficking The illegal trade of human beings for sexual exploitation or forced labor

humor style The ways individuals use humor in particular contexts and situations

hybrid (mixed) identity A sense of self with elements from multiple cultures

identity An individual's self-concept or sense of self

identity confusion An individual who moves from one environment to another may feel caught between two distinct worlds

identity expansion The broadening of one's sense of self through exposure to new ideas and practices

identity intensity The degree of significance of a particular identity

identity labels Terms used to categorize individuals or groups

identity salience The degree to which an identity is prominent in a particular situation

identity shock (confusion) Inconsistent, conflicting self-images, which can involve the loss of communication competence and self-confidence in a new environment

ideology A system of ideas which promotes the interests of a particular group of people

illustrators Nonverbal actions that shape/illustrate what is being said (e.g., pointing)

imagined community Individuals *assume* that people they associate with their group follow norms, practices, and beliefs similar to their own

immigration Moving from one's home country to reside in another country

inclusiveness General acceptance and appreciation of cultural diversity within a community or society

independent self-construal A self-perception that puts an emphasis on one's autonomy and separateness from others

indirect communication A style of communication that emphasizes the use of subtle, indirect forms of expression (e.g., hints, suggestions)

indirect conflict style A non-confrontational style of conflict management

indirect language The use of expressions that suggest or hint at ideas

individual racism A person's attitudes, beliefs, and actions which support or perpetuate racism

individualism The tendency to emphasize the rights, identities, responsibilities, and independent action of the individual rather than the group (*See also* collectivism)

inequality Unequal access to power and resources

information and communications technology (ICT) The role of unified communications and the integration of telecommunication (e.g., wireless signals), computers, middleware as well as necessary software, storage and audiovisual systems, which allow users to create, access, store, transmit, and manipulate information

information technology (IT) The application of computers and telecommunications equipment to store, retrieve, transmit, and manipulate data

ingroup A social or cultural group to which a person psychologically identifies as being a member

ingroup bias Situations in which people give preferential treatment to those who are perceived to be in the same ingroup

ingroup favoritism (ingroup bias) Situations in which people give preferential treatment to those who are perceived to be in the same ingroup

ingroup favoritism principle A positive attachment to and predisposition for norms that are related to one's ingroup

ingroup members People with whom you feel emotionally connected to

innate Existing in one from birth

institutional racism A kind of racism that can result in differential access to the goods, services, and opportunities of society

integration Immigrants take steps to maintain their cultural heritage and original cultural identity while developing harmonious relationships with host nationals

integration of difference According to the developmental model of intercultural sensitivity (DMIS), individuals in this phase do not have a definition of self that is central to any particular culture and they are able to shift from one cultural worldview to another

integrative communication theory of cross-cultural adaptation A theory proposed by Young Yun Kim (2001) to depict an individual's gradual adaption to a new environment

intensity The importance or strength of something (e.g., identity, value)

intentional communication Two or more people consciously engage in interaction with a specific purpose in mind

interaction The process of encoding and decoding messages

interactive communication A two-way process involving the sending and receiving of messages

intercultural adroitness *See* behavioral adroitness

intercultural attitudes (*savoir être*) Curiosity and openness, readiness to suspend disbelief about other cultures and belief about one's own intercultural attitudes

intercultural awareness *See* cognitive awareness

intercultural citizenship The development of the competencies necessary to engage in political activity with people who have a different linguistic and cultural background

intercultural communication Interpersonal communication that involves interaction between people who have a different cultural (and often linguistic) background

intercultural communication competence The ability to communicate appropriately and effectively with individuals who have a different cultural (and often linguistic) background

intercultural communication research Investigations of interpersonal interactions involving people who have diverse linguistic and cultural backgrounds (also studies of the adjustment of newcomers in unfamiliar cultural settings)

intercultural communication skills The skills needed to interact appropriately and effectively in intercultural interactions (e.g., adaptability, empathy, cross-cultural awareness, intercultural mediation, intercultural sensitivity)

intercultural communicative competence The abilities needed to communicate effectively and appropriately with people who are linguistically and culturally different from oneself

intercultural competence The ability to communicate effectively and appropriately in intercultural situations, drawing on one's intercultural attitudes, knowledge, and communication skills

intercultural conflict The perceived or actual incompatibility of cultural values, situational norms, goals, face orientations, scarce resources, styles/processes, and/or outcomes in a face-to-face (or mediated) context

intercultural conflict competence The mindful management of emotional frustrations and conflict interaction struggles largely due to cultural, linguistic, or ethnic group membership differences

intercultural conflict style model Devised by Mitch Hammer (2005), this model is based on two core dimensions that he maintains are influenced by cultural values and beliefs: (1) the degree of directness when dealing with conflicts and (2) divergent ways of coping with the affective dimension of conflict interaction

intercultural cyber or online romance Romantic relationships formed online

intercultural education Education designed to help prepare students for responsible intercultural citizenship in our global community

intercultural effectiveness The ability to interact with people from a different cultural background in ways that are respectful and appropriate

intercultural facework competence The ability to manage vulnerable identity-based conflict situations appropriately, effectively, and adaptively

intercultural friendship A personal connection or affiliation forged between people who have a different cultural background

intercultural gay (lesbian) romance A romantic relationship between two males or two females

intercultural identity orientation A flexible, open identity that is not rigidly tied to one's home culture or the host culture

intercultural interaction Communication between individuals from different subcultures, speech communities, discourse communities, etc.

intercultural intimate relationship A union between individuals who differ in terms of sociocultural background, ethnicity, race, religion, nationality, class, etc.

intercultural marriage A social union or legal contract between individuals from different cultural backgrounds who may possess differing values, worldviews, and personal philosophies

intercultural mediator An individual who is able to interact appropriately and effectively with someone who has a different linguistic and cultural background (*See also* intercultural speaker)

intercultural mind/mindset An open mindset capable of understanding from within and from without both one's own culture and other cultures (*See also* ethnorelativism)

intercultural offline romantic relationships Intercultural romances that are initiated and largely maintained through face-to-face interactions

intercultural political competence The ability to take part in community activity and service with people who have a different linguistic and cultural background

intercultural relationship A relationship between individuals who have a different cultural background

intercultural romance A close interpersonal relationship between individuals from diverse cultural backgrounds who share a romantic love for each other

intercultural (affective) sensitivity A positive emotion that enables individuals to acknowledge and respect cultural differences

intercultural sensitivity Within the context of the developmental model of intercultural sensitivity (DMIS), the developmental process that impacts an individual's psychological ability to deal with cultural differences

intercultural speaker A competent, flexible second language speaker who is able to establish positive intercultural relationships by drawing on/recognizing multiple identities and ways of being in intercultural interactions

intercultural transformation A process of change in which border crossers develop a broadened sense of self that is more inclusive and intercultural

interculturality The forging of respectful, equitable links between individuals and groups from different cultural (and linguistic) backgrounds

interdependent self-construal A self-perception that emphasizes one's relatedness to other people

interethnic conflict (ethnic conflict) A conflict situation between individuals or groups affiliated with different ethnic groups, whereby ethnicity is salient

interethnic marriage Marriage between people with different ethnic backgrounds

interethnic relationship A relationship between individuals affiliated with different ethnic groups

interfaith (interreligious) conflict (religious conflict) Disputes or conflict situations between individuals or groups affiliated with different faiths, whereby religion is a salient issue

interfaith (interreligious) friendship An interpersonal relationship or friendship bond between individuals who are affiliated with a different religion

interfaith (interreligious) identity One's sense of belonging to a particular religious group

interfaith (interreligious) marriage A religious or civil union between partners professing different religions

intergenerational conflict Disputes between individuals or groups from different generations, whereby age is a salient issue

intergroup conflict Disputes that arise between two or more groups of people

intergroup relations Relationships between groups of people (e.g., ethnic, national, religious)

intermediary *See* mediator

international (world) citizen *See* global citizen

international conflict Disputes between different countries, conflict between people and organizations from different nation-states, intergroup conflicts within a nation that impact other nations

International Criminal Court (ICC) A body established by the United Nations Security Council to try crimes against humanity (*See also* crimes against humanity)

international education Education that takes place outside one's home country

international intercultural relationship The ties that develop between people that bridge national, cultural, and citizenship differences

International Phonetic Alphabet (IPA) An alphabetic system of phonetic notation based primarily on the Latin alphabet that serves as a standardized representation of the sounds of spoken language

international relationship The ties that develop between individuals that bridge national cultural and citizenship lines

internationalization Any systematic sustained effort designed to make higher education more responsive to the requirements and demands of an interconnected, global world

'Internationalization at home' (IaH) The embedding of international/intercultural perspectives into local education systems to raise the global awareness, cultural understanding, and intercultural competence of faculty and students

Internet identity An online social representation that an internet user (or group) establishes in websites and other Internet-based communities

interpersonal communication A form of communication that involves a small number of people interacting with one another, usually for the purpose of managing relationships

interpersonal communication skills Communication strategies and techniques that can enhance relationships and be enhanced through knowledge, practice, feedback, and reflection

interpersonal conflict A conflict or a struggle between two or more people who may or may not have a similar linguistic and cultural background

interpersonal distance The psychological 'bubble' or distance that individuals stand from one another in a particular cultural context

interpersonal relationship Close personal ties between two or more people that may range in duration from brief to enduring

interpreting The act of translating spoken communication

interracial communication Interactions between two people in a situational context where racial difference is a salient issue

interracial conflict Individuals in a conflict situation whereby race or racial difference is a source of friction

interracial friendship A relationship between friends who are affiliated with a different race

interracial marriage A union between individuals who are regarded as members of different races

interracial relationship A relationship between individuals who are regarded as members of a different race

interfaith (interreligious) friendship An interpersonal relationship or friendship bond between individuals who are affiliated with a different religion

intimate intercultural couple A romantic union between partners from different cultural backgrounds who may possess divergent beliefs, assumptions, and values

intimate space The closest 'bubble' of space surrounding a person, which is reserved for private situations with those who are emotionally close and if others invade this space, the individual may feel threatened.

intracultural conflict A struggle between individuals with a similar linguistic and cultural background

intracultural interactions The exchange of messages between people who share the same cultural background

intracultural relationship Interpersonal bonds that form between individuals who share the same linguistic and cultural background

intrapersonal communication Language use or thought directed at oneself

intraracial relationship Interpersonal relationships between individuals from the same socially constructed racial group

involuntary migrant An individual is forced to move to another country or region

islamophobia The fear, hatred of, prejudice, discrimination, or racist acts against the Islamic religion or Muslims in general

kinesics A broad category of nonverbal actions, which encompasses the study of body movement, e.g., body posture, gestures, facial expressions and eye movements

Kluckhohn and Strodtbeck's cultural orientation framework A model developed by Kluckhohn and Strodtbeck (1961), which identifies five problems or challenges that all cultures face and may respond to in diverse ways

knowledge (*savoirs*) Knowledge of social groups and related products and practices in one's own culture as well as that of one's intercultural communication partner

knowledge industries Organizations that require a workforce with advanced scientific or technological knowledge and skills

language A system comprised of vocabulary and rules of grammar that allows people to engage in verbal communication

language affiliation One's attitudes toward and feelings about the language

language anxiety Degree of nervousness when using a second language

language death A process whereby a language that has been used in a speech community gradually dies out (language extinction, linguistic extinction or linguicide)

language expertise An individual's degree of proficiency in a particular language

language fatigue Exhaustion that may arise when communicating in a second language

language identity The relationship between one's sense of self and the language one uses to communicate

language inheritance Being born into a family or community where a particular language is spoken

language maintenance The preservation of a language or language variety in a context where there is significant pressure for speakers to use the more prestigious or politically dominant language

language or linguistic rights The right to choose the language(s) for communication in private and public places; the right to one's own language in legal, administrative and judicial acts, language education, and the media

language shock (confusion) The challenge of understanding and communicating in a second language in an unfamiliar environment

language socialization The acquisition of linguistic, pragmatic, and other cultural knowledge through social experience

'large culture' Prescribed ethnic, national, and international entities

lesbian A female who is sexually attracted to another female

lingua franca A language which is used as the medium of communication between speakers who have a different first language

linguistic competence The ability to apply knowledge of the rules of a standard version of the language to produce and interpret spoken and written language

linguistic determinism The strong form of the Sapir-Whorf Hypothesis which posits that the language we speak *determines* our ability to perceive and think about objects

linguistic relativity The weaker version of the Sapir-Whorf hypothesis which indicates that the language one speaks *influences* thinking patterns but does not determine them

linguistic similarity The degree of similarity between one's first language and the host language

linguistic style An individual's speaking pattern, including such features as degree of directness or indirectness, pacing and pausing, word choice, and the use of such elements as jokes, sarcasm, figures of speech (e.g., metaphors, irony, hyperbole), stories, questions, silence, and apologies

local self A regional or national identity

localism A political philosophy which prioritizes the local, e.g., the local production and consumption of goods, local control of government, promotion of local culture/customs, a local identity

long-term relationships Interpersonal ties that endure many years

long-term sojourner An individual who lives abroad for many years

low-contact culture In this context, touch occurs in limited circumstances and too much contact is viewed as intruding on an individual's privacy or personal space

low-context communication Explicit verbal messages are the norm, e.g., most of the information is conveyed directly in the transmitted message in order to make up for ambiguity in the context

low culture ('popular culture' or 'folk culture') Elements in society that have mass appeal, e.g., the sports, food, dress, manners, and other habits of the 'common people' who have limited education, money, and sophistication

majority identity An individual's identification with the dominant or majority group

marginality Living at the edges or margins of society

marginalization An acculturation strategy in which immigrants do not nurture their cultural heritage (e.g., first language, traditions) and also resist interacting with people in the host society

masculine cultures Distinct differences in the gender roles and responsibilities of men and women

masculinity The extent to which distinct gender roles are valued and certain qualities are regarded as characteristic of males (e.g., achievement, ambition, aggression)

mass media A message created by a person or a group of people sent through a transmitting device to a large audience or market (e.g., television, movies, the Internet)

mediation The settlement or negotiation of a conflict or dispute by an independent person or third party

mediator An independent or third party who facilitates negotiations and dialogue between the disputants

mental ability identity One's identity which is linked to one's cognitive abilities (e.g., degree of intelligence), mental health (e.g., stable, depressed), and ability to function in everyday life

message What is conveyed verbally (e.g., in speech, writing) or nonverbally from one person (the sender) to one or more persons (the receiver(s))

micro-term sojourner People who stay abroad for less than three weeks

mindful awareness Recognition of our own and others' cultural ways of knowing and being and their effect on our intercultural interactions

mindful fluency The ability to tune into our own cultural, linguistic, and personal habitual assumptions in intercultural interactions and learn from the unfamiliar other

mindful intercultural communicator A flexible individual who displays affective, cognitive, and behavioral flexibility in intercultural interactions.

mindfulness Being aware of our own assumptions, ideas, and emotions and those of our communication partners

minimization of difference According to the developmental model of intercultural sensitivity (DMIS), in this transitional phase, elements of one's own cultural world view tend to be experienced as universal and while more open-minded, one has not yet developed a sophisticated grasp and appreciation of cultural differences that may affect intercultural communication

minority identity One's sense of belong to a minority group

misattributions Inaccurate assumptions

monochronic time orientation A time system in which tasks tend to be done simultaneously and time is segmented into precise, small units

monocultural mindset *See* ethnocentric mindset

monogamy The practice of being married to only one person at a time

monolingual Fluent in only one language

multicultural Interculturally competent in multiple cultural contexts

multicultural identity A psychological state of not possessing or being owned by a single culture

multilingual The ability to speak more than two languages

multilingual identity A hybrid sense of self linked to the use of multiple languages

multinational An individual, group, or organization affiliated with multiple countries

mutual-face concern Concern for both parties' images and the well-being of the relationship

mutual facework The process of constructing a shared sense of identity

national identity An individual's affiliation with and sense of belonging to a state or nation

negative face The desire to have autonomy and not be controlled by others

negative facework The degree to which individuals protect their own privacy and freedom from interference

negotiation A process by which individuals or groups resolve a dispute by holding discussions and coming to an agreement that is mutually acceptable

netizens Individuals who actively engage in online interactions

netspeak (chatspeak or cyber-slang) An informal, concise, and expressive style

noise (interference) Any disturbance or defect which interferes with or distorts the transmission of the message from one person to another

nonverbal codes All symbols that are not words, e.g., bodily movements, use of space and time, clothing and adornments, sounds other than words

nonverbal communication Communication without words through various channels (e.g., gestures, clothing, use of personal space, touch)

nonverbal cues All potentially informative behaviors that are not purely linguistic in content

nonverbal expectancy violation theory A theory developed by Judee Burgoon (1978), which suggests that during the primary socialization process we build up expectations (mostly subconscious) about how others should behave nonverbally in particular situations and contexts and we respond negatively when people do not conform to these norms

oculesics A subcategory of kinesics, which is concerned with eye behavior as an element of communication

olfactics (olfaction) The study of how we use and perceive odors, e.g., perfume, cooking spices, body scent, deodorant

openness An internal posture that is receptive or open to new practices

operational competence The capacity for individuals in an unfamiliar environment to employ verbal and nonverbal acts that are considered appropriate in specific social transactions

organizational conflict Disputes that can arise within an organization due to competing needs, values, beliefs, and interests

organizational identity A sense of attachment to organizations, whether in one's social, educational, religious, or professional life

other-face concern The concern or consideration for the image or 'face' of the other conflict party in the conflict situation

Othering The labeling and degrading of people who are different from oneself

Otherization *See Othering*

outgroup Groups with whom one feels no emotional attachment

outgroup members Individuals with whom one feels no emotional or psychological attachment

outsourcing The contracting out of an internal business process to a third party organization

pacifism An approach in which individuals strive to avoid conflict situations

paralanguage (vocalics) The study of vocal cues, the nonphonemic qualities of language which convey meaning in verbal communication, e.g., accent, emphasis, loudness, rate of speech

particularism The application in which individuals may be treated differently depending on their social status, interpersonal relationships, and obligations

perception Becoming aware of, knowing, or identifying by means of the senses through a process involving selection, organization, and interpretation

perceptual understanding An individual's degree of open-mindedness, sophisticated cognitive processing, and resistance to stereotyping

peripheral beliefs Beliefs related to personal perceptions and tastes

personal identity An individual's sense of self, which differentiates him or her from others, e.g., personal interests or hobbies, gender, age, personality

personal space The distance most people feel comfortable standing from others in public

personal strength The quality of an individual's resilience, patience, hardiness, and persistence

personality predisposition Interrelated personality resources

personality strength A strong sense of self and degree of relaxation in social situations

phonetics A branch of linguistics concerned with the study of the sounds of human speech

physical ability identity A sense of self which is limited to an individual's physical capabilities and limitations

physical appearance An individual's outward appearance, e.g., skin color, facial features, hairstyle, dress

physical features Body type, deformities, eye shape, gender, height, skin color, weight

platonic intercultural relationship An affectionate, non-sexual friendship between individuals of the opposite sex who have a different cultural background

pluralistic society A society composed of people from numerous cultural and ethnic backgrounds, whereby cultural diversity among citizens is acknowledged and encouraged

politeness Demonstrating awareness and respect for another person's public self-image/ behaving in ways that are deemed socially acceptable in a particular cultural context

polychronic time orientation A system whereby several things tend to be carried out simultaneously and there is a fluid approach is taken to scheduling time

polygamy The practice of having more than one spouse at a time

populism A political approach that seeks to appeal to ordinary people who believe that their concerns have been ignored by established groups in power

positive discrimination Education, business, or employment policies that aim to redress the negative, historical impact of discrimination by taking factors such as race, sex, religion, gender, or national origin into consideration in hiring/promotion situations (*See also* affirmative action)

positive face A person's desire to gain the approval of other people

positive facework Actions that emphasize the need for acceptance, respect, and inclusion

positivity An optimistic outlook that enables individuals to better endure stressful events

posture An individual's bodily stance, e.g., slouching, towering, legs spread, jaw thrust, shoulders forward, arm crossing

power Authority or strength

power distance The degree to which less powerful members of a society or organization expect and accept the unequal distribution of power among members

power imbalance A situation in which an individual, group, or nation has great influence, control, or domination over others

power relations An imbalance of power between individuals or groups

power status One's degree of power in relation to others

prejudice Dislike or hatred of a person or group formed without reason that is often rooted in a person's early socialization

preparedness The degree of readiness of an individual to undertake the process of cross-cultural adaptation

primary socialization *See* enculturation

process model of intercultural competence Darla Deardorff's (1984) model that depicts the complexity of the development of intercultural competence

professional identity An individual's sense of belonging in a particular profession, e.g., teaching, nursing, business

professional identity formation The developmental process in which individuals develop a sense of what it means to be a member of a particular profession, which distinguishes them from other professional groups

proxemics The social use of space in a communication situation

psychological adaptation Feelings of personal well-being and self-esteem

psychological adjustment The ability to adapt to new situations

psychological health Mental well-being

public space The area of space beyond which individuals perceive interactions as impersonal and relatively anonymous

race A social construction that historically has privileged people in positions of power

racial discrimination The prejudicial or unequal treatment of certain individuals based on their membership, or *perceived* membership, in a particular racial group or category

racial identity An identity linked to one's biological or genetic makeup, e.g., Black, White, biracial

racial quotas Numerical requirements for the selection and promotion of people from a group that is disadvantaged

racial segregation The separation of people into racial groups in daily life

racism The belief in the inherent superiority of a particular race or ethnic group and the perceived inferiority of other races or ethnic groups

racist discourse Talk which has the effect of sustaining racist practices

racist ideologies The beliefs underpinning racism

racists Individuals who believe that people who have a different skin color (or ethnicity) are inferior; they may convey their hatred and bigotry in their nonverbal and verbal behavior (oral and written) and in extreme cases commit violent, racist acts

rapport Mutual empathy and understanding

rapport-challenge orientation A desire to challenge or weaken harmonious relations between interlocutors

rapport-enhancement orientation A desire to strengthen or enhance harmonious relations between interlocutors

rapport maintenance orientation A desire to maintain or protect harmonious relations

rapport-neglect orientation A lack of concern for the quality of interpersonal relations perhaps because of a focus on the self

'rapport-talk' Conversations in which people seek confirmation, offer support, and try to reach consensus

receiver The person (or persons) who is receiving a message that is being sent, whether intentional or not.

receiver response The verbal or nonverbal reaction, if any, of a receiver after decoding the message.

reductionism The tendency to ignore variations within cultures (*See also* essentialism)

reentry The process of returning home after spending time abroad

reentry (reverse) culture shock The process of readjusting and reacculturating to one's own home environment after living in a different cultural setting

reflective mindset The ability to revisit and make meaning from one's experience

refugee An individual who flees to another country to escape danger or persecution

regional identity The part of an individual's identity that is rooted in his or her region of residence

register Linguistically distinct varieties in which the language is systematically determined by the context

regulators Action (e.g., hand gestures, head nods, touching) which influences the flow of a conversation

relational bonds The interpersonal connection between individuals, which serves as the basis of social groups and society as a whole

relational identity The coordination of the attitudes, actions, and identities of communication partners in a close relationship

relational interdependence Mutual dependence or reliance on one other

relational intimacy The closeness one feels and displays toward one's friends

relational maintenance Communication which aims to keep relationships operating smoothly and satisfactorily

religious conflict *See* interfaith conflict

religious identity *See* interfaith identity

religious identity formation The process by which individuals decide what their relationship to religion will be

religious pluralistic society A society where many different religious beliefs, concepts, and ideologies coexist

'report-talk' Discourse that transmits information

resilience An individual's ability to cope with stress and adversity

resocialization The process of readjusting one's attitudes and behaviors to feel at ease in one's home environment after a period away

respect The display of positive regard for an individual from a different cultural background

reverse culture shock *See* reentry culture shock

reverse discrimination Perceived unfair treatment of the majority (or group that is generally considered to have more power and privilege) by providing advantages to minorities or other groups, which are deemed underprivileged

rituals A set of actions or rites performed for symbolic meaning

role shock (confusion) Lack of knowledge and confusion about the norms of behavior in a new cultural setting (e.g., what actions are expected in particular situations)

romantic relationship An intimate relationship of a romantic nature

same sex (gay) marriage A marital union between members of the same sex

Sapir-Whorf hypothesis The notion that differences in the way languages encode cultural and cognitive categories determines or affects the way the users of a particular language view the world around them (*See also* linguistic determinism, linguistic relativity)

second language socialization The process by which novices in an unfamiliar linguistic and cultural context enhance their intercultural communication as they gain exposure to and reflect on the linguistic conventions, sociopragmatic norms, cultural scripts, and other behaviors that are associated with the new culture (*See also* acculturation)

segregation *See* separation

self-awareness Knowledge about one's self-identities, strengths, and weaknesses

self-disclosure The process of deliberately revealing information about oneself that would not normally be known

self-face concern Protective concern for one's image when one's face is threatened in a conflict situation

self-presentation Information we disclose about ourselves through our discourse and nonverbal acts (e.g., dress, accent, gestures)

self-shock *See* identity shock (confusion)

sender The person who is intentionally or unintentionally sending a message (verbally or nonverbally)

separation The acculturation strategy in which individuals strive to maintain their cultural heritage and avoid participation in the larger or dominant society in their new country

service learning (community-engaged learning) A structured learning experience which combines community service with guided reflection

sex The biological and physiological characteristics that define males and females

sexism The behavior, conditions, or attitudes that promote stereotypes of social roles based on gender

sexist language The use of words or phrases that unnecessarily emphasize gender, or ignore, belittle, or stereotype members of either sex

sexual harassment Bullying or coercion of a sexual nature

sexual identity How one thinks of oneself in terms of who one is sexually and romantically attracted to

sexual orientation An individual's desires, fantasies, and attachments to sexual partners

short-term relationship An interpersonal relationship that is very brief, e.g., lasting a few weeks or months

short-term sojourner An individual who stays abroad for a few months or less

similarity-attraction hypothesis The belief that we are drawn to people we perceive to be similar to us

simultaneous interpreting The act of interpreting while the speaker is talking (e.g., at international business conference or meeting)

skills of discovery and interaction (*savoir apprendre/faire*) The ability to acquire new knowledge of a culture and to operate this knowledge in real time communication.

skills of interpreting and relating (*savoir comprendre*) The ability to interpret a document or event from another culture, to explain it and relate it to documents or events from one's own

'small culture' The notion of culture is attached to small social groupings or activities wherever there is cohesive behavior rather than large groups (e.g., ethnic groups)

social categorization The way we group people into conceptual categories in order to make sense of our increasingly complex social environment

social class A social grouping of people based on common characteristics (e.g., economic resource, educational level) determined by society and reflecting a social hierarchy

social class prejudice Negative personal attitudes toward individuals of another class

social distance The degree of solidarity or closeness between people

social exclusion The marginalization or barring of certain individuals or groups (e.g., disabled individuals, minority members) from participating in a group's or society's social activities

social identity How we identify ourselves in relation to others based on what we have in common

social identity theory (SIT) A theory developed by Tajfel and Turner (1979, 1986) that suggests that individuals tend to categorize people in their social environment into ingroups and outgroups

social inclusion The act of giving all people in society an opportunity to participate regardless of their background or characteristics (e.g., mental or physical disability, race, language, culture, gender, age, social status, etc.)

social justice The fair administration of laws to treat all people as equal regardless of ethnicity, religion, race, language, gender, origin, etc.

social marker An indicator of one's social status or position in society (e.g., accent, material possessions, level and source of education)

social media Internet-based applications that build on the ideological and technological foundations of Web 2.0 and permit the creation and exchange of content generated by users

social network The multiple web of relationships an individual forms in a society with other people who he or she is bound to directly or indirectly through friendship or other social relationships

social networking sites (SNSs) Web-based services that allow people to develop a public or semi-public profile and communicate with each other (e.g., Facebook, Twitter)

social penetration theory (SPT) A theory proposed by Irwin Altman and Dalmas Taylor (1973) which suggests that as self-disclosure increases in depth (degree of intimacy on a particular topic), amount, and breadth (the number of topics about which one self-discloses to one's communication partner), our relationships become more intimate

social responsibility The perceived level of interdependence and social concern for others, the society, and the environment

social sanctions The measures used by a society to enforce its rules or norms of acceptable behavior

social space The formal distance between individuals in a social setting or, more broadly, cultural space (e.g., the global community)

social status The honor or prestige attached to one's position or standing in society

socialization The process by which individuals learn to internalize and follow the conventions of behavior imposed by a society or social group (*See also* enculturation)

sociocultural adaptation Competence in dealing with social and cultural dimensions in one's environment

socioemotional support The psychological assistance provided by friendship circles, intracultural and intercultural relationships, and family members

sociolinguistic competence The ability to communicate verbally and nonverbally in ways that are deemed appropriate in a particular sociocultural setting

sociopragmatic awareness The awareness of how and why language is used in certain ways in social situations in a particular cultural context

sociopragmatic competence The ability to use language appropriately in specific social situations in a particular cultural context

sociopragmatic expectancy violation The use of language or nonverbal actions that are perceived to be inappropriate in relation to one's status or role identity in a particular social and cultural context

sociopragmatic norms Rules governing the appropriate use of discourse in specific social situations in a particular cultural context

sojourn A period of time spent living in a cultural setting different from one's home environment

sojourner An individual who is temporarily in a new environment for a specific purpose (e.g., study, work, business) and typically for a certain length of time (e.g., several days, months, years)

speech act The minimal unit of analysis of conversational interaction

speech community A group of individuals who use the same variety of a language and share specific rules for speaking and for interpreting speech

speech illustrators Gestures or movements that illustrate or emphasize a verbal message, even though the user may not be conscious of their use

speech style The way we talk, such as our use of vocabulary, syntactic patterns, volume, pace, pitch, register, and intonation

speech style preference The speech we are most comfortable using in interactions

stereotype A preconceived idea that attributes certain characteristics (e.g., personality traits, level of intelligence), intentions, and behaviors to all the members of a particular social class or group of people

stereotyping A strong tendency to characterize people from other cultural backgrounds unfairly, collectively, and usually negatively

stress-adaptation-growth dynamic Young Yun Kim's (2001) notion that acculturative stress (e.g., language and culture shock) can prompt intercultural learning and gradually lead to adaptation in border crossers

study abroad A subtype of education abroad that leads to progress toward an academic degree at a student's home institution; typically, this includes such activities as classroom study, research, internships, and/or service learning.

style shifting The process of adjusting or changing from one style of speech to another within the same language

subculture *See* co-culture

subtractive bilingualism A process whereby a second language is added at the expense of the first language and culture (*Also see* additive bilingualism)

superstition A belief, half-belief, or practice which is not based on scientific evidence

surface-level diversity Differences that are easily recognized through a quick assessment of physical characteristics, e.g., gender, age, race, ethnicity, etc.

symbol An artifact, word(s), gesture, sign, or nonverbal behavior that stands for something meaningful to individuals in a particular context

synchronous communication Direct communication whereby all parties involved in the communication are present and interacting at the same time (e.g., Skype, online chat rooms, Internet relay chat)

systemic racism The mistreatment of people of a particular race, religious, or ethnic group on a wide scale

telecommunication Communication at a distance via technological means, e.g., through electrical signals or electromagnetic waves

third culture building The blending of different cultural identities and practices to form an identity that is unique to the parties involved, i.e. the identity of a multicultural family

third culture individuals (TCIs) Individuals who have spent a significant part of their developmental years outside their parents' home country

third culture kids (TCKs) *See* third culture individuals (TCIs)

third gender People who are categorized as neither male nor female, either by themselves or by social consensus

time perception Views about such aspects as punctuality, willingness to wait, and number of tasks to carry out at the same time

tolerance Going along with behaviors that one does not necessarily respect or accept

tolerance of ambiguity One's ability to cope with situations that are not clear

tourism The movement of people to countries or places outside their usual environment for personal, recreational or business/professional purposes

tourist Visitors who usually stay abroad for only a short time (e.g., a few days to several weeks or months) to sight-see, enjoy themselves, and get a taste of a different linguistic and cultural environment

traditions The transmission of customs or beliefs from generation to generation

transactive communication People are consciously directing their messages to someone else

transformation The act or process of change

transformational learning theory A theory developed by Jack Mezirow (1994, 2000) which posits that adults who engage in critical reflection and self-examination may experience significant personal growth

transgender People whose gender identities are different from the expectations and social norms associated with their biological sex

transition shock (confusion) The state of loss, disorientation, and identity confusion that can occur when one enters a new situation, job, relationship, or physical location, e.g., the strain of adjusting to the unfamiliar

translation The act or process of translating from one written language to another

transnational competence *See* global competence

transnational identity See global identity

turn-taking The use of nonverbal or verbal means to start and finish a turn in a conversation

U-curve adjustment model A theory of cultural adaption which suggests that border crossers go through several phases as they adjust to a new cultural environment

uncertainty avoidance Feeling threatened by ambiguous situations, individuals take steps to avoid uncertainty and return to the familiar

uncertainty reduction theory (URT) A theory developed by Berger and Calabrese (1975) that posits that the greater our ability to predict and explain our communication partners' behavior, the greater the chance that our relationships will become more intimate

unintentional communication Messages that are unintentionally communicated to a receiver

universal Of, relating to, extending to, or affecting the entire world or all within the world; a worldwide phenomenon

universalism The application of the same rules for everyone regardless of their status or relationship

valence The positive or negative nature of something (e.g., values)

value Shared ideas about what is right or wrong

value orientation frameworks Models that identify, describe, and contrast the dominant value system in various cultures

vertical-based facework Formal-asymmetrical strategies/deferential treatment

virtual (cyber) identity *See* Internet identity

vocalics *See* paralanguage

voluntary migrant An individual who willingly chooses to settle abroad

W-curve adjustment model An extended version of the U-curve model of adjustment that suggests that sojourners go through predictable phases when adapting to a new cultural situation and returning home

ways of being A characteristic or frequent manner of acting or thinking

Web 2.0 Novel ways of creating, collaborating, editing, and sharing user-generated content online

'whole person' development The nurturing of emotional intelligence and resourcefulness, interpersonal communication skills, intercultural competence, independence, and maturity

willingness to communicate (WTC) An individual's readiness to enter into discourse at a particular time with a specific person or persons

work ethic A set of values based on hard work and discipline

workplace discrimination Unfair practices in hiring, promotion, job assignment, termination, and compensation

world citizen *See* global identity, global citizen

World Englishes Varieties of English in the world

worldview Our overall way of looking at the world, which serves as a filter to help us make sense of humanity

xenophobia An irrational fear of foreigners or strangers

Index

accent 3, 41, 42, 56, 67, 72, 82, 116, 118, 120, 124, 126, 127, 128, 137, 147, 148, 152, 186, 195, 214, 221
acceptance of difference 313; *see also* developmental model of intercultural sensitivity (DMIS)
accommodation (conflict) style 257
acculturation: definitions of 175; factors affecting 189–91; long-term *vs.* short-term adaptation 172–203; patterns 175–8; and second language socialization 175; strategies 176–8; temporary-permanent stays 172–4; transition shock 178–203
acculturative stress 178, 182, 202
acquaintance 223
active listening 219, 240, 320
'acts of identity' 127
adaptation 313; *see also* developmental model of intercultural sensitivity (DMIS)
adaptation to difference 313; *see also* developmental model of intercultural sensitivity (DMIS)
adaptor 93
additive bilingualism 128
affect display 91, 93
affective competence 202
affective conflict 248
affective display *see* affect display
affective sensitivity 311; *see also* intercultural sensitivity
affirmative action 156
age identity 132–4
ageism 150
ageist language 162
ageist stereotyping 150
Allport, G.W. 151, 165, 234
Anderson, B. 46–7

anti-Christian sentiments 160
anti-discrimination legislation 156
anti-racist legislation 212
anti-Semitism 159
anxiety/uncertainty management (AUM) theory 229–30, 233, 253
appearance message 103
'appropriate' communication 63, 64, 68, 82, 90, 146, 220, 252, 255–6, 278
'appropriate' intercultural communication 23, 80, 107, 185, 220, 230, 248–9, 254, 259, 303, 305, 308, 309, 312, 313, 314, *318*, 321, 322; *see also* sociopragmatic, competence
arbitrariness feature of language/nonverbal codes 61–2, 85
artifacts, cultural 27, 103
ascribed identity 116
ascription 116, 127
assertiveness 84, 286
assimilation 177
asylum seeker 171; *see also* refugee
asynchronous communication 224, 225
attitudes 152, 308; *see also* intercultural attitudes (*savoir être*), prejudicial attitudes
audience design framework 72–3; *see also* speech style
avoidance strategy 190; *see also* uncertainty avoidance
avoidance style of conflict management 256
avowal 116, 127–8
avowed identity 116, 127–8

behavioral flexibility 312, 320
behavioral (intercultural) adroitness 311, 312
behavioral uncertainty 253
beliefs: cultural 29; peripheral 29; religious 29, *30*, 32–6; superstitions 29; *see also* tradition; worldview

Bell, A. 72–3
Bennett, M.J. 312–13
Berry, J.W. 176–8
best friend 224
biases 150–2, 161–4, 290–1
bicultural 194, 198, 322
biculturalism 194, 198, 322; raising bi/
    multicultural children 39, 129, 177, 246
bilingual identity 118, 126, 128–30, 198, 214,
    271, 322
bilingualism 8, 128, 136, 214, 322; additive
    118, 126, 128; and biculturalism 198, 322;
    subtractive 128; see also code-mixing
biracial 212
bisexuality 132, 217
body language 58, 81, 88, 90, 91–8; see also
    kinesics
Buddhism 19, 20, 29, 32, 33, 34, 35, 135
Burgoon, J.K. 235, 252
business acumen 274
business ethics 290
business etiquette 280
business netiquette 280
business protocol 280
Byram, M. 305

casual friend 223, 224
casual intercultural dating 238
casual intercultural relationship 238
channel of communication 56
Chen and Starosta's model of intercultural
    communication competence 311–12
Chen, G.M. 311–12
Christianity 19, 33, 34–5
chronemics 104–5
citizenship: definitions of 297; global 298–303;
    intercultural 307–8; and sense of belonging 295
classism 214
class prejudice see social class, prejudice
climate 18
climate change 18, 19
close friend 223–4
co-culture 41
code-mixing 5, 270–1; and dual identity 128, 271
code of ethics 19–22
code-switching 72
cognitive competence 202
cognitive conflict 248

cognitive (intercultural) awareness 311–12
cognitive uncertainty 253
cohabitation 239
collaborating (conflict) style 256
collectivism 74–5, 113, 255, 256, 258, 259, 283, 284
communication, human: adaptability 262;
    appropriate 220; competence 220; components
    of 55–6; conflict styles 49, 55, 68–70; as
    cultural 68–70; definitions of 54–5; dynamic
    dimension of 54, 57; effective 220; high-
    context 74–5, 282–3; as intentional and
    unintentional 55, 63–4; interactive-transactive
    54, 57–8; low-context 74–5, 76, 282–3;
    nonverbal (see nonverbal communication);
    pervasiveness of 55, 68; and power 55, 66–8;
    as a process 54, 56–7; process model 55–6;
    properties of 56–70; situated and contextual
    55, 64–6; styles 18, 36, 71–6; symbolic
    dimension of 58–63
communication accommodation theory (CAT)
    71–2, 127, 214, 262
communication style typology 74–5
communication style typology, limitations of
    75–6
communicative competence 37, 309; see also
    intercultural (communicative) competence;
    sociopragmatic, competence
community of practice (CoP) 138, 193
computer-mediated communication (CMC) 221,
    224–7, 232
conational 222
conflict: affective 248; cognitive 248;
    cultural dimensions of 251–5; definitions
    of 245; domains; and face/facework
    254, 258–60 (see also conflict face
    negotiation theory); facework competence
    260; fluency 18; interaction style 256;
    intercultural conflict competence 260–2;
    managing language and intercultural
    conflict situations 262–4; mediation
    257; nature and characteristics of 245–6;
    negotiation strategies 252, 254, 257 (see
    also conflict face negotiation theory);
    script 249, 252–3, 260; sources of 245–6;
    styles 255–8; types of 247–51
conflict face negotiation theory 258–60
conflict facework competence 260
conflict interaction style 256

conflict management practices 291–2; *see also* conflict management style

conflict management style 259, 291–2

conflict types: gender 251, 255; intercultural 248–9; interethnic 250; interfaith (interreligious) 250–5; intergenerational 251; intergroup 247–8; interpersonal 249; interracial 249–50; international 250; intracultural 247; organizational 248

Confucian dynamism 286

consecutive interpreting 276

constructive communication skills 261

constructive conflict communication skills 261

contact hypothesis 234

contextual elements in communication: cultural 65; environmental 65; perceptual 65; physiological 65; psychological 65; relational 65; situational 65; social 66; sociorelational 66; temporal 66

convergence 72, 127, 214, 262; *see also* communication accommodation theory (CAT)

corporate culture 278

'crimes against humanity' 250

critical approach to intercultural business research/practice/education 288

critical cultural awareness/political education (*savoir s'engager*) *310*, 311

critical discourse analysis 48

critical intercultural communication 3, 47, 288

critical intercultural speaker 307

critical reflection 115, 311, 313–14, *318*, 320

cross-cultural communication research 3

cultural awareness 30–5; *see also* cognitive (intercultural) awareness

cultural difference frameworks 282–8; alternative approaches to 288; the GLOBE cultural framework 286; Hall's dimensions of cultural difference 282–3; Hampden-Turner and Trompenaars' value dimensions 283–4; Hofstede's value-orientations framework 284–6; impact on global business, research, and practice 287; Kluckhohn and Strodtbeck's cultural orientations framework 283; limitations and dangers 287–8

cultural display rules 96

cultural distance 189

cultural fluency 18

cultural identity formation 121

cultural intelligence 261

cultural maintenance 176

cultural membership 2, 3, 46, 121, 161

cultural norms 36, 39

cultural relativism 147

cultural schema 36–7, 63, 64, 74

cultural script 37–9, 42, 58, 63–4

cultural similarity 189, 286

cultural socialization *see* enculturation

cultural space 49

cultural synergy 273

culture: definitions of 27; facets of 28–49; text's conception of 49

'culture as nation' perspective 3, 44, 47, 287, 312; *see also* essentialism; reductionism

culture broker 277

culture brokering 277

culture-general intercultural education 306

'culture of learning' 64, 184–5, 196, 197–8

culture-sensitive knowledge 260

culture shock (confusion); coping with 203–4; degree of language and culture shock (confusion) 189–91; positive and negative effects 191–3; and reentry 194, 198–200; sources of language and culture shock (confusion) 180–8; stages of culture shock and adjustment 193–201; stress-adaptation-growth dynamic 202; symptoms 188–9; U-curve adjustment model 193–4; W-curve adjustment model 194–200

culture-specific intercultural education 306

cyberculture 139

cyber friendship 224–6, 227

cyber identity *see* internet identity

Deardorff, D.K. 308–9, 314–15, 317

decoding of messages 56

decorative ornamentation 103

deculturation 202

deep level diversity 269

defense against difference 313; *see also* developmental model of intercultural sensitivity (DMIS)

defense/reversal 313; *see also* developmental model of intercultural sensitivity (DMIS); polarization/defense/reversal

denial of difference 313; *see also* developmental model of intercultural sensitivity (DMIS)

developmental model of intercultural sensitivity
(DMIS) 312–14, 316

dialect 42

direct communication 75, 76

direct conflict style 256

direct eye contact 65, 97

direct language 277

discourse 48

discourse analysis 4; *see also* critical discourse
analysis

discourse community 41, 43, 259

discourse competence 310

discrimination: combatting discrimination
155–6; definition of 152; discriminatory
language 154–5; discriminatory practices 155;
employment 251, 281; gender 251, 281–2; and
identity labels; positive (affirmative action)
156; racial 152; sources of 155; types of
152–4; workplace 251, 281

discussion style of conflict 256–7

divergence 72, 127, 214; *see also* communication
accommodation theory (CAT)

diversity 269; deep-level 269; multicultural 269;
surface-level 269; *see also* pluralistic society

diversity benefits in the workplace 271–5;
enhanced relations with diverse customers/
clients 273–4; enhanced reputation and
competitive advantage 274; increased
adaptability and productivity 272–3;
international reach 274; personal growth and
intercultural development 274–5; synergy and
enhanced creativity 273

diversity challenges in the workplace
275–82; clash in values 278; conflict
278–9; conflicting communication styles
277–8; ethnocentricism and assumptions
of similarities 281; gender differences
280; language barrier 275–6; opposition
to change 279; prejudicial attitudes,
discrimination, harassment, and racism
281–2; religious differences 280; resistance
to integration 279; sociocultural differences
280–1; translation/interpreting limitations
276–7; variations in emotional display/
nonverbal codes 278

duration (in speech) 90

dynamic (conflict) code-switching 262

dynamic (conflict) style 256–7

economic justice 302

education abroad 10–11, 169–71, 172, 174, 291,
203–4, 312, 317; *see also* study abroad

effective communication 220, 322

effective intercultural communication 220,
308, *318*

e-identity *see* internet identity

emblem (emblematic gesture) *91*, 93–4; culture-general/
universal 94; culture-specific *95*

emblem of identity 125

emic perspective 308

emoticon 85

emotional display 87–9, 94–7, 236, 278

emotional expression 257; *see also* emotional
display

emotional expressiveness 257

emotional intelligence 162, 236

emotionally expressive (conflict) style 256, 257

emotionally restrained (conflict) style 256, 257

emotional restraint 257

emotion regulation 89, 236

empathy 146, 229, 259, 300, 303, *318*, 321–2

employment discrimination 281

encoding of messages 55, *56*

enculturation 28–9, 36; *see also* enculturation;
language, socialization; nonverbal
communication

engagement (conflict) style 256, 257

English as a lingua franca xv, 6, 214, 217, 224,
225, 226, 237, 269, 270

English as an international language 5, 69, 214,
270

English hegemony 270

Englishization 5, 7, 9, 10, 13, 14, 270–1; *see also*
English hegemony; English as a lingua franca

environmental context 56, *65*, 202

essentialism 44, 45, 76, 144, 288

ethical global citizens 317–18; *see also* global
ethics

ethical intercultural communication 22, 23–4, 321

ethics 19–22, 31; *see also* global ethics

ethnic cleansing 15, 250

ethnic conflict *see* interethnic conflict

ethnic group 40–1

ethnic group strength 202

ethnic identity 121, 123–4

ethnicity 121–4, 212, 250; *see also* ethnic
identity; ethnic group

ethnic proximity/distance 202; *see also* cultural distance
ethnic violence 250
ethnocentricism 43–4; overcoming ethnocentricism and identity biases 321ethnocentric mindset 44, 65, 146, 147, 281; *see also* ethnocentricism; monocultural mindset
ethnocentric stage of intercultural development 313; *see also* developmental model of intercultural sensitivity (DMIS)
ethnorelative mindset 45, 161–2, 164, 321; *see also* ethnorelativism
ethnorelative stage of intercultural development 313, 314; *see also* developmental model of intercultural sensitivity (DMIS)
ethnorelativism 44–5, 146–7, 161–2, 164, 192, 235, 281, 312, 321
etic perspective 308
expatriate 172
expectancy violation theory 105–6, 108, 235, 252, 253, 259; *see also* nonverbal expectancy violation theory
eye contact 58, 65, 75, 84, 90, 97–8, 155, 196; *see also* oculesics
eye movement 91; *see also* oculesics

face 236, 254, 258–60, 261, 263, 291; *see also* conflict face negotiation theory
face-giving *see* face-saving
face loss 259
face management 258
face rapport/maintenance 259
face-saving 286
face threat 259
face-threatening act 259
facework: definition of 254; horizontal 259; and (intercultural) conflict competence 259, 260; and intercultural conflict management 236, 259, 261 (*see also* intercultural conflict); mutual 230; negative 254; positive 254; and rapport 259; strategies 258–9, 260, 261, 263; style 260, 261; vertical-based 259
facial expressions 82, 83, 84, 85, 86, 89, 91, 94–7; *see also* kinesics
feedback (verbal/nonverbal) 23, 56
feminine cultures 285
femininity 131, 285

'friends with benefits' 238
friendship: cultural perceptions of 222–4; computer-mediated (cyber) 224–6; definitions of 223–4; *see also* intercultural friendship; interpersonal relationship; social networks
functional fitness 203

gay *see* homosexuality
gay marriage *see* same sex (gay) marriage
gaze 97
gender: and communication styles 67, 71, 130, 131, 216; conflict 251, 255; definition of 130; differences 216; discrimination 152, 153, 155–6, 251, 281–2; identity 2, 127, 130–1; and nonverbal communication 94, 97, 100, 101, 102; roles 16–17, 130, 285; *vs.* sex 130; socialization 67, 71, 130–1, 185, 216; stereotyping 149
gender-crossing 131
gender(ed) identities 130–1
generalization 13–16, 67, 71, 130, 131, 144, 147–8, 149, 151, 161, 258, 284; *see also* stereotyping
genocide 144, 160, 250
gestures 54, 55, 58, 62, 82, 84, 85, 87, 91, 93–4
gift giving 280–1
Giles, H. 71–2
glass ceiling 282
global business and English 7, 270–1, 288
global citizen 297–302, 318–23; *see also* global citizenship
global citizenship: activism 302–3; competency 303–4; conceptions/definitions of 298–302; conceptual model 298, *299*
global civic engagement 298
global competence 298, 303–4
global competence model 304
global consciousness 300
global English 10, 226, 303; *see also* English as an international language; Englishization
global ethics 302
globalization: definitions of 5; and diversity in the workplace 269; and English 5, 270–1 (*see also* Englishization; global English); and homogenization 7; and imperatives to study intercultural communication 5–8; and internationalization 8–9; resistance to 16; *see also* localism; populism; xenophobia

global knowledge 303
global nomad 129, 172, 200, 232; *see also* third
    culture individual (TCI)
global-ready graduates 304
global village 12
global warming 18, 246, 298, 302
GLOBE cultural framework 286
GLOBE dimensions 286
group membership 103, 114, 120, 145–6,
    229, 260
Gullahorn, J.E. 194
Gullahorn, J.T. 194

Hall, E.T. 74–6, 99–102, 282–3
Hall's dimensions of cultural difference 74–6,
    99–102, 104–5, 282–3
Hammer, M. 256–8
Hampden-Turner and Trompenaars' value
    dimensions 283–4
Hampden-Turner, C. 283–4
haptics 101–2
harassment 281–2; *see also* sexual, harassment
hedging 130, 277
hegemony, cultural 47; *see also* English
    hegemony
heritage 300; *see also* ethnicity
heritage language learning 128
heritage study abroad student 200
heterosexuality 132
heterosexual orientation 216–17
Hinduism 20, *30*, 32–3, 34, 35, *173*, *213*
high-contact cultures 101
high-context communication 74–5
high culture 27
Hofstede, G.H. 284–6
Hofstede's value-orientations framework 284–8
Holliday, A. 3, 41, 44, 48, 76, 145, 287
Holocaust 160
homogenization 7
homosexuality 132, 217
homosexual orientation 132
honeymoon period 193–5
honorifics 39, 68, 125–6, 133, 277
horizontal-based facework 259
host communication competence 202
host conformity pressure 202
host receptivity 202
humane orientation 286

human migration 14–15
human nature orientation 283
human rights 152–3, 156, 157, 159, 246, 302, 323
human trafficking 15
humor style 235–6

identity: avowed and ascribed 116–17; biases
    144, 161–4 (*see also* Othering); characteristics
    of 112–18; contested 48, 117, 122–3, 127–8,
    140, 234–5; definitions of 112; development
    of 112–13; dynamic nature 114–16; emblem
    125; expansion 175, 192–3, 205, 314;
    expressed verbally and nonverbally 118;
    intensity 117–18; and language 118, 126,
    126–30, 198, 214, 271, 322; multifaceted
    (multiple and complex) 114; reconstruction
    (*see* identity, expansion); salience 117; shock
    (confusion) (self shock) 180; and social
    categorization (*see* identity, biases; Othering)
identity types; age 118–40; bilingual 118, 126,
    128–30, 198, 214, 271, 322; class 124–6;
    cultural 120–1; dual 271; ethnic 121, 123–4;
    gender(ed) 130–1; global 115, 137, 298,
    300, 314; group 116, 124–6, 133, 146 (*see*
    also ingroups, outgroups); hybrid (mixed)
    41, 43, 114, 128, 200, 298, 312, 314; internet
    139; language 126–8; majority 123; mental
    ability 134–5; minority 123; multicultural
    128–30; multilingual 128–30; national 136;
    organizational 138; personal 120; physical
    ability 134–5; professional 138–9; racial
    121–3; regional 136–7; religious 134; sexual
    131–2; social 120; virtual (cyber and fantasy)
    139–40
ideology xvi, 48, 121, 144, 159
illustrator 93
imagined community 46–7, 115
immigration 15, 17, 173, 250
inclusion 215, 254; *see also* social inclusion;
    inclusiveness
inclusiveness 215; *see also* social inclusion
independent self-construal 113
indirect communication 74–5, 76, 87, 91, 152,
    190, 254, 255, 256, *257*, 261, 263, 277; *see*
    also high-context communication
indirect conflict style 254, 255, 256, 257, 261, 263
indirect language 277; *see also* high-context
    communication; indirect communication

individualism 74–5, 113, 259, 283, 284, 285
individualistic cultures 74, 75
individual racism 157
inequality 7, 131, 150, 159, 270, 280, 301
information and communications technology (ICT) 12
information technology (IT) 12
ingroup-favoritism (ingroup bias) 146
ingroup favoritism principle 146
ingroups 42, 63, 68, 72, 113, 120, 124–5, 132, 145–6, 164, 229, 234. 271
institutional racism 157
integration 177, 193, 279
integration of difference 313, 316; see also developmental model of intercultural sensitivity (DMIS)
integrative communication theory of cross-cultural adaptation 201–3
intentional communication 63
interactional sociolinguistics 288
interactive communication 54, 57–8
intercultural adroitness see behavioral (intercultural) adroitness
intercultural attitudes (savoir être) 310
intercultural awareness see cognitive (intercultural) awareness
intercultural citizenship 307–8
intercultural communication, defined 1
intercultural communication research 3–4
intercultural communication skills 220, 303, 318
intercultural (communicative) competence: definitions of 8, 220; and intercultural citizenship 307–8; and second language proficiency 315–17; see also nonverbal intercultural communicative competence
intercultural competence models 309–15; Byram's model of intercultural communicative competence 309–11; Chen and Starosta's model of intercultural communication competence 311–12; the developmental model of intercultural sensitivity (DMIS) 312–14; the process model of intercultural competence 314–15
intercultural conflict: competence 260–2; cultural dimensions 251–5; definition of 248–9; and face/facework 254, 258–60; management 256; managing language and intercultural conflict situations 262–4; mediation 257; negotiation 257; styles 255–8

intercultural conflict competence components: communication adaptability 262; constructive conflict communication skills 261; culture-sensitive knowledge 260; mindfulness 261
intercultural conflict cultural dimensions: ambiguity and uncertainty 253; differing perceptions and understandings of conflict 254–5; face and identity needs 254; language and nonverbal behaviors 253–4; mismatched expectations 252–3
intercultural conflict style model 256–8
intercultural conflict types: gender 251; interethnic (ethnic) 250; interfaith (interreligious) 250–1; intergenerational 251; international 250; interracial 249–50
intercultural cyber or online romance 238–9
intercultural dating 211, 212, 237, 238, 239
intercultural education 11, 17, 306; see also culture-general intercultural education; culture-specific intercultural education
intercultural facework competence 259
intercultural friendship: barriers to 231–7; benefits of 217–20; definition of 221; cultural perceptions of friendship 222–4; building/enhancing 226–31, 240–1; language and intercultural cyber friendship 224–6; and social networks 221
intercultural gay (lesbian) romance 238
intercultural identity orientation 203
intercultural intimate relationship 211; see also intercultural friendship; intercultural marriage
interculturality 314
intercultural marriage 239, 240–1
intercultural mediator 261, 307
intercultural mindset 315–16
intercultural offline romantic relationship 239
intercultural political competence 307
intercultural relationship benefits 217–20; acquisition of new skills and pursuits 219–20; the breaking down of stereotypes 218–19; enhanced appreciation of diversity 221; heightened self-awareness 218; more sensitivity towards identity issues 219; more understanding of different ways of being 218; the refinement of intercultural communication skills 220
intercultural relationships: benefits of 217–21; crossing boundaries in 211–17; definition of

211; and diverse social networks 221–2; and interpersonal communication 210–11; *see also* intercultural friendship; intercultural romance and marriage

intercultural relationship types/boundaries crossed: ability differences 215–16; age differences 215; gender differences 216; interethnic 212; interfaith (interreligious) 213; interracial 212; international 212–13; language differences 214–15; multifaceted 217; sexual orientation 216–17; social class differences 213

intercultural romance and marriage 237–41; barriers to 212, 213, 239–41 (*see also* intercultural friendship); common terms 238–9; enhancement of 240–1; facilitative factors 239, 240–1

intercultural sensitivity 311, 312; *see also* affective sensitivity; developmental model of intercultural sensitivity (DMIS)

intercultural speaker 306–7, 309, 310, 322; *see also* critical intercultural speaker; intercultural mediator

intercultural transformation 203

interdependent self-construal 13

interethnic conflict 250

interethnic marriage 239

interethnic relationship 212

interfaith (interreligious) conflict 250–1

interfaith (interreligious) friendship 213

interfaith (interreligious) marriage 239

interfaith (interreligious) relationship 213

intergenerational conflict 251

intergroup conflict 247–8

intergroup relations 18

intermediary *see* culture broker; mediator

international conflict 250

International Criminal Court (ICC) 250

international education 169

international English *see* global English

international intercultural relationship 212–13

internationalization 8–11, 172–3

internationalization at home' (IaH) 9–10

international language 69; *see also* global English

International Phonetic Alphabet (IPA) 61

international relationship 212–13

international students 169

international (world) citizen 300, 312, *318*; *see also* global citizen

internet identity 139

interpersonal communication 3, 210–11

interpersonal communication and intercultural relationships 210–11

interpersonal communication skills 210

interpersonal conflict 247

interpersonal distance 99, 100

interpersonal relationship 74, 210

interpreter 276–7

interpreting 276–7

interracial communication 212

interracial conflict 249–50

interracial friendship 212

interracial marriage 160, 239

interracial relationship 212

intimate space 99

intracultural conflict 247

intracultural interactions 83

intracultural relationship 211

intrapersonal communication 57

intraracial relationship 211

involuntary migrant 171

Islam 19–20, *21*, 29, 33, 35, 36, 118, 134

Islamophobia 159–60

Jackson, J. 42, 115, 200, 201, 208

Judaism 19, 32, 33, 36, 134

Kim, Y.Y. 175, 201–3

kinesics 91–6

Kluckhohn and Strodtbeck's cultural orientation framework 283

Kluckhohn, C. 283

knowledge, cultural 314, 317

knowledge industries 8

knowledge (saviors) 310, 314

language: affiliation 126; anxiety 229; and culture 29, 128, 180 (*see also* enculturation; second language socialization); and culture shock (confusion)/adaptation 180–204; death 303; expertise 126; fatigue 187; identity (*see* identity; language); inheritance 126; and the internet 85, 224–6; maintenance 176; and nonverbal communication 82–3; and perception (*see* Sapir-Whorf hypothesis); and power 3, 7, 48, 53, 55, 66–8, 71, 73, 76, 77, 126–7, 133, 149, 150, 155, 215, 258, 264,

270, 271, 275 (*see also* English hegemony; Englishization); rights 156, 302; socialization 37–9 (*see also* enculturation; second language socialization; sociopragmatic, awareness)
'large culture' 41, 287
lesbian 132, 217, 238
lingua franca 6, 214, 224, 225, 226, 237, 269, 270
linguistic competence 126, 307, 309, *310*, 311, 316
linguistic determinism 68
linguistic relativity 69
linguistic similarity 189
linguistic styles 71, 73; *see also* audience design framework; communication style; speech style
localism 16
local self 298
long-term relationship 210
long-term sojourner 185
loudness 84, 90
low culture 27
low-contact communication
low-contact cultures
low-context communication

marginality 129–30
marginalization 178
marginalized people 155, 178, 298; *see also* segregation
masculine cultures 131, 285
masculinity 131, 285
mass media 11, 94, 133, 215
mediation 257, 276
mediator 251; *see also* intercultural mediator
Mehrabian, A. 81–2, 94
mental ability identity 134–5
message 55
Mezirow, J. 313–14
micro-term sojourner 185
migration 14–15
mindful awareness 261, 290
mindful fluency 261
mindful intercultural communicator 320
mindfulness 261, 320
minimization of difference 313; *see also* developmental model of intercultural sensitivity (DMIS)
minority group 67, 123, 154, 160
misattribution 249, 254, 260, 278

monochronic time orientation 104–5
monocultural mindset 44, 146, 147
monogamy 239
monolingual 147
multicultural 128, 129, 322; *see also* multicultural identity
multicultural identity 128, 200
multiculturalism 15, 121; *see also* multicultural identity
multilingual identity 128
multilingualism 322; *see also* multilingual identity
multinational 222
mutual-face 258
mutual-face concern 258
mutual facework 230, 236, 258

national identity 46, 117, 136–7, 234–5, 298
nationalistic 16, 115, 201, 235
nature, orientation towards 283
negative face 254
negative facework 254
netizen 225
netspeak 225
noise (interference) 56
nonverbal codes 62, 82, 83, 85, 87, 103, 107, 108, 278; *see also* nonverbal communication
nonverbal communication 80–108; cues 92, 106, 107, 108; definitions of 81; functions of 83–9; importance of 81–2; nature of 81; relationship with verbal communication 82–3; types of 90–105
nonverbal communication functions 83–9; conflict; conveying relationship messages 84; displaying emotions 87–8; emphasizing verbal messages 85; regulating interactions 87; relaying awkward messages 85–6; repeating verbal messages 85; replacing verbal messages 84–5; rituals 89; self-presentation 83–4
nonverbal communication types: chronemics 104–5; facial expressions and emotional display 94–7; gestures 93; haptics 101–2; kinesics 91–6; oculesics 97–8; olfactics (olfaction) 102–3; paralanguage (vocalics) 90–1; physical appearance and artifacts 103–4; posture 94; proxemics 98–101
nonverbal expectancy violation theory 105–6
nonverbal intercultural communicative competence 105–6, 108

Oberg, K. 179, 182, 191, 193
oculesics 97–8
olfactics (olfaction) 102–3
openness 202, 303, 304, 310, 314, *318*, 321
operational competence 202
organizational conflict 248
organizational identity 138
other-face concern 258
Othering 22, 144–6, 288
Otherization *see* Othering
outgroups 42, 63, 67, 140, 145, 146, 148, 152, 159, 162
outsourcing 276

pacifism 255
paralanguage (vocalics) 90–1
particularism 283–4
perception in relation to social categorization 144
perceptual understanding 303
performance orientation 286
peripheral belief 29
personal identity 119–20
personality predisposition 202
personality strength 202–3, 305
personal strength 202–3
phonetics 59
physical ability identity 134
physical appearance and artifacts 103–4
physical feature 103, 134
platonic intercultural relationship 238
pluralistic society 213
polarization/defense/reversal 313; *see also* developmental model of intercultural sensitivity (DMIS)
politeness 18, 36, 37–9, 55, 58, 66, 68, 74, 76, 82–3, 87, 106, 127, 137, 146, 162, 179, 186, 235, 249
political system 136
polychronic time orientation 104–5
polygamy 239
popular culture *see* low culture
populism 16–17, 152
positive discrimination *see* affirmative action
positive face 254
positive facework 254
positivity 197, 203
posture 94
power 84

power distance 66, 87, 226, 259, 284–5, 286
power imbalance 160, 251, 264, 270, 275, 290
power relations 48, 71, 73, 158, 271, 288
power status 67, 84
prejudice 214
prejudicial attitudes 157, 216, 281
preparedness (for cross-cultural transitions) 181, 191, 202, 203, 317
primary socialization *see* enculturation; language, socialization
process model of intercultural competence 55–6
professional identity 138–9
professional identity formation 139
proxemics 98–101
psychological adaptation 178
psychological adjustment/adaptation 305; *see also* acculturative stress
psychological health 203
public space 100

race 40, 121–2, 156–7, 212; *see also* racial, identity; racism
racial: discrimination 152; identity 122–3; quota 156; segregation 158
racism 156–64, 212; definition of 157; types of 157–8; *see also* discrimination; ethnocentricism; power; prejudice; race
racism types: individual 157; institutional 157–8; systemic 158
racist discourse and behaviors 158–9; ideology 158–9
rapport 259
rapport-challenge orientation 259
rapport-enhancement orientation 259
rapport-maintenance orientation 259
rapport-neglect orientation 259
'rapport-talk' 67
reasons to study language and intercultural communication: advances in transportation and communication technologies 11–14; changing demographics 14–15; conflict and peace 17–18; ethics 19–22; globalization 15–18; internationalization 8–11; personal growth and responsibility 22–3; rise in populism, localism and xenophobia 16–17
receiver 56
receiver response 56

reductionism 3, 44, 144, 145, 288; *see also* 'culture as nation' perspective; essentialism

reentry 194, *195*, 198–200, 201, 204

reentry culture shock (confusion) 194, 198–201

refugee 171–2, 173, 175, *299*; *see also* asylum seeker

regional identity 136–7

register 42–3

regulators (of conversations) 87, 93

relational: bond 210–11; identity 230; interdependence 239–40; intimacy 230, 239; maintenance 230; orientation 283

religious: conflict (interfaith) 250–1; identity 230; identity formation 134; pluralistic society 213

'report talk' 67

resilience 185

resocialization 194, 199–200, 202; *see also* reentry

respect 97, 103, 105, 107, 115, 116–17, 120, 125–6, 132, 133, 134, 135, 136, 147, 149, 159, 161, 163, 254, 258, 321; *see also* honorifics

reverse culture shock *see* reentry culture shock (confusion)

reverse discrimination 156

ritual 89

role shock (confusion) 179

romantic relationship 238–40

same sex (gay) marriage 115, 239

Sapir, E. 68

Sapir-Whorf hypothesis 68–9; *see also* linguistic determinism; linguistic relativity

second language socialization 175; *see also* acculturation; sociopragmatic, awareness

segregation 177; *see also* racial; segregation

self-awareness 311–12

self-disclosure 230

self-face concern 258

self-presentation 83–4

self-shock *see* identity, shock (confusion) (self shock)

sender 56

separation 177

service learning (community-engaged learning) 170

sex 131–2

sex *vs.* gender 130

sexism 149

sexist language 149

sexual: harassment 155–6, 281

sexual identity 132

sexual orientation 132

short-term relationship 210

short-term sojourner 185

Sikhism 20, 34, 35, 118

silence 90

similarity-attraction hypothesis 228

simultaneous interpreting 276

skills of discovery and interaction (*savoir apprendre/faire*) *310*, 311

skills of interpreting and relating (*savoir comprendre*) *310*, 311

'small culture' 287

smiling (culture-specific/universal) 92–3

social categorization 144–6; *see also* essentialism; identity, biases; ingroups; Othering; outgroups; perception in relation to social categorization; social identity theory (SIT); stereotyping

social class 213–14; prejudice 214; *see also* classism

social context 66

social distance 38–9, 72, 81, 147, 151; *see also* proxemics

social exclusion 215

social identity 120

social identity theory (SIT) 145–6

social inclusion 215

socialization *see* enculturation

social justice 302, 323

social marker 214

social media 13, 14, 94, 112, 115, 234

social networking sites (SNSs) 13, 16, 89, 225–7, 232, 237

social networks 121, 200, 202, 203, 204, 221–2, 225; barriers to diverse social networks 190, 231–7; building diverse social networks 190, 226–31; *see also* social networking sites (SNSs)

social penetration theory (SPT) 230

social responsibility 298

social sanction 39, 237

social space 6, 41, 100, 101

social status 38, 39, 126, 214, 271

sociocultural adaptation 178

socioemotional support 185, 190, 202, 223

sociolinguistic competence 309, *310*

sociopragmatic: awareness 41, 187, 197; competence 38, 278, 322; expectancy violations 259; norms 58, 186

sojourn 172

sojourner 172

speech act 38, 74, 127, 235

speech community 41

speech illustrator 93

speech style 41, 67, 71, 72–5, 124, 130, 214, 216; and gender 67, 71, 130, 216; *see also* audience design framework; gender, and communication styles; linguistic styles

speech style preference 73

Starosta, W.J. 311–12

stereotype 147; *see also* generalization; stereotyping

stereotyping 17, 44, 71, 144, 147–50, 281, 287; definition of 147; examples 148, 149, 150; gender 149; harmful effects of 150; process of 147–9; pushing past 161–4; reasons for 148, 161; types of 148; *see also* essentialism; generalization; reductionism

stress-adaptation-growth dynamic 202; *see also* integrative communication theory of cross-cultural adaptation

strong ethnic identity 117, 250

strong national identity 298

Strodtbeck, F. 283

study abroad 170

style shifting 72

subculture *see* co-culture

subtractive bilingualism 128

superstition 29

surface-level diversity 269

symbol 27

synchronous communication 225

systemic racism 158

Tajfel, H. 120, 145, 146

Tannen, D. 67, 71, 130

telecommunication 11

third-culture building 129, 137, 239–40

third culture individual (TCI) 129, 137, 232–3

third culture kid (TCK) *see* third culture individual (TCI)

third gender 131

time: orientation 104–5; perception 104

Ting-Toomey, S. 120, 121, 258–60, 261

tolerance 321

tolerance of ambiguity 185, 253, 303, *318*, 320

tourism 169

tourist 172

tradition 34–6

transactive communication 54, 57–8

transformation 175, 203, 296, 311, 313, 314, 323

transformational learning theory 313–14

transgender 131

transition shock (confusion) 178–203; degree of 189–91; definition of 178; optimizing intercultural transitions 203–4; potential benefits of 181–3; sources of 180–8; symptoms of 188–9; types of 178–80; *see also* culture shock (confusion)

transition shock types: culture shock (confusion) 178–9; identity or self-shock 180; language shock 180; role shock 179

translation 276

transnational competence *see* global competence

transnational identity 137

Trompenaars, F. 283–4

turn-taking 87

U-curve adjustment model 193–4, 200–201; criticisms of 200–201

uncertainty avoidance 285, 286

uncertainty reduction 229, 253

uncertainty reduction theory (URT) 185, 229, 253

unintentional communication 63

universal facial expressions of emotion 94, 96

universalism 283–4

valence 30–1

value 30–1; *see also* value orientation framework; worldview

value orientations framework 282–8

verbal communication 59, 82–3; *see also* gender, and communication styles

vertical-based facework 259

virtual (cyber) identity *see* internet identity

vocal characterizer 90

vocalics *see* paralanguage (vocalics)

voice qualities 106

voluntary migrant 168–9

W-curve adjustment model 194–201; criticisms
      of 200–201
weak ethnic identity 117
weak national identity 298
Web 2.0 13–14
'whole person' development 192, 201
Whorf, B.L. 68
willingness to communicate (WTC) 228–9, 231, 233

work ethic 279
workplace discrimination 281
world citizen 300, 312, *318*
World Englishes 5, 69
worldview 31–4, 45, 69, 129, 139, 146, 147, 171,
      234, 304, 312, 313

xenophobia 16, 160, 164